'Like seemingly everything with business these days, corporate branding is undergoing a sea change in strategy and execution. This stimulating and insightful handbook assembles some of the sharpest thinking from around the world on the most important and compelling topics in this area.'

– *Kevin Keller, Senior Associate Dean for Marketing and Communications and E.B. Osborn Professor of Marketing, Tuck School of Business*

'Corporations are more than ever coming back, after being hidden by their brands during decades. Moreover the growth of the Benefit-corporation now adds a layer of purpose above the brands themselves. Clearly corporate branding needed to be reanalyzed. This is well done by this internationally co-created excellent book.'

– *Jean-Nöel Kapferer, Emeritus Professor, HEC Paris*

'*The Routledge Companion to Corporate Branding* provides a much-needed overview of the history and evolution of corporate branding as a distinct field of study and practice as well as offering insight into its possible futures. Embracing both theoretical and practical contributions, it promises much value for anyone drawn to this rapidly expanding field.'

– *Mary Jo Hatch, Professor Emerita, University of Virginia*

'When one wants to master a field, then what is really needed is a collection of high quality and well-crafted contributions from real and well recognised experts. This is exactly what the readers of *The Routledge Companion to Corporate Branding* will get. In this collection of articles top academics share their deep knowledge, offering important information and summarising the present and future of Corporate Branding. This collection of papers is an essential reading for those who want to understand, work, research or teach in Corporate Branding – a real "must have."'

– *Cleopatra Veloutsou, Professor of Brand Management, University of Glasgow*

# THE ROUTLEDGE COMPANION TO CORPORATE BRANDING

This companion is a prestige reference work that offers students and researchers a comprehensive overview of the emerging co-created, multi-stakeholder, and sustainable approach to corporate brand management, representing a paradigm shift in the literature.

The volume contains 30 chapters, organised into 6 thematic sections. The first section is an introductory one, which underscores the evolution of brand management thinking over time, presenting the corporate brand management field, introducing the current debates in the literature, and discussing the key dimensions of the emerging corporate brand management paradigm. The next five sections focus in turn on one of the key dimensions that characterize the emerging approach to corporate brand management: co-creation, sustainability, polysemic corporate narratives, transformation (history and future), and corporate culture. Every chapter provides a deep reflection on current knowledge, highlighting the most relevant debates and tensions, and offers a roadmap for future research avenues. The final chapter of each section is a commentary on the section, written by a senior leading scholar in the corporate brand management field.

This wide-ranging reference work is primarily for students, scholars, and researchers in management, marketing, and brand management, offering a single repository on the current state of knowledge, current debates, and relevant literature. Written by an international selection of leading authors from the USA, Europe, Asia, Africa, and Australia, it provides a balanced, authoritative overview of the field and convenient access to an emerging perspective on corporate brand management.

**Oriol Iglesias** is Associate Professor and Head of the Marketing Department at ESADE Business School, Universitat Ramon Llull. Oriol is member of the Scientific Committee of the Global Brand Conference and of the Editorial Board of the *Journal of Brand Management*. He has also been for 6 years a member of the Executive Committee of the European Marketing Academy (EMAC). His research focuses on corporate branding, conscientious brands, and co-creation and has been published in *California Management Review*, *Journal of Business Ethics*, *Business and Society*, *Industrial Marketing Management*, *Journal of Business Research*, and *European Journal of Marketing*, among others.

**Nicholas Ind** is Professor at Kristiania University College and Visiting Professor at ESADE Business School and Edinburgh Napier University. His main research interests are co-creation and conscientious brands. He is the author of 16 books and articles that have appeared in *California Management Review*, *Journal of Brand Management*, *European Business Review*, *Business Horizons*, and *Journal of Product and Brand Management*.

**Majken Schultz** is Professor of Management and Organization Studies at Copenhagen Business School. She is affiliated with the Centre for Organization and Time at the Department of Organization and is an international research fellow at the Centre for Corporate Reputation, Oxford University. Her work has focused on managerial and organizational issues related to identity, culture, and image, including the implications for corporate branding and use of history. She has published in the leading journals on organization studies and branding and co-written/edited more than a dozen books. She is one of the most cited professors at CBS and is Chair of Carlsberg Foundation.

# ROUTLEDGE COMPANIONS IN BUSINESS, MANAGEMENT AND MARKETING

Routledge Companions are prestige volumes which provide an overview of a research field or topic. Surveying the business disciplines, the books in this series incorporate both established and emerging research themes. Compiled and edited by an array of highly regarded scholars, these volumes also benefit from global teams of contributors reflecting disciplinary diversity.

Individually, *Routledge Companions in Business, Management and Marketing* provide impactful one-stop-shop publications. Collectively, they represent a comprehensive learning and research resource for researchers, postgraduate students and practitioners.

THE ROUTLEDGE COMPANION TO MARKETING RESEARCH
*Edited by Len Tiu Wright, Luiz Moutinho, Merlin Stone and Richard P. Bagozzi*

THE ROUTLEDGE COMPANION TO TALENT MANAGEMENT
*Edited by Ibraiz Tarique*

THE ROUTLEDGE COMPANION TO CORPORATE SOCIAL RESPONSIBILITY
*Edited by Thomas Maak, Nicola M. Pless, Sukhbir Sandhu and Marc Olitzky*

THE ROUTLEDGE COMPANION TO GLOBAL VALUE CHAINS
Reinterpreting and Reimagining Megatrends in the World Economy
*Edited by Renu Agarwal, Christopher Bajada, Roy Green and Katrina Skellern*

THE ROUTLEDGE COMPANION TO MARKETING AND FEMINISM
*Edited by Pauline Maclaran, Lorna Stevens and Olga Kravets*

THE ROUTLEDGE COMPANION TO CORPORATE BRANDING
*Edited by Oriol Iglesias, Nicholas Ind and Majken Schultz*

For more information about this series, please visit: www.routledge.com/Routledge-Companions-in-Business-Management-and-Marketing/book-series/RCBUS

# THE ROUTLEDGE COMPANION TO CORPORATE BRANDING

*Edited by Oriol Iglesias, Nicholas Ind and Majken Schultz*

LONDON AND NEW YORK

Cover image: © Getty Images

First published 2022
by Routledge
4 Park Square, Milton Park, Abingdon, Oxon OX14 4RN

and by Routledge
605 Third Avenue, New York, NY 10158

Routledge is an imprint of the Taylor & Francis Group, an informa business

© 2022 selection and editorial matter, Oriol Iglesias, Nicholas Ind and Majken Schultz; individual chapters, the contributors

The right of Oriol Iglesias, Nicholas Ind and Majken Schultz to be identified as the authors of the editorial material, and of the authors for their individual chapters, has been asserted in accordance with sections 77 and 78 of the Copyright, Designs and Patents Act 1988.

All rights reserved. No part of this book may be reprinted or reproduced or utilised in any form or by any electronic, mechanical, or other means, now known or hereafter invented, including photocopying and recording, or in any information storage or retrieval system, without permission in writing from the publishers.

*Trademark notice*: Product or corporate names may be trademarks or registered trademarks, and are used only for identification and explanation without intent to infringe.

British Library Cataloguing-in-Publication Data
A catalogue record for this book is available from the British Library

Library of Congress Cataloging-in-Publication Data
A catalog record has been requested for this book

ISBN: 978-0-367-47663-2 (hbk)
ISBN: 978-1-032-25259-9 (pbk)
ISBN: 978-1-003-03574-9 (ebk)

DOI: 10.4324/9781003035749

Typeset in Bembo
by Apex CoVantage, LLC

 Printed in the United Kingdom
by Henry Ling Limited

*We would like to dedicate the book to Marta, Vera, and Tor.*

# CONTENTS

List of contributors xiii
Acknowledgments xxii

**A**
**An introduction to the corporate brand management field** 1

1 Towards a paradigm shift in corporate branding 3
  *Oriol Iglesias, Nicholas Ind, and Majken Schultz*

2 Demarcating the field of corporate brand management 24
  *Russell Abratt and Michela Mingione*

3 Corporate brand management from a co-creative perspective 42
  *Hans Mühlbacher*

4 Welcome to the matrix: how to find and use your corporate brand's core identity 59
  *Mats Urde*

5 Commentary on 'Towards a paradigm shift in corporate brand management' 83
  *Joachim Kernstock and Shaun Powell*

## B
**Building brands together: Co-creating corporate brands with multiple stakeholders**    93

6   Embracing a co-creation paradigm of lived-experience ecosystem value creation    95
*Venkat Ramaswamy*

7   Brands in action: understanding corporate branding dynamics from an action net perspective    111
*Sylvia von Wallpach and Andrea Hemetsberger*

8   Reconceptualizing corporate brand identity from a co-creational perspective    131
*Catherine da Silveira and Cláudia Simões*

9   In search of corporate brand alignment: philosophical foundations and emerging trends    149
*Michela Mingione and Russell Abratt*

10   Commentary on 'Co-creating corporate brands with multiple stakeholders'    169
*Francisco Guzmán*

## C
**Building strong corporate brands: towards valuable and sustainable experiences**    175

11   B★Canvas 2.0: holistic and co-created brand management tool and use cases for corporate brands    177
*Carsten Baumgarth*

12   Brand experience co-creation at the time of artificial intelligence    195
*Federico Mangiò, Giuseppe Pedeliento, and Daniela Andreini*

13   Honey or condensed milk? Improving relative brand attractiveness through commercial and social innovations    211
*Seidali Kurtmollaiev, Line Lervik-Olsen, and Tor W. Andreassen*

| | | |
|---|---|---|
| 14 | A systematic literature review of sustainability in corporate services branding: identifying dimensions, drivers, outcomes, and future research opportunities<br>*Stefan Markovic, Yuqian Qiu, Cristina Sancha, and Nikolina Koporcic* | 228 |
| 15 | Building strong corporate brands: towards valuable and sustainable experiences<br>*Nicholas Ind* | 249 |

## D
## Polysemic corporate brand narratives: connecting internal and external communities — 257

| | | |
|---|---|---|
| 16 | Integrating multiple voices when crafting a corporate brand narrative<br>*Paul A. Argenti* | 259 |
| 17 | Corporate brand management and multiple voices: polyphony or cacophony?<br>*Line Schmeltz and Anna Karina Kjeldsen* | 281 |
| 18 | Polysemic corporate branding: managing the idea<br>*Alessandra Zamparini, Luca M. Visconti, and Francesco Lurati* | 300 |
| 19 | Visitors' destination brand engagement's effect on co-creation: an empirical study<br>*Raouf Ahmad Rather, Linda Hollebeek, Dale L.G. Smith, Jana Kukk, and Mojtaba Ghasemi* | 321 |
| 20 | Corporate brand narratives: polysemy, voice, and purpose<br>*Joep Cornelissen* | 338 |

## E
## The temporality of corporate branding: balancing the past and future — 343

| | | |
|---|---|---|
| 21 | Towards a co-creational perspective on corporate heritage branding<br>*Mario Burghausen* | 345 |
| 22 | Cross-fertilization of heritage between product and corporate branding<br>*Fabien Pecot* | 364 |

23  Closing corporate branding gaps through authentic internal brand
    strategies                                                              378
    *Michael B. Beverland and Pınar Cankurtaran*

24  When history inspires brand strategy: lessons for place brands and
    corporate brands                                                        395
    *Mihalis Kavaratzis*

25  Balancing the past and future in corporate branding                     408
    *Majken Schultz*

## F
## Branding inside-out: corporate culture and internal branding            417

26  Branding inside-out: development of the internal branding concept       419
    *Rico Piehler*

27  A co-creative perspective on internal branding                          442
    *Holger J. Schmidt and Pieter Steenkamp*

28  Exploring how to build a strong internal brand community and its
    role in corporate brand co-creation                                     459
    *Saila Saraniemi*

29  Co-creating conscientious corporate brands inside-out through
    values-driven branding                                                  480
    *Galina Biedenbach and Thomas Biedenbach*

30  Branding inside-out: corporate culture and internal branding            496
    *Ceridwyn King*

Index                                                                       505

# CONTRIBUTORS

**Russell Abratt** is Professor of Marketing in the School of Business at George Mason University. His research interests are in corporate identity, branding, and reputation management. His work has been published in the *Journal of Advertising Research, California Management Review, European Journal of Marketing, Industrial Marketing Management, Journal of Business Ethics, Tourism Management, Journal of Marketing Management, Journal of Brand Management*, and the *Journal of Product and Brand Management*, among others.

**Tor W. Andreassen** is Professor of Innovation, the previous Director of Center for Service Innovation, and the current Director of the Digital Innovation for Sustainable Growth (DIG) at NHH Norwegian School of Economics. Andreassen has published in several leading journals, such as *MIT Sloan Management Review, Marketing Science, Journal of Marketing*, and *Journal of Service Research*, in addition to eight books. For his research, Andreassen was elected Chair of INFORMS Service Science community and VP of Education and Professional Development at European Marketing Academy's Executive Committee. Andreassen is the founder of Service Forum (BI), the Norwegian Customer Satisfaction Barometer (BI), the Norwegian Innovation Index (NHH), and the annual Professor Johan Arndt Marketing Conference.

**Daniela Andreini** is Associate Professor in Marketing and Director of the Master in Digital Business Development at the University of Bergamo (Italy). She is Consulting Editor of *International Journal of Management Reviews*, a member of the editorial board of *Journal of Business Research, Journal of Product and Brand Management*, and *Italian Journal of Marketing* and of the editorial review board of the *International Journal of Information Management*. Her research appears in international journals such as *Journal of Advertising, Journal of Business Research, Industrial Marketing Management, Organization Studies, Journal of Advertising Research, Family Business Review, Journal of Business and Industrial Marketing, Journal of Business Ethics*, and *Journal of Service Theory and Practice*.

**Paul A. Argenti** is Professor of Corporate Communication at Tuck School of Business at Dartmouth. A pioneer in the field of corporate communication, he taught some of the earliest courses on the subject for Harvard Business School and Columbia Business School. He has also published widely in both academic and practitioner journals, wrote *Corporate Communication*, the first textbook in the field, now in its eighth edition, and has written hundreds of widely used cases. Argenti teaches in Tuck's MBA program, executive programs, and Master in Healthcare Delivery program. Professor Argenti is a Fulbright Scholar and a winner of the Pathfinder Award in 2007 from the Institute for Public Relations for the excellence of his research over a long career.

**Carsten Baumgarth** is Professor of Brand Management at the Berlin School of Economics and Law (Germany) and Adjunct Professor at the Ho-Chi-Minh-City Open University (Vietnam). Carsten has published more than 400 papers and books with a focus on brand management, B2B marketing, sustainable marketing, arts marketing, and empirical methods, and his work has been published in *Industrial Marketing Management, Journal of Business Research, European Journal of Marketing, Journal of Product and Brand Management*, and *International Journal of Arts Management*, among others. Carsten co-founded the Institute for Sustainability in Berlin (2012) and the Expert Council Technology Brands (2015).

**Michael B. Beverland** is Professor of Brand Management and Head of Department (Strategy and Marketing) at University of Sussex Business School. He is also Adjunct Professor of Marketing at Copenhagen Business School. Michael received his PhD from the University of South Australia and has authored numerous works on brand management and authenticity, including publications in the *Journal of the Academy of Marketing Science, Journal of Advertising, Journal of Consumer Research, Journal of Management Studies*, and *Journal of Product Innovation Management*. His practical work on brand authenticity has been published in two books: *Building Brand Authenticity: 7 Habits of Iconic Brands* (Kogan Page) and *Brand Management: Co-creating Meaningful Brands, 2nd Edition* (Sage, 2021).

**Galina Biedenbach** is Associate Professor in Marketing at Umeå School of Business, Economics, and Statistics, Umeå University. Her research interests include corporate branding, strategic marketing, and industrial marketing. Within her research projects, she has collaborated with small and large businesses, as well as governmental organizations. Her research has been published in *Industrial Marketing Management, Journal of Brand Management, Journal of Business & Industrial Marketing, Journal of Product and Brand Management, Marketing Intelligence and Planning, Public Management Review*, and *Qualitative Market Research: An International Journal*. She has also co-authored book chapters on business-to-business marketing, brand equity, and stakeholder branding.

**Thomas Biedenbach** is Associate Professor in Management at Umeå School of Business, Economics, and Statistics, Umeå University. His major research interests are innovation management, project management, temporary organizations, and organizing practices based on routines and capabilities. His research has been published in *International Journal of Managing Projects in Business, International Journal of Project Management, International Journal of Technology Management, Journal of Change Management*, and *Project Management Journal*. He has also written a book chapter on research philosophy and research paradigms.

*Contributors*

**Mario Burghausen** is Senior Lecturer (Associate Professor) at Essex Business School, University of Essex, UK. He is Co-Editor-in-Chief of the *Journal of Brand Management*, and he has ten years of industry experience outside academia. He holds the first-ever doctorate in corporate heritage (branding). His research interests are within the fields of corporate brand management and corporate marketing with a specific focus on multiple temporalities in organizational contexts and the various manifestations, interpretations, and representations of organizations and their brands more generally. Mario has published his work in the *Journal of Business Research, Marketing Theory, European Journal of Marketing*, and *Journal of Brand Management*, among others.

**Pinar Cankurtaran** is Assistant Professor of Brand Strategy at the Faculty of Industrial Design Engineering, Delft University of Technology. She holds a doctoral degree from Rotterdam School of Management, Erasmus University. Her current research focuses on brand authenticity, brand discourses, and brand-driven change. Her work has been published in the *Journal of Product Innovation Management, Industrial Marketing Management, Journal of Macromarketing*, and *Research In the Sociology of Organizations*. She has contributed three cases to the book *Brand Management: Co-creating Meaningful Brands, 2nd Edition* (authored by Michael B. Beverland, Sage, 2021).

**Joep Cornelissen** is Professor of Management at Rotterdam School of Management, Erasmus University, and Chair in Strategy and Organisation (part-time) at the *University of Liverpool* Management School. The main focus of his research involves studies of the role of corporate and managerial communication in the context of innovation, entrepreneurship, and change. He has written a textbook on corporate communication with Sage, which is now in its sixth edition (with a seventh edition planned for 2022).

**Catherine da Silveira** is Associate Professor at Nova School of Business and Economics, Portugal. Her fields of research encompass areas such as brand co-creation, brand identity management, and luxury branding. She has published in the *Journal of Business Research* and in practitioner-oriented publications. Academic Director of the CEMS Master's in International Management and Head of the Luxury Management field of specialization at Nova School of Business and Economics, she is also coordinating consulting projects for firms in brand strategy. Before joining the academic world, she worked for 13 years for the L'Oréal Group as a marketing executive across divisions, brands, and countries.

**Mojtaba Ghasemi** is a PhD candidate (marketing) at the Department of Business Management, Qazvin Branch, Islamic Azad University, in Iran. Mojtaba also completed a Master's degree from Allameh Tabataba'i University in Tehran, Iran. Mojtaba's research, which centres on customer engagement, destination brand engagement, and cocreation, has been published in the *Proceedings of the Fifth National Conference on Applied Research in Management and Accounting (ISC)*.

**Francisco Guzmán** is Professor of Marketing at the G. Brint Ryan College of Business and Distinguished Teaching Professor at the University of North Texas. He is Co-Editor-in-Chief of the *Journal of Product and Brand Management* and Associate Editor (consumer behaviour) of the

*Journal of Business Research*. He is a member of the Scientific Committee of the Global Brand Conference and Chair of the Cross-Cultural Research Conference. His research focuses on branding and social transformation, particularly on branding with purpose (sustainability, corporate social responsibility, socio-political activism), as well as brand equity, co-creation, public-private collaborations, and political branding. His more than 50 articles have been published in the *Journal of International Marketing, Journal of Business Research, European Journal of Marketing, Industrial Marketing Management, Journal of Marketing Management, Journal of Brand Management, Journal of Retailing and Consumer Services,* and *Harvard Business Review América Latina,* among many others.

**Andrea Hemetsberger** is Professor of Branding at the University of Innsbruck, Academic Director of the Brand Research Laboratory and Speaker of the Research Area EPoS (Economy, Politics, and Society). Her research focuses on branding and interpretive consumer research with a focus on CCT and social media. Her research has been published, for example, in the *Journal of Consumer Research, Consumption, Markets and Culture; Journal of Business Research; Organization Studies; Journal of Macromarketing; Journal of Marketing Management, Entrepreneurship, and Regional Development;* and *Management Learning*. She won the Shelby Hunt award 2012 and the Literati award 2017, and is a member of several review boards.

**Linda Hollebeek**, Ph.D, is Professor of Marketing at IPAG Business School, Vilnius University, and Tallinn University of Technology. Her research on customer, consumer, and stakeholder engagement has been published in the *Journal of the Academy of Marketing Science, Journal of Service Research,* and *International Journal of Research in Marketing,* among others. She has been named a Clarivate Highly Cited Researcher (2021, 2020) and is included on Stanford University's top 2% of researchers (2021, 2020). Linda also serves as Associate Editor of the *Journal of Service Research,* is the recipient of the 2020 SERVSIG Emerging Service Scholar Award, and is co-editor of *The Handbook of Research on Customer Engagement*.

**Mihalis Kavaratzis** is Professor of Place Marketing (Manchester Metropolitan University Business School), Co-Founder of the International Place Branding Association, and a Senior Fellow of the Institute of Place Management. He has published some of the most-cited work in the field of place branding in journals such as *Tourism Management, Journal of Travel Research,* and *Marketing Theory*. Mihalis has co-edited *Inclusive Place Branding* (with M. Giovanardi and M. Lichrou, 2017), *Rethinking Place Branding* (with G. Warnaby and G.J. Ashworth, 2015), and *Towards Effective Place Brand Management* (with G.J. Ashworth, 2010).

**Joachim Kernstock** is Head of the Centre of Competence for Brand Management in St. Gallen, Switzerland. He is an experienced corporate brand strategy advisor. He works with leading Swiss and European corporates and with SMEs. He has published leading publications about corporate brand management and brand behaviour in Germany and within international refereed journals. He lectures at the University of St. Gallen. Before this engagement he was responsible for the Lufthansa corporate marketing and brand portfolio. Joachim has been Co-Editor-in-Chief of the *Journal of Brand Management* since 2012.

*Contributors*

**Ceridwyn King** is Associate Professor in the School of Sport, Tourism, and Hospitality Management at Temple University, in the United States. Ceridwyn holds a Master of Marketing Management with Honours and a PhD in Marketing, both awarded at Griffith University in Australia, and she has several years of strategic marketing experience in a range of industries. She is a thought leader in internal brand management research. Her research can be found in leading international journals such as the *European Journal of Marketing, Journal of Services Management*, and the *Journal of Product and Brand Management*.

**Anna Karina Kjeldsen** concentrates on corporate communication, branding, co-creation, and corporate social responsibility in her research, especially in relation to public organizations and museums. She holds a PhD in strategic communication and is External Associate Professor at The Danish School of Media and Journalism (DMJX). Anna Karina has published her research in the *International Journal of Strategic Communication, Journal of Brand Management*, and *Public Relations Inquiry*, among others.

**Nikolina Koporcic**, PhD, is Senior Researcher at Laurea University of Applied Sciences and Visiting Assistant Professor at Luleå University of Technology. Nikolina is also affiliated with Åbo Akademi University and holds a title of a Docent (Adjunct Professor) at the University of Turku. Her research focuses on corporate branding, entrepreneurship, and co-creation of value in business-to-business relationships and networks. In particular, she is studying the importance of Interactive Network Branding for SMEs in business markets. Besides academic articles published in *Industrial Marketing Management, Technological Forecasting and Social Change,* and *Journal of Business and Industrial Marketing*, Nikolina has published two books.

**Jana Kukk**, PhD, is Senior Lecturer in Marketing at the Department of Business Administration, Tallinn University of Technology, Tallinn, Estonia. She defended her PhD in 2016. Her research is mainly focused on value creation in business services. In parallel to her academic career, Jana is active in the managerial sphere, consulting for companies on strategic marketing and service development.

**Seidali Kurtmollaiev** is Associate Professor at Kristiania University College and NHH Norwegian School of Economics. His main research interests are in strategic management and marketing with a focus on service innovation. His work on innovation management, innovation adoption, and organizational change appeared in, among others, the *Academy of Management Learning and Education Journal*, the *Journal of Service Research*, and the *Journal of Management Inquiry*. Kurtmollaiev is also one of the developers of Norwegian Innovation Index – the world's first customer-based ranking of the most innovative firms.

**Line Lervik-Olsen** is Professor of Marketing and the Head of the Department of Marketing at BI Norwegian Business School. Lervik-Olsen has been the research leader of the Norwegian Customer Satisfaction Barometer and is currently affiliated with the Digital Innovation for Growth (DIG) centre at NHH Norwegian School of Economics and the Norwegian Innovation Index. Her research interests are within the field of service marketing and strategic marketing, with a special focus on service innovation, consumer trends, customer satisfaction, and complaint behaviour. Lervik-Olsen has published her work in such journals as *Journal of Service Research*, the *Journal of Economic Psychology, Managing*

*Service Quality*, the *Journal of Service Theory and Practice*, *Journal of Business Research*, *PLOS One*, and *Marketing Letters*.

**Francesco Lurati** is Professor of Corporate Communication at USI, Università della Svizzera italiana in Lugano. He pursues research in the field of corporate communication, in particular, in the areas of organizational identity, corporate reputation, and crisis communication. He has published in the *Journal of Business Research*, *Strategic Organization*, *Corporate Reputation Review*, *Corporate Communications: an International Journal*, *International Journal of Strategic Communication*, and *Journal of Public Relations Research*. He is the Academic Director of the MS program in corporate communication. He is also the Director of the USI Startup Centre.

**Federico Mangiò** is a PhD candidate in marketing at the Department of Management of the University of Bergamo (Italy). He was a visiting PhD student at the Consumption, Culture, and Commerce research unit of the University of Southern Denmark. His research interests concern the consumption and market dynamics of privacy-enhancing technologies, brand communication, digital methods, and text mining. Early outputs of his research have been published in such journals as *Journal of Advertising*, among others.

**Stefan Markovic** is Associate Professor and Chair of the Marketing Ethics Research Cluster at the Department of Marketing, Copenhagen Business School, Frederiksberg, Denmark. He is also Chair of the SIG on Branding, Member of the Executive Committee, and National Representative of Denmark at the European Marketing Academy. Stefan's research addresses various intersections between marketing, innovation, and ethics. He published in several journals, including *Journal of Business Ethics*, *Journal of Business Research*, *Industrial Marketing Management*, and *IEEE Transactions on Engineering Management*. He is Co-Editor-in-Chief of *Business Ethics, the Environment and Responsibility* and Associate Editor for Interdisciplinary Research with *Industrial Marketing Management*.

**Michela Mingione** is Research Fellow in Marketing at the University of Rome Tor Vergata, Italy. Her current research interests are in corporate marketing, corporate identity, and branding. Her work has been published in the *Journal of Business Research*, *Journal of Marketing Management*, *Journal of Brand Management*, *Journal of Product and Brand Management*, and the *Journal of Marketing Communications*, among others. Moreover, she is an editorial board member of the *Journal of Marketing Analytics*.

**Hans Mühlbacher** is Prof. em. of Marketing at the International University of Monaco and Prof.i.R. of the University of Innsbruck School of Management. He served as President of the European Marketing Academy, as editor of Marketing – ZFP, and was the Associate Editor for International Business for the *Journal of Business Research*. He has published widely in academic journals, including the *International Journal of Research in Marketing*, the *Journal of Product Innovation Management*, the *Journal of Management Information Systems*, the *Journal of Business Research*, the *European Journal of Marketing*, and *Industrial Marketing Management*.

**Fabien Pecot** is Associate Professor at TBS Barcelona. His research interests involve the use of brand heritage in product brand management and the role of political ideology in anti-consumption phenomena. Fabien is a member of the editorial board of the *Journal of Advertising Research* and *Décisions Marketing*. His research has been published in journals such as the *Journal of*

Business Research, Marketing Theory, the Journal of Marketing Management, and Recherche et Applications en Marketing.

**Giuseppe Pedeliento** is Associate Professor of Marketing and Management at the Department of Management of the University of Bergamo (Italy). His articles have appeared in reputed international journals such as Organization Studies; Journal of Advertising; Family Business Review; Journal of Business Research; Industrial Marketing Management; Journal of Business Ethics; Journal of Business and Industrial Marketing, Consumption, Markets and Culture; Journal of Service Theory and Practice; Management Decision; Journal of Product and Brand Management, and in other academic outlets. Giuseppe serves on the editorial board of several journals such as Journal of Business Research, Journal of Product and Brand Management, Management Decision, and Italian Journal of Marketing; he is Associate Editor for Pearson Management and Marketing Cases and serves as a reviewer for several highly-ranked international journals.

**Rico Piehler** is Senior Lecturer in Marketing at Macquarie University in Sydney, Australia. He previously worked for the Chair of Innovative Brand Management and the Markstones Institute of Marketing, Branding & Technology at the University of Bremen in Germany. Rico gained practical experience as Consultant and Senior Consultant in numerous marketing and branding projects. His research focusses on internal and employer branding, brand communication, and social media marketing, city branding, brand competitiveness and the academic-practitioner gap. He has published in the Journal of Product and Brand Management, Journal of Brand Management, and European Journal of Marketing, among others.

**Shaun Powell** has worked within several universities in the UK and Australia following an extended period in industry. His research has appeared in various refereed international journals, often focused on interrelating aspects of corporate marketing, corporate brand management, and corporate social responsibility. He has also co-edited several books on corporate branding and luxury brand management within the Journal of Brand Management: Advanced Collections series. Shaun has been Co-Editor-in-Chief of the Journal of Brand Management since 2012, as well as a member of several other journal editorial boards.

**Yuqian Qiu** is a PhD candidate in management sciences at ESADE Business School, Spain. Yuqian holds a Master of Research degree from ESADE Business School and a Master of Science degree from the University of Manchester, UK. She is a keen researcher with interests covering areas such as branding, CSR, co-creation, and innovation. Her work has appeared in journals including Business and Society and Industrial Marketing Management. Before pursuing a career in academia, Yuqian had research and management experience in China National Petroleum Corporation (CNPC) for several years.

**Venkat Ramaswamy** is Professor at the Ross School of Business, University of Michigan, Ann Arbor, USA. Venkat is a globally recognized thought leader, idea practitioner, and eclectic scholar with wide-ranging interests in the theory and practices of value creation, innovation, strategy, marketing, branding, IT, operations, and the human side of organizations. [Visit www.venkatramaswamy.com.]

**Raouf Ahmad Rather**, PhD, is a marketing researcher, researcher/analyst at the Department of Management Studies (South Campus), University of Kashmir, Jammu and Kashmir, Srinagar,

India. His research interests centre on customer experience, co-creation, customer engagement, service innovation, and customer loyalty. His work to date has published in journals, including the *Journal of Travel Research*, *European Journal of Marketing*, and *Journal of Retailing and Consumer Services*, among others. Rather serves as an editorial team member and reviewer of several reputed SSCI journals.

**Cristina Sancha** is Lecturer at the Department of Operations, Innovation and Data Science at ESADE Business School; Academic Director of the MSc in Global Strategic Management; and member of the BuNeD research group (ESADE) and the Marketing Ethics Research Cluster (Copenhagen Business School). Cristina's research is centred on the extension of sustainability along supply chains. She has published in several journals, including *International Journal of Production Economics*, *Journal of Cleaner Production*, *International Journal of Production Research*, and *Industrial Marketing Management*, among others. She is Associate Editor of *Business Ethics, the Environment and Responsibility* and *International Journal of Shipping and Transport Logistics*.

**Saila Saraniemi** is Professor of Brand Marketing at Oulu Business School, University of Oulu, Finland. She also holds a title of docent (Adjunct Professor) at University of Eastern Finland. Her research interests include brand experiences and branding from contemporary perspectives, such as multiple stakeholders, digitalization, and sustainability, particularly in B2B, place, and health contexts. Her research has been published in *Industrial Marketing Management*, *Tourism Management*, *European Journal of Marketing*, *Journal of Product and Brand Management*, and *Corporate Reputation Review*, among others.

**Line Schmeltz** holds a PhD in strategic communication and is Senior Associate Professor of Strategic Communication and Director of Centre for Communication and Management at the Danish School of Media and Journalism (DMJX). Her research focuses on corporate social responsibility, sustainability communication, corporate branding and identity, brand co-creation, and strategic communication. Line's research has been published in *International Journal of Strategic Communication*, *Journal of Brand Management*, *Corporate Communications an International Journal*, *Public Relations Inquiry*, and *Social Responsibility Journal*, among others.

**Holger J. Schmidt** is Professor of Marketing at the Koblenz University of Applied Sciences. His research focuses on brand management, particularly on brand co-creation, brand orientation, internal branding, sustainable branding, technology branding, and brand purpose. He authored and edited various books, and his research has been published in the *Journal of Brand Management*, *Journal of Product and Brand Management*, *Journal of Retailing and Consumer Services*, *Business Research*, *Corporate Reputation Review*, and *Journal of Creating Value and Social Business*, among others.

**Cláudia Simões** is Professor of Management (Marketing and Strategy area) and Dean of the School of Economics and Management at the University of Minho in Portugal. Her research interests are in strategic marketing, corporate marketing (identity, brand and reputation), service management, and customer experience. She has published in the *Journal of Marketing*, *Journal of the Academy of Marketing Science*, *Industrial Marketing Management*, *Business Ethics Quarterly*, and others. Cláudia is Associate Editor of the *European Journal of Marketing* and member of the editorial board in other journals. She has participated in various industry-related projects in Portugal, Spain, and the UK.

*Contributors*

**Dale L.G. Smith**, M.Rehab, is a registered social worker. He works at Goodwood Park Health Group, Ltd. His research interest is in customer engagement as exhibited on both face-to-face and digital platforms. His research has been published in the *Journal of Services Marketing* and the *Journal of Retailing and Consumer Services*.

**Pieter Steenkamp** is Senior Lecturer, and he established and co-leads the Brand and Digital Research Hub within the Marketing Department of Cape Peninsula University of Technology (CPUT) in Cape Town, South Africa. His research focuses on brand management and has been published in, among others, the *Journal of Brand Management, Journal of Retailing and Consumer Services* and the *Journal of Business-to-Business Marketing*. He has presented at national and international conferences.

**Mats Urde** is Associate Professor, PhD, at Lund University in Sweden. As a researcher, teacher, and consultant in strategic brand management, Mats bridges theory and practice and is one of the pioneers in the field of corporate branding. He has a long track record of practical experience in projects with many companies, including Electrolux, ABB, and IKEA. He has published in *Harvard Business Review* and other leading journals. As Associate Professor, he heads the Lund Brand Management Group. He introduced the concept of brand orientation and has published field-based research on Volvo, the Nobel Prize Foundation, and the Swedish Monarchy. He has been voted "Teacher of the Year" and received the Case Center's case teaching award. Currently he is working on his own book on corporate brand management. In his spare time, Mats like sailing and Icelandic horse riding.

**Luca M. Visconti** is Professor of Marketing and Faculty Dean at USI, Università della Svizzera italiana in Lugano. He is Associate Editor of *Consumption Markets and Culture* and Co-Editor of the book *Marketing Management: A Cultural Perspective*. His research on brand storytelling and consumer vulnerability was published in the *Journal of Consumer Research, Journal of Business Research*, and *Marketing Theory*, among others.

**Sylvia von Wallpach**, SFHEA, is Professor MSO in branding and marketing management at the Department of Marketing of Copenhagen Business School (Denmark). Her main research interests are in the fields of branding, interpretative consumer research, and qualitative method development. Sylvia's publications have appeared in *Tourism Management; Journal of Business Ethics; Psychology and Marketing; Journal of Business Research; International Marketing Review;* and *Nonprofit and Voluntary Sector Quarterly*, among others. Currently, Sylvia serves as Associate Editor for Marketing with the *European Management Journal*.

**Alessandra Zamparini** is Lecturer and Researcher (MER) at the Institute of Marketing and Communication Management of USI, Università della Svizzera italiana in Lugano, Switzerland. Her research focuses on collective identity construction and change in organizational, urban, and regional contexts. She is particularly interested in how multiple modes of communication, time, and materiality inform these processes. She has conducted research in the wine, tourism, and creative industries. Her research has appeared in *Strategic Organization, Journal of Management Inquiry,* and *Corporate Communications: An International Journal*, among others.

# ACKNOWLEDGMENTS

We would like to thank Yuqian Qiu for helping us to put together the final book manuscript, Professors Mary Jo Hatch, Cleopatra Veloutsou, Kevin Lane Keller, and Jean-Nöel Kapferer for their valuable endorsements, and all the book co-authors for their excellent contributions to the *Routledge Companion to Corporate Branding*.

# A

# An introduction to the corporate brand management field

# 1
# TOWARDS A PARADIGM SHIFT IN CORPORATE BRANDING

*Oriol Iglesias, Nicholas Ind, and Majken Schultz*

### 1. The emergence of corporate branding

The foundational articles of the corporate branding literature were published in the mid-1990s and early 2000s (e.g., Balmer, 1995; Ind, 1997; Harris & de Chernatony, 2001; Hatch & Schultz, 2001). However, the branding academic field has a much longer history, and this rich heritage has been key to the emergence and later development and consolidation of the corporate branding domain. The first academic works in the area of branding appeared in the early 1900s when academics realized that brands were identifiers that could help build recognition and awareness of the manufacturer behind the product (Merz, 2009). This made researchers interested in understanding the potential impact of branded products vs. non-branded products in the consumer decision-making process (e.g., Copeland, 1923). It soon became evident that brands generate perceptions which influence consumer decisions. Consequently, brand image became a key construct (Gardner & Levy, 1955), and much research was developed attempting to understand its impact on the firm's competitive advantage and performance (Welcker, 1949). From this perspective, if managers wanted to build strong brands, they needed to develop relevant functional associations, such as product quality or convenience, that could connect with the utilitarian needs of customers (de Chernatony & McWilliam, 1989). Interestingly, researchers soon realized that in mature markets functional benefits alone couldn't sustain a relevant source of differentiation (Park et al., 1986). It was thus essential for brands to also provide consumers with symbolic benefits (Levy, 1959) such as the expression of identity and status within a community. Overall, in this foundational period, branding was primarily concerned with building product differentiation through consumer perceptions (Aaker, 1996) developed by the brand's communication activities (Di Mingo, 1988) as a way to simplify consumer choices (Jacoby et al., 1977).

During the 1970s and 1980s a group of researchers started to challenge the traditional perspective on branding and highlighted its limitations in the services context (e.g., Shostack, 1977; Knisely, 1979; Parasuraman, 1987). Unlike product brands, consumer evaluations of services brands are heavily influenced by the delivery process, where employees play a key role (Grönroos, 1990; Bitner, 1995; Vargo & Lusch, 2004). In fact, in service environments, employees are recognized by consumers as being part of the product (Knisely, 1979) or even personifying the brand itself (Bateson, 1995). Given that employees are the ones who can make or break the brand in services contexts (Gummesson, 1991), it is essential that they embrace the brand's ideology and beliefs (Parasuraman, 1987). This obviously gives a central role to internal branding, as organizations need to first recruit and induct employees whose personal values align with the brand values and later on train them so that they can effectively deliver the brand promise (Berry, 2000). Building a supportive culture which allows employees to live the brand became a central role for brand managers (Ind, 2007). Thus, the brand construct, which was initially conceptualized as an identifier that could help differentiate a product and build consumer preference, evolved to become a relational asset based on trust (de Chernatony & Dall'Olmo Riley, 1998).

The development of the services branding literature broadened the scope of branding from the product and the consumer to the organization, its employees, and its internal processes. In parallel, it also shifted the focus from individual transactions with customers to the establishment of long-term relationships. Consequently, it can be argued that the development of the services branding literature was instrumental to the emergence of corporate branding (e.g., Balmer, 1995; Ind, 1997; Harris & de Chernatony, 2001; Hatch & Schultz, 2001), which is more strategic and encompasses a much broader scope (Roper & Davies, 2007). While product branding aims to achieve customer satisfaction and services branding works to also build trusting relationships with customers, corporate branding considers the needs and expectations of many other stakeholders (Balmer, 1995; de Chernatony, 2002). According to Balmer and Gray (2003), corporate branding is about establishing an explicit covenant, a bilateral contract, between the organization behind a brand and its diverse set of stakeholders (Otubanjo et al., 2010; Balmer, 2012). Corporate brand stakeholders include founders, managers, employees, customers, investors, journalists, suppliers, and citizens, among others (Morsing & Kristensen, 2001; Davies et al., 2010).

Corporate brands were initially considered to be created, controlled, and managed by the senior management of the organization (Balmer, 2012). According to Aaker (2004), the corporate brand defines the firm that stands behind a certain offering, and it is manifested by a brand promise which encapsulates the organization's heritage, values, culture, people, strategy, and capabilities. Corporate brands build differentiation by developing organizational associations, which should be expressed in terms of functional, emotional, and self-expressive benefits (Aaker, 2004). Corporate brands are thus expressions of an organization's identity (Abratt & Kleyn, 2012). Corporate branding is about aligning the organization's strategic vision, culture, and image (Hatch & Schultz, 2003). Overall, the foundational literature in the field considers that the ultimate objective of corporate branding is to build a certain desired strong reputation by keeping the corporate brand promise (Argenti & Druckenmiller, 2004) and nurturing long-term relationships with the organization's diverse stakeholders (Balmer & Gray, 2003).

## 2. The megatrends that are re-defining corporate branding

While corporate branding as an area of research has developed significantly over the last 25 years, many of its key tenets have been undermined by changes in the business environment. Now, corporate branding is being re-thought and re-defined as a result of these changes and in particular by the impact of three megatrends.

The first megatrend is the massive growth during the last decade of digital technologies, which have progressively become mainstream and now play a central role in the daily lives of citizens and consumers worldwide. Just as an example, 2021 data shows that worldwide there are 5.22 billion unique mobile phone users, equivalent to two thirds of the global population; 4.66 billion internet users (59.5% of the worlds' population); and 4.2 billion active social media users (53.6%) (Datareportal.com, 2021). This massive growth in digital technologies has enabled individuals to develop many more connections with their peers, but also to have more opportunities for direct interaction with their favourite brands (Hanna et al., 2011). These connected consumers (Dolbec & Fischer, 2015), who have built communities of interest beyond limits imposed by proximity (Muniz & O'Guinn, 2001), want to know more about the brands that they like and to share their opinions and experiences. Additionally, some even want to exert influence on the brand's strategy. Consequently, consumers are increasingly willing to collaborate with their favourite brands to develop new products and services together (Ind et al., 2013) or to serve as brand ambassadors by sharing brand-related content through social media (Kumar & Mirchandani, 2012). Overall, digital technologies and social media have shifted the power from brands to consumers and other stakeholders, and have created more opportunities for interaction, collaboration, and co-creation (Iglesias & Bonet, 2012).

The second megatrend is the increasing servitization of business models, which were traditionally focused on manufacturing. This servitization is further transforming the global economy, which had already embraced a very significant services revolution during the 20th century. The United States, for example, shifted from a goods-based economy, where services accounted for just 43% of the GDP in 1950, to almost 77% in 2020.[1] This is a global phenomenon in developed countries, where services already account for three quarters of GDP.[2] Interestingly, emerging economies are also becoming services-based at an even faster pace. China's economy, which had come to be seen as the world's factory, has experienced a meteoric transformation, and services, which only represented 33% of GDP in 1960, now already account for more than half (54.3%). Very similar transformations are also happening in most emergent economies, such as India, Russia, and Brazil, where services now make up for 49.4%, 54%, and 63.3% of their GDP respectively.

This transition towards more service-based economies is currently being re-empowered by the servitization of the business models of many organizations and even of certain industries as a whole. Servitization is 'the transformational process of shifting from a product-centric business model and logic to a service-centric approach' (Kowalkowski et al., 2017, p. 7). Take as an example Rolls-Royce, a brand which for many decades focused on manufacturing and selling engines for planes and that a few years ago decided to servitize its business model. Instead of paying a certain amount of money to buy an engine, Rolls-Royce now offers its customers a TotalCare service package, which allows them to pay by the amount of time an engine is in flight. Additionally, by monitoring data from the engines, Rolls-Royce can also better decide when and how to conduct engine maintenance, thus reducing costs and maximizing the engine's total flying hours.

Business models are becoming servitized because (1) new digital technologies have given rise to multiple digital platforms that allow traditionally product-oriented value propositions to be turned into services (i.e., Netflix) and to maximize the use of a given asset (i.e., AirBnB, Uber, Signify); (2) consumers are realizing that it is cheaper to use a service when it is needed (i.e., car sharing) than to pay to own the asset (i.e., buying and maintaining a car); and (3) more conscientious consumers are recognizing that it is more sustainable to 'use' products than to 'buy and own' them. The challenge for corporate brands is that whenever a product becomes a service, the brand also becomes an experience (Prahalad & Ramaswamy, 2004).

The third megatrend is the exponential growth of ESG investment, which is based on environmental, social, and ethical governance criteria, and that responds to the growing demands from consumers and society for brands to embrace their broader responsibilities beyond profit. Consumers are rapidly becoming more conscious about the pressing challenges that humanity is facing, such as climate change, growing economic inequalities within societies and among countries, the increasing numbers of refugees, and the existence of racial and gender discrimination. Overall, research shows that ethical consumerism (Carrigan & Attalla, 2001; Shaw & Shiu, 2002) is already becoming mainstream rather than a fringe phenomenon (Carrington et al., 2014; Caruana et al., 2016). These conscientious consumers are deeply concerned as to how their consumption choices impact upon the environment and society (Shaw & Shiu,

2002; Caruana et al., 2016). Additionally, due to the hyperconnected and much more transparent environment that new digital technologies have created, consumers are also well-informed and aware of many of the irresponsible or harmful practices of corporate brands. In parallel, employees are also increasingly exerting pressure on their employer brands and demanding that they adopt more responsible and sustainable approaches to business (Smith, 2003).

Investors are echoing all of these pressures, and ESG investment reached a tipping point in 2020 by doubling the prior's year's figures on inflows.[3] However, 77% of the worldwide sustainable funds are still located in Europe while the USA represents an additional 14%,[4] making ESG investment a disrupting phenomenon but still largely limited to the occidental developed countries. Nevertheless, assets in sustainable investment products in Europe are expected to outnumber conventional funds by 2025, representing more than half (57%) of the European fund sector.[5] This exponential growth in ESG investments is already forcing corporate brands to rethink their traditional management models and to embrace more conscientious brand building approaches (Iglesias & Ind, 2020).

All in all, these three interconnected megatrends, the massive growth of digital technologies, the increasing servitization of business models, and the exponential growth in ESG investment are re-defining corporate branding. This is transforming the corporate branding field, heightening the relevance of corporate brand experience and promoting more co-creative and conscientious approaches to corporate brand building.

## 3. Re-defining corporate branding

Figure 1.1 visually summarizes the three megatrends that are driving a paradigm shift in corporate branding, together with the three key changes that are re-defining the corporate branding field.

### 3.1 Corporate branding as a co-creative process

The traditional literature sees corporate branding as an inside-out and top-down managerial process (e.g., Keller, 1993; Aaker, 1996; de Chernatony, 1996). From this perspective, corporate brands are managerial creations and the role of brand managers should be that of custodians of

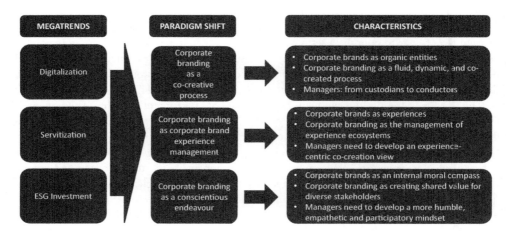

*Figure 1.1* Towards a paradigm shift in corporate branding

the purity of the corporate brand (Balmer, 1995; Kapferer, 2012). This is evident, for instance, in the early definitions of corporate brand identity, the main element of a corporate brand. Corporate brand identity is what makes a corporate brand unique, when compared to its competitors, and relevant to its stakeholders (Kapferer, 2012). The traditional literature tends to see corporate brand identity as how internal stakeholders 'perceive their company and how they aim to present it to the outside world' (Koporcic & Halinen, 2018). This of course emphasizes how managers unilaterally determine the corporate brand strategy and control the corporate brand building process (Iglesias et al., 2020a). Consequently, customers and other stakeholders are considered to be a rather passive audience (Balmer, 1995), while managers are concerned with building and maintaining a strong, clear, and consistent identity that can serve as a stable reference for consumers and other stakeholders over time (Aaker, 1996; Kapferer, 2012; da Silveira et al., 2013).

This traditional perspective of corporate branding has been challenged by the many new emerging digital technologies, including the internet and social media, which have developed a hyperconnected environment where customers and other stakeholders have many more opportunities for interaction among themselves and with corporate brands (Gyrd-Jones et al., 2013; Ramaswamy & Ozcan, 2016). In this hyperconnected context, the corporate brand-building process has moved beyond the scope of the organization (Iglesias & Bonet, 2012), making the idea of managerial control an illusion (Wider et al., 2018). Instead, corporate brands are socially constructed together with many stakeholders in a dynamic and ongoing process (Vallaster & von Wallpach, 2013; von Wallpach et al., 2017; Koporcic & Halinen, 2018). Here process is understood as 'a sequence of events or activities that describes how things change over time, or that represents an underlying pattern of cognitive transitions by an entity in dealing with an issue' (Van de Ven, 1992, p. 170). Building on this definition, corporate brands are developed through multiple interactions among very diverse stakeholders who jointly reinterpret, discuss, and negotiate corporate brand meanings (von Wallpach et al., 2017). This suggests that corporate brands are unstable and fluid (Csaba & Bengtsson, 2006) because brand meanings are 'always in circulation and flux' (Batey, 2008, p. 104). Accordingly, Iglesias et al. (2013) claim that corporate brands are organic entities, built in complex ecosystems, which continuously evolve through symbiotic relationships between the organization and its stakeholders (Ind, 2009), often in directions not intended by the corporate brand's managers (Iglesias et al., 2013). This development has also been discussed as the 'enterprise brand' embedded in an ecosystem of multiple, intertwined stakeholders (Hatch & Schultz, 2008). We summarize these developments in a perspective on corporate branding as a co-creative process.

As a consequence of these developments, the approach to corporate branding has to change: corporate brands need to inspire and guide, while at the same time open up and embrace stakeholders' inputs. Rather than the rigid corporate brand covenant (Balmer & Gray, 2003) or the classical corporate brand identity frameworks (Keller, 1993, Aaker, 1996; de Chernatony, 1996; Balmer & Soenen, 1999), there is a need for more flexible and fluid corporate brand-building models. Some scholars suggest that corporate brands need a corporate brand purpose (Gyrd-Jones, 2012; Iglesias & Ind, 2020), which should express the *raison d'être* of the brand and how it aims to create shared value for its diverse stakeholders. In essence, a corporate brand purpose should provide clarity and serve as an internal compass for managers to take better and more agile strategic decisions, while being sufficiently dynamic to inspire the corporate brand's stakeholders and engage them in further elucidating a shared evolved understanding of the corporate brand (Iglesias et al., 2020a).

This orientation is not without tension. Managers' goals are often to preserve the core essence of the corporate brand while at the same time to listen to stakeholders' needs and expectations and adapt accordingly (Kristal et al., 2020; Iglesias et al., 2020a). On one side, managers want to promote a more monolithic understanding of the corporate brand, while on the other, stakeholders create a rich and complex bundle of polysemic meanings (Michel, 2017). For example, in a study of a Nike online community, Kornum et al. (2017) showed that there is a synergic relationship between Nike and the community, while at the same time there is also a tension. The community accepts and supports Nike's identity, but in parallel also challenges it and develops its own set of values and practices. This implies that strong (monolithic) corporate brands are only temporary stabilizations in an ongoing process of change (Törmälä & Gyrd-Jones, 2017).

This perspective demands a rethink as to the role of managers, who should no longer see themselves as custodians of the corporate brand, in charge of rigidly preserving its essence and integrity (Iglesias et al., 2020a). Instead, they should see themselves as 'conductors' in charge of reconciling the desires and expectations of a diverse set of stakeholders (Michel, 2017). This demands a polyphonic perspective on corporate brands and corporate brand building, where managers need to ensure that they are capable of reinforcing and celebrating the corporate brand history and heritage (Balmer & Burghausen, 2015; Iglesias et al., 2020b) while allowing change and embracing the influence from the corporate brand's ecosystem of stakeholders. This also requires that organizations open up, see their stakeholders as strategic partners (Ind et al., 2017), and orchestrate a collaborative innovation network (Libert et al., 2015), while at the same time reinforcing and nurturing their own singular corporate culture (Ind & Schmidt, 2020). However, this will only be possible if managers adopt a new leadership mindset which is much more participatory and grounded in humility and empathy (Iglesias et al., 2013). Additionally, managers will need to promote much higher levels of organizational self-disclosure and transparency, while assuming higher risk (Hatch & Schultz, 2010).

Overall, there is a paradigm shift in the corporate branding academic domain, which acknowledges that corporate branding is a co-creative process. However, there is still the need to advance further our understanding of this co-creative perspective in corporate branding. We suggest that future research focus on the following four areas. First, more research is needed which truly adopts a multi-stakeholder perspective on corporate branding (von Wallpach et al., 2017). Most of the existing works either focus on internal stakeholders (e.g., Törmälä & Gyrd-Jones, 2017) or on external ones (e.g., Kornum et al., 2017), and only a few have attempted to provide a comprehensive multi-stakeholder perspective that includes both internal and external stakeholders along with the ecosystem in which stakeholders are embedded (Black & Veloutsou, 2017; von Wallpach et al., 2017; Essamri et al., 2019; Iglesias et al., 2020a). Second, more research should adopt a performative approach to corporate branding, where the key is to understand which stakeholder performances co-create the corporate brand. This is an approach derived from Goffman (1959, 1967), which has only been used in a few studies (da Silveira et al., 2013; Törmälä & Gyrd-Jones, 2017; von Wallpach et al., 2017; Iglesias et al., 2020a). Third, even if recent studies claim that companies need to define a corporate brand purpose (Gyrd-Jones, 2012; Iglesias & Ind, 2020), and many companies are already defining and embracing one, there is still a very significant lack of research regarding how corporate brands should define their purpose, what the potential benefits of doing so are, and how to encourage the organization to live it (Golob et al., 2020). Finally, most of the research on corporate branding from a co-creative perspective has been conducted in the business-to-consumer (B2C) domain. However, interactions and networks are the very essence of business-to-business (B2B) brands (Webster & Keller, 2004). Nevertheless, only a few studies have researched corporate brand co-creation processes in B2B environments (Mäläskä et al., 2011; Törmälä & Gyrd-Jones, 2017; Koporcic & Halinen, 2018; Iglesias et al., 2020a; Kristal et al., 2020).

## 3.2 Corporate branding as corporate brand experience management

Digital technologies have created a hyperconnected environment, which has transformed the business world, by decentring and democratizing the value creation process away from the goods and services provided by brands and the idea of traditional value chains toward individual experiences within ecosystems (Prahalad & Ramaswamy, 2004; Ramaswamy & Ozcan, 2018). If the industrial era entailed a brand logic which focused on the production of goods and services, the current stakeholder-focus brand era (Merz et al., 2009), where companies mostly compete in service-based economies with extremely high degrees of interconnectivity among different business partners, demands a shift towards a service-dominant logic (SDL) (Vargo & Lusch, 2004). Here the focus is on the (service) process instead of on the outcome (products-services). The key implication of this dynamic process perspective (Merz et al., 2009) is that the brand becomes the experience (Prahalad & Ramaswamy, 2004). Consequently, corporate branding should primarily be concerned with the ways in which it can construct, together with individuals and other organizations, a valuable, differentiated, and personalized/individualized corporate brand experience.

Brand experiences combine affective and intellectual dimensions (Brakus et al., 2009), such as the sensations, feelings, cognitions, and behavioural responses (Schmitt, 1999) that are evoked by many different stimuli that emerge when individuals directly, or indirectly, interact with a certain brand (Brakus et al., 2009). Direct interactions take place when stakeholders purchase, use, or experience the corporate brand offer. In parallel, indirect interactions occur when stakeholders are exposed to the corporate brand's communications and advertising, word-of-mouth recommendations, online reviews, and news in the media (Brakus et al., 2009). Overall, the corporate brand experience can be conceived of as a takeaway impression (Carbone & Haeckel, 1994) that is formed in the mind of customers and other stakeholders as a result of the many different interactions with the corporate brand (Klaus & Maklan, 2007).

The early conceptualization of the brand experience construct by Brakus et al. (2009) has become extremely influential, and most of the theoretical and empirical papers in the area rely on it without providing any critical perspective. However, Andreini et al. (2018) criticize this positivistic approach, which most academic researchers follow, and highlight that this traditional conceptualization overestimates the ability and power of managers to first design and deploy brand stimuli capable of generating a specific brand experience and then to link the designed positive experience to certain desirable outcomes. Instead, it can be argued that experiences occur when actors interact in a given context, activate resources, and initiate a process of value co-creation (Chandler & Vargo, 2011) that is influenced but not exclusively determined by the actions of managers. From this perspective, the corporate brand experience is socially constructed. Corporate brand experiences are co-created through a network of (not always structured) interactions among producers, customers, and other marketplace actors (Andreini et al., 2018). This perspective challenges the power of managers and undermines their ability to control the brand-building process. Instead, experiences are built through interactive and collaborative processes, where brands are operant resources (Merz et al., 2009) which contribute to the value co-creation process that always includes the beneficiary (i.e., the customer) (Vargo & Lusch, 2016).

While SDL has been fruitful in helping to evolve the branding domain, Prahalad and Ramaswamy (2004) claim that Vargo and Lusch haven't gone far enough and emphasize the need to develop a truly experience-centric co-creation view. This is about realizing that value co-creation can only happen when customers experience the service at hand. From this perspective, value is always value-in-use (Grönroos & Voima, 2013). This also means that the brand needs to be understood as a dynamic resource where value is co-created through contextual experience (Prahalad & Ramaswamy, 2004). Ramaswamy and Ozcan (2016) note that there needs to be an explicit recognition of the agency of individual human beings as experiencers alongside the creation of platforms that enable interactions. Additionally, this perspective requires challenging the intrinsic meaning of the brand construct and realizing that the brand is in fact the co-created experience. Finally, this implies conceiving the market as a forum where brands need to compete on experiences by designing the appropriate experience network/ecosystem (Prahalad & Ramaswamy, 2004). This entails much more than stressing the user experience of goods and services. Instead, this is about understanding the relevance of a 'broader emergent *lived-experience* space' in which individuals and smart, connected offerings connect in creating value (Ramaswamy & Ind, 2020). The implication of this new perspective is counter-intuitive in that while corporate brands increasingly rely on digital technology in designing experiences, the decentring of value creation makes brand experience more human-centric than before. Thus corporate branding has shifted from a chain of activities that flow out from the organization to a set of connected brand experiences that exist within an assemblage of relationships (Ind & Bjerke, 2007).

However, much more research is needed which allows for a better understanding of how brands need to be managed within these experience ecosystems, where there has been an acceleration in the shift in value creation towards individuals (Ramaswamy, 2020). Additionally, a second very relevant area for future research is that of the impact of the emergent digital technologies on the corporate brand experience. In fact, some of these technologies, such as artificial intelligence or virtual reality, are already having a disruptive impact and will progressively gain more relevance when designing and deploying brand experiences. Take for instance the Dalí Museum in Spain, where visitors can immerse themselves in the world of the surrealist master by using virtual reality. This technology enables visitors to become an active character in Dali's paintings, 'venturing into the towers, peering from them to distant lands and discovering surprises around every corner.'[6] More research should be conducted in this area because, as noted by Ramaswamy and Ozcan (2021), we are entering into the 'interactive live experience era,' which is powered by the unprecedented opportunities for interaction and personalization that new digital technologies offer.

### 3.3 Corporate branding as a conscientious endeavour

Conscientious and ethical consumption is rapidly becoming a mainstream phenomenon in developed societies (Caruana et al., 2016). In parallel, digital technologies are creating a much more connected and transparent world, where customers and other stakeholders can rapidly know about any corporate brand's harmful or unethical practices. Additionally, the burgeoning of ESG investment is reinforcing this more demanding context for corporate brands and putting significant pressure on all organizations to embrace their broader responsibilities beyond profit. Finally, the COVID-19 pandemic has further emphasized that corporate brands need to give an adequate response to the challenges that humanity faces. Corporate brands are a key agent within the complex network of collaborations which needs to be articulated to solve complex and urgent problems in an efficient and timely manner.

Many corporate brands have long embraced corporate social responsibility (CSR) as a tool which has allowed them to tackle their broader responsibilities (Golob & Podnar, 2019). However, CSR has been heavily criticized because of three significant shortcomings. First, empirical research shows that most corporate brands which have embraced CSR still consider their shareholders as the key stakeholder group to serve (Jurgens et al., 2010). This idea of shareholder primacy, that Milton Friedman proselytized (1970), and which has long been influential, has been challenged by institutions (the Business Roundtable, World Economic Forum) and by researchers who have argued for a more balanced stakeholder perspective (Freeman et al., 2007; Smith & Rönnegard, 2016) capable of encouraging long-term strategic thinking (Ind & Ryder, 2011).

Second, CSR is still too often disconnected from the core of the business strategy. As Golob and Podnar (2019) argue, only a minority of corporate brands place CSR at the core of the corporate brand strategy and positioning and consider it to be a key dimension of the corporate brand identity (Kitchin, 2003; van Rekom et al., 2013). This means that CSR tends to be tangential to the business, instead of embedded into its core (Iglesias & Ind, 2020). The reality is that many corporate brands still do not relate their CSR activities to the corporate brand strategy, or they simply view it as a supplement to the brand positioning (Golob & Podnar, 2019). This disconnection between CSR and the corporate strategy has also prevented corporate brands from developing measures that can help them to understand the value that their CSR activities provide for their different stakeholders (Knox & Maklan, 2004). Nevertheless, if corporate brands want to serve their stakeholders strategically, they should rethink how to measure value beyond traditional financial measures and instead develop a holistic and integrated system of financial and non-financial indicators which could measure how the firm's corporate strategy evolves, together with its resulting performance (Harrison & Wicks, 2013).

Third, CSR has progressively lost legitimacy (Joyner & Payne, 2002; Pope & Wæraas, 2016). The key issue is that too many organizations have embraced CSR as a mechanism to reduce and manage potential risks (Walsh & Beatty, 2007), with the primary goal to reburnish their corporate reputations (Maxfield, 2008). This non-essential interest in CSR, which is merely a passive reaction to external pressures, has of course led to stakeholders perceiving CSR as a non-authentic endeavour (Mazutis & Slawinski, 2015).

Overall, the CSR limitations, together with increasing pressures from stakeholders (including consumers, employees, NGOs, and investors, among others), demand going beyond CSR. This is the rationale for the need for conscientious corporate brands (Ind & Ryder, 2011; Ind & Horlings, 2016; Iglesias & Ind, 2016).

The first key trait of conscientious corporate brands is that they define, promote, and live a transformative corporate brand purpose, which aims at creating shared value beyond profit (Iglesias & Ind, 2020). This purpose should be grounded in the corporate brand's heritage and history and in the organization's distinctive capabilities. The corporate brand purpose serves as a moral compass for strategic decision-making and should not only drive all the company's strategic decisions but also its operations and relationships with its diverse stakeholders (Rindell et al., 2011). Take for instance, Patagonia – the American outdoors sports clothing company founded by Yvon Chouinard. Yvon was a mountain climber who realized that the pitons he was using to climb were destroying the mountain surfaces when hammering them. This is why he instead adopted aluminium chocks that didn't need to be hammered and thus were much more respectful to the environment. This commitment to our home planet has been driving Patagonia's business during the last 45 years. Patagonia's purpose, 'Build the best product, cause no unnecessary harm, use business to inspire and implement solutions to the environmental crisis,' encapsulated very well the underlying philosophy of the company and served as a moral compass for strategic decision-making, even when doing the right thing could have very significant costs. This year Patagonia has decided to modify its purpose, which now reads 'Patagonia is in business to save our home planet.' The new more direct and clear purpose underscores a very important sense of urgency, highlighting that we all need to act now and fight against the climate crisis.

The second characteristic of conscientious corporate brands is that they adopt and promote a balanced stakeholder perspective, which ensures that they consider the needs and expectations of their customers, shareholders, employees, partners, and society. Additionally, they also consider the earth as another key stakeholder that they need to serve and preserve (Iglesias & Ind, 2020). Danone, the French dairy company, has been one of the pioneer corporate brands to promote this balanced, multi-stakeholder approach to business. In fact, Danone became the first listed company in France to adopt the 'Entreprise à Mission' model, which represents a commitment to run a business by developing an organization with a transformative purpose and a balanced stakeholder perspective. In the words of Emmanuel Faber, the former Danone CEO who led this transition towards a more conscientious approach to business, we are on the threshold of a time when what we mean by 'in the ordinary course of business' will change forever. This is an extraordinary moment . . . as employees, consumers, customers, partners, governments and shareholders now see the critical importance of a balanced multi-stakeholder approach to value creation and sharing.

However, Emmanuel Faber was recently dismissed by the board, because of growing concerns from certain shareholders who were expecting a better short-term financial performance. This underscores that there is a powerful underlying tension between purpose and profit and that companies and managers willing to embrace a transformative purpose and a balanced stakeholder perspective need to find a way to deliver profits while also bringing the purpose alive. Nevertheless, the good news is that empirical research shows that conscientious corporate brands which embrace a balanced stakeholder perspective can perform financially as well as (Edmans, 2020) or even better than other brands. According to Unilever (which has developed a value creation model which considers their consumers and customers, their internal people, society, the planet, and their shareholders), the brands within their portfolio that have already embraced a transformative purpose and a balanced stakeholder perspective are outperforming the average of their portfolio both in terms of growth and profitability.

A third key trait of conscientious corporate brands is that they are not only committed to listening to the needs, concerns, and expectations of their diverse stakeholders. Conscientious corporate brands also engage their stakeholders with the co-creation of the organization's strategic priorities and work with them to find novel and innovative solutions to deliver on their purpose and build shared value. This is extremely important as, unfortunately, there is still too often a 'disconnection of many salient stakeholders from company decisions on CSR' (Mason & Simmons, 2014, p. 77). To overcome this, Danone launched its 'One person, One voice' initiative, which engaged Danone's 100,000 employees worldwide to co-create the company's 2030 strategic goals. Danone also regularly involves employees, customers, and some other external stakeholders in the co-creation of their social, environmental, and governance strategies. This of course implies seeing stakeholders as key strategic partners (Ind et al., 2017) with whom to develop long-term collaborative relationships based on mutual trust. This is about considering stakeholders as value co-creators, 'rather than as entities to be merely managed by the enterprise' (Ramaswamy & Ozcan, 2014, p. 249). Overall, this also demands more open and participative corporate cultures (Kazadi et al., 2015; Ind et al., 2013) and executives that embrace transformative, participatory, and empathetic leadership styles (Iglesias & Ind, 2020).

Conscientious corporate brands are a growing managerial reality but still an emerging academic field of study, which demands much more theoretical and empirical research. First, there is still a dearth of research regarding how corporate brands should define and embrace a transformative purpose (Golob et al., 2020). Second, future research should study how corporate brands can promote a balanced multi-stakeholder perspective and what the role of the different stakeholders can be in promoting conscientious corporate brands. Finally, more research is needed in order to better understand which governance models, reward systems, and leadership styles can better allow corporate brands to open up and adopt more co-creative and conscientious approaches to business.

## 4. An introduction to the book sections and chapters

### 4.1 Section A: an introduction to the corporate brand management field

This first section of the book introduces the corporate brand management field, its evolution, its key characteristics, and the main changes that are driving a paradigm shift.

In Chapter 2, Russell Abratt and Michela Mingione demarcate the corporate branding academic field. Abratt and Mingione first define corporate branding as the process aimed at building a certain image and reputation by developing long-term relationships with diverse stakeholders. They also present the three constructs that are at the core of corporate branding: brand identity, brand values, and brand positioning. Abratt and Mingione argue that these three constructs are interrelated. Brand identity defines 'who we are' as an organization and 'what makes us unique' and thus should influence the organization's core values, while brand positioning will leverage on the organization's distinct capabilities by considering its unique identity and core values. Abratt and Mingione also discuss what the key characteristics of corporate brands are and their potential outcomes. Here, it is interesting to note the key role that they assign to corporate brand heritage as it legitimates future strategy. Finally, they argue that there is a trend towards more co-creative and conscientious approaches to corporate branding.

In Chapter 3, Hans Mühlbacher challenges the traditional sender-oriented managerial corporate branding paradigm. Instead, building on the trends already introduced by Abratt and Mingione, he proposes that corporate brands are co-created by a multiplicity of stakeholders. This is an ongoing process of interrelated exchanges where stakeholders shape brand meaning through collaborative co-creation, but also through co-destructive interventions. The challenge for managers is to accept that they cannot control the corporate brand-building process. Mühlbacher argues that managers need to act as conductors of this co-creative process and establish the basis for a consistent pattern of organizational behaviour. Here, internal branding should of course play a key role. Mühlbacher finalizes the chapter by suggesting that future research should adopt a historical analyses perspective in order to better grasp how the co-creative process takes place.

In Chapter 4, Mats Urde presents his perspective on corporate brands and corporate branding, putting a special focus on how the corporate brand identity influences the corporate brand-building process. Urde claims that the Identity Matrix is a key tool that managers should use to position the corporate brand in the marketplace and to communicate its mission and values to employees, customers, and other stakeholders. According to the Identity Matrix, the key internal elements that establish the foundation of corporate brand identity are the organization's mission and vision, its culture, and its unique capabilities. From an external perspective, the key elements to be managed are the value proposition, outside relationships, and positioning. Finally, there are some elements that bridge internal and external aspects, such as the organization's personality, its distinctive ways of communicating, and its brand core. Urde also discusses how to manage the tension between continuity and change by reviewing, and if necessary updating, the brand's logos-ethos-pathos appeals. Interestingly, he also suggests that corporate brand-building processes are becoming more collaborative and co-creative.

In Chapter 5, Joachim Kernstock and Shaun Powell provide a commentary on the evolution of corporate brand management and the perspectives presented in this section.

## 4.2 Section B: building brands together: co-creating corporate brands with multiple stakeholders

This second section of the book discusses how corporate branding is evolving towards a co-creative perspective, which recognizes that corporate brands are organic and fluid entities, co-created by multiple stakeholders in an ongoing process.

Venkat Ramaswamy discusses in Chapter 6 how digital technologies have favoured a dual de-centring and democratization of corporate brands, within the broader umbrella of co-creative brand-management systems. Ramaswamy argues that this demands that managers develop a human and experience-centric perspective, instead of the traditional product-centric one, because the life journeys of all experiencers in the value co-creation system matter. A key implication of this perspective is that the experience becomes the brand. Accordingly, Ramaswamy claims that corporate brands should compete on experiences and that corporate branding from a co-creative paradigm implies supporting the co-creative configuration of experience ecosystems and the relational engagement with multiple stakeholders.

In Chapter 7, Sylvia von Wallpach and Andrea Hemetsberger show how even if the current branding literature is well equipped with co-creative conceptualizations of corporate branding, more complex assemblage perspectives are needed. First, because non-human actors, such as historical buildings, which are traditionally considered as resources without a voice, should also be recognized as key actors in the brand-building process. Second, because when the focus is on actors and network dynamics, then the role of actions in the corporate brand-building process becomes much more prominent. Accordingly, von Wallpach and Hemetsberger suggest an action net perspective to the study of corporate branding. This novel perspective adopted by von Wallpach and Hemetsberger allows them to show how corporate brands are built and evolve in dynamic action nets. Additionally, von Wallpach and Hemetsberger's empirical results emphasize how a continuous flow of brand actions contributes to spanning the corporate brand action net across organizational boundaries, time, space, and spheres. Consequently, heterogeneity and instability foster dynamic brand-identity construction.

Corporate brand identity is the very essence of a corporate brand. In Chapter 8 Catherine da Silveira and Cláudia Simões add to the current debate on the nature and features of corporate brand identity by reconciling the traditional perspective with the co-creative perspective that has gained increasing relevance. Da Silveira and Simões argue that corporate brand identity dimensions become more or less salient over time according to the context and to the stakeholders' self-identity enactments and focus. Additionally, they also claim that the more traditional internal corporate brand-building orientation is not antagonistic to the multi-stakeholder perspective. Instead, the two are complementary because managers' behaviours trigger stakeholders' performativity. Overall, da Silveira and Simões show how corporate brand identity can be both enduring and dynamic by bringing a corporate brand-identity pattern that combines preservation and adaptation.

In the last chapter (9) of this second section of the book, Michela Mingione and Russell Abratt discuss the philosophical foundations of corporate brand alignment theory, paying special attention to the ontological and epistemological underpinnings of two different competing paradigms, the functionalist and interpretivist. According to Mingione and Abratt, the functionalist paradigm views corporate brands as strong assets owned and uniformly managed by the organization. Hence, under the functionalist paradigm, corporate brand alignment is seen as a tool to verify the fit between internal and external stakeholders' perceptions of the corporate brand. Of course, the role of managers is to minimize any potential gap. The interpretivist paradigm takes a different perspective and views corporate brands as a set of symbols which are socially constructed and continuously reinterpreted by multiple stakeholders. Given this, Mingione and Abratt suggest that under the interpretivist paradigm, corporate brand alignment is a process calling for coherent relationships between internal and external constituents to strategically manage the corporate brand. To bridge the boundaries between both paradigms, Mingione and Abratt take a meta-paradigm perspective that allows them to suggest that corporate brand alignment can be understood as a strategic enabler to build a more coherent and elucidated corporate brand. This perspective underscores the key relevance of corporate brand alignment for corporate brands to co-create value with its diverse stakeholders.

In his commentary in Chapter 10, Francisco Guzmán brings together the themes developed by the different writers in this section and outlines the growing orientation towards a co-creative perspective.

## 4.3 Section C: building strong corporate brands: towards valuable and sustainable experiences

The chapters in this section focus on the central role of experience in corporate brand building, from a managerial planning model to the role of artificial intelligence to the connectedness of innovation and sustainability to the importance of a holistic approach to corporate service branding.

In Chapter 11, Carsten Baumgarth guides the reader through the workings of a corporate brand management model called B★Canvas 2.0. This is a comprehensive model that has been created to enable brand managers of both established businesses and start-ups to enhance brand equity. Moving beyond a marketing communications focus, the model incorporates a broad range of elements. Using the example of the German SME, Werkhaus, Baumgarth shows how three key elements, which he labels 'Brand Foundations, Brand Touchpoints, and Brand Performance,' come together to deliver equity for the public and customers. This view of equity then encompasses what Baumgarth calls 'Final Performance,' which includes organizational purpose and economic and social impacts.

Chapter 12 represents a change of emphasis, as it investigates an under-explored aspect of corporate brand management: the increasingly powerful role that artificial intelligence (AI) plays in brand building and the delivery of the brand experience. Frederico Mangiò, Giuseppe Pedeliento, and Daniela Andreini's chapter charts the positives and negatives of AI, from the opportunities it creates to enhance experiences to the way it can treat stakeholders as passive recipients rather than as active co-creators. The authors' argument is that AI is evolving rapidly and can make significant contributions to corporate brand experience, but to do so it must have a strong human-centric focus rather than allowing the technology itself to dominate.

From the potential of AI, in Chapter 13 we move to a focus on the impact of brand innovations on stakeholders. Drawing on their work in creating a stakeholder-led Innovation Index, Seidali Kurtmollaiev, Line Lervik-Olsen, and Tor W. Andreassen show the power of brands that combine innovation and sustainability either by transferring knowledge from one sphere to the other or by integrating social and economic innovation and commercial innovation. Their recommendation then is not to see these different types of innovation as distinct, but rather to recognize the potential to unify innovation so that it delivers value by working together with stakeholders through all the stages of the innovation process.

In Chapter 14, Stefan Markovic, Yuqian Qiu, Cristina Sancha, and Nikolina Koporcic provide an analysis of an under-researched area – sustainability strategies in corporate service brands. They demonstrate the fragmented nature of most studies and the lack of a holistic approach to the economic, environmental, and social dimensions of corporate brands that can be found in the 'Triple Bottom Line of People, Planet, and Profit.' In spite of the research gap, Markovic et al. note that sustainability in corporate services branding can provide such benefits as positive stakeholder perceptions, service excellence and service innovation, brand image and reputation, customer trust and satisfaction, customer purchase behaviour, and reduced corporate hypocrisy.

In Chapter 15, Nicholas Ind summarises the ways the different writers in the section interpret brand building and the emphasis some of them give to sustainability.

## 4.4 Section D: polysemic corporate brand narratives

In the first chapter of this section (16), Paul A. Argenti describes how the emergence of the internet and digital technologies have created a hyperconnected world which has completely transformed corporate brands' competitive environment and has forced them to adapt their competitive strategy. All in all, managers have lost control over the corporate brand-building process and have learnt that it is not possible to develop monolithic communication messages.

Consequently, corporate brand communications have adapted, and messages are now built in collaboration with key constituencies, including customers, employees, investors, and communities. According to Argenti, this co-creative corporate brand-building process implies that companies must accept that their corporate brands are polysemous, while ensuring alignment on foundational issues, such as core values. This perspective suggests that companies need to ask how they will engage with constituencies and co-create the corporate brand narrative together with them. However, at the same time, Argenti emphasizes that even if consistency takes on new meaning, it is still key, and a strong corporate culture is the driver to achieve it.

In Chapter 17, Line Schmeltz and Anna Karina Kjeldsen draw on the literature from critical theory and organization studies on polyphony (the idea of multi-voices) to challenge traditional views of the one corporate brand voice. Instead, they suggest that the diversity of voices within organizations and the multiplication of the points of contact between an organization and its diverse stakeholders inevitably leads to a loss of unity. Does this diminish the corporate brand or enrich it? Using the example of the National Gallery of Denmark/Statens Museum for Kunst (SMK), they show how an organization can use co-creative methods to design a brand, but also the complexity that comes with trying to implement it when the voices inside an organization come from very different perspectives. Whether the result is harmony or cacophony is determined by the ability of managers to orchestrate multiple and diverse voices.

With echoes of Schmeltz and Kjeldsen's work, in Chapter 18 Alessandra Zamparini, Luca M. Visconti, and Francesco Lurati explore the multiple meanings of signs inherent in the idea of polysemy within another cultural entity: the Locarno Film Festival. Again there is the challenge of diversity, which in part represents the appeal of the Festival, but there is also the challenge of trying to manage a corporate brand. By combining an ethnographic case study with semi-structured interviews with festival managers, employees, and festival goers, they show 'the extreme polysemic richness' of the brand alongside the competing interests of the stakeholders. The authors both identify the three main axes that corporate brand managers can use to manage brand polysemy and the decision areas that are critical in managing the resulting tensions.

In Chapter 19, Raouf Rather, Linda Hollebeek, Dale Smith, Jana Kukk and Mojtaba Ghasemi. emphasize how even if the emergent technologies such as social media and online brand communities have revolutionized consumer brand engagement, there is still the need to better understand the consumer brand-engagement dynamics in certain contexts. This is for instance the case of destination brands, which is the context of their study, that aims at exploring the relationships between visitors' destination brand engagement and its key antecedents and outcomes. Their findings show that the higher the level of involvement that the visitors of a destination have with the destination brand-related social media content, the higher their destination brand engagement will be. Additionally, the authors also find that there is a positive impact of visitors' destination brand engagement on brand co-creation. These findings are very relevant to destination branding organizations as they should help them to improve their destination brand performance.

In Chapter 20, Joep Cornelissen charts the transition from a perspective rooted in the idea of a corporate brand as a single voice to one that is multi-voiced.

## 4.5 Section E: the temporality of corporate branding: balancing the past and future

In Chapter 21, Mario Burghausen applies a co-creation perspective to the field of corporate heritage branding scholarship and offers a framework for how scholars may analyse the processes of co-creating for corporate heritage brands. The chapter argues how multiple stakeholders actively shape the temporal relations between past, present, and future that are constitutive of corporate heritage brands. The chapter outlines key co-creation processes characteristic of corporate heritage brands: valorizing, (re)interpreting, manifesting, appropriating, and augmenting the past in the present and for the future as heritage. These processes are linked to temporal co-creation as an additional generic form of corporate brand co-creation stressing the importance of co-creating the temporality of corporate branding in addition to the co-creation of value, meaning, identity, and experience. The chapter concludes with a conceptual framework that shows the links between these different processes and dimensions of co-creation as they apply to corporate heritage brands.

While the chapter by Burghausen addresses the importance of heritage to corporate brands, Chapter 22 by Fabien Pecot extends the discussion of brand heritage by comparing insights from both product and corporate branding research. Although brand heritage exists at the corporate level, in many organizations product brands often have a heritage of their own. The chapter offers a review of brand heritage at the product and at the corporate brand levels, showing that both streams of research are interested in the broader question of permanence in brand management. Pecot identifies six areas for their cross-fertilization. These can lead to the development of new methods in the quantification of corporate brand heritage principles and a more focused approach to studies of the co-creation processes at play in product brand heritage research. In conclusion, the chapter calls for more collaborations between product brand and corporate brand scholars to advance brand management research.

In contrast to a focus on multiple stakeholders in the first two chapters of the section, Chapter 23 by Michael Beverland and Pinar Cankurtaran focuses on the internal aspects of corporate branding. Research suggests that consumers display greater brand engagement when they can place themselves in the brand's narrative, that is, experience the brand's claims as authentic. This chapter argues that the same holds for employees, and it extends work on authenticity into internal branding. The authors explore the internal branding challenges in relation to three forms of authenticity: consistency, conformity, and connection. The chapter particularly contributes to authenticity as connection and discusses how it poses challenges for placeless global brands. Together these three forms of authenticity identify the need for programmes that enable employees to operate as cultural insiders among stakeholders and build connections between brand narratives and the collective historical identity of the organization. The chapter concludes with a discussion of managerial implications and issues for future research.

The importance of connection of brands is further elaborated in Chapter 24 by Mihalis Kavaratzis' discussion of how elements from the past are used in the branding of places. Acknowledging that both places and corporations often rely on their pasts in their branding strategies, the chapter shows how this prompts a number of questions. What are the reasons that make the past an appealing source of resources and inspiration for branding? What elements of the past are appropriate for use, and who makes that choice? What is the process that turns elements of the past into a heritage that is both relevant in the present and can be used to craft a strategy that relates to the future? The chapter explicates the various ways in which heritage is used within place branding. The process of turning history into heritage and heritage into strategy is scrutinized in order to reach a better understanding of the decisions involved as well as the tensions caused. The chapter draws parallels between corporate branding and place branding and reflects on possible mutual lessons.

In Chapter 25, Majken Schultz provides a commentary on the section authors' views on temporality, history, and heritage.

## 4.6 Section F: branding inside-out: corporate culture and internal branding

Over the last 20 years, internal branding as an area of practice and research within corporate brand management has expanded rapidly. It has been suggested that the field is highly fragmented, but as Rico Piehler points out in Chapter 26, this is hardly surprising given the variety of conceptual bases used in its exploration. Internal branding not only draws on marketing but also management, psychology, sociology, and organizational behaviour. In a comprehensive overview of the field – with the exception of the developing role of co-creation, which Piehler largely leaves to Schmidt and Steenkamp to cover in the next chapter – he covers the way internal branding has become woven into the fabric of corporate brand management. His wide-ranging analysis enables him to demonstrate the breadth and depth of the field and to conclude with a new and richer definition of internal branding.

At the beginning of Chapter 27, Holger J. Schmidt and Pieter Steenkamp note that while the literature on internal branding has expanded significantly, little attention has been paid to the role of employees in co-creating brands. The chapter tries to fill this gap by offering a co-creative view on internal branding. In addition to discussing relevant research issues, Schmidt and Steenkamp review some 31 articles which identify the central role that employees play as the co-creators of brand meaning. However, they not only pinpoint the nature of a co-creative approach, but they also raise valuable questions around how managers can understand the concept of brand-oriented behaviour, how consistency can be developed in a world where brand meaning is multidirectional, and finally how corporate brands can reconcile potential conflicts of interest among stakeholders.

In Chapter 28, Saila Saraniemi explores how internal brand communities are becoming a key stakeholder in the corporate brand co-creation process. This is especially relevant in remote working environments, where the physical distance of employees creates a unique context to building a brand community. The empirical study by Saraniemi identifies the set of dynamic interactions that positively influence the development of an internal brand community and those ones that inhibit it. Saraniemi also identifies six key roles that any internal brand community can play in the corporate brand co-creation process: an enactor of corporate brand values, a negotiator of corporate brand meanings, a contributor to corporate brand design, a communicator of the corporate brand, a creator of corporate brand value, and a maintainer of the corporate brand. Interestingly, this chapter contributes to the still very-scarce literature of corporate brand co-creation in business-to-business contexts.

Chapter 29 by Galina Biedenbach and Thomas Biedenbach explores how conscientious corporate brands can be co-created inside-out through values-driven branding. The chapter provides insights as to the opportunities and challenges related to establishing a conscientious organization and to implementing values-driven branding. The chapter explains how organizations can commit to internal branding with a conscience and build a conscientious corporate brand inside-out. The chapter introduces a novel categorization of corporate brands based on a conscience, which includes (1) a spiritual corporate brand; (2) a hypocritical corporate brand; (3) a toxic corporate brand; and (4) a destructive corporate brand. The chapter provides an illustrative practical case demonstrating how an organization can make a long-term commitment to building continuously its conscientious brand inside-out by engaging, inspiring, and empowering employees.

In Chapter 30, Ceridwyn King charts the evolution of internal branding and the different perspectives that have developed.

## Notes

1 https://data.worldbank.org/indicator/NV.SRV.TOTL.ZS
2 www.wto.org/english/res_e/booksp_e/02_wtr19_1_e.pdf
3 www.cnbc.com/2021/02/11/sustainable-investment-funds-more-than-doubled-in-2020-.html
4 www.credit-suisse.com/about-us-news/en/articles/news-and-expertise/coronavirus-brings-esg-investing-to-the-fore-202005.html
5 www.ft.com/content/5cd6e923-81e0-4557-8cff-a02fb5e01d42
6 https://thedali.org/exhibit/dreams-of-dali-in-virtual-reality/

# Bibliography

Aaker, D. A. (1996). *Building strong brands*. New York: The Free Press.

Aaker, D. A. (2004). Leveraging the corporate brand. *California Management Review*, 46(3), 6–18. https://doi.org/10.1177/000812560404600301

Abratt, R., & Kleyn, N. (2012). Corporate identity, corporate branding and corporate reputations: Reconciliation and integration. *European Journal of Marketing*, 46(7/8), 1048–1063. https://doi.org/10.1108/03090561211230197

Andreini, D., Pedeliento, G., Zarantonello, L., & Solerio, C. (2018). A renaissance of brand experience: Advancing the concept through a multi-perspective analysis. *Journal of Business Research*, 91, 123–133.

Argenti, P., & Druckenmiller, B. (2004). Reputation and the corporate brand. *Corporate Reputation Review*, 6, 368–374. https://doi.org/10.1057/palgrave.crr.1540005

Balmer, J. M. T. (1995). Corporate branding and connoisseurship. *Journal of General Management*, 21(1), 24–46.

Balmer, J. M. T. (2012). Corporate brand management imperatives: Custodianship, credibility, and calibration. *California Management Review*, 54(3), 6–33. https://doi.org/10.1525/cmr.2012.54.3.6

Balmer, J. M. T., & Burghausen, M. (2015). Explicating corporate heritage, corporate heritage brands and organisational heritage. *Journal of Brand Management*, 22(5), 364–384.

Balmer, J. M. T., & Gray, E. R. (2003). Corporate brands: What are they? What of them? *European Journal of Marketing*, 37(7/8), 972–997.

Balmer, J. M. T., & Soenen, G. B. (1999). The ACID test of corporate identity management. *Journal of Management*, 15, 69–92.

Bateson (1995). SERVQUAL: Review, critique, research agenda. *European Journal of Marketing*, 30, 8–32.

Batey, M. (2008). *Brand meaning*. New York: Routledge.

Berry, L. L. (2000). Cultivating service brand equity. *Journal of the Academy of Marketing Science*, 28(1), 128–137.

Bitner (1995). Building service relationships: It's all about promises! *Journal of the Academy of Marketing Science*, 23(4), 246–251. https://doi.org/10.1177%2F009207039502300403

Black, I., & Veloutsou, C. (2017). Working consumers: Co-creation of brand identity, consumer identity and brand community identity. *Journal of Business Research*, 70, 416–429.

Brakus, J. J., Schmitt, B. H., & Zarantonello, L. (2009). Brand experience: What is it? How is it measured? Does it affect loyalty? *Journal of Marketing*, 73(3), 52–68.

Carbone, L. P., & Haeckel, S. H. (1994). Engineering customer experiences. *Marketing Management*, 3(3), 9–19.

Carrigan, M., & Attalla, A. (2001). The myth of the ethical consumer – Do ethics matter in purchase behaviour? *Journal of Consumer Marketing*, 18(7), 560–578.

Carrington, M. J., Neville, B. A., & Whitwell, G. J. (2014). Lost in translation: Exploring the ethical consumer intention-behavior gap. *Journal of Business Research*, 67(1), 2759–2767.

Caruana, R., Carrington, M. J., & Chatzidakis, A. (2016). 'Beyond the attitude-behaviour gap: Novel perspectives in consumer ethics': Introduction to the thematic symposium. *Journal of Business Ethics*, 136(2), 215–218.

Chandler, J. D., & Vargo, S. L. (2011). Contextualization and value-in-context: How context frames exchange. *Marketing Theory*, 11(1), 35–49.

Copeland, M. T. (1923). Relation of consumers' buying habits to marketing methods. *Harvard Business Review*, 1(3), 282–289.

Csaba, F. F., & Bengtsson, A. (2006). *Rethinking identity in brand management*. London: Routledge.

da Silveira, C., Lages, C., & Simões, C. (2013). Reconceptualizing brand identity in a dynamic environment. *Journal of Business Research*, 66(1), 28–36.

Datareportal.com. (2021). Retrieved from https://datareportal.com/reports/digital-2021-global-overview-report

Davies, G., Chun, R., & Kamins, M. A. (2010). Reputation gaps and the performance of service organizations. *Strategic Management Journal*, 31(5), 530–546.

de Chernatony, L. (1996). 2001 – The brand management odyssey. *Journal of General Management*, 21(4), 15–30.

de Chernatony, L. (2002). Living the corporate brand: Brand values and brand enactment. *Corporate Reputation Review*, 5(2), 113.

de Chernatony, L., & Dall'Olmo Riley, F. (1998). Defining a "Brand": Beyond the literature with experts' interpretations. *Journal of Marketing Management*, 14(5), 417–443. https://doi.org/10.1362/026725798784867798

de Chernatony, L., & McWilliam, G. (1989). The strategic implications of clarifying how marketers interpret 'Brands'. *Journal of Marketing Management*, *5*(2), 153–171.

Di Mingo, E. (1988). The fine art of positioning. *The Journal of Business Strategy*, *9*, 34–38. https://doi.org/10.1108/eb039211

Dolbec, P. Y., & Fischer, E. (2015). Refashioning a field? Connected consumers and institutional dynamics in markets. *Journal of Consumer Research*, *41*(6), 1447–1468.

Edmans, A. (2020). *Grow the pie. How great companies deliver both purpose and profit*. Cambridge: Cambridge University Press.

Essamri, A., McKechnie, S., & Winklhofer, H. (2019). Co-creating corporate brand identity with online brand communities: A managerial perspective. *Journal of Business Research*, *96*, 366–375.

Freeman, R. E., Harrison, J. S., & Wicks, A. C. (2007). *Managing for stakeholders: Survival, reputation, and success*. New Haven, CT: Yale University Press.

Friedman, M. (1970, September 13). The social responsibility of business is to increase its profits. *The New York Times Magazine*. p. 17. https://www.nytimes.com/1970/09/13/archives/a-friedman-doctrine-the-social-responsibility-of-business-is-to.html

Gardner, B. B., & Levy, S. J. (1955). The product and the brand. *Harvard Business Review*, *33*, 33–39.

Goffman, E. (1959). *The presentation of self in everyday life*. New York: Anchor Books.

Goffman, E. (1967). *On face-work, an analysis of ritual elements in social interaction. Interaction ritual, essays on face-to-face behavior*. Chicago, IL: Aldine Publisher.

Golob, U., Davies, M. A. P., Kernstock, J., & Powell, S. M. (2020). Trending topics plus future challenges and opportunities in brand management. *Journal of Brand Management*, *27*, 123–129.

Golob, U., & Podnar, K. (2019). Researching CSR and brands in the here and now: An integrative perspective. *Journal of Brand Management*, *26*,1–8.

Grönroos, C. (1990). Relationship approach to marketing in service contexts: The marketing and organizational behavior interface. *Journal of Business Research*, *20*(1), 3–11.

Grönroos, C., & Voima, P. (2013). Critical service logic: Making sense of value creation and co-creation. *Journal of the Academy of Marketing Science*, *41*, 133–150.

Gummesson, E. (1991). Marketing-orientation revisited: The crucial role of the part-time marketer. *European Journal of Marketing*, *25*(2), 60–75.

Gyrd-Jones, R. (2012). Five ways branding is changing. *Journal of Brand Management*, *20*(2), 77–79.

Gyrd-Jones, R., Merrilees, B., & Miller, D. (2013). Revisiting the complexities of corporate branding: Issues, paradoxes, solutions. *Journal of Brand Management*, *20*(7), 571–589.

Hanna, R., Rohm, A., & Crittenden, V. L. (2011). We're all connected: The power of the social media ecosystem. *Business Horizons*, *54*(3), 265–273.

Harris, F., & de Chernatony, L. (2001). Corporate branding and corporate brand performance. *European Journal of Marketing*, *35*(3/4), 441–456.

Harrison, J. S., & Wicks, A. C. (2013). Stakeholder theory, value, and firm performance. *Business Ethics Quarterly*, *23*(1), 97–124.

Hatch, M. J., & Schultz, M. (2001, February). Are the strategic stars aligned for your corporate brand? *Harvard Business Review*, 128–134.

Hatch, M. J., & Schultz, M. (2003). Bringing the corporation into corporate branding. *European Journal of Marketing*, *37*(7–8), 1041–1064.

Hatch, M. J., & Schultz, M. (2008). *Taking brand initiative: How companies can align strategy, culture, and identity through corporate branding*. New York: John Wiley & Sons.

Hatch, M. J., & Schultz, M. (2010). Toward a theory of brand co-creation with implications for brand governance. *Journal of Brand Management*, *17*(8), 590–604.

Iglesias, O., & Bonet, E. (2012). Persuasive brand management: How managers can influence brand meaning when they are losing control over it. *Journal of Organizational Change Management*, *25*(2), 251–264.

Iglesias, O., & Ind, N. (2016). How to be a brand with a conscience. In N. Ind & S. Horlings (Eds.), *Brands with a conscience* (pp. 203–211). London: Kogan Page.

Iglesias, O., & Ind, N. (2020). Toward a theory of conscientious corporate brand co-creation. The next key challenge in brand management. *Journal of Brand Management*, *6*(27), 710–720.

Iglesias, O., Ind, N., & Alfaro, M. (2013). The organic view of the brand: A brand value co- creation model. *Journal of Brand Management*, *20*(8), 670–688.

Iglesias, O., Ind, N., & Schultz, M. (2020b). History matters: The role of history in corporate brand strategy. *Business Horizons*, *63*(1), 51–60.

Iglesias, O., Landgraf, P., Ind, N., Markovic, S., & Koporcic, N. (2020a). Corporate brand identity co-creation in Business-to-business contexts. *Industrial Marketing Management, 85*, 32–43.

Ind, N. (1997). *The corporate brand*. London: Palgrave Macmillan.

Ind, N. (2007). *Living the brand: How to transform every member of your organization into a brand champion*. London: Kogan Page Publishers.

Ind, N. (2009). *The organic organisation: Freedom, creativity and the search for fulfilment*. New York: Atropos Press.

Ind, N., & Bjerke, R. (2007). *Branding governance: A participatory approach to the brand building process*. New York: John Wiley & Sons.

Ind, N., & Horlings, S. (2016). *Brands with a conscience: How to build a successful and responsible brand*. London: Kogan Page.

Ind, N., & Ryder, I. (2011). Conscientious brands editorial. *Journal of Brand Management, 18*(9), 635–638.

Ind, N., Iglesias, O., & Markovic, S. (2017). The co-creation continuum: From tactical market research tool to strategic collaborative innovation method. *Journal of Brand Management, 24*(4), 310–321.

Ind, N., Iglesias, O., & Schultz, M. (2013). Building brands together: Emergence and outcomes of co-creation. *California Management Review, 55*(3), 5–26.

Ind, N., & Schmidt, H. (2020). *Co-creating brands: Brand management from a co-creative perspective*. London: Bloomsbury.

Jacoby, J., Chestnut, R. W., & Silberman, W. (1977). Consumer use and comprehension of nutrition information. *Journal of Consumer Research, 4*(2), 119–128.

Joyner, B. E., & Payne, D. (2002). Evolution and implementation: A study of values, business ethics and corporate social responsibility. *Journal of Business Ethics, 41*(4), 297–311.

Jurgens, M., Berthon, P., Papania, L., & Shabbir, H. A. (2010). Stakeholder theory and practice in Europe and North America: The key to success lies in a marketing approach. *Industrial Marketing Management, 39*(5), 769–775.

Kapferer, J. N. (2012). *The new strategic brand management: Advanced insights and strategic thinking*. London: Kogan Page.

Kazadi, K., Lievens, A., & Mahr, D. (2015). Stakeholder co-creation during the innovation process: Identifying capabilities for knowledge creation among multiple stakeholders. *Journal of Business Research*, 1–16.

Keller, K. L. (1993). Conceptualizing, measuring, and managing customer-based brand equity. *Journal of Marketing, 57*(1), 1–22.

Kitchin, T. (2003). Corporate responsibility: A brand extension. *Journal of Brand Management 10*(4–5), 312–326.

Klaus, P., & Maklan, S. (2007). The role of brands in a service-dominated world. *Journal of Brand Management, 15*(2), 115–122.

Knisely, G. (1979). Listening to consumer is key to consumer or services marketing. *Advertising Age, 50*, 54–60.

Knox, S., & Maklan, S. (2004). Corporate social responsibility: Moving beyond investment towards measuring outcomes. *European Management Journal, 22*(5), 508–516.

Koporcic, N., & Halinen, A. (2018). Interactive network branding: Creating corporate identity and reputation through interpersonal interaction. *IMP Journal, 12*(2), 392–408.

Kornum, N., Gyrd-Jones, R., Al Zagir, N., & Brandis, K. A. (2017). Interplay between intended brand identity and identities in a Nike related brand community: Co-existing synergies and tensions in a nested system. *Journal of Business Research, 70*, 432–440.

Kowalkowski, C., Gebauer, H., Kamp, B., & Parry, G. (2017). Servitization and deservitization: Overview, concepts, and definitions. *Industrial Marketing Management, 60*, 4–10.

Kristal, S., Baumgarth, C., & Henseler, J. (2020). Performative corporate brand identity in industrial markets: The case of German prosthetics manufacturer Ottobock. *Journal of Business Research, 114*, 240–253.

Kumar, V., & Mirchandani, R. (2012). Increasing the ROI of social media marketing. *MIT Sloan Management Review, 54*(1), 55–61.

Levy, S. J. (1959). Symbols for sale. *Harvard Business Review, 37*(4), 117–124.

Libert, B., Wind, Y., & Beck Fenley, M. (2015). What Apple, Lending Club, and AirBnB know about collaborating with customers. *Harvard Business Review*. Retrieved from http://hbr.org/2015/07/what-apple-lending-club-and-airbnb-know-about-collaborating-with-customers

Mäläskä, M., Saraniemi, S., & Tähtinen, J. (2011). Network actors' participation in B2B SME branding. *Industrial Marketing Management, 40*(7), 1144–1152.

Mason, C., & Simmons, J. (2014). Embedding corporate social responsibility in corporate governance: A stakeholder systems approach. *Journal of Business Ethics, 119*, 77–86.

Maxfield, S. (2008). Reconciling corporate citizenship and competitive strategy: Insights from economic theory. *Journal of Business Ethics, 80*(2), 367–377.

Mazutis, D. D., & Slawinski, N. (2015). Reconnecting business and society: Perceptions of authenticity in corporate social responsibility. *Journal of Business Ethics, 131*(1), 137–150.

Merz, M. A., He, Y., & Vargo, S. L. (2009). The evolving brand logic: A service dominant logic perspective. *Journal of the Academy of Marketing Science, 37*, 328–344.

Michel, G. (2017). From brand identity to polysemous brands: Commentary on "Performing identities: Processes of brand and stakeholder identity co-construction". *Journal of Business Research, 70*, 453–455.

Morsing, M., & Kristensen, J. (2001). The question of coherency in corporate branding – Over time and across stakeholders. *Journal of Communication Management, 6*(1), 24–40. https://doi.org/10.1108/13632540210806919

Muniz, A. M., & O'Guinn, T. C. (2001). Brand community. *Journal of Consumer Research, 27*, 412–432.

Otubanjo, O., Abimbola, T., & Amujo, O. (2010). Conceptualising the notion of corporate brand covenant. *Journal of Product and Brand Management, 19*(6), 410–422. https://doi.org/10.1108/10610421011085721

Parasuraman, A. (1987). Customer-oriented corporate cultures are crucial to services marketing success. *Journal of Services Marketing, 1*(1), 39–46.

Park, C. W., Jaworski, B. J., & MacInnis, D. J. (1986). Strategic brand concept-image management. *Journal of Marketing, 50*(4), 135–145. https://doi.org/10.2307/1251291

Prahalad, C. K., & Ramaswamy, V. (2004). *The future of competition: Co-creating unique value with customers*. Boston, MA: Harvard Business School Press.

Ramaswamy, V. (2020). Leading the experience ecosystem revolution: Innovating offerings as interactive platforms. *Strategy & Leadership, 48*(3), 3–9.

Ramaswamy, V., & Ind, N. (2020). Company brands as purpose-driven lived experienced ecosystems. *European Business Review*. Retrieved from www.europeanbusinessreview.com/company-brands-as-purpose-driven-lived-experience-ecosystems/

Ramaswamy, V., & Ozcan, K. (2014). *The co-creation paradigm*. Stanford: Stanford University Press.

Ramaswamy, V., & Ozcan, K. (2016). Brand value co-creation in a digitalized world: An integrative framework and research implications. *International Journal of Research in Marketing, 33*(1), 93–106.

Ramaswamy, V., & Ozcan, K. (2018). What is co-creation? An interactional creation framework and its implications for value creation. *Journal of Business Research, 84*, 196–205.

Ramaswamy, V., & Ozcan, K. (2021). Brands as co-creational experience ecosystems – An integrative theoretical framework of interactional creation. In S. Markovic, R. Gyrd-Jones, S. von Wallpach, & A. Lindgreen (Eds.), *Research handbook on brand co-creation: Theory, practice, and ethical implications*. London: Edward Elgar.

Rindell, A., Svensson, G., Mysen, T., Billström, A., & Wilén, K. (2011). Towards a conceptual foundation of 'Conscientious Corporate Brands'. *Journal of Brand Management, 18*(9), 709–719.

Roper, S., & Davies, G. (2007). The corporate brand: Dealing with multiple stakeholders. *Journal of Marketing Management, 23*(1–2), 75–90.

Schmitt, B. (1999). Experiential marketing. *Journal of Marketing Management, 15*(1–3), 53–67.

Shaw, D., & Shiu, E. (2002). The role of ethical obligation and self-identity in ethical consumer choice. *International Journal of Consumer Studies, 26*(2), 109–116.

Shostack, G. L. (1977). Breaking free from product marketing. *Journal of Marketing*, 73–90. https://doi.org/10.1177/002224297704100219

Smith, N. C. (2003). Corporate social responsibility: Whether or how? *California Management Review, 45*(4), 52–76.

Smith, N. C., & Rönnegard, D. (2016). Shareholder primacy, corporate social responsibility, and the role of business schools. *Journal of Business Ethics, 134*(3), 463–478.

Törmälä, M., & Gyrd-Jones, R. I. (2017). Development of new B2B venture corporate brand identity: A narrative performance approach. *Industrial Marketing Management, 65*, 76–85.

Vallaster, C., & von Wallpach, S. (2013). An online discursive inquiry into the social dynamics of multi-stakeholder brand meaning co-creation. *Journal of Business Research, 66*(9), 1505–1515.

Van de Ven, A. H. (1992). Suggestions for studying strategy process: A research note. *Strategic Management Journal, 13*(1), 169–188.

Van Rekom, J., Berens, G., & Van Halderen, M. (2013). Corporate social responsibility: Playing to win, or playing not to lose? Doing good by increasing the social benefits of a company's core activities. *Journal of Brand Management, 20*(9), 800–814.

Vargo, S. L., & Lusch, R. F. (2004). Evolving to a new dominant logic for marketing. *Journal of Marketing, 68*(1), 1–17.

Vargo, S. L., & Lusch, R. F. (2016). Institutions and axioms: An extension and update of service-dominant logic. *Journal of the Academy of Marketing Science, 44*, 5–23.

von Wallpach, S., Hemetsberger, A., & Espersen, P. (2017). Performing identities: Processes of brand and stakeholder identity co-construction. *Journal of Business Research, 70*, 443–452.

Walsh, G., & Beatty, S. E. (2007). Customer-based corporate reputation of a service firm: Scale development and validation. *Journal of the Academy of Marketing Science, 35*(1), 127–143.

Webster, F. E., & Keller, K. L. (2004). A roadmap for branding in industrial markets. *Journal of Brand Management, 11*(5), 388–402.

Welcker, J. W. (1949). The community relations problem of industrial companies. *Harvard Business Review, 49*(6), 771–780.

Wider, S., von Wallpach, S., & Mühlbacher, H. (2018). Brand management: Unveiling the delusion of control. *European Management Journal, 36*(3), 301–305.

# 2
# DEMARCATING THE FIELD OF CORPORATE BRAND MANAGEMENT

*Russell Abratt and Michela Mingione*

## 1. Introduction

As a concept, corporate branding has become an established business strategy and can be seen in large, medium, and small organizations. Corporate branding differs from product branding, which relies more on the efforts of marketing and advertising departments. Corporate branding draws its value from all of an organization's stakeholders, including its funders, owners, managers, and personnel (Balmer & Gray, 2003). It is related to the multiple stakeholders interacting with the organization's employees, such as shareholders, media, competitors, and governments, to build and maintain positive perceptions.

Although the concept is well established, corporate branding has different conceptualizations. According to Aaker (2004), the corporate brand is represented as a proposition, a 'brand promise' that represents the organization and reflects its heritage, values, culture, people, and strategy. A corporate brand relates to the 'visual, verbal, and behavioural expression of an organisation's unique business model' (Knox & Bickerton, 2003, p. 998). The corporate brand, according to Hatch and Schultz (2003), is based on collaborative activities through which the strategic vision, organizational culture, and brand image are aligned to ensure that the brand promise is delivered in the day-to-day activities of the organization. Thus, corporate brand is a systematic process by an organization to create a good brand image and reputation through interaction with all stakeholders (Einwiller & Will, 2002). It is a process of building the desired reputation of an organization in its markets (Abratt & Kleyn, 2012).

## 2. The core of the corporate brand

Three constructs are at the core of the corporate brand: corporate identity, core values, and brand positioning.

### 2.1 Corporate identity

The corporate brand identity is what makes a corporate brand different and most suitable to its stakeholders, when compared to the competition (Kapferer, 2008). Brand identity is historically an internal perspective, typically created before presenting the brand to external stakeholders,

DOI: 10.4324/9781003035749-3

and managed by the brand management team. The traditional view sees corporate brand identity as stable and unilaterally determined by managers and other internal stakeholders (Essamri et al., 2019). Brand identity is defined as the set of unique brand associations that producers aspire to create or maintain and the symbols they use to identify the brand to people (Aaker, 1996). A corporate brand identity can establish points-of-difference that might help to reflect the organization's benefits, such as quality, reliability, and performance, and enhance perceived levels of corporate intangible associations, such as credibility, authenticity, or trustworthiness. The dimensions of brand identity include the emblematic, observable, and physical representation; the product and service characteristics; and the brand personality. It could be argued that brands have always been co-created by diverse stakeholders, and the literature now acknowledges this reality. New emerging technologies that favour stakeholders' connection have also fostered the relevance and opportunities offered by co-creation. Consumers and other stakeholders are playing a role in the development of brands, and they make decisions about these brands. The internet provides opportunities for individuals to communicate with others regarding brands through brand communities, blogs, and social media platforms.

## 2.2 Brand values

Core brand values are the beliefs that an organization stands for. They serve as the compass that guides the brand promise, behaviours, and decision-making process. Urde (2009, p. 621) defines them as 'mindsets rooted within an organisation and the essential perceptions held by customers and non-customer stakeholders defining the identity of a brand.' Core values are a central facet of the identity of a corporate brand, and they generally come from the brand's origin and founders (Urde, 2003). Values are defined as enduring beliefs that are personally or socially preferable to converse beliefs, which eclipse specific situations, and which influence selection or evaluation of behaviour (Rokeach, 1973). Core values can be defined as boundless terms that sum up the identity of the brand as well as being the guiding principles for all brand-building processes, both internal and external. Knowing 'what values we stand for' and 'what values customers and other stakeholders over time have come to appreciate us for' is vital for the management of brands. The values entrenched in the organization need to reverberate with the values perceived and appreciated by the customers over time, and vice versa (Urde, 2009).

This can be seen in the brand values of American Express and Coca-Cola.

American Express core brand values (American Express, 2020) are:

Customer Commitment
Quality
Integrity
Teamwork
Respect for People
Good Citizenship
A Will to Win
Personal Accountability

Coca-Cola's core brand values (Coca-Cola, 2020) are listed as:

Leadership: The courage to shape a better future
Collaboration: Leverage collective genius

Integrity: Be real
Accountability: If it is to be, it's up to me
Passion: Committed in heart and mind
Diversity: As inclusive as our brands
Quality: What we do, we do well

These examples of the corporate brand core values are the centre around which the organizations' strategies revolve.

## 2.3 Brand positioning

Brand positioning is the act of designing an organization's offering and image to occupy a special place in the mind of the target market as well as its other stakeholders. A well-positioned brand should appeal to the needs of a target market because a differential value proposition is conceived. Positioning the corporate brand is also about creating a unique position and distinguishing the organization from its competitors. All aspects of a company's behaviour affect the position in stakeholders' minds. Segmentation, targeting, and positioning are too often treated as separate concepts in the literature. However, corporate brand positioning has no value unless it is appropriate for the target market and other stakeholders. Effective positioning of the corporate brand differentiates the organization and its products and services in terms of quality, innovation, and knowledgeable employees, among other benefits. Starbucks' positioning is focused on the consumer experience. What the brand wants is to make the simple act of buying a coffee as pleasant as possible. The company has relied on technology; for example, it is possible for a customer to make a request through a mobile phone by using its application. The customer experience is fast and efficient, reinforcing the positioning of the company. Another example of good positioning is Apple. Apple is positioned as a brand that offers elegance, luxury, and exclusivity. This positioning is expressed through the Apple Store and its various products and services. The company dominates the technology market. Positioning serves as the basis for all of Apple's marketing campaigns.

Brand identity, core values, and brand positioning are interrelated. Brand identity should answer the questions, 'Who are we?' and 'What makes us different from other organizations?' This will influence the organization's core values. The brand positioning will use the firm's distinct capabilities that distinguish it from others by taking into account the organization's unique brand identity and core values.

## 3. Outcomes of corporate brand management

An advantage of corporate branding is the opportunity for achieving a coherent focus for all products and conveying consistent messages to all stakeholders (Dall'Olmo Riley & de Chernatony, 2000). The corporate brand helps an organization differentiate itself from the competition; it gives the organization credibility and trust from stakeholders; and it helps stakeholders to form an image and reputation of the organization. The top 30 brands on the Interbrand (2020) Global top 100 brands list for 2020 are all corporate brands, highlighting their value.

### 3.1 Brand differentiation

Corporate brands involve establishing differentiation and preference at the level of the organization rather than individual products or services and can differentiate themselves in the organizational associations. This is implemented through brand positioning, as discussed earlier.

Differentiation involves seeking points of difference from other organizations that the firm competes with, and at the same time capitalizing on the points of parity with other organizations.

## 3.2 Credibility and trust

Corporate brand credibility covers the need for the brand promise to be demonstrably bona fide in terms of an organization's activities, purposes, products and services, and behaviours (Balmer, 2012). Brand credibility is the believability of the product position information embedded in a brand depending on consumers' perceptions of whether the brand has the ability and willingness to continuously deliver what has been promised, and it is thought to consist of two main components: trustworthiness and expertise (Erdem & Swait, 2004). It is a critical element affecting an organization's market share.

Brand trust reflects a stakeholder's expectation that a corporate brand's behaviour reflects the promises the organization has made. Brand trust is conceptualized as having two dimensions: brand intentions and brand reliability (Delgado-Ballester, 2004). Trust evolves out of perceived risk; consumers seek trustworthy brands when they feel uncertain or insecure about a purchase decision (Delgado-Ballester & Luis Munuera-Alemán, 2001). Greenberg (2014) deduced that trust is the belief that an organization can accomplish their objectives, as they are both competent and have sound intentions. To build brand credibility and trust, the corporate brand must first get to know customers and other stakeholders. This should be done through two-way communication, listening to what they say and want, and then giving them what they want. Corporate brands must be consistent when it comes to brand promises. If stakeholders have issues, these need to be addressed instantly, if possible. An example of a credible and trustworthy corporate brand is Warby Parker. This eyeglass manufacturer has about 50 stores in the USA and Canada, but the majority of its business is done online. Consumers like to try on frames before they purchase. However, Warby Parker has changed this and has gained the trust of consumers. They have their 'Home Try-On' program where users can easily select five different frames and test them out for five days at home. The company ships the glasses for free to users and allows the customer to do a free return once the trial period ends. This leads to greater credibility and trust for the brand.

## 3.3 Reputation and image

The brand image of an organization represents the current and immediate reflection that the stakeholders have towards an organization (Bick et al., 2003). It is related to the various physical and behavioural attributes of the organization, including its name, architecture, products and service portfolio, heritage, ideology, and the quality cues communicated by the organization. Consumers and other stakeholders construe their imagery of a brand through brand experiences, brand relationships, brand communities, and social media. Brand image is related to the various physical and behavioural attributes of the firm, such as its name, brand architecture, products and services assortments, tradition, ideology, and to the quality cues communicated by the firm's products, services, and people (Nguyen & Leblanc, 2001).

Reputation is an outcome of interactions between stakeholders and the organization over time (Argenti & Druckenmiller, 2004). Abratt and Kleyn (2012) define corporate reputation as a stakeholder's overall evaluation of an organization over time. This evaluation is based on the stakeholder's experiences with the corporate brand and product brands, relationships with these and the organization's employees and representatives, memberships of brand communities, social media, blogs, and any other perceived communication and symbolism that provide information about the organization's actions and/or a comparison with the organization's competitors.

Table 2.1 The 10 most visible corporate brands in the USA

| Rank | Corporate Brand |
| --- | --- |
| 1 | Clorox |
| 2 | Amazon |
| 3 | Publix |
| 4 | Wegmans |
| 5 | Costco |
| 6 | Procter & Gamble |
| 7 | Kroger |
| 8 | UPS |
| 9 | Chick-fil-A |
| 10 | 3M |

Source: Adapted from the Harris Poll, 2020

An organization that seeks to create a positive reputation amongst its various stakeholders must understand the dimensions on which they evaluate reputation. These include, but are not limited to, the organization's performance, its goods and services, its citizenship activities, its sustainability and environmental practices, service, innovation, the workplace, governance, and ethics (Abratt & Kleyn, 2012).

The Harris Poll® releases an annual Reputation Quotient® (RQ®) report every year, revealing corporate reputation ratings for the 100 most visible companies in the USA, as perceived by the general public (Harris Poll-Axios, 2020). In 2020, their study revealed the reputation ranking as follows (Table 2.1):

## 4. Evolution of corporate brand management

The body of literature on corporate brand has evolved significantly in recent years (Powell, 2014). The modern concept of corporate brand management emerged in the mid-1990s when Balmer (1995) and Aaker (1996) saw the need to evolve the idea of product and service brands to the perspective of a brand as an organization. Even before this, some aspects of corporate brand were discussed by academics and practitioners in the 1950s. The writings of Martineau (Balmer, 1995) and Ogilvy (Shee & Abratt, 1989) made important contributions, and in the 1960s research in the area expanded greatly (see, for example, the work of Greenberg, 1961, and Spector, 1961). In the 1970s, Kennedy (1977) highlighted the importance of employees in corporate brand building. Also in the 1970s, the complexity of strategic brand management was discussed, and the work of Wally Olins was prominent (Ind, 1998 Gray, 1986; Jenkins, 1991). The 1980s saw a growth in the work highlighting the role of corporate identity in strategic brand management. Management recognized that the corporate brand had a positive impact on performance (Worcester, 1986). The 1990s saw the growth of the corporate brand concept, with Balmer and Ind making substantial contributions to the field (Balmer, 1995; Ind, 1998). In the 2000s, corporate brand knowledge expanded both conceptually and empirically with major work by Balmer (2008, 2009) and Hatch and Schultz (2001, 2003, 2008). More recently, corporate brand has become a mainstream concern for both scholars and practitioners, and it is a valuable resource for every organization (Balmer et al., 2016, 2017).

The purpose of organizations themselves acting as brands is to ensure a sustainable competitive advantage (Balmer & Gray, 2003; Knox & Bickerton, 2003). They are distinguishable from brands owned by products and are differentiated as having a multitude of stakeholders rather than a simple customer orientation. While product brands are reliant on the perceptions that customers have of them, corporate brands are reliant on stakeholder perceptions, and these stakeholders vary widely in their representation of different target markets (Hatch & Schultz, 2003).

3M is a multinational manufacturing company with a turnover of over $30 billion in 2020. It continually looks at its stakeholders to help increase understanding, broaden awareness, seek technical input and expertise, and evaluate possible collaborations and strategic partnerships. It relies on their counsel and expertise to help guide it. 3M believes stakeholder engagement should be based on candid and authentic dialogue – grounded in the company's values – and should contribute to the evolution of its strategic priorities. 3M serves multiple stakeholders. Whether it is regarding technology, manufacturing, global capabilities, or the brand, the company is committed to connecting its fundamental strengths to its customers. 3M engages its customers and delves into its own processes, problems, and promises to its customers. It brings technology to the customer, along with a deep domain of expertise, and further deepens this expertise by working side by side with customers as partners. For the community, 3M has a long-standing commitment to sustainability. Its industry leadership is evident in the establishment of the ground-breaking Pollution Prevention Pays program in 1975, as well as more recent initiatives, including the shift to renewable energy sources, reducing greenhouse gas emissions, increasing circular solutions, and growing their skills-based volunteering programs. Together with its employees, customers, partners, governments, and communities, 3M is committed to a science-based, collaborative approach to solving shared global challenges and improving lives. For employees, 3M knows that a diverse, global workforce – people with different experience, ethnicity, age, gender, sexual orientation, personality, style, and ways of thinking – helps it relate more closely to the needs of all 3M customers, suppliers, and channel partners around the world. (www.3m.com/3M/en_US/sustainability-us/annual-report/)

## 5. Characteristics of strong corporate brands

### 5.1 Cultivate a valuable brand heritage

Brand heritage has been addressed as the feature of a brand's identity related to its history, core values, and use of brand elements like symbols (Balmer, 2011) under the tacit assumption that a long tradition can be connected with legitimacy and authenticity (Balmer & Burghausen, 2015). Heritage scholars usually follow an omni-temporal perspective that centres on the past, present, and prospective future concurrently. The meanings attached to the character of an organization's identity can vary over the passage of time. Consumers and other stakeholders might identify signals of brand heritage both in the brand's past (Wiedmann et al., 2011) and in its communications (Urde, 1994). The reason organizations with heritage should use it is to take advantage of differentiation that is valuable for all stakeholders. It is also distinctive for the brand and difficult for competitors to imitate (Urde et al., 2007). Iglesias et al. (2020a) show how the use of a systematic approach can enable the progressive institutionalization of history in corporate brand strategy development. There are four stages: first, managers should uncover history and bring it from latency to focus; second, managers should promote those organizational structures and processes that help history to be remembered; third, managers should promote the curation of history in order to make it relevant for the current context; and fourth, managers should embed history to support the future strategy. Balmer and Burghausen

(2019, p. 221) suggest the past can variously be characterised as serving different purposes in the present, such as:

- Authentication: probing the veracity of the past
- Documentation: archiving/systematizing the remnants of the past
- Interpretation: understanding (the relevance of) the past
- Narration: disseminating (a version of) the past
- Manifestation: performing/(re)enacting the past (e.g., commemoration)
- Valorization: ratifying/ennobling the past
- Identification: defining the individual, collective or institutional 'self' vis-à-vis the past
- Contestation: addressing the inequities and injuries of the past

Heritage brands stand for longevity and sustainability. Heritage is acknowledged as a key organizational resource imparting long-lasting strategic value; companies are unique in terms of their heritage, and heritage can provide the basis for superior performance (Balmer, 2009). Unlocking the potential hidden value of a brand's heritage may be one way of harnessing the past and the present in order to safeguard the future (Urde et al., 2007). Balmer (2013) states that brand heritage is about long-term commitment and continuity, which adds to both the organization's and its stakeholders' positive values. There are six traits an organization should possess to be regarded as having a corporate heritage, including organization trait constancy (e.g., in terms of organizational culture; product, process, and quality focus; location; group and class associations; design, style and sensory utilization; and corporate communications) (Balmer, 2013).

For example, Wells Fargo was founded in 1852 by Henry Wells and William Fargo. The company has survived for 169 years and evokes emotional ties in many customers whose families have long been connected to the business. The brand Wells Fargo is linked with the image of a six-horse stagecoach thundering across the American West, loaded with gold. Its history is rich in detail with great events in America's history. From the Gold Rush to the early 20th century, through prosperity, depression, and war, Wells Fargo earned a reputation of trust due to its attention and loyalty to customers. Wells Fargo delivered business by the fastest means possible, whether it was by stagecoach, steamship, railroad, pony rides, or telegraph. In 1858, Wells Fargo helped to start the Overland Mail Company. After the completion of the Transcontinental Railroad in 1869, Wells Fargo increasingly rode the rails. In 1888, after expanding along the new steel network across the Northeast into New York, Wells Fargo became the country's first nationwide express company. It adopted the motto 'Ocean-to-Ocean' to describe its service that connected over 2,500 communities in 25 states, and 'Over-the-Seas' to highlight its lines linking America's increasingly global economy. By 1918, Wells Fargo was part of 10,000 communities across the country. The famous image of the stagecoach and the reputation of the name saw Wells Fargo well through the mighty events and fantastic growth of the 20th century. In the 1910s and 1920s, Wells Fargo served as a commercial bank in San Francisco, supporting the West's growing business and agriculture, including fledgling auto, aerospace, and film industries. The Wells Fargo stagecoach became a regular actor in Hollywood westerns. After the Second World War, new banking concepts not only changed where people banked, but how they banked. Drive-up tellers, banking by phone, express lines, credit cards, automated teller machines, and online banking are some of the innovative solutions to modern customers' needs. As in the stagecoach days, Wells Fargo has been a pioneer in bringing banking convenience to its customers. Today in the 21st century, with extensive and diversified financial services, the Wells Fargo name once again extends 'Ocean-to-Ocean,' 'Over-the-Seas,' and, of course, online. (www.wellsfargo.com/about/corporate/history/)

## 5.2 Leverage on the organizational core competencies

A corporate brand has the perception among stakeholders that it has the assets and skills to add value to them. Although every organization has a corporate brand and develops a reputation over time, strong corporate brands and reputations are impossible to imitate in totality owing to the unique sets of assets, skills, and choices made by organizations and the broad number of dimensions used across stakeholders to evaluate corporate brands and reputations (Abratt & Kleyn, 2012).

Walmart is the largest retail department store chain in the world, with global sales of over $524 billion in 2020. The company has more than 11,500 locations in the US and internationally. Its core capabilities include excellent supply chain management and massive buying power (Walmart, 2019). In fiscal 2020, it launched Next Day Delivery to more than 75 percent of the US population, launched Delivery Unlimited from 1,600 locations in the US, and expanded Same Day Pickup to nearly 3,200 locations. Its eCommerce efforts and innovation have also led to omni-channel offerings in many of its markets, including grocery pick up and/or delivery in nearly a dozen countries outside the US.

## 5.3 Embrace corporate social responsibility and environmental programmes

What kind of values and people are behind the corporate brand? This is a question that stakeholders ask. Is the organization concerned about the environment, sustainability, and the community?

Ferrell and Geoffrey (2000) define corporate social responsibility (CSR) as the corporate behaviour in relation to business ethics' fulfilment that includes corporate obligations and commitments to society. The corporate brand relates more strongly to the relationship of consumer stakeholders and CSR than the product brand. Given stakeholders' attitudes towards the corporate brand and their intention to interact with it versus the individual brand, they may be more willing to reward and/or punish the corporate brand than the individual brand (Sweetin et al., 2013). According to Vesal et al. (2021, p. 2), environmental sustainability is defined as 'an organizational activity directed at reducing pollution and increasing the efficient use of energy and other resources to diminish the detrimental effects of firms' activities on the environment.' They suggest that this denotes that environmental sustainability reveals in environmental remediation and economic efficiency. Environmental remediation examines reducing air emissions, wastewater, solid waste, consumption of hazardous materials, and environmental accidents, whereas economic efficiency involves the efficient utilization of energy and other resources.

Examples of companies that have strong CSR programmes include Ben & Jerry's ice-cream. In 1989, they first opposed the Recombinant Bovine Growth Hormone use in cows. The company created the Ben & Jerry's Foundation, which encourages their employees to give back to their communities and offers grants for social justice programmes.

The LEGO Group was slated as one of the top examples of social responsibility by the Reputation Institute, which lists the most highly regarded companies in the world (Global RepTrak, 2020). In addition to partnerships with organizations like the World Wildlife Fund, LEGO has also made a commitment to reduce its carbon footprint and is working towards 100% renewable energy capacity by 2030. LEGO has used environmentally friendly processes in its manufacturing with the creation of LEGO's Sustainable Materials Center, which works to find sustainable alternatives to current materials and packaging (Gaus, 2020).

## 6. Building the corporate brand

### 6.1 Employee and internal branding

A corporate brand can be built through the internal actions that seek to promote the brand for the purpose of ensuring that its employees accept the value that the brand represents and transform it into reality when serving customers (Punjaisri & Wilson, 2007). Customers' experience of a brand is often shaped by the way employees act and perform on the job (de Chernatony et al., 2003). 'Brand ambassadors' (Vallaster & de Chernatony, 2006), 'brand champions' (Morhart et al., 2009), and 'living the brand' (Burmann & Zeplin, 2005) have been used to gain the spirit of the desired employee behaviour.

### 6.2 Multiple stakeholder involvement

In positioning stakeholder theory within the corporate brand building context, there are a variety of stakeholders, all of whom require the corporation to communicate with them in order to deliver on the objectives (Donaldson & Preston, 1995). The corporate brand contributes to the images formed and held by all its stakeholders including employees, customers, investors, suppliers, partners, regulators, special interests, and local communities (Hatch & Schultz, 2003). Although corporate brands are born in organizations, their value is only accomplished when they are comprehended by stakeholders (Fournier, 1998).

### 6.3 The role of corporate communications

Corporate communication is defined by Cornelissen (2004, p. 185) as 'the functions and process of managing communications between an organization and important stakeholder groups (including markets and publics in its environment).' Balmer (1995) states that total corporate communication is imperative to building a corporate brand. This requires an alignment or congruence of symbolism, behaviour, planned and unplanned communication, and, by extension, all communication between third parties (Gregory, 2007). Battacharya and Sen (2003) provide many activities that convey an organization's corporate identity ranging from controlled communication, such as official documents, through to uncontrolled third party communication, such as media activity.

### 6.4 Importance of relationship building

It is important to build good relationships with all stakeholders, including customers. The development of brand meaning and values has shifted somewhat as consumers and other stakeholders are playing an increasing role in shaping the brand (Mingione & Abratt, 2020).

### 6.5 Enhancing corporate brand alignment

Hatch and Schultz (2001) state that to build a corporate brand, an organization must align three interdependent elements: vision, culture, and image. Vision is the top management's aspirations for the organization. Culture is the organization's values, behaviours, and attitudes: the way employees feel about the organization. Image is the external stakeholder's impression of the organization. In building the corporate brand, all three elements need to be aligned. Managers must always assess the relationships between vision, culture, and image; integrate the organization behind the corporate brand; and know how stakeholders will interpret the brand symbols (Hatch & Schultz, 2003).

## 6.6 Brand experience

Brakus et al. (2009, p. 52) conceptualize brand experience as 'subjective, internal consumer responses (sensations, feelings, and cognitions) and behavioural responses evoked by brand-related stimuli that are part of a brand's design and identity, packaging, communications, and environments.' When stakeholders, including customers, experience a corporate brand, they are judging whether it is delivering on the brand covenant or promise to them. Brakus et al. (2009) suggest that brand experience can be broken down into four dimensions (sensory, affective, intellectual, and behavioural) which are differentially evoked by various brands. Consumers and other stakeholders want the corporate brand to employ their senses and 'move' them. Thus, an organization's distinctive corporate brand must be directed towards consumer and other stakeholder senses with the goal of providing them an emotional, mental, social, and physical way to engage with them and to consume their product or service. The consequences of brand experience include customer and stakeholder satisfaction, loyalty, and brand commitment (Iglesias et al., 2011).

## 6.7 Brand authenticity

Authentic brands put their organizational values at the core of their practices and actions (Eggers et al., 2013). The key dimensions of brand authenticity are individuality, originality, naturalness, credibility, reliability, consistency, continuity, integrity, and symbolism.

> The definitions of the general concept of authenticity differ. Nevertheless, the following conclusions can be drawn for the specific context of brand authenticity: (1) Authenticity in the context of brands deals with the authenticity of market offerings (objects and services) in contrast to the authenticity of human beings; (2) Brand authenticity is based on the evaluations of individuals rather than being solely related to the inherent attributes of the brand; (3) Brand authenticity corresponds to a variety of attributes since there is no unique definition of the authenticity concept, particularly in the branding context.
>
> (Bruhn et al., 2012, p. 567)

Consumers co-create the meaning of brand authenticity according to their own understanding of what is genuine, sincere, real, and true (Beverland & Farrelly, 2010).

# 7. Corporate brand applications and future directions

## 7.1 Corporate brand applications

Corporate brand and corporate brand management for goods and services for profit industries are well documented (see for example Aaker, 2004; Balmer, 1995; Hatch & Schultz, 2003; Kay, 2006). However, corporate brand also applies to non-profit, state-owned, social, city, and place contexts.

### Government

Government (also known as state-owned) organizations offer a number of discretionary and non-discretionary services and products, and exhibit market activities, such as the employment of marketing and branding techniques, but their business goals and, therefore, their strategies in attempting to deliver on those business goals are different (Hansen & Ferlie, 2016; Högström et al., 2016). There are, however, many challenges as public organizations are by nature inconsistent and complex entities that are difficult to include under one, single identity definition (Wæraas, 2008). Osborne and Brown (2005) describe corporate brand building in government organizations as more challenging in context compared with private sector companies due to public policy issues and rate of change that are dominant influencing factors. In a study of the South African Broadcasting Corporation, it was found that there were unclear corporate identities as well as fragmented corporate branding strategies, which needed to be orchestrated and aligned through a formal corporate branding process (Cullinan et al., 2020).

## Universities

Corporate branding applies to universities (Curtis et al., 2009). They embody an evolving sense of identity and represent a specific and measurable community (Drori et al., 2013). As a result, universities have implemented corporate branding to differentiate themselves from other universities and to have an integrated marketing communication strategy from which to declare their reputation. The different stakeholders that a university must manage include funders, academics, employees, students, and alumni. Harvard and Yale in the United States, and Oxford and Cambridge in the United Kingdom, are good examples of universities with very strong corporate brands.

## Monarchy

Balmer et al. (2006) concluded that the monarchy is an institution very much like a corporate brand steeped in heritage. Though monarchies are not organizations, they are brand-like institutions (Balmer et al., 2006). The following 'brand-like qualities' are pointed out with reference to monarchies: able and willing to adapt to change; financially valuable in terms of benefits (to the country and tourism); adds value to key constituencies (including foreign investors); amenable to being managed; creates a consistent image that garners support from a community; symbolizes stability; generates revenue from endorsed products; and is represented by numerous members and managed by even more members. A very distinct difference between organizations and monarchies is that while organizations build their corporate brands to leverage them for financial gain and shareholder value, a monarchy does so to improve the country's social balance sheet and value system.

The British monarchy is a good example of a corporate brand that benefits the United Kingdom. The contribution includes the Monarchy's indirect effect on different industries. The esteem for the institution boosts the price and volume premium of brands boasting a Royal Warrant or a Coat of Arms; the appeal of the grandeur set in living royal residences draws millions of tourists; the awe surrounding the Monarchy adds to the popularity of shows like 'The Crown' and 'Victoria' that offer a glimpse of the private lives of the Royal Family. (https://brandfinance.com/wp content/uploads/1/brand_finance_monarchy_press_release.pdf)

## Place branding

Place branding is considered the most prevalent example of corporate brand in the public sector (Hankinson, 2010; Klijn et al., 2012). Like corporate brands, place brands act as umbrella brands for a number of smaller product and service brands and, like all organizations, managers involved in promotion of destinations and places have identified that creating a unique identity is a way of standing out from competitive cities, countries, and sites (Hankinson, 2010). Place branding involves both public and private parties ranging from tourist boards and hotels to chambers of commerce and municipalities. In the classical sense, branding of places is about communicating carefully selected physical, utilitarian, and emotional attributes that translate into meaning for the target audience (Hankinson, 2010). Balmer et al. (2020) suggest that nascent corporate brands can be enhanced through positive associations with places. According to Kavaratzis and Hatch (2021, p. 10):

> There are various phases of the place branding process. These are the *Analytical* Phase (research and analysis of the place, its resources, its image and perceptions), the *Strategic* Phase (development of strategic actions and tactical measures to create or influence the place brand), the *Articulative* phase (expression and communication of brand identity and other elements) and the *Participatory* phase (engagement with various groups of stakeholders).

## Social marketing

In social marketing, corporate brands assist individuals to indicate to themselves and others that they identify with a specific behaviour (Kirby, 2001) and, in doing so, may speed up the exchange process, with more immediate benefits and positive reinforcement (Lefebvre, 2013). Komen Race for the Cure, Oxfam, American Cancer Society, the Sierra Club, and UNICEF are examples of well-known social corporate brands (Naidoo & Abratt, 2018).

## 7.2 Future directions

In the future, corporate branding is likely to move in three interrelated directions. In an environment of financial uncertainty, and increased scrutiny as far as corporate branding is concerned, there will be stakeholder co-creation, increased ethical compliance, and sustainability in decision-making.

## Stakeholder co-creation and corporate brands

The emerging thinking in corporate brand research reflects the increasing permeability of organizations, where both internal and external stakeholders are involved in the corporate brand identity co-creation process (Iglesias et al., 2020b). Co-creation is a process that brings consumers, managers, employees, and other stakeholders together to participate in corporate brand development and to create new products and services. Through co-creation activities, organizations can develop relationships with stakeholders, and together they can explore their emotions, feelings, and memories while generating deep insights (Ind et al., 2013). A corporate brand has different aspects that satisfy different stakeholders, and it has to be managed with sensitivity towards these differences (Roper & Davies, 2007). The traditional perspective on corporate brand identity is represented by (1) a belief that it emanates unilaterally and top-down from the organization's management; and (2) stability over time (da Silveira et al., 2013). In contrast to the traditional approach, there is an emerging and increasingly influential perspective, which considers corporate brand identity to be subject to a co-creation process in which many different stakeholders take part. These interactions unfold as a co-creation process of brand-identity construction whereby brand managers and other stakeholders, individually and collectively, 'use, talk about, and construct brand identity while enacting their own identities' (von Wallpach et al., 2017, p. 443). The corporate brand meanings ascribed by these stakeholders help to legitimize the corporate brand. These exchanges are the basis on which corporate brand identity is negotiated and how the meaning of the corporate brand can be accentuated for individual stakeholders (Essamri et al., 2019). This requires a cooperative style of leadership that is more open, humble, and capable of embracing the inputs of multiple stakeholders (Iglesias et al., 2020b).

## Ethics and corporate brands

Corporate brands are facing an ever-increasing pressure to integrate ethical values into their identities and to display their ethical commitment (Iglesias et al., 2020b). Organizations can be identified as being relatively more or less ethical by evaluating the extent to which they embrace social connectedness, openness, critical reflexivity, and responsiveness (Fukukawa et al., 2007). Corporate ethical identity may be defined as 'the set of behaviours, communications, and stances that are representative of an organization's ethical attitudes and beliefs' and includes its 'ethical values, behaviours, and communications on ethical commitments,' all of which 'may enhance corporate performance' (Berrone et al., 2007, p. 35). According to Kleyn et al. (2012), developing an ethical identity cannot begin without acknowledgement on the part of organization leadership of the importance of building trusted relationships with all stakeholders. There is evidence that excellent organizations appear to be more ethical, implying a relationship between excellence and ethics (Bendixen & Abratt, 2007).

An example of ethical marketing is TOMS, a shoe company. It states that 'Through the TOMS COVID-19 Global Giving Fund, you've helped generate $2 million in support of global relief efforts. Over the next few months, we'll continue to distribute these funds to partners that remain on the frontlines, delivering supplies, building hygiene stations, and so much more' (TOMS, 2020).

## Sustainability and corporate social responsibility

Corporate social responsibility and corporate sustainability (CS), as concepts, share the same vision, which intends to balance economic responsibilities with social and environmental ones. Some scholars identify corporate sustainability as an approach to conceptualizing CSR or vice versa, and from a practical point of view, companies use both CSR and CS as interchangeable concepts (Montiel, 2008). Research suggests that adoption of environmental sustainability practices, such as pollution prevention and reducing the consumption of energy and natural resources, induces firms to strengthen their corporate brand and reputation (Slotegraaf & Atuahene-Gima, 2011). Sustainability is defined as contributing to one or more of the following aspects: an economic component (fair price to both producer and consumer), an ecological component (care for the environment, quality of life for humans and farmed animals, careful management of natural resources), and a social component (being the integration of agriculture into the needs of society) (Vermeir & Verbeke, 2008). Sustainability has also been defined as 'development that meets the needs of the present without compromising the ability of future generations to meet their own needs' (World Commission on Environment and Development, 1987).

Corporate social responsibility, on the other hand, concerns organizations' activities aimed at fulfilling important societal obligations and is widely recognized as a vital business practice contributing to the long-term success of companies (Sen & Bhattacharya, 2001). Research suggests that CSR brings about employees' ethical behaviours, which in turn enhance organizational efficiency (Laczniak & Murphy, 1991). Consumers' perceptions of the corporate brand relative to CSR may affect their corporate associations, which reflect what they know about the organization (Sweetin et al., 2013). There is evidence that CSR communications have been found to have a positive impact on brand reputation (Du & Vieira, 2012) and also evidence suggesting that CSR may influence consumer support for a brand (Green & Peloza, 2011).

An example of a company that is committed to sustainability is IKEA. It is the world's largest furniture retailer, and it plans to use only renewable and recycled materials in its products by 2030, in the latest commitment by a global store group to reducing its impact on the environment (Ringstrom, 2018).

An example of CSR is Starbucks. It is looking to diversify its workforce and provide opportunities for certain communities. By 2025, it has pledged to hire 25,000 veterans as part of its socially responsible efforts. This hiring initiative will also look to hire more younger people with the aim of 'helping jump-start careers by giving them their first job' (Starbucks, 2019).

The traditional perspective on ethics and CSR is currently being challenged. Despite many organizations having a corporate code of ethics, unethical practices in many organizations continue. CSR practice in many organizations has been in response to stakeholder pressure rather than based in the organization's brand identity and core values. The COVID-19 crisis, climate change, increasing inequalities, and racism in society are among the challenges facing humanity. Corporate brands are under pressure to embrace a more conscientious approach to management. The idea is that 'conscience' should be at the core of the corporate brand identity. A brand with a conscience indicates both a truth to self and a commitment to social responsibility and fairness (Iglesias & Ind, 2020).

The American outdoor clothing company Patagonia is a good example of a brand with a conscience. It has a long history of being environmentally friendly and being a company with high integrity and quality. Its mission statement is 'We're in business to save our home planet.' Its benefit purposes include: 1% for the planet; build the best product with no unnecessary harm; conduct operations causing no unnecessary harm; sharing best practices with other companies; transparency; and providing a supportive work environment. (www.patagonia.com/on/demandware.static/-/Library-Sites-PatagoniaShared/default/dwf14ad70c/PDF-US/PAT_2019_BCorp_Report.pdf)

## References

Aaker, D. A. (1996). *Building strong brands*. New York: Free Press.
Aaker, D. A. (2004). Leveraging the corporate brand. *California Management Review*, 46(3), 6–18. https://doi.org/10.1177/000812560404600301
Abratt, R., & Kleyn, N. (2012). Corporate identity, corporate branding and corporate reputations: Reconciliation and integration. *European Journal of Marketing*, 46(7), 1048–1063. https://doi.org/10.1108/03090561211230197
American Express. (2020). *Our blue box shared values*. Retrieved from www.americanexpress.com/us/supplier-management/supplier-standards/our-blue-box-shared-values.html
Argenti, P. A., & Druckenmiller, B. (2004). Reputation and the corporate brand. *Corporate Reputation Review*, 6(4), 368–374. https://doi.org/10.1057/palgrave.crr.1540005
Balmer, J. M. T. (1995). Corporate branding and connoisseurship. *Journal of General Management*, 21(1), 22–46. https://doi.org/10.1177/030630709502100102
Balmer, J. M. T. (2008). Identity based views of the corporation. Insights from corporate identity, organisational identity, social identity, visual identity, corporate brand identity, and corporate image. *European Journal of Marketing*, 42(9/10), 879–906. http://dx.doi.org/10.1108/03090560810891055
Balmer, J. M. T. (2009). Scrutinising the British monarchy: The corporate brand that was shaken, stirred and survived. *Management Decision*, 47(4), 639–675. https://doi.org/10.1108/00251740910959468
Balmer, J. M. T. (2011). Corporate heritage identities, corporate heritage brands and the multiple heritage identities of the British Monarchy. *European Journal of Marketing*, 45(9/10), 1380–1398. https://doi.org/10.1108/03090561111151817

Balmer, J. M. T. (2012). Strategic corporate brand alignment: Perspectives from identity based views of corporate brands. *European Journal of Marketing*, 46(7/8), 1064–1092. https://doi.org/10.1108/03090561211230205

Balmer, J. M. T. (2013). Corporate heritage, corporate heritage marketing, and total corporate heritage communications. What are they? What of them? *Corporate Communications: An International Journal*, 18(3), 290–326. https://doi.org/10.1108/CCIJ-05-2013-0031

Balmer, J. M. T., Abratt, R., & Kleyn, N. (2016). Corporate brands and corporate marketing: Emerging trends in the big five eco-system. *Journal of Brand Management*, 23(1), 3–7. https://doi.org/10.1057/bm.2015.51

Balmer, J. M. T., & Burghausen, M. (2015). Explicating corporate heritage, corporate heritage brands and organisational heritage. *Journal of Brand Management*, 22(5), 364–384. https://doi.org/10.1057/bm.2015.26

Balmer, J. M. T., & Burghausen, M. (2019). Marketing, the past and corporate heritage. *Marketing Theory*, 19(2), 217–227. https://doi.org/10.1177/1470593118790636

Balmer, J. M. T., & Gray, E. R. (2003). Corporate brands: What are they? What of them? *European Journal of Marketing*, 37(7/8), 972–997. https://doi.org/10.1108/03090560310477627

Balmer, J. M. T., Greyser, S. A., & Urde, M. (2006). The crown as a corporate brand: Insights from monarchies. *Journal of Brand Management*, 14(1/2), 137–161. https://doi.org/10.1057/palgrave.bm.2550031

Balmer, J. M. T., Mahmoud, R., & Chen, W. (2020). Impact of multilateral place dimensions on corporate brand attractiveness and identification in higher education: Business school insights. *Journal of Business Research*, 116, 628–641. https://doi.org/10.1016/j.jbusres.2019.03.015

Balmer, J. M. T., Powell, S. M., Kernstock, J., & Brexendorf, O. (2017). *Advances in corporate branding*. London: Palgrave Macmillan.

Battacharya, C. B., & Sen, S. (2003). Consumer-company identification: A framework for understanding consumer's relationships with companies. *Journal of Marketing*, 67(2), 76–88. https://doi.org/10.1509/jmkg.67.2.76.18609

Bendixen, M., & Abratt, R. (2007). Corporate identity, ethics and reputation in supplier-buyer relationships. *Journal of Business Ethics*, 76(1), 69–82. https://doi.org/10.1007/s10551-006-9273-4

Berrone, P., Surroca, J., & Tribó, J. A. (2007). Corporate ethical identity as a determinant of firm performance: A test of the mediating role of stakeholder satisfaction. *Journal of Business Ethics*, 76, 35–53. https://doi.org/10.1007/s10551-006-9273-4

Beverland, M., & Farrelly, F. (2010). The quest for authenticity in consumption: Consumers' purposive choice of authentic cues to shape experienced outcomes. *Journal of Consumer Research*, 36(5), 838–856. https://doi.org/10.1086/615047

Bick, G., Jacobson, M. C., & Abratt, R. (2003). The corporate identity management process revisited. *Journal of Marketing Management*, 19(7/8), 835–855. https://doi.org/10.1080/0267257X.2003.9728239

Brakus, J. J., Schmitt, B. H., & Zarantonello, L. (2009). Brand experience: What is it? How is it measured? Does it affect loyalty? *Journal of Marketing*, 73, 52–68. https://doi.org/10.1509/jmkg.73.3.052

Bruhn, M., Schoenmüller, V., Schäfer, D., & Heinrich, D. (2012). Brand authenticity: Towards a deeper understanding of its conceptualization and measurement. *Advances in Consumer Research*, 40, 567–576.

Burmann, C., & Zeplin, S. (2005). Building brand commitment: A behavioural approach to internal brand management. *Journal of Brand Management*, 12(4), 279–300. https://doi.org/10.1057/palgrave.bm.2540223

Coca-Cola. (2020). *Coca-Cola mission and vision statement analysis*. Retrieved from https://mission-statement.com/coca-cola/

Cornelissen, J. (2004). *Corporate communications theory and practice*. Los Angeles, CA: SAGE.

Cullinan, J., Abratt, R., & Mingione, M. (2020). Challenges of corporate brand building and management in a state owned enterprise. *Journal of Product & Brand Management*, 30(2), 293–305. https://doi.org/10.1108/JPBM-08-2019-2522

Curtis, T., Abratt, R., & Minor, W. (2009). Corporate brand management in higher education: The case of ERAU. *Journal of Product & Brand Management*, 18(6), 404–413. https://doi.org/10.1108/10610420910989721

da Silveira, C., Lages, C., & Simões, C. (2013). Reconceptualizing brand identity in a dynamic environment. *Journal of Business Research*, 66(1), 28–36. https://doi.org/10.1016/j.jbusres.2011.07.020

Dall'Olmo Riley, F., & de Chernatony, L. (2000). The service brands as relationships builder. *British Journal of Management*, 11(2), 137–150. https://doi.org/10.1111/1467-8551.t01-1-00156

de Chernatony, L., Dizerury, S., & Segal-Horn, S. (2003). Building a services brand: Stages, people and orientations. *Service Industries Journal, 23*(3), 1–21. https://doi.org/10.1080/714005116

Delgado-Ballester, E. (2004). Applicability of a brand trust scale across product categories: A multigroup invariance analysis. *European Journal of Marketing, 38*(5/6), 573–592. https://doi.org/10.1108/03090560410529222

Delgado-Ballester, E., & Luis Munuera-Alemán, J. (2001). Brand trust in the context of consumer loyalty. *European Journal of Marketing, 35*(11/12), 1238–1258. https://doi.org/10.1108/EUM0000000006475

Donaldson, T., & Preston, L. E. (1995). The stakeholder theory of the corporation: Concepts, evidence and implications. *Academy of Management Review, 20*(1), 65–91. https://doi.org/10.5465/amr.1995.9503271992

Drori, G. S., Delmestri, G., & Oberg, A. (2013). Branding the university: Relational strategy of identity construction in a competitive field. In L. Engwall & P. Scott (Eds.), *Trust in higher education institutions* (pp. 134–147). London: Portland Press.

Du, S., & Vieira, E. T. (2012). Striving for legitimacy through corporate social responsibility: Insights from oil companies. *Journal of Business Ethics, 110*(4), 413–427. https://doi.org/10.1007/s10551-012-1490-4

Eggers, F., O'Dwyer, M., Kraus, S., Vallaster, C., & Güldenberg, S. (2013). The impact of brand authenticity on brand trust and SME growth: A CEO perspective. *Journal of World Business, 48*(3), 340–348. https://doi.org/10.1016/j.jwb.2012.07.018

Einwiller, S., & Will, M. (2002). Towards an integrated approach to corporate branding: Findings from an empirical study. *Corporate Communications: An International Journal, 7*(2), 100–109. https://doi.org/10.1007/978-3-8349-9772-2_13

Erdem, T., & Swait, J. (2004). Brand credibility, brand consideration, and choice. *Journal of Consumer Research, 31*(1), 191–198. https://doi.org/10.1086/383434

Essamri, A., McKechnie, S., & Winklhofer, H. (2019). Co-creating corporate brand identity with online brand communities: A managerial perspective. *Journal of Business Research, 96*, 366–375. https://doi.org/10.1016/j.jbusres.2018.07.015

Ferrell, O. C., & Geoffrey, H. (2000). *Business: A changing world*. New York: McGraw-Hill Education.

Fournier, S. (1998). Consumers and their brands: Developing relationship theory in consumer research. *Journal of Consumer Research, 24*, 343–373. https://doi.org/10.1086/209515

Fukukawa, K., Balmer, J. M. T., & Gray, E. R. (2007). Mapping the interface between corporate identity, ethics and corporate social responsibility. *Journal of Business Ethics, 76*, 1–5. https://doi.org/10.1007/s10551-006-9277-0

Gaus, A. (2020). *6 Socially responsible companies to applaud*. Retrieved from www.classy.org/blog/6-socially-responsible-companies-applaud/

Global RepTrak. (2020). *2020's most reputable companies worldwide*. Retrieved from www.reptrak.com/global-reptrak-100/

Gray, J. (1986). *Managing the corporate image*. Westport, CT: Quorum Books.

Green, T., & Peloza, J. (2011). How does corporate social responsibility create value for consumers? *Journal of Consumer Marketing, 28*(1), 48–56. https://doi.org/10.1108/07363761111101949

Greenberg, A. (1961). Frame of reference of image responses. *Journal of Marketing, 25*(4), 62–64. https://doi.org/10.1177/002224296102500413

Greenberg, M. R. (2014). Energy policy and research: The underappreciation of trust. *Energy Research & Social Science, 1*, 152–160. https://doi.org/10.1016/j.erss.2014.02.004

Gregory, A. (2007). Involving stakeholders in developing corporate brands: The communication dimension. *Journal of Marketing Management, 23*(1–2), 59–73. https://doi.org/10.1362/026725707X178558

Hankinson, G. (2010). Place branding research: A cross-disciplinary agenda and the views of practitioners. *Place Branding and Public Diplomacy, 6*(4), 300–315. https://doi.org/10.1057/pb.2010.29

Hansen, J. R., & Ferlie, E. (2016). Applying strategic management theories in public sector organisations: Developing a typology. *Public Management Review, 18*(1), 1–19. https://doi.org/10.1080/14719037.2014.957339

Harris Poll-Axios. (2020). *The 100 most visible companies*. Retrieved from www.axios.com/axios-harris-poll-corporate-reputations-2020-7fe2c572-ba60-4897-b470-0a60ec96fb9e.html

Hatch, M. J., & Schultz, M. (2001). Are the strategic stars aligned for your corporate brand? *Harvard Business Review, 79*(2), 128–134.

Hatch, M. J., & Schultz, M. (2003). Bringing the corporation into corporate branding. *European Journal of Marketing, 37*(7–8): 1041–1064. https://doi.org/10.1108/03090560310477654

Hatch, M. J., & Schultz, M. (2008). *Taking brand initiative: How companies can align strategy, culture, and identity through corporate branding.* San Francisco, CA: Jossey Bass.

Högström, C., Davoudi, S., Löfgren, M., & Johnson, M. (2016). Relevant and preferred public service: A study of user experiences and value creation in public transit. *Public Management Review, 18*(1), 65–90. https://doi.org/10.1080/14719037.2014.957343

Iglesias, O., & Ind, N. (2020). Towards a theory of conscientious corporate brand co-creation: The next key challenge in brand management. *Journal of Brand Management, 27*, 710–720. https://doi.org/10.1057/s41262-020-00205-7

Iglesias, O., Ind, N., & Schultz, M. (2020a). History matters: The role of history in corporate brand strategy. *Business Horizons, 63*, 51–60. https://doi.org/10.1016/j.bushor.2019.09.005

Iglesias, O., Landgraf, P., Ind, N., Markovic, S., & Koporcic, N. (2020b). Corporate brand identity co-creation in business-to-business contexts. *Industrial Marketing Management, 85*, 32–43. https://doi.org/10.1016/j.indmarman.2019.09.008

Iglesias, O., Singh, J. J., & Foguet, B. (2011). The role of brand experience and affective commitment in determining brand loyalty. *Journal of Brand Management, 18*(8), 570–582. https://doi.org/10.1057/bm.2010.58

Ind, N. (1998). An integrated approach to corporate branding. *Journal of Brand Management, 6*(5), 323–329. https://doi.org/10.1057/bm.1998.20

Ind, N., Iglesias, O., & Schultz, M. (2013). Building brands together: Emergence and outcomes of co-creation. *California Management Review, 55*(3), 5–26. https://doi.org/10.1525/cmr.2013.55.3.5

Interbrand. (2020). *Best global brands.* Retrieved from https://interbrand.com/best-brands/

Jenkins, N. (1991). *The business image.* London: Kogan Page.

Kapferer, J.-N. (2008). *The new strategic brand management, creating and sustaining brand equity long term.* London: Kogan Page.

Kavaratzis, M., & Hatch, M. J. (2021). The elusive destination brand and the ATLAS wheel of place brand management. *Journal of Travel Research, 60*(1), 3–15. https://doi.org/10.1177/0047287519892323

Kay, M. J. (2006). Strong brands and corporate brands. *European Journal of Marketing, 40*(7–8), 742–760. https://doi.org/10.1108/03090560610669973

Kennedy, S. H. (1977). Nurturing corporate images: Total communication or ego trip? *European Journal of Marketing, 11*(1), 120–164.

Kirby, S. D. (2001). Focus on branding: Introduction and overview. *Social Marketing Quarterly, 7*(2), 4–7. https://doi.org/10.1080/15245004.2001.9961149

Kleyn, N., Abratt, R., Chipp, K., & Goldman, M. (2012). Building a strong corporate ethical identity: Key findings from suppliers. *California Management Review, 54*(3), 61–76. https://doi.org/10.1525/cmr.2012.54.3.61

Klijn, E., Eshuis, J., & Braun, E. (2012). The influence of stakeholder involvement on the effectiveness of place branding. *Public Management Review, 14*(4), 499–519. https://doi.org/10.1080/14719037.2011.649972

Knox, S., & Bickerton, D. (2003). The six conventions of corporate branding. *European Journal of Marketing, 37*(7–8), 998–1016. https://doi.org/10.1108/03090560310477636

Laczniak, G., & Murphy, P. (1991). Fostering ethical marketing decisions. *Journal of Business Ethics, 10*(4), 259–271. https://doi.org/10.1007/BF00382965

Lefebvre, R. C. (2013). *Social marketing and social change.* New York: John Wiley &Sons.

Mingione, M., & Abratt, R. (2020). Building a corporate brand in the digital age: Imperatives for transforming born-digital startups into successful corporate brands. *Journal of Marketing Management, 36*(11–12), 981–1008. https://doi.org/10.1080/0267257X.2020.1750453

Montiel, I. (2008). Corporate social responsibility and corporate sustainability: Separate pasts, common futures. *Organisation & Environment, 21*(3), 245–269. https://doi.org/10.1177/1086026608321329

Morhart, F. M., Herzog, W., & Tomczak, T. (2009). Brand-specific leadership: Turning employees into brand champions. *Journal of Marketing, 73*(5), 122–142. https://doi.org/10.1509/jmkg.73.5.122

Naidoo, C., & Abratt, R. (2018). Brands that do good: Insight into social brand equity. *Journal of Brand Management, 25*, 3–13. https://doi.org/10.1057/s41262-017-0072-2

Nguyen, N., & Leblanc, G. (2001). Corporate image and corporate reputation in customers' retention decisions in services. *Journal of Retailing and Consumer Services, 8*(4), 227–36. https://doi.org/10.1016/S0969-6989(00)00029-1

Osborne, S. P., & Brown, K. (2005). *Managing change and innovation in public sector organisations.* London: Routledge.

Powell, S. (2014). Twenty-one years of the *Journal of Brand Management*: A commemorative review. *Journal of Brand Management, 21*(9), 689–701. https://doi.org/10.1057/bm.2015.3

Punjaisri, K., & Wilson, A. (2007). The role of internal branding in the delivery of employee brand promise. *Journal of Brand Management, 15*(1), 57–70. https://doi.org/10.1057/978-1-352-00008-5_6

Ringstrom, A. (2018, June 7). *IKEA to use only renewable and recycled materials by 2030*. Retrieved from www.reuters.com/article/us-ikea-sustainability/ikea-to-use-only-renewable-and-recycled-materials-by-2030-idUSKCN1J31CD

Rokeach, M. (1973). *The nature of human values*. New York: Free Press.

Roper, S., & Davies, G. (2007). The corporate brand: Dealing with multiple stakeholders. *Journal of Marketing Management, 23*(1–2), 75–90. https://doi.org/10.1362/026725707X178567

Sen, S., & Bhattacharya, C. B. (2001). Does doing good always lead to doing better? Consumer reactions to corporate social responsibility. *Journal of Marketing, 38*(2), 225–243. https://doi.org/10.1509/jmkr.38.2.225.18838

Shee, P., & Abratt, R. (1989). A new approach to the corporate image management process. *Journal of Marketing Management, 5*(1), 63–76. https://doi.org/10.1080/0267257X.1989.9964088

Slotegraaf, R., & Atuahene-Gima, K. (2011). Product development team stability and new product advantage: The role of decision-making processes. *Journal of Marketing, 75*(1), 96–108. https://doi.org/10.1509/jm.75.1.96

Spector, A. J. (1961). Basic dimensions of the corporate image. *Journal of Marketing, 25*(6), 47–51. https://doi.org/10.1177/002224296102500608

Starbucks. (2019). *2019 report on global social impact*. Retrieved from www.starbucks.com/responsibility/global-report

Sweetin, V. H., Knowles, L. L., Summey, J. H., & McQueen, K. S. (2013). Willingness-to-punish the corporate brand for corporate social irresponsibility. *Journal of Business Research, 66*(10), 1822–1830. https://doi.org/10.1016/j.jbusres.2013.02.003

TOMS. (2020). *TOMS global giving fund Covid-19. $2 million, made possible by you*. Retrieved from www.toms.com/uk/global-giving-fund.html

Urde, M. (1994). Brand orientation – A strategy for survival. *Journal of Consumer Marketing, 11*(3), 18–32. https://doi.org/10.1108/07363769410065445

Urde, M. (2003). Core value-based corporate brand building. *European Journal of Marketing, 37*(7–8), 1017–1040. https://doi.org/10.1108/03090560310477645

Urde, M. (2009). Uncovering the corporate brand's core values. *Management Decision, 47*(4), 616–638. https://doi.org/10.1108/00251740910959459

Urde, M., Greyser, S. A., & Balmer, J. M. T. (2007). Corporate brands with a heritage. *Journal of Brand Management, 15*(1), 4–19. https://doi.org/10.1057/palgrave.bm.2550106

Vallaster, C., & de Chernatony, L. (2006). Internal brand building and structuration: The role of leadership. *European Journal of Marketing, 40*(7–8), 761–784. https://doi.org/10.1108/03090560610669982

Vermeir, I., & Verbeke, W. (2008). Sustainable food consumption among young adults in Belgium: Theory of planned behaviour and the role of confidence and values. *Ecological Economics, 64*(3), 542–553. https://doi.org/10.1016/j.ecolecon.2007.03.007

Vesal, M., Siahtiri, V., & O'Cass, A. (2021). Strengthening B2B brands by signalling environmental sustainability and managing customer relationships. *Industrial Marketing Management, 92*, 321–331. https://doi.org/10.1016/j.indmarman.2020.02.024

von Wallpach, S., Hemetsberger, A., & Espersen, P. (2017). Performing identities: Processes of brand and stakeholder identity co-construction. *Journal of Business Research, 70*, 443–452. https://doi.org/10.1016/j.jbusres.2016.06.021

Wæraas, A. (2008). Can public sector organisations be coherent corporate brands? *Marketing Theory, 8*(2), 205–221. https://doi.org/10.1177/1470593108093325

Walmart. (2019). *2019 Annual report. Defining the future of retail*. Retrieved from https://s2.q4cdn.com/056532643/files/doc_financials/2019/annual/Walmart-2019-AR-Final.pdf

Wiedmann, K. P., Hennigs, N., Schmidt, S., & Wuestefeld, T. (2011). The importance of brand heritage as a key performance driver in marketing management. *Journal of Brand Management, 19*(3), 182–194. https://doi.org/10.1057/bm.2011.36

Worcester, B. (1986). Corporate image research. In R. Worcester & J. Dowham (Eds.), *Consumer market research handbook* (3rd ed., pp. 601–616). New York: McGraw Hill.

World Commission on Environment and Development. (1987). *Our common future*. Oxford: Oxford University Press.

# 3
# CORPORATE BRAND MANAGEMENT FROM A CO-CREATIVE PERSPECTIVE

*Hans Mühlbacher*

## 1. The emergence of the co-creation paradigm in corporate brand management

### 1.1 The traditional brand paradigm

Perspectives on corporate brand management, brand-management decisions, and actions very much differ depending on the way researchers and brand managers conceive brands. Traditional brand research is either sender- or consumer-focused (Kotler & Armstrong, 2006); is object-, cognition-, or experience-oriented (Aaker, 1996; Keller, 1998; Richards et al., 1998); is mostly dyadic (Hult et al., 2011); focuses in particular on interactions with customers; and takes an individual (Elliott & Davis, 2005) or a social-level approach (Kozinets, 2002; McAlexander et al., 2002).

Sender-focused, object-oriented researchers and managers conceive brands as material objects comprising intangible components. A corporate brand is either a name, a trademark, a logo, or a combination thereof to identify and differentiate an organization from others (e.g., Aaker, 1996; Kotler, 1991), or the brand is the entire organization (Aaker & Joachimsthaler, 2000; de Chernatony & Harris, 2000; Hatch & Schultz, 2001; Kapferer, 2004). Corporate brand management taking the first perspective focuses on brand name awareness and perceptual effects of brand name and logo.

If management considers the organization to be the brand, managers develop, implement, and manage the brand through organizational characteristics and behaviour. Customers and other stakeholders are a rather passive audience (Balmer, 1995). They react in a predetermined way to stimuli provided by a firm. Early literature in this stream of brand conceptualization treats the corporate brand as corporate identity consisting of corporate personality, communication, design, and behaviour that trigger a corporate image in the minds of customers (Birkigt & Stadler, 1986). From this perspective, the Red Bull brand, for example, represents a young, adventurous, risk-taking, fun-loving male who is not mainstream. Corporate brand communication consists mainly of events such as 'Flugtag,' air races, free skiing competitions, cliff jumping, or participation in Formula 1 races. The corporate design of the Red Bull brand has become iconic through the slick blue and silver can and the red bull. And teamwork of staff, extensive sponsorship of extreme sports such as the Rally Dakar in parallel to ownership of teams in mainstream sports like soccer or ice hockey, and financial support of research on heavy sport injuries are typical for Red Bull's corporate behaviour.

Broadening this predominantly communication-oriented approach, Kapferer (2008) calls brand identity the 'essence' of a brand that can be illustrated through a prism encompassing a corporate brand's material representations, such as the look of a Louis Vuitton flagship shop or the design of KTM motorcycles, values and norms of behaviour of people representing the company to other stakeholders, personality traits of the brand, the way of treating relationships, self-reflection, and a reflection of the typical consumer or brand user. Consequently, corporate brand management deals with typical attributes of the organization, organizational values (Balmer, 2001), their presentation through staff, communication devices and activities (de Chernatony & Segal-Horn, 2001), the monitoring of how the company is perceived by customers and other stakeholders (Ballantyne & Aitken, 2007), and the evolution of corporate image (Hatch & Schultz, 2003).

Seen from this perspective, strategic corporate brand management searches for, determines, and disseminates objectives concerning the corporate brand; it defines the intended image of the brand to customers, the central manifestations of intended brand meaning, and the most important partners in generating the intended meaning. Brand management develops or acquires the capabilities to support the development of brand meaning, manifestations, and relationships with important communication partners; allocates scarce resources of the organization in a coordinated way; and monitors the outcomes of all of those activities. Based on a control-centric mindset (Iglesias & Bonet, 2012; Iglesias & Ind, 2020), the managerial perspective ascribes active brand creation and development to the firm, and a rather passive, receptive role to customers, who derive functional, emotional, and self-expression benefits (Aaker & Joachimsthaler, 2000). The customers continually make direct or indirect, real or virtual experiences with the organization (Ballantyne & Aitken, 2007; Payne et al., 2009), store the interpretations of those experiences as associations in their memories, and develop company-related attitudes and images.

Consumer-focused, cognition-oriented brand researchers consider corporate brands as mental representations like perceived attributes and benefits, corporate image, and related attitudes (Keller, 2008). Corporate managers following this view tend to influence consumers' associations with the brand, related emotions, and behaviour. In comparison, consumer culture researchers are mainly interested in social relationships (Elliott & Davis, 2005) between members of brand communities (Muñiz & O'Guinn, 2001) or tribes (Cova & Cova, 2002), and in experiential aspects of brands (Arvidsson & Caliandro, 2016; Roux, 2007). Corporate brand managers following this approach observe and participate in the discussions concerning their brand in social media, launch events to fuel discourse on important matters, or provide bloggers with information to lead their contributions in the intended direction.

## 1.2 The co-creation paradigm

Challenging the traditional idea of value created by companies in exchanges with customers (Bagozzi, 1975; Hunt, 1976), the Scandinavian school of services marketing introduced the notion of interactive marketing (Grönroos, 1982; Gummesson, 1987) in parallel to the French school of 'servuction' (Eiglier & Langeard, 1987), whose members remarked that 'prosumers' consume and participate in the production of services in closely interwoven manners. However, it took until the turn of the century until American authors picked up the idea and suggested replacing the exchange paradigm in marketing literature by value co-creation, i.e., value formed in interaction between co-creating actors (Prahalad & Ramaswamy, 2004; Ramirez, 1999; Vargo & Lusch, 2004). Kozinets et al. (2004) introduced the notion of 'interagency' that refers to the interaction of marketers and consumers. Vargo and Lusch (2016, p. 9) define this interaction as a 'mutual or reciprocal action or influence' which can take place face-to-face or virtually. Ind et al. (2013) define co-creation as 'an active, creative, and social process based on collaboration between organizations and participants that generates benefits for all and creates value for stakeholders' (p. 9).

First applications of the co-creative paradigm can be found in 'open innovation' (Chesbrough, 2006; Prahalad & Ramaswamy, 2000), that is the idea of making customers participate in new product development processes. The participation can reach from online customer communities' acceptance to be observed in their exchanges about company-related experiences to collaborative product development projects between focal firms and their suppliers or customers (Ind et al., 2017). Prahald and Ramaswamy (2004, p. 16) describe this process of value co-creation as the consumer and the firm being 'intimately involved in jointly creating value that is unique to the individual consumer.' The created value is not simply monetary but an 'interactive relativistic preference experience' (Holbrook, 2006, p. 212) on the basis of attitudes, affections, and judgements. In a certain contrast to this mainstream of views that sees value arising in reciprocal or mutual processes of companies and customers (Vargo & Lusch, 2016), Scandinavian authors underline that value is always personal as 'value-in-use for the customer' (Grönroos & Voima, 2013, p. 135) and 'value-in-social-context' constructed as part of a social system (Edvardsson et al., 2011) at the same time.

In parallel to the idea of value created in interactions between co-creating actors, Muñiz and O'Guinn (2001) or Kates (2004) were first to show how customers socially co-construct brand meaning. Pitt et al. (2006) described 'open brands' as a new window of opportunity. Mühlbacher and Hemetsberger (2008) defined brands as (1) systems of interrelated meanings, manifestations, and individuals as well as organizations interested in those meanings, manifestations, individuals and organizations; and (2) the social discourse from which that system continuously emerges in an evolving socio-cultural context. Merz et al. (2009) state that 'the logic of brands and branding . . . has shifted from the conceptualization of brand as a firm-provided property of goods to brand as a collaborative, value co-creation activity of firms and all of their stakeholders' (p. 328f.).

The ideas of customers co-creating brands and of customer engagement (van Doorn et al., 2010) radically altered previous views on the creation and development of brands. A large stream of literature on co-creative branding has developed over the last 20 years (e.g., Iglesias et al., 2013, 2020; Lucarelli & Hallin, 2015; von Wallpach et al., 2017; Wider et al., 2018). This literature provides abundant empirical evidence of active consumers (Diamond et al., 2009; Schau et al., 2009) who intensively follow the actions of brand managers, comment on brand management decisions, negotiate the meaning of new brand manifestations (Brodie et al., 2013; Kozinets et al., 2010; Schroll et al., 2018), or even become 'brand developers' (Füller et al., 2008) taking the initiative in creating new brand manifestations (Berthon et al., 2015; Fisher & Smith, 2011; Füller et al., 2013; O'Sullivan et al., 2011) or creating their own brands independent of companies (Füller et al., 2008). Consumers communicate about the joy or disappointment of working for a brand (Brodie et al., 2013; Sarkar & Banerjee, 2020). Fans of brands disseminate brand knowledge, expectations, evaluations, and experiences (Stieler & Germelmann, 2018) and enact brand meaning through 'performances' (Lucarelli & Hallin, 2015; von Wallpach et al., 2017).

## *1.3 A multi-stakeholder perspective*

A customer-centric perspective has traditionally dominated brand research. However, an increasing number of marketing researchers recognize that other stakeholders can have a major impact on a company's market success (Frow & Payne, 2011; Gummesson, 2006; Hult et al., 2011; Koll et al., 2005; Kornum & Mühlbacher, 2013; Vargo & Lusch, 2016). Stakeholders of corporate brands may be entrepreneurs and managers, consumers, staff and service personnel, distributors, retail sales personnel, celebrities, journalists, media agents and suppliers, legislators, public administrations, consumer advocates, and even fans of competing brands. These stakeholders can play several roles in parallel. In the case of SWARCO, one of the world's leading suppliers of mobility solutions to make travel experiences more convenient, safer, and environmentally sound, for example, public administrators and legislators are customers, norm setters, and supervisors. Car manufacturers play the roles of development partners and competitors.

Stakeholders directly or indirectly, virtually or physically take part more or less intensively in the formation of brand meaning; in the creation, production, consumption, and use of brand manifestations; and in the social construction of other brand stakeholders. Active stakeholders express their beliefs and convictions about brands and other stakeholders (Kozinets et al., 2010; Schau, et al., 2009); share their experiences through narrations, talk, and visualizations (Bal et al., 2009); engage (Brodie et al., 2013; Hollebeek et al., 2021), create (Berthon et al., 2008; Ertimur & Gilly, 2012;), and produce (Berthon et al., 2015; Ritzer et al., 2012) or simply use brands (Dion & Arnould, 2016); and coincidentally observe others consuming or acting in a context relevant to the brand (Kozinets et al., 2004).

Corporate branding literature has been among the first to recognize the importance of other stakeholders in branding processes (Gregory, 2007; Hatch & Schultz, 2003, 2010). Leitch and Richardson (2003) criticized the traditional company-centric view (Balmer & Grey, 2003; de Chernatony & Segal-Horn, 2001; Schultz & de Chernatony, 2002) and emphasized the mutuality in interactions between companies and their stakeholders. Jones (2005) provided empirical evidence of stakeholders sometimes taking the initiative in corporate branding. Neville and Menguc (2006) showed stakeholder actions to be interrelated. Schau et al. (2009) and Vallaster and von Wallpach (2013) documented the active participation and interaction of various stakeholders in public discourses concerning company-related events. Ingenbleek and Imminik (2010) found diverse, partly conflicting interests of stakeholders concerning the formulation of corporate social responsibility standards. Thus, corporate brand co-creation research and management must stay incomplete and distant from reality without a careful account of the influence of various stakeholders.

Brand co-creation in dynamic social processes involving various stakeholder groups raises the issue of brand governance. Ind and Bjerke (2007) see organizations co-creating their brand with stakeholders sharing control over the brand. Hatch and Schultz (2010) suggest to manage such control-sharing through an integration of stakeholder/company engagement, i.e., facilitating access of selected stakeholders and company management to information through dialogue, and organizational self-disclosure, i.e., taking and managing higher risks in exchange to increased transparency. However, because co-creation of corporate brands can take place between stakeholders without the intervention of the company (Hatch & Schultz, 2010), Fournier and Avery (2011, p. 194) suggest that brand co-creation forces managers to 'relinquish control.' Wider et al. (2018) go even a step further, unmasking the idea of management's control of brand processes as an illusion. In sum, company management is only one of the central stakeholders in interaction processes between a fluctuating number of active brand stakeholders with changing influence on the brand process. Corporate brands continuously form under limited control of brand management as ongoing interaction processes and the outcome of these processes at a certain point in time (Mühlbacher & Hemetsberger, 2013).

## 2. Key characteristics of corporate brand co-creation

### 2.1 Co-creation engagement as process and state

Co-creative interactions of stakeholders concerning corporate brands take place in complex systems of relationships. These systems are not the sum of all dyadic relationships of a firm with individual stakeholders or groups of stakeholders. Interacting stakeholders in corporate branding represent a continuous multiplicity (Hillebrand et al., 2015), i.e., a heterogeneous social entity constituted by the conjunctive synthesis of a number of stakeholders that cannot be considered independently (Deleuze, 1988). The actions and interactions of stakeholders simultaneously influence or have delayed effects on all other stakeholders. Even when stakeholders do not participate in interactions, these interactions influence their stake in a direct or indirect manner. Take the example of Amazon. If legislators would force the company to pay higher wages to their workers in the logistics centres, the company might increase the amount taken from cooperating producers and retailers to assure profits for Amazon shareholders and premiums for top management. The partners might reduce their number of personnel to secure margins, and Amazon might lose these laid-off people as their customers. All of this would affect the meaning of Amazon's corporate brand. Thus, in line with Brodie et al. (2019), who conceive the engagement of actors in co-creation as a process, corporate brand co-creation is an ongoing process of interrelated exchanges of multiple stakeholders. All stakeholder activities shape brand meaning and manifestations, and they may range from collaborative co-creation to co-destructive interventions.

Hollebeek et al. (2021) underline the state-based nature of stakeholder engagement in parallel to the process view of co-creation. Stakeholders' perception and interpretation of the particular state of the co-creation process and its socio-political context influence the level of participation in corporate brand co-creation. Additionally, role-related social norms of behaviour (Vargo & Lusch, 2016) and personality characteristics (Hollebeek et al., 2021) influence the level of stakeholder engagement. When a consumer enters a Hermès shop, for example, sales assistants do not play the role of informers and servants of potential clients only. They also have to personally represent the brand and to teach consumers appropriate brand-related behaviour. In this case, consumers who might possess a high multiple of personal wealth compared to the sales persons agree to subordinate themselves in order to become part of the Hermès brand universe.

The intensity of stakeholders' engagement in brand co-creation fluctuates (Hollebeek et al., 2021). It is not always volitional and can be inadvertent (Hollebeek et al., 2018). As the example of the launch of esports by AS Monaco presented by Bertschy et al. (2020) shows, stakeholders such as football and esports fans, players, and club management and media participate in the brand-cocreation process in a more or less active manner, more or less intentionally, in varying roles (von Wallpach et al., 2017), with diverse goals (Kornum et al., 2017), and at different times (Vallaster & von Wallpach, 2013). Football fans tend to simply ignore the launch in their brand-related social media communication. They protest against decisions taken by club management but do not lose their deep engagement in the brand. Their goal is to feel being part of a community of brand enthusiasts. Esports fans are rather reactive communicators who love to consume the games and esports-related content provided by management and professional players. The professionals are not only players unintentionally influencing the brand, but they act intentionally as content providers to fans at the same time. Club management acts in various roles such as informers, norm setters, or content providers with the goal of strengthening the brand relationships of other stakeholders.

### 2.2 Role-related stakeholder participation

Stakeholders of corporate brands engage in role-related decision-making (Hollebeek et al., 2021). They construct their own roles (Crane & Ruebottom, 2011; Carlson et al., 2008) depending on the perceived relevance of the brand to them (Johnson et al., 2011), perceived brand meaning (Dong & Tian, 2009), and the roles ascribed to other stakeholders. Some stakeholders construe themselves as 'belonging' to the brand because this membership is functional for the development and maintenance of their individual and social identity (Carlson et al., 2008). According to Mühlbacher and Hemetsberger (2013), stakeholders considered being most relevant to a brand by other stakeholders form an inner circle. As a 'living example' of what the brand stands for, these core stakeholders serve as representatives and ambassadors of the brand (Hemetsberger & Reinhardt, 2006). They discursively assign roles, such as mentor, learner, storyteller, historian, talent scout, or celebrity to other stakeholders (Beverland et al., 2010) depending on perceived stakeholder legitimacy (Hollenbeck & Zinkhan, 2010; Santana, 2012) and the perceived relationship of these stakeholders with manifestations of the brand (Beverland et al., 2010). Some participants in brand processes actively search for potential other actors to convince them to join the community of engaged stakeholders (Brodie et al., 2013), whereas other stakeholders organize partners for distinct brand destructive actions (Hollenbeck & Zinkhan, 2010; Roux, 2007).

## 2.3 Drivers of stakeholder engagement

Stakeholders can have quite diverse agendas making them participate in corporate brand co-creation processes (Robson & Farquhar, 2021). They can have competing or even contradictory goals, interests, expectations, responsibilities, and rights (Hollebeek et al., 2021) influenced by issues of the socio-political context such as power structures, administrative hurdles, information asymmetry, perceived agendas of other stakeholders, conflict, threat, or defamation (Freeman et al., 2018; Jordan et al., 2019; Letaifa et al., 2016).

Managers, employees, intermediaries, bloggers but also customers engage in impression management (Schlenker, 1980). They act as gatekeepers of information aiming to actively communicate brand values, symbols, or signs to other social actors. They actively recommend branded products, services, or the entire organization (Johnson & Rapp, 2010; Brodie et al., 2013) and communicate brand meanings to inspire others to become committed brand stakeholders (Schau et al., 2009). Brand antagonists use the same impression management tools and practices as brand enthusiasts to reach their oppositional goals. They influence the judgement and actions of others to resist dominant or to spread oppositional brand meanings (Krishnamurthy & Kucuk, 2009; Luedicke et al., 2010). The case of Danone yogurt has shown that management wanted to promote a new product with some positive effects for the wellness of consumers. Consumers expected to be able to contribute to their health without having to give up the pleasure of consumption. Defenders of consumer health interest tested the product and – as a result – strongly opposed the health claims of Danone's advertising. The Danone brand was hurt by their claims of misleading communication. Consumers refrained from positive word-of-mouth in fear of potentially doing wrong.

## 2.4 Simultaneous value creation and value destruction

Most of co-creation literature has a positive bias in the sense of demonstrating the deliberate active engagement of consumers or other stakeholders in launching or participating in reciprocal value co-creation processes for mutual benefit (Brodie et al., 2013). Ind et al. (2013) see brand building as 'an organic process that brings the parties closer together to co-create value' (p. 21). Merz et al. (2009, p. 340) talk about a 'collaborative, value co-creation activity.' Referring to Hatch and Schultz (2010), Törmälä and Saraniemi (2018, p. 36) report that shared expectations and mutual benefits 'are the central drivers of business partner's corporate brand co-creation.' Iglesias et al. (2020) modify that positive view. They find multiple internal and external stakeholders participating in processes of corporate brand co-creation through communication, internalization, elucidation, and contestation. Contestation potentially leads to value destruction, as stakeholders might share their negative views on the brand. Earlier empirical research concerning co-creation processes of corporate brand meaning (Vallaster & von Wallpach, 2013) and brand identity (da Silveira et al., 2013) provides indications that co-creation processes must neither be collaborative nor driven by intrinsic motivation, shared expectations, mutual benefits and trust, nor do they necessarily create value for all stakeholders.

According to their specific interests and goals, multiple stakeholders act in relation to corporate brands, always creating value for themselves and maybe for some others but potentially destructing more or less value for other stakeholders at the same time (Clark et al., 2020). Echeverri and Skålén (2011) report that interaction partners in a service delivery act as value co-creators and -recoverers as well as value co-reducers and -destroyers. Cabiddu et al. (2019) and Dolan et al. (2019) find value co-creation and co-destruction happening in parallel during supplier and customer interactions. Thus, brand co-creation processes are not necessarily beneficial for the focal company. Critical accounts of value co-creation (Bonsu & Darmody; 2008, Cova & Dalli, 2009; Zwick et al., 2008), negative contributions to interactive value creation (Cova & White, 2010; Hemetsberger, 2006; Hollenbeck & Zinkhan, 2010; Holt, 2002; Kashif & Zarkada, 2015), and reports of value and brand co-destruction (Andriopoulou et al., 2019; Grégoire & Fisher, 2006; Järvi et al., 2018; Kashif & Zarkada, 2015; Makkonen & Olkkonen, 2017; Parmentier & Fischer, 2015; Prior & Marcos-Cuevas, 2016) provide increasing evidence of the commonly unnoticed 'dark side of co-creation.' Value co-creation presumes a shared understanding of proper procedures, understandings, and engagements. In value co-destruction the interaction partners draw on incongruent elements (Echeverri & Skålén, 2011). Cabiddu et al. (2019) suggest to conceptually situate the simultaneous positive and negative contributions to value creation (seen from the company perspective) in a value variation space rather than see them as being mutually exclusive. Plé and Chumpitaz Caceres (2010) suggest replacing the term *value co-creation* for the process of simultaneous co-creation and co-destruction by 'interactive value formation.'

While brand co-creation and co-destruction are obvious in stakeholder behaviour, they are often grounded in differences in brand meaning. The meaning of corporate brands is not consensual. Differing or even conflicting elements of brand meaning (Gyrd-Jones & Kornum, 2013) can co-exist without being harmful (Bertschy et al., 2020; Thompson et al., 2006), but this might also be detrimental when core elements of meaning are subject to disillusionment and become contested (Parmentier & Fischer, 2015) or are interpreted along diametrically opposed moral standards (Kozinets & Handelman, 2004). As Luedicke et al. (2010) documented, fans and antagonists of AM General's Hummer brand hold diametrically opposed meanings of the brand. The brand is a sign of freedom deserved by members of a nation blessed by God for the fans, and it stands for unprecedented waste of resources by irresponsible egocentrics for antagonists. The communicative fight between the two groups becoming sometimes even physical forced General Motors to close the Hummer production in 2010 to avoid negative effects on their corporate brand. The brand stayed dormant before GMC launched the electrical Hummer EV 2022 that tries to combine the interests of both groups of highly engaged stakeholders.

Depending on contextual conditions (Aaker et al., 2004) and the importance of the brand relationship to the self (Johnson et al., 2011) or to the social group (Luedicke et al., 2010), active stakeholders may tend to sustain the coherence of brand meaning (Canniford & Shankar, 2013) but may also bring forward diverse or even conflicting ideas (Gebauer et al., 2013), feel betrayed, disengage, or even become brand antagonists (Grégoire & Fisher, 2006) who destroy value of other stakeholders (Kozinets & Handelman, 2004). Recently, Engen et al. (2020) found that brand destruction might occur in the interaction of several types of stakeholders due to inability, mistakes, lack of functional competence, and lack of transparency. Even organizational branding activities can destroy value for stakeholders when discursive closure or hypocrisy take over, marginalizing or neglecting essential operations or shortcomings of the organization (Bertilsson & Rennstam, 2018).

## 3. Managerial consequences of the co-creation paradigm for corporate brand management

### 3.1 The challenge

Independent of their perspective on branding – whether it is traditional or co-creative – managers of corporate brands face the difficulty of managing the tension between adapting company actions to collective norms of the industry to safeguard the legitimacy gained from membership in a specific category of organizations and differentiating the company's role behaviour as employer, supplier, customer, communicator, etc. to successfully compete with rivals. Corporate brand management needs to establish and maintain what Leitch & Motion (2007) call 'unified diversity' – that is, a distinct recognizable pattern of organizational behaviour which allows the corporate brand to be multifaceted and to fluctuate with contexts but to have a core meaning (Michel, 2017) shared by the majority of stakeholders. Context specific interpretations of brand elements, such as products, advertisement, service delivery, or social media content differ between various stakeholders. They are peripheral to brand meaning and result in multiple context-dependent interpretations of the corporate brand that can become potentially decisive for stakeholder behaviour (Michel & Donthu, 2014).

Corporate brand management based on a co-creation perspective differs from traditional managerial approaches to branding by embracing a multiplicity of stakeholders which potentially take an active role in brand formation and cannot be closely governed. Co-creative corporate brand formation is not primarily driven by shareholder and customer interests, the creation of financial value to shareholders and of functional and emotional value to customers. A more balanced perspective of differing stakeholder interests and a sincere intent to co-create shared value must dominate corporate brand management. To firmly establish such a mindset, a number of organizational conditions must be in place (Mühlbacher & Böbel, 2019). Top management needs to have a shared value-oriented entrepreneurial vision that reinforces co-creative processes. Managers must have strong networking capabilities to establish, sustain, and influence co-creation processes with and between various stakeholders for mutual benefit. Management decisions and actions must be aligned with corporate strategy that contains the intended meaning of the corporate brand, basic rules of behaviour, and communicative action as well as the media to be used. Finally, corporate brand management needs to continuously monitor the impact of stakeholders' brand-related communication.

### 3.2 The role of top management

Corporate brands continually form from the actions and experiences of stakeholders internal and external to focal organizations. Thus, corporate brand management becomes a strategic management issue that cannot be delegated to lower ranks in the organization, a public relations department, or to an external agency. Top managers who are aware of the positive and negative potentials of brand co-creation take care that stakeholders experience the personal and physical manifestations of the organization in a manner representing and enacting the intended corporate brand. Managers cannot control the formation of their corporate brand but – similar to conductors of an orchestra – they have an important influence on brand formation processes.

Management's role in corporate brand formation is to establish the basis for a consistent pattern of organizational behaviour recognizable by all stakeholders. Consistency of organizational behaviour is achieved through dynamic stability of actions, i.e., behaviour adapted to specific contexts but following recognizable basic rules that assure self-resemblance over time despite a high diversity of actors and situations. Such basic rules must be defined by top management to reinforce the dominant self of the organization. Managers are role models in the process of establishing and reinforcing those basic rules. Entrepreneurial leaders such as Steve Jobs, Elon Musk, or Giorgio Armani often represent the brand through their strong personality, highly visible to the public but also marking the internal environment of the company. Company leaders should reinforce brand-adequate behaviour of staff members by positive feedback and rethink existing incentives in the light of their impact on the intended corporate brand.

## 3.3 *Internal corporate branding*

How the intended corporate brand translates into actual behaviour of people representing the company to external stakeholders strongly influences the experiences of those stakeholders and their brand-related actions. Every member of a business organization is a part-time manager of the corporate brand (Gummesson, 1991). Thus, selection of staff and training with lively examples for context specific adaptations of behaviour become important tools of corporate brand management. For example, millions of customers who visit Disney theme parks in the US, France, and Japan every year personally experience the Disney brand together with many other visitors. Staff playing the famous roles of Mickey, Goofy, and all the other characters are intensively trained during several weeks to act exactly according to their roles whatever happens around them when they are 'on scene.' Disney carefully selects the technical staff and trains them intensively to assure perfect visitor illusions. Celebrations of success, storytelling, the way of resource allocation, and total quality management can strengthen the corporate brand experience of staff members. IKEA, for example, invites its high-potential local managers to training camps in Sweden, where they can personally experience the Swedish lifestyle with its values and norms of behaviour the brand stands for. Over several years the HILTI Culture Journey has stimulated brand-related discourse among top managers and all levels of staff. Top management regularly invited employees to share breakfast and had lunch together with staff at the canteen. The BMW Academy provides intensive opportunities for participants to discuss and experience the meanings of BMW, Mini, and Bentley.

Leadership style, organizational structure, and time horizon of management decisions influence the corporate brand. Even if corporate brand management is not really a democratic undertaking as suggested by some literature (Asmussen et al., 2013), transactional leadership based on rather strict supervision, organization, and performance will not be able to come up to the demands of co-creative branding. Functionally structured organizations and short-term, success-oriented decision-makers will have some difficulties in reaching the goal of unified brand diversity. Driven by short-term, function-specific objectives set by top management, staff members in charge of specific business functions tend to perceive differing corporate role identities, different self-classifications, and different goals of their organization. Such staff members jeopardize the generation of a coherent pattern of company behaviour recognizable by external stakeholders. If Amazon managers, for example, set a goal to provide customers with reliable and fast services and shareholders with high profits but exploit their employees by paying very low wages and creating immense work pressure, and at the same time evade tax payment in Europe, the corporate brand tends to become loaded with discrepant core associations that risk becoming a source of destructive energy for the future development of the brand.

A transformative leadership style that relies on a shared vision, a high level of shared values, basic norms of behaviour, and the execution of brand-related actions in cooperation with committed staff members will more easily embrace brand co-creation. Transformative leaders invite co-creative, situationally adapted actions concerning the corporate brand inside the frame of corporate brand strategy. Process-oriented organizational structures facilitate close cooperation of functional specialists who have a shared objective. In conjunction with long-term-oriented transformative management, process-oriented structures facilitate the development of a dominant organizational self that is shared and enacted by most members of the organization.

## 3.4 External corporate branding

A perspective on corporate brands as complex, social, co-creation processes comprises collaborative to controversial, constructive to destructive, individual to interactive, intended to unintended but always interrelated actions of a continuous multiplicity of stakeholders including company managers. In light of this complexity, it appears rather problematic to conceive corporate brand management as a collaborative value co-creation activity driven by brand management. Corporate brands are continuously forming in a rather unpredictable manner as social processes and their outcome at certain points in time. The impact of brand managers' actions is limited as external stakeholders take over important functions in the process. When the French administration banned the Red Bull brand from its markets, the brand profited from the reluctance of public food administrations to approve product sales. French adolescents drove to Belgium to take home whole trunk loads of the energy drink. Mothers expressing fear for the health of their children increased the attractiveness of the brand to adolescents. Rumours spread by media about taurine made from bulls' testicles further increased the popularity of the brand. Stakeholders such as customers, intermediaries, suppliers, or media do not wait to be invited for participation. They can take the initiative and be multipliers in positive and negative terms. Corporate brands need both positive and negative contributions to brand-related public discourse for their vigorous development because both fuel interactions. Through organized bike rides across the USA, Harley-Davidson, for example, has been able to attract the active engagement of consumers, distributors, employees, and media representatives in a way that makes them feel part of a community. Members of these stakeholder groups virtually exchange experiences with each other, personally spend time together, and express their brand enthusiasm or criticism.

Brand managers can stimulate brand-related interactions through launching and contributing to them and by influencing the social context of the interactions. Dove's famous campaign for 'Real Beauty' of women or Snapple's original approach to communication demonstrated impressively how brand management can gain public attention for an issue; popularize the issue with the help of media, spokespeople, and interest groups; let consumers personally relate to the issue; and even empower stakeholders to create individual communicative contributions. KTM managers increased the involvement of media in the rally Paris-Dakar by personal invitations to try-outs of new bikes on the island of Elba together with motocross and endurance-race stars. Caterpillar brings together their staff, distributors, and suppliers to create personal relationships and reinforce shared interest. Ducati offers an internet platform for all interested stakeholders where they can meet and exchange their knowledge and experiences.

To reach the desired level of corporate brand communication consistency externally is more difficult than internally. Management can offer one or several communication platforms to specific stakeholder groups, feed highly active stakeholders with excusive information, support these stakeholders with latest products well ahead of their market launch, or provide the stakeholders with communication devices easy to handle. To avoid flaming by communities or shitstorms, stakeholders should never feel urged or pressed to orient their evaluations and communication in a manner prespecified by the company. As the examples of LEGO and Alfa Romeo show, companies can very successfully cooperate with stakeholders in co-creating the corporate brand or lose stakeholders' interest in cooperation. LEGO successfully established LEGO Ideas, a platform for creative stakeholders interested in the latest information and willing to exchange and provide product ideas. More recently LEGO launched a platform called LEGO World Builder, a story-development platform where fans can pitch ideas for new LEGO stories and contribute artwork, characters, or storylines. LEGO management promises to give feedback and even to purchase the rights to the best contributions. In contrast, Alfa Romeo tried to make their highly engaged fan community, the Alfisti, not only work for the company in organizing events but also tried to dictate the content of their media communication. The highly disappointed fans decided to cease cooperation and to go their own way concerning the brand. Thus, management should not attempt to control consumers as if they were staff members. They should rather engage in establishing and sustaining social and emotional relationships with external stakeholders in addition to reliable information sources (Cova et al., 2015).

### 3.5 Corporate brand monitoring

Corporate brand management with a co-creation perspective monitors how external and internal stakeholders interact directly or indirectly in which roles – how they influence each other concerning the meanings they attribute to the organization, concerning which specific subjects and with which impact. Because interacting stakeholders may have differing brand perceptions and expectations or may be the same individuals in different roles depending on context, brand managers need to know if expectations and perceptions of stakeholders at various contact points are in conflict with each other. Not every stakeholder group can be fully satisfied. Brand managers needs to analyse the potential influence of stakeholders on the corporate brand and their own potential to influence the stakeholders' expectations, experiences, and communication. Brand managers determine the importance of contact points with stakeholders they can influence and how the configuration of these contact points affects stakeholder experiences, brand perceptions, and behaviour. The goal is to find solutions that do not disappoint or even repel the more powerful stakeholders and to compensate less-influential stakeholders who cannot be fully satisfied. The development of brand contact points of stakeholders which management cannot influence needs to be continuously monitored to be warned of and to act against negative evolutions in time. As long as stakeholder perceptions only differ in terms of peripheral elements of the corporate brand, no major problems for the brand should occur.

## 4. Potential future research

Traditionally, brand research has been characterized by a dyadic focus and a managerial or consumer perspective. Most often researchers study the impact of company actions on consumers or vice versa. Corporate brand literature has embraced a broader stakeholder perspective since the early works of Hatch and Schultz (2003) and Leitch and Richardson (2003). The co-creation perspective on corporate brands entails an even higher complexity of relationships. Brands continuously form through the interaction of a continuous multiplicity of stakeholders. Thus, future research should take that complexity into account and analyse corporate brand formation in its totality: Who is acting how, with which effect on whom, and does it matter for the brand? Network analysis (de Nooy & Mrvar, 2005; Goldenberg et al., 2009) can help to discover which stakeholders are more or less active, who tends to take the initiative or to react, and how strongly stakeholders relate to each other. Content analysis of stakeholders' (re-)actions can show how the stakeholders influence each other and which wave-like effects corporate brand management actions can generate.

To find sequences of actions and reactions caused by stakeholder interrelatedness, longitudinal analyses should increasingly replace cross-sectional studies. Additionally, structural equation modelling finds its limits in highly complex relationships between interrelated antecedent conditions and their outcome. Regression algorithms assume sufficiency of every antecedent condition and do not consider necessary minimum levels of the conditions for the outcome. Therefore, future research should increasingly apply Necessary Condition Analysis (Dul, 2016) and Qualitative Comparative Analysis (Mello, 2021) in parallel to methods based on regression algorithms.

It will become increasingly important for research to replace a purely managerial perspective on corporate brands by a position of observers. Brand co-creation outcomes of stakeholder interactions on brand touchpoints not directly controllable to brand management need increased monitoring. In addition to highly interesting descriptions of how stakeholders enact corporate brands for their own purposes, researchers should develop tools easily applicable by brand managers for monitoring the effects of such enactments on the formation of the brand.

In view of the limited control of corporate brand managers over ongoing brand co-creation processes, future research should analyse how brand managers can keep positive brand discourse alive over longer time periods. Historical analyses (Argyres et al., 2020) of the evolution of strong corporate brands could produce interesting insights on how brand managers can contribute to making positive discourse more resilient against a loss of stakeholder interest or attacks from brand antagonists.

# References

Aaker, D. A. (1996). *Building strong brands*. New York: University of Michigan; Free Press.
Aaker, D. A., & Joachimsthaler, E. (2000). *Brand leadership*. New York: Free Press.
Aaker, J., Fournier, S., & Brasel, A. S. (2004). When good brands do bad. *Journal of Consumer Research*, *31*, 1–16.
Andriopoulou, A., Skourtis, G., Giannopoulos, A., Strapchuk, S., & Koniordos, M. (2019). Understanding value co-destruction in tourism service ecosystem. 11th International Scientific Conference, Mecavnik-Drvengrad, Uzice, Serbia.
Argyres, N. S., De Massis, A., Foss, N. J., Frattini, F., Jones, G., & Silverman, B. S. (2020). History-informed strategy research: The promise of history and historical research methods in advancing strategy scholarship. *Strategic Management Journal*, *41*, 343–368. https://doi.org/10.1002/smj.3118
Arvidsson, A., & Caliandro, A. (2016). Brand public. *Journal of Consumer Research*, *42*(5), 727–748.
Asmussen, B., Harridge-March, S., Occhiocupo, N., & Farquhar, J. D. (2013). The multi-layered nature of the internet-based democratization of brand management. *Journal of Business Research*, *66*(9), 1473–1483. https://doi.org/10.1016/j.busres.2012.09.010
Bagozzi, R. P. (1975). Marketing as exchange. *Journal of Marketing*, *39*(4), 32–39. https://doi.org/10.2307/1250593
Bal, A. S., Pitt, L. F., Berthon, P., & DesAutels, P. (2009). Caricatures, cartoons, spoofs and satires: Political brands as butts. *Journal of Public Affairs*, *9*(4), 229–237.
Ballantyne, D., & Aitken, R. (2007). Branding in B2B markets: Insights from the service-dominant logic of marketing. *Journal of Business & Industrial Marketing*, *22*(6), 363–371.
Balmer, J. M. T. (1995). Corporate branding and connoisseurship. *Journal of General Management*, *21*(1), 24–46.
Balmer, J. M. T. (2001). Corporate identity, corporate branding and corporate marketing – Seeing through the fog. *European Journal of Marketing*, *35*(3), 248–291.
Balmer, J. M. T., & Grey, E. R. (2003). Commentary – Corporate brands. What are they? What of them? *European Journal of Marketing*, *37*(7–8), 972–997.

Berthon, P., Pitt, L. F., & Campbell, C. (2008). Ad lib: When customers create the ad. *California Management Review, 50*(4), 6–32.

Berthon, P., Pitt, L. F., Kietzmann, J., & McCarthy, I. P. (2015). CGIP: Managing consumer-generated intellectual property. *California Management Review, 57*(4), 43–62.

Bertilsson, J., & Rennstam, J. (2018). The destructive side of branding: A heuristic model for analyzing the value of branding practice. *Organization, 25*(2), 260–281.

Bertschy, M., Mühlbacher, H., & Desbordes, M. (2020). Esports extension of a football brand: Stakeholder co-creation in action? *European Sport Management Quarterly, 20*(1), 47–68.

Beverland, M. B., Farrelly, F., & Quester, P. G. (2010). Authentic subcultural membership: Antecedents and consequences of authenticating acts and authoritative performances. *Psychology & Marketing, 27*(7), 698–716. https://doi.org/10.1002/mar.20352

Birkigt, K., & Stadler, M. (1986). *Corporate identity: Grundlagen, Funktionen und Beispiele*. Landsberg am Lech: Verlag Moderne Industrie.

Bonsu, S. K., & Darmody, A. (2008). Co-creating second life: Market-consumer cooperation in contemporary economy. *Journal of Macromarketing, 28*(4), 355–368.

Brodie, R. J., Fehrer, J. A., Jaakkola, E., & Conduit, J. (2019). Actor engagement in networks: Defining the conceptual domain. *Journal of Service Research, 22*(2), 173–188.

Brodie, R. J., Ilic, A., Juric, B., & Hollebeek, L. (2013). Consumer engagement in a virtual brand community: An exploratory analysis. *Journal of Business Research, 66*(1), 105–114.

Cabiddu, F., Frau, M., & Lombardo, S. (2019). Toxic collaborations: Co-destroying value in the B2B context. *Journal of Service Research, 22*(3), 241–255.

Canniford, R., & Shankar, A. (2013). Purifying practices: How consumers assemble romantic experiences of nature. *Journal of Consumer Research, 39*, 1051–1069.

Carlson, B. D., Suter, T. A., & Brown, T. J. (2008). Social versus psychological brand community: The role of psychological sense of brand community. *Journal of Business Research, 61*(4), 284–291.

Chesbrough, H. W. (2006). *Open innovation: The new imperative for creating and profiting from technology*. Boston, MA: Harvard Business Press.

Clark, M., Lages, C., & Hollebeek, L. (2020). Friend or foe? Customer engagement's value-based effects on fellow customers and the firm. *Journal of Business Research, 12s1*. https://doi.org/10.1016/j.jbusres.2020.03.011

Cova, B., & Cova, V. (2002). Tribal marketing: The tribalisation of society and its impact on the conduct of marketing. *European Journal of Marketing, 36*(5–6), 595–620.

Cova, B., & Dalli, D. (2009). Working consumers: The next step in marketing theory? *Marketing Theory, 9*(3), 315–339.

Cova, B., Pace, S., & Skålén, P. (2015). Marketing with working consumers: The case of a carmaker and its brand community. *Organization, 22*(5), 682–701.

Cova, B., & White, T. (2010). Counter-brand and alter-brand communities: The impact of web 2.0 on tribal marketing approaches. *Journal of Marketing Management, 26*, 256–270.

Crane, A., & Ruebottom, T. (2011). Stakeholder theory and social identity: Rethinking stakeholder identification. *Journal of Business Ethics, 102*(1), 77–87.

Da Silveira, C., Lages, C., & Simões, C. (2013). Reconceptualizing brand identity in a dynamic environment. *Journal of Business Research, 66*(1), 28–36.

de Chernatony, L., & Harris, F. (2000). Developing corporate brands through considering internal and external stakeholders. *Corporate Reputation Review, 3*(3), 268–74.

de Chernatony, L., & Segal-Horn, S. (2001). Building on services' characteristics to develop successful services brands. *Journal of Marketing Management, 17*(7), 645–669.

de Nooy, W., & Mrvar. A. (2005). *Exploratory social network analysis with pajek*. New York: Cambridge University Press.

Deleuze, G. (1988). *Bergsonism*. New York: Zone Books.

Diamond, N., Sherry, J. F., Muñiz, A. M., McGrath, M. A., Kozinets, R. V., & Borghini, S. (2009). American girl and the brand gestalt: Closing the loop on sociocultural branding research. *Journal of Marketing, 73*, 118–134.

Dion, D., & Arnould, E. (2016). Persona-fied brands: Managing branded persons through persona. *Journal of Marketing Management, 32*, 121–148.

Dolan, R., Seo, Y., & Kemper, J. (2019). Complaining practices on social media in tourism: A value co-creation and co-destruction perspective. *Tourism Management, 73*, 35–45.

Dong, L., & Tian, K. (2009). The use of western brands in asserting Chinese national identity. *Journal of Consumer Research, 36*(3), 504–523.

Dul, J. (2016). Necessary Condition Analysis (NCA). Logic and methodology of "Necessary but Not Sufficient" causality. *Organizational Research Methods, 19*(1), 10–52.

Echeverri, P., & Skålén, P. (2011). Co-creation and co-destruction: A practice theory based study of interactive value formation. *Marketing Theory, 11*, 351–373.

Edvardsson, K., Tronvoll, B., & Gruber, T. (2011). Expanding understanding of service exchange and value co-creation: A social construction approach. *Journal of the Academy of Marketing Science, 39*(2), 327–339.

Eiglier, P., & Langeard, E. (1987). *Servuction – Le marketing des services*. Paris: McGraw-Hill.

Elliott, R., & Davies, A. (2005). Symbolic brands and authenticity of identity performance. In J. Schroeder & M. Salzer-Morling (Eds.), *Brand culture*. London: Routledge.

Engen, M., Fransson, M., Quist, J., & Skålén, P. (2020). Continuing the development of the public service logic: A study of value co-destruction in public services. *Public Management Review, 22*.

Ertimur, B., & Gilly, M. C. (2012). So whaddya think? Consumers create ads and other consumers critique them. *Journal of Interactive Marketing, 26*(3), 115–130.

Fisher, D., & Smith, S. (2011). Cocreation is chaotic: What it means for marketing when no one has control. *Marketing Theory, 11*(3), 325–350.

Fournier, S., & Avery, J. (2011). The uninvited brand. *Business Horizons, 54*(3), 193–207.

Frow, P., & Payne, A. (2011). A stakeholder perspective of the value proposition concept. *European Journal of Marketing, 45*(1–2), 223–240.

Freeman, R. E., Harrison, J., & Zyglidopoulos, S. (2018). *Stakeholder theory: Concepts and strategies* (Cambridge Elements in Organization Theory). Cambridge: Cambridge University Press.

Füller, J., Lüdicke, M. K., & Jawecki, G. (2008). How brands enchant: Insights from observing community driven brand creation. *Advances in Consumer Research, 35*, 359–366.

Füller, J., Schroll, R., & von Hippel, E. (2013). User generated brands and their contribution to the diffusion of user innovations. *Research Policy, 42*(6–7), 1197–1209.

Gebauer, J., Füller, J., & Pezzei, R. (2013). The dark and the bright side of co-creation: Triggers of member behavior in online innovation communities. *Journal of Business Research, 66*(9), 1516–1527.

Goldenberg, J., Han, S., Lehmann, D. R., & Hong, J. W. (2009). The role of hubs in the adoption process. *Journal of Marketing, 73*(2), 1–13.

Grégoire, Y., & Fisher, R. J. (2006). The effects of relationship quality on customer retaliation. *Marketing Letters, 17*(1), 31–46.

Gregory, A. (2007). Involving stakeholders in developing corporate brands: The communication dimension. *Journal of Marketing Management, 23*(1–2), 5973.

Grönroos, C. (1982). An applied service marketing theory. *European Journal of Marketing, 16*(7), 30–41.

Grönroos, C., & Voima, P. (2013). Critical service logic: Making sense of value creation and co-creation. *Journal of the Academy of Marketing Science, 41*(2), 133–150.

Gummesson, E. (1987). The new marketing – Developing long-term interactive relationships. *Long Range Planning, 20*(4), 10–20.

Gummesson, E. (1991). Marketing-orientation revisited: The crucial role of the part-time marketer. *European Journal of Marketing, 25*(2), 60–75.

Gummesson, E. (2006). *Many-to-many marketing as grand theory: A nordic school contribution*. New York: Sharpe.

Gyrd-Jones, R., & Kornum, N. (2013). Managing the co-created brand: Value and cultural complementarity in online and offline multi-stakeholder ecosystems. *Journal of Business Research, 66*(9), 1484–1493.

Hatch, M. J., & Schultz, M. (2001). Are the strategic stars aligned for your corporate brand. *Harvard Business Review, 79*(2), 128–34.

Hatch, M. J., & Schultz, M. (2003). Bringing the corporation into corporate branding. *European Journal of Marketing, 37*(7), 1041–1064.

Hatch, M. J., & Schultz, M. (2010). Toward a theory of brand co-creation. *Brand Management, 17*(8), 590–604.

Hemetsberger, A. (2006). When David becomes goliath: Ideological discourse in new online consumer movements. In C. Pechmann & L. Price (Eds.), *Advances in consumer research* (Vol. 33, pp. 494–500) Provo, Utah: Association for Consumer Research.

Hemetsberger, A., & Reinhardt, C. (2006). Learning and knowledge-building in open-source communities – A social-experiential approach. *Management Learning, 37*(2), 187–214.

Hillebrand, B., Driessen, P. H., & Koll, O. (2015). Stakeholder marketing: Theoretical foundations and required capabilities. *Journal of the Academy of Marketing Science*, *43*(4), 411–428.

Holbrook, M. B. (2006). Consumption experience, customer value, and subjective personal introspection: An illustrative photographic essay. *Journal of Business Research*, *59*(6), 714–725.

Hollebeek, L. D., Andreassen, T., Smith, D., Grönquist, D., Karahasanovic, A., & Marquez, A. (2018). Service innovation actor engagement: Am integrative model. *Journal of Services Marketing*, *32*(1), 95–100.

Hollebeek, L. D., Kumar, V., & Srivastava, R. K. (2021). From customer-, to actor-, to stakeholder engagement: Taking stock, conceptualization, and future directions. *Journal of Service Research*. https://doi.org/10.1177/1094670520977680

Hollenbeck, C. R., & Zinkhan, G. M. (2010). Anti-brand communities, negotiation of brand meaning, and the learning process: The case of Wal-Mart. *Consumption Markets & Culture*, *13*(3), 325–345.

Holt, D. B. (2002). Why do brands cause trouble? A dialectical theory of consumer culture and branding. *Journal of Consumer Research*, *29*(1), 70–90.

Hult, G. T. M., Mena, J. A., Ferrell, O. C., & Ferrell, L. (2011). Stakeholder marketing: A definition and conceptual framework. *Academy of Marketing Science Review*, *1*(1), 44–65.

Hunt, S. D. (1976). The nature and scope of marketing. *Journal of Marketing*, *40*(3), 17–28.

Iglesias, O., & Bonet, E. (2012). Persuasive brand management: How mangers can influence brand meaning when they are losing control over it. *Journal of Organizational Change Management*, *25*(2), 251–264.

Iglesias, O., & Ind, N. (2020). Towards a theory of conscientious corporate brand co-creation: The next key challenge in brand management. *Journal of Brand Management*, *27*, 710–720. https://doi.org/10.1057/s41262-020-00205-7

Iglesias, O., Ind, N., & Alfaro, M. (2013). The organic view of the brand: A brand value co-creation model. *Journal of Brand Management*, *20*(8), 670–688.

Iglesias, O., Landgraf, P., Ind, N., Markovic, S., & Koporcic, N. (2020). Corporate brand identity co-creation in business-to-business contexts. *Industrial Marketing Management*, *85*, 32–43. https://doi.org/10.1016/j.indmarman.2019.09.008

Ind, N., & Bjerke, R. (2007). *Branding governance*. London: Wiley & Sons.

Ind, N., Iglesias, O., & Markovics, S. (2017). The co-creation continuum: From tactical market research tool to strategic collaborative innovation method. *Journal of Brand Management*, *24*(1–2), 1–12. https://doi.org/10.1057/s41262-017-0051-7

Ind, N., Iglesias, O., & Schultz, M. (2013). Building brands together: Emergence and outcomes of co-creation. *California Management Review*, *55*(3), 5–26.

Ingenbleek, P. T. M., & Imminik, V. M. (2010). Managing conflicting stakeholder interests: An exploratory case analysis of the formulation of corporate social responsibility standards in the Netherlands. *Journal of Public Policy & Marketing*, *29*(1), 52–65.

Järvi, H., Kähkönen, A.-K., & Torvinen, H. (2018). When value co-creation fails: Reasons that lead to value co-destruction. *Scandinavian Journal of Management*, *34*(1), 63–77.

Johnson, A. R., Thomson, M., & Matear, M. (2011). Coal in the heart: Self-relevance as a post-exit predictor of consumer anti-brand actions. *Journal of Consumer Research*, *38*, 108–125.

Johnson, J. W., & Rapp, A. (2010). A more comprehensive understanding and measure of customer helping behavior. *Journal of Business Research*, *63*(8), 787–792.

Jones, R. (2005). Finding sources of brand value: Developing a stakeholder model of brand equity. *Brand Management*, *13*(1), 10–32.

Jordan, T., Gibson, F., Sinnett, B., & Howard, D. (2019). Stakeholder engagement in event planning: A case study of one rural community´s process. *Event Management*, *23*(1), 61–74.

Kapferer, J. N. (2004). *The new strategic brand management*. London and New York: Kogan Page.

Kapferer, J. N. (2008). *The new strategic brand management: Creating and sustaining brand equity long term* (4th ed.). London and New York: Kogan Page.

Kashif, M., & Zarkada, A. (2015). Value co-destruction between customers and frontline employees: A social system perspective. *International Journal of Bank Marketing*, *33*(6), 672–691.

Kates, S. M. (2004). The dynamics of brand legitimacy: An interpretive study in the gay men's community. *Journal of Consumer Research*, *31*(2), 455–465.

Keller, K. L. (1998). *Strategic brand management – Building, measuring, and managing brand equity*. Upper Saddle River, NJ: Prentice-Hall.

Keller, K. L. (2008). *Strategic brand management: Building, measuring, and managing brand equity*. Englewood Cliffs, NJ: Pearson; Prentice Hall.

Krishnamurthy, S., & Kucuk, U. S. (2009). Anti-branding on the internet. *Journal of Business Research*, 62(11), 1119–1126.

Koll, O., Woodside, A. G., & Mühlbacher, H. (2005). Balanced versus focused responsiveness to core constituencies and organizational effectiveness. *European Journal of Marketing*, 39(9–10), 1166–1183.

Kornum, N., Gyrd-Jones, R., Al Zagir, N., & Brandis, A. (2017). Interplay between intended brand identity and identities in a Nike related brand community: Co-existing synergies and tensions in a nested system. *Journal of Business Research*, 70(1), 432–440.

Kornum, N., & Mühlbacher, H. (2013). Multi-stakeholder virtual dialogue: Introduction to the special section. *Journal of Business Research*, 66(9), 1460–1464.

Kotler, P. (1991). *Marketing management*. Englewood Cliffs, NJ: Prentice Hall.

Kotler, P., & Armstrong, G. (2006). *Principles of marketing* (11th ed.). Upper Saddle River, NJ: Prentice Hall.

Kozinets, R. V. (2002). Can consumers escape the market? Emancipatory illuminations from burning man. *Journal of Consumer Research*, 29(1), 20–38.

Kozinets, R. V., de Valck, K., Wojnicki, A. C., & Wilner, S. J. S. (2010). Networked narratives: Understanding word-of-mouth marketing in online communities. *Journal of Marketing*, 74(2), 7s1–89.

Kozinets, R. V., & Handelman, J. M. (2004). Adversaries of consumption: Consumer movements, activism, and ideology. *Journal of Consumer Research*, 31(3), 691–704.

Kozinets, R. V., Sherry Jr., J. F., Storm, D., Duhachek, A., Nuttavuthisit, K., & Deberry-Spence, B. (2004). Ludic agency and retail spectacle. *Journal of Consumer Research*, 13(3), 658–72.

Leitch, S. R., & Motion, J. (2007). *Retooling the corporate brand: A foucauldian perspective on normalisation and differentiation*. Faculty of Commerce – Papers (Archive), University of Wollogong. Retrieved from https://ro.uow.edu.au/commpapers/522

Leitch, S. R., & Richardson, N. (2003). Corporate branding in the new economy. *European Journal of Marketing*, 37(7–8), 1065–1079.

Letaifa, B., Edvardsson, B., & Tronvoll. B. (2016). The role of social platforms in transforming service ecosystems. *Journal of Business Research*, 69, 1933–1938.

Lucarelli, A., & Hallin, A. (2015). Brand transformation: A performative approach to brand regeneration. *Journal of Marketing Management*, 31(1–2), 84–106.

Luedicke, M. K., Thompson, C. J., & Giesler, M. (2010). Consumer identity work as moral protagonism: How myth and ideology animate a brand-mediated moral conflict. *Journal of Consumer Research*, 36(6), 1016–1032.

Makkonen, H., & Olkkonen, R. (2017). Interactive value formation in interorganizational relationships: Dynamic interchange between value co-creation, no-creation, and co-destruction. *Marketing Theory*, 17(4), 517–535.

McAlexander, J. H., Schouten, J. W., & Koenig, H. F. (2002). Building brand community. *Journal of Marketing*, 66(1), 38–54.

Mello, P. A. (2021). *Qualitative comparative analysis: An introduction to research design and application*. Washington, DC: Georgetown University Press.

Merz, M., He, Y., & Vargo, S. L. (2009). The evolving brand logic: A service dominant logic perspective. *Journal of the Academy of Marketing Science*, 37(3), 328–344.

Michel, G. (2017). From brand identity to polysemous brands: Commentary on "Performing identities: Processes of brand and stakeholder identity co-construction". *Journal of Business Research*, 70, 453–455.

Michel, G., & Donthu, N. (2014). Why negative brand extension evaluations do not always negatively affect the brand: The role of central and peripheral brand associations. *Journal of Business Research*, 67(12), 2611–2619.

Mühlbacher, H., & Böbel, I. (2019). From zero-sum to win-win – Organisational conditions for successful shared value strategy implementation. *European Management Journal*, 37(3), 313–324.

Mühlbacher, H., & Hemetsberger, A. (2008). Cosa diamine è un brand? Un tentativo di integrazione e le sue conseguenze per la ricerca e il management. *Micro & Macro Marketing*, 2, 271–292.

Mühlbacher, H., & Hemetsberger, A. (2013). Brands as processes, a social representations Perspective. In J. Scholderer & K. Brunso (Eds.), *Marketing, food and the consumer* (pp. 31–46). Festschrift in Honour of Klaus G. Grunert: Pearson.

Muñiz Jr, A. M., & O'Guinn, T. C. (2001). Brand community. *Journal of Consumer Research*, 27(4), 412–432.

Neville, B. A., & Menguc, B. (2006). Stakeholder multiplicity: Toward an understanding of the interactions between stakeholders. *Journal of Business Ethics*, 66(4), 377–391.

O'Sullivan, S. R., Richardson, B., & Collins, A. (2011). How brand communities emerge: The beamish conversion experience. *Journal of Marketing Management*, 27(9–10), 891–912.

Parmentier, M.-A., & Fischer, E. (2015). Things fall apart: The dynamics of brand audience dissipation. *Journal of Consumer Research, 41*, 1228–1251.

Payne, A., Storbacka, K., Frow, P., & Knox, S. (2009). Co-creating brands: Diagnosing and designing the relationship experience. *Journal of Business Research, 62*(3), 379–389.

Pitt, L. F., Watson, R. T., Berthon, P., & Zinkhan, D. W. G. (2006). Corporate brands from an open-source perspective. *Journal of the Academy of Marketing Science, 34*(2), 115–127.

Plé, L., & Chumpitaz Cáceres, R. (2010). Not always co-creation: Introducing interactional co-destruction of value in service-dominant logic. *Journal of Services Marketing, 24*(6), 430–437.

Prahalad, C. K., & Ramaswamy, V. (2000). Co-opting customer competence. *Harvard Business Review, 78*(1), 79–90.

Prahalad, C. K., & Ramaswamy, V. (2004). Co-creation experiences: The next practice in value creation. *Journal of Interactive Marketing, 18*(3), 5–14.

Prior, D., & Marcos-Cuevas, J. (2016). Value co-destruction in interfirm relationships: The impact of actor engagement styles. *Marketing Theory, 16*(4), 533–552.

Ramirez, R. (1999). Value co-production: Intellectual origins and implications for practice and research. *Strategic Management Journal, 20*(1), 49–65.

Richards, L., Foster, D., & Morgan, R. (1998). Brand knowledge management: Growing brand equity. *Journal of Knowledge Management, 2*(1), 47–54.

Ritzer, G., Paul, D., & Jurgenson, N. (2012). The coming of age of the prosumer. *American Behavioral Scientist, 56*(4), 379–398.

Robson, J., & Farquhar, J. D. (2021). Recovering the corporate brand: Lessons from an industry crisis. *European Journal of Marketing.* https://doi.org/10.1108/EJM-09-2019-0698

Roux, D. (2007). Consumer resistance: Proposal for an integrative framework. *Recherche et Applications en Marketing, 22*(4), 59–79.

Santana, A. (2012). Three elements of stakeholder legitimacy. *Journal of Business Ethics, 105*(2), 257–265.

Sarkar, S., & Banerjee, S. (2020). Brand co-creation through participation of organizations, consumers, and suppliers; an empirical validation. *Journal of Product and Brand Management.* https://doi.org/10.1108/JPBM-01-2020-2732

Schau, H. J., Muñiz, A. M., & Arnould, E. J. (2009). How brand community practices create value. *Journal of Marketing, 73*, 30–51.

Schlenker, B. (1980). *Impression management: The self concept, social identity and interpersonal relations.* Monterrey: Brooks-Cole.

Schroll, R., Schnurr, B., & Grewal, D. (2018). Humanizing products with handwritten typefaces. *Journal of Consumer Research, 45*(3), 648–672.

Schultz, M., & de Chernatony, L. (2002). Introduction: The challenges of corporate branding. *Corporate Reputation Review, 5*(2), 105–112.

Stieler, M., & Germelmann, C. C. (2018). Actor engagement practices and triadic value co-creation in the team sports ecosystem. *MARKETING ZFP – Journal of Research and Management, 40*(4), 30–43.

Thompson, C. J., Rindfleisch, A., & Arsel, Z. (2006). Emotional branding and the strategic value of the Doppelgänger brand image. *Journal of Marketing, 70*(1), 50–64.

Törmälä, M., & Saraniemi, S. (2018). The roles of business partners in corporate brand image co-creation. *Journal of Product & Brand Management, 27*(1), 29–40.

van Doorn, J., Lemon, K. N., Mittal, V., Nass, S., Pick, D., Pirner, P., & Verhoef, P. C. (2010). Customer engagement behavior: Theoretical foundations and research directions. *Journal of Service Research, 13*(3), 253–266.

Vallaster, C., & von Wallpach, S. (2013). An online discursive inquiry into the social dynamics of multi-stakeholder brand meaning co-creation. *Journal of Business Research, 66*(9), 1505–1515.

Vargo, S. L., & Lusch, R. F. (2004). Evolving to a new dominant logic for marketing. *Journal of Marketing, 68*(1), 1–17.

Vargo, S. L., & Lusch, R. F. (2016). Institutions and axioms: An extension and update of service-dominant logic. *Journal of the Academy of Marketing Science, 44*(1), 5–23.

Von Wallpach, S., Hemetsberger, A., & Espersen, P. (2017). Performing identities: Processes of brand and stakeholder identity co-construction. *Journal of Business Research, 70*(1), 443–452.

Wider, S., von Wallpach, S., & Mühlbacher, H. (2018). Brand management: Unveiling the delusion of control. *European Management Journal, 36*, 301–305.

Zwick, D., Bonsu, S. K., & Darmody, A. (2008). Putting consumers to work: 'Co-creation' and new marketing govern-mentality. *Journal of Consumer Culture, 8*(2), 163–196.

# 4
# WELCOME TO THE MATRIX*
## How to find and use your corporate brand's core identity

*Mats Urde*

### 1. The corporate brand

All companies have a corporate brand, even if its role and function may differ. One thing all corporate brands have is a unique identity core, defined or not. Finding the identity core and using it is an opportunity to communicate and position your corporate brand, build its reputation, and thereby leverage the organization's brands and grow the entire business. The identity core is a point of departure and home base in understanding and managing your corporate (organizational) brand.

The very term *corporate brand* signals that you have an organization behind your brand and that it is a vital part of the brand (Abratt & Kleyn, 2012; Balmer, 2008; Boulding, 1956; Ind, 1998; Kennedy, 1977; King, 1991; Urde, 1994). Fundamentally, a brand is a promise, and a strong brand is one with a clear positioning and an earned reputation for keeping its promise. A promise kept builds trust and helps an organization reach its goals and stay true to its purpose.

I like to think of the corporate brand as a mother and its product/service brands as daughters. Corporations often have portfolios of brands (Gardner & Levy, 1955; Kapferer, 2012; Olins, 1989). Typically, they are organized according to one of four principal strategies: (1) corporate brand; (2) corporate brand with product brands; (3) product brands endorsed by corporate brand; and (4) individual brands with the corporate brand in the shadow. No matter what brand strategy a company applies, there is always a corporate brand to consider.

There is a trend toward placing more focus on the corporate brand (De Wit & Meyer, 2010; Balmer, 2008; Hatch & Schultz, 2003). Consider $58 billion Unilever and its portfolio of 400 brands. The Unilever corporate brand's role and function have changed. Once, Unilever was the mother standing in the background of its daughters. Today Unilever has a clearly defined identity core that is communicated both internally and externally, and the company is an endorser of its own product brands. For example, Unilever communicates on topics such as sustainability that have relevance for all its brands, and it actively supports its brands, such as Dove, Magnum, Rexona, and Hellman's.

Procter & Gamble's brand strategy is focused on individual product brands such as Gillette, Ariel, and Pampers. However, at international sponsorship events, the corporate brand may step into the limelight. P&G's Olympics advertising theme 'Thank you, Mom,' celebrating mothers supporting kids doing sports, showed the kinship between the well-known P&G daughters and their mother.

---

* This chapter is based on my forthcoming book on corporate branding.

Where would you place your corporate brand on the spectrum ranging from a focus on the corporate brand to a focus on product branding (Figure 4.1)? What do you envision the role and function of your corporate brand to be in the future?

IKEA focuses strongly on its corporate brand even as it expands into new product categories; Samsung highlights its corporate brand but positions its daughter brands, such as Galaxy, as spearheads in the market; Kevlar, a prominent ingredient brand, has its own identity and position, which are strengthened by the DuPont corporate brand; and P&G generally remains in the wings while its product brands take centre stage.

Corporate – *corpus* in Latin – stands for 'body and entity.' Viewed as a whole, a corporate brand has an internal side, an external side, and a core. Its meaning, relevance, and uniqueness are created in an ongoing interaction among the organization standing behind the brand and its customers and non-customer stakeholders (Urde, 1999, 2003). The brand is continuously shaped and positioned in people's minds and hearts in a cultural setting and competitive environment (Figure 4.2).

Brand meaning and value are moulded by internal and external forces, influences, and initiatives (Bately, 2016; Holt & Cameron, 2010; Santos, 2012; Morgan & Smircich, 1982). Internally,

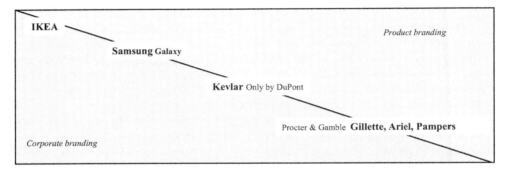

*Figure 4.1* The corporate branding gamut

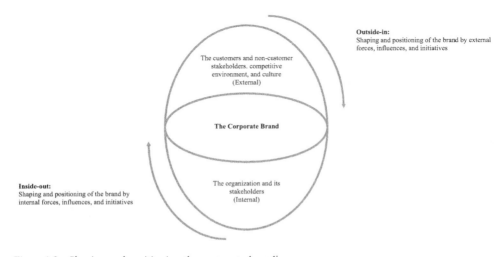

*Figure 4.2* Shaping and positioning the corporate brand[1]

*Welcome to the matrix*

the corporate brand is shaped and positioned by characteristics such as its purpose, values, and goals. In practice, the intent is to create appealing value propositions to bond the corporate brand with its targeted audiences. Simultaneously, external forces influence the brand's meaning and position, beyond the appreciation of its value propositions. For example, a Mercedes owner, a Zara blogger, a Spotify playlist-creator, the Scania truck fleet-owner, and a Nobel Laureate all influence the image, communication, and even the identity core of brands they relate to or feel to be part of. Consider the role of the Trek mountain bikers, the IKEA family of customers, and Wikipedia contributors in these confident corporate brands' inception and identities.

Counter-intuitively, the better you know who your corporate brand is and what it stands for, the more open you may find it to influences and relationships with others. All brands are, to various degrees, co-created since brands are not lonely islands. A question for management is: How do we work together to build brand value and still be at the helm? The management of brands is the management of meaning and value-creation; I believe this is especially true for corporate brands.

## 1.1 *Fusing the layers of corporate brand management*

Identity, communication and positioning, and reputation together form the territory of corporate brand management. The challenge is to fuse these three layers of a brand into a single entity – a corporate brand (Figure 4.3).

The *Corporate Brand Identity Matrix* framework and its two outer layers serve, in combination, as a guide to the territory, the ongoing interactions, and its management:

The **identity matrix** is about answering, on behalf of your organization's brand, nine crucial questions: What are our key offerings? What should be the nature of our stakeholder relationships? What is our intended position in the market? What is distinctive about how we communicate? What do we promise? What is our corporate character? What engages and inspires us? What are our attitudes? What are we particularly good at?

The **communication and positioning** layer is about expressing your brand's identity by telling its story and making it stand out in the marketplace. Your brand needs to appeal to reason (*logos*), to instil trust (*ethos*), and to stir emotions among its audiences (*pathos*). By looking at your brand's identity from the three rhetorical modes of persuasion, the identity matrix's communication and positioning layer guides your corporate brand's activation.

The **reputation** layer, the identity matrix's outermost layer, is about what customers and non-customer stakeholders think of your corporate brand. Your words and deeds influence the reputation you earn. Reputation is not something you *have*; it is something that is attributed to

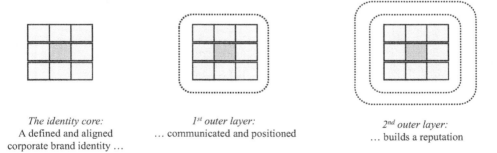

*The identity core:*       *1ˢᵗ outer layer:*      *2ⁿᵈ outer layer:*
A defined and aligned     ... communicated and positioned     ... builds a reputation
corporate brand identity ...

*Figure 4.3* The territory of corporate brand management

your corporate brand by others. Perceived reality is reality. That is to say, your brand's reputation is your business reality.

Companies are usually expert at defining and articulating their product and service brands – think of the iPhone or the VISA card. But they often struggle to figure out what the corporate brand stands for – or what it *should* stand for – in the minds of people both inside and outside the company.

After Volvo broke out its truck brands into separate units a few years ago, the company seemed uncertain about its identity. Employees of the new units weren't sure about their corporate mission, values, or capabilities: What should they tell customers about their mission and values? How closely should these match Volvo Group's mission and values? What was the units' relationship with the Volvo corporate brand?

By using the Corporate Brand Identity Matrix, the Volvo Group and its spinoffs were able to figure out how they should position themselves in the marketplace and how they should communicate their mission and values to employees, customers, and the world. Like many other companies, Volvo found that a clear, unified corporate brand is critical to competitive strategy. It serves as the company's North Star, providing direction, enhancing the image of individual products and brands, helping the firm recruit and retain employees, and providing protection against reputational damage in times of trouble. A powerful corporate brand engenders pride, meaning, and commitment as it invites people to participate in the organization's endeavours.

The corporate brand identity matrix, the result of more than ten years of engagement and research with hundreds of executives in organizations around the world, has helped not only Volvo but also Electrolux, the Nobel Foundation, and many other organizations to understand and strengthen their corporate brands.[2] It serves as a framework to guide executive teams through a structured set of questions focusing on one element of the organization's identity at a time. There are nine elements in total, and in the identity matrix, we stack them in three rows, with internally oriented elements on the bottom, those that are both internal and external in the middle, and externally focused elements on top.

## *Internal elements*

Forming the foundation of a corporate brand identity are the firm's mission and vision, which engage and inspire its people and stakeholders; culture, which includes employees' work ethic and attitudes; and competences, or unique capabilities. Good examples of these elements can be seen in Johnson & Johnson's credo, which is carved in stone at the entrance of the company's headquarters. It describes J&J's top priority – the needs and well-being of doctors, nurses, patients, and their families; how it will serve them, by providing high quality at reasonable cost; and the creation of a work environment based on dignity, safety, and fairness.

## *External elements*

At the top of the identity matrix, you will find elements related to how the company wants to be perceived by customers and other external stakeholders: its value proposition, outside relationships, and positioning. Nike, for instance, wants to be known for helping customers achieve their personal best, a goal that shapes its product offerings and is captured in its marketing tagline 'Just Do It.' The engineering company ABB's 'Power and productivity for a better world' is translated into value propositions about 'energy efficiency,' 'lower environmental impact,' and 'long-term customer partnerships.'

*Welcome to the matrix*

## Elements that bridge internal and external aspects

In the middle row of the matrix, these elements include the organization's personality, its distinctive ways of communicating, and its 'brand core' – what it stands for and the enduring values that underlie its promise. The brand core is the essence of the corporate brand's identity. Patagonia's is summed up in its promise to provide the highest-quality products and to support and inspire environmental stewardship. IKEA's promise to create a better life for everyone is reinforced by its core values of simplicity and common sense and its encouragement of both employees and customers to create 'difference with a meaning.' Audi captures its brand core with the phrase *Vorsprung Durch Technik* – 'Ahead through technology.' 3M describes its core as 'Science. Applied to life.'

When a corporate brand identity is coherent, each of the eight other elements informs and echoes the brand core at the centre of the matrix, resonating with the company's values and what the brand stands for. The brand core, in turn, shapes the other elements (Figure 4.4).

The matrix is a holistic structure that allows an organization to see its corporate persona, the promises it makes to itself and its stakeholders, the value it generates, and how that value is created. In a sense, it is a historical record, showing where the organization has been and what it has done, but it is also a map, pointing the way for the future. It shows *why* you are engaged in doing what you are doing, *how* you go about working in line with that why, *what* your value proposition is, and *by whom* that value proposition is generated – the audience needs to know the speaker in order to trust what is promised.[3]

A tool for capturing a corporate brand's identity needs to be as simple as possible; accordingly, the identity matrix asks questions and shows fundamental relationships for you and your

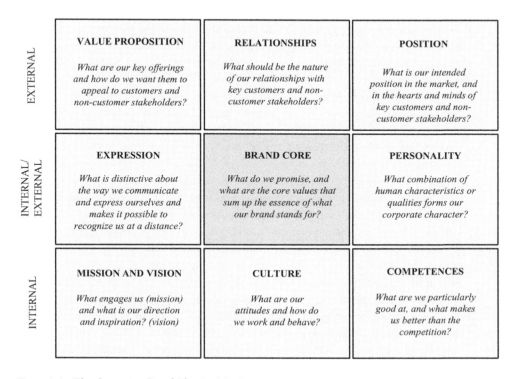

*Figure 4.4* The Corporate Brand Identity Matrix

organization to consider. In practice, it's an iterative and co-creative process taking into account your stakeholders and the world around you. It's not about paint by numbers since the matrix's elements and layers represent an infinite number of combinations and relationships. You and your teams are not in full control of all the elements, but this does not diminish your role (Iglesias et al., 2020). On the contrary, you have a very important role in leading the organization to manage its brands. Albert Einstein said: 'Everything should be made as simple as possible, but not simpler.'

Although brands may share some elements with other organizations – McDonald's and Hilton Hotels share a passion for customer service, for example – every brand is unique, just as every tree is unique despite similarities to others of its species (Norrmann, 2001).

---

### Exercise 1: Mapping the identity elements

The exercise that follows can reveal whether your corporate brand identity is well integrated and, if it isn't, show where problems and opportunities lie and help you address them. While this process can be done by an individual, it's most useful when undertaken by an executive team. By repeating the process with other groups, you will engage more people and gain deeper insights.

First, answer the questions in each of the nine elements. When conducting identity-matrix workshops, I often advise participants to follow these guidelines:

1. **Be concise.** Respond in short phrases, not paragraphs, as Starbucks does when describing its mission, or purpose: 'To inspire and nurture the human spirit – one person, one cup, and one neighborhood at a time.' Think of these phrases as headings under which you will later write more detailed descriptions fleshing out the brand identity and story.
2. **Be straightforward.** Avoid jargon and keep your responses uncomplicated. Less is more. IKEA describes its relationships as 'Hello!' – a single word that reflects a down-to-earth attitude in line with its core values.
3. **Seek what is characteristic.** Capture words or concepts that resonate within your organization, words or concepts that signal 'This is us.' A real-estate company answered the personality question this way: 'We are not sitting on a high horse.' The Ritz Hotel in Paris has a work description for its staff: 'We are ladies and gentlemen, serving ladies and gentlemen.' This expression perfectly captures the essence of the staff's self-image and the respectful relationship with guests. A newly opened hotel in Oslo lives by the motto: 'We treat rock stars as guests and guests as rock stars' – promising a different reception from that signalled by the Paris Ritz.
4. **Stay authentic.** Some elements of your identity may already be firmly rooted in your organization. Be careful to be honest in your expression of them. Some elements may be aspirational, calling for adaptation within the company if they are to ring true. For start-up companies, an identity matrix is dominantly about aspirations – 'This is what we seek to stand for and offer.' Such an internal agreement can guide business development and help place the company on the map.

5 **Seek what is timeless.** For a British monarch, '*Dieu et mon Droit*' ('God and my Right') is the motto still in use after almost a millennium. 'Liberty, equality, fraternity' are the eternal values of the French Revolution. A corporate brand's identity should be lasting – like this signature expression of one watchmaker: 'You never actually own a Patek Philippe. You merely look after it for the next generation.' Forward-looking but rooted in the past, it has stood the test of time.

To get a sense of what a finalized matrix looks like, consider the one my colleague Stephen A. Greyser of Harvard Business School and I helped the Nobel Prize organization produce (Figure 4.5). The Nobel Foundation, which is responsible for safeguarding the Prize's 'standing and reputation,' needed to clarify its corporate brand identity – a considerable challenge, given that laureates are actually chosen by four independent institutions: the Royal Swedish Academy of Sciences, the Norwegian Nobel Committee, the Karolinska Institute, and the Swedish Academy (Urde & Greyser, 2015; Greyser & Urde, 2018a, 2018b). Each of these organizations has its own long history and well-developed identity. The identity matrix helped the Foundation and the four other institutions find a shared brand core in the goal of rewarding people who had provided 'the greatest benefit to humankind,' a phrase directly from Alfred Nobel's will.

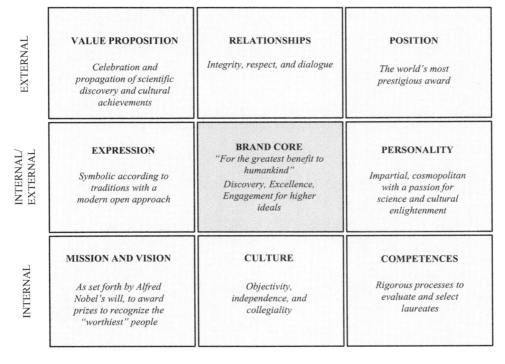

*Figure 4.5* The Nobel Prize brand identity matrix

## 1.2 Walk the paths

One of the most useful aspects of the matrix is that it can help you understand, visually, four key kinds of organizational capability (Figure 4.6). Consider the diagonal path from lower left to upper right. This path includes mission and vision, brand core, and position – essential elements of *strategy* capability. A diagonal path from upper left to the lower right passes through value proposition, brand core, and competences – *competition*. A vertical path through the middle touches relationships, brand core, and culture – *interaction*. And a midlevel horizontal path touches expression, brand core, and personality – *character*. Note that all four paths, or axes, pass through brand core at the centre of the matrix.

After you have answered the questions in the nine elements, combine the answers into a script for a short presentation on your corporate brand identity. (See the exercise 'Does your matrix measure up?')

Ask yourself: Does the presentation hang together? Are there gaps or inconsistencies? If so, the next job is to examine the weak links and explore how to strengthen them, so that the elements harmonize coherently. The stronger the connections along each axis, the more stable the matrix.

For example, if you are a fashion company and your brand core and position are about being the first with new trends, yet your mission is about achieving sustainability, how can you alter your promises to customers to achieve better alignment along the strategy axis? If you are an automaker and your value proposition and brand core are about being a technology leader, yet your competence in autonomous navigation lags behind others, what capabilities do you need to develop in order to achieve better alignment along the competition axis? Strengthening the connections among the identity elements and increasing the matrix's stability is a never-ending process.

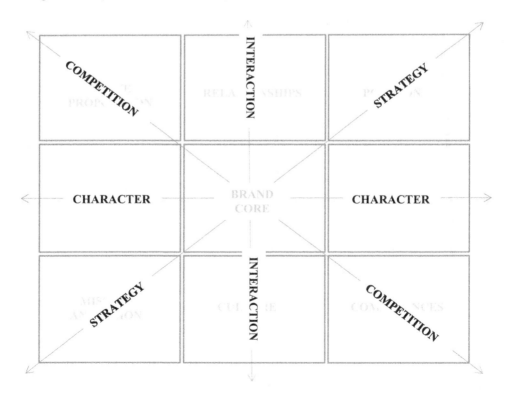

*Figure 4.6* The four paths

## Exercise 2: Does your matrix measure up?

Use the following exercise to assess the coherence of your answers to the questions in the identity matrix. As you fill in the blanks, you'll create a narrative about your strategy (the first diagonal path), your competitive approach (the second diagonal path), and the basis and nature of your external interactions (the vertical path) and character (the horizontal path). With all four paths, you'll want to confirm that each element logically follows the one before it, regardless of which direction you're moving. The clearer and more logical your narrative is, the more stable the matrix is, and the stronger your corporate brand identity.

**The first diagonal path focuses on strategy:**

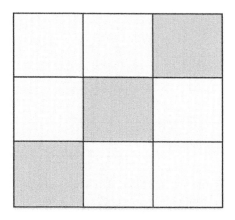

Our mission is _____

Our vision is _____

We promise _____

Our core values are _____

Our intended position in the market is _____

Do your mission and vision engage and inspire people in your own organization and, ideally, beyond it? Do they translate into a promise that the organization will fulfil? Is that promise manifest in the company's positioning? Finally, does the logic also flow in the other direction: Does your positioning resonate with your promise and values, which align with the corporate mission and vision?

**The second diagonal path focuses on competition:**

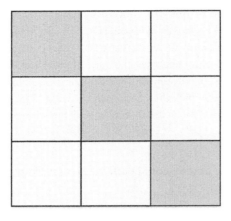

Our competences are _____

We promise _____

Our core values are _____

Our value proposition is _____

Do the items in this list fit well together? Do your current competences allow you to keep your promise and provide a solid basis for competitive and appealing value propositions?

**The vertical path focuses on interaction:**

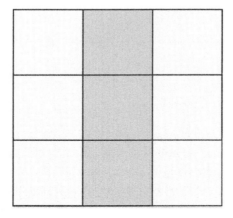

Our culture is _____

We promise _____

Our core values are _____

The kinds of relationships we strive for are _____

This section reveals how well your organizational values and culture resonate with and engage people inside and outside your company. Employees are your most important resource for ensuring the authenticity of the corporate brand. If they don't embrace these elements of your identity core, then your outside relationships, whether with customers, partners, communities, or other stakeholders, will suffer.

**The horizontal path focuses on character:**

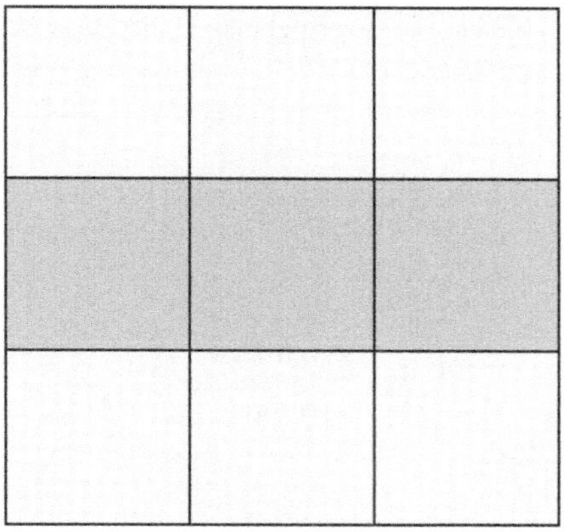

Our corporate personality traits are_____

We promise _____

Our core values are _____

Our communication style is _____

The corporate personality underpins the company's brand core and is expressed in myriad ways, from product design and the architecture of the headquarters to the corporate logo and marketing taglines. Assess how well that personality comes through in all communications, both internally and externally.

## 2. The first outer layer: communicating and positioning

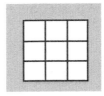

In managing and leading your corporate brand, to what extent should your organization be guided by its identity, and to what extent should it be responsive to others' views and wishes? If you opt for a brand-oriented approach, your point of departure is from the inside out, with identity as your primary focus; if you opt for a market-oriented approach, your point of departure is from the outside in, with image as your main focus (Baumgarth et al., 2013; Gromark & Melin, 2011). You will probably find that the two approaches are synergetic and not an either-or proposition, but it is better to focus on the identity core as a point of departure (Urde et al., 2010). Brand-oriented companies start from the inside.

Your identity matrix has shown your corporate brand's *why*, *how*, *what*, and *by whom*; now it is time to choose how to communicate and position your brand for maximum impact. Let us look at the first outer layer around the matrix.

If you are to persuade anyone about anything, first you need to explain with the help of language and facts. Aristotle's three modes of persuasion are *logos*, *ethos*, and *pathos*: logic, trust, and emotion – a universal triad (Aristotle, 2004; Inglesias & Bonet, 2012; McCloskey, 1998). To find a balance among logos, ethos, and pathos, ask these questions:

- What are our appeals to reason and understanding?
- What are our appeals to build trust by character and personality?
- What are our appeals to stir emotions? (Figure 4.7)

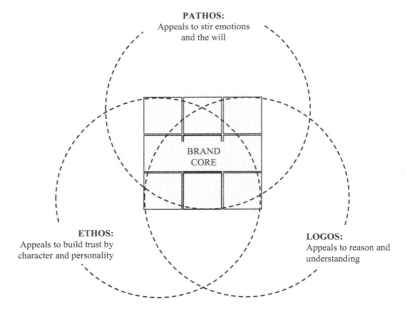

*Figure 4.7* Finding the corporate brand's appeals

In your search for arguments, you are outlining the corporate brand's value proposition and its positioning (Ries & Trout, 1981; Bourdieu, 1992). The aim is to build a bond between your corporate brand and its customers and non-customer stakeholders. At the same time, you position the corporate brand in the minds and hearts of people and make it stand out against the competition. All communication and positioning efforts express and influence the perception of the corporate brand's ethos.

Once the analytical groundwork is concluded, the next step is addressing the world. 'What is the secret of capturing an audience?' a journalist asked the Nobel literature laureate Isaac Singer. His succinct answer was: 'Tell them a good story.' The novelist E.M. Forster explains what a story is: 'If you are told that the king died and then the queen died, that is a sequence of events. If you are told that the king died and that the queen then died of grief, that is a story.' Your brand's identity is not a set of facts or a list of features; it's a source of stories about its past, present, and future.

## 2.1 What's your signature story?

What are the stories that are told and retold about your brand? What are the stories you tell when you want to share something that is important about your company? These stories typically have a beginning, a middle, and an end with a meaningful message that people listen to, like, and remember (Ogilvy, 1983). What you are looking for is a special kind of story – a *signature story* – that is of particular value in the communication and positioning of your corporate brand.

A signature story is an intriguing, authentic, involving narrative resonating with the essence of a corporate brand's identity (Aaker, 2018; Fog et al., 2005). A signature story stands for the corporate brand in some respect or capacity, functioning much like a logotype or other trademarked sign. Each Patek Philippe watch is said to be personally inspected by the company's CEO before it is delivered. This story can be interpreted as attention to quality but also as a watchmaker's passion for the trade. A signature story addresses someone – it creates in the mind and heart of that person an equivalent story, or perhaps a more developed story.[4]

To determine whether a story could become a signature story, ask:

- Does it grab the attention of your audiences?
- Is it authentic?
- Is it involving to your key audiences, and ideally beyond?
- Does it resonate with the essence of your corporate brand?

It is not surprising that Volvo Cars' story is about commitment to safety, that the Spotify story relates to unlocking music, and that the Johnson & Johnson story places top priority on patients.

It is striking how varied signature stories can be. Most are based on real people, real events, and real settings, but they can be about imaginary figures too. Think of Coca-Cola's ads showing Santa Claus enjoying a refreshing drink while steering his reindeer.

While many signature stories are *we-stories*, they can also be *they-stories* – stories told about your brand by others, whether customers or non-customer stakeholders. The *Volvo Saved My Life Club* is a community of grateful drivers and passengers with dramatic stories about car accidents. These accounts are not told by the company, but they resonate with the brand's identity and positioning, reinforcing its credibility and building its track record (Ind et al., 2013).

By searching for and selecting resonating stories about your brand's value proposition, you are activating critical aspects of the corporate brand's identity. You can, for example, tell stories about your way of working (culture), your ambitions (position), the origin of your name or logotype (expression), or customer service (relations). As illustrated by the communication and positioning layer of the matrix (Figure 4.8), the signature story is placed in the centre square of the framework, superimposed on the identity matrix, echoing other stories about the corporate brand.

Your corporate brand's narrative ideally tells an engaging story that makes people want to know more. The variations on the signature story told by you, your colleagues, customers, and others in different settings and to different audiences make storytelling a versatile and powerful way to communicate. The ability to naturally tell the brand's signature story is an essential part of your leadership.

How do you find clarity, coordination, and consistency in corporate communications and positioning? I asked the CEO of an international shipping corporation. He compared a corporate brand to a work of music, emphasizing that its 'melody' must be recognizable in all internal and external communications. He explained that his favourite song, 'My Way,' had been performed by Frank Sinatra, the French star Claude François, Elvis Presley, Luciano Pavarotti, and even the punk rocker Sid Vicious, and though their voices, styles, and audiences all differed, the melody remained the same. 'In our company,' the CEO said, 'we too have different voices and communicate through multiple channels, telling the world about our brand and what it stands for. The key is for everyone to follow the same melody.'

## 2.2 *Continuity* and *change?*

As the world changes, companies face the challenge of adapting to new trends, technologies, and competitors while preserving the brand's promise and core values (Urde, 2016). A workable solution to the paradox of changing while maintaining continuity can be found in the perspective of rhetoric. Start by interpreting or reinterpreting your brand's core identity in light of the current market situation and the world around you. Review and update, if necessary, your brand's logos-ethos-pathos appeals: 'To be the same, you sometimes need to change.' Doing so will help you adapt or change your communication and positioning while keeping your brand's core identity stable and enrich it.

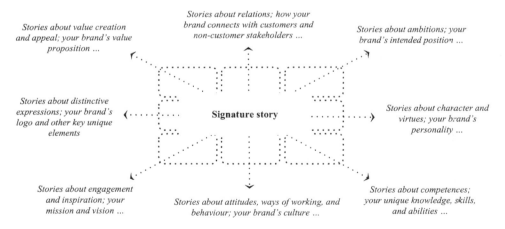

*Figure 4.8* A signature story as communication and positioning theme

*Welcome to the matrix*

The Volvo brand, with its safety positioning, has remained surprisingly stable.[5] In the 1960s, safety was about technical design; in that era, Volvo communicated with a focus on logos arguments. After interpreting and reinterpreting its identity core in 1976, Volvo took a big step and presented its first safety-concept car. The new car series positioned Volvo as an organization with an ethos committed to safety. The longstanding communication theme 'Volvo – For Life' fortified the safety positioning. More recently, the advertising theme 'Made by Sweden,' with the Swedish footballer Zlatan Ibrahimovic, added a strong dose of pathos to the Volvo brand. Thus, over time, safety has evolved from technical design, to commitment to car safety, to caring with a humanistic approach (Figure 4.9).

The idea is to focus creativity on how to express and communicate your brand's core identity, not necessarily to create a new one. At Volvo, there are always voices arguing that 'the safety message is received,' and, therefore, 'let's move on.' However, the message of safety provides reinforcement to existing Volvo customers and is fresh for prospects and new customers.

Another company that faced a need to reinterpret its identity core is IKEA. In doing so, the home-furnishings company opted for an approach to open up its business model for co-creation.

From the family-owned company's beginnings more than 75 years ago, IKEA has been a closed organization, keeping its value chain and decision-making tightly controlled. But a few years ago, the company's leaders, worried that IKEA might one day lose its ability to create products and services that are highly relevant to customers, decided that the business model and brand identity needed to evolve. The company wanted its identity to better speak to and respond to social and environmental challenges that were affecting customers' lives.

The company's leaders concluded that this could not be done by the IKEA organization alone. IKEA, therefore, made a momentous shift: opening up its value chain to co-create.

At IKEA, co-creation is a way to engage with 'the many people' and give its identity core and communication greater legitimacy and acceptance among stakeholders. By opening up and

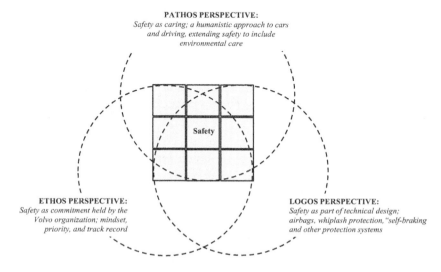

*Figure 4.9* Continuity with change

interacting with customers and non-customer stakeholders, the company listens, learns, and shares in creating more relevant products and services. IKEA studies people's everyday lives and involves customers and suppliers in the development process, aiming to find 'the right solution for the right problem.'

In some collaborations, IKEA's role is to be the host, inviting star artists to its scene. Early examples are designer collections with Tom Dixon and Virgil Abloh. These product lines, internally called 'curious collections,' are introduced rapidly in limited editions – a contrast to typical new-product introductions, which slowly work their way through IKEA's production and logistical system.

Co-creation changes IKEA's perspective. Rather than making self-contained decisions defining the 'ideal home' or 'better' products, the company allows customers to define 'better' and focuses on developing solutions in line with their views. However, IKEA doesn't blindly follow the market or trends. Internally the company is guided by the statement 'What is better is defined by the many, and figured out by us.' The combination of the two parts of that sentence clarifies IKEA's role in partnerships and other forms of cooperation. It guides the company to know when and how to respond to the customer needs and wants that emerge from various forms of cooperation and helps to align the IKEA product range with the company's identity and culture.

The co-creation shift was not easy for the company at first. For example, managers had trouble incorporating community input into their concept of the identity core and corporate culture. IKEA discovered what many other companies have found in attempting co-creation: there is often tension between stakeholders' input and managers' reluctance to change. Nevertheless, IKEA has been able to absorb and incorporate stakeholder insights, with the result that the identity core and how it is communicated have been adjusted – or at least nudged a bit.

Here I use the identity matrix to illustrate changes with implications for communication and positioning. Figure 4.10 summarizes the IKEA identity core based on my analysis. Changes are in boldface.

A first observation is that the mission and vision, the brand core, and the position are nudged to have slightly different meanings. A second finding is that there were ripple effects in which one change led to others. For example, the introduction of sustainability as a new democratic-design criterion led to additions to the IKEA personality and culture. A third insight is that much remains unchanged. Noticing what has *not* changed is as important as seeing what *has* changed.

At IKEA, it is often said, 'The IKEA values inspire you. You share many of the core values, and you can live with the rest. This way, you participate in the development of new values for IKEA. When you develop, IKEA does too.' This is a pragmatic and progressive view that incorporates the shift toward co-creation.

## 3. The second outer layer: reputation

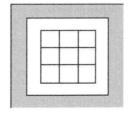

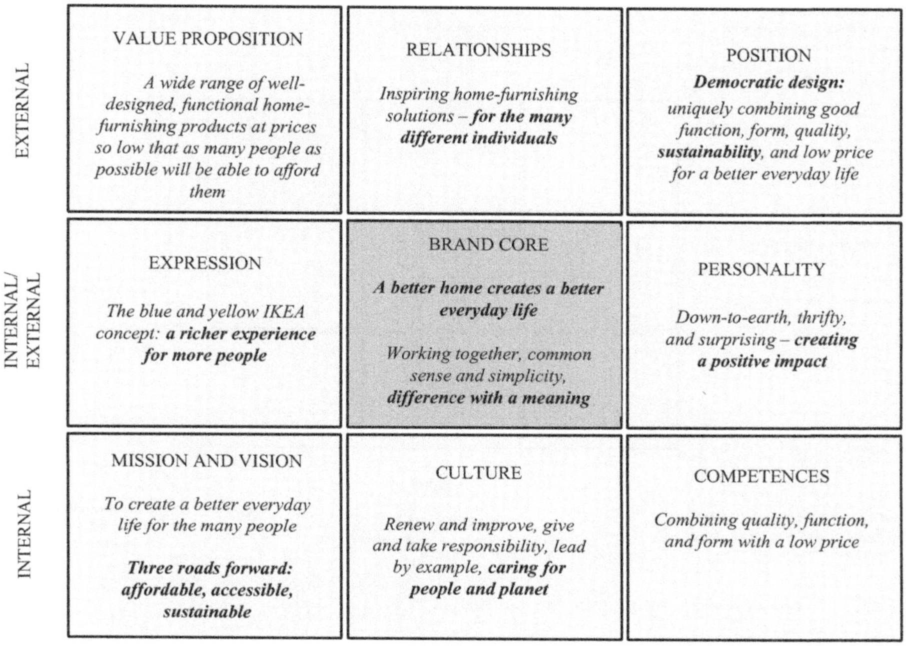

*Welcome to the matrix*

| | | |
|---|---|---|
| **VALUE PROPOSITION**<br><br>*A wide range of well-designed, functional home-furnishing products at prices so low that as many people as possible will be able to afford them* | **RELATIONSHIPS**<br><br>*Inspiring home-furnishing solutions – for the many different individuals* | **POSITION**<br>**Democratic design:**<br>*uniquely combining good function, form, quality, sustainability, and low price for a better everyday life* |
| **EXPRESSION**<br><br>*The blue and yellow IKEA concept: a richer experience for more people* | **BRAND CORE**<br><br>*A better home creates a better everyday life*<br><br>*Working together, common sense and simplicity, difference with a meaning* | **PERSONALITY**<br><br>*Down-to-earth, thrifty, and surprising – creating a positive impact* |
| **MISSION AND VISION**<br><br>*To create a better everyday life for the many people*<br><br>**Three roads forward:** *affordable, accessible, sustainable* | **CULTURE**<br><br>*Renew and improve, give and take responsibility, lead by example, caring for people and planet* | **COMPETENCES**<br><br>*Combining quality, function, and form with a low price* |

Rows (left labels): EXTERNAL / INTERNAL-EXTERNAL / INTERNAL

*Figure 4.10* The evolving IKEA identity core

We now further shift the perspective of the corporate brand. We move from communication and positioning to reputation. The outermost layer of the identity matrix is about how others think of your corporate brand when all is said and done. The corporate brand's reputation is a collective representation of personal judgements based on past and present words and deeds and future prospects (Fombrun, 1996; Roper & Fill, 2012). Image upon image, together and over time, give your corporate brand its reputation. It is not whether the perception of your corporate brand is fair. As noted earlier, what others think of your corporate brand affects your business reality. The question is, how can you influence your corporate brand's image and reputation by its identity and performance?

This layer surrounding the identity matrix emphasizes the connections between your identity core and the impression of your communication and positioning as perceived by others. The reputational layer can be used for alignment and troubleshooting, but also for exploration of new business opportunities.

The reputational layer can serve as a guide to help an executive team go through a structured set of questions about the corporate brand's stature (Figure 4.11). Each question focuses on one reputational element that mirrors an element in the identity matrix and connects with an element in the communication and positioning layer (Urde & Greyser, 2016). The brand core remains at the centre. There are eight elements in total, and the reputational layer extends the strategy diagonal, the competition diagonal, the interaction vertical, and the character horizontal. The dotted square illustrates how communication and positioning shape the reputation of the corporate brand. Let's look at each set of reputational questions in turn.

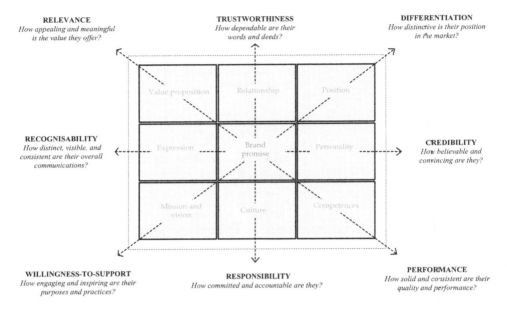

*Figure 4.11* The corporate brand reputational matrix

The **extended strategy diagonal**: *Willingness-to-support* and *differentiation* are the endpoints of the extended strategy diagonal. Willingness-to-support is your customers' and non-customers' answer to 'How engaging and inspiring are the company's purposes and practices?' Willingness-to-support is closely related to the company's mission and vision in the identity matrix and to your activation efforts in the communication and positioning layer.

Here is an example of how the reputational layer was used for troubleshooting. A municipal waste-disposal and recycling company struggled with a low level of willingness-to-support. Market research revealed that customers and non-customer stakeholders were not engaged with or inspired by the company. This surprised managers, who thought they were doing the right thing by contributing to 'a sounder environment' at a time of growing societal engagement with sustainability. The solution was to better communicate the corporate brand's identity. In this case, solving the reputation-layer problem involved addressing a communication-and-positioning layer issue, rather than an identity issue.

At the opposite end of the strategy diagonal across the reputation layer is *differentiation*, which represents your customers' and non-customer stakeholders' answer to 'How distinctive is the brand's position in the market?' In your identity matrix, you have carved out a niche with the intent to make your corporate brand stand out. The reputational input gives you an indication of how uniquely you have managed to position your corporate brand.

Consider Volvo Cars' safety-related position in the identity matrix and safety-related communication and positioning strategy. Annual reputational studies show that safety is, in fact, closely associated with the corporate brand. Management is evaluated on how the safety track record is maintained and built over time to ensure the brand's position and differentiation.

The **extended competition diagonal**: Stakeholders' answer to the *performance* question (lower right of the competition diagonal) – 'How solid and consistent are the brand's quality and performance?' – reflects a corporate brand's competences. Louis Vuitton is known for skilled leather craftmanship, Hilti Tools is known for precision and customer support, and Swedish Rail is known for not being on time. A reputation can give your brand fair winds and following seas, but it can also present persistent headwinds and choppy water. In most cases, issues with performance call for a review of competences. The Irish building company Kingspan takes it one step further by co-creating with its clients and stakeholders to strengthen and continuously update its competences (Impeciati & Ostermann, 2020).

Turning to *relevance* (upper left in the competition diagonal), the question is: 'How appealing and meaningful is the value that the brand offers?' A hotel group with a stellar reputation found that with the rise of Airbnb, the relevance of its value proposition was rapidly declining. The hotel group had to rethink its entire competition diagonal to trace the root of the problem. It invested in digitalization (competences) and developed a digital platform with features and value propositions similar to those of its new competitors.

The **extended interaction vertical**: *Trustworthiness* (the upper element of the vertical) is about the answer to 'How dependable are the brand's words and deeds?' Having trust is a sign of good relations (Light & Kiddon, 2015). Pre-orders of Tesla cars and Apple devices, as well as early signups for stock in companies going public, are examples of how people place their trust in brands.

*Responsibility* (the lower element of the vertical) mirrors your organization's culture, embracing ways of working, behaviour, and attitudes. Your customers and non-customers are asked: 'How committed and accountable is the corporate brand?'

An analysis of Volkswagen's reputation before, during, and after Dieselgate showed how the corporate brand was affected by the crisis. The disappointment and anger among many customers and non-customer stakeholders – including VW employees and business partners – resulted in a significant loss of trustworthiness. Other tarnished reputational elements were responsibility, credibility, and willingness-to-support. The relevance of the company's products, its value-for-money position, and its performance remained fairly stable. Recognizability turned sharply up, but for all the wrong reasons.

This reputational analysis served as a damage report similar to that of a submarine captain calling for an 'all-sections-report' after a collision or nearby explosion. The damage report helped management develop an overview of the situation, prioritize, and take action. In the aftermath of the scandal, Volkswagen's initiatives included a review of its identity core and its communication and positioning. Among the changes to rebuilding the company's reputation as a more open culture, the Volkswagen slogan 'Das Auto' was replaced, and the vision now focuses on electric vehicles.

The **character horizontal**: *Credibility* (the right side of the horizontal) is closely related to how your corporate brand's personality is perceived. The reputational question to follow is: 'How convincing and believable is the brand?' McDonald's Japan was hit by a food-security scandal when pieces of plastic were found in chicken nuggets, causing sales and reputation to plummet (Ku et al., 2018). The CEO publicly apologized, bowing deeply in the Japanese way, and presented a detailed plan to prevent a recurrence. This is an example of how credibility can be lost but also regained.

Turning to *recognizability* (the left side of the vertical), the question you are seeking an answer to is: 'How distinct, visible, and consistent are the brand's overall communications?' The answer reflects the distinctiveness of your brand's expression, including, for example, your logotype, graphic designs, advertising themes, and iconic products. Consider how the Porsche emblem, the company's advertising focus on performance driving, and the lineage of nine generations of the 911 series together make the brand instantly identifiable.

> ### Exercise 3: Mapping the reputational elements
>
> The exercise that follows can reveal whether, in your view, your corporate brand identity is well reflected in the minds and hearts of your customers and non-customer stakeholders – and, if not, it can show where problems and opportunities lie and help you address them.
>
> Starting with any of the eight reputational elements, formulate imagined answers to the related question in the matrix's outermost layer. Since corporate brands typically have multiple stakeholders, it's a good idea to start by focusing on your customers. For example, if you begin with willingness-to-support, you will answer the questions on behalf of a customer: 'How engaging and inspiring are the company's purposes and practices?'
>
> Asking your team members for a ballpark figure often sparks a good discussion: 'Give a number from 1 to 5, with 5 indicating very strong.' The responses may initially be based on your and the team's experience; later in the process, they may be supported by market and customer data, including comments on social media. In your team's discussion of each question, a picture of your corporate brand's reputation gradually emerges.
>
> In imagining customers' and non-customer stakeholders' responses to the questions, follow these guidelines, which are based on suggestions listed previously in the discussion of identity:
>
> 1. **Be concise.** Respond in short phrases and think of these phrases as headings under which you will later write more detailed descriptions fleshing out your brand's image.
> 2. **Be straightforward.** Keep your responses uncomplicated. Less is more.
> 3. **Seek what is characteristic.** Capture words or concepts that resonate with your customers' views, that signal 'this is how they see us.'
> 4. **Stay authentic.** Dare to take a hard look in the mirror. Some elements of your reputation may not be flattering. However, do not fall into the trap of becoming overly critical or defensive; instead, strive to provide a balanced picture.
> 5. **Include what's timeless.** Don't overlook obvious aspects of the brand's image or uniqueness only because they are widely known, such as the triangular shape of the Toblerône chocolate.

Returning to the Nobel Prize example: Figure 4.12 shows the reputational layer that professor Greyser and I helped the organization produce. It is based on interviews with former Nobel laureates, comments by a Stanford University president, and input from other stakeholder groups influencing the reputation of the Nobel Prize.

Lars Heikensten, CEO of the Nobel Foundation, explains the importance of the prestige and standing of the Nobel Prize: 'The reputation is the value and foundation of the Nobel Prize, and it is instrumental for its impact on the world – for the benefit of humankind.'

Our work with the Nobel Foundation took place in 2016. But events in subsequent years demonstrated that there is no such thing as a guaranteed position or reputation. You constantly have to monitor what people say and think about your corporate brand and be prepared to take responsibility and act.

> **Exercise 4: Does your reputational layer measure up?**
>
> The assessment of your corporate brand's reputation provides an overall picture. Most likely, there will be discrepancies between your views and your customers' and stakeholders' perceptions of the corporate brand. There will be gaps where you are doing better than expected and others where there are disappointments. Some gaps are to be expected as a result of strategic repositioning or change processes.
>
> All kinds of gaps and tensions merit further investigation. For example, when you find ratings higher than expected on a reputational element, such as *performance*, ensure that the finding is not based solely on your track record. After a Danish company producing automobile trailers for hauling bulky items reduced the thickness of the steel to save costs, performance ratings remained high among loyal long-time customers, but not among new ones, who complained that the trailers weren't rugged enough.
>
> When you are looking into reputational gaps, a systematic approach is to backtrack.
>
> Appraising your communication and positioning, along with relevant identity elements, including the brand core itself, helps you find possible roots to the problem.
>
> You have earlier asked and interpreted the eight reputational questions from your customer and non-customer stakeholders' perspective. Taking a hard look in the mirror also means answering the same questions *yourself* from your company's perspective:
>
> 1. How engaging and inspiring are our purposes and practices?
> 2. How distinctive is our position in the market?
> 3. How solid and consistent are our quality and performance?
> 4. How appealing and meaningful is the value we offer?
> 5. How committed and accountable are we?
> 6. How dependable are our words and deeds?
> 7. How believable and convincing are we?
> 8. How distinct, visible, and consistent are our overall communications?
>
>    Managing a corporate brand requires the ability to ask penetrating questions and to be able to shift perspectives.

In the spring of 2018, the Swedish Academy was engulfed in a scandal that threatened its reputation, especially its reputation as the organization that awards the Nobel Prize in Literature. A person with close ties to the Academy was accused of and sentenced for sexual harassment and rape. The investigation revealed that members of the Academy had known about the misbehaviour while showing an inability to act. The Swedish Academy's role in awarding one of the Nobel Prizes became part of the battleground of the scandal.

Heikensten put pressure on the Swedish Academy to protect its reputation, and by extension, the Nobel Prize's reputation. 'A loss of reputation is a sign that we, in fact, are not doing our job,' Heikensten said. The 2018 literature award was postponed, the statutes of the Swedish Academy were changed, and new members were elected. The actions have proven to help in the process of rebuilding the reputations of both the Swedish Academy and the Nobel Prize.

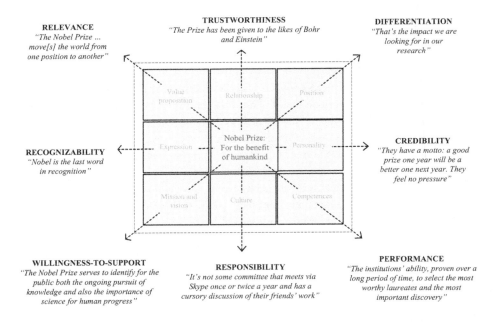

*Figure 4.12* The Nobel Prize reputation

In times of crisis, ask whether the problem comes from your organization or the outside. Next, does the crisis touch the brand's essence? And does the situation affect a part of your business or the entire business?

The corporate brand identity matrix and its two outer layers, with all their deep connections, map your territory. The understanding, branding, and management of a corporate brand are ongoing and iterative processes with pitfalls to avoid, lessons to be learned and shared, and opportunities to grasp. Each layer of the matrix is defined with the help of questions. These are questions you can ask yourself and discuss with your colleagues, customers, and stakeholders. Corporate brand leadership is about engaging and connecting people with something meaningful that is built to last.

Ultimately, you and your organization need to converge on a shared narrative about the corporate brand identity so that the stories the company tells will be engaging, unified, and consistent throughout the organization and beyond.

## Notes

1  This framework was an outcome of my case study of the Nicorette brand dating back to my PhD thesis on brand orientation (1997). Later, it became a foundation for the Brand Identity Matrix presented in this chapter.
2  The Corporate Brand Identity Matrix was first published in the *Journal of Brand Management* (Urde, 2013) and later further developed and enriched by applications in practice, and published in *Harvard Business Review* (Greyser & Urde, 2019).

3 Simon Sinek (2009) asks in sequence the why, how, and what questions. Starting with 'why?' is an inside-out approach that emphasizes the importance of being purpose-driven. I add a fourth question: By whom?
4 Inspired by Charles Sanders Peirce's study of signs and the forming of a symbol.
5 I have worked with Volvo as a brand strategy consultant and followed the brand as a researcher since 1995. The safety positioning, and how it came about, inspired a longitudinal case study (Urde, 2009) and, later, an investigation into the management of a corporate brand over time (Urde, 2016).

# References

Aaker, D. A. (2018). *Creating signature stories*. New York: Free Press.
Abratt, R., & Kleyn, N. (2012). Corporate identity, corporate branding and corporate reputations: Reconciliation and integration. *European Journal of Marketing, 46*(7), 1048–1063.
Aristotle (2004). *The art of rhetoric*. London: Pinguine Classics (Translated with an introduction and notes by H. C. Lawson-Tancred).
Balmer, J. M. T. (2008). Identity-based views of the corporation. *European Journal of Marketing, 42*(9–10), 879–906.
Bately, M. (2016). *Brand meaning: Meaning, myth, and mystique in today's brands*. London: Routledge.
Baumgarth, C., Merrilees, B., & Urde, M. (2013). Brand orientation: Past, present, and future. *Journal of Marketing Management, 29*(9–10), 973–980.
Boulding, K. E. (1956). *The image: Knowledge in life and society*. Ann Arbor, MI: University of Michigan Press.
Bourdieu, P. (1992). *Distinction: A social critique of the judgment of taste*. London: Routledge.
De Wit, B., & Meyer, R. (2010). *Strategy: Process, content, context*. Andover: South-Western Cengage.
Fog, K., Budtz, C., & Yakaboylu, B. (2005). *Storytelling: Branding in practice*. Heidelberg: Springer.
Fombrun, C. J. (1996). *Reputation: Realizing value from the corporate image*. Boston, MA: Harvard Business School Press.
Gardner, B. B., & Levy, S. J. (1955, March–April). The product and the brand. *Harvard Business Review*, 33–39.
Greyser, S. A., & Urde, M. (2018a). The reputation of the 'world's most prestigious award': The Nobel Prize. *Harvard Business School*, Case number 9–919–401 with Teaching Note.
Greyser, S. A., & Urde, M. (2018b). The Swedish Academy #MeToo scandal and the reputation of the Nobel Prize. *Harvard Business School*, Case number 9–919–409 with Teaching Note.
Greyser, S. A., & Urde, M. (2019, January/February). What does your corporate brand stand for? *Harvard Business Review*.
Gromark, J., & Melin, F. (2011). The underlying dimensions of brand orientation and its impact on financial performance. *Journal of Brand Management, 18*, 394–410.
Hatch, M. J., & Schultz, M. (2003, February). Are the strategic stars aligned for your corporate brand? *Harvard Business Review*, 129–134.
Holt, D., & Cameron, D. (2010). *Cultural strategy*. Oxford: Oxford University Press.
Iglesias, O., & Bonet, E. (2012). Persuasive brand management. *Journal of Organizational Change Management, 25*(2), 252–264.
Iglesias, O., Landgraf, P., Ind, N., & Markovic, S. (2020). Corporate brand identity co-creation in business-to-business. *Industrial Marketing Management, 85*, 32–43.
Impeciati, E., & Ostermann, A.-M. (2020). *Under pressure: Tensions in the acquiring firms corporate brand identity* (Master Thesis). Lund University School of Economics and Management, Lund.
Ind, N. (1998). An integrated approach to corporate branding. *Journal of Brand Management, 5*(5), 323–329. https://doi.org/10.1057/bm.1998.20.
Ind, N., Iglesias, O., & Schultz, M. (2013). Building brands together: Emergence and outcomes of co-creation. *California Management Review, 55*(3), 5–26.
Kapferer, J.-N. (2012). *The new strategic brand management*. London: Kogan Page.
Kennedy, S. H. (1977). Nurturing corporate images. *European Journal of Marketing, 11*(3), 119–164. https://doi.org/10.1108/EUM0000000005007.
King, S. (1991). Brand building in the 1990s. *Journal of Consumer Marketing, 8*(4), 43–52. https://doi.org/10.1108/07363769110035144.

Ku, H. E., Fiorini, R., & Huang, R. (2018). *When the golden arches lose their shine: McDonald's Japan food Scandal* (Corporate Brand Management and Reputation: Master Cases Series). Lund: Lund University School of Economics and Management.

Light, L., & Kiddon, J. (2015). *New brand leadership: Managing at the intersection of globalization, localization, and personalization*. Old Tappan: Pearson Education.

McCloskey, D. N. (1998). *The rhetoric of economics*. Madison, WI: The University of Wisconsin Press.

Morgan, G., & Smircich, L. (1982). Leadership: The management of meaning. *Journal of Applied Behavioral Science, 18*(3), 257–273.

Norrmann, R. (2001). *Reframing business: When the map changes the landscape*. New York: John Wiley & Sons.

Ogilvy, D. (1983). *Ogilvy on advertising*. London: Pan Books.

Olins, W. (1989). *Corporate identity*. London: Thames and Hudson.

Ries, A., & Trout, J. (1981). *Positioning: The battle for your mind*. New York: McGraw-Hill.

Roper, S., & Fill, C. (2012). *Corporate reputation: Brand and communication*. London: Pearson.

Santos, F. P. (2012, September). The semiotic conception of brand and the traditional marketing view. *Irish Journal of Management*, 95–108.

Sinek, S. (2009). *Start with why*. London: Pearson.

Urde, M. (1994). Brand orientation: A strategy for survival. *Journal of Consumer Marketing, 11*(3), 18–32.

Urde, M. (1999). Brand orientation: A mindset for building brands into strategic resources. *Journal of Marketing Management, 15*(1–3), 117–133.

Urde, M. (2003). Core value-based corporate brand building. *European Journal of Marketing, 37*(7–8), 1017–1040.

Urde, M. (2009). Uncovering the corporate brand's core values. *Management Decision, 47*(4), 616–638.

Urde, M. (2013). Corporate brand identity matrix. *Journal of Brand Management, 20*(9), 742–761.

Urde, M. (2016). The brand core and its management over time. *Journal of Product and Brand Management, 25*(1), 26–42.

Urde, M., Baumgarth, C., & Merrilees, B. (2010). Brand orientation and market orientation: From alternatives to synergy. *Journal of Business Research, 66*(1), 13–20.

Urde, M., & Greyser, S. A. (2015). The Nobel Prize: The identity of a corporate heritage brand. *Journal of Product and Brand Management, 24*(4), 319–332.

Urde, M., & Greyser, S. A. (2016). The corporate brand identity and reputation matrix – The Nobel Prize case. *Journal of Brand Management, 23*(1), 89–117.

# 5
# COMMENTARY ON 'TOWARDS A PARADIGM SHIFT IN CORPORATE BRAND MANAGEMENT'

*Joachim Kernstock and Shaun Powell*

## 1. Introduction

We begin our commentary by first considering the branding of organizations and outlining some key facets of corporate brand management. These are based on an extrapolation of themes and concepts from across three chapters in this section of the book by Russell Abratt and Michela Mingione, Hans Mühlbacher, and Mats Urde.

Next, in Section 3 we discuss what we have termed the 'co-creative school of thought.' In Section 4 we reflect on what co-creation might mean for leadership. In Section 5 we consider tools for applying corporate brand management with a focus on the Corporate Brand Identity Matrix.

In the final section we conclude by delineating some avenues for ongoing and future research in the field of corporate brand management.

## 2. Key facets of corporate brand management

There has been an amplification of interest in the branding of organizations and corporations during the last 25 years (Powell et al., 2007; Golob et al., 2020). For example, in 1995 John Balmer published in the *Journal of General Management* on 'Corporate branding and connoisseurship' (Balmer, 1995), and David Aaker (1996) published an editorial in the *Journal of Brand Management* entitled 'Misconceptions about brands,' considering the need to broaden the brand concept beyond a product or service, to a brand-as-organization perspective (Powell, 2014, p. 695).

In their chapter, Russell Abratt and Michela Mingione usefully demarcate much of the corporate brand management terrain to date. The scope of their discussion brings to light a number of concepts that researchers and managers consider, including: the relevance of corporate identity, brand values, brand positioning and differentiation, credibility and trust, reputation and image, organizational core competencies and corporate social responsibility. Amongst other things they also address considerations related to 'top management and founder involvement,' 'multiple stakeholder involvement,' 'internal branding,' the role of 'corporate communications,' 'brand experience,' and 'brand authenticity,' as well as 'brand heritage.' Several of these concepts and themes have resonance and intertwine with other chapters in this section of the book.

For example, Hans Mühlbacher in the illuminating chapter on 'Corporate brand management from a co-creative perspective' considers the need for internal corporate branding, as well as the relevance of the top management role – which he indicates is similar to that of conducting an orchestra. This orchestration view of top management aligns with the chapters by Russell Abratt and Michela Mingione, as well as Mats Urde, who outlines the need for a common 'melody' when creating a signature story as part of corporate brand management.

Additionally, Mats Urde in his chapter and excellent discussion on the application of the Corporate Brand Identity Matrix encapsulates many of the concepts considered by Russell Abratt and Michela Mingione – including once again the need to consider corporate identity, credibility and trust, reputation (reputational matrix), communications, positioning, trustworthiness, authenticity, multiple stakeholders and brand heritage.

We believe these unifying themes and concepts – plus other astute aspects discussed within this section of the book, collectively provide readers with a broad and evolutionary insight for many of the key facets of corporate brand management to date.

## 3. Introduction of the co-creative school of thought

Previously, Leitch and Motion (2007), while drawing partially on work from the concept of 'corporate marketing,' which also takes a stakeholder perspective (Balmer, 1998, 2001a, 2001b; Balmer & Greyser, 2003), have called for academics and practitioners to radically reappraise how they envision the management of organizational and corporate brands.

Other authors have proposed and discussed the need to better integrate a co-creation perspective with various stakeholders for corporate brand management (e.g., Gregory, 2007; Hatch & Schultz, 2010; Helm & Jones, 2010; Cova & Paranque, 2012; Gyrd-Jones & Kornum, 2013; Iglesias et al., 2013; Ind et al., 2013; Ind & Iglesias, 2016; Ind & Schmidt, 2019), which we pick up on in this section of our commentary.

The informative chapter by Hans Mühlbacher also unpacks corporate brand management from a co-creative perspective. His discussion includes the viewpoint that 'the logic of brands and branding . . . has shifted from the conceptualization of brand as firm-provided property of goods to brand as a collaborative, value co-creation activity of firms and all their stakeholders' (Merz et al., 2009, pp. 328–329).

As we have reflected upon previously (Kernstock & Powell, 2018, pp. 489–493), Balmer (2013) has discussed a variety of perspectives within the brand orientation canon which have relevance for corporate brand management – as characterized via nine symptomatic schools of thought that had emerged up until that point. These schools of thought also reflect on the stakeholder view, addressing stakeholders as relevant for the development of the corporate brand. The nine schools of thought (Balmer, 2013, p. 729) are outlined here:

1 **The philosophical school:** Relates to the importance of the (corporate) brand as an organizational-wide mindset. This perspective has been adopted by demanding a 'purpose' orientation rather than 'positioning' when thinking about brand management within an organization (Jones, 2012). We note that Mats Urde in his chapter discussing the corporate brand identity matrix addresses the key questions raised by the philosophical school, focussing on understanding of the corporate brand as 'body and entity.'
2 **The behavioural school:** Relates to the importance of the (corporate) brand in guiding behaviour. This school relates to the influence on customer behaviour, i.e., purchasing behaviour or customer loyalty, and employee behaviour showing to be on-brand. This school connects the brand management discussion with the wide field of brand experience.

3   **The hybrid school:** Relates to both philosophical and behavioural schools. This school relates to a brand-focussed organizational-wide philosophy and organizational behaviours.
4   **The cultural school:** Relates to an organizational-wide brand-focussed culture, and recently there have been research achievements in bridging research on organizational culture with research on brand management. The chapter by Russell Abratt and Michela Mingione highlights this convergence – by addressing the specific role of corporate heritage for corporate brand management. The relevance and impact of internal brand management has also been highlighted by several researchers.
5   **The performance school:** Relates to branding effects vis-a-vis overall organizational performance. This school is associated with the improvement of corporate performance linked to the brand.
6   **The strategic school:** Relates to the central role of brands in formulating an organization's strategy. For example, brand portfolio management and the development of brand architecture strategies are profound fundamentals of a corporate strategy, including for strategic corporate actions such as mergers and acquisition. In their chapter, Russell Abratt and Michela Mingione also refer to the importance of the strategic view in the emergence of the field of corporate brand management.

7   **The marketing school:** Relates to the role of brands regarding the marketing function and marketing strategy and has its origin in considering brand management as a part of product brand management, as well as in relation to the role of the brand in packaging. This view brings corporate brands closer to the consumer or customer, adding the corporate brand as endorsement or ingredient and communicating product brands and corporate brand as a joint entity.
8   **The omni-brands school:** Relates (inferred) to an organization's brands in their entirety and reflects on the specific role of the brand for its business and the corporation, its structure and processes, and defining its customer relationship. For example, in luxury brand management, where brand management is the warranty for success and performance, this is done by creating a specific customer-brand and customer-corporation relationship. Luxury brand management is a concept, an industry, and a very specific strategy at the same time (Kapferer, 2014).
9   **The corporate brands school:** Relates to the corporate brand per se (IMPLICIT). This school considers the stakeholder orientation of the brand and includes all perspectives of all these schools and builds on their achievements in research and management practice. The corporate brand management school especially considers and builds on the contribution of the corporate brand to the leadership of the company (Balmer et al., 2013).

Building on these schools we have earlier proposed an additional school of thought to be added, named the 'co-creative school of thought' (see also Schmidt & Redler, 2018):

10  **The co-creative school:** Relates to 'collaborative processes with customers, users or other stakeholders for an evolutionary development of the brand' (Kernstock & Powell, 2018, pp. 491–492). We outline our view from a broader base in the next section, where we consider co-creation from a leadership perspective.

We feel the proposal to add the co-creative school is warranted given some other more recent developments in the field. These include, for example, evolving digital technologies and online activity which 'supports co-creation by providing internal and external stakeholders that never met offline with unprecedented opportunities for joint brand-related interaction' (Kristal et al., 2020, pp. 240–241). Co-creation can also help to 'open up a brand to the outside world and help it to generate relevant innovations' (Ind et al., 2017, p. 310).

The co-creative school could lead to an insightful stream of research, adding to the previous results of the other nine schools while not replacing them, and can provide inspiration for investigation of potential gaps in some of the other schools (Kernstock & Powell, 2018).

## 4. Co-creation and leadership

In our view, the co-creation perspective on corporate brand management is also strictly connected with the leadership perspective – leading us to consider whether the co-creation context also necessitates a change in approach to leadership. And by *leadership*, we mean two different views: either the leadership of the corporation itself or the leadership of the corporate brand. We are aware that both perspectives on leadership are inter-connected. However, they are also two different things.

In the current 'mainstream' of co-creation brand management research and management practice, *co-creation* often means acknowledging the influence of consumers and stakeholders on the product or corporate brand development. Presently, the discussion within this stream tends to focus on how an empathic view or approach of brand development might occur, for example either in relation to brand identity, brand goals, brand value, or brand purpose. If successful, the main objective is to edge closer to a relevant group of customers and/or other relevant stakeholders, becoming a respected, desired member of the targeted community. In this context, the corporate, or the product brand, if co-creating successfully, is at least accepted by the community and perhaps better desired and purchased.

However, this strategy of co-creation comes with a risk of failure. For as we have noted elsewhere (Powell, 2014; Kernstock & Powell, 2018), Hatch and Schultz (2010) have identified that

> as brand management grows in sophistication, it engages not just all stakeholders, but also all parts of the organization, ultimately becoming an amalgam of all these interests . . . to the extent that dialogue leads to access and access to transparency, the real risk that companies take when they move to the full stakeholder model of enterprise branding is to recognize the extent to which the larger world determines their value(s).
> (Hatch & Schultz, 2010, p. 603)

Co-creation often requires quite a different approach – as one example, perhaps encouraging co-creation by totally giving up any control of the outside perception of the corporate brand and focussing only on the core product itself. A co-creation approach might also necessitate a significant change in corporate culture – and as a consequence disrupt previously well researched and executed management practices, which had been successful in the past, which might then be lost, or weakened moving forward, potentially leading to some associated problems.

A similar strategy has been deployed by Bottega Veneta, a luxury fashion brand owned by Kering, a French luxury conglomerate. After several initial approaches to co-work with and influence the 'influencers' who have a focus on the luxury fashion industry and community, Bottega Veneta subsequently switched approaches and cancelled any marketing and brand management activity directed towards social media, influencers, and fashion activists. Bottega Veneta management decided to stop all such communication in alignment with parent company Kering.

This step acknowledges the reality of social media activism, in this case fashion influencers, as its own business reality with its own rules. The new goal of Bottega Veneta is creating products and its own fashion events, which are of such high quality that luxury fashion influencers must talk about them and participate, if not wishing to be off-loaded by the community, the fashionistas.

The shift of power becomes obvious when we look at social media fashion influencers. One of the most popular, if not the most important is Chiara Ferragni, former student at Bocconi University, Milano. She started 'The Blonde Salad,' now the most influential fashion blog and the role model for blog creation at the Harvard Business School. Together with her husband Fedez, a famous Italian rapper, Chiara has around 40 million followers worldwide. She was asked by the Italian Prime Minister Giuseppe Conte to support Coronavirus restrictions and explain them to the community, which she did. She also asked their community to support the Italian rock newcomers Måneskin to win the Eurovision Song Contest in 2021 by voting for them, with Måneskin winning the contest.

Hence, the balance of power has shifted. One strategy has been deployed by Bottega Veneta: focus on excellence of the product so that influencers like Chiara Ferragni are expected to comment on it, like a good old luxury fashion magazine, but not to be the 'fashion magazine' itself. Another strategy might be to invite the influencer into the supervisory board of the company, crossing the border into the corporate world. This is what Tod's, another Italian luxury fashion brand has done with Chiara Ferragni, who is now on the board of directors.

We also note that the relatively recent and insightful co-creation continuum research by Ind et al. (2017) has led to 'findings indicating most brands currently tend to use co-creation as a tactical market research tool. However, some have successfully transitioned to the other end of the continuum and engage customers and other stakeholders potentially in all stages of the co-creation process – enabling differentiation and competitive advantage' (Powell, 2017, p. 509).

This leads us to reflect: What do we need for product and brand development in a co-creation business environment and context? We may need to decide on whether to have direct, indirect, or else perhaps no communicative interaction with any influencers and the community itself. Erasing all corporate social media channels and acknowledging the existence of a clear borderline between corporate action and social media reality and activity might not be the only approach an organization can take – but it is one way that has been taken by some organizations at present. In these cases, only the product communicates by itself. Finally, as touched upon earlier:

> The co-creation perspective is not without its risks, challenges or potential pitfalls for corporate brand management. It may be difficult to orchestrate, at least for some organisations . . . hence, while in our view the co-creative school is a worthy avenue for future corporate brand management research and holds great promise, research will need to approach the topic rigorously and from a number of perspectives and contexts, to ensure adequate clarity is achieved in the area.
> (Kernstock & Powell, 2018, p. 492)

## 5. Tools for applying corporate brand management

There are a number of models and tools available to aid with corporate brand identity management. These include, for example, the AC$^4$ID test (Balmer, 2012) and the 'brand steering wheel' (Esch, 2019). Each of these work on different levels towards the management of the corporate brand identity. The AC$^4$ID test undertakes an assessment of the situation for a corporation regarding its corporate identity via an analysis of potential gaps, aiming where possible to reduce any gaps uncovered. We could also see the AC$^4$ID test as a meta level analysis tool that requires the additional application of a specific tool for identity development. The 'brand steering wheel' supports brand identity development by raising a number of questions to consider in five interrelated areas, either functional or emotional. Amongst other things this tool considers the brand essence, which at the corporate brand level could also include the issue of 'brand purpose.'

In his chapter, Mats Urde discusses a comprehensive tool for corporate brand development: the Corporate Brand Identity Matrix. This matrix is a holistic approach to corporate brand management which builds upon and successfully integrates different levels of analyses, as well as for application. The matrix integrates internal and external views on corporate brand development and provides a set of challenging questions in nine core fields of development for the corporate brand which bridges both the meta level and the core identity level. The full and complete set of questions leads to a description of the corporate brand identity, which is also highly applicable in management practice. Mats gives an assessment, plus advice on how to use – as well as challenge – the matrix. He recommends challenging the matrix by asking: Does your matrix measure up? The elements of the matrix should be challenged in four different directions, the 'paths': strategy, competition, interaction, communication. All paths are areas of assessment and address the quality of development of an explicit corporate brand identity, based on the matrix tool. The Corporate Brand Identity Matrix is a fully developed tool for brand management practice, experts, and researchers that considers different levels that need integrating.

Mats also takes the Corporate Brand Identity Matrix a stage further on the road towards application by introducing the Corporate Brand Reputational Matrix. This second set of questions takes the corporate brand management discussion to the 'second outer layer' – reputation. If 'brand purpose' is considered as one of the key elements within corporate brand identity development, then the reputation of the corporate brand is the final answer to the key question and challenge of 'Does your matrix measure up?' After developing the corporate brand identity and applying the brand identity in the ongoing business, management and researchers might identify gaps between ideal or desired identity and the actual behaviour of the company and its representatives. The additional set of questions provided by the Corporate Brand Reputational Matrix provides advice to close any reputational gap. The Corporate Brand Reputational Matrix is an assessment and steering tool to help direct the corporate brand towards achieving a positive reputation.

## 6. Current and future research

In conclusion, and extending on some of our and colleagues previous work (Balmer et al., 2017), we have undertaken a recent (though limited) literature review, spanning the last five years, to identify some streams of research for ongoing/upcoming exploration and application of corporate brand management. For the purpose of brevity each are briefly outlined here, along with citation of some sources for further reading. It is also important to note that corporate brand management research and practice are not limited to these streams. We are also aware of other insightful research avenues and applications underway within the domain.

### 6.1 Business-to-business

One growing research stream of note including during the past five years is anchored within the context of business-to-business (B2B) and corporate brand management (see for example: Törmälä & Gyrd-Jones, 2017; Törmälä & Saraniemi, 2018: Balmer et al., 2020; Iglesias et al., 2020b; Mingione & Leoni, 2020; Ozdemir et al., 2020; Pranjal & Sarkar, 2020).

## 6.2 Heritage and history

Another established and growing stream of interest within corporate brand management has been that of heritage and history (see for example: Balmer, 2017; Balmer & Chen, 2017; Wilson, 2018; Balmer & Burghausen, 2019; Iglesias et al., 2020a; Sammour et al., 2020; Sørensen et al., 2021).

## 6.3 Online and digital

A third stream of interest which has been increasingly active is the management and role of the corporate brand in social media and other online or digital contexts (see for example: Balmer & Yen, 2017: Nobre & Ferreira, 2017; Leitch & Merlot, 2018; Schniederjans et al., 2018; Tarnovskaya & Biedenbach, 2018; Tuškej & Podnar, 2018; Cooper et al., 2019; Essamri et al., 2019; Meek et al., 2019; Mingione & Abratt, 2020; Schivinski et al., 2020).

## 6.4 CSR and ethics

A fourth stream of established and growing research is related to corporate brand management and corporate social responsibility, as well as ethics (see for example: Wegerer & Munro, 2018; Golob & Podnar, 2019; Vollero et al., 2021).

## 6.5 Co-creation

Finally, as already discussed, the co-creation perspective also offers a promising avenue for ongoing/upcoming research in the field (see for example: Biraghi et al., 2017; Ind et al., 2017; Uncles & Ngo, 2017; Schmeltz & Kjeldsen, 2019; Renton & Richard, 2019; Stach, 2019; France et al., 2020; Iglesias & Ind, 2020; Ind et al., 2020; Kristal et al., 2020; Lahtinen & Närvänen, 2020).

## References

Aaker, D. (1996). Misconceptions about brands. *Journal of Brand Management, 3*(4), 212–214. https://doi.org/10.1057/bm.1996.1

Balmer, J. M. T. (1995). Corporate branding and connoisseurship. *Journal of General Management, 21*(1), 24–46. https://doi.org/10.1177/030630709502100102

Balmer, J. M. T. (1998). Corporate identity and the advent of corporate marketing. *Journal of Marketing Management, 14*(8), 963–996. https://doi.org/10.1362/026725798784867536

Balmer, J. M. T. (2001a). The three virtues and seven deadly sins of corporate brand management. *Journal of General Management, 27*(1), 1–17. https://doi.org/10.1177/030630700102700101

Balmer, J. M. T. (2001b). Corporate identity, corporate branding and corporate marketing – Seeing through the fog. *European Journal of Marketing, 35*(3/4), 248–291. https://doi.org/10.1108/03090560110694763

Balmer, J. M. T. (2012). Strategic corporate brand alignment: Perspectives from identity based views of corporate brands. *European Journal of Marketing, 46*(7–8), 1064–1092. https://doi.org/10.1108/03090561211230205

Balmer, J. M. T. (2013). Corporate brand orientation: What is it? What of it? *Journal of Brand Management, 20*(9), 723–741. https://doi.org/10.1057/bm.2013.15

Balmer, J. M. T. (2017). Advances in corporate brand, corporate heritage, corporate identity and corporate marketing scholarship. *European Journal of Marketing, 51*(9–10), 1462–1471. https://doi.org/10.1108/EJM-07-2017-0447

Balmer, J. M. T., Brexendorf., T. O., & Kernstock, J. (2013). Corporate brand management – A leadership perspective. *Journal of Brand Management, 20*(9), 717–722. https://doi.org/10.1057/bm.2013.20

Balmer, J. M. T., & Burghausen, M. (2019). Marketing, the past and corporate heritage. *Marketing Theory, 19*(2), 217–227. https://doi.org/10.1177/1470593118790636

Balmer, J. M. T., & Chen, W. (2017). Corporate heritage brands, augmented role identity and customer satisfaction. *European Journal of Marketing, 51*(9–10), 1510–1521. https://doi.org/10.1108/EJM-07-2017-0449

Balmer, J. M. T., & Greyser, S. A. (2003). *Revealing the corporation: Perspectives on identity, image, reputation, corporate branding and corporate-level marketing*. London: Routledge.

Balmer, J. M. T., Lin, Z., Chen, W., & He, X. (2020). The role of corporate brand image for B2B relationships of logistics service providers in China. *Journal of Business Research, 117*, 850–861. https://doi.org/10.1016/j.jbusres.2020.03.043

Balmer, J. M. T., Powell, S. M., Kernstock, J., & Brexendorf, T. O. (2017). Introduction: Current state and future directions for research on corporate brand management. In J. M. T. Balmer, S. M. Powell, J. Kernstock, & T. O. Brexendorf (Eds.), *Advances in corporate branding. Journal of Brand Management: Advanced Collections*. London: Palgrave Macmillan. https://doi.org/10.1057/978-1-352-00008-5_1

Balmer, J. M. T., & Yen, D. A. (2017). The Internet of total corporate communications, quaternary corporate communications and the corporate marketing Internet revolution. *Journal of Marketing Management, 33*(1–2), 131–144. https://doi.org/10.1080/0267257X.2016.1255440

Biraghi, S., Gambetti, R. C., & Schultz, D. E. (2017). Advancing a citizenship approach to corporate branding: A societal view. *International Studies of Management & Organization, 47*(2), 206–215. http://doi.org/10.1080/00208825.2017.1256168

Cooper, T., Stavros, C., & Dobele, A. R. (2019). The levers of engagement: An exploration of governance in an online brand community. *Journal of Brand Management, 26*(3), 240–254. https://doi.org/10.1057/s41262-018-0132-2

Cova, B., & Paranque, B. (2012). Value creation versus destruction: The relationship between consumers, marketers and financiers. *Journal of Brand Management, 20*(2), 147–158. https://doi.org/10.1057/bm.2012.46

Esch, F. R. (2019). Identität der Corporate Brand entwickeln und schärfen. In F. R. Esch, T. Tomczak, J. Kernstock, T. Langner, & J. Redler (Eds.), *Corporate brand management* (pp. 89–105). Wiesbaden: Springer Gabler. https://doi.org/10.1007/978-3-658-24900-7_5

Essamri, A., McKechnie, S., & Winklhofer, H. (2019). Co-creating corporate brand identity with online brand communities: A managerial perspective. *Journal of Business Research, 96*, 366–375. https://doi.org/10.1016/j.jbusres.2018.07.015

France, C., Grace, D., Lo Iacono, J., & Carlini, J. (2020). Exploring the interplay between customer perceived brand value and customer brand co-creation behaviour dimensions. *Journal of Brand Management, 27*(4), 466–480. https://doi.org/10.1057/s41262-020-00194-7

Golob, U., Davies, M. A. P., Kernstock, J., & Powell, S. M. (2020). Trending topics plus future challenges and opportunities in brand management. *Journal of Brand Management, 27*(2), 123–129. https://doi.org/10.1057/s41262-019-00184-4

Golob, U., & Podnar, K. (2019). Researching CSR and brands in the here and now: An integrative perspective. *Journal of Brand Management, 26*(1), 1–8. https://doi.org/10.1057/s41262-018-0112-6

Gregory, A. (2007). Involving stakeholders in developing corporate brands: The communication dimension. *Journal of Marketing Management, 23*(1–2), 59–73. https://doi.org/10.1362/026725707X178558

Gyrd-Jones, R. I., & Kornum, N. (2013). Managing the co-created brand: Value and cultural complementarity in online and offline multi-stakeholder ecosystems. *Journal of Business Research, 66*(9), 1484–1493. https://doi.org/10.1016/j.jbusres.2012.02.045

Hatch, M., & Schultz, M. (2010). Toward a theory of brand co-creation with implications for brand governance. *Journal of Brand Management, 17*(8), 590–604. https://doi.org/10.1057/bm.2010.14

Helm, C., & Jones, R. (2010). Extending the value chain – A conceptual framework for managing the governance of co-created brand equity. *Journal of Brand Management, 17*(8), 579–589. https://doi.org/10.1057/bm.2010.19

Iglesias, O., & Ind, N. (2020). Towards a theory of conscientious corporate brand co-creation: The next key challenge in brand management. *Journal of Brand Management, 27*(6), 710–720. https://doi.org/10.1057/s41262-020-00205-7

Iglesias, O., Ind, N., & Alfaro, M. (2013). The organic view of the brand: A brand value co-creation model. *Journal of Brand Management, 20*(8), 670–688. https://doi.org/10.1057/bm.2013.8

Iglesias, O., Ind, N., & Schultz, M. (2020a). History matters: The role of history in corporate brand strategy. *Business Horizons, 63*(1), 51–60. https://doi.org/10.1016/j.bushor.2019.09.005

Iglesias, O., Landgraf, P., Ind, N., Markovic, S., & Koporcic, N. (2020b). Corporate brand identity co-creation in business-to-business contexts. *Industrial Marketing Management, 85*, 32–43. https://doi.org/10.1016/j.indmarman.2019.09.008

Ind, N., Coates, N., & Lerman, K. (2020). The gift of co-creation: What motivates customers to participate. *Journal of Brand Management, 27*(2), 181–194. https://doi.org/10.1057/s41262-019-00173-7

Ind, N., & Iglesias, O. (2016). *Brand desire: How to create consumer involvement and inspiration*. London: Bloomsbury.

Ind, N., Iglesias, O., & Markovic, S. (2017). The co-creation continuum: From tactical market research tool to strategic collaborative innovation method. *Journal of Brand Management, 24*(4), 310–321. https://doi.org/10.1057/s41262-017-0051-7

Ind, N., Iglesias, O., & Schultz, M. (2013). Building brands together: Emergence and outcomes of co-creation. *California Management Review, 55*(3), 5–26. https://doi.org/10.1525/cmr.2013.55.3.5

Ind, N., & Schmidt, H. J. (2019). *Co-creating brands: Brand management from a co-creative perspective*. London: Bloomsbury.

Jones, R. (2012). Five ways branding is changing. *Journal of Brand Management, 20*(2), 77–79. https://doi.org/10.1057/bm.2012.51

Kapferer, J. N. (2014). The future of luxury: Challenges and opportunities. *Journal of Brand Management, 21*(9), 716–726. https://doi.org/10.1057/bm.2014.32

Kernstock, J., & Powell, S. M. (2018). Twenty-five years of the Journal of Brand Management. *Journal of Brand Management, 25*(6), 489–493. https://doi.org/10.1057/s41262-018-0138-9

Kristal, S., Baumgarth, C., & Henseler, J. (2020). Performative corporate brand identity in industrial markets: The case of German prosthetics manufacturer Ottobock. *Journal of Business Research, 114*, 240–253. https://doi.org/10.1016/j.jbusres.2020.04.026

Lahtinen, S., & Närvänen, E. (2020). Co-creating sustainable corporate brands: A consumer framing approach. *Corporate Communications: An International Journal, 25*(3), 447–461. https://doi.org/10.1108/CCIJ-11-2019-0121

Leitch, S., & Merlot, E. (2018). Power relations within brand management: The challenge of social media. *Journal of Brand Management, 25*(2), 85–92. https://doi.org/10.1057/s41262-017-0081-1

Leitch, S., & Motion, J. (2007). Retooling the corporate brand: A Foucauldian perspective on normalisation and differentiation. *Journal of Brand Management, 15*(1), 71–80. https://doi.org/10.1057/palgrave.bm.2550111

Meek, S., Ogilvie, M., Lambert, C., & Ryan, M. M. (2019). Contextualising social capital in online brand communities. *Journal of Brand Management, 26*(4), 426–444. https://doi.org/10.1057/s41262-018-00145-3

Merz, M. A., He, Y., & Vargo, S. L. (2009). The evolving brand logic: A service-dominant logic perspective. *Journal of the Academy of Marking Science, 37*, 328–344. https://doi.org/10.1007/s11747-009-0143-3

Mingione, M., & Abratt, R. (2020). Building a corporate brand in the digital age: Imperatives for transforming born-digital startups into successful corporate brands. *Journal of Marketing Management, 36*(11–12), 981–1008. https://doi.org/10.1080/0267257X.2020.1750453

Mingione, M., & Leoni, L. (2020). Blurring B2C and B2B boundaries: Corporate brand value co-creation in B2B2C markets. *Journal of Marketing Management, 36*(1–2), 72–99. http://doi.org/10.1080/0267257X.2019.1694566

Nobre, H., & Ferreira, A. (2017). Gamification as a platform for brand co-creation experiences. *Journal of Brand Management, 24*(4), 349–361. https://doi.org/10.1057/s41262-017-0055-3

Ozdemir, S., Gupta, S., Foroudi, P., Wright, L. T., & Eng, T.-Y. (2020). Corporate branding and value creation for initiating and managing relationships in B2B markets. *Qualitative Market Research, 23*(4), 627–661. https://doi.org/10.1108/QMR-12-2017-0168

Powell, S. M. (2014). Twenty-one years of the Journal of Brand Management: A commemorative review. *Journal of Brand Management, 21*(9), 689–701. https://doi.org/10.1057/bm.2015.3

Powell, S. M. (2017). Journal of Brand Management: Year end review 2017. *Journal of Brand Management, 24*(6), 509–515. https://doi.org/10.1057/s41262-017-0078-9

Powell, S., Balmer, J. M. T., & Melewar, T. C. (2007). Corporate marketing and the branding of the organisation. *Journal of Brand Management, 15*(1), 1–3. https://doi.org/10.1057/palgrave.bm.2550105

Pranjal, P., & Sarkar, S. (2020). Corporate brand alignment in business markets: A practice perspective. *Marketing Intelligence & Planning, 38*(7), 907–920. https://doi.org/10.1108/MIP-10-2019-0539

Renton, M., & Richard, J. E. (2019). Exploring brand governance in SMEs: Does socialisation provide a means to value creation? *Journal of Brand Management, 26*(4), 461–472. https://doi.org/10.1057/s41262-018-00143-5

Sammour, A. A., Chen, W., & Balmer, J. M. T. (2020). Corporate heritage brand traits and corporate heritage brand identity: The case study of John Lewis. *Qualitative Market Research, 23*(3), 447–470. https://doi.org/10.1108/QMR-03-2018-0039

Schivinski, B., Langaro, D., Fernandes, T., & Guzmán, F. (2020). Social media brand engagement in the context of collaborative consumption: The case of AIRBNB. *Journal of Brand Management, 27*(6), 645–661. https://doi.org/10.1057/s41262-020-00207-5

Schmeltz, L., & Kjeldsen, A. K. (2019). Co-creating polyphony or cacophony? A case study of a public organization's brand co-creation process and the challenge of orchestrating multiple internal voices. Journal of Brand Management, 26(3), 304–316. https://doi.org/10.1057/s41262-018-0124-2

Schmidt, H. J., & Redler, J. (2018). How diverse is corporate brand management research? Comparing schools of corporate brand management with approaches to corporate strategy. *Journal of Product & Brand Management, 27*(2), 185–202. https://doi.org/10.1108/JPBM-05-2017-1473

Schniederjans, D. G., Atlas, S. A., & Starkey, C. M. (2018). Impression management for corporate brands over mobile media. Journal of Product & Brand Management, 27(4), 385–403. https://doi.org/10.1108/JPBM-09-2016-1309

Sørensen, A. R., Korsager, E. M., & Heller, M. (2021). A bittersweet past: The negative equity of corporate heritage brands. Journal of Consumer Culture, 21(2), 200–218. https://doi.org/10.1177/1469540518773803

Stach, J. (2019). Meaningful experiences: An embodied cognition perspective on brand meaning co-creation. Journal of Brand Management, 26(3), 317–331. https://doi.org/10.1057/s41262-018-0133-1

Tarnovskaya, V., & Biedenbach, G. (2018). Corporate rebranding failure and brand meanings in the digital environment. Marketing Intelligence and Planning, 36(4), 455–469. https://doi.org/10.1108/MIP-09-2017-0192

Törmälä, M., & Gyrd-Jones, R. (2017). Development of new B2B venture corporate brand identity: A narrative performance approach. Industrial Marketing Management, 65, 76–85. https://doi.org/10.1016/j.indmarman.2017.05.002

Törmälä, M., & Saraniemi, S. (2018). The roles of business partners in corporate brand image co-creation. Journal of Product & Brand Management, 27(1), 29–40. https://doi.org/10.1108/JPBM-01-2016-1089

Tuškej, U., & Podnar, K. (2018). Consumers' identification with corporate brands: Brand prestige, anthropomorphism and engagement in social media. Journal of Product & Brand Management, 27(1), 3–17. https://doi.org/10.1108/JPBM-05-2016-1199

Uncles, M., & Ngo, L. V. (2017). Introduction to the special issue: Harnessing the power of brand and co-created innovation. Journal of Brand Management, 24(4), 307–309. https://doi.org/10.1057/s41262-017-0052-6

Vollero, A., Palazzo, M., Siano, A., & Foroudi, P. (2021). From CSR to CSI: Analysing consumers' hostile responses to branding initiatives in social media-scape. Qualitative Market Research, 24(2), 143–160. https://doi.org/10.1108/QMR-12-2017-0184

Wegerer, P., & Munro, I. (2018). Ethics of ambivalence in corporate branding. Organization, 25(6), 695–709. https://doi.org/10.1177/1350508417749736

Wilson, R. T. (2018). Transforming history into heritage: Applying corporate heritage to the marketing of places. Journal of Brand Management, 25(4), 351–369. https://doi.org/10.1057/s41262-017-0087-8

B

# Building brands together
Co-creating corporate brands with multiple stakeholders

# 6
# EMBRACING A CO-CREATION PARADIGM OF LIVED-EXPERIENCE ECOSYSTEM VALUE CREATION

*Venkat Ramaswamy\**

## 1. Introduction

Ubiquitous information and communication technologies in a hyperconnected and interdependent digitalized world of interactional flows of engagements have transformed the business and societal landscape, accelerating the *de-centring* of value creation away from the goods-services activities of firms and institutions toward the experiences of individuals (Ramaswamy & Ozcan, 2020). Think of some global brands today: Amazon, Airbnb, Alibaba, Apple, Burberry, Disney, Facebook, Google, IBM, LEGO, Marriott, Microsoft, Netflix, Nike, Philips, Salesforce, ServiceNow, Starbucks, Twitter, and Uber, just to name a few. What do they all have in common? While they are all company brands, they all entail the management of offerings, what Ramaswamy and Ozcan (2018a) refer to as 'Digitalized Interactive Platforms' (DIPs) – evolving networked arrangements of artifacts, persons, processes, and interfaces (or APPI, for short), 'platformiz-ed' by digital technology enabling new types of networked interactions and digitalized experiences of value to individuals. Ramaswamy and Ozcan (2020) formally define such platformization as framing of interactional flows across instantiations of socio-technical agencial assemblages composed of APPI components entailing interactive structures-agencies. As they discuss, the term *agencial assemblage* connotes more than an ensemble and captures the intentionality behind and around brands in interactive system-environments, from creating individual identities and crafting value propositions to shaping an enterprise's innovation, strategy, and performance. DIP brand offerings don't just have fixed value in the traditional sense, but 'constitute more of a "means" for ongoing creation of new and enhanced forms of value through interactions' (Ramaswamy & Ozcan, 2018a, p. 19). As this de-centring of value creation accelerates, it is increasingly spurring an 'experience-first' frame of reference in value creation, not to mention 'digitally native' business models, centred on flows of networked interactions through DIP offerings (Ramaswamy, 2020).

As emphasized by Ramaswamy (2005, 2006, 2008, 2009, 2011, 2020), following the original work of Prahalad and Ramaswamy (2004a, 2004b, 2004c), this movement toward creation of experience value through interactional flows of DIP offerings, simultaneously entails an increasing *democratization* in the process of value creation as a 'co-creation.' Prahalad and Ramaswamy originally articulated co-creation as a process of individuals and enterprises jointly creating customer experience value, where the individual was involved in this process (Leavy, 2013; Prahalad &

Ramaswamy, 2004a; Randall & Leavy, 2014). They heralded a new frontier of co-creation of interactive experience value creation based on the engagement of individuals through their environments of experiences on the one hand and access to resources, skills, and capabilities of networks of firms and communities on the other hand. They articulated how this was more than a mere focus on the user experience of goods and services, instead entailing a broader emergent *lived experience* space of which individuals themselves were an integral part (in their specific situational contexts with their preferred levels of involvements, in ways that are meaningful to them), personally and collectively, along with the rapidly evolving smart connected offerings that engaged them through multiple modes of interactions – spurred today by new cloud-enabled mobile applications of artificial intelligence (AI), the Internet of Things (IoT), and augmented/virtual reality (AR/VR). Following this view, as noted by Ramaswamy (2020), the innovation of (APPI) platformed environments of lived experiences offers opportunities for stake-holding individuals as co-creators (whether as customers, employees, suppliers, citizens, financiers, partners, or regulators) to engage and co-shape personalized experienced outcomes based on their own life journeys as experiencers and mutually valuable developmental impacts in markets, economies, and societies.

Over the past two decades, there has been growing recognition of this dual de-centring and democratization of company brands in the literature, within the broader umbrella of co-creating brands and co-creative brand management systems (Ind & Schmidt, 2020), with the active participation of stake-holding individuals in creating brands and valuable impacts together (see for instance, Arvidsson, 2006; da Silveira et al., 2013; Gyrd-Jones & Kornum, 2013; Hatch & Schultz, 2010; Iglesias & Bonet, 2012; Iglesias & Ind, 2020; Iglesias et al., 2020a; Ind, 2003, 2007; Ind & Bjerke, 2007a; Ind et al., 2013, 2017; Lury, 2004; Markovic & Bagherzadeh, 2018; Merz et al., 2009; Payne et al., 2009; Price & Coulter, 2019; Ramaswamy & Ozcan, 2016; Schembri, 2009; Stach, 2019; Swaminathan et al., 2020; Tormala & Gyrd-Jones, 2017; Wider et al., 2018). Ramaswamy and Ozcan (2018b, 2020) provide a novel, unifying perspective of co-creation by anchoring its theorization in a relational ontology of '"experience ecosystems," i.e., interactive system-environments whose heterogeneous relations of emergent experiences can be configured via interactive platforms anywhere in the "value creational system," i.e., regardless of whether it concerns activities of "producing," "exchanging," or "using" goods and services.' In a digitalized and increasingly hyperconnected and interdependent world of digitalized interactional flows of engagements, this perspective of co-creation forms the basis of the conceptualization and theoretical development of an interactional creation framework of value creation of lived-experience ecosystems, or a co-creation paradigm (CCP) for short (Ramaswamy & Ozcan, 2014, 2018b, 2020). In the CCP (Ramaswamy & Ozcan, 2021), co-creation is explicitly defined and theorized as the enactment of interactional creation via flows of engagements across ecosystem environments, enabled by purpose-built platformization of resourced capabilities, engendering developmental impacts of experienced outcomes, through the life journeys of individuals-as-experiencers (as captured stylistically in the outer diamond of Figure 6.1).

In the next section, we summarize the essentials of the CCP, emphasizing the shifts in the locus of innovation, value, strategy, and performance, and its implications for brand (value) co-creation, beyond conventional value creation (as captured by the inner diamond of Figure 6.1). We conclude by discussing some of the key challenges in embracing a brand CCP.

## 2. Co-creation paradigm

About two decades ago, Prahalad and Ramaswamy (2004a, 2004b, 2004c) put forth 'co-creation' as a new frame of reference of interactive value creation based on individual experiences. They argued that 'the use of *interactions* as a basis for co-creation is at the crux of our emerging reality,'

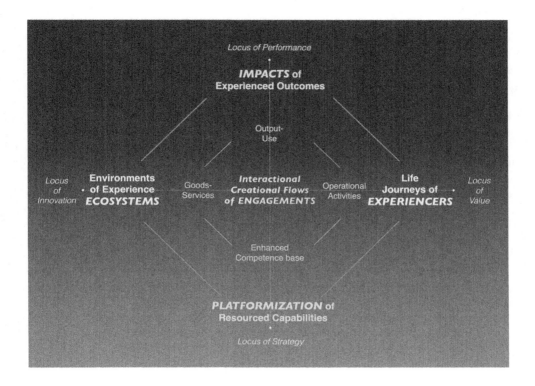

anticipating an evolving movement in interactive value creation towards individuals and their experiences, in an internetworked world. They urged managers to go beyond conventional thinking of business-to-business and business-to-consumer value creation toward an individual and experience-centric view of value creation, 'whether that individual is a fork-lift operator, a pilot, a design engineer, a beautician, a clinical researcher, an instructor, a contractor, a paralegal, or a civic worker' (Prahalad & Ramaswamy, 2004c, p. 12). They discussed the changing locus of innovation from products to environments of experiences based on the engagement of individuals on the one hand and access to resources, skills, and capabilities of networks of firms and communities on the other hand. In addition, they also discussed the changing locus of competence from an internal view of the firm toward an enhanced network of competence including customers and other stakeholders. Hence, Prahalad and Ramaswamy (2004c) emphasized both collaborative value creation (Prahalad & Ramaswamy, 2000, 2002) and simultaneously expanding the scope of the value creation space beyond the conventional 'product' output of firms to the experience space of individuals (Prahalad & Ramaswamy, 2003). In their new frame of reference (Prahalad & Ramaswamy, 2004c, p. 14), they emphasized how 'co-creation supplants the exchange process' toward creation of value entailing interactive experiences. In today's digitalized world of connected and smarter DIP offerings, value is dynamically created through interactional flows of engagements (Ramaswamy & Ozcan, 2018b) versus one where value is simply the exchange of a fixed offering between a firm and its customers (Ramaswamy & Ozcan, 2018a).

The goods-services industrial era entailed an output orientation of brand logic that focused on production of goods and services (Merz et al., 2009). Adopting a process orientation ('service') perspective, or 'service-dominant logic' (SDL) (Lusch & Vargo, 2014; Vargo & Lusch, 2004, 2008, 2016), Vargo (2008, p. 214) noted that 'firm activity is best understood in terms of *input* for the *customer's resource integrating, value-creation activities,'* with firms seen as merely 'proposing' value and 'creation' of value happening in the customer's (i.e., beneficiary's) process. This was later modified (Vargo & Lusch, 2016) to say that 'value is cocreated by multiple actors, always including the beneficiary,' placing 'value co-creation' at the centre of the 'narrative and process' of SDL.[1]

Although Vargo and Lusch (2004) noted that 'marketing inherited a model of exchange from economics,' their SDL remained tethered to a view of exchange, with service as its foundational basis, to the exclusion of directly focusing on interactional flows (Ramaswamy & Ozcan, 2020). Grönroos and Gummerus (2014, p. 217) note that 'co-creation is not problematized in SDL.' The dynamics of the very act of creation (through flows of interactions in DIP offerings) requires further conceptualization (Ramaswamy & Ozcan, 2018a, 2018b), especially through interactivity across various interfaces in business networks (Håkansson & Snehota, 2017). By reducing interactional service environments 'metaphorically' (Grönroos & Gummerus, 2014) to an actor-to-actor service exchange (as in SDL), the very constitution of services (and goods) in practices of enactment of interactional creation is lost (Orlikowski & Scott, 2015). As noted by Orlikowski and Scott (2015, p. 203), in a critique of SDL: 'Both the goods and service-dominant logics overlook the ways in which producing and consuming outputs – at the level of practices – are relatively similar, in the sense that they entail a range of activities, bodies, and artifacts.' This has become more evident in a digitalized world of platformed interactional flows and DIP offerings of interactive experience value creation. In an invited commentary following the original SDL article, Prahalad (2004) noted that Vargo and Lusch 'do not go far enough' and that in moving further to an 'experience-centric co-creation view, new and exciting opportunities unfold,' although this required also challenging 'deeply held assumptions about marketing staples, such as the meaning of brand (experience is the brand), the role of exchange and the market (market as a forum), and innovation (innovating experience environments)' in the internetworked economy as it was becoming.

Sheth and Uslay (2007, p. 305), in their discussion of the limits of exchange (Bagozzi, 1975), emphasize that 'the need for and desire of actors to *cocreate* value *preempts and supersedes* the need for *exchange* [italics ours].' By theorizing co-creation ontologically and epistemologically as a joint agency and experience creation, Ramaswamy and Ozcan (2021) discuss how the CCP, with an *experience ecosystem ontology* entailing agencial assemblages, interactive system-environments, and platformed networks, transcends the service exchange of SDL. Following their comparative discussion of CCP in light of the axioms of SDL, Table 6.1 provides an adapted

*Table 6.1* The co-creation paradigm: beyond service-dominant logic*

| *Co-creation paradigm (CCP)* | *Service-dominant logic (SDL)* |
|---|---|
| Enactment of creation via flows of interactive agencing-structuring experiences is the fundamental basis of co-creation. | Service is the fundamental basis of exchange. (Axiom 1) |
| Interactional creation occurs via experience ecosystems always including the experiencer. | Value is cocreated by multiple actors, always including the beneficiary. (Axiom 2) |
| Actor-networked flows engender experienced outcomes of interactional creation. | All social and economic actors are resource integrators. (Axiom 3) |
| Valuation is a function of impacts of lived experienced outcomes. | Value is always uniquely and phenomenologically determined by the beneficiary. (Axiom 4) |
| Interactional value creation is dynamically configured via interactive platformization of lived experience ecosystems. | Value cocreation is coordinated through actor-generated institutions and institutional arrangements. (Axiom 5) |

*Source:* *Adapted from Ramaswamy and Ozcan (2021)

summary. In the CCP, co-creation is seen as entailing mediated interactions (Callon, 2016) wherein traditional 'exchange'-based views are insufficient in recognizing the new dynamism of creation through interactional flows and the sustainability of their developmental impacts (Ramaswamy & Ozcan, 2014). While still remaining relevant in the CCP, the exchange of goods and services become special cases of the broader enactment of creation via interactional flows of 'agencing-structuring,' i.e., the conjugation of agency and structure in an enacted process of creation. In an economy of interactive experiences, connected and smarter offerings entail platformized mediated flows of interactions (Callon, 2016) where the offering is also endogenous, as it were, in 'hybrid collectives' of nonhuman and human actors implicated in relational experience ecosystems always including the experiencer (Ramaswamy, 2020; Ramaswamy & Ozcan, 2016). As discussed by Ramaswamy and Ozcan (2021), the 'Interactive Lived Experience' Brand Era (2010+) that we are in now entails a further evolution of brands, as connected smart offerings amplify personal agency in creating interactive lived experiences together with stake-holding individuals. The concept of a lived-experience ecosystem in the CCP is a broader notion than the service (eco)system of firms, customers, communities, and other stakeholders (Merz et al., 2009), comprising brands as assemblages of agency and lived experience entailing interactional flows with other assemblages (Ramaswamy & Ozcan, 2016, 2018a, 2020). Thus, the brand CCP, entailing a 'joint agency and experience creation of brands, branding, and brand value creation' provides a theoretically grounded integrative framework (Ramaswamy & Ozcan, 2021), which resonates with brands seen as complex processual phenomena in a continuous flux (Wider et al., 2018), with stakeholders shaping brands by participating in brand-related interaction and creating brands and brand experiences together, and increasingly with sustainable impact considerations (Iglesias & Ind, 2016; Ind, 2014; Ind & Schmidt, 2020).

## 2.1 Locus of innovation: beyond goods-services to experience ecosystem environments

In an age of ubiquitous connectivity, as argued by Prahalad and Ramaswamy (2004c), value is interactively created through spatiotemporal contextual engagement in an increasingly individual-centric world, 'creating new market space by innovating the consumer 'experience' together' (Leavy, 2019). This shift has been accelerated by the fourth industrial revolution (Ramaswamy, 2020). The third industrial revolution heralded an information age with the advent of information technology (IT) driven competition with automation of activities in the value chain, to new levels of co-ordination and integration across the firm's goods-service supply chain. In the fourth industrial revolution, IT became an integral part of the product itself. Products have become 'complex systems that combine hardware, sensors, data storage, microprocessors, software, and connectivity in myriad ways. These "smart, connected products" – made possible by vast improvements in processing power and device miniaturization and by the network benefits of ubiquitous wireless connectivity – have unleashed a new era of competition' (Porter & Heppelmann, 2014, p. 4). Anticipating this shift toward connected smart offerings, Prahalad and Ramaswamy (2003, 2004c) introduced the novel concept of 'experience innovation' (in contrast to conventional goods-services innovation) and discussed how managers have to build an 'experience network' to effectively 'compete on experiences' (Prahalad & Ramaswamy, 2004c, p. 93). They discussed a shift in the locus of innovation from the traditional goods-service market space to an 'experience space' centred around individuals and events in the context of space and time, and derivation of personal meaning. They elaborated upon the resulting transformation from a firm-centric view of the value creation process represented by the traditional supply of good-services value chain system to one centred around individuals and their interactive experiences.

The transformational shift of offerings and organizations toward experience innovation and networks of experiences to create experience value, and with experience ecosystems increasingly entailing Internet of Things (IoT) based experiences (Hoffman & Novak, 2018; Ramaswamy, 2020; Yoo, 2010), calls for a rethinking of the boundaries of branding in an ever more hyperconnected world (Swaminathan et al., 2020) where brands, brand-related experiences, and meanings have to be co-created, heightening the need for practitioners and academics to see brand creation and brand management from a co-creative perspective (Ind & Schmidt, 2020).

Consider the case of the John Deere brand, which is almost two centuries old with its roots in agriculture. As Docherty and Porter (2019) note:

> John Deere talked with local farmers, who spoke of their frustrations with their old plows, most of which were designed for the sandy soils common in the eastern United States and were therefore unable to shed the sticky soil of the Midwest. John Deere built a new plow of highly polished steel that was self-scouring, allowing farmers to plow their fields uninterrupted. In 1837 he created the company that bears his name.

John Deere's focus on helping farmers ultimately built a brand trusted by farmers.

Fast forward to the early 2000s, when Deere began experimenting with global positioning systems (GPS) and a wide variety of biosensors on their combines and tractors with on-board sensors that can measure the oil content of grain or tell the difference between weeds and crops (Prahalad & Ramaswamy, 2004c). GPS-guided steering of tractors and other machines establishes repeatable accuracy and eliminates overlaps in the treatment of farm areas, reducing costs to the farmer in time, fuel, labour, and chemicals, while fertilizers and herbicide can be applied according to the needs of the soil in a farmer's area. Farmers could be more productive, make the best use of capital investments, and reduce machinery costs per acre due to greater efficiency. They could work longer hours with less stress for field preparation, cultivation, and spraying. Today, the farmer can keep track of equipment remotely, access remote diagnostics integrated into the system, and use predictive analytics to avoid costly surprises during the planting or harvesting seasons. John Deere created the Intelligent Solutions Group (ISG), comprising 'hundreds of system architects and developers centered on developing advanced farming technologies' to help capitalize on 'the use of technologies such as GPS, vision, sensors, robotics, and machine learning' and provide 'software and data-based solutions that work with equipment and analyze outcomes to solve complex problems on the farm' (Docherty & Porter, 2019, p. 266). Deere is connecting not only farm machinery but also an ecosystem of connected services through irrigation systems, combined with weather data and seed optimization for an advanced 'precision farming lived brand experience ecosystem.' Lived brand experience ecosystem environments are interactive system-environments composed of heterogeneous networked relations of emergent and embodied brand experiences (Ramaswamy & Ozcan, 2021b), as discussed next.

## 2.2 *Locus of value: beyond operational activities to life journeys of experiencers*

Conventional value chain thinking 'divides a firm into the discrete activities it performs in designing, producing, marketing, and distributing its product,' and which is 'embedded in a larger stream of activities' that Michael Porter originally dubbed the 'value system' (Porter, 1985, p. 33). At the core is its assumption that activities create value. However, as the locus of innovation shifts toward experience ecosystems, it demands a concomitant shift beyond activity chains to the *life journeys of individuals-as-experiencers*. As Prahalad and Ramaswamy (2004c) note, the network of experiences underlying experience ecosystems have to be built around experiencers. The Deere brand offering as a precision farming experience ecosystem has to be 'farmer-centric.' As a farmer, it has to champion 'my farm, my farming productivity, and my unique experiences,' and the 'choices are the farmers', not dictated by the company.'

Remarkably, Deere has made such digitalized transformation based on an experience ecosystem configured toward the lived journeys of farmers as experiencers. Over the past decade, it has systematically become focused on the individual jobs a farmer has throughout the entire growing season, starting with the process of field preparation, planting or seeding, applying (nurturing and protecting), and harvesting, including all the analysis and planning that goes into farm management to assist farmers, even as they stand on their fields or sit in their combines, on how their businesses could be run better overall using mobile interactive platforms. Farmers can harness machine and agronomic data to enhance the long-term health and sustainability of their operations, while promoting their stewardship of the land. They have a sense of control over *their* data and can share it with whomever they choose to with appropriate access and decision rights.

Value creation through the CCP often requires a fresh look at experiencer journeys across the entire value creational system, from downstream to upstream, into the enterprise and its supply and partner base, as it 'opens up' one entity's activities to other entities, often in cascading fashion in an increasingly digitalized world of platformed interactions. It also invariably implies different roles of actors in configuring DIP brand offerings and how we come to understand interactive relations of smart connected offerings (Novak & Hoffman, 2019; Ramaswamy & Ozcan, 2018a) in a joint sphere of value creational interactivities and interdependencies. In the case of Deere, it has transformed the journey of dealers as experiencers in order to support farmer-centric value creation. Likewise, it has transformed its internal teams to be more cross-functional, cross-platform, and collaborative across its product groups and regions, opening up these teams to stakeholders from a variety of functional areas ranging from engineering and marketing to supply management, operations, and finance.

The importance of going beyond the activities of actors toward interactivities in business networks of value co-creation has been increasingly recognized in the literature from industrial marketing and purchasing (IMP) studies of business interactions (Ford, 2011; Ford & Mouzas, 2013; Håkansson et al., 2009; Håkansson & Snehota, 2017) to practices of strategic collaborative innovation (Ind et al., 2017; Ostendorf et al., 2014) and digital innovation management (Nambisan et al., 2017). However, there has been less emphasis on paying attention to 'individuals as experiencers from within the enterprise' (Prahalad & Ramaswamy, 2004c) in the co-creation literature (Gummesson et al., 2014; Leclercq et al., 2016), which has tended to focus more on customers and external stakeholders, as such. In the CCP, the life journeys of *all* experiencers in the value co-creation system matter, as do their *inter*activities within and across the activity (value) chain. In addition to activities and resources as being interactively defined, Ramaswamy and Ozcan (2020) discuss how experience value co-creation through the CCP explicitly recognizes the interactivities and the lived experiences of all individuals through creational flows of relational engagements (i.e., drawing on the affective developmental capacities of agencial assemblages in which individuals are entangled). The CCP applies at both the individual and enterprise levels, of agencial assemblages, or more generally at any level of agglomeration, as the creational and relational logics are applicable at varying levels of scale across system-environment boundaries. Hence, interactive experience value creation in the (professional) life journeys of employees and managers as experiencers must undergo a continuous process of re-framing of interactional flows to engender more 'valuable' co-creational impacts. In doing so, it also draws attention to the heterogeneous ways in which impacts of experienced outcomes are 'valorized' by different actors, beyond conventional economic output-based metrics of performance. Iglesias and Ind (2020) discuss a more balanced stakeholder perspective in this regard.

### 2.3 Locus of strategy: beyond an enhanced competence base to digitalized interactive platformization of resourced capabilities

Multi-stakeholder engagement with a CCP logic of joint agency and experience creation requires a shift beyond traditional processes of service exchange, toward paying attention to the *con*-figuration (i.e., figuring together) of developmental capacities of multiple focal and connected platforms of interactional creation (Ramaswamy & Gouillart, 2010a; Ramaswamy & Ozcan, 2014, 2016) and network governance and strategic risk management of interactive experience value creation (Prahalad & Ramaswamy, 2004c; Ramaswamy & Ozcan, 2014). This puts a strategic emphasis on the co-design of strategic architectures of interactive platforms and how capabilities are resourced via knowledge and skills in actualizing opportunities of interactive experience value creation.

Prahalad and Ramaswamy (2004c) discuss the shifting locus of core competencies from the firm to a family/network of companies and an enhanced network of the company, suppliers, partners, and customers/consumers. Building on their work, Ramaswamy and Ozcan (2013, 2014) discuss the shift in perspective on resources, opportunities, and value creation, from the 1960s to the 2000s, from allocation of resources in the product space until the early 1980s, to resource leverage in the services and solutions space in the late 1980s to 1990s, to access to competence (resources on demand) in the individual experience space at the turn of the millennium, with the advent of the worldwide web and information and communications infrastructures on the one hand, and digital technology making its way into the hands of individuals. From the early 2000s, the value creation process began to shift from one being unilaterally defined by the enterprise to jointly by the enterprise and stake-holding individuals, including consumers and citizens. Since then, there have been dramatic advances in digital technology from computer storage, networking, and miniaturization to cloud computing, big data, analytics, and machine learning to embedded intelligence, IoT, and extended (augmented and virtual) reality. As of this writing, while established corporate brands like John Deere and Philips from the first and second industrial revolutions had navigated the daunting transition in digitally transforming their offerings and organizational activities, others like Kodak had disappeared, while icons like General Electric struggled. Meanwhile, there has been a simultaneous unprecedented rise of *digitally native enterprises*, which have capitalized on global access to competence (and capital) and leveraged enhanced network resources by making digitalized interactive platformization the very basis of their business strategy and brand development in an increasingly digitally savvy society.

Digitally native enterprises from Alibaba to Lemonade to Ping An and Zillow have been shaking up traditional industries by using platformized business models entailing interactive resourced capabilities that transform impacts of customer and other stakeholder-experienced outcomes via digitalized experience ecosystems, continuously expanding the *scope* of enterprise capabilities, even as they *scale* existing interactive experience value-creation opportunities. For instance, Lemonade insurance has opened up its software application programming interface (API) to its ecosystem so other enterprising entities can easily incorporate insurance into their own experience, alongside their products, while offering easy quoting, policy creation, and payment. From e-commerce websites to property management companies, and IoT platforms to payment software processors, Lemonade offers seamless integration with its API, expanding the scope of its interactive experience value-creation opportunities. Ping An, a giant Chinese insurer has become a digitalized ecosystem orchestrator by offering healthcare consultations (Ping An

Good Doctor), banking services (Ping An Bank), auto sales, and real estate listings to more than 350 million online customers through a single customer portal called the One Account.

Just being digitally native is, of course, not in any way a key success factor, as the business landscape is littered with failed start-ups and those that are unable to survive for various reasons (from Brandless to Webvan). On the other hand, while established companies have an installed base of customers, deeply etched ways of business logic and systems are often formidable barriers to transformational change. Indeed, a new class of enterprises are emerging, signifying a morphing and evolution of incumbents and start-ups as such. Whether established or start-up, the ability to configure digitalized experience ecosystems of capabilities toward expanding value co-creation with stakeholders in 'all win more' fashion is a key success factor. The rise of 'meta' cloud-based infrastructure corporate brands from Microsoft, Amazon, and Google to Salesforce and IBM, and Alibaba to Tencent, is propelling a digitalized experience ecosystem revolution with 'capabilities as a service' (Ramaswamy, 2020). For instance, Microsoft's vision is to is 'to empower every person and every organization on the planet to achieve more through its digital platforms and tools.' Digital infrastructures (Tilson et al., 2010) are also fostering new organizational designs of company brands. For instance, Haier has transformed itself (Frynas et al., 2018) under the leadership of Zhang Ruimin, using a co-creative management system it calls *Rendanheyi* (which can be loosely translated as a 'win-win model of individual-goal combination'). *Rendanheyi* is a platform management innovation entailing a bundle of management systemic practices through multiple online engagement platforms that aim for 'zero distance' with individuals. Systematic interactions among experiencers (customers, employees, and partners) on Haier's platforms drive the co-creative development of new DIP brand offerings in the Haier experience ecosystem, building direct brand relationships and 'living the corporate brand' (Ind, 2007). Such digitalized transformation and developmental platformization is key to co-creating the future of interactive experience value-creation together with stake-holding individuals.

## 2.4 Locus of performance: beyond outputs-uses to impacts of experienced outcomes

The CCP goes beyond the locus of performance based on outputs-uses of goods and service exchanges in the co-creation literature (Guzmán et al., 2019) to emergent experiences (Prahalad & Ramaswamy, 2004b), interactional creation of experienced outcomes, and its *impacts* on wellbeing of interactive system-environments whether psychological, economic, social, communal, cultural, or natural, as valorized by actors (Ramaswamy & Ozcan, 2014, 2018a, 2020, 2021). By 'valorization' is meant 'giving worth to,' wherein a 'performance' (Callon, 2007; Kjellberg & Helgesson, 2006, 2007) is implied, as is the case on an 'evaluation' (Vatin, 2013). Such a multi-faceted performative view is relevant in all aspects of the brand (value) creational process and its management (Ind et al., 2017; Ind & Schmidt, 2020). While outputs-use of goods-services call attention to what activities have been undertaken and the use cases of service exchange, impacts of experienced outcomes go beyond to call attention to the effects of what has changed, as experienced by actors in their domains of brand experiences (Ramaswamy & Ozcan, 2016). Moreover, the CCP recognizes heterogeneous and varied aspects of valuation of actors by drawing attention to how valorization is implicated and structured in the enactment of interactional creation in focal and supporting platforms and their developmental capacities.

In the case of John Deere, through engagements with farmers, the core essence of its brand has been imbibed by management as 'helping farmers feed a growing world,' as sustainability is deeply rooted in John Deere's higher purpose of serving those linked to the land (see Docherty & Porter, 2019, p. 265). John Deere helps its customers assess impact of precision agriculture on farm productivity to produce more with less and works together with dealers, partners, and communities on the one hand, and its employees and managers on the other hand, to advance mechanization and entrepreneurship, facilitate customer 'stewardship of the land' through use of data driven decision-making, natural resource conservation through integrated crop-livestock-forest farming, and achieving sustainable outcomes of plant-level management and job automation as experienced by farmers.

With growing recognition of the importance of the United Nations Sustainable Development Goals (SDGs) to achieve a better and more sustainable future for all, there is increasing emphasis on focusing on multi-stakeholder impacts with the recent U. S. Business Roundtable Compact (signed by over 180 CEOs) and the Davos Manifesto 2020, which states that the 'purpose of a company is to engage all its stakeholders in shared and sustained value creation,' and that in creating such value, 'a company serves not only its shareholders, but all its stakeholders – employees, customers, suppliers, local communities and society at large.' The company is

> more than an economic unit generating wealth. It fulfils human and societal aspirations as part of the broader social system. Performance must be measured not only on the return to shareholders, but also on how it achieves its environmental, social and good governance objectives.

Ramaswamy and Ozcan (2016) discuss the concept of a 'co-creational enterprise' (Ramaswamy & Gouillart, 2010a, 2010b) in the brand value creation process as 'assemblage systems engaged in organizing the practice of brand value co-creation,' whereby 'organizing' means both the enabling and constraining of joint agency of stake-holding individuals as co-creating experiencers in brand value co-creation. Co-creational enterprises entail a shift in the strategic management of brands (Lucarelli & Hallin, 2015; Wider et al., 2018) toward orchestrating platformized lived brand experience ecosystems in connecting brand value-creation opportunities with resourced capabilities, which allow engaging stakeholders as co-creating experiencers and organizing actors to co-design environments of emergent experiences and enact valuable embodied experiences through those environments over space and time. In the brand CCP, stakeholders have a more active role in brand value co-creation, contributing through their differences in views of brand value expressed through their joint agency in creating impacts of experienced outcomes together. Co-creational experiences (Prahalad & Ramaswamy, 2004b, 2004c) as the foundation of brand value co-creation imply that stake-holding individuals, whether 'inside or outside' a focal enterprise experience ecosystem, are integral to the differential articulation of experiential agencies in jointly defining and creating valuable brand impacts together. It requires considerable organizational transformation in 'letting go' of traditional unilateral control over the management process and instead shifting to the intersection of stake-holding individuals and organizations and designing and developing new organizational management systems around it (Ind & Ramaswamy, 2021).

Multi-stakeholder perspectives of brand valuation, corporate social responsibility, and sustainability considerations have gained increased recognition in the brand co-creation literature (Iglesias et al., 2020a, 2020b; Markovic & Bagherzadeh, 2018; von Wallpach et al., 2017), building on earlier emphases of brand value as a 'multifarious construct that is affected by, or the sum of, a gamut of relationships' (Jones, 2005), involvement of employees, customers, and other stakeholders in the development of a brand (Ind & Bjerke, 2007a, 2007b), and contributions of all stakeholders in the enterprise network to a 'negotiated' brand, wherein brand value develops over time (Gregory, 2007). They also draw attention to balancing heterogeneous matters of concern, dealing with the loss of control over brand evolution, finding the middle ground between polyphony and cacophony, positive and negative freedom, and cultivating trust and ethics, and nurturing a sense of meaningful brand purpose. In addition, technological advances, such as in machine learning and artificial intelligence, also raise important questions of inclusiveness, privacy, and ethics in decision-making that impact brand relations in experience ecosystems.

## 3. Discussion

Embracing a CCP of value creation requires expanding simultaneously across all the four loci of innovation, value, performance, and strategy in interactive experience value creation, which is a challenge for practitioners and academics alike, schooled in conventional ways of thinking and doing value creation (Prahalad & Ramaswamy, 2004c), from the third industrial revolution, if not the second, which still lingers. Value creation in the fourth industrial revolution is not a 'linear extension' from the inner diamond to the outer one, stylistically depicted in Figure 6.1. Rather, it entails a whole new set of premises that starts with the five facets of interactive experience value creation, viz., experiencers, interactions, platforms, ecosystems, and impacts, (Ramaswamy, 2020) and the enactment of *creation via flows of agencing-structuring interactions* at its conceptual core (Ramaswamy & Ozcan, 2021). In other words, the CCP (outer diamond), with is logic of joint agency and experience creation, transcends and subsumes *both* goods and service-dominant logic. Put simply, in the fourth industrial revolution, 'flows' of interactivities, resourced capabilities, and 'interacted' (nonhuman and human) actors in platformized experience ecosystems of emergent and embodied experienced outcomes, which endogenize stakeholders and enterprises, characterize the new digitalized world of value creation. It calls for a creational philosophy wherein one has to start with relations 'independent' of its terms, as it were (Ramaswamy & Ozcan, 2021). The conventional approach of starting with human actors in 'atomistic' fashion (whether dyadic, triadic, or otherwise), in activity chains (or even pre-conceived agent networks) of discrete goods and services that ignores their interdependencies and interactivities in 'thick' interactions (Hakansson & Waluszewski, 2020) along with a resource-based view that overlooks agile access to dynamic digital infrastructure capabilities (Teece, 2018) has become insufficient in inquiring into the phenomena of interactive experience value creation in digitalized society (Couldry & Hepp, 2017; Van Dijck et al., 2018; Yablonsky, 2018).

For instance, the word *user* implicitly suggests use of something, in contrast to *experiencer*, which suggests an 'experience-first' perspective. As Ramaswamy and Gouillart (2010b, p. 248) note: 'The commonly used term *users* limits people's potentially creative roles, as well as the significance of their personal human experiences. The language that managers use often reinforces a mindset, in this case of design being enterprise- and product-centric, rather than *human- and experience-centric*. The latter is what constitutes co-creative design.' Similarly, the word *platform* often characterizes 'autonomous and separate "blocs" of supply and demand' as exogenous to the exchange of goods and services (Callon, 2016), let alone creation of experiences (which often excludes how the experiencer is implicated in formation of experience), which has long been the dominant view in 'marketing as exchange' (Bagozzi, 1975). In contrast, the outer diamond of Figure 6.1, taken as a whole, is constituted in enactment of creation through interactional flows of agencing-structuring, directing our attention to how agencial assemblages of non-human and human actors exercise interactive agency in creative enactment of potentially mutually valuable experienced outcomes through interactional flows, whose structures are framed by digital technology platforms in experience ecosystems.

From the perspective of enterprises, starting with a brand CCP entails the ongoing co-creative transformation of brand management systems (Ind & Schmidt, 2020) that support the co-creative configuration of platformized experience ecosystems of offerings and relational engagement with multiple stakeholders in joint creation of valuable brand impacts. A significant challenge is to configure platformed lived brand experience ecosystems together with partners and other stakeholders, as they plug into or proactively build out focal digital infrastructures, while enhancing its developmental capacities. In addition to the co-creation of environments of emergent experiences, co-creational enterprises have to simultaneously pay attention to the lived experiences of individuals through those environments to not only gain a deeper understanding of the involvements of people but also their contexts of engagements, the events that give rise to their brand experiences through their practices in activated environments, and what is meaningful to experiencers in their domain of embodied experiences.

Sustaining the valuable orchestration of experience ecosystems requires continued emphasis on the positive generation and modification of its capacities to produce 'surplus' effects of wellbeing-risk management. In contrast to the economization of brand 'surplus' through conventional exchange value creation management of goods-services, a CCP-based brand management requires *re-thinking 'surplus'* through the lens of co-creational experiences of value. As Chakrabarti and Ramaswamy (2014) note: 'The surplus in the new co-creative economy is not restricted to the surplus that conventional economic thinking identifies with.' This has significant implications for the performativity of brand management systems and practices in a digitalized world of interactional flows of brand value co-creation. It also has organizational implications entailing transformational changes in 'flows' of work in brand management, including infusion of design thinking and Agile methods, and a CCP-based mindset that is truly experiencer-centric so that networked interactions can be orchestrated anywhere and everywhere in the value creation system (Ramaswamy, 2020).

A CCP-based orchestration of a lived brand experience ecosystem entails the configuration of a multiplicity of networked focal and supporting platformized environments of engagements and organizations across various sociotechnical assemblages of agencies instantiated in the value creational system, constituting co-creational experience capabilities together with stake-holding individuals in 'all-win more' ways (Ramaswamy & Gouillart, 2010a; Ramaswamy & Ozcan, 2014, 2016). Stakeholders shape brands by participating in brand-related interaction together with brand management (Iglesias et al., 2020a; Ind et al., 2017; Markovic & Bagherzadeh, 2018; Wider et al., 2018). Ramaswamy and Ozcan (2016, p. 99) note that in brand value co-creation, 'stakeholders have a more active role, contributing through their differences in views of brand value expressed through their joint agency in creating brand value together.' While the embracing of 'brands as processes of continuous becoming is a perspective widely unknown to brand research and management' (Wider et al., 2018, p. 304), in the CCP, brands are assemblages of agency and experience whose rhizomic constitutions flourish in an interplay of agencing-structuring interactions of content and expression. Wider et al. (2018, p. 303) note that rhizomic brands '"require a total *re-orientation* of management practice altogether," with a shift in the underlying managerial mindset of delusion of control, . . . "Brand reality is heterogeneous by nature at the individual level and, at the same time, is manifested in assemblages, creating collective spheres of shared understanding, which are constitutive of multiple and interrelated brand forms."' In the CCP, as we have discussed, this re-orientation is one of an *experience ecosystem orientation*. Ramaswamy and Ozcan (2016, p. 104) note:

> Brands now co-evolve with co-creation experiences, challenging traditional brand management orthodoxies. The rise of digitally empowered consumers has upset the conventional model of brand management from a one-way process (with feedback) to a (more complex) multi-sided, multi-stakeholder, joint creation process. This means a focus on

not managing the brand per se, but managing the quality of co-creation infrastructures that facilitate (and constrain) joint agency in creation of brand experience value and managing the quality of co-creation experiences, especially across multiple channels of interactions, while simultaneously enabling personalized co-creation experiences.

The immense power of brand co-creation arises from combining digitalized interactive platforms of brand offerings and engagements, experiences, and a collaborative innovation process that harnesses the insights, knowledge, skills, and ingenuity of all participants, in a mutually valuable manner, which requires co-creative design of organizations and brand management systems, which must constantly co-evolve as a function of the co-creative interactions it fosters. As Ramaswamy and Gouillart (2010b, p. 252) note in their co-creation manifesto: 'The co-creative enterprise has the power to transform relationships among individuals and institutions. The evolution toward a co-creative economy rests on the convergence of private, social, and public sector enterprises around productive and meaningful human experiences, and the realization of human potential.' In a post-COVID economy of digitalized society, the *co-creation advantage* of company brands will increasingly revolve around the becoming of enterprises as 'conscientious co-creational living enterprises' (Ramaswamy & Ind, 2021; Ramaswamy & Pieters, 2021) entailing valuable adaptive interactional creation of biological, psychological, social, cultural, ecological, and economic wellbeing.

## Notes

* Venkat Ramaswamy (venkatr@umich.edu) is Professor, Ross School of Business, University of Michigan, Ann Arbor, MI 48109, USA.
1 Note that in their original article Vargo and Lusch (2004), the second premise was originally "the customer is always a co-producer." In their update two years later, Vargo and Lusch (2006) changed the premise to "the customer is always a co-creator of value." Since then, following their consolidated Vargo and Lusch (2008) article, a multitude of papers cited "SD-logic" as implying that "value is co-created" (Grönroos & Gummerus 2014; Saarijärvi et al., 2013; Galvagno & Dalli, 2014).

## References

Arvidsson, A. (2006). *Brands: Meaning and value in media culture*. New York: Psychology Press.
Bagozzi, R. P. (1975). Marketing as exchange. *Journal of Marketing*, *39*(4), 32–39.
Callon, M. (2007). What does it mean to say that economics is performative? In D. MacKenzie, F. Muniesa, & L. Siu (Eds.), *Do economists make markets? On the performativity of economics* (pp. 310–357). Princeton, NJ: Princeton University Press.
Callon, M. (2016). Revisiting marketization: From interface-markets to market-agencements. *Consumption Markets & Culture*, *19*(1), 17–37.
Chakrabarti, A., & Ramaswamy, V. (2014). Re-thinking the concept of surplus: Embracing co-creation experiences in economics. *The BE Journal of Economic Analysis & Policy*, *14*(4), 1283–1297.
Couldry, N., & Hepp, A. (2017). *The mediated construction of reality*. Cambridge: Polity Press.
da Silveira, C., Lages, C., & Simões, C. (2013). Reconceptualizing brand identity in a dynamic environment. *Journal of Business Research*, *66*(1), 28–36.
Docherty, D., & Porter, M. (2019). Transforming a historic brand for a hyper-connected world: The John Deere story. In A. M. Tybout & T. Calkins (Eds.), *Kellogg on branding in a hyper-connected world*. Hoboken, NJ: John Wiley & Sons.
Ford, D. (2011). IMP and service-dominant logic: Divergence, convergence and development. *Industrial Marketing Management*, *40*(2), 231–239.
Ford, D., & Mouzas, S. (2013). Service and value in the interactive business landscape. *Industrial Marketing Management*, *42*(1), 9–17.
Frynas, J. G., Mol, M. J., & Mellahi, K. (2018). Management innovation made in China: Haier's Rendanheyi. *California Management Review*, *61*(1), 71–93.

Gregory, A. (2007). Involving stakeholders in developing corporate brands: The communication dimension. *Journal of Marketing Management*, 23(1–2), 59–73.

Grönroos, C., & Gummerus, J. (2014). The service revolution and its marketing implications: Service logic vs service-dominant logic. *Managing Service Quality*, 24(3), 206–229.

Gummesson, E., Mele, C., Polese, F., Galvagno, M., & Dalli, D. (2014). Theory of value co-creation: A systematic literature review. *Managing Service Quality*, 24(6), 643–683.

Guzmán, F., Paswan, A. K., & Kennedy, E. (2019). Consumer brand value co-creation typology. *Journal of Creating Value*, 5(1), 40–52.

Gyrd-Jones, R. I., & Kornum, N. (2013). Managing the co-created brand: Value and cultural complementarity in online and offline multi-stakeholder ecosystems. *Journal of Business Research*, 66(9), 1484–1493.

Håkansson, H., Ford, D., Gadde, L.-E., Snehota, I., & Waluszewski, A. (2009). *Business in networks*. Chichester: John Wiley & Sons.

Håkansson, H., & Snehota, I. (2017). *No business is an island: Making sense of the interactive business world*. Bingley: Emerald Publishing Limited.

Hakansson, H., & Waluszewski, A. (2020). "Thick or thin"? Policy and the different conceptualisations of business interaction patterns. *Journal of Business & Industrial Marketing*, 35(11), 1849–1859.

Hatch, M. J., & Schultz, M. (2010). Toward a theory of brand co-creation with implications for brand governance. *Journal of Brand Management*, 17(8), 590–604.

Hoffman, D. L., & Novak, T. P. (2018). Consumer and object experience in the internet of things: An assemblage theory approach. *Journal of Consumer Research*, 44(6), 1178–1204.

Iglesias, O., & Bonet, E. (2012). Persuasive brand management how managers can influence brand meaning when they are losing control over it. *Journal of Organizational Change Management*, 25(2), 251–264.

Iglesias, O., & Ind, N. (2016). How to be a brand with a conscience. In S. Horlings & N. Ind (Eds.), *Brands with a conscience: How to build a successful and responsible brand* (pp. 203–211). London: Kogan Page.

Iglesias, O., & Ind, N. (2020). Towards a theory of conscientious corporate brand co-creation: The next key challenge in brand management. *Journal of Brand Management*, 27(6), 710–720.

Iglesias, O., Landgraf, P., Ind, N., Markovic, S., & Koporcic, N. (2020a). Corporate brand identity co-creation in business-to-business contexts. *Industrial Marketing Management*, 85, 32–43.

Iglesias, O., Markovic, S., Bagherzadeh, M., & Singh, J. J. (2020b). Co-creation: A key link between corporate social responsibility, customer trust, and customer loyalty. *Journal of Business Ethics*, 163(1), 151–166.

Ind, N. (2003). *Beyond branding*. New York: Kogan Page.

Ind, N. (2007). *Living the brand: How to transform every member of your organization into a brand champion*. New York: Kogan Page.

Ind, N. (2014). How participation is changing the practice of managing brands. *Journal of Brand Management*, 21(9), 734–742.

Ind, N., & Bjerke, R. (2007a). *Branding governance: A participatory approach to the brand building process*. Chichester: John Wiley & Sons.

Ind, N., & Bjerke, R. (2007b). The concept of participatory market orientation: An organisation-wide approach to enhancing brand equity. *Journal of Brand Management*, 15(2), 135–145.

Ind, N., Iglesias, O., & Markovic, S. (2017). The co-creation continuum: From tactical market research tool to strategic collaborative innovation method. *Journal of Brand Management*, 24(4), 310–321.

Ind, N., Iglesias, O., & Schultz, M. (2013). Building brands together: Emergence and outcomes of co-creation. *California Management Review*, 55(3), 5–26.

Ind, N., & Ramaswamy, V. (2021). How enterprises can create meaningful purpose together with their stakeholders. *The European Business Review*, January–February, 76–80.

Ind, N., & Schmidt, H. (2020). *Co-creating brands: Brand management from a co-creative perspective*. London: Bloomsbury Business.

Jones, R. (2005). Finding sources of brand value: Developing a stakeholder model of brand equity. *The Journal of Brand Management*, 13(1), 10–32.

Kjellberg, H., & Helgesson, C.-F. (2006). Multiple versions of markets: Multiplicity and performativity in market practice. *Industrial Marketing Management*, 35(7), 839–855.

Kjellberg, H., & Helgesson, C.-F. (2007). On the nature of markets and their practices. *Marketing Theory*, 7(2), 137–162.

Leavy, B. (2013). Venkat Ramaswamy-a ten-year perspective on how the value co-creation revolution is transforming competition. *Strategy and Leadership*, 41(6), 11–17.

Leavy, B. (2019). Thriving in the era of the "connected customer". *Strategy & Leadership*, 47(5), 3–9.

Leclercq, T., Hammedi, W., & Poncin, I. (2016). Ten years of value cocreation: An integrative review. *Recherche et Applications en Marketing (English Edition), 31*(3), 26–60.

Lucarelli, A., & Hallin, A. (2015). Brand transformation: A performative approach to brand regeneration. *Journal of Marketing Management, 31*(1–2), 84–106.

Lury, C. (2004). *Brands: The logos of the global economy*. London: Routledge.

Lusch, R. F., & Vargo, S. L. (2014). *Service-dominant logic: Premises, perspectives, possibilities*. New York: Cambridge University Press.

Markovic, S., & Bagherzadeh, M. (2018). How does breadth of external stakeholder co-creation influence innovation performance? Analyzing the mediating roles of knowledge sharing and product innovation. *Journal of Business Research, 88*, 173–186.

Merz, M. A., He, Y., & Vargo, S. L. (2009). The evolving brand logic: A service-dominant logic perspective. *Journal of the Academy of Marketing Science, 37*(3), 328–344.

Nambisan, S., Lyytinen, K., Majchrzak, A., & Song, M. (2017). Digital innovation management: Reinventing innovation management research in a digital world. *MIS Quarterly, 41*(1), 223–238.

Novak, T. P., & Hoffman, D. L. (2019). Relationship journeys in the internet of things: A new framework for understanding interactions between consumers and smart objects. *Journal of the Academy of Marketing Science, 47*(2), 216–237.

Orlikowski, W. J., & Scott, S. V. (2015). The algorithm and the crowd: Considering the materiality of service innovation. *MIS Quarterly, 39*(1), 201–216.

Ostendorf, J., Mouzas, S., & Chakrabarti, R. (2014). Innovation in business networks: The role of leveraging resources. *Industrial Marketing Management, 43*(3), 504–511.

Payne, A., Storbacka, K., Frow, P., & Knox, S. (2009). Co-creating brands: Diagnosing and designing the relationship experience. *Journal of Business Research, 62*(3), 379–389.

Porter, M. E. (1985). *Competitive advantage: Creating and sustaining superior performance*. New York: Free Press.

Porter, M. E., & Heppelmann, J. E. (2014). How smart, connected products are transforming competition. *Harvard Business Review, 92*(11), 11–64.

Prahalad, C. K. (2004). The cocreation of value. *Journal of Marketing, 68*(1), 23.

Prahalad, C. K., & Ramaswamy, V. (2000). Co-opting customer competence. *Harvard Business Review, 78*(1), 79–87.

Prahalad, C. K., & Ramaswamy, V. (2002). The co-creation connection. *Strategy and Business 27*, 50–61.

Prahalad, C. K., & Ramaswamy, V. (2003). The new frontier of experience innovation. *MIT Sloan Management Review, 44*(4), 12–18.

Prahalad, C. K., & Ramaswamy, V. (2004a). Co-creating unique value with customers. *Strategy & Leadership, 32*(3), 4–9.

Prahalad, C. K., & Ramaswamy, V. (2004b). Co-creation experiences: The next practice in value creation. *Journal of Interactive Marketing, 18*(3), 5–14.

Prahalad, C. K., & Ramaswamy, V. (2004c). *The future of competition: Co-creating unique value with customers*. Boston, MA: Harvard Business School Press.

Price, L. L., & Coulter, R. A. (2019). Crossing bridges: Assembling culture into brands and brands into consumers' global local cultural lives. *Journal of Consumer Psychology, 29*(3), 547–554.

Ramaswamy, V. (2005). Co-creating experiences of value with customers – New paradigm. *Tata Journal of Management*, 6–14.

Ramaswamy, V. (2006). Co-creating experiences of value with customers. *SETLabs Briefings, 4*(1), 25–36.

Ramaswamy, V. (2008). Co-creating value through customers' experiences: The Nike case. *Strategy & Leadership, 36*(5), 9–14.

Ramaswamy, V. (2009). Co-creation of value – Towards an expanded paradigm of value creation. *Marketing Review St. Gallen, 26*(6), 11–17.

Ramaswamy, V. (2011). It's about human experiences . . . and beyond, to co-creation. *Industrial Marketing Management, 40*(2), 195–196.

Ramaswamy, V. (2020). Leading the experience ecosystem revolution – Innovating offerings as interactive platforms. *Strategy & Leadership, 48*(3), 3–9.

Ramaswamy, V., & Gouillart, F. J. (2010a). Building the co-creative enterprise. *Harvard Business Review, 88*(10), 100–109.

Ramaswamy, V., & Gouillart, F. J. (2010b). *The power of co-creation: Build it with them to boost growth, productivity, and profits*. New York: The Free Press.

Ramaswamy, V., & Ind, N. (2021). Company brands as purpose-driven lived-experience ecosystems. *The European Business Review*, May–June, 59–67.
Ramaswamy, V., & Ozcan, K. (2013). Strategy and co-creation thinking. *Strategy & Leadership*, 41(6), 5–10.
Ramaswamy, V., & Ozcan, K. (2014). *The co-creation paradigm*. Stanford, CA: Stanford University Press.
Ramaswamy, V., & Ozcan, K. (2016). Brand value co-creation in a digitalized world: An integrative framework and research implications. *International Journal of Research in Marketing*, 33(1), 93–106.
Ramaswamy, V., & Ozcan, K. (2018a). Offerings as digitalized interactive platforms: A conceptual framework and implications. *Journal of Marketing*, 82(4), 19–31.
Ramaswamy, V., & Ozcan, K. (2018b). What is co-creation? An interactional creation framework and its implications for value creation. *Journal of Business Research*, 84(March), 196–205.
Ramaswamy, V., & Ozcan, K. (2020). The 'interacted' actor in platformed networks: Theorizing practices of managerial experience value co-creation. *Journal of Business & Industrial Marketing*, 35(7), 1165–1178.
Ramaswamy, V., & Ozcan, K. (2021). Brands as co-creational lived experience ecosystems – An integrative theoretical framework of interactional creation. In S. Markovic, R. Gyrd-Jones, S. von Wallpach, & A. Lindgreen (Eds.), *Research handbook on brand co-creation: Theory, practice, and ethical implications* (pp. 49–66). Cheltenham: Edward Elgar.
Ramaswamy, V., & Pieters, M. K. (2021). How companies can learn to operate as co-creational, adaptive, "living" enterprises. *Strategy & Leadership*, 49(2), 3–8.
Randall, R., & Leavy, B. (2014). Venkat Ramaswamy – How value co-creation with stakeholders is transformative for producers, consumers and society. *Strategy & Leadership*, 41(6), 11–17.
Schembri, S. (2009). Reframing brand experience: The experiential meaning of Harley-Davidson. *Journal of Business Research*, 62(12), 1299–1310.
Sheth, J. N., & Uslay, C. (2007). Implications of the revised definition of marketing: From exchange to value creation. *Journal of Public Policy & Marketing*, 26(2), 302–307.
Stach, J. (2019). Meaningful experiences: An embodied cognition perspective on brand meaning co-creation. *Journal of Brand Management*, 26(3), 317–331.
Swaminathan, V., Sorescu, A., Steenkamp, J.-B. E. M., O'Guinn, T. C. G., & Schmitt, B. (2020). Branding in a hyperconnected world: Refocusing theories and rethinking boundaries. *Journal of Marketing*, 84(2), 1–23.
Teece, D. J. (2018). Profiting from innovation in the digital economy: Enabling technologies, standards, and licensing models in the wireless world. *Research Policy*, 47(8), 1367–1387.
Tilson, D., Lyytinen, K., & Sorensen, C. (2010). Digital infrastructures: The missing IS research agenda. *Information Systems Research*, 21(4), 748–759.
Tormala, M., & Gyrd-Jones, R. I. (2017). Development of new B2B venture corporate brand identity: A narrative performance approach. *Industrial Marketing Management*, 65, 76–85.
Van Dijck, J., Poell, T., & De Waal, M. (2018). *The platform society: Public values in a connective world*. Oxford: Oxford University Press.
Vargo, S. L. (2008). Customer integration and value creation: Paradigmatic traps and perspectives. *Journal of Service Research*, 11(2), 211–215.
Vargo, S. L., & Lusch, R. F. (2004). Evolving to a new dominant logic for marketing. *Journal of Marketing*, 68(1), 1–17.
Vargo, S. L., & Lusch, R. F. (2008). Service-dominant logic: Continuing the evolution. *Journal of the Academy of Marketing Science*, 36(1), 1–10.
Vargo, S. L., & Lusch, R. F. (2016). Institutions and axioms: An extension and update of service-dominant logic. *Journal of the Academy of Marketing Science*, 44(1), 5–23.
Vatin, F. (2013). Valuation as evaluating and valorizing. *Valuation Studies*, 1(1), 31–50.
von Wallpach, S., Voyer, B., Kastanakis, M., & Muhlbacher, H. (2017). Co-creating stakeholder and brand identities: Introduction to the special section. *Journal of Business Research*, 70, 395–398.
Wider, S., von Wallpach, S., & Muhlbacher, H. (2018). Brand management: Unveiling the delusion of control. *European Management Journal*, 36(3), 301–305.
Yablonsky, S. (2018). *Multi-sided platforms (MSPs) and sharing strategies in the digital economy: Emerging research and opportunities: Emerging research and opportunities*. Hershey, PA: IGI Global.
Yoo, Y. (2010). Computing in everyday life: A call for research on experiential computing. *MIS Quarterly*, 34(2), 213–231.

# 7
# BRANDS IN ACTION
## Understanding corporate branding dynamics from an action net perspective

*Sylvia von Wallpach and Andrea Hemetsberger*

**Acknowledgements**

We thank Laura Enzinger, Denise Gossner, and Verena Pirkl for their support during the data-collection phase and Sabrina Gabl for her input to this chapter.

## 1. Introduction

Societal and technological shifts have radically altered the understanding of brands and branding. The proliferation of digitalization, the growing number of digital natives, global nomadism, or the recent pandemic situation bring consumers, stakeholders, and brands much closer together in diverse digital (public) spheres. Online platforms, social media, and collaboration technology also allow consumers and stakeholders to act out their participatory, agentic aspirations; they share brand-related content, address brands directly, and organize themselves into larger, collective actors that can have great power over brands (von Wallpach et al., 2017). Researchers acknowledge the waning power of corporate brand management (Gyrd-Jones et al., 2013; Hemetsberger & Mühlbacher, 2009; Iglesias et al., 2013), and Asmussen et al. (2013) even forecasted a democratization of brand management enabled through online technologies. On the internet, brand co-creation can take on unprecedented scales and produce multi-faceted, polyvocal, and dynamic narratives of brands. The development of platform brands like Google, Facebook, Uber, AirBnB in combination with AI, blockchain, and other disruptive technology provokes an even more radical view on corporate brands as ever-evolving, dynamic, intensely networked entities, and branding as radically co-created by various actors in hybrid firm-stakeholder nets and assemblages.

    Current branding literature is well equipped with co-creative conceptualizations of branding that go far beyond firm-centric views, instead highlighting the potential of brand co-creation in a dense network of stakeholders (e.g., Hatch & Schultz, 2010; Lusch & Webster, 2011; Merz et al., 2009), or assemblage-like brand formations, wherein branding is viewed as a process of assembling culture (Lury, 2009) and shaping markets (Onyas & Ryan, 2014). This view shifts the focus of attention from a structuralist, essentialist, and actor-centric perspective towards a perspective that regards brands as fluid, dynamic, and inherently unstable, and branding as co-creative, continuous, and conscientious practice (Csaba & Bengtsson, 2006; Hemetsberger & Mühlbacher, 2009; Iglesias & Ind, 2020; von Wallpach et al., 2017). To make that point, branding research adopted different theoretical views – from service-dominant logic as theoretical underpinnings (Payne et al., 2009), an action-centric orientation (Lucarelli & Hallin, 2015), to network and assemblage perspectives (Christiansen et al., 2009; Parmentier & Fischer, 2015). But how do internal and external stakeholders co-create? Even though co-creation has become the prime concept for brand building among stakeholders and firms, co-creation itself, what it includes, and how it happens still needs further attention. Iglesias et al. (2020a) highlight that co-creation among stakeholders occurs through four different performances, that is communication, internalizing, contesting, and elucidating. In their seminal articles, Kozinets et al. (2008) and Schau et al. (2009) presented 12 common practices of value creation related to impression management, social networking, community engagement, and brand use, and Hemetsberger (2012) highlighted activation, participation, and collaboration as central creative practices of co-creation in online communities and crowds. Recently, several scholars highlighted the performative character of brand co-creation (Kristal et al., 2020; Lucarelli & Hallin, 2015; von Wallpach et al., 2017), thereby illuminating important co-creative processes that help us understand stakeholders' performances in brand co-creation. Despite the fervent, authentic belief in the importance of stakeholder integration and engagement, however, literature still draws a firm distinction between internal and external stakeholders (Merz et al., 2009) – a view which does not quite correspond with the daily business of corporate brands (Iglesias & Ind, 2020) nor reflect the innumerable co-creative activities during events, or on social media, amongst many other co-creative activities of stakeholders. It further also ignores non-human actors' performative impact on brands – for example, technology's impact on the spreading of co-created brand communication.

More complex assemblage perspectives are different in that they include non-human actors in their conceptualization – a radically different way of thinking about brands and branding. An assemblage view of brands dismantles the internal-external distinction and introduces a holistic perspective instead, one that includes all actors in the brand assemblage (e.g., Lury, 2009; Mühlbacher & Hemetsberger, 2008). Hence, these views acknowledge stakeholders and non-human actors as integral parts of brands, which adds to a more considerate, ethical, and responsible account of brands in that not only stakeholders become equivalent contributors to brands but also earthly resources, or historical buildings, for example, which firms commonly treat as resources 'without a voice.' Yet, these approaches put more emphasis on actors and network dynamics, thus leaving much room for inquiry into actual brand co-creation activities as forms of action exhibiting typicality (Schütz, 1953) in the sense of a brand, that is, how they contribute to corporate brands.

This chapter proposes an action net perspective, rooted in a 'sociology of translation' perspective based on narratology. It accounts for both – actions and networks – and guides researchers' and practitioners' attention towards brand-related actions and their interrelations. This perspective is inherently intersubjective and relational (cf. Löbler, 2011), acknowledging that what is real or – in this context, what is a brand – is the 'outcome of social relations' (Gergen, 1999, p. 237). This makes action net theory explicitly suitable to study brands and branding in co-creative multi-stakeholder brand ecosystems (Gyrd-Jones & Kornum, 2013). It further assumes no solid boundaries, or internal-external distinction between actors, and introduces the notion of actants to include non-human actors in the conceptualization and analysis of action nets. Our theoretical and empirical discussions in this chapter aim to contribute to branding theory with an integrated, theoretical conceptualization of stakeholder action in brand networks that are in constant flux.

## 2. Corporate brands as action nets

Studying brands from an action net perspective puts stakeholder action as well as non-human agency centre stage and draws attention towards the interconnectedness of these actions in a more or less stable net (Czarniawska, 1997, 2008). Table 7.1 summarizes, defines, and exemplifies the most important key concepts and terms of action net theory.

Table 7.1 Definition of key terms and concepts

| Key term | Definition and source | Example |
|---|---|---|
| Assemblage/ agencement | Agencement is an arrangement of connections among concepts that gives the concepts their sense. (Phillips, 2006, p. 108). Assemblage is the English translation of agencement and is used interchangeably to denote Deleuze et al.'s philosophy in *A Thousand Plateaus* (1987). | A brand, its elements, and connections can be considered an assemblage. |
| Action nets | The concept of action nets 'is founded on the idea that in each time and place it is possible to speak of an 'institutional order,' a set (not a system) of institutions (not necessarily coherent) prevalent right then and there. Such institutions shape organizing inasmuch as they dictate which actions, conventionally, should be tied together' (Czarniawska, 2004, p. 780). | The complex interrelations of helping institutions and actants within the breast health centre (BHC), which develop a particular plan of action at a given time and place, which makes the BHC a branded institution. |
| Action | 'A movement or an event, to which an intention can be attributed by relating the event to the social order in which it takes place' (Czarniawska, 2004, p. 782). | The intentional implementation of COVID measures by public authorities; vice versa, Coronavirus infection statistics inducing political action. |
| Actant | 'Objects and abstract concepts can be actants just as much as humans, as long as they can be identified as "that which accomplishes or undergoes an act"' (Schleifer, 1987, p. 88) | Greta Thunberg, her speeches, the perceived consequences of climate change, and regular demos powerfully mobilize politicians to take action. Greta, speeches, climate change, and demos are all actants. |
| Non-human actor | An entity that is not human and undergoes an act | A branded event induces visitors to come and engage in communal brand action. |
| Translation | Translation is the process of establishing connections, of forming a passage between two spheres, or of enabling communication (Serres, 1982). When 'travelling' from one context to another, an idea, object or practice needs to be de-contextualized and re-contextualized, which involves the process of translation (Czarniawska & Joerges, 1996); a mediation, construction and transformation of ideas, objects, and practices into a different context (Mica, 2013). | Metaphorical and charismatic speeches of the Waldviertler CEO, establishing connections between his illegal savings club and how it helped an economically weak region to prosper. |

*(Continued)*

*Table 7.1* (Continued)

| Key term | Definition and source | Example |
|---|---|---|
| Knotting | Knotting is some form of connecting, for example through translating (Lindberg & Czarniawska, 2006). | Asking, storytelling, mediating among mountain enthusiasts in order to create the typicality of the IMS brand |
| Dispatcher | Dispatchers build and maintain action nets; organizations as legal personalities of action nets (Czarniawska, 2004). | Organizations as dispatchers of brands in a legal sense; social media and press as dispatchers of brand communication among stakeholders. |
| Boundary object | Boundary objects allow coordination in that they allow an actor's local understanding to be reframed in the context of a wider collective activity (Bechky, 2003). | Tangible branded products with brand labels (Waldviertler) that reflect environmental consciousness |
| Boundary procedure | 'A means for sharing meaning across borders and among different social worlds' (Dietrich et al. Czarniawska, 2011, p. 6) | Storytelling and lecturing of climbing experts at the IMS to enable common understanding of mountaineering risks |

Rather than looking at corporate brands from a static perspective, an action net's theoretic perspective emphasizes the fluid, temporary effects of ongoing organizing (Czarniawska, 2008). This view is radical in that it supposes that corporate brands are not corporate brands by definition but become brands only through typical branding activities – no matter who or what is taking action in branding. Consequentially, actions are the focal interest in action net theory. Action net theory proposes a major reversal of the centrality of actors (Czarniawska, 2007) as it assumes that actions come first, construct actors, and provide them with identity. Based on Harré (1982), Czarniawska (2004) defines *action* as 'a movement or an event, to which an intention can be attributed by relating the event to the social order in which it takes place' (Czarniawska, 2004, p. 782). The intentionality of an action is only ascribed to it in retrospect and is often subject to interpretation. In contrast to behaviour, action is full of meaning and intention – action is relevant in a particular context but also beyond the immediate time and space in which the action is performed, implying that action nets are not restricted in time and space (Czarniawska, 1997; Lindberg & Czarniawska, 2006). Collective actions concerned need not necessarily be performed within the boundaries of a specific 'organization.' On the contrary, an action net may involve a great variety of organizations or organized groups of people of a loose or temporary nature (Czarniawska, 2004). Organizations or corporate brands, specifically start-up brands, multinational platform brands and online retailers, for example, depend on the interagency of multiple, global activities, which compose the brand at a specific point in time. Any action – no matter if it is performed by (assemblies of) human or non-human actors within the boundaries of a formal organization or outside – can be of importance, as long as it exhibits some typicality in the sense of the construct (Schütz, 1953), that is, the corporate brand. Lucarelli and Hallin (2015), and von Wallpach et al. (2017), for example, adopt this perspective to brands as entities that are being constantly, materially, and discursively created. Though many brands consist of a number of repetitive core actions usually situated within the boundaries of a corporate brand, multi-stakeholder co-creation renders them fluid, adaptive, and ever-changing entities. The case of the LEGO fan community, which is in permanent contact, exchanging their innovative creations, selling LEGO parts and eventually becoming even certified LEGO dealers, is a prime example of a corporate brand in permanent flux (von Wallpach et al., 2017). Actions, interactions, and associations performatively constitute the action net (cf. Czarniawska, 2004; Lucarelli & Hallin, 2015), that is, the brand. According to Lash and Lury (2007), brands are brought into being not only through ongoing actions of stakeholders but also shaped by actions that are materializing in a certain space-time frame (Lash & Lury, 2007) 'in ongoing transformations of a socio-technical agencement' (Onyas & Ryan, 2014, p. 142). What the authors emphasize here is that any brand materialization – be it a product, a sales channel, a formalized procedure, anything tangible – also exerts agentic power over humans.

Action net theory assumes that objects are continuously constructed and acted upon, but it also ascribes them agency in performing action (cf., Greimas & Courtes, 1982). According to action net theory, actions can be performed by human *actants*, non-human actants such as material or even concepts, or assemblies of these (Czarniawska, 1997, 2004). In a branding context, the material product, a brand myth, or a corporate brand as a whole can perform brand-related actions. A LEGO brick triggers building and creative activities and so becomes a branding actant, for example. Through these actions, actants acquire an 'actorial' identity from actions, not the other way around (Czarniawska, 2004, p. 9). Corporate brands, according to this view, derive their identity from actions of relevant actants in their action net, be it human or non-human actants. Moreover, 'past actions build up an actor's reputation, and it is the stability of their identities that gives "character" to "actants"' (Lindberg & Czarniawska, 2006, p. 294). The Exxon Valdez oil spill disaster of 1989, for example, dramatically illustrates how visuals of oil-covered birds and beaches produce a long-lasting identity of a corporate actor. Most importantly, actants as part of an established action net are exchangeable. As long as the actions performed by the actant (and connections between actions) are kept up, the action net is not going to break down.

Inspired by Actor-Network Theory (ANT), action net theory conceptualizes *translation* as the glue between two actions. According to Serres (1982), translation is the process of establishing connections, of forming a passage between two spheres, or of enabling communication. Any successful brand encounter at any touchpoint would qualify as such a translation between brands and related actors. Translations connect one action to another and thus, enable the action net to spread across time and space. If an action is not (successfully) translated, it might become disconnected from the net and will most probably not be continued (cf. Kjellberg & Helgesson, 2007). A brand can be regarded as an assemblage of connected actions (Lury, 2009), but it takes more for it to be considered a stable action net. Organizations, that is, corporate brands, are important as 'a *dispatcher* (Latour, 1998) and a *translator* . . . that is given a legal personality, thus acquiring the right to an identity, a will, an image' (Czarniawska, 2004, p. 780). *Dispatcher* and *translator* are dependent on one another and are central to the building and maintenance of the action net. Organizational brands as dispatchers send objects and humans (e.g., products and sales staff) to the right place (consumer domain) with the help of translators (retailers). They are responsible for the continuous knotting and re-knotting of the net. This understanding highlights that someone initiated a brand, that an 'institutional order' exists at a certain time and place. 'Such institutions, like corporate brands, shape [practices such as] organizing [management or branding] inasmuch as they dictate which actions, conventionally, should be tied together' (Czarniawska, 2004, p. 780; Lindberg & Czarniawska, 2006; parentheses added). Yet, at some point the brand starts to have a life of its own and constructs humans, objects, and non-material concepts, as the abundance of branded content in social media demonstrates.

*Boundary objects* (Bechky, 2003; Lindberg & Czarniawska, 2006; Star & Griesemer, 1989) and *boundary procedures* (Dietrich et al., 2011; Lindberg & Czarniawska, 2006) allow coordination and shared understandings across different social realms. Thus, they facilitate translations, and enable and even stabilize connections. Boundary objects 'have different meanings in different social worlds but their structure is common enough to more than one world to make them recognizable' (Star & Griesemer, 1989, p. 393). They are 'simultaneously concrete and abstract, specific and general, conventionalized and customised' (Star & Griesemer, 1989, p. 408). Lindberg and Czarniwska (2006) found three different types of *connections* – cognitive, emotional, and mimetic – that can be facilitated through boundary objects or procedures. Unlike emotional interactions, cognitive connections do not necessarily involve face-to-face contact and include information or knowledge objects. As an example of an emotional connection, Lindberg and Czarniawska (2006) point out the 'we-feeling' among different actants, and Briers and Chua (2001) suggest that visionary objects can evoke strong emotions. In the case of mimetic connections, boundary procedures such as storytelling can play an important role in triggering mimetic behaviour.

Storytelling is actually one of the major boundary procedures identified in action nets (Dietrich et al., 2011; Lindberg & Czarniawska, 2006). According to Dietrich et al. (2011), storytelling is crucial in coordinating and 'connecting different social realities and competing interests, thereby enabling and coordinating joint action across social worlds' (4). Storytelling can establish a common understanding which is not based on actual shared experience, but rather on the sharing of a story. In many cases, the function of stories as connectors of actions is not confined to a single occasion. Stories, like ideas, can travel through time and space and thus, serve as boundary procedure for many more actions (Czarniawska & Joerges, 1996; Lindberg & Czarniawska, 2006). In branding, brand stories have, for example, been studied as important ingredient for an inspiring brand experience (Lundkvist et al., 2013) or as important ritual of identity-building in brand subcultures (Schouten & McAlexander, 1995) and communities (Muñiz & O'Guinn, 2001). By accessing existing action nets and through boundary procedures, such as storytelling, actants recreate and stabilize connections between brand actions.

Action net theory challenges traditional views in brand management that brands and brand communication, specifically, should be cohesive and consistent over time (e.g., Keller, 1993). Repeated actions developing into patterns of actions can stabilize the net; however, brand action nets are only temporarily stable. In practice, brands also proved to be inconsistent, complex, and impossible to tame (Berthon et al., 2009; Payne et al., 2009). Stability in action nets only exists from a static perspective. Actants' continuous engagement in forming new connections through processes of translation initiates change, since the identity of anything involved in translation (e.g., knowledge, people, or things) is in constant flux and uncertain (Czarniawska, 2009). While boundary objects (e.g., a branded object) and boundary procedures (e.g., storytelling in brand communities) help to stabilize connections between actions, the simultaneous presence of different narratives in the action net (e.g., brand memes on Instagram) lead to a constant state of paradox (Czarniawska, 1997) and necessity to negotiate typicality. Yet, incompatibilities or disconnections between actions do not necessarily lead to a breakdown of the net but rather trigger necessary change. So, brand action nets are inherently unstable but also permanently stabilized by continuous processes of translation at various brand touchpoints.

Action net theory as firmly anchored in actions at centre stage is actually a radical perspective and puts corporate actors and stakeholders back to what they are – important actants in a net of actions, forming and recreating connections through translations, among many, also non-human actants in an action net. While the inclusion of non-human actants is quite prominently discussed in ANT, assemblage-based conceptualizations of brands (e.g., Lury, 2009), theorizations based on performativity approaches, and the socio-materiality of brands (Lucarelli & Hallin, 2015; von Wallpach et al., 2017), action net theory puts particular emphasis on knotting – connections and processes of translation – among actions in order to become relevant for corporate brand development and identity. Orchestrating corporate brands, then, is a matter of orchestrating action and acting as formal 'dispatcher,' creating boundary objects, connecting actants, and shaping processes of translation across time and space. With three extended corporate branding cases, this chapter aims to demonstrate how brand action nets are formed by brand-related actions of multiple stakeholders, and how they connect and (de)materialize in certain time-space frames.

## 3. Research context and methods

In order to trace brand-related actions, the connections between them and the related (de)materialization of brand action nets, we investigated three different cases adopting an exploratory research design, including participant observation, taking field notes, narrative interviewing, netnography, and secondary data analysis (Czarniawska, 2002, 2004; Kozinets, 2002). In order to cover a broader range of corporate branding activities, we purposefully sampled three different types of corporate brands: (a) a commercially oriented corporate brand; (b) a non-profit oriented corporate brand; and (c) an event brand as an extreme case of a temporary corporate brand. All three brands appeared particularly relevant for the study at hand due to their strong focus on their active involvement of multiple stakeholders in brand-related actions and time-space frames that transcend conventional corporate boundaries. The three focal brands are located in the same cultural context (Austria and the German-speaking areas in Northern Italy), which makes them more comparable. In the following, we briefly introduce the three case brands, highlighting their relevance as focal cases for this study and the data collection methods adopted for each case study.

*Waldviertler:* The Austrian corporate brand Waldviertler is well known for its traditional, handmade shoe brand, but also for furniture or bags. The regionally and sustainably manufactured products are sold through Waldviertler's own distribution channel, the GEA shops. Waldviertler had intense media coverage in 2012 when the company was violating the banking law. Waldviertler's CEO collected € 3 million in a crowdfunding project from family and friends after credit refusal from his principal bank. Waldviertler issued shares, so-called GEA 'Sonnen-Gut Scheine,' founded a savings club and used the collected money to finance a photovoltaic installation as well as a storehouse. While this savings club was already founded in 2003, only in 2012 the CEO was taken to court by the Financial Market Authority (FMA). The CEO of Waldviertler refused to pay the fine of € 20.000 and even called for a demonstration in front of the parliament. With his 'savings club,' the CEO fought against the banking law, advocated civil rights, and tried to revitalize the troubled area around company headquarters ('FMA vs. GEA – Pressemeldungen' 2014). This incident involved various (new) stakeholders outside the daily business of a shoe manufacturer and considerably enlarged and changed the brand action net of Waldviertler.

The focus of investigation was narrowed down to the period between October 2012 and the beginning of 2013. Within this period the most impactful events in this episode took place, and media coverage reached its peak. Online media articles from Austrian newspapers with the highest national coverage were sampled, and online comments from a variety of brand-interested stakeholders were downloaded to get a first overview of the chronology of events, actants involved, and activities in the action net. A netnographic approach (Kozinets, 2002) was adopted to collect relevant additional data from online forums, Facebook pages, and the commentary section of videos that were available online. In line with Czarniawska (2002), 18 semi-structured narrative interviews with core actants (including the CEO) complemented the data collection and helped explore chronological and spatial relations of activities.

*Breast Health Centre (BHC) Tyrol*: The BHC Tyrol is a non-profit organization located in Innsbruck (Austria) and represents the first certified centre for breast health in Austria. More than half of all breast cancer cases in Tyrol are treated here. The certification requires that every action from diagnosis to last treatment is standardized and documented. This means that everyone in the BHC, irrespective of their position, knows what actions need to be performed and in what sequence. While the patient is at the core of the BHC, the department of Obstetrics and Genecology represents the face of the centre and the brand. This department is mostly involved with patients and coordinates all procedures for the patient. Like most other non-profit organizations, the BHC is dependent on the actions of a multitude of brand stakeholders in order to be able to offer a high-quality service to beneficiaries. Many different partners temporarily engage in brand-related patient-focused actions at different points in time and in different spaces (e.g., physiotherapists, dieticians).

Data collection spanned from late 2013 to early 2014. Thirteen semi-structured narrative interviews with relevant actants (including patients, employees, management, and one sponsor) provide insights into different actants' actions and relations between them. Participant observation, including taking field notes, complemented interview data.

*International Mountain Summit (IMS):* Between 2009 and 2018, the IMS served as a platform for mountain enthusiasts from all over the world.

> The mountain festival is an independent and international platform at which the Lebensraum Mountain is illuminated, discussed and celebrated in all its facets. The Mountain is as diverse as its visitors and admirers. It is simultaneously Lebensraum, market factor and personal challenge or simply just a natural wonder. It opens the eyes of individuals and coins whole cultures. At the IMS topics as well as generations and perceptions are linked. Within this variety every visitor of the IMS has something in common with the others: everyone is enthusiastic about mountains.
> (Official Concept Folder IMS)

The idea behind the IMS was to revive the tradition of '*abklettern*.' *Abklettern* came up in the 1930s and was practiced until the 1970s. Mountaineers met in November every year after a long season of expeditions for challenging their latest routes together and sharing and exchanging experiences. The IMS was supposed to create a place for modern *abklettern* and attracted mountain enthusiasts including professionals as well as regular climbers, united by their passion for mountains. The IMS catered to different ways of expressing and living this passion, for instance in the form of actual hikes and activities in the mountains, meeting professional mountaineers and climbers, or enjoying mountain-related artwork. Furthermore, the IMS was obviously also a place where mountain equipment producers, sponsors, and media specialized on mountaineering as well as general media could meet. Instead of providing tangible products, the IMS provided time and space for brand enthusiasts to get together and share their passion about mountains.

Data collection took place before, during, and after the IMS in October 2011. Thirty-nine semi-structured narrative interviews provided us with an in-depth understanding of different actants' actions and how they relate to actions of other actants. More informal and shorter conversations with individuals, IMS participants, or small groups during the IMS, as well as participant observation, including taking field notes, complemented the data collection.

Data material resulting from the three case studies was largely textual in nature. In our analysis, we followed an inductive categorization process (Spiggle, 1994) by: (a) independently analysing the data material resulting from each case study and inductively deriving major themes; (b) independently engaging in a cross-case analysis, identifying similarities and differences in major themes arising in different cases; and (c) comparing and discussing the independent coding to jointly agree on a catalogue of major themes characterizing the (de)materialization of corporate brand action nets. The first outcome of the data analysis was a snapshot of each brand action net, illustrating case-specific brand-related actions and connections between them as well as actants involved in performing brand-related actions. In a second step, actions and connections between them were, where possible, traced over time and across spaces in order to gain a more dynamic understanding of corporate brand action nets. The next section presents the outcome of the second step of this analysis.

## 4. Brand action nets in action

### 4.1. Spanning boundaries – across time, space, and spheres

Adopting an action net perspective to brands as processual phenomena, this study finds streams of brand-relevant actions and connections between them that flow continuously, intensifying and materializing in certain time and space frames, while dematerializing and eventually vanishing completely in others. Our findings further show that connections between brand-relevant actions span boundaries across time and space and additionally, across different spheres (e.g., political, legal, and economic spheres; leisure versus professional spheres). Figure 7.1 captures these dynamics and boundaries spanning characteristics of brand action nets.

#### 4.1.1. Time in brand action nets

Understanding time in the context of action nets requires 'a reversal of the time perspective' (Czarniawska, 2004, p. 773). 'Brand' is not the 'starting or end-point' of the investigation (cf. Czarniawska, 2004), but lies in and comes to life through a continuous flow of brand-related actions and its temporary brand manifestations (Wider et al., 2018). Understanding 'brand' thus requires following this flow, observing (or collecting accounts on) the instantaneous kindling of a brand-related action that either vanishes again in that instance or can repeatedly be observed in other instances, which can indicate an institutionalization of a brand-related action, at least for the time being.

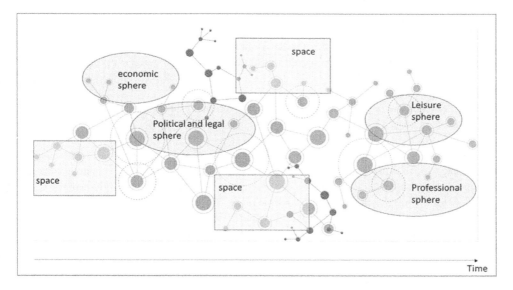

*Figure 7.1* The dynamics and boundaries spanning characteristics of brand action nets.

The IMS case was an extreme case of a brand action net that (de)materialized in constant intervals over the 10 years of its existence, with a peak in actions and connections between them at the annual events. During these events, time and space was structured into five main institutional actions initiated by the brand management team: the IMS talk (i.e., speeches by well-known mountaineers and other experts), IMS discussion (i.e., discussion sessions with well-known mountaineers and other experts), IMS congress (i.e., gatherings of interested parties representing different perspectives on mountaineering), IMS walks (i.e., walk and talk with well-known mountaineers), and IMS climbing (i.e., climbing sessions with well-known climbers). This action-oriented structuring of the IMS led to the temporary development of a large net of actions, which drastically shrank in between events, only consisting of core institutional actions (e.g., managing, communicating) that kept the net alive until the next summit.

Our tracing of actions in the context of the three case studies confirms that attempts to study time in strict mechanical terms (i.e., using chronological measurements, which build on the assumption that time is linear and measurable) are not expedient in the context of action nets (Czarniawska, 2004). Action nets are mainly characterized by kairotic time ordering. Kairos is defined as a 'propitious moment for decision or action' (Stevenson, 2010, p. 954). 'Kairos jumps and slows down, omits long periods and dwells on others' (Czarniawska, 2004, p. 775). This becomes especially evident in our respondents' accounts of their perspective and contribution to the respective action net: Different respondents' accounts focus on different points in time, highlighting different sequences of actions as relevant. Particularly in the highly institutionalized context of the BHC, which due to its certification requires every action from diagnosis to last treatment to be standardized and documented, such differences in temporal perceptions are striking.

When asked about critical points in time and related brand actions in the net, one patient does, for instance, focus on actions concerning her breast cancer diagnosis:

> It was the first time, when I met him because for me that was the most dramatic time and this was between mammography and actually going to him and meeting him and it's not like, . . . I mean, he knew how serious it was and that he immediately had to operate and react, but he still took the time the first time at least two hours, three hours and then I came back two days later and it was the same amount of time and he just takes the time and you never had the feeling that he's gotta be somewhere else. He just took the time and unfortunately for him, I am a patient who reads everything, underlines everything and asks a million questions and he answered everything.
>
> (BHC 1)

A doctor, on the contrary, highlights brand-related actions regarding post-illness follow-ups as most critical:

> Not just the therapy is an aspect of the illness, but also the follow-up. That's what represents the biggest problems. Cutting the tumour out and doing chemo therapy is quite a short time period, but the woman needs to live with the consequences and also with the knowledge that she had that illness and that a relapse might happen, her whole life. And that's why the follow-ups are that important. It's often underestimated which impact that has. With just cutting out the tumour it's not done, the patient needs the follow-up her whole life.
>
> (BHC 3)

The rather different temporal focus of accounts regarding the same action net demonstrates another core characteristic of kairotic time, 'individual timing' (Czarniawska, 2004, p. 777), which allows brand actants to highlight which brand-related actions are most relevant for them and at what point in time.

While kairotic timing characterizes in particular individual perceptions and accounts of actants, brand action nets do also require some degree of chronological structuring of actions in order to function; or as Czarniawska (2004, p. 777) puts it: 'If, however, organizations ran on kairotic time only, no train would ever leave on time.' This is reflected in the following comment by an assistant doctor at the BHC:

> One employee in our administration department works a lot, because he arranges all investigations. Immediately as soon as he gets the information from the radiologist that a new diagnosis is coming, he arranges all investigations, before the patient is coming to us. That's really pleasant for her as a patient and she already gets in touch with this net. She knows tomorrow I need to go here and then there, I think that's very important for her.
> (BHC 4)

Ultimately, Kairos and Chronos co-exist, contributing to maintaining the flow of brand-related actions over time.

### 4.1.2. The intertwining of time and space in brand action nets

While often separated in theory, 'time and space are irreversibly intertwined in practice: . . . Modern organizing takes place in a net of fragmented, multiple contexts, through multitudes of kaleidoscopic movements' (Czarniawska, 2004, p. 786). Especially new social media support the simultaneousness of brand-related actions in many places, not necessarily requiring physical presence (cf. Vallaster & von Wallpach, 2013). These new dynamics also add to today's unprecedented mobility and flexibility that allow brand actants to move across time and space with very few restrictions.

Intersections between time and space become apparent in different constellations throughout the three cases. The IMS is an extreme case, providing a temporary space in which brand-related actions were performed, contributing to the enactment of the macro actor 'IMS brand.' A core characteristic of this time and space frame was its boundlessness: actants were brought together at the same time and in the same space and enabled to interact freely, based on their shared passion: mountaineering. One participant describes this as follows:

> It's of huge value because the IMS brings interested persons together outside associations.
> (IMS 1)

The mountain plays a key role in this action net, being the central non-human actant. Very much like a human actant, the mountain seemingly acts according to its own will, creating the space and the conditions for brand-related actions to take place (e.g., by making the ascent to Mount Everest impossible due to bad weather conditions). The mountain is the object of love and hate; he is ascribed human-like qualities such as 'being unforgiving' and serves as a surface on which other brand actants can project their (shared) passions.

Boundary objects and boundary procedures present in the context of the IMS time and space frame enabled boundary spanning, that is, the overcoming of classical boundary-creating characteristics such as culture, heritage, background, ethnicity, education, employment, etc. As outlined earlier, the purpose of boundary objects and procedures is to support the development of a shared understanding across different social realms, thus enabling and eventually stabilizing connections between actions (Lindberg & Czarniawska, 2006). In the context of the IMS, core institutionalized actions serving as boundary procedures were *walking*, *talking*, and *lecturing*. Famous mountaineers, such as Reinhold Messner, became boundary objects. Through their lectures, narratives, and joint walks professional mountaineers translated actions originating in a different sphere, namely the professional 'extreme sports sphere' to the social realm of 'normal' mountain enthusiasts (i.e., leisure sphere). Making extreme sports actions more accessible through translation implied making them compatible with actions of the regular mountain enthusiast. During walks or after lectures, mountain enthusiasts could connect by performing actions such as asking questions, telling own narratives about mountaineering experiences, or just walking together. One participant describes this connecting and translating during walks as follows:

> For me the walk is central. In combination with the talk in the evening. In the evening you join a talk and the next day you go walking with this person. . . . Everyone has an image of the celebrity. A constructed image. This image is complemented or eventually completely torn down while talking or asking questions during the walk. But for sure it has changed.
>
> (IMS 2)

Another example by the same respondent shows how mountain enthusiasts could connect with the extreme sports sphere by asking questions that made actions more accessible:

> A woman asked Alexander Huber [famous mountaineer] whether he knows how to cook. And he said, yes of course, otherwise I would not survive in the camps. At home he cooks as well once in a while, it is just that the time is often missing. Then he talked about diverse recipes. Profane everyday stories become meaningful.
>
> (IMS 2)

The same respondent perceives his own role as translator as follows:

> I'm a mediator. In my normal work life, I'm the middleman between wild, dangerous nature and the people coming from the city. Now, here [at the IMS] among my colleagues – the climbers – . . . a kind of bridge is established through me [between professionals and non-professionals].
>
> (IMS 2)

These joint actions contributed to the knotting of the IMS brand action net in the specific time and space frame and to the development of a common institutionalized thought structure, implying shared understanding and emotions and thus cognitive and emotional connections (Lindberg & Czarniawska, 2006):

> Share feelings, share emotions, share tips and, life in the mountains. Live mountains. . . . I think people come here looking for, mainly for these emotions . . . and at the end share the same emotions.
>
> (IMS 3)

In the case of the BHC and Waldviertler, brand-related actions are more dispersed in time and space. This might come as a surprise, since – contrary to the IMS – both corporate brands work in a more conventional way, operating from a corporate headquarter and working permanently throughout the years to deliver their branded products or services. Studying the BHC case from an action net perspective, we learn that offering breast cancer treatment requires the performance of a multitude of sequential as well as partially simultaneous actions that involve a multitude of actants. The BHC accordingly relies on an array of partners that temporarily engage in brand-related patient-focused or supportive actions at different points in time and in different places. Patients do, for instance, receive physiotherapy or dietary consultation at different intervals, usually at the specialists' facilities. Actual breast cancer operations are performed at the local hospital. Furthermore, the BHC is partnering with the pharmaceutical industry. As money provided by the government is not sufficient to cover the costs of research, the BHC depends heavily on the pharmaceutical industry in order to finance research. The pharmaceutical industry, on the other hand, is dependent on the BHC for getting patient access for their studies. By adopting an action net approach, it is possible to capture such entanglements and temporary constellations of multiple, diverse actions that are more or less related to the core activities of the brand but nonetheless essential for the brand's existence (cf. Czarniawska, 2004). Also, in the context of the BHC, boundary objects and procedures are crucial to connect actions originating in different professional spheres (e.g., research versus different professional spheres of involved specialists). The core boundary object in the case of the BHC is the patient, who is ultimately the core focus of all brand-related actions. The centre's certification underlying all brand-related actions is another central boundary object, serving as a collective basis for brand-related action and facilitating connections between actions over time and space. Finally, the so-called tumour-board is the core boundary procedure, translating and spanning boundaries across spheres:

> You look for one central interface with all disciplines and that is this tumour board. That is eventually the most important part of the centre.
>
> (BHC 3)

At this meeting, all partners and specialists are sitting at one table and discuss every single patient based on patient protocols. All decisions regarding patient treatment as well as patient recruitment for studies are discussed in these meetings.

Finally, in terms of temporal and spatial structuring, the Waldviertler case can again be perceived as an extreme case. At first sight, this corporate brand appears to be the most conventional in the sample, characterized by a net of institutional brand-related actions that are typical for a production company (e.g., management, production, supply, marketing) and repeatedly performed in a certain chronological sequence, mainly in the company's facilities and stores. The conventional temporal and spatial structuring was shaken by the credit case incident described earlier. This incident led to a drastic intensification of brand-related actions in the period of investigation. Actions were no longer only performed by conventional company internal and external actants (economic sphere) but all of a sudden involved new actants appertaining also to the legal and the political sphere. While the company and its related actants had so far mainly engaged in brand-related actions in offline spaces and communicated via traditional media and channels, this incident led to a fast adoption of brand-related actions in online spaces. Since this case is also an excellent illustration of a brand action net in change, the development of the Waldviertler brand action net and the spanning of boundaries within this net will be discussed in more detail in the next sub-section.

## 4.2. Oscillations between stability and change

Oscillations between stability and change are a core characteristic of brand action nets. These oscillations are largely subtle and thus not easy to trace. In the context of an extreme case of a brand in crisis, such as Waldviertler, changes in the brand action net are more pronounced, which also facilitates identifying oscillations between stability and change. Figure 7.2 illustrates the brand action net of Waldviertler after the credit case incident, including old and new actions and involved actants.

While established and institutionalized brand-related actions were carried out as previously, new actions and connections between them emerged, enlarging the action net, spanning boundaries across time, space, and spheres. Spanning boundaries again required translation. The company's CEO was a central boundary object, translating the brand, while the general media served as dispatchers and translators of communicative brand actions. Talking publicly about his company, its philosophy, and his neglect of any wrongdoing relating to the credit case and the charge that he refused to pay, as well as by purposefully staging events (e.g., after the hearing in front of the court room or in his GEA shops), the CEO translated his actions for more and less involved audiences. (Social) media turned out as a main (non)human actor, broadcasting speeches, interviews and events, further contributing to the translation of the CEO's brand-related actions for the general public. The circle of brand actants was enlarged by new brand supporters and critics, who might never have and might also not plan to buy the brand's products but who fully support the brand's values guiding its CEO's actions. Old and new brand supporters in turn engaged in own brand-related actions, mainly re-narrating and re-interpreting stories they had heard from different sources, thus drastically changing the brand action net and eventually recruiting further brand actants.

The core driving force behind this outlined change process, where paradoxical tensions that provide a basis for argumentation and energized discussions, related to the Waldviertler brand. Waldviertler's core brand values, reviving an old, almost extinct craft and thereby creating jobs in an economically weak region, established the basis for old and new brand actants to connect with the brand and its actions. A main paradox underlying the action net at the point of investigation was the fact that legal restrictions by the FMA kept a brand from acting in an economically sound (i.e., what is best for the brand and its core stakeholders, e.g., employees) and societally sound

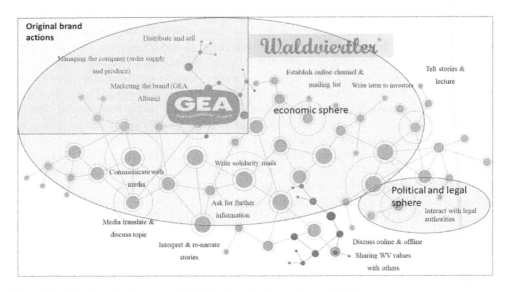

*Figure 7.2* The brand action net of Waldviertler after the credit case incident

(contributing to the development of an economically weak region by reviving an old handicraft) manner, as well as citizens from supporting the brand by lending money for this endeavour.

> *What is known* from discussion until now in media and press puts dim light on the FMA, up to now shining by inability or idleness, absolutely failing in critical situations with deceitful and balance faking banks from Kommunalkredit till HypoAlpe Adria. . . . Now the wish of the citizen, to support something meaningful with their honest acquired money . . . is prosecuted by the FMA with wrong arguments in terms of content, where [the CEO] pursues banking transactions.
>
> (WV 7)

Brand-related discussions in different online and offline spaces illustrate how outlawing the 'savings club' causes a lack of understanding and initiates brand-supportive actions. The CEO uses the same rationale in his argumentation:

> And then I said to the judge 'Don't you think this is funny? There is a great hearing against me, while banks lose billions; with me no one has lost a cent.' He looked at me and said 'well, anyway' . . . what should I do, the law compels me to do so?
>
> (WV 1)

The fact that even a representative of the legal sphere had to admit that the law underlying the credit case was problematic, provided a strong argument uniting the community of brand actants in solidarity in their fight against the banking law and for the preservation of civil rights. Solidarity in its extreme form involved brand actants announcing their willingness to enrich the brand action net by going to jail for the brand:

> BRAVO, keep up [CEO]and if you need someone who serves one day in prison for you I am happy to step in for you.
>
> (WV 8)

The general public's agreement and solidarity with a brand accused of illegal funding sparks online discussions and furthers changes in the brand action net. These discussions advance to debates on fundamental principles concerning the current law. In many ways, the law is an important non-human actant in this temporary brand action net and forces the FMA as well as other actors to act for, or against, a brand action net.

> Even if he produces in the Waldviertel [area], does not rip people off, but instead creates real value. . . . It does not free him from the obligation to comply with the law. If he thinks that these laws do not make sense, he should act politically.
>
> (WV 10)

> Are these really meaningful laws which should be enforced with power????
>
> (WV 11)

The credit case and the related problematic legal situation found resolution in a paradoxical solution: the subordinated loan. Waldviertler investors needed to sign a document stating that they accept not to be entitled to make any claims in case of bankruptcy. This solution led again to heated discussion related to the brand:

> Insanely enough, this result with the subordinated loan has no conditions AT ALL. Except that the loaner signs that he is without rights.
>
> (WV 1)

> Please, everybody, who lends money to Staudinger with the knowledge that no bank is behind it and he does not get his money back in the case of bankruptcy, is well aware of his risk.
>
> (WV 12)

> I do not understand the excitement, or not quite. . . . People seem to want to take a risk, because the repayment of the loan is not a sure thing.
>
> (WV 13)

The fact that their money was at risk did not discourage old and new brand supporters. They continue supporting the brand until today. With the resolution of various paradoxes, the development of the action net slowed down and newly introduced actions across new spaces and spheres were partially institutionalized. These changes had far reaching economic consequences for the brand, in terms of (a) a general increase in brand awareness and popularity; (b) more demand for branded products; and (c) growth, which created new work places in the region.

## 5. Conclusion

In a networked world and times of technological disruption, corporate brands find themselves entangled in assemblages of a myriad of actants (e.g., stakeholders, influencers, and the wider public, COVID-19, AI technology, chatbots, blockchains, virtual assistants) impacting brands by spreading various narratives (e.g., on Facebook, Twitter, Instagram, Whatsapp, on the street) and spinning nets of actions (e.g., tweets, open innovation, recommendations). As the cases of the IMS, Waldviertler, and the BHC demonstrate, corporate brands become conglomerates of people, objects, ideas, and their translations into a more or less fluid or stable net of actions. Consequently, corporate brand management should be concerned with the identification of brand action in diverse fields and domains, connecting them in meaningful ways and sustain brands by knotting together actions of various actants.

Action Net Theory helps us navigating brands in this new environment by challenging established categories and forcing us to think in radical new ways in a radically new world.

*Primacy of brand-related action:* Looking at branding from an action-centric perspective offers an array of new insights into how branding works in a radically transformed world. First, brand action refocuses our viewpoint to the many brand stakeholders, who take part in brand co-creation, specifically in the development of corporate brands (Gregory, 2007). Second, it also ascribes agency to contemporary disruptive technology and pandemic situations. As the recent COVID pandemic has taught us, some brands (e.g., Biontech Pfizer, producers of facial masks) ultimately are becoming saviours of global mankind, whilst others (event brands; music festivals, and more) were quickly sent on entire hold. Or take the example of platforms, which act upon consumers and brands in an either empowering or constraining manner through network effects, algorithms, and affordances (Kozinets et al., 2021). However, neither stakeholders nor technological affordances per se create brands but rather their agentic potencies and typicality regarding brands.

*Sources of brand-related action:* In line with recent branding literature, advocating a process-oriented perspective on branding (e.g., Merz et al., 2009; Wider et al., 2018), action net theory suggests a shift in focus from 'stable' actors as sources of action towards fluid and dynamic nets of actions producing *collective actors*, such as networks of brand-interested stakeholders (Hillebrand et al., 2015), as temporarily stable outcomes. This is not to say that stakeholders are to lose their importance. Assumingly, they will gain importance by a renewed engagement in translating and connecting actions.

In line with an assemblage perspective (e.g., Lury, 2009), an action net perspective adopts a more holistic approach, emphasizing and enriching our analyses with explicit integration of *non-human actants*, some of which are about to become even humanized, for example, the mountain as exemplified in the case of the IMS presented in this chapter, or, more digital humanized but still non-human actants, who gain momentum and impact many brands today, such as robots and chatbots. Those digital(ized) actants have become important connectors, translators, and boundary objects for corporate brand communication. But also less human technologies and procedures, as exemplified in the case of the BHC, or the focal importance of the law and institutions like the FMA in the Waldviertler case, proved to be central actants in the sphere of corporate brands. By integrating non-human actants in investigations of corporate branding, we enlarge our view of brand-related action and are better able to incorporate and foresee powerful influencers in the wider brand assemblage. Non-human actants often act as translators who spread, automatize, multiply, or mediate human brand action without being ultimately manageable. The case of tweets or fake news spreading on the Net is just one of many examples of unforeseen consequences of non-human action.

*Spatiality and temporality of brand-related action:* Focusing on brand action nets also implies rethinking conventional categories such as space and time in relation to brands. Corporate brands as assemblages (e.g., Lury, 2009) or processual phenomena (Hemetsberger & Mühlbacher, 2009) have no starting point and no end and are no longer confined by corporate boundaries. The continuous flow of brand actions contributes to spanning the corporate brand action net across organizational boundaries, time, space, and spheres. Brand actions and connections between them accumulate and materialize in certain time and space frames, while decomposing and dematerializing in others. Continuous oscillations between composition and decomposition, materialization and dematerialization, stability (and related institutionalization) and change thus characterize corporate brands as processual phenomena.

*Continuity and change of brand-related action:* We conclude that action net theory provides a profound theoretical basis for further investigating into contemporary corporate brands as fluid, dynamic nets of stakeholder action in highly fragmented and mediated markets. In a world characterized by instability, change, and heterogeneity, brand action is both a core driving force, contributing to dynamic corporate brand identity development (von Wallpach et al., 2017), as well as an important stabilizing element for corporate brands. Defining typical brand actions and connecting core actants is important to the omni-temporal – establishing a specific transtemporal continuity between past, present, and future (Balmer & Burghausen, 2015) – and ubiquitous character of brands as action nets. As our cases demonstrate, corporate brands constitute themselves through brand actions and connections, and if brand action is not maintained, e.g., in the form of the international mountain summit, the brand ceases to exist. Understanding corporate brands as action nets and adopting related new perspectives on time and space prepares corporate brand management for navigating corporate brands in process.

# References

Asmussen, B., Harridge-March, S., Occhiocupo, N., & Farquhar, J. (2013). The multilayered nature of the internet-based democratization of brand management. *Journal of Business Research, 66*(9), 1473–1483. http://doi.org/10.1016/j.jbusres.2012.09.010

Balmer, J. M. T., & Burghausen, M. (2015). Introducing organizational heritage: Linking corporate heritage, organisational identity and organisational memory. *Journal of Brand Management, 22*, 385–411. http://doi.org/10.1057/bm.2015.25

Bechky, B. A. (2003). Sharing meaning across occupational communities: The transformation of understanding on a production floor. *Organization Science, 14*(3), 312–330. http://doi.org/10.1287/orsc.14.3.312.15162

Berthon, P., Pitt, L. F., & Campbell, C. (2009). Does brand meaning exist in similarity or singularity? *Journal of Business Research, 62*(3), 356–361. http://doi.org/10.1016/j.jbusres.2008.05.015

Briers, M., & Chua, W. F. (2001). The role of actor-networks and boundary objects in management accounting change: A field study of an implementation of activity-based costing. *Accounting Organizations and Society, 26*(3), 237–269. http://doi.org/10.1016/S0361-3682(00)00029-5

Christiansen, J. K., Varnes, C., Hollensen, B., & Blomberg, B. C. (2009). Co-constructing the brand and the product. *International Journal of Innovation Management, 13*(3), 319–348.

Csaba, F. F., & Bengtsson, A. (2006). Rethinking identity in brand management. In J. E. Schröder & M. Mörling (Eds.), *Brand culture* (pp. 118–135). London: Routledge.

Czarniawska, B. (1997). *Narrating the organization – Dramas of institutional identity*. Chicago, IL: The University of Chicago Press Ltd. http://doi.org/10.2307/2655183

Czarniawska, B. (2002). Remembering while forgetting: The role of automorphism in city management in Warsaw. *Public Administration Review, 62*(2), 163–173. http://doi.org/10.1111/0033-3352.00167

Czarniawska, B. (2004). On time, space, and action nets. *Organization, 11*(6), 773–791. http://doi.org/10.1177/1350508404047251

Czarniawska, B. (2007). Complex organizations still complex. *International Public Management Journal, 10*(2), 137–151. http://doi.org/10.1080/10967490701323662

Czarniawska, B. (2008). *A theory of organizing*. Cheltenham: Edward Elgar.

Czarniawska, B. (2009). Emerging institutions: Pyramids or anthills? *Organization Studies, 30*(4), 423–441. http://doi.org/10.1177/0170840609102282

Czarniawska, B., & Joerges, B. (1996). Travels of ideas. In B. Czarniawska & G. Sevón (Eds.), *Translating organizational change* (pp. 13–48). de Gruyter. http://doi.org/10.1016/S0956-5221(97)84646-5

Deleuze, G., Guattari, F., & Massumi, B. (1987). *A thousand plateaus: Capitalism and schizophrenia*. Minneapolis, MN: University of Minnesota Press.

Dietrich, A., Walter, L., & Czarniawska, B. (2011). Boundary stories: Constructing the validation centre in west Sweden. *Scandinavian Journal of Public Administration, 15*(1), 3–20.

Gergen, K. J. (1999). *An invitation to social construction*. London: Sage.

Gregory, A. (2007). Involving stakeholders in developing corporate brands: The communication dimension. *Journal of Marketing Management, 23*(1–2), 59–73. http://doi.org/10.1362/026725707X178558

Greimas, A. J., & Courtés, J. (1982). *Semiotics and language: An analytical dictionary*. Bloomington, IN: Indiana University Press.

Gyrd-Jones, R. I., & Kornum, N. (2013). Managing the co-created brand: Value and cultural complementarity in online and offline multi-stakeholder ecosystems. *Journal of Business Research, 66*(9), 1484–1493. http://doi.org/10.1016/j.jbusres.2012.02.045

Gyrd-Jones, R., Marrilees, B., & Miller, D. (2013). Revisiting the complexities of corporate branding: Issues, paradoxes, solutions. *Journal of Brand Management, 20*(7), 571–589. http://doi.org/10.1057/bm.2013.1

Harré, R. (1982). Theoretical preliminaries to the study of action. In M. von Cranach & R. Harré (Eds.), *The analysis of action: Recent theoretical and empirical advances* (pp. 5–33). Cambridge: Cambridge University Press.

Hatch, M. J., & Schultz, M. (2010). Toward a theory of brand co-creation with implications for brand governance. *Journal of Brand Management, 17*(8), 590–604. http://doi.org/10.1057/bm.2010.14

Hemetsberger, A. (2012). The democratization of markets through participative and collaborative practices. In C. Lynne, A. Ostendorf, M. Thoma, & W. G. Weber (Eds.), *Democratic competences and social practices in organizations* (pp. 17–33). Springer. http://doi.org/10.1007/978-3-531-19631-2

Hemetsberger, A., & Mühlbacher, H. (2009). Do brands have an identity? A critical reflection and extension of the brand identity construct. Proceedings of the European Marketing Academy Conference, Nantes.

Hillebrand, B., Driessen, P., & Koll, O. (2015). Stakeholder marketing: Theoretical foundations and consequences for marketing capabilities. *Journal of the Academy of Marketing Science, 43*(4), 411–428. http://doi.org/10.1007/s11747-015-0424-y

Iglesias, O., & Ind, N. (2020). Towards a theory of conscientious corporate brand co-creation: The next key challenge in brand management. *Journal of Brand Management, 27*, 710–720. http://doi.org/10.1057/s41262-020-00205-7

Iglesias, O., Ind, N., & Alfaro, M. (2013). The organic view of the brand: A brand value co-creation model. *Journal of Brand Management, 20*(8), 670–688. http://doi.org/10.1057/bm.2013.8

Iglesias, O., Landgraf, P., Ind, N., Markovic, S., & Koporcic, N. (2020a). Corporate brand identity co-creation in business-to-business contexts. *Industrial Marketing Management, 85*, 32–43. http://doi.org/10.1016/j.indmarman.2019.09.008

Keller, K. L. (1993). Conceptualizing, measuring and managing customer-based brand equity. *Journal of Marketing, 57*(1), 1–22. http://doi.org/10.1177/002224299305700101

Kjellberg, H., & Helgesson, C.-F. (2007). On the nature of markets and their practices. *Marketing Theory, 7*(2), 137–162. http://doi.org/10.1177/1470593107076862

Kozinets, R. V. (2002). The field behind the screen: Using netnography for marketing research in online communities. *Journal of Marketing Research, 39*(1), 61–72. http://doi.org/10.1509/jmkr.39.1.61.18935

Kozinets, R. V., Abrantes Ferreira, D., & Chimenti, P. (2021). How do platforms empower consumers? Insights from the affordances and constraints of Reclame Aqui. *Journal of Consumer Research*s. http://doi.org/10.1093/jcr/ucab014

Kozinets, R. V., Hemetsberger, A., & Schau, H. J. (2008). The wisdom of consumer crowds: Collective innovation in the age of networked marketing. *Journal of Macromarketing, 28*(4), 339–354. http://doi.org/10.1177/0276146708325382

Kristal, S., Baumgarth, C., & Henseler, J. (2020). Performative brand identity in industrial markets: The case of German prosthetics manufacturer Ottobock. *Journal of Business Research, 114*, 240–253. http://doi.org/10.1016/j.jbusres.2020.04.026

Lash, S., & Lury, C. (2007). *Global culture industry: The mediation of things.* Cambridge: Polity Press.

Latour, B. (1998). Artefaktens återkomst. Stockholm: Nerenius & Santerus. https://libris.kb.se/bib/7771504

Lindberg, K., & Czarniawska, B. (2006). Knotting the action net, or organizing between organizations. *Scandinavian Journal of Management, 22*(4), 292–306.

Löbler, H. (2011). Position and potential of service-dominant logic – Evaluated in an 'ism' frame for further development. *Marketing Theory, 11*(1), 51–73. http://doi.org/10.1177/1470593110393711

Lucarelli, A., & Hallin, A. (2015). Brand transformation: A performative approach to brand regeneration. *Journal of Marketing Management, 31*(1–2), 84–106. http://doi.org/10.1080/0267257X.2014.982688

Lundkvist, A., Liljander, V., Gummerus, J., & van Riel, A. (2013). The impact of storytelling on the consumer brand experience: The case of a firm-originated story. *Journal of Brand Management, 20*(4), 278–283. http://doi.org/10.1057/bm.2012.15

Lury C. (2009). Brands as assemblage; assembling cultures. *Journal of Cultural Economy*, 2(1–2), 67–82. https://doi.org/10.1080/17530350903064022

Lusch, R. F., & Webster Jr., F. E. (2011). A stakeholder-unifying, cocreation philosophy for marketing. *Journal of Macromarketing, 31*(2), 129–134. https://doi.org/10.1177/0276146710397369

Merz, M. A., He, Y., & Vargo, S. L. (2009). The evolving brand logic: A service dominant logic perspective. *Journal of the Academy of Marketing Science, 37*(3), 328–344. https://doi.org/10.1007/s11747-009-0143-3

Mica, A. (2013). From diffusion to translation and back. Disembedding – Re-embedding and re-invention in sociological studies of diffusion. *Polish Sociological Review, 181*(1), 3–19.

Mühlbacher, H., & Hemetsberger, A. (2008). Cosa diamine è un brand? Un tentativo diintegrazione e le sue consequenze per la ricerca e il management. *Micro & Macro Marketing, 2*, 271–292.

Muñiz Jr., A. M., & O'Guinn, T. C. (2001). Brand community. *Journal of Consumer Research, 27*(4), 412–432. https://doi.org/10.1086/319618

Onyas, W. I., & Ryan, A. (2014). Exploring the brand's world-as-assemblage: The brand as a market shaping device. *Journal of Marketing Management, 31*(1–2), 141–166. https://doi.org/10.1080/0267257X.2014.977333

Parmentier, M.-A., & Fischer, E. (2015). Things fall apart: The dynamics of brand audience dissipation. *Journal of Consumer Research, 41*(5), 1228–1251. https://doi.org/10.1086/678907

Payne, A. F., Storbacka K., Frow, P., & Knox, S. (2009). Co-creating brands: Diagnosing and designing the relationship experience. *Journal of Business Research, 62*(3), 379–389. https://doi.org/10.1016/j.jbusres.2008.05.013

Phillips, J. W. P. (2006). Agencement/assemblage. *Theory Culture & Society, 23*(2–3), 108–109. https://doi.org/10.1177/026327640602300219

Schau, H. J., Muñiz Jr., A. M., & Arnould, E. J. (2009). How brand community practices create value. *Journal of Marketing, 73*(5), 30–51. https://doi.org/10.1509/jmkg.73.5.30

Schleifer, R. (1987). *A.J. Greimas and the nature of meaning: Linguistics, semiotics and discourse theory*. London & Sydney: Croom Helm.

Schouten, J. W., & McAlexander, J. H. (1995). Subcultures of consumption: An ethnography of the new bikers. *Journal of Consumer Research*, *22*(1), 43–61. https://doi.org/10.1086/209434

Schütz, A. (1953). Common-sense and scientific interpretation of human action. *Philosophy and Phenomenological Research*, *14*(1), 1–38. https://doi.org/10.1007/978-94-010-2851-6_1

Serres, M. (1982). *Hermes: Literature, science, philosophy* (J. V. Harari & D. F. Bell, Eds.). Baltimore, MD: Johns Hopkins University Press.

Spiggle, S. (1994). Analysis and interpretation of qualitative data in consumer research. *Journal of Consumer Research*, *21*(3), 491–503. https://doi.org/10.1086/209413

Star, S. L., & Griesemer, J. R. (1989). Institutional ecology, 'translations' and boundary objects: Amateurs and professionals in Berkeley's museum of vertebrae zoology, 1907–1939. *Social Studies of Science*, *19*, 387–420. https://doi.org/10.1177/030631289019003001

Stevenson, A. (2010). *Oxford dictionary of English* (3rd ed.). Oxford: Oxford University Press. https://doi.org/10.1093/acref/9780199571123.001.0001

Vallaster, C., & von Wallpach, S. (2013). An online discursive inquiry into the social dynamics of multi-stakeholder brand meaning co-creation. *Journal of Business Research*, *66*(9), 1505–1515. https://doi.org/10.1016/j.jbusres.2012.09.012

von Wallpach, S., Hemetsberger, A., & Espersen, P. (2017). Performing identities: Processes of brand and stakeholder identity co-construction. *Journal of Business Research*, *70C*, 443–452. https://doi.org/10.1016/j.jbusres.2016.06.021

Wider, S., von Wallpach, S., & Mühlbacher, H. (2018). Brand management: Unveiling the delusion of control. *European Management Journal*, *36*(3), 301–305. https://doi.org/10.1016/Ej.emj.2018.03.006

# 8
# RECONCEPTUALIZING CORPORATE BRAND IDENTITY FROM A CO-CREATIONAL PERSPECTIVE

*Catherine da Silveira and Cláudia Simões*

## 1. Introduction

Until recently, the branding literature has defined brand identity (BI) as an *internal* and *enduring* concept, providing direction, meaning, and stability for the brand (Aaker, 1996; de Chernatony, 1999; Kapferer, 1997). From an *internal* perspective, BI was conventionally defined as an aspirational construct that emanates unilaterally from the organization – i.e., what the internal stakeholders aspire the brand to be. The *enduring* aspect captured the idea that if BI was fixed and constant over time, brands could act as anchors of meaning and as long-lasting references for customers (Aaker, 1996; Kapferer, 1997). A high degree of BI stability and permanency was therefore recommended as a precondition for brand continuity and credibility. This reasoning was particularly relevant for corporate brands that entail additional challenges when compared to product brands. The corporate BI expresses the uniqueness of the company and acts as a behavioural compass for the organization's stakeholders. Corporate BI is expected to provide direction not only to customers, but also to employees, to product brands, and ultimately to all the company's stakeholders (Balmer & Greyser, 2003; Balmer & Gray, 2003; Davies et al., 2010).

Yet, the market context from which initial BI definitions were established has changed. Of particular relevance are two intertwined transformations: brand shared ownership and co-creation. The technological and market evolution are converting corporate brands from single to shared ownership between the company's managers and other stakeholders. Under such context, the generation of brand meanings emerges across networks of stakeholders, alongside those who market the brand (Swaminathan et al., 2020; Vallaster & von Wallpach, 2013). In parallel, there is an increasing focus on co-creation, as 'the practice of developing systems, products, or services through collaboration with customers, managers, employees, and other stakeholders' (Ramaswamy, 2011, p. 195). As widely acknowledged, co-creation is engendering a paradigm shift in many domains of research. Branding is one of them. Co-creation is transforming the nature and the essence of the brand (Merz et al., 2018). Brands are shifting from a firm input concept to differentiate products and influence consumers (e.g., Gardner & Levy, 1955; Aaker, 1991) to a 'dynamic and social process' (Merz et al., 2009, p. 338) shaped collectively by the firm, consumers, and other stakeholders.

As a result, the previously mentioned features of initial BI definitions – *internal* and *enduring* – have evolved in the literature and in practice. Under the co-creation logic, research extends the notion of corporate brand internal stakeholders to customers and other active players (von Wallpach et al., 2017). Accordingly, corporate BI is conceptualized from a dynamic viewpoint as a socially constructed notion that develops through a process allowing organizations to continuously adjust and incorporate the co-creational context (Iglesias et al., 2020b). However, the transition from an internal and enduring perspective to a multi-stakeholder and dynamic approach is much more complex than it may appear at first sight.

A deeper analysis of the traditional perspective on BI suggests that BI has never been fully internal and enduring as has been claimed (da Silveira et al., 2013). While the branding literature was defining BI as a predominantly internal concept, most foundational academic and practitioner-oriented BI frameworks were already incorporating inputs from the market, aside from the (expected) management's aspirational dimensions. Similarly, in some early research, the enduring feature of BI had evolved into a more dynamic perspective, in which BI experiences continuous (partial) adjustments to environmental changes, while maintaining a sense of consistency over time (e.g., Collins & Porras, 1994). Moreover, the static/internal and the dynamic/multi-stakeholder perspectives of corporate BI appear as less antagonistic than conceptualized in recent approaches to co-creation. Early academic studies on identity already recommended combining stability and change (Hatch & Schultz, 2002; Gioia et al., 2000). In practice, corporate BI frameworks have been balancing adaptation and preservation.

This chapter constitutes a preliminary attempt to shed light into the understanding of the concept of corporate BI in the new market context. We add to the current debate amongst researchers and practitioners on the nature and features of corporate BI. First, we present the tensions in the initial notion of BI. Second, we explain how the debate has evolved into a cocreational perspective and examine how corporate BI became conceptualized as dynamic in nature, involving multiple stakeholders in its development. Finally, we develop the argument that the aspiration for an internal static/permanent identity (mainly suggested in early research), and the aspiration for a multistakeholder-dependent adaptive identity (predominantly developed in the co-creation context), are reconcilable. Considering that a strong corporate identity protects 'against [brand] reputational damage in times of troubles' (Greyser & Urde, 2019, p. 5), reconciling BI preservation and adaptation might be particularly relevant in the current context. The world is facing interlinked predicaments that reshape the implicit contract between brands and their stakeholders. As 'crises make reputations' (Interbrand, 2020, p. 23), corporate brands are expected to do more for people, and BI should lead the way.

## 2. Tensions in the conventional notion of corporate brand identity

### 2.1. Internal and enduring foundational definition

The conventional definitions of BI have established two main features: *internal* and *enduring*. Academic and practitioner-oriented literature in BI (e.g., Aaker, 1996; de Chernatony, 1999; Balmer & Gray, 2003; Kapferer, 2012) has traditionally emphasized the *internal* component. In the earlier studies, corporate BI refers to an organization's unique characteristics that are rooted in the internal member perceptions of the organization (van Riel & Balmer, 1997) and as the tool representing the substance that the organization aspires to develop for the corporate brand. BI is conventionally defined as an aspirational construct that emanates unilaterally from the managers and staff, rather than being externally determined. From this perspective, BI has been interpreted as a form of managers' and employees' group identity, expressed by a set of shared values that determine the substance of the brand (Burmann et al., 2009). Underlying this conventional internal orientation is the belief that if the organization allows consumers and other stakeholders to define the brand, it may lose its identity. Aaker, for example, challenges the external orientation, because it would 'let the customer dictate what you [the brand] are' (1991, p. 70).

## 2.2. Discrepancy between definitions and frameworks

### 2.2.1 Dual orientation – internal and external – of the foundational frameworks

A particularity of the BI domain is the discrepancy between conventional definitions and frameworks regarding the *internal* (vs. external) aspect of BI. Since the foundation of the BI concept and despite the internal orientation of conventional definitions, an external market-determined expression of BI has been present in the branding literature and in practice through influential frameworks that incorporate managers' inputs. Table 8.1 illustrates the twofold basis – internal and external – of the academic BI frameworks. For example, Kapferer's prominent framework (1986) simultaneously incorporates managers' and consumers' inputs. In fact, the *self-image* facet of Kapferer's *Brand Identity Prism* framework is defined as the target's own internal mirror, which

*Table 8.1* Internal vs. external components of brand identity frameworks in the branding literature

| BI frameworks usual components | Kapferer (1986) | Aaker (1996) | Upshaw (1995) | de Chernatony (1999) |
|---|---|---|---|---|
| *Managers' inputs (internal components)* | | | | |
| Vision | | | | √ |
| Physical interpretation of the brand | √ | √ (e.g., brand-as- product perspective, visual imagery, functional benefits) | √ (i.e., brand elements) | |
| Relationship | √ | √ (i.e., brand- customer relationships) | √ (i.e., how the brand relates to current and future consumers) | √ (i.e., staff to staff; staff to customers; staff to other stakeholders) |
| Personality | √ | √ | √ | √ |
| Brand culture | √ | √ (e.g., brand heritage) | | √ |
| Organization | | √ | | |
| Positioning | | | | √ |
| Reflection | √ | | | |
| *Consumers' inputs (external components)* | | | | |
| Consumers' self-image | √ | √ (e.g., self-expressive benefits) | | √ (e.g., 'internal self-images of the brand's stakeholders', de Chernatony, 1999, p. 169) |
| 'Power positioning' (Upshaw, 1995, p. 39) | | | √ (i.e., how consumers position the brand, based on their own perceptions of the brand) | |

*Source:* Authors, based on Kapferer (1986), Upshaw (1995), Aaker (1996) and de Chernatony (1999)

the author describes as the inner relationship that consumers develop with themselves through consuming, purchasing, or using the brand (Kapferer, 1986). Aaker's (1996) *Brand Identity System* framework provides a value proposition that includes self-expressive benefits – the expression of the consumers' self-identity, aside from internally determined functional benefits, and internally/externally combined emotional benefits. Aaker's (1996) BI framework is such an accurate illustration of interconnected internal and external influences that it has been described as 'predating the emergence of the term co-creation' (Ind et al., 2013, p. 8).

Practitioners' early frameworks also incorporate market-based inputs in addition to the expected management-based contributions. Table 8.2 examines the components of five practitioner foundational frameworks: Unilever, Nestlé, Diageo, BP, and Heineken.

The analysis confirms the combination of the internal vision – what managers aspire the brand to be – and the external vision – what the brand is, according to the market – of the frameworks. For example, the Unilever 'Brand Key' framework (provided by Unilever in 2013) incorporates the consumer-based component 'competitive environment,' together with the combined – management and consumer – component 'consumer insight' and several internally determined dimensions.

### 2.2.2 'Constant yet flexible' conventional brand identity frameworks

Both practitioner and academic BI frameworks, and their discrepancy with the initial BI definitions, reflect the tensions in the conventional *internal* grounding of BI. Comparable tensions can be found in the *enduring* original feature of BI. Conventional definitions of BI stress the importance of a high degree of stability and permanency of BI as a precondition for the brand continuity and credibility (e.g., Aaker, 1996; Kapferer, 1997). While acknowledging that BI may change in certain circumstances, brands have traditionally been recommended to maintain a constant identity over time to serve as anchor of meanings to the organization's stakeholders. This has been particularly emphasized for corporate BI, which is expected to provide direction not only to customers, but also to employees, to product brands, and to all company stakeholders (Bick et al., 2003; Hatch & Shultz, 2003; Balmer & Greyser, 2003; Simões et al., 2015).

*Table 8.2* Examples of foundational practitioner frameworks to define brand identity

| Framework/Source | Management-based components* | Consumer-based components* | Combined – management and consumer – components* |
|---|---|---|---|
| **Nestlé Brand Essence** Provided by Nestlé in 2009** | • Core brand promise<br>• Brand personality<br>• Type of consumers | • Brand benefit<br>• Products: 'How I would describe the products' (as a consumer) | |
| **Diageo Brand Essence Wheel** Provided by Diageo in 2010** | • Core brand promise<br>• Facts and symbols | • Brand personality<br>• **Rational aspects:** 'What the product does for me,' 'How I would describe the product'<br>• **Emotional aspects**: 'How the brand makes me feel,' 'How the brand makes me look' | |

*(Continued)*

Table 8.2 (Continued)

| Framework/Source | Management-based components* | Consumer-based components* | Combined – management and consumer – components* |
|---|---|---|---|
| **Unilever Brand Key** Provided by Unilever in 2013** | • Root strengths<br>• Target<br>• Benefits (i.e., key consumer benefits that drive the purchase)<br>• Brand values and personality<br>• Reasons to believe<br>• 'Discriminator'<br>• Essence (core brand promises) | • Competitive environment 'as seen by the consumer' | • Consumer insight (i.e., the consumer need 'that opens the door to an opportunity for the brand') |
| **BP** (British Petroleum) **Brand Bridge** Provided by BP in 2013** | • Market space<br>• Core target (including insight)<br>• Proposition (i.e., statement of brand offer including functional and emotional benefits)<br>• Reasons to believe<br>• Brand personality<br>• 'Summary positioning' | • Key differentiator 'in eyes of target' | • Essence (core meaning of the brand) |
| **Heineken®** **Brand Architecture framework** Provided by Heineken in 2013** | • Brand promise<br>• Brand essence<br>• Brand values<br>• Brand personality<br>• Emotional benefits<br>• Functional benefits<br>• Source of authority<br>• Key visual features | • Brand proposition<br>• Consumer insight<br>• Emotional needs<br>• Functional needs<br>• Reference occasion<br>• Reference consumer<br>• Mind set | |

Source: Authors

Notes:
The criteria used to include a framework in the table are: (1) effective use of the framework by brand managers as a tool to develop and/or manage their corporate brand; and (2) corporate brands with high awareness in the market.
Components defined as 'core' by framework's providers are underlined.
*The decision about whether a component in the framework is internal, external, or a combination of both, was taken on the basis of discussions with the framework's adopters (i.e., firm brand managers and staff) and information provided by the company.
**Information provided by the company is publicly unavailable.

Handelman has exemplified the expected leading role of the corporate BI by stating that 'as companies increasingly turn to corporate branding to present their corporate personas and values, it is corporate brands in particular that serve as beacons for the voices and actions of societal constituents who challenge corporate marketers' identity-building efforts' (2006, p. 107).

In practice, two approaches to enduring corporate BI have co-existed: (1) static, steady, and constant as time goes by, so that BI acts as a long-lasting reference for stakeholders (cf. Harley Davidson); and (2) 'constant yet flexible' (Interbrand, 2007), in which BI experiences continuous adjustments to environmental changes, while maintaining consistency over time (*cf.* Unilever, L'Oréal). The latter perspective has been supported by influential BI frameworks and practitioner-oriented literature that proposes *enduring* as a notion that combines stability with ongoing adaptations to the market context (e.g., Collins & Porras, 1994). For example, the 'constant yet flexible' feature of Aaker's BI framework is apparent, as his *Brand Identity System* is organized according to the 'enduring patterns of meaning' (1996, p. 85) of the identity elements. Aaker differentiates 'the core identity,' which contains the 'associations that are most likely to remain constant as the brand travels to new markets and products' (1996, p. 86), and 'the extended identity,' which contains elements subject to change. In essence, the widely accepted internal and fixed features of the initial approaches to BI have been challenged since the foundation of the BI concept. The original perspective of BI, exclusively founded on managers' and employers' inputs, is rather fragile. BI has never been fully internally determined and static, as typically portrayed.

## 3. Corporate brand identity from a co-creational perspective

### 3.1. New market context

#### 3.1.1 Hyper-connected digital environment

The branding domain is engaged in a profound adjustment process. The new hyper-connected market context is transforming brands from single to shared ownership (Swaminathan et al., 2020; Vallaster & von Wallpach, 2013). The expansion of networks and online platforms enables consumers and other brand stakeholders (e.g., digital influencers) to collectively produce brand meanings alongside from the internal entities that market the brand (e.g., managers, employees). Firms' members are not the only stakeholders who convey branded contents and shape brand meanings. Through social networks, customers and other key stakeholders can promote, reshape, or contest contents produced by the brand-internal stakeholders, especially as customers tend to give more attention to brand meanings produced by their peers than to branded messages generated by the brand managers (Fournier & Avery, 2011). The brand meaning construction process has moved beyond the full control of the firm, turning 'the idea of managerial control an illusion' (Iglesias & Ind, 2020, p. 711).

#### 3.1.2 Stakeholder-focus brand era

Firms are moving from an organization-centric approach of branding to one that is participative (Ind et al., 2013). The current brand era is founded on a stakeholder-centric approach. Brands become a form of 'collaborative, value co-creation activity of firms and all of their stakeholders' (Merz et al., 2009, p. 329). The focus is on the stakeholders who 'form network, rather than only dyadic, relationships with brands' (Merz et al., 2009, p. 337). Consequently, the idea of corporate brand internal stakeholder extends to multiple interrelated market actors (Iglesias et al., 2013; von Wallpach et al., 2017). This new focus shifts the branding domain into a process that has a stakeholder orientation at its heart.

### 3.2. New multi-stakeholder and dynamic corporate brand identity definition

The increasingly connected and participative market context substantiates the growing motivation for a co-creation approach, both in companies and among scholars. Although the boundaries of the co-creation definition are not fully stabilized, some common grounds can be found within the multiplicity of approaches. Corporate BI is conceptualized through a dynamic viewpoint as a socially constructed concept that develops as an organizational work in progress (Iglesias et al., 2020b). Under a co-creation perspective, corporate BI departs from the internally determined and stable primary delineation into a *multi-stakeholder* and *on-going/dynamic* definition.

### 3.2.1 Multi-stakeholder corporate brand identity

Brands increasingly emerge from collaborative creation activities of firms and their stakeholders. Brand co-creation is conceptualized as a process occurring through network relationships and social interactions among the ecosystem of all brand stakeholders (Merz et al., 2018). This multi-stakeholder approach to brand co-creation is particularly relevant for corporate brands that engage and develop with multiple interrelated social constituents (e.g., product brand managers, consumers, corporate managers, employees, distributors, influencers, investors, detractors), whose voice matters in the construction of the corporate brand (Handelman, 2006; Gregory, 2007; Cornelissen et al., 2012).

The literature traditionally considers two types of stakeholders: the internal stakeholders, including the corporate brand owners and managers, and the external stakeholders, including the consumers. The co-creation paradigm and the hyper-connected digital environment challenge this demarcation as well as the nature of stakeholders' engagement in corporate BI co-creation.

From a co-creational perspective, corporate BI emerges as constructed over time through performative co-constructions involving multiple stakeholders. Internal and external stakeholders intertwine in developing and managing the corporate BI (Hatch & Schultz, 2003; Handelman, 2006; Cornelissen et al., 2012). Both become endogenous to the co-creation process. Indeed, influential research in brand co-creation expands the traditional stakeholder scope by conceptualizing external stakeholders and particularly the customers as endogenous to the process of brand management (Merz et al., 2009; Ranjan & Read, 2016; Ind et al., 2013), reflecting a foundational co-creation principle (Vargo & Lusch, 2008). Under such lenses, the principle that co-creation of identity is an action voluntarily performed (rather than a received/given feature) by participative stakeholders gains traction (da Silveira et al., 2013; von Wallpach et al., 2017 Iglesias et al., 2020b). Stakeholders engage in BI co-creation performances with a 'self-other relationality' (von Wallpach et al., 2017, p. 445) purpose (i.e., to enact their self-identity in relation to other performers).

Ramaswamy and Ozcan (2016, 2018) suggest a multi-sided and experiential view of the stakeholder, shedding light on the understanding of the engaged stakeholder in the age of digitalized interactions. The authors propose two 'sides' of stakeholders within the co-creation spectrum. On the one side, there are the 'organizing' stakeholders (Ramaswamy & Ozcan, 2016, p. 95), who enable and support physical or digital platforms of brand co-engagement. On the other side are the 'experiencers' who develop 'conscious agencial experiences' by engaging in those platforms (Ramaswamy & Ozcan, 2016, p. 94). Within such perspective, stakeholders are experiential co-creators, whether managers, customers, employees, suppliers, partners, or shareholders. The nature of the stakeholder engagement in corporate BI co-creation becomes dependent on the experience. Consumers' actions range from 'just posting comments and evaluations at one end of a continuum to actually determining the nature and direction of a brand at the other end,' while companies 'may merely provide a platform at one end of the continuum to also actively participating in their platform at the other end' (Ramaswamy & Ozcan, 2016, p. 96). This 'agency' approach to the stakeholder as an individual who chooses what actions to take adds to the previous understandings of the notion of stakeholder as an actor or as an active participant in brand-related narratives (Vallaster & van Wallpach, 2013).

### 3.2.2 Dynamic corporate brand identity

Within the emerging co-creation paradigm, corporate BI is conceptualized as an inherently dynamic process that evolves over time. Corporate BI evolves as multiple brand stakeholders support, reshape or contest branded contents according to their self-identity and self-representation aspirations. BI development is reciprocally triggered by those aspirations. In their study on the co-construction of LEGO's BI, von Wallpach et al. (2017) demonstrate the bi-directionality of the corporate BI dimensions' adjustments and the stakeholders' self-identity enactment performances. An example of the stakeholder identity influence on the BI is the evolution of the LEGO 'construction and creativity' BI dimension to a more adult orientation triggered by the hedonic aspirations of the adult fans playing with LEGO. Reciprocally, an example of the BI impact on the stakeholder identity is the strengthening of the stakeholders' creative self-representation prompted by the 'creativity' dimension of LEGO's BI. By playing with LEGO and showcasing their achievements to their peers, adult LEGO players reinforce the creative dimension of their identity towards others. Corporate BI is constantly (re)produced and adapted according to the stakeholders' self-identity aspirations. Reciprocally, stakeholders draw on corporate BI to develop their self-identity, and, in doing so, arise as active co-creators of BI. As a result, corporate BI is 'in constant flux' (Iglesias et al., 2020b, p. 33).

Moreover, corporate BI evolves, prompted by the stakeholders' pressure. Nestlé is a good example of such corporate BI evolution process: Nestlé is known for its long-term approach to market and its steady corporate BI orientation. However, confronted with intense pressure from consumers and other stakeholders, Nestlé shifted its BI in 2000, from a 'processed food and beverages' position to the aspiration of becoming 'the leading nutrition, health and wellness company in the world' (Henderson & Johnson, 2012). Accordingly, in 2005, the company embraced an approach termed 'Creating Shared Value,' to improve nutrition, water conservation, and rural development (Porter et al., 2017). Nestlé communicated its (internally) redefined identity, as exemplified by Nestlé CEO's quote: 'The vision of Nestlé is to be the leading nutrition, health and wellness company in the world. When you have a good vision, you don't change it dramatically each year' (Paul Bulcke – Nestlé CEO from 2008 to 2016 – cited by Henderson & Johnson, 2012, p. 1). Despite large investments in R&D to develop new products and reformulate existing ones meeting nutritional recommendations and improving health benefits, Nestlé struggled to legitimize its new corporate BI. Confronted with public awareness on supply chain issues and contradictions inherent in its confectionary and prepared food product brands, Nestlé faced stakeholders' adverse reactions. Consumers and NGOs pressured the company to intensify its commitments to the 'Creating Shared Value' engagements and to take actions to make the new BI more tangible. Simultaneously, activist investors put pressure for higher share performance (*cf.* Porter et al., 2017). Although driven by different motivations, investors, consumers, and NGOs were converging on urging Nestlé to reshape its product brand portfolio towards a greater focus on its BI key dimensions – nutrition, health, and wellness. As a result, Nestlé reconsidered its internal corporate BI orientation and shifted to a more dynamic and participative approach to corporate BI management. Some corporate BI dimensions were revised to incorporate inputs from the various stakeholders. Relevant actions were undertaken, such as the company's disinvestment from its USA confectionary business.

From a co-creational perspective, corporate BI is multi-stakeholder determined and in constant flux. However, the shift from internal and enduring to multi-stakeholder and dynamic is much more complex than appears at first sight. The hyperconnected market context and the brand-shared ownership paradigm are gaining strength. But firms are still searching for ways to handle the resulting corporate BI transformations. In the next section, we explore a possible integration of the internal and static perspective of corporate BI with the multi-stakeholder adaptive approach.

## 4. Reconciling the multi-stakeholder/dynamic and internal/static aspirations for corporate brand identity

### 4.1. *Dynamic* or *static?* Or *dynamic* and *static?*

Should one look at corporate BI as 'dynamic *or* static' or as 'dynamic *and* static'? Should identity be fixed over time to serve as a stable reference or be adaptive in order to respond to environmental transformations and stakeholders' self-identity changing aspirations? These questions have been extensively studied in different fields of research. The organizational studies domain provides relevant insights for this chapter. The organizational studies field first looked at organizational identity from a static delineation to provide stakeholders with a stable reference of their organization. It then evolved into the dynamic viewpoint of identity as a socially constructed concept that develops as an organizational work-in-progress to allow organizations to adapt to their changing environment.

#### 4.1.1 Initial perspectives

Early seminal works (e.g., Albert & Whetten, 1985) considered organizational identity as immutable. Organizational identity should persist and be preserved over time to serve as a stable reference to the organization's stakeholders. An important concern of this initial research was to develop theory to help organizations adapt to their changing environment while maintaining their organizational identity constant. Albert and Whetten (1985, p. 97) defended that the more stable the identity of an organization, the better, 'since change may involve loss.' Dutton and Dukerich (1991) laid foundations for a more flexible approach to organizational identity's evolution in their research based on how the Port Authority of New York and New Jersey' stakeholders dealt with the homelessness matter. Internal stakeholders' early response to the issue (i.e., denial, contain damage, move homeless out – *cf.* Dutton & Dukerich, 1991, p. 521, Figure 1) was triggered by the objective of preserving the organization's identity, characterized as 'professional . . . with a unique technical expertise . . . altruistic . . . provider of superior quality . . . first class institution . . . highly committed to the welfare of the region' (pp. 526–527). When it became clear that the identity was constraining the actions taken on the issue, and consequently damaging the organization's image, internal stakeholders sought cooperation with external stakeholders (e.g., social services) to collectively undertake opposing actions (e.g., build shelters, educate employees about the special needs of homeless people). Those actions triggered the adjustment of the organizational identity, giving salience to certain identity features (e.g., altruistic) while down-playing others (e.g., technical expertise). Although Dutton and Dukerich (1991) advocated for identity preservation, they recognized that stakeholders' collective actions can 'transform the organization's identity (and image) through individual's sense making efforts' and that 'the process of adaptation [is] continuous' (p. 543). Their work opened up a way to conciliate identity preservation and change by gradually modifying the organization's identity as a result of 'making certain features more or less salient' (Dutton & Dukerich, 1991, p. 520).

### 4.1.2 Adaptive instability perspectives

The initial viewpoints on identity preservation vs. change were later supplemented with the belief that a more dynamic identity may better capture the need for organizations to adapt to their changing environment than a static and enduring identity (Gioia et al., 2000). According to this more dynamic perspective, stability and change can co-exist through 'adaptive instability,' which means that organizations can undergo changes while maintaining a sense of continuity of their identity. Furthermore, the changeable aspect of identity is necessary in order to adapt to the demands of a market that is undergoing continuous transformations. Under this perspective, to preserve the character of the organization over time, identity paradoxically must change. Without such adaptation process, 'an organization would find itself trapped with an inevitably stagnant identity, unprepared to address demands that might have survival implications' (Gioia et al., 2000, p. 74). This standpoint reconciles identity preservation and change.

Drawing on Gioia et al.'s (2000) perspective, academic and practical studies on identity in different streams of research recommend combining stability and change (e.g., Hatch & Schultz, 2004; de Chernatony et al., 2004; Interbrand, 2007). The model of corporate BI construction and management balancing preservation and adjustments arises as the most appropriate approach (Greyser & Urde, 2019). However, the process proposed by the balanced approach advocates – keeping the core aspects of the identity constant while adjusting the peripheral ones – might not be appropriate under the co-creation perspective. Consider the Nestlé case. Nestlé shifted its corporate brand mission in 2000 from a processed food and beverages position to the stance of the leading nutrition, health, and wellness company in the world. By doing so, Nestlé actually altered a key BI element – its brand mission and vision – that is commonly assumed as a core dimension of the corporate BI. This example suggests that corporate BI might not evolve through its peripheral dimensions in a context of co-creation.

### 4.1.3 Reconciling dynamic and static aspirations

The corporate BI core dimensions are crucial because they ground and help define the remaining BI dimensions. This does not imply that BI core dimensions should be the most lasting elements of the BI. Gioia et al.'s (2000) early statement that 'even the core can shift' (p. 76) corroborates this idea. We propose a process that mirrors the organizational identity configuration projected by Dutton and Dukerich (1991). The process balances adaptation and preservation. It suggests a scheme of corporate BI development where identity dimensions become more or less salient over time, gaining or losing strength as stakeholders enact their self-identity and as the market environment evolves. Key elements gain relevance (e.g., nutrition in the Nestlé corporate BI) while obsolete elements progressively vanish (e.g., processed/industrial food in the Nestlé corporate BI).

Recent research on the role of history in corporate brand strategy supports our configuration. The study analyses how the corporate brand Adidas rejected part of its history at a certain point in time, then reused it later to refocus its corporate strategy (Iglesias et al., 2020a). Two external consultants were asked by the CEO to instigate a new corporate brand strategy when the brand was facing serious financial issues in 1989. Together with other stakeholders, they reconstructed the founder's original BI to build a renewed BI inspired by the original brand athletic spirit and the 1960's and 1970's core legendary products such as the Stan Smith model. The corporate BI was recreated out of the brand's history, intersecting and balancing past and future. The Adidas case is an example of our suggested BI evolution scheme, where identity dimensions become more or less salient over time. As reflected in the case, identity dimensions lose and gain strength according to the context and to the stakeholders' self-identity enactments and focus.

In a similar vein, Starbucks key corporate BI dimensions were reactivated in 2008, when Howard Schultz, CEO until 2000, returned from his eight-year retirement to help the company fight the 2008/2009 financial crisis and address the weakening profitability of the business model. After visiting many stores and interacting with stakeholders (e.g., customers, partners, baristas), Schultz launched a transformation agenda to bring the brand back to its initial values and unique corporate culture. Original brand identity attributes such as 'emotional attachment with customers,' '[make] each store the heart of a local neighbourhood' or 'baristas' inspired' had lost strength over the years – although not disappearing – to make room for features such as 'fast customer service' or 'leading the coffee sector' (Schultz & Gordon, 2012). The transformation agenda provided renewed salience to initial brand values that had made Starbucks special, while later-introduced features were revised. For example, 'leading the coffee sector' was not abandoned but reinterpreted as 'leading the coffeehouse customer experience.' This dimension is still gaining strength in Starbucks' current corporate BI. The Starbucks case exemplifies how BI components develop over time, becoming more or less salient according to the stakeholders' indirect or direct performances and aspirations. By stretching its identity to a rapidly expanding coffeehouse chain offering a fast service to more clients, Starbucks disenchanted its customers and partners (e.g., baristas) who distanced themselves from the brand. Their disengagement triggered the corporate BI (re)transformation.

Corporate heritage brands are also acknowledged as following a 'turbulent' BI journey (Cooper et al., 2015, p. 449). The corporate heritage brands Burberry and Tiffany are both described as having experienced BI core dimensions' decline, followed by the same dimensions' revival (Cooper et al., 2015). The case of Burberry is particularly instructive. Burberry started in 1856 and prospered thanks to a strong BI, underpinned by values of excellent quality and classic British luxury. Quality was primarily expressed in the functionality and durability of the patented trench coat and outwear gabardines, while classic British luxury was reflected in the iconic check pattern introduced in the 1920s. The brand faced a sharp decline in the 1990s, primarily triggered by its gradual disconnection from its BI core values. In particular, the management decided in 1995 to disinvest in the rainwear and outwear division, leaving aside the trench coat, one of the most iconic expressions of Burberry's original BI. When the Design Director Christopher Bailey was appointed Creative Director in 2004, the biggest concern was the brand dilution, partially caused by the over-licensing of the Burberry's check pattern for all sorts of products including bikinis and household appliances. The brand dilution issue was also embedded in the progressive (re)interpretation of the check pattern as a fashion statement by multiple stakeholders. Initially popular among the British elite, the Burberry's check pattern had become a status symbol for the young working class 'chavs' and football soccer fans (Gallagher, 2017). Two of the first strategic moves decided by the team appointed to restore the brand success were: (1) to refocus on the legendary trench coat; and (2) to minimize the iconic check pattern in the BI and in the collections. Four years later, Bailey decided to team up with the streetwear designer Gosha Rubchinskiy on his spring/summer 2018 collection to create pieces that 'lean into the check's "chav" reputation' (Gallagher, 2017). This move merged references of Burberry's past working-class appeal with high fashion and rehabilitated the check pattern as a strong BI dimension. The check pattern was reinterpreted as luxury street fashion. The trench coat and the check pattern, respectively core expressions of the Burberry iconic quality, and of its classic British luxury heritage, lost and gained salience over the BI's turbulent journey. The check pattern successively expanded, vanished, and re-developed according to multiple stakeholders' (e.g., managers, designers, cultural agents, upper class customers, young working class 'chavs,' football soccer fans) self-representation performances.

The Nestlé, Adidas, Starbucks, and Burberry cases suggest that BI components – assumed as core elements – evolve over time, contrasting with the generalized view that BI mainly evolves through its peripheral dimensions. The process commonly proposed for describing BI components' evolution – the BI peripheral components adjust over time while the core aspects of the identity remain constant – does not fully capture the brand dynamics and contexts of co-creation.

### 4.1.4 Incorporating new dimensions into the corporate brand identity

In the co-creational paradigm, while corporate BI evolves through (de-)emphasizing selected existing dimensions, it also develops by incorporating new elements, driven by the brand's stakeholders' performances and aspirations. Co-creation is about giving and receiving (Cova & Dalli, 2009). Stakeholders contribute to the corporate BI construction. In this sense, brands capture value from stakeholders. In turn, corporate brands create value for their diverse stakeholders (Iglesias & Ind, 2020). Value creation spans from stock price maximization (for shareholders) to making a positive impact on the planet and people (being consumers and other stakeholders). As such, corporate brands need to address broader issues including social responsibility and sustainability (Swaminathan et al., 2020) that go beyond conventional firm performance requirements (e.g., profit and growth). Organizations are increasingly required to fulfil a wider mission towards society. They are expected to incorporate NGOs' and consumers' aspirations for a better world into their corporate BI. In parallel, investors call upon increasing value for shareholders. Thus, in order to create value for the brand's multiple stakeholders, corporate BI needs to incorporate new dimensions. At this stage, and although externally influenced, the adjusted BI is still an internally shaped aspiration. To become *true to self*, the corporate BI new dimensions need to be legitimized together with the organization's stakeholders. Otherwise, the internally defined incremental alterations to BI are seen as a 'supplement' to BI (Golob & Podnar, 2019, p. 4) rather than embedded in the BI. This process of *becoming true to self* is described as 'internalizing – [a performance] concerned with bringing the corporate BI to life, turning it into actual behaviours aligned with the corporate BI, and embedding it into the corporate brand's routines and actions' (Iglesias et al., 2020b, p. 38). If the (new) corporate BI resonates with the brand's stakeholders, they legitimate and 'endorse' it (Iglesias et al., 2020b, p. 38). Otherwise, brand stakeholders 'contest' and challenge the BI. According to Iglesias et al. (2020b), contesting can occur when there is a gap between BI and brand image. As the Nestlé case illustrates, contesting also emerges when there is an inconsistency between the internally shaped new BI and the brand's actions developed to bring the BI to life. If actions do not match the BI, BI is neither legitimized nor internalized. The process of legitimation lead to new BI dimension adjustments. This move might encompass emphasizing selected BI dimensions while downplaying others, and/or creating new dimensions, as depicted in the Unilever case that we present next.

The Unilever CEO, Alan Jope, recently disclosed the new Unilever corporate BI – 'Unilever Compass' (Unilever, 2021a). The Unilever Compass is presented as a multi-stakeholder model involving 'Our People, Consumers, Customers [i.e., retailers], Suppliers and Business Partners, Society, Planet, Shareholders' (Unilever, 2021a). The underlying vision is 'to be the global leader in sustainable business. We will demonstrate how our purpose-led, future-fit business model drives superior performance, consistently delivering financial results in the top third of our industry' (Unilever, 2021a). An analysis of the proposed corporate BI suggests that the Unilever corporate BI evolution dynamics supports our proposed BI evolution process: some existing dimensions, labelled '[d]imensions to do more' (Unilever, 2021a) become salient (e.g., heathy nutrition, diversity, and inclusion) while other dimensions lose strength (e.g., equality). New dimensions, such as 'equity,' are introduced.

Analysing the process that led Unilever to downplay the notion of 'equality' and incorporate the new 'equity' dimension in the corporate BI brings insights into our argument. First, following the worldwide 'Black Lives Matter' movement, consumers and society confronted the beauty and personal care companies with the definition of beauty that they were projecting. Similar to other firms (e.g., L'Oréal), Unilever declared its opposition to racism and banned the words *fair/fairness*, *white/whitening*, and *light/lightening* from product packaging and advertisings (Taylor, 2021). The underlying rationale was the adjustment of the company's BI towards more diversity and inclusion. Such actions were controversial among some stakeholders who argued that [words] adjustments were 'scratching the surface on what needs to be done more broadly' (Taylor, 2021). In order to further legitimate the adjusted BI, Unilever conducted a global market research to investigate people's experiences with, and expectations towards, the beauty industry, and to uncover positive actions demanded to foster a more globally inclusive beauty culture (Unilever, 2021b). The corporate BI was then re-adjusted, according to consumers' and society's expectations. The objective was to '[tackle] harmful norms and stereotypes and [shape] a broader, far more inclusive definition of beauty' (Sunny Jain, President Beauty & Personal Care Division, Unilever, 2021b). The 'equality' dimension was restrained as, according to Unilever, equality calls for a 'normal' behaviour, which might lead to the idea of a world where everyone would have the same beauty, thus excluding many, while the 'diversity and inclusion' dimensions were reinforced, and 'equity' was raised. Together with its stakeholders, Unilever is now taking actions to bring the new BI to life (e.g., remove the word *normal* from products and advertisings).

In the co-creation perspective, corporate BI needs to evolve to keep creating and delivering value for multiple stakeholders and for the brand. This evolution combines emphasizing existing dimensions, downplaying others, and incorporating new ones to address stakeholders' aspirations and needs. In order to embed both the newly reinforced as well as the entirely new dimensions into the BI, stakeholders engage in a co-creational process of legitimization. Such process entails stakeholders' engagement in actions that might involve new BI changes. In this sense, we concur with Iglesias et al.'s (2020b) view that corporate BI construction is a value creation process that 'unfolds over time through a series of interactions that take place between multiple internal and external stakeholders' (p. 33). Those interactions entail different but interrelated stakeholder performances, whose objective is to reach an 'evolved shared understanding of the corporate brand' (Iglesias & Ind, 2020, p. 711).

## 4.2. Multi-stakeholder or *internal orientation*? Or multi-stakeholder and *internal orientation*?

### 4.2.1 Role of the managers in balancing stability and change: guardians or conductors?

Recent research suggests that the dual orientation of corporate BI – enduring and dynamic – is driven by the tension between the internal stakeholders, who protect the corporate brand's core values and nurture a stable BI, and the external stakeholders who generate an evolving BI by continually reperforming brand meanings (Iglesias et al., 2020b). Other studies encourage managers to maximize corporate BI stability (e.g., Greyser & Urde, 2019). Such insights raise the role of the managers in balancing stability and change. Are managers the 'guardians' (Michel, 2017, p. 454) of the corporate BI? Some managers might manage BI in a rather static way because they intuitively feel that this approach will preserve both their and the brand's credibility. In this case, their steady protection of the brand's expressions operates against corporate BI drastic transformations and 'lead[s] to more progressive and subtle changes in corporate BI'

(Iglesias et al., 2020b, p. 40). Or are managers the 'conductors' (Michel, 2017, p. 454) of the corporate BI? In this case, managers co-produce and harmonize brand meanings enacted by brand stakeholders, enabling a more fluid BI.

This discussion raises an important question regarding how management leadership affects the corporate BI construction process. The type of management leadership undeniably affects the internal vs. multi-stakeholder orientation of the corporate BI. Literature on brand co-creation demonstrates that the potential of co-creation is more soundly realized when managers adopt a 'conductor' leadership behaviour rather than a 'guardian' behaviour (Ind et al., 2017). 'Conductors' embrace an open and participatory approach to management. They envision brand stakeholders as partners with whom they can build a trusting and equitable relationship and assume customers as 'living the brand' in a way that is similar to them (Ind et al., 2013, p. 23). Trust (Ind et al., 2013) and humility (von Wallpach et al., 2017) are required to develop the 'conductor' approach. Managers generate trust not only by being receptive but also by sharing knowledge in a transparent way. Such approach to brand management – humble, honest, and transparent – 'converts co-creation into a strategic resource' (Ind et al., 2017, p. 318), which in turn promotes a multi-stakeholder corporate BI management. Brand managers' performativity impacts the corporate BI orientation. By adopting a co-creational approach to brand management, managers provide customers, employees, and all other company stakeholders with opportunities to enact their self-identity construction projects and activities and consequently contribute to the corporate BI they aspire to. Multi-stakeholder BI co-creation seems only possible if managers adopt a 'conductor' leadership behaviour. The internal and multi-stakeholder orientations are not antagonistic. They are complementary as the latter engenders the former. The managers' role becomes more prominent in co-creating corporate BI, not necessarily because managers contribute more to the process but because their leadership behaviour triggers stakeholders' performativity.

### 4.2.2 All stakeholders or some stakeholders?

Literature in brand co-creation tends to use the term *all brand stakeholders* (e.g., Merz et al., 2018). Yet, several studies highlight that although corporate BI is co-created by multi-stakeholder networks, there are disparities in stakeholder salience (Vallaster & von Wallpach, 2013; Michel, 2017). Co-creation is a voluntary performance in the sense that stakeholders take the initiative to participate. Participation in co-creation depends on the stakeholders' willingness and motivation (Cova & Dalli, 2009; Vallaster & von Wallpach, 2013). Hence, corporate BI co-creation is limited in essence to the stakeholders who wish to engage.

## 5. Implications and future research

This study debates from academic and practitioner perspectives the nature and profiling of corporate BI features in the new market context. We contrast the search for an internal static/permanent identity (mainly suggested in early research) and the aspiration for a multi-stakeholder and adaptive identity (predominantly developed in more recent research on co-creation). We propose that these perspectives are reconcilable, showing that BI preservation and adaptation might be particularly relevant in the current business context featuring hyper-connected and multi-stakeholder environments. The static/internal and the dynamic/multi-stakeholder perspectives of corporate BI are less antagonistic than conceptualized both in early and recent research.

In early research, our study demonstrates that, despite the internal orientation of foundational BI definitions, an external stakeholder-determined expression of BI has always been present in the branding literature and in practice through influential frameworks. Comparable tensions can be found in the enduring original feature of BI. Taking a closer look, corporate BI has never been fully internally determined and static, as originally portrayed. The simultaneously static and dynamic perspective of corporate BI is present in the market and in research since the earlier stages of the study and use of BI, although it was generally out of the scope of most research.

In recent research, corporate BI is conceptualized from a co-creational perspective as multi-stakeholder determined and in constant flux. However, literature on identity in different streams of research recommends combining stability and change (e.g., Hatch & Schultz, 2004; Greyser & Urde, 2019). Additionally, tensions between managers – who tend to resist to disruptive changes by protecting and maintaining the corporate BI core values, and other stakeholders – and experiential co-creators who generate brand meanings (Ramaswamy & Ozcan, 2016) call for a subtle balance between the enduring and the dynamic aspirations of corporate BI (Iglesias et al., 2020b).

This study corroborates the argument that the enduring and the dynamic aspects of BI can co-exist by bringing a corporate BI pattern that combines preservation and adaptation. Grounded on the organizational identity configuration projected by Dutton and Dukerich (1991) and on the analysis of the evolution of leading corporate brand Bis (i.e., Nestlé, Adidas, Starbucks, Burberry, Unilever), we propose a process where BI dimensions become more or less salient over time, gaining or losing strength as stakeholders enact their self-identity and as the market environment evolves. Key elements gain relevance while obsolete elements progressively vanish. Additionally, stakeholders' performances and aspirations drive the introduction of new BI dimensions. These interchanges are embedded in the role that corporate brands are expected to play in society. Corporate brands are accountable to their stakeholders. They need to create value for all their diverse stakeholders, among which are the planet, its people, and society as a whole; and creating value implies a dynamic BI.

Such rationale challenges the process commonly proposed for describing BI components' evolution supported by advocates of the balanced approach to BI, that is the BI peripheral components adjust over time while the core aspects of the identity remain constant (Aaker, 1996; Collins & Porras, 1994; Greyser & Urde, 2019). We defend the lack of precision in the general assumption of preserving BI core elements while adjusting peripheral components. The Nestlé, Adidas, Starbucks, and Burberry cases exemplify how corporate brands primarily adjust the core dimensions and then infuse those adjustments into the remaining BI dimensions. These cases also demonstrate that the core attributes are not static. They may persist but with different importance over time. In this sense, they are simultaneously enduring and dynamic.

Our work builds on the approach to corporate BI development depicted in recent BI co-creation literature (Iglesias et al., 2020b) and further suggests how the process reflects upon the BI dimensions' construction. Existing dimensions may be rekindled and/or new dimensions introduced. Yet, stakeholders ought to legitimize any new dimensions so that they can be internalized into the corporate BI. Such process turns the evolution more complex than commonly expected.

Our study has relevant implications for managers and shareholders. Corporate BI construction is a value creation process. Corporate brands are expected to create value for all their stakeholders (Iglesias & Ind, 2020), including their shareholders. The Nestlé case illustrates the increasingly active participation of investors in the process of corporate BI evolution. Within the current context where most investors present themselves as 'the true owners of [the] companies' (Fink, 2017), how can managers/CEOs achieve a 'conductor' role, promoting a co-creational multi-stakeholder corporate BI management? The question became recently highly relevant when the board of one of the most prominent B Corporation certified companies, Danone, dismissed its CEO and Chairman, Emmanuel Faber. The board acted under pressure from activist shareholders, concerned with the underperformance of the Danone share and the perceived financial risks of Faber's multi-stakeholder driven strategy (Abboud, 2021).

By balancing preservation and change, the corporate BI evolution process proposed in this chapter might give confidence to investors. It also offers founders and managers with a 'guardian' behaviour (Michel, 2017), the assurance that the brand's heritage and foundational values they have contributed to establish will not be eclipsed. Rather than occulted, corporate BI original dimensions might be renewed and strengthened over time.

The discussion presented in this chapter opens avenues for future research. The way corporate BI dimensions develop in a co-creation context remains a relevant line of inquiry. Although the corporate BI process proposed in this chapter advances knowledge on how to conciliate stability and change, more specific insights ought to be captured. For example, it is important to further investigate how foundational BI dimensions can co-exist with newly introduced dimensions.

Questions remain on how to integrate multiple stakeholders with diverse and sometimes opposed aspirations in the multi-stakeholder co-creational corporate BI construction. There is a need to further investigate: (1) how shareholders' objectives can be reconciled with other stakeholders' (e.g., community, consumers, managers) expectations; (2) how managers can fully achieve their 'conductor' role in such a complex context; and (3) what role employees should play to facilitate the multi-stakeholder corporate BI co-construction. Although capturing the complexity of such connections is a challenge for research, it remains a rich platform for multiple quests to address in future studies.

# References

Aaker, D. (1991). *Managing brand equity*. New York: The Free Press.
Aaker, D. (1996). *Building strong brands*. New York: The Free Press.
Abboud, L. (2021, March 15). Danone board ousts Emmanuel Faber as chief and chairman. *Financial Time*. Retrieved from www.ft.com/content/8e7ae718-eb18-4d2f-bd18-59e6349540f2
Albert, S., & Whetten, D. A. (1985). Organizational identity, research in organizational behavior. In M. J. Hatch & M. Schultz (Eds.), *Organizational identity, a reader* (pp. 89–118, 2004, Vol. 7). Oxford: Oxford University Press.
Balmer, J. M. T., & Gray, E. R. (2003). Corporate brands: What are they? What of them? *European Journal of Marketing*, 37(7–8), 972–997. https://doi.org/10.1108/03090560310477627
Balmer, J. M. T., & Greyser, S. A. (2003). *Revealing the corporation. Perspectives on identity, image, reputation, corporate branding and corporate-level marketing*. London: Routledge. https://doi.org/10.4324/9780203422786
Bick, G., Jacobson, M. C., & Abratt, R. (2003). The corporate identity management process revisited. *Journal of Marketing Management*, 19, 835–855. https://doi.org/10.1080/0267257X.2003.9728239
Burmann, C., Hegner, S., & Riley, N. (2009). Towards an identity-based branding. *Marketing Theory*, 9, 113–118. https://doi.org/10.1177/1470593108100065
Collins, J. C., & Porras, J. L. (1994). *Built to last: Successful habits of visionary companies*. New York: Harper Collins Publishing.
Cooper, H., Miller, D., & Merrilees, B. (2015). Restoring luxury corporate heritage brands: From crisis to ascendency. *Journal of brand Management*, 22(5), 448–466. https://doi.org/10.1057/bm.2015.9
Cornelissen, J., Christensen, L. T., & Kinuthia, K. (2012). Corporate brands and identity: Developing stronger theory and a call for shifting the debate. *European Journal of Marketing*, 46(7–8), 1093–1102. https://doi.org/10.1108/03090561211230214
Cova, B., & Dalli, D. (2009). Working consumers: The next step in marketing theory? *Marketing Theory*, 9(3), 315–339. https://doi.org/10.1177/1470593109338144
da Silveira, C., Lages, C., & Simões, C. (2013). Reconceptualizing brand identity in a dynamic environment. *Journal of Business Research*, 66, 28–36. https://doi.org/10.1016/j.jbusres.2011.07.020
Davies, G., Chun, R., & Kamins, M. A. (2010). Reputation gaps and the performance of service organizations. *Strategic Management Journal*, 31(5), 530–546. https://doi.org/10.1002/smj.825
de Chernatony, L. (1999). Brand management through narrowing the gap between brand identity and brand reputation. *Journal of Marketing Management*, 15(1–3), 157–179. https://doi.org/10.1362/026725799784870432

de Chernatony, L., Drury, S., & Segal-Horn, S. (2004). Identifying and sustaining services brands' values. *Journal of Marketing Communications, 10*(2), 73–93. https://doi.org/10.1080/13527260410001693785

Dutton, J. E., & Dukerich, J. M. (1991). Keeping an eye on the mirror: Image and identity in organizational adaptation. *The Academy of Management Journal, 34*(3), 517–554. https://doi.org/10.5465/256405

Fink, L. (2017, January 24). *Annual Letter to CEOs*. Retrieved from www.businessinsider.com/blackrock-ceo-larry-fink-letter-to-ceos-2017-1

Fournier, S., & Avery, J. (2011). The uninvited brand. *Business Horizons*, Special Issue on Web 2.0, Consumer-Generated Content and Social Media, 54, 193–207. https://doi.org/10.1016/j.bushor.2011.01.001

Gallagher, B. (2017, December 7). *The history of Burberry's check*. Retrieved from www.grailed.com/drycleanonly/history-of-the-burberry-check

Gardner, B. B., & Levy, S. J. (1955, March–April). The product and the brand. *Harvard Business Review*, 33–39.

Gioia, D. A., Schultz, M., & Corley, K. G. (2000). Organizational identity, image, and adaptive instability. *Academy Management Review, 25*(1), 63–81. https://doi.org/10.5465/amr.2000.2791603

Golob, U., & Podnar, K. (2019). Researching CSR and brands in the here and now: An integrative perspective. *Journal of Brand Management, 26*, 1–8. https://doi.org/10.1057/s41262-018-0112-6

Gregory, A. (2007). Involving stakeholders in developing corporate brands: The communication dimension. *Journal of Marketing Management, 23*(1–2), 59–73. https://doi.org/10.1362/026725707X178558

Greyser, S. A., & Urde, M. (2019, February). What does your corporate brand stand for? *Harvard Business Review*, 82–89. Retrieved from https://hbr.org/2019/01/what-does-your-corporate-brand-stand-for

Handelman, J. M. (2006). Corporate identity and the societal constituent. *Journal of the Academy of Marketing Science, 34*(2), 107–114. https://doi.org/10.1177/0092070305284970

Hatch, M. J., & Schultz, M. (2002). The dynamics of organizational identity. *Human Relations, 55*(8), 989–1018. https://doi.org/10.1177/0018726702055008181

Hatch, M. J., & Schultz, M. (2003). Bringing the corporation into corporate branding. *European Journal of Marketing, 37*(7), 1041–1064. https://doi.org/10.1108/03090560310477654

Hatch, M. J., & Schultz, M. (2004). *Organizational Identity*. Oxford: Oxford University Press. Retrieved from https://global.oup.com/ushe/product/organizational-identity-9780199269471?cc=fr&lang=en&

Henderson, R. M., & Johnson, R. (2012). *Nestlé SA: Nutrition, health and wellness strategy* (HBS No. 9-311-119). Boston, MA: Harvard Business School Publishing.

Iglesias, O., & Ind, N. (2020). Towards a theory of conscientious corporate brand co-creation: The next key challenge in brand management. *Journal of Brand Management, 27*, 710–720. https://doi.org/10.1057/s41262-020-00205-7

Iglesias, O., Ind, N., & Alfaro, M. (2013). The organic view of the brand: A brand value co-creation model. *Journal of Brand Management, 20*(8), 670–688. https://doi.org/10.1057/978-1-352-00008-5_9

Iglesias, O., Ind, N., & Schultz, M. (2020a). History matters: The role of history in corporate brand strategy. *Business Horizons, 63*(1), 51–60. https://doi.org/10.1016/j.bushor.2019.09.005

Iglesias, O., Landgraf, P., Ind, N., Markovic, S., & Koporcic, N. (2020b). Corporate brand identity co-creation in business-to-business contexts. *Industrial Marketing Management, 85*, 32–43. https://doi.org/10.1016/j.indmarman.2019.09.008

Ind, N., Iglesias, O., & Markovic, S. (2017). The co-creation continuum: From tactical market research tool to strategic collaborative innovation method. *Journal of Brand Management, 24*(4), 310–321. https://doi.org/10.1057/s41262-017-0051-7

Ind, N., Iglesias, O., & Schultz, M. (2013). Building brands together: Emergence and outcomes of co-creation. *California Management Review, 55*(3), 5–26. https://doi.org/10.1525/cmr.2013.55.3.5

Interbrand. (2007). *Building a powerful and enduring brand: The past, present, and future of the energy star ® brand*. Interbrand Publication for the U.S. Environmental Protection Agency.

Interbrand. (2020). *Best global brand 2020 Report*. Retrieved from https://interbrand.com/thinking/best-global-brands-2020-download/

Kapferer, J.-N. (1986, June 4–6). *Beyond positioning, retailer's identity*. Esomar Seminar Proceedings. Brussels, 167–176.

Kapferer, J.-N. (1997). *Strategic brand management: Creating and sustaining brand equity long term* (2nd ed.). London: Kogan Page.

Kapferer, J.-N. (2012). *The new strategic brand management: Advanced insights and strategic thinking*. London: Kogan Page. Retrieved from www.koganpage.com/product/the-new-strategic-brand-management-9780749465155

Merz, M. A., He, Y., & Vargo, S. L. (2009). The evolving brand logic: A service-dominant logic perspective. *Journal of the Academy of Marketing Science, 36*(1), 1–10. https://doi.org/10.1007/s11747-009-0143-3

Merz, M. A., Zarantonello, L., & Grapi, S. (2018). How valuable are your customers in the brand co-creation process? The development of a customer co-creation value (CCCV) scale? *Journal of Business Research, 82*, 79–89. https://doi.org/10.1016/j.jbusres.2017.08.018

Michel, G. (2017). From brand identity to polysemous brands: Commentary on 'Performing identities: Processes of brand and Stakeholder identity co-construction'. *Journal of Business Research, 70*, 453–455. https://doi.org/10.1016/j.jbusres.2016.06.022

Porter, M. E., Kramer, M. R., Herman, K., & Mcara, S. (2017). *Nestlé's creating shared value strategy* (HBS No. 8-716–422). Boston, MA: Harvard Business School Publishing.

Ramaswamy, V. (2011). It's about human experiences . . . and beyond, to co-creation. *Industrial Marketing Management, 40*, 195–196. https://doi.org/10.1016/j.indmarman.2010.06.026

Ramaswamy, V., & Ozcan, K. (2016). Brand value co-creation in a digitalized world: An integrative framework and research implications. *International Journal of Research in Marketing, 33*(1), 93–106. https://doi.org/10.1016/j.ijresmar.2015.07.001

Ramaswamy, V., & Ozcan, K. (2018). Offerings as digitalized interactive platforms: A conceptual framework and implications. *Journal of Marketing, 82*(July), 19–31. https://doi.org/10.1509/jm.15.0365

Ranjan, K. R., & Read, S. (2016). Value co-creation: Concept and measurement. *Journal of the Academy of Marketing Science, 44*, 290–315. https://doi.org/10.1007/s11747-014-0397-2

Schultz, H., & Gordon, J. (2012). *Onward: How Starbucks fought for its life without losing its soul*. New York: Rodale.

Simões, C., Singh, J., & Perin, M. (2015). Corporate brand expressions in business-to-business companies' websites: Evidence from Brazil and India. *Industrial Marketing Management, 51*, 59–68. https://doi.org/10.1016/j.indmarman.2015.05.017

Swaminathan, V., Sorescu, A., Steenkamp, J-B. E. M., O'Guinn, T. C. G., & Schmitt, B. (2020). Branding in a hyperconnected world: Refocusing theories and rethinking boundaries. *Journal of Marketing, 84*(2), 24–46. https://doi.org/10.1177/0022242919899905

Taylor, D. B. (2021, March 9). Maker of Dove soap will drop the world 'Normal' from beauty products. *The New York Times*. Retrieved from www.nytimes.com/2021/03/09/business/unilever-normal-positive-beauty.html

Unilever. (2021a, March 9–10). Conference 'The Unilever Compass – Our sustainable business strategy'. Virtual event hosted by Alan Jope, CEO & Annemarieke de Haan, EVP Benelux. Retrieved from https://unilever.6connex.eu/event/VirtualEvents/theunilevercompass/login

Unilever. (2021b, March 9). Unilever says no to 'normal' with new positive beauty vision. *Unilever Website*. Retrieved from www.unilever.com/news/press-releases/2021/unilever-says-no-to-normal-with-new-positive-beauty-vision.html

Upshaw, L. (1995). *Building brand identity*. New York: John Wiley. Retrieved from www.wiley.com/en-us/Building+Brand+Identity%3A+A+Strategy+for+Success+in+a+Hostile+Marketplace-p-9780471042204

Vallaster, C., & von Wallpach, S. (2013). An online discursive inquiry into the social dynamics of multi-stakeholder brand meaning co-creation. *Journal of Business Research, 66*(9), 1505–1515. https://doi.org/10.1016/j.jbusres.2012.09.012

van Riel, C. B. M., & Balmer, J. (1997). Corporate identity: The concept, its measurement and management. *European Journal of Marketing, 31*(5–6), 340–355. https://doi.org/10.1108/eb060635

Vargo, S. L., & Lusch, R. F. (2008). Service-dominant logic: Continuing the evolution. *Journal of the Academy of Marketing Science, 36*(1), 1–10. https://doi.org/10.1007/s11747-007-0069-6

von Wallpach, S., Hemestsberger, A., & Espersen, P. (2017). Performing identities: Processes of brand and stakeholder identity co-construction. *Journal of Business Research, 70*, 443–452. https://doi.org/10.1016/j.jbusres.2016.06.021

# 9
# IN SEARCH OF CORPORATE BRAND ALIGNMENT
## Philosophical foundations and emerging trends

*Michela Mingione and Russell Abratt*

### 1. A philosophical premise

For decades, with seminal works suggesting the pivotal importance of consistently managing the corporate identity/corporate image interface (Shee & Abratt, 1989; Bernstein, 1984; Dowling, 1986; Kennedy, 1977), a growing interest by academics and practitioners has been devoted to the theory of corporate brand alignment; a strategic process to successfully manage corporate brands through the assessment of coherency between internal and external corporate brand constituencies (Mingione, 2015). Over time, scholars have assumed two main philosophical stances (i.e., objective and interpretive assumptions) to nurture the construct, starting from defining it, then exploring its dimensions, and finally giving guidelines for its management.

In general, the philosophical foundations of organizational, management, and marketing research are implicit, with authors usually not disclosing their assumptions. In the field of marketing, this is a 'seriously neglected issue' (Hunt, 2003, p. 5), and scholars are called to be more 'aware of the philosophical assumptions embedded in their research outputs' (Tadajewski, 2004, p. 307). The under-evaluation of ontological and epistemological assumptions might have serious consequences for both practical and theoretical advancements in social science, mainly because they foster theory-building and support theories (Gioia & Pitre, 1990; Peters et al., 2014).

Concerns about ontology and epistemology represent the pillars of almost every science (Addis & Podestà, 2005). Ontology can be described as what can be considered as real. Etymologically, it combines two words, the past participle of the verb *èinai* (i.e., εἶναι) 'to be' (i.e., óntos; ὄντος) and *lógos* (i.e., λόγος) 'science, doctrine, discourse.' Thus, it literally means discourse about being (i.e., the science of being). Similarly, the word *epistemology* stems from the Greek words *epistéme* (i.e., ἐπιστήμη), which is composed of the prefix *èpi* (i.e., ἐπί) 'on, about, over' and the verb *histémi* (i.e., ἵστημι) 'to establish, to determine, to create, to generate,' and logos. Hence, the word *epistemology* can be literally conceived as a discourse about creation (i.e., the science of generation), generally translated with the term *knowledge*. Ontological and epistemological stances are intertwined because what is considered as 'real' strongly influences how scholars approach the generation of knowledge (Hatch & Cunliffe, 2012).

Specific philosophical stances determine different paradigms mapped on the basis of ontological and epistemological assumptions (Hunt, 1994; Lewis & Kelemen, 2002; Schultz & Hatch,

1996). In particular, Burrell and Morgan (1979) highlighted four main paradigms, namely the functionalist, interpretivist, radical structuralist, and radical humanist, which dominate the management and organization fields of study. Amongst these paradigms, organizational scholars have traditionally devoted their attention towards the debate on the functionalist vs. the interpretivist paradigms, both grounded into juxtaposed philosophical assumptions (Annells, 1996; Gioia & Pitre, 1990). Of note is that the functionalist paradigm has been alternatively labelled as orthodox, modernist, and positivist, especially when related to philosophical assumptions, whereas the interpretivist paradigm has also been named as constructivist and symbolic. The 'schism' between these paradigms strongly characterizes the marketing domain, as highlighted by Tadajewski (2004) in his literature review on the philosophy of science in marketing research.

The functionalist paradigm is grounded on objective ontology and positivistic epistemology. This means that the nature of reality (i.e., ontology) is conceived as objective, which in turn denotes that reality is an object and that all events of interest are objectified (Hatch & Cunliffe, 2012; Hunt, 1991; Morgan & Smircich, 1980). Positivistic epistemological underpinnings of research require a scientific method (i.e., formal logic) to create knowledge about the observed object (Anderson, 1983; Lee, 1991). The goal is to allow generalization of knowledge and to provide rules and predictive models (Savigny, 2007). Conversely, the interpretivist paradigm is grounded on subjective ontology and interpretivist epistemology. Subjective ontological assumptions indicate that the nature of reality is subjective and inter-subjectively constructed (Tadajewski, 2004). Shifting towards epistemological concerns, knowledge is 'gained through social interactions,' thus it is socially constructed (Hatch & Cunliffe, 2012; Point et al., 2017, p. 188). The goal is to discover 'how a particular social reality is constructed and maintained' to 'generate descriptions, insights and explanations of events so that the system of interpretations of meanings, and the structuring and organising processes, are revealed' (Gioia & Pitre, 1990, p. 588).

Given this information, the present chapter presents a more comprehensive view of the theory of corporate brand alignment by fostering the awareness of its philosophical foundation and by offering a meta-theoretical model that bridges the boundaries between the functionalist and the interpretivist paradigms. Afterwards, special attention is devoted to the role of corporate brand alignment to successfully co-create value across multiple stakeholders. Finally, this chapter offers a conclusive discussion and potential avenues for future research.

## 2. Fundamental underpinnings of corporate brand alignment

This section details the particularities of each paradigm on the basis of the underpinned philosophical stances. In particular, differences between paradigms followed two criteria: (1) the terminology used to mean alignment; and (2) the methodology used to develop knowledge and build theory.

First, since the inception of corporate brand alignment theory, a proliferation of terms has characterized this domain of research, indicating scholars' interest as well as the richness of the construct. Over time, scholars have used terms such as *uniform, consistent, similar, homogeneous*, and *unified corporate brand constituencies* (de Chernatony, 1999; de Chernatony & Cottam, 2008; Harris & de Chernatony, 2001; Urde, 2003). Further terms for the construct have been added, namely: *fit, consistency, reconciliation, calibration, coherence*, and *orchestration* (Balmer, 2012a, 2012b, 2009; Balmer & Gray, 2003; Hatch & Schultz, 2009, 2008, 2003, 2001), as well as *coherency, consistency, synchronization, fit, match, deviations*, and *discrepancies* (Anisimova & Mavondo, 2014, 2010; Chun & Davies, 2006; Davies & Chun, 2002; Verčič & Verčič, 2007).

In order to line up the philosophical assumptions with the used terminology (Scherer & Steinmann, 1999), this study included positivist research when scholars used terms such as *fit*, *match*, *uniform*, *homogeneous*, and *deviations*, whereas the terms *coherency*, *orchestration*, and *calibration* are suggested for the interpretivist paradigm. In fact, whilst the first cluster of terminology implies control of corporate brand messages, by highlighting the unique objectified characteristics of corporate brands, the second cluster respects multiple stakeholders' interpretative differences referring to the capacity of mutual understanding, or at least communication, between actors that might view the corporate brand in different ways.

Second, in the functionalist paradigm, knowledge and theory building are generated in a deductive manner, whereas inductive reasoning is completely denied (Hunt, 1994, 1991). Consequently, researchers first create hypotheses based on previous theories on the phenomenon of interest, then collect data typically through pre-determined questionnaires, and apply mainly quantitative analysis (Hatch & Cunliffe, 2012). Typical 'proofs of rigor' are principles such as validity, reliability, explanatory power, falsifiability, and logical consistency (Lee, 1991; Point et al., 2017, p. 189). In opposition, in the interpretivist paradigm, theory building traditionally takes place inductively and makes use of methods such as ethnography and hermeneutics (Gioia & Pitre, 1990). Research mainly deals with qualitative data collected by means of unstructured and open-ended interviews, and observations including aspects such as participants' feelings (Carson et al., 2001; Mayan, 2009). Typical proofs of rigor are the production of documents discussing the sense-making and sense-giving related to the resulting process, and the researchers' 'shared linguistic, social, and cultural knowledge, as well as human sensitivity and capacity for information processing' (Gioia et al., 1989, p. 510).

## 2.1 The quest for fit in the functionalist paradigm: calculating distances between corporate brand constituencies

In the functionalist paradigm, corporate brands represent strong assets unambiguously and uniquely representing the organization, its products, and services (Aaker, 2004; Balmer & Gray, 2003). Being an asset/thing/object, a corporate brand is legally owned by the company and can be turned into a liquid asset with financial value (Aaker, 2004; Balmer, 2012a). Therefore, it is potentially transferrable and can be further acquired and 'sold or borrowed, as in the case of franchise arrangements' (Balmer, 2008, p. 894).

To understand how to leverage the corporate brand into being more profitable (Aaker, 2004), scholars have aimed mainly at uncovering and describing corporate brand sub-constituencies. In general, corporate brands have been conceived as the result of internal and external constituencies (i.e., sub-constituencies/sub-assets), mainly defined as (internal) identity and (external) image or reputation (Chun & Davies, 2006; Davies & Chun, 2002; Davies et al., 2004; Verčič & Verčič, 2007). In particular, differences (i.e., distances) between internal and external perceptions of the same corporate brand are conceived as suboptimal outcomes that managers are forced to deal with (Anisimova, 2010; Anisimova & Mavondo, 2014).

Therefore, to ensure consistency of the corporate brand's performance and to avoid biases, the externalization of internal corporate brand components (i.e., delivery of the corporate brand identity) should be 'uniform' at each organization's touch point (Harris & de Chernatony, 2001, p. 446) to unambiguously represent the 'organization's unique model' (Knox & Bickerton, 2003, p. 998). In other words, the identity elements should be 'homogeneous' to match the organization's reputation (de Chernatony, 1999, p. 157) because the lack of fit between them negatively affects the corporate brand's performance and introduces biases that decrease stakeholders' satisfaction and loyalty (Anisimova, 2010; Anisimova & Mavondo, 2014; Davies & Chun, 2002).

Corporate brand research in the functionalist paradigm has been developed through the scientific method, thus testing hypotheses based on previous theories through quantitative analyses. In line with positivist assumptions, the main research goal is to find general laws on corporate branding and to provide explanatory and predictive corporate brand models to reveal cause-and-effect relationships. According to Davies and Chun (2002, p. 146), 'quantification is inevitable' to make advancements on corporate branding, especially because the interpretive method limits the generalizability of findings and only generic scales include 'dimensions that can be used to assess any target.'

Driven by the specific research aim of verifying the fit between internal and external corporate brands' sub-constituencies/sub-assets, Davies and colleagues (Chun & Davies, 2006; Davies & Chun, 2002; Davies et al., 2004) developed and applied the Corporate Personality Scale to measure the fit between corporate brand internal stakeholders' perceptions (i.e., CEO, top and middle managers and/or employees) and those of external stakeholders (i.e., the customers). In using a corporate personality metaphor, the scale includes 49 items to objectify corporate brands into seven personality dimensions (i.e., agreeableness, competence, enterprise, chic, ruthlessness, machismo, and informality). In particular, gaps between internal and external perceptions and their impact on staff and customers' satisfaction have been measured by means of a MultiGroup structural equation modelling analysis (Davies & Chun, 2002; Davies et al., 2004). In addition to employees and customers, some authors added other stakeholder groups to the analysis, such as students (Roper & Davies, 2007), journalists, and experts (Verčič & Verčič, 2007). Despite these authors having hypothesized similar stakeholder perceptions' of corporate brands because 'driving forces of corporate brand satisfaction are the same for all stakeholder groups' (Roper & Davies, 2007, p. 77), the findings highlighted significant differences between stakeholder groups, which did not affect the corporate brands' performance (Chun & Davies, 2006; Davies & Chun, 2002; Roper & Davies, 2007; Verčič & Verčič, 2007).

Moving beyond the Corporate Personality Scale, some scholars have embraced positivist epistemological assumptions to 'help marketing managers to understand the branding process more objectively' (Anisimova, 2010; Anisimova & Mavondo, 2014, 2010; Roy & Banerjee, 2014, p. 207). For instance, Anisimova and colleagues investigated corporate brand misalignment by using Venkatraman's (1989) measure of fit to verify the distances (i.e., gaps) of stakeholders' perceptions from the corporation's point of view (Anisimova, 2010; Anisimova & Mavondo, 2014, 2010). In particular, they hypothesized that the greater the deviation of external stakeholders' perceptions – such as customers' (Anisimova, 2010), salespeople's (Anisimova & Mavondo, 2010), or dealers' (Anisimova & Mavondo, 2014) – from those of top managers, the worse the stakeholders' satisfaction and loyalty. In particular, Anisimova and colleagues created the following formula to verify corporate brand misalignment, which includes the stakeholders' score (i.e., $x_{sj}$), and top managers' ideal profile of corporate branding (i.e., $x_{mgmt}$):

$$\text{MISALIGN} = \sqrt{\sum_{J}^{N}(X_{SJ} - \overline{X}_{mgmt})^2}$$

Findings are discordant. For three stakeholder groups (i.e., customers, dealers, and channel members), corporate brand alignment constitutes a source of positive performance (Anisimova, 2010; Anisimova & Mavondo, 2014; Roy & Banerjee, 2014). In particular, customers' satisfaction and loyalty are negatively associated with company-customer misalignment (Anisimova, 2010), and the misalignment between manufacturers and dealers negatively impacts on dealers' satisfaction and commitment (Anisimova & Mavondo, 2014). On the contrary, deviation from top managers' perceptions seems to represent a source of satisfaction and commitment for sales people (Anisimova & Mavondo, 2010). However, the authors specify that this result indicates that 'salespeople have a more favorable corporate brand perception and are perhaps less conservative than senior management in their evaluation of the corporate brand' (Anisimova & Mavondo, 2010, p. 785). To note, satisfaction is measured as external stakeholders' perceptions over sales growth, new product market opportunities, potential profits, return on equity and service level, whereas stakeholders' commitment reflects their willingness to maintain and continue the relationship with the corporate brand (Anisimova & Mavondo, 2014).

Based on these findings, a key question arises: How much is misalignment acceptable? In this regard, scholars propose a hybrid approach to corporate brand management and suggest aligning core dimensions and undertaking a stakeholder-specific approach when considering peripheral elements (Chun & Davies, 2006; Gyrd-Jones et al., 2013).

On the basis of the present framework, corporate brand alignment is defined as 'a tool to verify the fit between internal and external stakeholders' perceptions of the same corporate brand.'

## 2.2 The quest for coherency in the interpretivist paradigm: nurturing corporate brand symbolic connections

Corporate brands are conceived as symbols (Hatch & Schultz, 2009). Being a perceptual construct (i.e., a symbolic expression), a corporate brand's real value resides within all actors interacting with it, namely its stakeholders, who are the true owners of its emotional value (Balmer, 2017, 2012b; Balmer & Thomson, 2009). In particular, the corporate brand is conceived as a 'set of symbols' socially constructed and continuously interpreted by multiple stakeholders (Hatch & Schultz, 2003, p. 1059; Hatch & Rubin, 2006; Iglesias et al., 2013; Jones, 2005; Morsing & Kristensen, 2001).

Drawing on the key tenets of the interpretivist paradigm, the aim of corporate brand alignment is to enquire into relational gaps as a means to achieve corporate brand symbolic connections, especially related to shared responsibility, participation, and conversations and dialogue between internal and external corporate brand stakeholders. Corporate brand constituencies constantly (and simultaneously) interact and influence each other, resulting in them being interrelated and interdependent (Balmer, 2012b; Hatch & Schultz, 2003, 2001). Thus, corporate brand constituencies should not be considered separately or in isolation (Abratt & Mingione, 2017; Balmer et al., 2009; Schultz & Hatch, 2003).

The main goal of scholars belonging to this paradigm is to explore how corporate brands are developed in order to reveal the strategic processes supporting the management of corporate brands. Research has been mainly conducted by means of qualitative data and qualitative analysis. In particular, scholars embracing this paradigm used soft data (e.g., interviews or observations) to provide interpretative explorations, mainly by contact with those who use corporate brand symbolism (Balmer & Soenen, 1999; Foreman & Argenti, 2005; Urde, 2003). Grounded theory and action research based on qualitative case studies characterizes the methodological stances embraced to answer interpretivist epistemic queries (Chong, 2007; de Chernatony & Cottam, 2008; Urde, 2009, 2013). Most research questions and research aims deal with 'how' concerns, thus scholars mainly aim to explore the processes that construct, maintain, and change corporate brands (Balmer & Thomson, 2009; Balmer et al., 2009; Golant, 2012; Hatch & Schultz, 2001, 2003; Knox & Bickerton, 2003; Morsing & Kristensen, 2001). In particular, to gain knowledge of corporate brand alignment, scholars have mainly used single and multiple case studies, such as LEGO (Gyrd-Jones & Kornum, 2013; Hatch & Schultz, 2009, 2008, 2001; Schultz & Hatch, 2003), British Airways (Balmer et al., 2009; Hatch & Schultz, 2003), the British Monarchy (Balmer, 2011), universities (Balmer & Liao, 2007; Curtis et al., 2009), Volvo

(Urde, 2009, 2003), and the Oticon Company (Morsing & Kristensen, 2001). The selection of the qualitative single case study as a method of research particularly satisfies the interpretivist goal of achieving rich descriptions (Siggelkow, 2007) in order to reveal the processes triggered and enacted by corporate brand multiple constituencies.

A longitudinal approach has been applied in some studies, for instance LEGO (Hatch & Schultz, 2010, 2009, 2008, 2001; Schultz & Hatch, 2003) and British Airways (Balmer et al., 2009; Hatch & Schultz, 2003). In using Hatch and Schultz's VCI (Vision-Culture-Image) Model and Balmer's ACID (Actual-Communicated-Ideal-Desired) Test, these case studies show a complex and dynamic process of alignment over time and across the multiple constituencies that interact with the corporate brand. To enquire into the corporate brand process, scholars suggested specific questions to assess corporate brand alignment, such as: 'How do your employees interact with stakeholders?' (i.e., Image-Culture gap); 'What do your stakeholders want from your company?' (i.e., Image-Vision gap); 'How do vision, culture, and image interconnect?' and 'Are you realizing synergies, or are the elements independently conceived and possibly incoherent?' (Hatch & Schultz, 2001, p. 131). Answers to these questions require triangulation of data between multiple data sources, for the main observations, internal strategic documents and reports, and interviews to explore managers', consumers', stakeholders', and experts' opinions and perceptions (Balmer & Soenen, 1999; Hatch & Schultz, 2008, 2001). Thus, drawing on the key tenets of the interpretivist approach, the aim of these models is mainly explorative.

In involving, listening, understanding, and responding to all their stakeholders, corporate brand managers should narrow relational gaps whose presence may indicate a lack of interaction and connection between top managers, employees, and external stakeholders, each driving corporate brand elements, namely vision, culture, and image (Hatch & Schultz, 2009, 2003). Relationships between corporate brand constituents should be aligned and coherent in order to share the same corporate brand symbolism without sharing the same interpretation of meanings (Balmer & Thomson, 2009; Hatch & Schultz, 2008, 2003, 2001; Schultz & Hatch, 2003).

Given this framework, corporate brand alignment is defined as: 'a process that calls for coherent relationships between internal and external corporate brand constituents to strategically manage the corporate brand.'

## 3. Bridging boundaries between paradigms: a meta-paradigm perspective

Despite fundamental differences between opposite paradigms, 'polarization of paradigms can inhibit researchers' from broader understanding and theory advancements (Gioia & Pitre, 1990; Lewis & Kelemen, 2002, p. 253; Schultz & Hatch, 1996). Thus, some authors refused the incommensurability thesis of irreconcilable barriers between these divergent paradigms, and a multiple paradigm perspective was embraced (Combe, 1999; Hunt, 1994; Lowe et al., 2004, 2005).

At a meta level, paradigms meet and inform each other (Gioia & Pitre, 1990; Scherer & Steinmann, 1999; Schultz & Hatch, 1996). To bridge the paradigm boundaries, structuration theory is relevant, which 'considers social construction processes together with the objective characteristics of the social world' (Gioia & Pitre, 1990, p. 592). Accordingly, scholars are encouraged to make use of a stratified ontology and a pluralist epistemology, where the 'reality is at once made and in the making' (Lewis & Kelemen, 2002, p. 258), which highlights the *in fieri* characteristics of objects.

*In search of corporate brand alignment*

## 3.1 A meta-paradigm model

In order to bridge (Gioia & Pitre, 1990) interplay and cross (Schultz & Hatch, 1996), and transcend the incommensurability (Lowe et al., 2004, 2005) of competitive paradigms, the meta-theoretical position underpinned in this chapter frames the mutual relationship between paradigms into a circular process (Figure 9.1) that simultaneously considers the objectified corporate brand (Stage 1) and the corporate branding process (Stage 2).

The process starts with the recognition of the corporate brand as a uniform and unique object that exists independently from the interpretivist process of stakeholders' sense-making and sense-giving (Stage 1). The recognition of an indisputable object, stable in its features, represents the starting point of stakeholders' relationship with the corporate brand itself. At this stage, managers create the desired corporate brand identity and activate an *inside-out process* of meaning-making. The mission and vision of the corporate brand are initially determined by management and implemented by employees. External stakeholders have little influence on the corporate brand at this stage and begin to interpret brand meaning as they use the corporate brand's products and services, start having brand relationships, and observe its behaviour and citizenship.

As stakeholders enter into a relationship with the corporate brand (Stage 2), they start an *outside-in process* of meaning-making, attaching to the corporate brand both rational and emotional meanings, triggering a process of cognitive (i.e., rational-based meanings) and affective (i.e., emotional-based meanings) symbolization that represents the basis of his/her past, present, and future relationship with the corporate brand. Hence, the object corporate brand becomes a

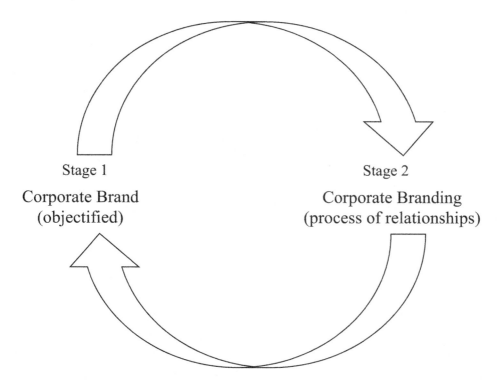

*Figure 9.1* A meta-paradigm model: bridging the functionalist and the interpretivist approaches

symbol that triggers a dynamic process of collective symbolization (i.e., interpretation of meanings, process of objects' sense-giving, and sense-making). Thus, during the corporate branding process enacted in Stage 2, there are many interpretations of meanings of the same object coexisting, all part of the same symbolic process. In this scenario, multiple stakeholders unceasingly co-create dynamic and fluid corporate brand meanings.

The circularity of the model indicates that the corporate brand firstly acts as a managerially defined object (Stage 1), which then generates stakeholders' relationships (from Stage 1 to Stage 2). These influence the corporate brand meanings, which are modified and co-created by the external stakeholders' interpretations and processes of meaning-making during Stage 2. Stakeholders' sense-making and co-creation represent a basis to reify the corporate brand from Stage 2 to Stage 1, where managers adjust the corporate brand to address stakeholders' raised issues. Hence, the revised corporate brand in Stage 1 represents a historical artefact of the corporate brand processes enacted during Stage 2 by embedding the refined corporate brand meanings into the culture of the corporation. Based on this model, the foundational definition of the corporate brand identity is conceived as a top-down internal process started in Stage 1. However, it is important to recognize that – in some specific cases – the first corporate brand identity definition can be the result of an open and participatory process where different stakeholders play a key role. For instance, born-digital corporate brand start-ups, which raise from a digital context, may take a bottom-up approach by co-creating their meaning with their brand communities since the very initial stages of the corporate brand identity-building process (Mingione & Abratt, 2020).

## 3.2 The role of corporate brand alignment in the meta-paradigm model

In the meta-paradigm model, corporate brand alignment plays a key role in evolving across stages, as it triggers a virtuous process of value creation and co-creation by fostering dialogue and connections between entities (corporate brands) and processes (corporate branding). Conversely, the absence of alignment can create relational bottlenecks in progressing from one stage to the other (Figure 9.2).

In particular, in Stage 1, managers trigger an inside-out process by developing the corporate brand, which generates a managerial-driven value creation and sets the basis to enable co-creation (Grönroos & Voima, 2013). However, in the transition from Stage 1 to Stage 2, the management will begin to realize that it is necessary to engage and collaborate with stakeholders to gain a deeper understanding of their demands. Thus, the search for alignment from Stage 1 to Stage 2 is key to designing powerful relationship enablers (Payne et al., 2009) and successfully co-creating value in Stage 2. For instance, managers may plan and organize specific encounters, such as online platforms (e.g., corporate website, corporate blogs, brand communities, and brand-owned social media) to facilitate aligned connections with external stakeholders (Iglesias & Bonet, 2012). In doing so, they set the potential to create, manage, and adapt coherent interactions and dialogue fostering the interplay between functional, symbolic, and emotional ties that characterize the relationship between the corporation and its multiple stakeholders (Mingione et al., 2020).

In Stage 2, external stakeholders relate with the corporate brand and trigger an outside-in process of value co-creation. The search for alignment from Stage 2 to Stage 1 is fundamental because aligned corporate brand stakeholders' collective representations may coherently develop the corporate brand as an object, which is the result of a dynamic process and reciprocal sense-making (Törmälä & Gyrd-Jones, 2017) enacted in Stage 2. Hence, after engaging with stakeholders on a continuous basis, management is in a position to redefine the corporate brand to be aligned with the brand meanings of stakeholders (Iglesias et al., 2020). Thus, the renewed

*In search of corporate brand alignment*

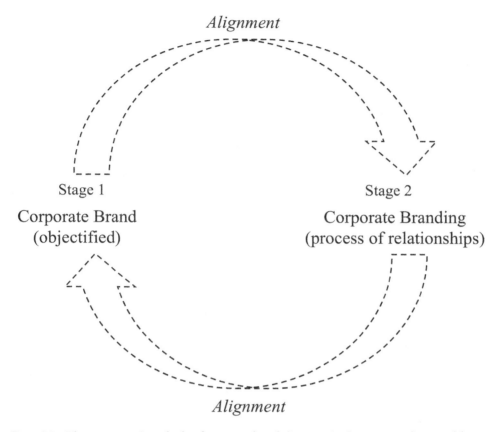

*Figure 9.2* The progress-oriented role of corporate brand alignment in the meta-paradigm model

corporate brand in Stage 1 is developed thanks to a feedback loop started in Stage 2. In this scenario, the corporate brand alignment with external stakeholders allows managers to coherently adapt to their needs and embed them into the culture of the corporation. In do, managers' aim is to anchor the changes made according to stakeholders' evolving demand, so as the newly co-created corporate brand is formulated to develop a stronger alignment between the managers' desired corporate brand and what constitutes desirable for external stakeholders. Brand relationships and engagement are now an accepted routine, and the alignment of corporate brand symbolisms helps in the delivery of the objectified corporate brand, transforming it back into a stable referral point for stakeholders and an asset to be sold or acquired.

Given the new meta-theoretical framework, corporate brand alignment can be defined as 'a strategic enabler to develop a more coherent and elucidated representation of multiple corporate brand symbolisms.'

## 4. Developing corporate brand-aligned relationships to successfully co-create value with multiple stakeholders

The corporate brand process requires social construction by multiple internal and external stakeholders (i.e., top managers, employees, business partners, consumers, and other external stakeholders), who, in relating to it, trigger a dynamic co-creation process (Hatch & Schultz, 2009, 2010; Iglesias et al., 2013). Consequently, knowledge of the corporate brand is co-created via multiple interpretations by all stakeholders who contribute to its multiple meanings (Ind et al., 2013; Törmälä & Saraniemi, 2018; Vallaster & von Wallpach, 2013). In particular, multiple and dynamic interpretations and interactions between the corporate brand internal and external constituents constantly influence each other by being embedded into corporate brand dynamic processes (Balmer, 2012b; Holt, 2002; Schultz & Hatch, 2003). Hence, corporate brand alignment is key to successfully co-creating value between the multiple stakeholders, with whom a corporate brand interfaces with daily. Conversely, corporate brand misalignment may indicate an absence of connections during interactions and potentially reduce the speed of the dialogue between entities (i.e., corporate brand internal and external constituencies) and processes (i.e., corporate brand management). In other words, and in line with a holistic and full stakeholder approach, where the corporate brand value is co-created through the interactions between the various stakeholders (Iglesias et al., 2013; Jones, 2005; Merz et al., 2009; Prahalad & Ramaswamy, 2004), alignment may help in achieving synergistic and mutual outcomes.

### 4.1 Corporate brand internal alignment

Employees are called to live the corporate brand and coherency helps in achieving a mutual understanding that enhances the co-creation of authentic corporate brand values (Golant, 2012). Corporate brand alignment with employees – even if it is difficult to attain – is crucial to reach a common corporate identity, otherwise problems may arise (Kay, 2006). For example, LEGO created the LEGO Brand School in order to engage employees and make them part of the decision-making process (Hatch & Schultz, 2009). In particular, employees used to meet with senior managers, who listened to their ideas and problems, involving them in authentic conversations (Hatch & Schultz, 2009). Thus, marketing managers cannot use traditional control mechanisms to ensure cultural alignment but are called to use persuasion in order to increase employees' willingness to be aligned with the corporate brand vision (Iglesias & Bonet, 2012). In fact, according to Iglesias et al. (2013, p. 673): 'when employees understand and share the brand vision, then their actions can be easily aligned with the brand.' Hence, listening and dialoguing with your stakeholders and including them collaboratively in the corporate ecosystem can be considered an alternative form of control that helps marketing managers to develop successful corporate brands in the digital era (Mingione & Abratt, 2020).

The crucial importance of internal alignment increases if we take into consideration those employees who are used to being in contact with consumers during a service exchange. For instance, Glanfield et al. (2018) suggest a coherent management of the corporate brand, especially when related to the experience delivered (by employees) and lived (by consumers) at a point of sale. In particular, they highlight the key role of interactions between FLEs (front-line employees) and consumers, suggesting that they successfully co-create the brand value when messages are not conflicting and, remarkably, when the corporate brand stakeholders are connected by a common purpose. If so, employees and consumers may pro-actively co-create solutions to problems and, more in general, behave similarly to achieve mutual outcomes (Glanfield et al., 2018; Iglesias et al., 2013).

### 4.2 Corporate brand external alignment

#### 4.2.1 Co-creating value with consumers and brand communities

According to Helm and Jones (2010, p. 585), the corporate brand 'value-generating resources are aligned to meet consumers' value-seeking processes.' For the most, scholars suggesting that external alignment is crucial to achieving successful value co-creation focus on brand communities. As scholars observed, brand value is co-created through the sharing of community-based practices such as rules, skills, and emotional features (Schau et al., 2009), and procedures and understandings (Skålén et al., 2015), which should be aligned in order to be successful. In particular, the LEGO Group successfully aligned the corporate brand with external brand communities and co-created long-term value (Gyrd-Jones & Kornum, 2013; Hatch & Schultz, 2009). For instance, fans belonging to the LUGNET (LEGO User Group Network) community created a website where they could share ideas, also proposing new products and collaborating with the R&D team in the corporation (Hatch & Schultz, 2009). When ideas successfully transformed into products, the LEGO Group acknowledged the role of the community, by reporting on the co-created products the label 'Designed by LEGO fans' (Hatch & Schultz, 2009, p. 124). Another community aligned with the values and culture of the corporate brand over entrepreneurial and passion-driven traits is the LEGO Mindstorm community, which included lead users who built LEGO programmable robots (Gyrd-Jones & Kornum, 2013).

It is interesting to outline the case of the AFOL (Adult Fans of LEGO) community, which shared with LEGO the values of the 'love for the brick' and created an open-source website. Despite their value-based alignment, when LEGO created a 'Non-disclosure Agreement,' fans strongly reacted and mobilized against this strategic choice, forcing LEGO to re-align with their values, based on open ideas and the sharing of knowledge (Gyrd-Jones & Kornum, 2013). This example shows that when stakeholders are not aligned, the corporate brand is called to enact strategies of re-alignment and negotiation. In fact, failure in co-creation may occur if there is corporate brand misalignment (Gyrd-Jones & Kornum, 2013; Thompson et al., 2006; Skålén et al., 2015). However, marketing managers can use misalignment information and insights to accomplish re-alignment strategies that are suggested by scholars, such as compliance, interpretation, and orientation (Thompson et al., 2006; Skålén et al., 2015). In fact, listening and use feedback is one of the crucial drivers of brand value co-creation (Ind et al., 2013; Hatch & Schultz, 2010). For instance, corporate brand managers could also decide to design points of connection with brand communities aligned with consumers' expectations and co-create experiences with the brand community itself (Payne et al., 2009).

In the broader context of online consumers (i.e., users), Mingione et al. (2020) analysed 7,605 interactions on Twitter between 18 corporate brands and their users. In particular, they conceptually defined and quantitatively explored – through the ECCS (Emotional Co-Creation Score) – the emotional value of the brand co-created during brand-consumer dyadic interactions. The study revealed that corporate brands search for emotional alignment, which works as a key strategic tool to manage consumers' extreme polar emotions. Specifically, when consumers displayed extreme negative emotions, corporate brands tended to show higher values of positive emotions, whereas in the presence of consumers' extreme positive emotions, they offered less emotional value. Hence, the study demonstrates that to successfully manage the co-created emotional value stemming from online interactions, emotional exchanges should be aligned in order to avoid relational collapses between the corporate brand and its external stakeholders (Mingione et al., 2020).

### 4.2.2 Co-creating value with B2B stakeholders

More recently, scholars are directing their attention towards the crucial importance of B2B (business-to-business) relationships, which include a wide range of stakeholders, such as business clients, suppliers, and distributors, amongst others (Balmer et al., 2020; Gupta et al., 2019; Lambert & Enz, 2012; Mingione & Leoni, 2020). Co-creation opportunities can be developed by activating cross-functional B2B relationships aligned toward an established goal, thus corporate brand managers should collaboratively work together with stakeholders to develop value propositions that respect both parties' expectations (Lambert & Enz, 2012). Similarly, in exploring buyer-seller relationships, Gupta et al. (2019) underlined the importance of a collaborative orientation process, where continuous interactions and mutual understanding of problems are designed to align strategic goals and to co-create value between business stakeholders.

Interestingly, Mingione and Leoni (2020) explored how corporate brands co-create value in B2B2C (business-to-business-to-consumers) markets. Strategic alignment was found to be – amongst others – a key driver to successfully manage the value co-creation process in this specific marketplace. The authors highlight the crucial role of vision alignment in the GlobTechCompany (i.e., 'A world where technology-based operations are safer and easier'), where all stakeholders of the B2B2C value chain joined initiatives to achieve the same broad goal. In particular, the corporate brand created formal partnerships with those companies strategically aligned and divided stakeholders on the basis of the objective to be achieved; whilst with banks, merchants, and governments, they collaboratively worked to increase consumers' willingness to pay electronically, with NGOs sharing the goal of enhancing financial inclusion. Remarkably, the research discovered that when visions are aligned, it is possible to co-create value with competitors. For instance, the GlobTechCompany created ad hoc events involving all the actors of the corporate brand ecosystem to join the 'battle against cash' (Mingione & Leoni, 2020). It is important to underline the need for a structured approach to pursue strategic alignment, where senior managers orchestrate strategic relationships, also including continuous meetings to ensure coherency and synergy between the actions and strategies of the different actors belonging to the corporate ecosystem (Mingione & Leoni, 2020).

## 5. Final remarks

This chapter contributes to the corporate branding domain by offering knowledge on corporate brand alignment theory. In particular, this chapter makes two main contributions to the extant literature on corporate brands. First, it illustrates a multi-paradigmatic framework on corporate brand alignment by highlighting three diverse perspectives (Table 9.1). Second, it outlines emerging trends of the corporate brand alignment theory, by highlighting the role of alignment in the paradigm of value co-creation.

Corporate brand alignment in the functionalist approach reflects the extent of a 'a tool to verify the fit between internal and external stakeholders' perceptions of the same corporate brand,' suggesting that alignment requires unity of interpretations. Hence, the ontological status is static because the corporate brand internal and external constituents have uniform and unique interpretations of the same corporate brand. Its ultimate aim is to strategically leverage the corporate brand, which implies clear attention devoted to the outcomes that alignment allows to be achieved (i.e., outcome-oriented). This is related to the epistemological aim of objectivist lens, which is to predict cause-and-effect relationships between internal and external corporate brand constituents. In particular, our conceptual analysis shows that internal constituents should be synchronized to match the organization's external image and reputation because the lack of fit between them may negatively affect the corporate brand's performance. In line with this, scholars mainly provided explanatory models.

When assuming interpretivist lens, corporate brand alignment is conceived as 'a process that calls for coherent relationships between internal and external corporate brand constituents,' signifying the symbolic sharing and connection between multiple stakeholders' interpretations. In particular, there may be as many realities as there are observers. Thus, multiple realities and interpretations of their meanings, even contradictory, co-exist and are influenced by continuous

*Table 9.1* Fundamental underpinnings of corporate brand alignment: demarcating multi-paradigmatic differences between perspectives

| Fundamentals | Functionalist* | Interpretivist** | Meta-paradigmatic |
|---|---|---|---|
| Definition | Corporate brand alignment is a tool to verify the fit between internal and external stakeholders' perceptions of the same corporate brand. | Corporate brand alignment is a process that calls for coherent relationships between internal and external corporate brand constituents. | Corporate brand alignment is a strategic enabler to develop a more coherent and elucidated representation of multiple corporate brand symbolisms. |
| Aim | How to strategically leverage the corporate brand (outcome-oriented) | How to strategically manage the corporate brand (process-oriented) | How to evolve the corporate brand (progress-oriented) |
| Ontological status | Static | Dynamic | Static and dynamic |
| Epistemological aims | To predict cause-and-effect relationships between internal and external corporate brand constituents | To explore how internal and external corporate brand constituencies relate to each other | To offer both explanatory and exploratory models |

interactions between diverse actors. Hence, the ontological status is dynamic because the corporate brand is continuously shaped by multiple interpretations of its stakeholders. The overarching aim of this approach is to strategically manage the corporate brand, in order to explore how internal and external corporate brand constituencies relate to each other (process-oriented). Thus, explorative models are provided in order to inquire into relational gaps between multiple stakeholders. In particular, most research questions and research aims deal with 'how' concerns, implying that scholars mainly aim to explore the processes that construct, maintain, and change corporate brands. Accordingly, most studies offered exploratory models.

The conceptual analysis of the philosophical foundations of the corporate brand alignment theory has a threefold implication. First, despite many scholars having emphasized the dominance of the functionalist paradigm in management, organization (Gioia & Pitre, 1990; Schultz & Hatch, 1996) and marketing research (Hunt, 2003; Savigny, 2007), where quantitative methods are preferred (Addis & Podestà, 2005; Hanson & Grimmer, 2007), the present analysis recognizes the relevance of both the functionalist and interpretivist paradigms. This is not surprising because brands have an intrinsic interpretivist nature, where individuals' (i.e., consumers, stakeholders) perceptions assume major importance as brand meaning makers (Hatch & Rubin, 2006; Salzer-Mörling & Strannegård, 2004). Second, our review reveals that scholars do not stick to a single paradigm and rather may embrace diverse paradigmatic lenses to shed light on different aspects of interest. Thus, they can change their perspective over time or can have 'a foot in more than one paradigm' (Gioia & Pitre, 1990, p. 595; Tadajewski, 2004), such as Balmer's and de Chernatony's studies. Third, our study clarifies the debate on corporate brand alignment models, namely Hatch and Schultz's VCI model and Balmer's ACID Test. In particular, our conceptual analysis on philosophical assumptions unveils that these are based on socio-constructionist (i.e., interpretivist) assumptions, which contradicts Cornelissen et al.'s (2012) critique on alignment models, deemed to be based on objectivist and positivistic assumptions. Thus, this review runs counter to scholars claiming that these models require predetermined and fixed meanings, and uniform and standardized strategies (Cornelissen et al., 2012; Gyrd-Jones et al., 2013; Morsing, 2006).

Going beyond the boundaries imposed by the philosophical differences embedded in the functionalist and the interpretivist approaches, the present study proposes a conceptual meta-paradigm model reconciling opposite views. In particular, the circular model discerns two stages, where corporate brand meaning-making is initially fixed and determined by managers (i.e., first stage, triggered by inside-out processes) and then, when meeting stakeholders, it is shaped by their interpretations (second stage, generated by outside-in processes). In this scenario, alignment plays a key role as 'a strategic enabler to develop a more coherent and elucidated representation of multiple corporate brand symbolisms.' In particular, the alignment of cognitive and affective symbolism helps in the evolution of the circular process of corporate brand interpretation and objectification. Hence, its ultimate role is devoted to how to evolve the corporate brand from one stage to another (progress-oriented). Accordingly, the ontological status is both dynamic and static. Whilst flexibility and adaptability address a reference to a dynamic dialogue with the multifaceted subjectivity and sense-making of all individuals who co-create the corporate brand, the stability embedded in an indisputable corporate brand, stable in its features, represents a key ground for the maintenance of stakeholders' relationship with the corporate brand itself. Finally, the epistemological aim is twofold: to develop both explanatory research, when scholars make use of quantitative methodology, and exploratory research, when studies are grounded on qualitative methodology.

The new conceptual model advances two main implications. First, it answers the call for more 'complementary, rather than alternative mechanisms for developing and managing corporate brands' (Melewar et al., 2012, p. 602) by offering 'a more sophisticated or nuanced understanding, rather than a narrow, one-sided view' of corporate brands (Balmer et al., 2016, p. 212). Second, it highlights the need for both dynamic and stable elements of the corporate brand. In particular, the corporate brand, being both open to change and stable in its features, can endure in the long-term and engage its multiple stakeholders over time. In fact, being dynamic respects the complexity of the corporate brand, which deals with a multiplicity of stakeholders who have various – and sometimes contradictory – needs (Gyrd-Jones et al., 2013; Melewar et al., 2012; Urde, 2013). On the other hand, the corporate brand requires stable elements during periods of equilibrium to offer corporations a clear strategic orientation and guide consistent behaviour over time (Abratt & Mingione, 2017). In fact, after a change the renewed corporate brand needs to be institutionalized and be part of the corporate culture, which should commit its resources and activities in accordance with the adjusted corporate brand (Maon et al., 2009). Moreover, stability serves as a unique point of reference for every stakeholder, who needs to maintain stable relationships with the corporate brand itself (Baumeister & Leary, 1995). Hence, the stability of the corporate brand embedded into a coherent symbolic representation makes the corporate brand a unique and hardly replicable asset to differentiate from competitors (Aaker, 2004). However, as we live in a VUCA world (i.e., volatile, uncertain, complex, and ambiguous, Bennet & Lemoine, 2014), one key issue is related to understanding how long this stabilization holds true. The longitudinal case studies of British Airways (Balmer et al., 2009; Hatch & Schultz, 2003) and LEGO (Schultz & Hatch, 2003) expose their evolutionary path and suggest that a corporate brand is stable until external triggers (i.e., privatization, diverse consumers' needs) or internal ones (i.e., CEO's vision) force the corporate brand change. However, the extent to which corporate brand alignment is beneficial in a stable manner needs a finer-graded understanding, thus representing valuable food for thought for future research.

The second contribution of this chapter is attributed to the emerging trends of corporate brand alignment theory, by exploring the co-creative approach to corporate brand building. In particular, we offer a multiple stakeholders' perspective, by showing that a symbolic common (i.e., aligned) ground is needed to successfully co-create corporate brands with internal and external stakeholders. Hence, corporate brand alignment means realizing synergies between inside and outside corporate brand interdependent constituents and requires shared knowledge. In particular, the corporate brand should involve multiple stakeholders to develop an aligned corporate brand and collaboratively work together with them to achieve mutual outcomes and to co-create long-term value.

Co-creation is a central tenet of conscientious corporate brands, which are purpose-led and call for broader responsibilities across all the multiple stakeholders a corporate brand daily deals with (Iglesias & Ind, 2020; Ind & Horlings, 2016). Recently, research has considered the role of corporate brand alignment with the growing expectations from stakeholders for brands to embrace their broader responsibilities. In particular, studies have pointed out that whilst misalignment between internal (e.g., corporate identity) and external dimensions (e.g., image and reputation) may lead to stakeholders' scepticism (Grossman, 2005) and pertains to CSR (corporate social responsibility) greenwashing (Pope & Wæraas, 2016), alignment is associated with corporate enlightenment (Lahtinen & Närvänen, 2020) and reduces the risks associated with practices of decoupling (Maon et al., 2021). In doing so, corporate brand alignment helps in increasing not only external-driven outcomes (i.e., consumers' perceptions of corporate authenticity, Vredenburg et al., 2020) but also increases employees' performance (Carlini & Grace, 2021). However, despite the fact that scholars have acknowledged the key role of alignment within a more conscientious approach to corporate branding (Rindell et al., 2011), further research is needed. Accordingly, a finer-graded understanding of how corporate brand alignment should work for conscientious corporate brands represents a fertile ground for future research. In particular, what is the role of alignment in driving a transformative purpose-led change? Moreover, scholars are called to explore the role of alignment in the management of a purpose-led network. Accordingly, how can corporations ensure that all the stakeholders participating to the co-creation of value are aligned with the corporate brand purpose? Finally, follow-up research is needed to inquire into the role of alignment in delivering an authentic purpose.

## Acknowledgements

The authors would like to thank Emeritus Professor M. J. Hatch and Professor L. M. Visconti for their helpful comments on earlier drafts of this research.

## References

Aaker, D. A. (2004). Leveraging the corporate brand. *California Management Review*, *46*(3), 6–18. https://doi.org/10.1177/000812560404600301

Abratt, R., & Mingione, M. (2017). Corporate identity, strategy and change. *Journal of Brand Management*, *24*(2), 129–139. https://doi.org/10.1057/s41262-017-0026-8

Addis, M., & Podestà, S. (2005). Long life to marketing research: A postmodern view. *European Journal of Marketing*, *39*(3–4), 386–412. https://doi.org/10.1108/03090560510581836

Anderson, P. F. (1983). Marketing, scientific progress, and scientific method. *The Journal of Marketing*, *47*(4), 18–31. https://doi.org/10.1177/002224298304700403

Anisimova, T. (2010). Corporate brand: The company-customer misalignment and its performance implications. *Journal of Brand Management*, *17*(7), 488–503. https://doi.org/10.1057/bm.2010.7

Anisimova, T., & Mavondo, F. (2010). The performance implications of company-salesperson corporate brand misalignment. *European Journal of Marketing 44*(6), 771–795. https://doi.org/10.1108/03090561011032711

Anisimova, T., & Mavondo, F. (2014). Aligning company and dealer perspectives in corporate branding: Implications for dealer satisfaction and commitment. *Journal of Business-to-Business Marketing, 21*(1), 35–56. https://doi.org/10.1080/1051712X.2014.857501

Annells, M. (1996). Grounded theory method: Philosophical perspectives, paradigm of inquiry, and postmodernism. *Qualitative Health Research, 6*(3), 379–393. https://doi.org/10.1177/104973239600600306

Balmer, J. M. T. (2008). Identity based views of the corporation. Insights from corporate identity, organisational identity, social identity, visual identity, corporate brand identity, and corporate image. *European Journal of Marketing, 42*(9–10), 879–906. https://doi.org/10.1108/03090560810891055

Balmer, J. M. T. (2009). Corporate marketing: Apocalypse, advent and epiphany. *Management Decision, 47*(4), 544–572. https://doi.org/10.1108/00251740910959413

Balmer, J. M. T. (2011). Corporate heritage brands and the precepts of corporate heritage brand management: Insights from the British Monarchy on the eve of the royal wedding of Prince William (April 2011) and Queen Elizabeth II's Diamond Jubilee (1952–2012). *Journal of Brand Management, 18*(8), 517–544. https://doi.org/10.1057/bm.2011.21

Balmer, J. M. T. (2012a). Corporate brand management imperatives: Custodianship, credibility, and calibration. *California Management Review, 54*(3), 6–33. https://doi.org/10.1525/cmr.2012.54.3.6

Balmer, J. M. T. (2012b). Strategic corporate brand alignment: Perspectives from identity based views of corporate brands. *European Journal of Marketing, 46*(7–8), 1064–1092. https://doi.org/10.1108/03090561211230205

Balmer J. M. T. (2017). Explicating corporate brands and their management: Reflections and directions from 1995. In J. M. T. Balmer, S. M. Powell, J. Kernstock, & T. O. Brexendorf (Eds.), *Advances in corporate branding. Journal of brand management: Advanced collections*. London: Palgrave Macmillan. https://doi.org/10.1057/978-1-352-00008-5_2

Balmer, J. M. T., & Gray, E. R. (2003). Corporate brands: What are they? What of them? *European Journal of Marketing, 37*(7/8), 972–997. https://doi.org/10.1108/03090560310477627

Balmer, J. M. T., Johansen, T. S., & Ellerup Nielsen, A. (2016). Guest editors' introduction. Scrutinizing stakeholder thinking: Orthodoxy or heterodoxy? *International Studies of Management & Organization, 46*(4), 205–215. https://doi.org/10.1080/00208825.2016.1140517

Balmer, J. M. T., & Liao, M. N. (2007). Student corporate brand identification: An exploratory case study. *Corporate Communications: An International Journal, 12*(4), 356–375. https://doi.org/10.1108/13563280710832515

Balmer, J. M. T., Lin, Z., Chen, W., & He, X. (2020). The role of corporate brand image for B2B relationships of logistics service providers in China. *Journal of Business Research, 117*, 850–861. https://doi.org/10.1016/j.jbusres.2020.03.043

Balmer, J. M. T., & Soenen, G. B. (1999). The acid test of corporate identity management™. *Journal of Marketing Management, 15*(1–3), 69–92. https://doi.org/10.1362/026725799784870441

Balmer, J. M. T., Stuart, H., & Greyser, S. A. (2009). Aligning identity and strategy: Corporate branding at British Airways in the late 20th century. *California Management Review, 51*(3), 6–23. https://doi.org/10.2307/41166491

Balmer, J. M. T., & Thomson, I. (2009). The shared management and ownership of corporate brands: The case of Hilton. *Journal of General Management, 34*(4), 15–37. https://doi.org/10.1177/030630700903400402

Baumeister, R. F., & Leary, M. R. (1995). The need to belong: Desire for interpersonal attachments as a fundamental human motivation. *Psychological Bulletin, 117*(3), 497–529.

Bennett, N., & Lemoine, G. J. (2014). What a difference a word makes: Understanding threats to performance in a VUCA world. *Business Horizons, 57*(3), 311–317. https://doi.org/10.1016/j.bushor.2014.01.001

Bernstein, D. (1984). *Company image and reality: A critique of corporate communications*. New York: Rinehart and Winston Holt.

Burrell, G., & Morgan, G. (1979). *Sociological paradigms and organisational analysis*. London: Heinemann Educational Books.

Carlini, J., & Grace, D. (2021). The corporate social responsibility (CSR) internal branding model: Aligning employees' CSR awareness, knowledge, and experience to deliver positive employee performance outcomes. *Journal of Marketing Management*, 1–29. https://doi.org/10.1080/0267257X.2020.1860113

Carson, D., Gilmore, A., Perry, C., & Gronhaug, K. (2001). *Qualitative marketing research*. Los Angeles, CA: SAGE.

Chong, M. (2007). The role of internal communication and training in infusing corporate values and delivering brand promise: Singapore Airlines' experience. *Corporate Reputation Review, 10*(3), 201–212. https://doi.org/10.1057/palgrave.crr.1550051

Chun, R., & Davies, G. (2006). The influence of corporate character on customers and employees: Exploring similarities and differences. *Journal of the Academy of Marketing Science, 34*(2), 138–146. https://doi.org/10.1177/0092070305284975

Combe, L. A. (1999). Multiple strategy paradigms: An integrational framework. *Journal of Marketing Management, 15*(5), 341–359. https://doi.org/10.1362/026725799784870289

Cornelissen, J., Christensen, L. T., & Kinuthia, K. (2012). Corporate brands and identity: Developing stronger theory and a call for shifting the debate. *European Journal of Marketing, 46*(7–8), 1093–1102. https://doi.org/10.1108/03090561211230214

Curtis, T., Abratt, R., & Minor, W. (2009). Corporate brand management in higher education: The case of ERAU. *Journal of Product & Brand Management, 18*(6), 404–413. https://doi.org/10.1108/10610420910989721

Davies, G., & Chun, R. (2002). Gaps between the internal and external perceptions of the corporate brand. *Corporate Reputation Review, 5*(2–3), 144–158. https://doi.org/10.1057/palgrave.crr.1540171

Davies, G., Chun, R., da Silva, R. V., & Roper, S. (2004). A corporate character scale to assess employee and customer views of organization reputation. *Corporate Reputation Review, 7*(2), 125–146. https://doi.org/10.1057/palgrave.crr.1540216

de Chernatony, L. (1999). Brand management through narrowing the gap between brand identity and brand reputation. *Journal of Marketing Management, 15*(1–3), 157–179. https://doi.org/10.1362/026725799784870432

de Chernatony, L., & Cottam, S. (2008). Interactions between organisational cultures and corporate brand. *Journal of Product & Brand Management, 17*(1), 13–24. https://doi.org/10.1108/10610420810856477

Dowling, G. R. (1986). Managing your corporate images. *Industrial Marketing Management, 15*(2), 109–115. https://doi.org/10.1016/0019-8501(86)90051-9

Foreman, J., & Argenti, P. A. (2005). How corporate communication influences strategy implementation, reputation and the corporate brand: An exploratory qualitative study. *Corporate Reputation Review, 8*(3), 245–264. https://doi.org/10.1057/palgrave.crr.1540253

Gioia, D. A., Donnellon, A., & Sims Jr, H. P. (1989). Communication and cognition in appraisal: A tale of two paradigms. *Organization Studies, 10*(4), 503–529. https://doi.org/10.1177/017084068901000403

Gioia, D. A., & Pitre, E. (1990). Multiparadigm perspectives on theory building. *Academy of Management Review, 15*(4), 584–602. https://doi.org/10.5465/amr.1990.4310758

Glanfield, K., Ackfeldt, A. L., & Melewar, T. C. (2018). Corporate branding's influence on front-line employee and consumer value co-creation in UK household consumer markets. *Journal of General Management, 43*(2), 63–69. https://doi.org/10.1177/0306307017740184

Golant, B. D. (2012). Bringing the corporate brand to life: The brand manager as practical author. *Journal of Brand Management, 20*(2), 115–127. https://doi.org/10.1057/bm.2012.44

Grönroos, C., & Voima, P. (2013). Critical service logic: Making sense of value creation and co-creation. *Journal of the Academy of Marketing Science, 41*(2), 133–150. https://doi.org/10.1007/s11747-012-0308-3

Grossman, H. A. (2005). Refining the role of the corporation: The impact of corporate social responsibility on shareholder primacy theory. *Deakin Law Review, 10*(2), 572–596.

Gupta, S., Polonsky, M., & Lazaravic, V. (2019). Collaborative orientation to advance value co-creation in buyer – Seller relationships. *Journal of Strategic Marketing, 27*(3), 191–209. https://doi.org/10.1080/0965254X.2017.1384747

Gyrd-Jones, R. I., & Kornum, N. (2013). Managing the co-created brand: Value and cultural complementarity in online and offline multi-stakeholder ecosystems. *Journal of Business Research, 66*(9), 1484–1493. https://doi.org/10.1016/j.jbusres.2012.02.045

Gyrd-Jones, R. I., Merrilees, B., & Miller, D. (2013). Revisiting the complexities of corporate branding: Issues, paradoxes, solutions. *Journal of Brand Management, 20*(7), 1–19. https://doi.org/10.1057/bm.2013.1

Hanson, D., & Grimmer, M. (2007). The mix of qualitative and quantitative research in major marketing journals, 1993–2002. *European Journal of Marketing, 41*(1–2), 58–70. https://doi.org/10.1108/03090560710718111

Harris, F., & de Chernatony, L. (2001). Corporate branding and corporate brand performance. *European Journal of Marketing, 35*(3/4), 441–456. https://doi.org/10.1108/03090560110382101

Hatch, M. J., & Cunliffe, A. L. (2012). *Organization theory: Modern, symbolic and postmodern perspectives.* Oxford: Oxford University Press.

Hatch, M. J., & Rubin, J. (2006). The hermeneutics of branding. *Journal of Brand Management, 14*(1–2), 40–59. https://doi.org/10.1057/palgrave.bm.2550053

Hatch, M. J., & Schultz, M. (2001). Are the strategic stars aligned for your corporate brand? *Harvard Business Review*, *79*(2), 128–134.

Hatch, M. J., & Schultz, M. (2003). Bringing the corporation into corporate branding. *European Journal of Marketing*, *37*(7–8), 1041–1064. https://doi.org/10.1108/03090560310477654

Hatch, M. J., & Schultz, M. (2008). *Taking brand initiative: How companies can align strategy, culture, and identity through corporate branding*. San Francisco, CA: Jossey-Bass.

Hatch, M. J., & Schultz, M. (2009). Of bricks and brands: From corporate to enterprise branding. *Organizational Dynamics*, *38*(2), 117–130. https://doi.org/10.1016/J.ORGDYN.2009.02.008

Hatch, M. J., & Schultz, M. (2010). Toward a theory of brand co-creation with implications for brand governance. *Journal of Brand Management*, *17*(8), 590–604. https://doi.org/10.1057/bm 2010.14

Helm, C., & Jones, R. (2010). Extending the value chain – A conceptual framework for managing the governance of co-created brand equity. *Journal of Brand Management*, *17*(8), 579–589. https://doi.org/10.1057/bm.2010.19

Holt, D. B. (2002). Why do brands cause trouble? A dialectical theory of consumer culture and branding. *Journal of Consumer Research*, *29*(1), 70–90. https://doi.org/10.1086/339922

Hunt, S. D. (1991). Positivism and paradigm dominance in consumer research: Toward critical pluralism and rapprochement. *Journal of Consumer Research*, *18*(1), 32–44. https://doi.org/10.1086/209238

Hunt, S. D. (1994). On rethinking marketing: Our discipline, our practice, our methods. *European Journal of Marketing*, *28*(3), 13–25. https://doi.org/10.1108/03090569410057263

Hunt, S. D. (2003). *Controversy in marketing theory: For reason, realism, truth and objectivity*. Armonk, NY: M. E. Sharpe.

Iglesias, O., & Bonet, E. (2012). Persuasive brand management: How managers can influence brand meaning when they are losing control over it. *Journal of Organizational Change Management*, *25*(2), 251–264. https://doi.org/10.1108/09534811211213937

Iglesias, O., & Ind, N. (2020). Towards a theory of conscientious corporate brand co-creation: The next key challenge in brand management. *Journal of Brand Management*, *27*(6), 710–720. https://doi.org/10.1057/s41262-020-00205-7

Iglesias, O., Ind, N., & Alfaro, M. (2013). The organic view of the brand: A brand value co-creation model. *Journal of Brand Management*, *20*(8), 670–688. https://doi.org/10.1057/978-1-352-00008-5_9

Iglesias, O., Landgraf, P., Ind, N., Markovic, S., & Koporcic, N. (2020). Corporate brand identity co-creation in business-to-business contexts. *Industrial Marketing Management*, *85*, 32–43. https://doi.org/10.1016/j.indmarman.2019.09.008

Ind, N., & Horlings, S. (2016). *Brands with a conscience: How to build a successful and responsible brand*. New York: Kogan Page.

Ind, N., Iglesias, O., & Schultz, M. (2013). Building brands together: Emergence and outcomes of co-creation. *California Management Review*, *55*(3), 5–26. https://doi.org/10.1525/cmr.2013.55.3.5

Jones, R. (2005). Finding sources of brand value: Developing a stakeholder model of brand equity. *Journal of Brand Management*, *13*(1), 10–32. https://doi.org/10.1057/palgrave.bm.2540243

Kay, M. J. (2006). Strong brands and corporate brands. *European Journal of Marketing*, *40*(7–8), 742–760. https://doi.org/10.1108/03090560610669973

Kennedy, S. H. (1977). Nurturing corporate images. *European Journal of Marketing*, *11*(3), 119–164. https://doi.org/10.1108/EUM0000000005007

Knox, S., & Bickerton, D. (2003). The six conventions of corporate branding. *European Journal of Marketing*, *37*(7–8), 998–1016. https://doi.org/10.1108/03090560310477636

Lahtinen, S., & Närvänen, E. (2020). Co-creating sustainable corporate brands: A consumer framing approach. *Corporate Communications: An International Journal*, *25*(3), 447–461. https://doi.org/10.1108/CCIJ-11-2019-0121

Lambert, D. M., & Enz, M. G. (2012). Managing and measuring value co-creation in business-to-business relationships. *Journal of Marketing Management*, *28*(13–14), 1588–1625. https://doi.org/10.1080/0267257X.2012.736877

Lee, A. S. (1991). Integrating positivist and interpretive approaches to organizational research. *Organization Science*, *2*(4), 342–365. https://doi.org/10.1287/orsc.2.4.342

Lewis, M. W., & Kelemen, M. L. (2002). Multiparadigm inquiry: Exploring organizational pluralism and paradox. *Human Relations*, *55*(2), 251–275. https://doi.org/10.1177/0018726702055002185

Lowe, S., Carr, A. N., & Thomas, M. (2004). Paradigmapping marketing theory. *European Journal of Marketing*, *38*(9–10), 1057–1064. https://doi.org/10.1108/03090560410548861

Lowe, S., Carr, A. N., Thomas, M., & Watkins-Mathys, L. (2005). The fourth hermeneutic in marketing theory. *Marketing Theory, 5*(2), 185–203. https://doi.org/10.1177/1470593105052471

Maon, F., Lindgreen, A., & Swaen, V. (2009). Designing and implementing corporate social responsibility: An integrative framework grounded in theory and practice. *Journal of Business Ethics, 87*(1), 71–89. https://doi.org/10.1007/s10551-008-9804-2

Maon, F., Swaen, V., & De Roeck, K. (2021). Corporate branding and corporate social responsibility: Toward a multi-stakeholder interpretive perspective. *Journal of Business Research, 126*, 64–77. https://doi.org/10.1016/j.jbusres.2020.12.057

Mayan, M. J. (2009). *Essentials of qualitative inquiry*. Walnut Creek, CA: Left Coast Press.

Melewar, T. C., Gotsi, M., & Andriopoulos, C. (2012). Shaping the research agenda for corporate branding: Avenues for future research. *European Journal of Marketing, 46*(5), 600–608. https://doi.org/10.1108/03090561211235138

Merz, M. A., He, Y., & Vargo, S. L. (2009). The evolving brand logic: A service-dominant logic perspective. *Journal of the Academy of Marketing Science, 37*(3), 328–344. https://doi.org/10.1007/s11747-009-0143-3

Mingione, M. (2015). Inquiry into corporate brand alignment: A dialectical analysis and directions for future research. *Journal of Product & Brand Management, 24*(5), 518–536. https://doi.org/10.1108/JPBM-05-2014-0617

Mingione, M., & Abratt, R. (2020). Building a corporate brand in the digital age: Imperatives for transforming born-digital startups into successful corporate brands. *Journal of Marketing Management, 36*(11–12), 981–1008. https://doi.org/10.1080/0267257X.2020.1750453

Mingione, M., Cristofaro, M., & Mondi, D. (2020). 'If I give you my emotion, what do I get?' Conceptualizing and measuring the co-created emotional value of the brand. *Journal of Business Research, 109*, 310–320. https://doi.org/10.1016/j.jbusres.2019.11.071

Mingione, M., & Leoni, L. (2020). Blurring B2C and B2B boundaries: Corporate brand value co-creation in B2B2C markets. *Journal of Marketing Management, 36*(1–2), 72–99. https://doi.org/10.1080/0267257X.2019.1694566

Morgan, G., & Smircich, L. (1980). The case for qualitative research. *Academy of Management Review, 5*(4), 491–500. https://doi.org/10.5465/amr.1980.4288947

Morsing, M. (2006). Corporate moral branding: Limits to aligning employees. *Corporate Communications: An International Journal, 11*(2), 97–108. https://doi.org/10.1108/13563280610661642

Morsing, M., & Kristensen, J. (2001). The question of coherency in corporate branding – Over time and across stakeholders. *Journal of Communication Management, 6*(1), 24–40. https://doi.org/10.1108/13632540210806919

Payne, A., Storbacka, K., Frow, P., & Knox, S. (2009). Co-creating brands: Diagnosing and designing the relationship experience. *Journal of Business Research, 62*(3), 379–389. https://doi.org/10.1016/j.jbusres.2008.05.013

Peters, L. D., Löbler, H., Brodie, R. J., Breidbach, C. F., Hollebeek, L. D., Smith, S. D., & Varey, R. J. (2014). Theorizing about resource integration through service-dominant logic. *Marketing Theory, 14*(3), 249–268. https://doi.org/10.1177/1470593114534341

Point, S., Fendt, J., & Jonsen, K. (2017). Qualitative inquiry in management: Methodological dilemmas and concerns in meta-analysis. *European Management Review, 14*(2), 185–204. https://doi.org/10.1111/emre.12097

Pope, S., & Wæraas, A. (2016). CSR-washing is rare: A conceptual framework, literature review, and critique. *Journal of Business Ethics, 137*(1), 173–193. https://doi.org/10.1007/s10551-015-2546-z

Prahalad, C. K., & Ramaswamy, V. (2004). *The future of competition: Co-creating unique value with customers*. Cambridge, MA: Harvard Business School Press.

Rindell, A., Svensson, G., Mysen, T., Billström, A., & Wilén, K. (2011). Towards a conceptual foundation of 'Conscientious Corporate Brands'. *Journal of Brand Management, 18*(9), 709–719. https://doi.org/10.1057/bm.2011.38

Roper, S., & Davies, G. (2007). The corporate brand: Dealing with multiple stakeholders. *Journal of Marketing Management, 23*(1–2), 75–90. https://doi.org/10.1362/026725707X178567

Roy, D., & Banerjee, S. (2014). Identification and measurement of brand identity and image gap: A quantitative approach. *Journal of Product & Brand Management, 23*(3), 207–219. https://doi.org/10.1108/JPBM-01-2014-0478

Salzer-Mörling, M., & Strannegård, L. (2004). Silence of the brands. *European Journal of Marketing, 38*(1–2), 224–238. https://doi.org/10.1108/03090560410511203

Savigny, H. (2007). Ontology and epistemology in political marketing: Keeping it real? *Journal of Political Marketing*, 6(2–3), 33–47. https://doi.org/10.1300/J199v06n02_03

Schau, H. J., Muñiz Jr, A. M., & Arnould, E. J. (2009). How brand community practices create value. *Journal of Marketing*, 73(5), 30–51. https://doi.org/10.1509/jmkg.73.5.30

Scherer, A. G., & Steinmann, H. (1999). Some remarks on the problem of incommensurability in organization studies. *Organization Studies*, 20(3), 519–544. https://doi.org/10.1177/0170840699203006

Schultz, M., & Hatch, M. J. (1996). Living with multiple paradigms the case of paradigm interplay in organizational culture studies. *Academy of Management Review*, 21(2), 529–557. https://doi.org/10.5465/amr.1996.9605060221

Schultz, M., & Hatch, M. J. (2003). The cycles of corporate branding: The case of the LEGO Company. *California Management Review*, 46(1), 6–26. https://doi.org/10.2307/41166229

Shee, P. S. B., & Abratt, R. (1989). A new approach to the corporate image management process. *Journal of Marketing Management*, 5(1), 63–76. https://doi.org/10.1080/0267257X.1989.9964088

Siggelkow, N. (2007). Persuasion with case studies. *The Academy of Management Journal*, 50(1), 20–24. https://doi.org/10.5465/amj.2007.24160882

Skålén, P., Pace, S., & Cova, B. (2015). Firm-brand community value co-creation as alignment of practices. *European Journal of Marketing*, 49(3–4), 596–620. https://doi.org/10.1108/EJM-08-2013-0409

Tadajewski, M. (2004). The philosophy of marketing theory: Historical and future directions. *The Marketing Review*, 4(3), 307–340. https://doi.org/10.1362/1469347042223373

Thompson, C. J., Rindfleisch, A., & Arsel, Z. (2006). Emotional branding and the strategic value of the doppelgänger brand image. *Journal of Marketing*, 70(1), 50–64. https://doi.org/10.1509/jmkg.70.1.050.qxd

Törmälä, M., & Gyrd-Jones, R. I. (2017). Development of new B2B venture corporate brand identity: A narrative performance approach. *Industrial Marketing Management*, 65, 76–85. https://doi.org/10.1016/j.indmarman.2017.05.002

Törmälä, M., & Saraniemi, S. (2018). The roles of business partners in corporate brand image co-creation. *Journal of Product & Brand Management*, 27(1), 29–40. https://doi.org/10.1108/JPBM-01-2016-1089

Urde, M. (2003). Core value-based corporate brand building. *European Journal of Marketing*, 37(7–8), 1017–1040. https://doi.org/10.1108/03090560310477645

Urde, M. (2009). Uncovering the corporate brand's core values. *Management Decision*, 47(4), 616–638. https://doi.org/10.1108/00251740910959459

Urde, M. (2013). The corporate brand identity matrix. *Journal of Brand Management*, 20(9), 742–761. https://doi.org/10.1057/bm.2013.12

Vallaster, C., & von Wallpach, S. (2013). An online discursive inquiry into the social dynamics of multi-stakeholder brand meaning co-creation. *Journal of Business Research*, 66(9), 1505–1515. https://doi.org/10.1016/j.jbusres.2012.09.012

Venkatraman, N. (1989). Strategic orientation of business enterprises: The construct, dimensionality, and measurement. *Management Science*, 35(8), 942–962. https://doi.org/10.1287/mnsc.35.8.942

Verčič, A. T., & Verčič, D. (2007). Reputation as matching identities and images: Extending Davies and Chun's (2002) research on gaps between the internal and external perceptions of the corporate brand. *Journal of Marketing Communications*, 13(4), 277–290. https://doi.org/10.1080/13527260701300151

Vredenburg, J., Kapitan, S., Spry, A., & Kemper, J. A. (2020). Brands taking a stand: Authentic brand activism or woke washing? *Journal of Public Policy & Marketing*, 39(4), 444–460. https://doi.org/10.1177/0743915620947359

# 10
# COMMENTARY ON 'CO-CREATING CORPORATE BRANDS WITH MULTIPLE STAKEHOLDERS'

*Francisco Guzmán*

The world has changed at a pace that few would have predicted. While businesses were focusing on fully understanding the impact of the rapid digital and technological transformation driving the disruption of the status quo during the last decade, the COVID-19 pandemic brought another catalyst for change. As a consequence, corporate brands have had to quickly react to this tsunami of change that has affected life, business, and society (Lehmann, 2020). The digital transformation has allowed for stakeholders to be engaged with brands more than ever (Harmeling et al., 2017; Ramaswamy & Ozcan, 2016). Although brand co-creation as a strategy was already growing to build brand value and engagement, much in part due to the digitized and hyperconnected world in which we live (Ramaswamy & Ozcan, 2020; Swaminathan et al., 2020), the need to connect due to the pandemic has further increased this trend; 'new and accelerated customer interactions have upended the "rules of engagement"' (Accenture, 2020). Higher levels of stakeholder engagement in recent years have led to brands being defined collectively through the assemblage of heterogonous human and nonhuman actors (Price & Coulter, 2019).

The higher levels of stakeholder engagement are also altering the strategic direction of many corporate brands. On one hand, corporate brands are increasingly developing strategies with purpose (Iglesias & Ind, 2020) and taking socio-political stances (Moorman, 2020; Schmidt et al., 2021; Vredenburg et al., 2020) as a response to stakeholders' expectations (Bhagwat et al., 2020; Merrilees et al., 2021). On the other hand, the marketing discipline as a whole is at a cross point where there are calls for exploring how marketing can work for creating a better world and enable win-win actions that benefit multiple stakeholders (Chandy et al., 2021). Co-creation is a natural response to these challenges. The interaction of multiple stakeholders whilst co-creating value naturally leads to enabling win-win strategies for all involved. Multiple recent studies have explored the impact of brand co-creation in generating social value – i.e., creating a better world (e.g., Gilal et al., 2021; Iglesias et al., 2020b; Lahtinen & Närvänen, 2020; Simpson et al., 2020; Sreejesh et al., 2019).

What motivates stakeholder brand co-creation? Kennedy and Guzmán (2016) categorize firm and consumer motivational factors that lead to brand co-creation. From the firm's perspective, they identify organizational and brand goals as the firms' motivation to co-create. Obtaining a higher return on investment, conducting research, increasing available resources, aligning with a brand's mission statement, and enhancing their service, are the organizational goals, whereas building brand value, increasing brand loyalty and brand awareness, differentiating from competitors, and strengthening the brand experience, are the brand goals. From a consumer perspective, they identify how co-creation affects consumers' social status, how fun they find co-creating to be, how compatible the brand is to them in terms of values, how appealing they find brand communication to be, and how committed they are to a particular brand as the factors that influence consumers to co-create with a brand. Multi-stakeholder co-creation is motivated by reputation enhancement, experimentation, and relationship building (Pera et al., 2016). Other stakeholders, such as employees, are motivated to co-create by professional identity, financial, recognition, and career opportunities benefits (Amin et al., 2021). Furthermore, co-creation as a business strategy has also been explored, as it can occur non-prompted, driven by stakeholders, or prompted, driven by the brand (Kennedy & Guzmán, 2017). Whereas before the digital transformation of the past decade co-creation could only happen 'organically,' nowadays firms can orchestrate the brand co-creation process (Merz et al., 2018).

Corporate brands have historically represented an important source of value (Balmer & Gray, 2003). As focus shifted from product to corporate brands in order to leverage value across a firm's brand portfolio, corporate brands became the insignia for firms, and stakeholder co-creation of corporate brands also increased (Iglesias et al., 2020a; Mingione & Leoni, 2020). Corporate brand identity co-creation is an ongoing dynamic process where multiple internal and external stakeholders engage (Iglesias et al., 2020a). Corporate brands engage with different partners to co-create that perform any of the following roles: co-innovator, co-marketer, brand specialist, knowledge provider, referee, intermediary, or advocate (Törmälä & Saraniemi, 2018). The corporate brand experience has been identified to play a critical role for developing customers' involvement in value co-creation activities (Shamim et al., 2016). Given that the work on corporate brand co-creation can still be considered to be in its nascent stages, the four chapters included in this section shed light on corporate brand co-creation. All agree that co-creation is driven by the increase in technological advancements in the current hyperconnected world we live in and the increasing levels of stakeholder brand co-ownership, which implies a democratization of the value creation process.

In Chapter 6, Ramaswamy details how corporate brands are managing digital interactive platforms (DIP) that allow for the creation of value through interactions and highlights the democratization of the value creation process and the importance of the brand experiences provided to all participating stakeholders through these platforms. According to Ramaswamy, these interactional experience ecosystems lead to the theoretical conceptualization of the co-creation paradigm that can be defined as the interactional creation of value through the experience a stakeholder has within a digital ecosystem. The model he presents suggests that a co-creation paradigm of value creation requires focusing simultaneously on four business aspects: innovation, value, performance, and strategy. Ramaswamy concludes that an active engagement of stakeholders on these four business aspects will be critical for corporate brands to create value in the future.

In Chapter 7, von Wallpach and Hemetsberger conceptualize how corporate brands form, change, and develop in dynamic action nets, and how heterogeneity and instability foster the construction of dynamic brand identities. They argue that this is a radical way to conceptualize corporate brands given that, from an action net perspective, corporate brands are not so by definition, but become one through their branding activities regardless of the stakeholders that are interacting. In other words, corporate brand identity is the result of unstable and heterogeneous interactions between corporate actors and stakeholders in a dynamic and fluid digitized environment. In sum, von Wallpach and Hemetsberger's conceptualization highlights the challenge of balancing heterogeneous stakeholders' perspectives to craft a consistent corporate brand identity.

In Chapter 8, da Silveira and Simões also argue that corporate brand identity is dynamic and co-created by multiple stakeholders. They analyse and discuss the tension between the conventional and more recent conceptualizations of corporate brand identity and argue that the more conventional aspiration for an internal static/permanent identity and the more recent aspiration for a multi-stakeholder adaptive identity are both well-founded and reconcilable. They demonstrate that corporate brand identity changes gradually, gaining and losing salience over time. In other words, corporate brand identity is simultaneously enduring and dynamic, adaptive but not in constant flux, and determined by multiple stakeholders although more heavily influenced by managers' leadership behaviour. Their approach highlights the long-term challenge that co-ownership and democratizing the value creation process presents to corporate brands.

In Chapter 9, Mingione and Abratt discuss the theory of corporate brand alignment and its role in co-creating value for multiple stakeholders. They present a meta-paradigm model that simultaneously considers the corporate brand itself and the corporate branding process and describe the importance of both internal and external corporate brand alignment. By comparing an objectivist and interpretivist approach to interpreting corporate brand alignment, they explain how the former suggests that alignment requires unity of interpretations, whereas the latter suggests alignment means sharing, coherency, and connection between internal and external stakeholders. Their meta-paradigm model reconciles these opposing views and claims that corporate brand meaning is initially fixed and determined by managers and then shaped by its stakeholders' interpretations.

Overall, the four chapters in this section highlight the important role of corporate brands in generating firm value. Moreover, they highlight the shift – or democratization – in the process of value creation. As stakeholders interact in experiential digital brand platforms, value is co-created. These unstable and heterogenous multi-stakeholder interactions create corporate brand identities that are adaptive and that managers reconcile with their internal views. This process leads to the co-creation of corporate brand identity by coalescing value for multiple stakeholders and generating a win-win scenario for everyone involved. It is imperative that corporate brand strategies consider this process of value co-creation in the future (Swaminathan et al., 2020).

Although democratizing the process of value creation seems to be the present imperative, for brands to 'let go' is not easy. The challenge arises from two perspectives. On one hand, brand managers have to find a balance between crafting a consistent brand identity and allowing for multiple perspectives to build value. They have to overcome their egos and let other stakeholders have more control, which requires a certain level of executive maturity and trust in the data and process. On the other, corporate brands have to truly embrace technological change in order for stakeholders to fully engage in a win-win value creation process.

Ramaswamy argues in Chapter 6, 'the power of brand co-creation arises from combining brand's DIP experiences, and a collaborative innovation process that harnesses the insights, knowledge, skills, and ingenuity of all participants, in a mutually valuable manner.' In this type of interaction, however, the ever-present tension between brand identity and brand image comes to play; what the company wants their brand to represent versus what customers actually view of the brand. Moreover, in a democratized value creation process this tension is exacerbated, because the identity itself is being co-created by multiple stakeholders, and in the current market, in real-time. Brand managers are thus forced to let go and relinquish control while still being responsible for guiding the value creation process – to ensure consistency while embracing diverse perspectives. Therefore, the key takeaway for brand managers is that they must focus on shifting their managerial approach from crafting to guiding. In other words, brand managers should embrace an orchestra conductor or, even better, jazz ensemble leader mentality where their role is to direct the input of all of the performers and be open to a bit of improvisation.

Moving forward, with the understanding that corporate branding depends on the integration of stakeholders to create value, brands must focus on continuous learning, innovation, and successful utilization of the evolving technology (Hollebeek et al., 2019). Ultimately, technology enables stakeholder-brand connections (van der Westhuizen, 2018) and increases the perceived ability to influence (Kennedy & Guzmán, 2017) and co-create value with a brand (Kaufmann et al., 2016). Corporate brands must thus keep exploring how to leverage technology and benefit from the digitization of brand experiences to achieve higher levels of stakeholder advocacy, co-creation, engagement, and repurchase. Purpose-driven strategies allow for stakeholders to have higher levels of trust that boost co-creation (Iglesias et al., 2020b), which could also allow corporate brands to rebound faster in case of committing a transgression (Kennedy & Guzmán, 2021). Given the long-term technological, socioeconomic, and geopolitical trends that are reshaping the marketplace (Rust, 2020), leveraging technology and embracing purpose-driven strategies is essential for corporate branding.

## References

Accenture (2020). A new era in customer engagement. Retrieved May 5, 2021 from www.accenture.com/_acnmedia/PDF-125/Accenture-A-New-Era-in-Customer-Engagement.pdf

Amin, M., Shamim, A., Ghazali, Z., & Khan, I. (2021). Employee motivation to co-create value (EMCCV): Construction and validation of scale. *Journal of Retailing and Consumer Services*, 58, 102334.

Balmer, J. M. T., & Gray, E. R. (2003). Corporate brands: What are they? What of them? *European Journal of Marketing*, 37(7–8), 972–997.

Bhagwat, Y., Warren, N. L., Beck, J. T., & Watson IV, G. F. (2020). Corporate sociopolitical activism and firm value. *Journal of Marketing*, 84(5), 1–21.

Chandy, R. K., Johar, G. V., Moorman, C., & Roberts, J. H. (2021). Better marketing for a better world. *Journal of Marketing*, 85(3), 1–9.

Gilal, F. G., Paul, J., Gilal, N. G., & Gilal, R. G. (2021). Strategic CSR-brand fit and customers' brand passion: Theoretical extension and analysis. *Psychology & Marketing*, 38(5), 759–773.

Harmeling, C. M., Moffett, J. W., Arnold, M. J., & Carlson, B. D. (2017). Toward a theory of customer engagement marketing. *Journal of the Academy of Marketing Science*, 45(3), 312–335.

Hollebeek, L. D., Sprott, D. E., Andreassen, T. W., Costley, C., Klaus, P., Kuppelwieser, V., Karahasanovic, A., Taguchi, T., Ul Islam, J., & Rather, R. A. (2019). Customer engagement in evolving technological environments: Synopsis and guiding propositions. *European Journal of Marketing*, 53(9), 2018–2023.

Iglesias, O., & Ind, N. (2020). Towards a theory of conscientious corporate brand co-creation: The next key challenge in brand management. *Journal of Brand Management*, 27(6), 710–720.

Iglesias, O., Landgraf, P., Ind, N., Markovic, S., & Koporcic, N. (2020a). Corporate brand identity co-creation in business-to-business contexts. *Industrial Marketing Management*, 85, 32–43.

Iglesias, O., Markovic, S., Bagherzadeh, M., & Singh, J. J. (2020b). Co-creation: A key link between corporate social responsibility, customer trust, and customer loyalty. *Journal of Business Ethics*, 163(1), 151–166.

Kaufmann, H. R., Loureiro, S. M. C., & Manarioti, A. (2016). Exploring behavioural branding, brand love and brand co-creation. *Journal of Product & Brand Management*, 25(6), 516–526.

Kennedy, E., & Guzmán, F. (2016). Co-creation of brand identities: Consumer and industry influence and motivations. *Journal of Consumer Marketing*, 33(5), 313–323.

Kennedy, E., & Guzmán, F. (2017). When perceived ability to influence plays a role: Brand co-creation in Web 2.0. *Journal of Product and Brand Management*, 26(4), 342–350.

Kennedy, E., & Guzmán, F. (2021). No matter what you do, I still love you: An examination of consumer reaction to brand transgressions. *Journal of Product & Brand Management*, 30(4), 594–608.

Lahtinen, S., & Närvänen, E. (2020). Co-creating sustainable corporate brands: A consumer framing approach. *Corporate Communications: An International Journal*, 25(3), 447–461.

Lehmann, D. (2020). The evolving world of research in marketing and the blending of theory and data. *International Journal of Research in Marketing*, 35, 27–42.

Merrilees, B., Miller, D., & Yakimova, R. (2021). Building brands through internal stakeholder engagement and co-creation. *Journal of Product & Brand Management*. https://doi.org/10.1108/JPBM-03-2020-2784.

Merz, M. A., Zarantonello, L., & Grappi, S. (2018). How valuable are your customers in the brand value co-creation process? The development of a customer co-creation value (CCCV) scale. *Journal of Business Research*, 82, 79–89.

Mingione, M., & Leoni, L. (2020). Blurring B2C and B2B boundaries: Corporate brand value co-creation in B2B2C markets. *Journal of Marketing Management, 36*(1–2), 72–99.

Moorman, C. (2020). Commentary: Brand activism in a political world. *Journal of Public Policy & Marketing, 39*(4), 388–392.

Pera, R., Occhiocupo, N., & Clarke, J. (2016). Motives and resources for value co-creation in a multistakeholder ecosystem: A managerial perspective. *Journal of Business Research, 69*(10), 4033–4041.

Price, L. L., & Coulter, R. A. (2019). Crossing bridges: Assembling culture into brands and brands into consumers' global local cultural lives. *Journal of Consumer Psychology, 29*(3), 547–554.

Ramaswamy, V., & Ozcan, K. (2016). Brand value co-creation in a digitalized world: An integrative framework and research implications. *International Journal of Research in Marketing, 33*(1), 93–106.

Ramaswamy, V., & Ozcan, K. (2020). The 'interacted' actor in platformed networks: Theorizing practices of managerial experience value co-creation. *Journal of Business & Industrial Marketing, 35*(7), 1165–1178.

Rust, R. (2020). The future of marketing. *International Journal of Research in Marketing, 37*, 15–26.

Schmidt, H., Ind, N., Guzmán, F., & Kennedy, E. (2021). Sociopolitical brand activism. *Journal of Product & Brand Management*. https://doi.org/10.1108/JPBM-03-2020-2805

Shamim, A., Ghazali, Z., & Albinsson, P. A. (2016). An integrated model of corporate brand experience and customer value co-creation behavior. *International Journal of Retail & Distribution Management, 44*(2), 139–158.

Simpson, B., Robertson, J. L., & White, K. (2020). How co-creation increases employee corporate social responsibility and organizational engagement: The moderating role of self-construal. *Journal of Business Ethics, 166*(2), 331–350.

Sreejesh, S., Sarkar, J. G., & Sarkar, A. (2019). CSR through social media: Examining the intervening factors. *Marketing Intelligence & Planning, 38*(1), 103–120.

Swaminathan, V., Sorescu, A., Steenkamp, J. B. E., O'Guinn, T. C. G., & Schmitt, B. (2020). Branding in a hyperconnected world: Refocusing theories and rethinking boundaries. *Journal of Marketing, 84*(2), 24–46.

Törmälä, M., & Saraniemi, S. (2018). The roles of business partners in corporate brand image co-creation. *Journal of Product & Brand Management, 27*(1), 29–40.

van der Westhuizen, L-M. (2018). Brand loyalty: Exploring self-brand connection and brand experience. *Journal of Product & Brand Management, 27*(2), 172–184.

Vredenburg, J., Kapitan, S., Spry, A., & Kemper, J. A. (2020). Brands taking a stand: Authentic brand activism or woke washing? *Journal of Public Policy & Marketing, 39*(4), 444–460.

# C

# Building strong corporate brands
Towards valuable and sustainable experiences

# 11
# B*CANVAS 2.0
## Holistic and co-created brand management tool and use cases for corporate brands

*Carsten Baumgarth*

### 1. Corporate branding as a holistic and co-created management concept

Compared with classic brand management for products or services, corporate branding is much more complex due to the larger number of stakeholders, the greater importance of employees and corporate culture, and the broader consideration of all corporate actions (Harris & de Chernatony, 2001; Balmer & Gray, 2003). A strong corporate brand is made up of many single building blocks and the totality is more than the sum of its parts. Hence, corporate branding is based on a holistic view of the whole company, its stakeholders, its competitive environment, and its brand.

In addition, a corporate brand is not the result of decisions made by a single or a few managers, but a continuous process of co-creation. An increasing number of researchers discuss the concept of co-creation for corporate brands (Iglesias et al., 2013, 2020; Hatch & Schulz, 2010; Juntunen, 2012; Gregory, 2007). Most of these papers focus on the co-creation of the corporate brand by the interaction with external stakeholders, such as customers, but one important and often neglected stakeholder group for corporate branding is the employees and external professional service companies, like advertisement agencies and brand consultants. The development of a strong corporate brand is based on a common understanding of the corporate brand by all these 'brand co-creators.'

Corporate brand equity depends on the interaction of all elements and their synergies (holistic approach) and a common internal understanding of all 'brand co-creators.' Therefore, it is important for research, teaching, and management practice to have models and tools available that allow a holistic approach for all 'brand co-creators' that delivers an easy-to-understand view of the corporate brand elements. The goal of this chapter is to present the latest brand canvas version B★Canvas 2.0 as such a tool. Additionally, this chapter further discusses different B★Canvas 2.0 use cases in brand management practice and teaching.

### 2. Brand canvas

#### 2.1 Business model canvas and more

The idea of mapping complex issues onto one single canvas is not really new. Osterwalder and Pigneuer published their Business Model Canvas in 2010 (Osterwalder & Pigneuer, 2010; see also Osterwalder, 2014), which quickly became widespread, especially in corporate practice and the start-up scene. Google currently returns around 3,330,000 hits for the search term 'Business Model Canvas' (Google, 2021), and in 2020, the platform Strategyzer reported more than 5 million users of the Business Model Canvas (Strategyzer, 2020). The Business Model Canvas is often associated with concepts such as Design Thinking (Stickdorn & Schneider, 2011; Lewrick et al., 2017) and Lean Start-up (general Ries, 2011; see also Felin et al., 2020; Onken & Campeau, 2016).

There are also a number of publications on the application of the original or slightly adapted Business Model Canvas for industries and individual companies (e.g., Mobile Payment Service: Zolonowski et al., 2014; Artists: Carter & Carter, 2020, Social Business: Sparviero, 2019). Based on the classic Business Model Canvas, the idea has also been adapted to various management fields. Joyce and Paquin (2016) proposed an adapted Business Model Canvas that integrates sustainability in particular. Ahmed et al. (2014) presented an innovation canvas including an instructor guide at the American Society for Engineering Education (ASEE) conference. Habermann (2014) and Habermann and Schmidt (2018, 2020) have developed a comprehensive Project Canvas.

The canvas models listed earlier, and others, have certain characteristics in common:

- Clear visualization of a complex management field on a single canvas
- Mental decomposition of the overall problem into individual building blocks and elements that are, however, interrelated
- Tools for groups with different backgrounds and expertise
- Visual mapping
- Use of a simple language and easy-understandable symbols
- Flexibility (e.g., Canvas can be taken anywhere, and content is often recorded on Post-it®, making it shareable and modifiable).

Corporate branding can also be characterized as complex, consisting of many individual elements and involving multiple (internal) stakeholders from different fields (e.g., C-level, marketing, R&D, HR, etc.) and backgrounds, which is why the Canvas methodology is fundamentally suitable for (corporate) brand management. The next section presents the B★Canvas 2.0.

## 2.2 Brand Canvas B*Canvas 2.0

### 2.2.1 Overview

In 2018, the first version of the B★Canvas was published as open source under a Creative Commons license at the B★lab, a laboratory for researching and testing new brand approaches located at the Berlin School of Economics and Law (also Baumgarth, 2019). The B★Canvas is based on a brand management model, which was developed in a research project for the description and evaluation of corporate brands in the context of cultural institutions such as museums and opera houses (Baumgarth et al., 2016), as well as the earlier-mentioned general characteristics of the canvas method. In general, the development process followed the design thinking philosophy with direct user-integration, feedback, and trial-and-error processes. The result of this process was a tool, which from a practitioner's perspective was better than existing solutions. The first version of the brand canvas was tested in several master and MBA brand courses at universities in Germany and Switzerland. On the basis of own observations of the groups and the group results, and grounded in explicit user feedback, the tool was improved over several loops. At the beginning of 2018, we reached, similar to the idea of theoretical saturation in the context of the Grounded Theory (Glaser & Strauss, 1967), a 'stable' version. The student and management participants of several workshops, training, and consulting projects understood this version could work with the tool and produced meaningful and relevant descriptions and evaluations of their corporate brands. Additionally, the satisfaction of the participants reached a high level. Therefore, we published the B★Canvas online (2018) and in an article (Baumgarth, 2019). In the next years, we used and improved this version in various consulting and teaching projects for corporate brands in the technology, sustainability, and cultural sector, among others. In January 2021, the improved B★Canvas 2.0 was published. Figure 11.1 shows the current version of the B★Canvas, which can be used for free under the Creative Commons license CC BY-SA 4.0.

### 2.2.2 Building blocks and elements

The B★Canvas 2.0 consists of three groups of building blocks and a total of 14 elements. In the following, the individual building blocks cannot be dealt with in detail, as this would go beyond the scope of this chapter (see classical branding textbooks, Keller/Swaminathan, 2020; de Chernatony et al., 2011; Beverland, 2021; Baumgarth, 2014). Rather, key questions and some selected references are intended to illustrate the respective building block and its elements.

1. BRAND FOUNDATION

Brand foundation is invisible to customers and external stakeholders since this building block is made out of the brand's internal factors. However, they form the necessary prerequisites for a

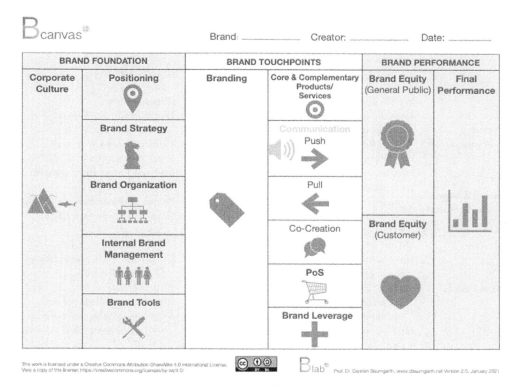

Figure 11.1   B★Canvas 2.0

brand to be managed professionally and successfully. As individual elements, the brand foundation factors include the corporate culture, the brand positioning, the brand strategy, the brand organization, the internal brand management, as well as the implementation of brand tools. Table 11.1 summarizes the elements of the potential factors.

*Table 11.1* Elements of the brand foundation

| Elements | Key questions | Selected theoretical reference points and references |
|---|---|---|
| Corporate culture | How important is the branding concept for our top management? Are the values of our company the guiding principles for all our decisions and behaviours? Do we follow an inside-out (brand orientation) or outside-in (market orientation) approach? | **Corporate culture** Schein (1999, 2004), Cameron and Quinn (2006), Hatch and Schultz 2008) **Brand orientation** Urde (1994, 1999), Baumgarth (2010), Balmer (2017) |
| Positioning | Do we have a written brand positioning statement? Is our brand positioning relevant for our main stakeholders (e.g., customers, potential employees)? Do we differentiate ourselves from the competition? Is our brand positioning authentic? | **Brand positioning** Koch (2014) **Authenticity** Gilmore and Pine (2007), Beverland (2009) |
| Brand strategy | Do we follow a clear and logical mapping of our brands to our products and services? Is our brand strategy simple and comprehensible for external stakeholders? Is the fit between our corporate brand and our products and services high? | **Brand architecture** Laforet and Saunders (2007); Aaker and Joachimsthaler (2000), Strebinger (2014), Nguyen et al. (2018) **Brand extension** Völckner and Sattler (2006) |
| Brand organization | Who is responsible for the brand management? Does the top management support the brand management? What is the expertise of the responsible persons? Do the people in charge have a power base? | **Organization** Low and Fullerton (1994), Kernstock et al. (2014) **Skills of brand manager** Brexendorf and Daecke (2012) |
| Internal brand management | How do we anchor the brand inside the company? Is our internal brand management professional and effective? Have we implemented an internal network of brand ambassadors? Do our employees know and live our brand values? | **Internal brand management** Ind (2007, 2017) **Brand ambassadors** Schmidt and Baumgarth (2018), Hesse et al. (2020) |
| Brand tools | Have we implemented rules and guidelines for the implementation of a corporate design? Have we implemented rules and guidelines for the integration of brand values in all our operations? Have we implemented tools for tracking the short- and long-term brand performance (e.g., brand equity, brand image, brand trust)? Have we legally protected our trademarks? | **Corporate design (guidelines) and brand books** Wheeler (2006) **Brand controlling system** Kriegbaum (2011); Tomczak et al. (2014); Baumgarth and Douven (2018) **Trademark management** Lemper (2012) |

## 2. BRAND TOUCHPOINTS

The brand touchpoints form the interface to the customer and other external stakeholder groups, making the brand perceptible and tangible for them. Here, too, a broad approach to brand management is taken, since brand touchpoints encompass far more than pure (media) communication. The basis of all brand touchpoints is branding, because signs like brand name, logo, slogan, architecture, design among others, are integrated in all other brand touchpoints. The external stakeholder cannot directly perceive the branding without a brand touch point. The B★canvas 2.0 differentiates with products and services, communication, Point-of-Sale (PoS) and brand leverage, four different categories of direct brand touchpoints (see Table 11.2).

*Table 11.2* Elements of Brand Touchpoints

| Elements | Key questions | Selected theoretical reference points and references |
|---|---|---|
| Branding | By which signs is our brand recognizable? Is it easy to learn and remember our brand signs? Are our brand signs different to our competitors? Do our brand signs express our positioning? Do the brand signs fit well together? | **Single brand elements** Klink (2003), Machado et al. (2015), Henderson and Cote (1998), Raffelt (2012), **Integrated branding** Langner (2003) |
| Core and complementary products/services | What products and services do we offer to the market? Is the user experience of our product and services high? Do our products and services express our positioning? | **User and brand experience** Brakus et al. (2009) **Product and service design** Kreuzbauer (2013), Bloch (1995) |
| Communication | Do we reach our relevant stakeholders with our push communication? Do we offer interesting and relevant content for our relevant stakeholders? Do our communication tools follow the integrated communication approach? Do we interact and collaborate with our relevant stakeholders? Does our brand communication express our positioning? | **Brand communication** Rossiter et al. (2018) **Content marketing/brand journalism** Arrese and Pérez-Latre (2017) **Co-creation** Ind and Schmidt (2019), Ramaswamy and Ozcan (2014) |
| PoS | Are we achieving a high level of distribution with our own and indirect distribution channels? Do our distribution channel express our positioning? | **Store** Spence et al. (2014); Ebster and Garaus (2011) **Online store** Ha and Lennon (2010) **Pop-up-store** Baumgarth and Kastner (2012) |

(*Continued*)

Table 11.2 (Continued)

| Elements | Key questions | Selected theoretical reference points and references |
|---|---|---|
| ✛<br>**Brand leverage** | With which other image objects such as brands, regions, testimonials, influencers, sports, art, etc. do we visibly connect our brand?<br>Do these partners drive our visibility and reach?<br>Are the collaborations for our stakeholder credible?<br>Do our partners express our positioning? | **Brand leveraging (overview)**<br>*Michel and Willing (2020), Keller and Swaminathan (2020), pp. 291–326)*<br>**Single options**<br>*Blackett and Boad (1999), Erdogan et al. (2001); Thakor and Kohli (1996); Lim and O'Cass (2001); Lou and Yuan (2019), Knoll and Matthews (2017)* |

### 3. BRAND PERFORMANCE

The third and last building block of the B★Canvas 2.0 is brand performance, which is divided in three elements: general public-based brand equity, customer-based brand equity, and final performance. In contrast to the other two building blocks (brand foundation and brand touchpoints), this dimension is not a management task but answers the question about the output of all brand management activities. In particular, the final performance depends on the company type and the motives of the top management and/or the company owners. For example, for a conventional company, key performance indicators like the financial brand value, profit, or market share are typical aspects of this element. In contrast for a social business, indicators like financial survival and social impact are the main goals. Table 11.3 summarizes the three elements of brand performance.

Table 11.3 Elements of brand performance

| Elements | Key questions | Selected theoretical reference points and references |
|---|---|---|
| **Brand equity (General public)** | What is the reputation of our brand in society?<br>How do opinion leaders (e.g., critics, influencers) and the media rate our brand?<br>Do we win prizes and awards for our brand? | **Sentiment analysis**<br>*Liu (2020), Kübler et al. (2020)*<br>**Reputation**<br>*Fombrun et al. (2000)* |
| **Brand equity (Customer)** | How well known (recognition, recall) is our brand among customers?<br>How do customers and non-customers evaluate our brand (e.g., attitude, sympathy, trust)?<br>How strong is customer loyalty and the willingness to recommend our brand? | **Brand metrics**<br>*Fetscherin (2020)*<br>**Customer-based brand equity**<br>*Keller (1993), Yoo and Donthu (2001), Salinas (2009)*<br>**Brand loyalty**<br>*Keiningham et al. (2008), Odin et al. (2001)* |
| **Final performance** | What final goals are we pursuing with our company?<br>How high is the economic brand value?<br>How well do we meet economic goals such as price premium, profit, market shar, or return on investment?<br>How strong is our social impact? | **Brand value**<br>*Salinas (2009)*<br>**Impact on society**<br>*Florman et al. (2016)* |

## 3. Use cases of the B★Canvas 2.0

Building on this overview of the B★Canvas 2.0, this chapter outlines some applications of the tool in brand management practice and teaching in the form of four different use cases. This section describes four scenarios for the practical use of the B★Canvas 2.0: description, evaluation, development, and teaching of corporate branding. In reality, a corporate brand project often combines two or more of these use cases. The goal of this section is to clarify the flexibility of the B★Canvas 2.0 tool as well as the presentation of concrete, real-world-tested recommendations and routines.

### 3.1 Use case 1: description of corporate brands – the Werkhaus case

The first use case for the B★Canvas 2.0 is the description and basic understanding of existing corporate brands. This application can be the basis for (internal or external) brand projects, because the B★Canvas 2.0 supports a common understanding of the status quo of a corporate brand in the brand project team. This is particularly important and challenging for corporate brands because a lot of different departments and people with a different professional background work together in a corporate brand project. In addition to that, the structure of the B★Canvas 2.0 ensures the common understanding of all members of the project team, and the recognition that corporate branding is more than the brand name, logo, and communication. The goal of the first application is the pure systematic and holistic description without any evaluation of the single elements.

The company and corporate brand Werkhaus (www.werkhaus.de) was selected as a brand to illustrate this use case. This corporate brand was chosen because it is a medium-sized company with a limited level of complexity, which makes it easier to present the B★Canvas 2.0 of this brand in the context of this chapter. Furthermore, the author knows the brand and the owner family well, which allowed good access to internal information. The case study is based on publicly available materials (e.g., sustainability report, catalogue, website, social media channels), their own observations (e.g., stores, factory and headquarter), internal materials (e.g., photos), and an interview with the two founders and owners. The company and brand Werkhaus was founded in 1992 by Eva and Holger Danneberg and is located in Bad Bodenteich (Germany). It produces mainly from medium-density fibreboard (MDF) in E1 quality, various products for the office and living areas, toys and displays for retailers and trade fairs. The first products were kaleidoscopes in 1992. This product is still produced and sold today. However, currently the B-to-B sector (displays for the trade, trade fair construction) forms the main field of the company's activities with a share of sales of about 70%. The company started in 1992 with 15 employees. In 2020, the company employed around 180 employees. Figure 11.2 shows a condensed version of the B★Canvas 2.0 with the most important information about the corporate brand. The sketch of the Werkhaus B★Canvas illustrates the content of the single canvas elements. The complete Werkhaus B★Canvas includes more detailed information, additional visual artifacts, and concrete numbers.

### 3.2 Use case 2: holistic evaluation of corporate brands – brand audit approach

A second use case for the B★Canvas 2.0 is brand controlling and in particular the brand audit approach. Brand controlling, as the informational basis of professional brand management, is, on the whole, a strongly neglected area, both in brand science and in practice. For many years, this has created a legitimization crisis for brand management and brand-oriented marketing in

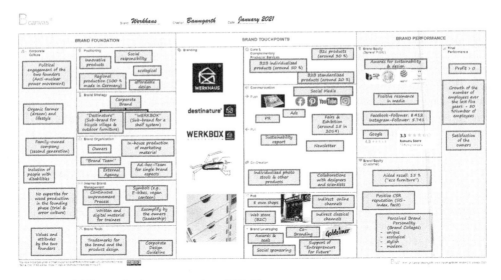

*Figure 11.2* B★Canvas for the corporate brand Werkhaus

many companies. Without 'hard' figures, internal acceptance at the top management level and the influence of brand management and marketing is severely jeopardized. Despite the repeatedly postulated emphasis on the company-wide philosophy claim of marketing ('customer orientation') and brand ('brand orientation'), in practice, the range of brand management tasks is often limited to communication. This loss of importance has been sufficiently addressed in the literature and empirically proven (Verhoef & Leeflang, 2009, Verhoef et al., 2011; Homburg et al., 2015).

Therefore, brand and marketing departments are increasingly trying to make their activities measurable and comparable with key figures. For some years now, digitization has been meeting this concern, by providing a large number of 'hard' key performance indicators (KPIs), such as visits or conversion rates, that are almost automatically part of the associated tools, such as the company's own website, social media applications, marketing automation, etc. However, these performance-oriented KPIs are usually campaign-oriented, short-term in nature, and limited to individual marketing tools. Holistic fields of activity such as the management of a corporate brand can hardly be controlled by such KPIs. Therefore, the necessary development of a stronger number orientation of brand management through KPIs must be supplemented by holistic brand controlling approaches.

Such a holistic view of the corporate brand is made possible by a brand audit. Historically, brand audits can be seen as a further development of marketing audits. A classic definition of marketing audits comes from Kotler et al. (1977, p. 27):

> A marketing audit is a comprehensive, systematic, independent, and periodic examination of a company's – or business unit's – marketing environment, objectives, strategies, and activities with a view to determining problem areas and opportunities and recommending a plan of action to improve the company's performance.

Important characteristics of marketing audits are the comprehensive, systematic, independent assessment of the quality of marketing, repeated over time, and the derivation of suggestions for improvement based on this assessment. These characteristic features also formed the starting point for developing a definition of brand audits. With the change in perspective from marketing to brand management and from market or customer orientation to brand orientation (Urde et al., 2013), the basic principles of marketing audits can be transferred to the area of brand. According to these, a brand audit can be defined as follows (Baumgarth et al., 2016, p. 55; similar to Jenner, 2005, p. 200):

> A brand audit is a comprehensive, systematic, independent assessment of the quality of the brand, repeated at intervals, and based on this, the derivation of improvement approaches.

Such a brand audit fulfils the following functions:

1  Identification and reduction of weaknesses of the brand
2  Identification of opportunities for strengthening and/or growing the brand
3  Promotion of learning processes within the company
4  Thinking in contexts as well as understanding and acting across departments.

The core of every brand audit is a brand model that comprehensively depicts the most important facets of a brand. This brand model can be provided by the B★Canvas 2.0, which thus represents the core of a brand audit. In addition to the pure description of the brand with the help of the B★Canvas 2.0 (see Section 3.1), the individual elements must be evaluated as part of the brand audit in order to identify strengths and weaknesses. For this purpose, a methodology with the following features has proven successful in practice (for details, see Baumgarth et al., 2016):

- Formation of an external brand audit group with diverse expertise (e.g., brand management, human resource management, industry knowledge, design and legal aspects)
- Derivation of 6–7 assessment criteria per element of the B★Canvas 2.0 (in total, usually around 70–100 criteria)
- Development of a scoring model for each assessment criterion (see Table 11.4)
- Weighting of the criteria and elements by the external audit group
- Collection of qualitative and quantitative data (primary and secondary research, mixed-method approach, triangulation of the data)
- Evaluation of each criterion and documentation of rationale (see last column in Table 11.4).
- Calculation of the values for the elements, building blocks, and the overall brand.

To illustrate the practical implementation of a brand audit for corporate brands, a project from the cultural sector is outlined in the following text. In order to maintain the anonymity of the project partner, in the following, the museum will be referred to as ARTMUSEUM. The ARTMUSEUM is a small private museum in a large European capital, which is dedicated to a female artist. In a first step, the B★CANVAS was adapted and tailored to the specifics of this industry. For example, 'museum store and gastronomy' was integrated as an additional brand touch point and the final brand performance was concretized by visitor numbers. In a second step, a total of 98 assessment criteria were derived for the 15 elements of the B★Canvas. Experts from academia and cultural practice estimated the importance of each dimension, which was used as a weighting factors in the scoring model. In the third step, information was collected by the external audit team (five persons). In particular, the following data were taken into account:

- Internet presence of the ARTMUSEUM and the most important competitors
- ARTMUSEUM communication materials (e.g., flyers, posters, exhibition catalogues)

*Carsten Baumgarth*

Table 11.4 Sample worksheet of the B★Canvas 2.0-Brand Audit

| | The corporate brand X... | 100 % (positive) | 75 % | 50 % | 25 % | 0 % (negative) | Sources and justification |
|---|---|---|---|---|---|---|---|
| .... | | | | | | | |
| **Element 3: Brand strategy (Brand foundation)** | | | | | | | |
| **Fortification of the corporate brand** | ... Offers all products and services with a strong and clear link to the corporate brand. | All products and services offer under the corporate brand. | All products and services show a clear link to the corporate brand. | Most product and services show a clear link to the corporate brand. | Most products and services show only a moderate link to the corporate brand. | All products and services operate more or less with independent product brands, with no link to the corporate brand. | |
| ... | | | | | | | |
| **Element 13: Brand equity (customer) (Brand Performance)** | | | | | | | |
| **Brand recall** | ... Is well known (unaided brand recall) on the market. | highest unaided brand recall in the market. | leading with other brands regarding the unaided brand recall. | among the top 30 % regarding the unaided brand recall | among the 75 % regarding the unaided brand recall. | is more or less unknown on the market. | |
| ... | | | | | | | |

- Social media channels of the ARTMUSEUM and the most important competitors
- Guest book
- Travel guide and travel platforms
- Employee survey (n = 7, primary research)
- Visitor survey (n = 213, primary research)
- Online branding test (n = 27, primary research)
- Management interviews with the director, the curator, and the marketing manager
- Observations and field notes in the museum

This information was used by the brand audit team in a fourth step to systematically describe and score the brand using the B★Canvas. Using a scoring model, the 98 individual assessments were condensed into 15 elements, three dimensions and an overall score. In the fifth and final step, the information was prepared for a workshop and the project documentation, with the central representation, the 'pie diagram' presented in Figure 11.3. The different widths of the 'pie pieces' symbolize the varying importance of the elements and are based on the expert survey from Step 2. In order to communicate the assessment quickly and easily, the cake pieces were marked with the colours green (more than 75 %), yellow (50–75 %), and red (0–49 %) depending on the assessment result ('traffic-light metaphor'). During the workshop, not only were the results presented (approx. 20 % of the workshop time), but suggestions for improvement were

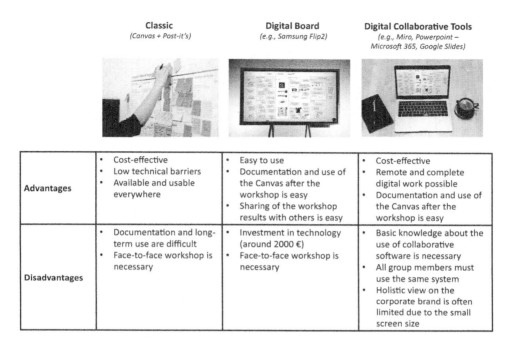

|  | Classic<br>(Canvas + Post-it's) | Digital Board<br>(e.g., Samsung Flip2) | Digital Collaborative Tools<br>(e.g., Miro, Powerpoint – Microsoft 365, Google Slides) |
|---|---|---|---|
| Advantages | • Cost-effective<br>• Low technical barriers<br>• Available and usable everywhere | • Easy to use<br>• Documentation and use of the Canvas after the workshop is easy<br>• Sharing of the workshop results with others is easy | • Cost-effective<br>• Remote and complete digital work possible<br>• Documentation and use of the Canvas after the workshop is easy |
| Disadvantages | • Documentation and long-term use are difficult<br>• Face-to-face workshop is necessary | • Investment in technology (around 2000 €)<br>• Face-to-face workshop is necessary | • Basic knowledge about the use of collaborative software is necessary<br>• All group members must use the same system<br>• Holistic view on the corporate brand is often limited due to the small screen size |

*Figure 11.3* Brand audit results of the ARTMUSEUM

worked out with the whole team of the ARTMUSEUM. In a second workshop after half a year, it was evaluated whether, and how, the improvements were realized.

### 3.3 Use Case 3: developing start-up brands – classic, digital, and micro-boards for start-ups

The third-use case is the development and/or the improvement of a corporate brand in a brand project. This section describes the use case by the example of workshops for start-up brands.

New companies are currently emerging in the digital environment, but also in traditional fields such as food, mobility, and clothing, which as start-ups also regularly build a corporate brand explicitly or, more frequently, implicitly. Although the topic of brand was still considered of little importance by founders and start-ups years ago (Rode, 2004), start-ups are increasingly recognizing the strategic relevance of the corporate brand for market success, for the search for investors and the exit, as well as for employer branding (Rus et al., 2018; Konecnik Ruzzier/Ruzzier, 2015; Bresciani and Eppler, 2010). These companies also often lack a deep understanding and know-how as to the complexity and holistic nature of brand management due to the background of the founding team (e.g., technology, natural sciences, engineering, computer science) as well as the contextual factors of the start-up such as investors and start-up philosophies (e.g., lean start-up approach) (Rode and Vallaster, 2005). The start-up team is also frequently confronted with a time allocation challenge, and in many cases brand management is not the first priority (Wong and Merrilees, 2005). This regularly leads to start-ups changing their brand assets (e.g., name, logo) multiple times, building multiple brands, not fully exploiting the potential of their business idea, or even failing in the end. The proposed B*Canvas 2.0 can help start-ups systematically conceptualize and implement their brand even without decades of experience in

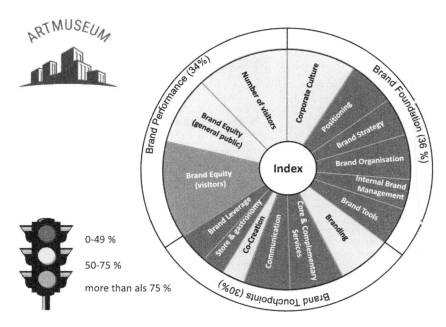

*Figure 11.4* Technological tools for the development of a start-up brand via B★Canvas 2.0

branding and marketing. In addition to that, the B★Canvas 2.0 is flexible and can incorporate future adaption and developments, which are typical for start-ups (Sommer et al., 2009). In contrast to the two application fields presented in the previous sections, this application starts with the development of something new. Two formats have proven themselves in practice: (1) 'Sprint' and (2) 'Living Document.' Based on Google Sprint (Knapp, 2016), the development of a brand concept can be organized with the help of the B★Canvas 2.0 in a 3–4-hour 'Sprint' workshop, in which the individual tasks are very tightly timed and the focus is more on completion than on perfection in detail. The 'Living Document' approach is more about using and developing the B★Canvas 2.0 over a long period of time. This can be useful, for example, when individual elements such as brand positioning, branding, or brand leverage have been developed and/or changed. It is also often a good idea to combine both approaches in order to develop an overview and a uniform understanding of corporate brand management in the founding team in a first sprint and then to develop the open or unclear elements in projects and workshops and then to complete or change the B★Canvas 2.0 over time. In both cases, it is a good idea to design the B★Canvas so that it is visible and available to all participants and changes can be made easily. Three technologies are recommended as possible solutions, as summarized in Figure 11.4.

### 3.4 Use case 4: teaching brand management – the one-semester student project

A final use case of the B★Canvas 2.0 is its use in courses at universities and in management training. The author has been using the B★Canvas in master's courses on brand management for several years. This is a combination of classic input sessions and a student project. In a one-semester course with 14 weeks (each with four semester hours per week), the sequence shown in Table 11.5 has proven to be a successful framework.

*Table 11.5* Blueprint for a one-semester master course, 'Brand Management'

| Week | Content | Format |
|---|---|---|
| 1 | Overview and presentation of B★Canvas 2.0 and presentation of the sector and the project brands, group building (optimal group size: 5–6 students) | Lecture |
| 2 | Theoretical background to brand foundation* | Lecture |
| 3 | Theoretical background to brand touch points* | Lecture |
| 4 | Theoretical background to brand performance*, description of the selected project brand by using the B★Canvas | Lecture and group work |
| 5–6 | Development of a brand audit methodology on the basis of the B★Canvas | Coaching and group work |
| 7–9 | Collection of data for the evaluation of the brand (e.g., interviews with the management, secondary research, sentiment analysis, customer surveys, etc.) | Coaching and group work |
| 10 | Conduction of the brand audit and identification of strengths and weaknesses | Group work |
| 11 | Development of ideas for improving the project brand | Group work |
| 12 | Final Event with the presentation (TED Talk-Format; Anderson, 2016) in front of the brand managers of the project brands & direct group feedback by the companies | Class event |

*Source:* * Tables 1–3 summarize important sub-topics and recommend some selected references for the lecturer and as the basis for self-study

In order to increase the realism of university education as well as increase motivation, the fun and the engagement, a cooperation with real corporate brands is recommended for this course. They then have their brand evaluated by the B★Canvas 2.0 and a brand audit (see subcchapter 3.2) and are available to the student groups with background materials and interview partners. Furthermore, the project partners pinpoint the importance of the final presentation through their presence and direct feedback to the groups. To avoid overburdening the student groups in terms of complexity and resources (time, personnel), it is recommended to select medium-sized corporate brands as project brands. It has also proved useful to select an 'industry' (e.g., sustainability or technology brand) as the overarching theme, of the course as this allows a reduction of the brand management content (week 1–4) to topics that are particularly relevant to the industry in question.

## 4. Discussion

Corporate branding is not a pure communication task, but it encompasses many individual areas that must mesh like the cogs in a good mechanical watch. In order to take this multitude and variety of elements of corporate branding into account, tools are needed that on the one hand allow a holistic and systematic view in a diverse team of employees and external service partners, but on the other hand are not too detailed and complex. Building on the basic principles of the Business Model Canvas approach, the chapter at hand presented and discussed the B★Canvas 2.0 as such a tool. The B★Canvas 2.0 divides brand management for corporate brands into the three dimensions of brand foundation, brand touchpoints, and brand performance with a total of 14 elements. The tool, which has proven itself for years in practical brand work and training, can be used practically in various use scenarios. The chapter outlined four use cases: (1) description and common understanding of a corporate brand,;(2) evaluation of a corporate brand by a brand audit; (3) development of a corporate brand for start-ups as well; as and (4) a teaching framework for a master lecture 'Brand Management.'

Although the presented tool is holistic, easy to understand even for non-specialists in branding and/or marketing, available for free and flexible to use, it only provides a first overview of the brand. Therefore, it makes sense to combine this tool with more detailed tools such as brand positioning models, UX-, CX- and BX-tests or brand equity models.

Furthermore, it is important to understand that the proposed B★Canvas 2.0 often needs to be extended and reduced by elements before concrete application. For example, in the case of many B-to-B brands, it might make sense to include sales as the most important brand touchpoint as an additional element and, if necessary, to eliminate the PoS element for this purpose.

The B★Canvas 2.0 is also more a tool for joint discussion, evaluation, and development in a team (internal co-creation). It is not a 'mathematical optimization model' that automatically leads to good corporate brand management, so to speak. After all, the tool was developed for corporate branding or at least for brands with a comprehensive range of products and services, where elements such as corporate culture or internal brand management play a pivotal role. For companies with strongly defined product brands without a corporate brand or a weak link to the corporate brand, the B★Canvas 2.0 in the form presented is only suitable to a limited extent.

## References

Aaker, D. A., & Joachimsthaler, E. (2000). *Brand leadership*. New York: The Free Press.

Ahmed, J., Rogge, R., Kline, W., Bunch, R. Mason, T., Wollowski, M., & Livesay, G. (2014). The innovation canvas: An instructor's guide. 121st ASEE Annual Conference and Exposition (pp. 1–12).

Anderson, C. (2016). *TED talks – the official TED guide to public speaking*. London and Boston, MA: Nicholas Brealey.

Arrese, Á., & Pérez-Latre, F. J. (2017). The rise of brand journalism. In G. Siegert, B. M. Rimscha, & S. Grubenmann (Eds.), *Commercial communication in the digital age information or disinformation?* (pp. 121–140). Berlin: De Gruyter.

Balmer, J. M. T. (2017). Corporate brand orientation: What is it? What of it? *Journal of Brand Management*, 20(9), 723–741

Balmer, J. M. T., & Gray, E. R. (2003). Corporate brands: What are they? What of them? *European Journal of Marketing*, 37(7–8), 972–997.

Baumgarth, C. (2010). "Living the brand": Brand orientation in the business-to-business sector. *European Journal of Marketing*, 44(5), 653–671.

Baumgarth, C. (2014). *Markenpolitik: Markentheorien, Markenwirkungen, Markenführung, Markencontrolling, Markenkontext* [Brand management: Brand theories, brand efect, brand management, brand controlling, brand contexts] (4th ed.). Wiesbaden: SpringerGabler.

Baumgarth, C. (2019). Brand Canvas: Hin zur ganzheitlichen Markenführung [Brand canvas: Towards holistic brand management]. *markenartikel, 81*(1–2), 58–61.

Baumgarth, C., & Douven, S. (2018). *B-to-B-Markencontrolling: Überblick und Instrumente* [B-to-B-brand controlling: Overview and tools]. Baumgarth, C. (Ed.): B-to-B-Markenführung [B-to-B-brand management], (pp. 761–787, 2nd. ed.). Wiesbaden: Springer.

Baumgarth, C., Kaluza, M., & Lohrisch, N. (2016). Brand audit for cultural institutions (BAC): A validated and holistic brand controlling tool. *International Journal of Arts Management, 19*(1), 54–68.

Baumgarth, C., & Kastner, O. L. (2012). Pop-up-Stores im Modebereich: Erfolgsfaktoren einer vergänglichen Form der Kundeninspiration [Pop-up stores in the fashion sector-success factors of an ephemeral form of customer inspiration]. *Marketing Review St. Gallen, 29*(5), 34–45.

Beverland, M. B. (2009). *Building brand authenticity: 7 Habits of iconic brands.* Houndmills: Palgrave Macmillan.

Beverland, M. B. (2021). *Brand management: Co-creating meaningful brands* (2nd ed.). Los Angeles, CA: SAGE.

Blackett, T., & Boad, B. (Eds.). (1999). *Co-branding – The science of alliance.* Houndmills: Macmillan.

Bloch, P. H. (1995). Seeking the ideal form: Product design and consumer response. *Journal of Marketing, 59*(3), 16–29.

Brakus, J. J., Schmitt, B. H., & Zarantonello, L. (2009). Brand experience: What is it? How is it measured? Does it affect loyalty? *Journal of Marketing, 73*(3), 52–68.

Bresciani, S., & Eppler, M. J. (2010). Brand new ventures? Insights on start-ups branding practices. *Journal of Product & Brand Management, 19*(5), 356–366.

Brexendorf, T. O., & Daecke, N. (2012). The brand manager – Current tasks and skill requirements in FMCG companies. *Marketing Review St. Gallen, 29*(6), 32–37.

Cameron, K. S., & Quinn, R. E. (2006). *Diagnosing and changing organizational culture.* San Francisco, CA: Jossey-Bass.

Carter, M., & Carter, C. (2020). The creative business model canvas. *Social Enterprise Journal, 16*(2), 141–158.

De Cherantony, L., McDonald, M., & Wallace, E. (2011). *Creating powerful brands* (4th ed.). Amsterdam: Elsevier.

Ebster, C.& Garaus, M. (2011). *Store design and visual merchandising: Creating store space that encourages buying.* New York: Businessexpert.

Erdogan, B. Z., Baker, M. J., & Tagg, S. (2001). Selecting celebrity endorsers. *Journal of Advertising Research, 41*(3), 39–49.

Felin, T., Gambardella, A., Stern, S., & Zenger, T. (2020). Lean startup and the business model: Experimentation revisited. *Long Range Planning, 53*(4), 101953.

Fetscherin, M. (2020). *The brand relationship playbook.* Brand Relationship Book.

Florman, M., Klingler-Vidra, R., & Facada, M. J. (2016). *A critical evaluation of social impact assessment methodologies and a call to measure economic and social impact holistically through the External Rate of Return platform* (Working Paper #1602). LSE Enterprise, London.

Fombrun, C. J., Gardberg, N. A., & Sever, J. M. (2000). The reputation quotient: A multi-stakeholder measure of corporate reputation. *Journal of Brand Management, 7*(4), 241–255.

Gilmore, J. H., & Pine, B. J. (2007). *Authenticity – What consumers really want.* Boston, MA: Harvard Business School.

Glaser, B. G., & Strauss, A. L. (1967). *The discovery of grounded theory: Strategies for qualitative research.* New York: Aldine.

Google. (2021). Search "Business Model Canvas". Last access on January 17, 2021.

Gregory, A. (2007). Involving stakeholders in developing corporate brands: The communication dimension. *Journal of Marketing Management, 23*(1–2), 59–73.

Ha, Y., & Lennon, S. J. (2010). Online visual merchandising (VMD). cues and consumer pleasure and arousal: Purchasing versus browsing situation. *Psychology & Marketing, 27*(2), 161–165.

Habermann, F. (2014). Der Projekt Canvas – Eine gemeinsame Sprachplattform für Business und IT [The project canvas – A common language platform for management and IT]. *Praxis der Wirtschaftsinformatik, 51*(5), 568–579.

Habermann, F., & Schmidt, K. (2018). *Over the fence.* Berlin: Becota.

Habermann, F., & Schmidt, K. (2020). The project canvas: Five years evolution of a project management instrument. *International Journal of Management Practice, 13*(2), 216–236.

Harris, F.& de Chernatony, L. (2001). Corporate branding and corporate brand performance. *European Journal of Marketing, 35*(3–4), 441–456.

Hatch, M. J., & Schultz, M. (2008). *Taking brand initiative: How companies can align strategy, culture, and identity through corporate branding*. San Francisco, CA: Jossey-Bass.

Hatch, M. J., & Schultz, M. (2010). Toward a theory of brand co-creation with implications for brand governance. *Journal of Brand Management, 17*(8), 590–604.

Henderson, P. W., & Cote, J. A. (1998). Guidelines for selecting or modifying logos. *Journal of Marketing, 62*(2), 14–30.

Hesse, A., Schmidt, H. J., & Baumgarth, C. (2020). Practices of corporate influencers in the context of internal branding: The case of Pawel Dillinger from Deutsche Telekom. *Corporate Reputation Review, 24*, 191–204.

Homburg, C., Vomberg, A., Enke, M., & Grimm, P. H. (2015). The loss of the marketing department's influence. *Journal of the Academy of Marketing Science, 43*(1), 1–13.

Iglesias, O., Ind, N., & Alfaro, M. (2013). The organic view of the brand: A brand value co-creation model. *Journal of Brand Management, 20*(8), 670–688.

Iglesias, O., Landgraf, P., Ind, N., Markovic, S., & Koporcic, N. (2020). Corporate brand identity co-creation in business-to-business contexts. *Industrial Marketing Management, 85*, 32–43.

Ind, N. (2007). *Living the brand – How to transform every member of your organization into a brand champion* (3rd ed.). London and Philadelphia, PA: Kogan Page.

Ind, N. (Ed.). (2017). *Branding inside out: Internal branding in theory and practice*. London: Kogan Page.

Ind, N., & Schmidt, H. J. (2019). *co-creating brands – Brand management from a co-creative perspective*. London: Bloomsbury Business

Jenner, T. (2005). Funktionen und Bedeutung von Marken-Audits im Rahmen des Marken-Controllings [Functions and relevance of brand audits in the context of bran controlling]. *Marketing ZFP, 27*(3), 197–207.

Joyce, A., & Paquin, R. L. (2016). The triple layered business model canvas. *Journal of Cleaner Production, 135*(1), 1474–1486.

Juntunen, M. (2012). Co-creation corporate brands in start-ups. *Marketing Intelligence & Planning, 30*(2), 230–249.

Keiningham, T. L., Aksoy, L., Cooil, B., Andreassen, T. W., & Williams, L. (2008). A holistic examination of net promoter. *Journal of Database Marketing & Customer Strategy Management, 15*(2), 79–90.

Keller, K. L. (1993). Conceptualizing, measuring, and managing customer-based brand equity. *Journal of Marketing, 57*(1), 1–22.

Keller, K. L., & Swaminathan, V. (2020). *Strategic brand management: Building, measuring, and managing brand equity* (5th ed.). Harlow: Pearson.

Kernstock, J., Esch, F.-R., & Tomczak, T. (2014). Management-Verantwortung, Prozesse und Strukturen für das Corporate Brand Management klären [Clarify management responsibilities, processes and structures for corporate brand management]. In F.-R. Esch, T. Tomczak, J. Kernstock, T. Langner, & J. Redler (Eds.) *Corporate brand management* (pp. 129–138, 2nd ed.). Wiesbaden: SpringerGabler.

Klink, R. R. (2003). Creating meaningful brands: The relationship between brand name and brand mark. *Marketing Letters, 14*(3), 143–157.

Knapp, J. (2016). *Sprint – How to solve big problems and test new ideas in just five days*. New York: Simon & Schuster.

Knoll, J., & Matthes, J. (2017). The effectiveness of celebrity endorsements: A meta-analysis. *Journal of the Academy of Marketing Science, 45*(1), 55–75.

Koch, C. (2014). *Corporate brand positioning – Case studies across firm levels and over time*. Lund: Lund University Press.

Konecnik Ruzzier, M., & Ruzzier, M. (2015). Startup branding funnel: A new approach for developing startup brands. Proceedings of the 4th Annual International Conference on Enterprise Marketing and Globalization (EMG 2015). and 5th Annual International Conference on Innovation and Entrepreneurship (IE 2015) (pp. 32–34). Singapore.

Kotler, P., Gregor, W., & Rodgers, W. (1977). The marketing audit comes of age. *Sloan Management Review, 18*(2), 25–43.

Kreuzbauer, R. (2013). *Design and brand: The influence of product form on the formation of brands*. Wiesbaden: DUV.

Kriegbaum, C. (2011). *Markencontrolling: Bedeutung und Steuerung von Marken als immaterielle Vermögenswerte im Rahmen eines unternehmerischen Controlling* [Brand controlling: Relevance and management of brands as intangible assets in the context of a company-oriented controlling]. München: Vahlen.

Kübler, R. V., Colicev, A., & Pauwels, K. H. (2020). Social media's impact on the consumer mindset: When to use which sentiment extraction tool? *Journal of Interactive Marketing, 50*, 136–155.

Laforet, S., & Saunders, J. (2007). How brand portfolios have changed: A study of grocery suppliers brands from 1994 to 2004. *Journal of Marketing Management, 23*(1–2), 39–58.

Langner, T. (2003). *Integriertes Branding: Baupläne zur Gestaltung erfolgreicher Marken* [Integrated Branding: Blueprints for designing successful brands]. Wiesbaden: Deutscher Universitäts-Verlag.

Lemper, T. A. (2012). Five trademark law strategies for managing brands. *Business Horizons, 55*(2), 113–117.

Lewrick, M., Link, P., Leifer, L., & Langensano, N. (2017). *Das design thinking playbook* [The design thinking playbook]. München: Vahlen.

Lim, K., & O'Cass, A. (2001). Consumer brand classifications: An assessment of culture-of-origin versus country-of-origin. *Journal of Product & Brand Management, 10*(2), 120–136.

Liu, B. (2020). *Sentiment analysis: Mining opinions, sentiments, and emotions* (2nd ed.). Cambridge: Cambridge University Press.

Lou, C., & Yuan, S. (2019). Influencer marketing: How message value and credibility affect consumer trust of branded content on social media. *Journal of Interactive Advertising, 19*(1), 58–73.

Low, G. S., & Fullerton, R. A. (1994). Brands, brand management, and the brand manager system: A critical-historical evaluation. *Journal of Marketing Research, 31*(2), 173–190.

Machado, J. C., de Carvalho, L. V., Torres, A., & Costa, P. (2015). Brand logo design: Examining consumer response to naturalness. *Journal of Product & Brand Management, 24*(1), 78–87.

Michel, G., & Willing, R. (2020). *The art of successful brand collaborations: Partnerships with artists, designers, museums, territories, sports, celebrities, science, good causes . . . and more*. London and New York: Routledge.

Nguyen, H. T., Zhang, Y., & Calantone, R. J. (2018). Brand portfolio coherence: Scale development and empirical demonstration. *International Journal of Research in Marketing, 35*, 60–80.

Odin, Y., Odin, N., & Valette-Florence, P. (2001). Conceptual and operational aspects of brand loyalty: An empirical investigation. *Journal of Business Research, 53*(2), 75–84.

Onken, M., & Campeau, D. (2016). Lean startups: Using the business model canvas. *Journal of Case Studies, 34*(1), 95–101.

Osterwalder, A. (2014). *The business model ontology*. Lausanne: University of Lausanne.

Osterwalder, A., & Pigneuer, Y. (2010). *Business model generation*. Hoboken, NJ: John Wiley & Sons.

Raffelt, U. (2012). *Architectural branding: Understanding and measuring its relevance for brand communication*. München: FGM.

Ramaswamy, V.& Ozcan, K. (2014). *The co-creation paradigm*. Stanford, CA: Stanford Business Books.

Ries, E. (2011). *The lean startup: How today's entrepreneurs use continuous innovation to create radically successful businesses*. New York: Crown Books.

Rode, V. (2004). *Corporate Branding von Gründungsunternehmen* [Corporate branding of startups]. Wiesbaden: Springer.

Rode, V., & Vallaster, C. (2005). Corporate branding for start-ups: The crucial role of entrepreneurs. *Corporate Reputation Review, 8*(2), 121–135.

Rossiter, J. R., Percy, L., & Bergkvist, L. (2018). *Marketing communications: Objectives, strategy, tactics*. Los Angeles, CA: SAGE.

Rus, M., Koecniak Ruzzier, M., & Ruzzier, M. (2018). Startup branding: Empirical evidence among slovenian startups. *Managing Global Transitions, 16*(1), 79–94.

Salinas, G. (2009). *The international brand valuation manual*. Chichester: Wiley.

Schein, E. H. (1999). *The corporate culture survival guide*. San Francisco, CA: Jossey-Bass.

Schein, E. H. (2004). *Organizational culture and leadership* (3rd ed.). San Francisco, CA: Jossey-Bassey.

Schmidt, H. J., & Baumgarth, C. (2018). Strengthening internal brand equity with brand ambassador programs: Development and testing of a success factor model. *Journal of Brand Management, 25*(3), 220–265.

Sommer, S., Loch, C. H., & Dong, J. (2009). Managing complexity and unforeseeable uncertainty in startup companies: An empirical study. *Organization Science, 20*(1), 118–133.

Sparviero, S. (2019). The case for a socially oriented business model canvas: The social enterprise model canvas. *Journal of Social Entrepreneurship, 10*(2), 232–251.

Spence, C., Puccinelli, N. M., Grewal, D., & Roggeven, A. L. (2014). Store Atmosphere: A multisensory perspective. *Psychology & Marketing, 31*(7), 472–488.

Stickdorn, M., & Schneider, J. (2011). *This is service design thinking*. Amsterdam: BIS Publishers.

Strategyzer (2020). *Over 5 million people use our business model canvas*. Retrieved March 30, 2020 from www.strategyzer.com.

Strebinger, A. (2014). Rethinking brand architecture: A study on industry, company- and product-level drivers of branding strategy. *European Journal of Marketing, 48*(9–10), 1782–1804.

Thakor, M., & Kohli, C. S. (1996). Brand origin: Conceptualization and review. *Journal of Consumer Marketing, 13*(3), 2–42.

Tomczak, T., Kernstock, J., & Brexendorf, O. (2014). Ziele, Leistungsgrößen und Erfolgsfaktoren identifizieren udn stuern [Identify and control goals, performance measures and success factors], In. F.-R. Esch, T. Tomczak, J. Kernstock, T. Langner, & J. Redler (Eds.), *Corporate brand management* (2nd ed., pp. 565–582). Wiesbaden: Springer.

Urde, M. (1994). Brand orientation: A strategy for survival. *Journal of Consumer Marketing, 11*(3), 18–32.

Urde, M. (1999). Brand orientation: A mindset for building brands into strategic resources *Journal of Marketing Management, 15*(1–3), 117–133.

Urde, M., Baumgarth, C., & Merrilees, B. (2013). Brand orientation and market orientation, *Journal of Business Research, 66*(1), 13–20.

Verhoef, P. C., & Leeflang, P. S. H. (2009). Understanding the marketing department's influence within the firm. *Journal of Marketing, 73*(1), 14–37.

Verhoef, P. C., Leeflang, P. S. H., Reiner, J., Natter, M., & Baker, W. (2011). A cross-national investigation into the marketing department's influence within the firm. *Journal of International Marketing, 19*(3), 59–86.

Völckner, F., & Sattler, H. (2006). Drivers of brand extension success. *Journal of Marketing, 70*(2), 18–34.

Wheeler, A. (2006). *Designing brand identity: A complete guide to creating, building, and maintaining strong brands* (2nd ed.). Hoboken, NJ: John Wiley & Sons.

Wong, H. Y., & Merrilees, B. (2005). A brand orientation typology for SMEs: A case research approach. *Journal of Product & Brand Management, 14*(3), 155–162.

Yoo, B., & Donthu, N. (2001). Developing and validating a multidimensional consumer-based brand equity scale. *Journal of Business Research, 52*(1), 1–14.

Zolonowski, A., Weiß, C., & Böhmann, T. (2014). Representing service business models with the service business model canvas. Proceedings of the 24th Hawaii International Conference on System Science, 718–727.

# 12
# BRAND EXPERIENCE CO-CREATION AT THE TIME OF ARTIFICIAL INTELLIGENCE

*Federico Mangiò, Giuseppe Pedeliento, and Daniela Andreini*

## 1. Introduction

With the turn of the new millennium and the 'experience economy' hype (Pine & Gilmore, 1999), research on brand experience flourished (Andreini et al., 2018). Building on Brakus et al.'s (2009) conceptualization of the brand experience construct, scholars gradually adopted a more critical approach to brand experience issues and shifted their focus from marketers' ability to design and deploy brand stimuli in order to generate specific and positive brand experiences (Brakus et al., 2009; Schmitt, 1999) to the process through which consumers and brands are jointly involved in the co-creation of brand experiences (Andreini et al., 2018). Scholars soon realized that brand experience is more than a set of 'subjective, internal consumer responses (sensations, feelings, and cognitions) and behavioural responses evoked by brand-related stimuli that are part of a brand's design and identity, packaging, communications, and environments' (Brakus et al., 2009). Subsequently, the concept of brand experience has been enlarged, elaborated upon, and framed as a socially constructed phenomenon, co-created by a myriad of purposeful, albeit not necessarily structured, interactions among producers, consumers, and other marketplace actors (Andreini et al., 2018; Brodie, 2017; Merz et al., 2009).

With the development of consumer-sensitive approaches to brands and brand experiences, non-deterministic approaches to commercial exchanges, such as 'service-dominant logic' (SDL) (Vargo & Lusch, 2004, 2008, 2011), became valuable analytical lenses (Merz et al., 2009). SDL postulates that the role of consumers is to co-author brand experiences, and it views the same brand experience as a series of contexts defined by unique actors and their links (Chandler & Vargo, 2011). Nonetheless, there is a specific actor which, despite its disruptive potential, has been neglected in the current exploration of the processes leading to brand experience co-creation: artificial intelligence (AI). Apart from being most recognizable among the new millennium buzzwords, AI broadly refers to the substitution of human intelligence by computational tools when performing certain tasks. Actually, although brand co-creation research in technology-mediated contexts has flourished (Gidhagen et al., 2017), we still know little about how and to what extent AI-powered emerging technologies can be involved in the process of creating brand experiences. Undoubtedly, AI can play a pivotal role in facilitating the creation of new, different, or untapped forms of brand experience, especially since AI – due to its agency-deploying ability in interactive dynamics – is both a technological context *and* a technological actor (Kaartemo & Helkkula, 2018). For this reason, the emergence and diffusion of AI poses exceptional and novel challenges to marketing and branding scholars. Although widely recognized as being able to provide substantial benefits to both consumers and brands, AI always contains negative aspects. Its design and functioning pose certain intrinsic threats to consumers' expression of autonomy, self-determination, and free will (André et al., 2018). This inevitably undermines individuals' perceived control and self-efficacy (Bandura, 1977), which are core ingredients of the participative dynamics of brand management and development, as well as of brand experience co-creation (Merrilees, 2016). Stated differently, although AI can create new forms of brand experience, it simultaneously downgrades the consumers' role as co-authors or co-producers of experiences to a set of options (irrespective of its range) that is predetermined by technology. In response to this 'technological paradox,' the aim of this chapter is to theoretically explore this *terra incognita* by constructing an updated framework of brand experience co-creation that combines recent conceptual and theoretical refinements of the brand experience notion (Andreini et al., 2018). This is done within a unique conceptual framework that combines the service dominant logic (SDL) of markets (Vargo & Lusch, 2004, 2008, 2011) and Actor Network Theory (ANT) (Callon, 1999; Latour, 1992, 2005).

The remainder of this chapter is structured as follows: as a starting point, we review the SDL approach and its relevance in order to refine the concept of brand experience co-creation. Thereafter, we define and provide a taxonomy of AI before shedding light on the benefits of and the threats posed by AI to brands and brand experiences. This will be followed by the outline of our theoretical elaboration. In conclusion, we identify certain theoretical and practical implications and propose directions for future research.

## 2. Brand experience co-creation: the SDL approach

The service-dominant logic (SDL) of markets is a well-established framework that provides explanations of how and why market exchanges take place. SDL relies on a dualistic ontology (Schembri, 2009), focuses on a phenomenological view of value (Akaka & Vargo, 2015), and considers consumers and companies to be intertwined in a mutual process of value co-creation where services are positioned as the basis of commercial exchanges (Vargo & Lusch, 2004, 2008, 2011). According to SDL, market value is always co-created by a service beneficiary (i.e., a customer) through the use of a market offering (Vargo & Lusch, 2004, 2008). Therefore, within the SDL frame of reference, the complex value co-creation mechanisms are bounded by a service ecosystem (Akaka et al., 2012), which extends firm-consumer dyads and emphasizes the influence of institutions and institutional logics (Vargo & Lusch, 2011). Two main resource types guide actions and interactions among actors: *operant* resources, i.e., dynamic and influential resources like knowledge, skills, and competencies; and *operand* resources, i.e., static-state resources like money and goods (Vargo & Lusch, 2004; Vargo & Lusch, 2008). Because the former sources are much rarer and more difficult to acquire than the latter, *operant* resources are generally considered superior to, or more valuable than, *operand* resources.

Halliday (2016) argued that brands are *operant* resources. Merz et al. (2009) similarly argued that marketplace interactions among consumers, brands, and other audiences, are also *operant* resources. Chandler and Vargo (2011) and Edvardsson et al. (2011) stated that the intricate web of interactions between marketplace actors can be considered both as a (*operant*) resource and as the context in which actors co-create value. For this reason, Andreini et al. (2018) recently claimed that 'defining the context as a set of unique actors with reciprocal links implies that under SDL, interactions are always event and context-specific, and that the context affects the way in which actors integrate or use resources and therefore develop experiences' (p. 126).

The context is neither static nor neutral but affects the process of value co-creation and the creation and development of experiences (Payne et al., 2009; Vargo et al., 2008). Experiences occur when actors activate resources (including brands) in contextual interaction, and when these resources initiate a process of value co-creation (Akaka et al., 2012; Chandler & Vargo, 2011; Edvardsson et al., 2011). For example, consumers' positive experience during a brand fest (McAlexander et al., 2002) manifests itself, insofar as consumers and marketers are jointly involved in the process of leveraging a set of interactional layers that contribute value to both consumers (in the form of relational bonds) and marketers (in the form of, for instance, higher loyalty rates). However, despite experience being a central tenet of markets' SDL (e.g., Schau et al., 2009; Vargo & Lusch, 2008; Vargo et al., 2008), previous studies included only a few isolated contributions focusing on brand experience (Brodie et al., 2006) or, in general, did not explicitly mention brand experience (Andreini et al., 2018).

Although different terms are used to define the experience construct (Jaakkola et al., 2015), SDL scholars agree that experience is the foundation of the co-creation of value-in-use (Gummerus, 2013). Experience is conceived as the context in which all actors meet, interact, and activate service-for-service social exchanges. Therefore, in line with SDL, value creation can only be achieved to the extent that consumers experience the service at hand, and only when its domain-spanning nature, comprising affective, cognitive, and behavioural value, is considered (Mohd-Any et al., 2015; Salomonson et al., 2012). This phenomenological characterization implies that experiences are 'internal, subjective, event-specific and context-specific' (Helkkula, 2011, p. 375) in customers' everyday lives. Collectively, experiences can be interpreted as a primary platform that fosters direct and/or indirect interactions between the actors within a system (McColl-Kennedy et al., 2012; Schau et al., 2009; Vargo & Lusch, 2011).

In summary, the framing of brands and brand experiences through the lens of SDL informs us that a brand is anything but a static and neutral resource: it is a dynamic *operant* resource that exists adjacent to the market offering; the value of which is co-created through *contextual* experiences. Accordingly, brand experience is an objective and subjective platform, of a direct and indirect nature, where actors – with consumers at the forefront – interact and cooperate with the aim of co-creating value-in-use. Apart from the specific conceptualization of brand experience, the SDL's contextual emphasis offers interesting and promising avenues for this theoretical perspective's application to gain a fine-grained understanding of brand experience co-creation in highly technology-mediated contexts (Gidhagen et al., 2017). Indeed, SDL is deemed well suited to shed light on the brand co-creation practices and processes (Hatch & Schultz, 2010) that are situated in digital contexts (Iglesias et al., 2013; Ind et al., 2013; Vallaster & von Wallpach, 2013; Iglesias et al., 2019). However, to date no research has specifically dealt with issues of brand co-creation dynamics in a technology-mediated context created or enabled by AI, despite the latter being used in a myriad of business practices and applications. Although there is a dire need for empirical research on AI's effect on brand experience, the development of a general ontology and the provision of a solid theoretical understanding of AI are equally imperative. As we argue, AI's very nature should encourage scholars to desist from considering AI and AI-powered technologies as 'contexts' of specific brand experiences, or as mere 'tools' that enable brands and customers to build better or more valuable brand experiences. Rather, being designed and deployed to be interactive, adaptive, contextual, and user-sensitive, AI is actually an *actant* agent that plays an active role in the process of brand experience co-creation. Subsequently, we describe AI's agentic nature and its varying degrees of agency.

## 3. What is in a name? A definition and a taxonomy of AI

From the word-autocompletion ability of our smartphones to targeted advertisements that match recipients' interests and tastes, AI is omnipresent, even if we often fail to notice this. From its first appearance in the early 1950s (Turing, 1950), the term *AI* denoted those technological agents with the ability to exhibit or mimic some degrees of human intelligence (Huang & Rust, 2018; Syam & Sharma, 2018). In particular, the *intelligence* of these agents allows them to take into account both the goals they are designed to achieve and the environment where they operate. In this way, they can promptly act and respond to the multiple stimuli of the context in which they are embedded (Russell & Norvig, 2016). Accordingly, it is unsurprising that AI's controversial nature (McCarthy & Hayes, 1981) does not refer to its *artificial* attribute but instead to its supposed human-like *intelligence*, as 'it is not easy to distinguish thinking from purely mechanical processing' (Wirth, 2018, p. 436).

As AI comprises a vast array of applications that differ in scope and use – ranging from the spam-detecting systems installed on email accounts to virtual digital assistants such as Amazon's Alexa or more complex systems like IBM's Watson – we provide a taxonomic primer of these technological systems (see Table 12.1) based on the most recent, extant research (e.g., Chui et al., 2018; Davenport et al., 2020; De Bruyn et al., 2020; Du & Xie, 2020; Ma & Sun, 2020; Puntoni et al., 2021).

A first form of AI-powered technologies comprises computer vision (CV). CV encompasses a set of artificial applications with the ability to extract and analyse data and information from images (Huang & Vandoni, 1996; Russell & Norvig, 2016). Commercial applications of CV range from Facebook's auto-tagging to advanced image recognition services like Clarifai's face-based, instant check-in payments and personalized customer services (www.clarifai.com). Besides CV, natural language processing (NLP) is another form of AI comprising those programs and applications that enable machines to understand the hierarchical structure of natural language and the logical relationships of sentences' different parts (Jurafsky & Martin, 2000). Not only does NLP interpret and transform human language into data, but it also creates human-like language outputs (Syam & Sharma, 2018). NLP is currently used in many practical applications, and it also powers text-mining software available for both academic and business uses. Machine learning (ML) is another form of AI that enables computers to learn without being explicitly programmed for this purpose. Since ML caused a paradigmatic shift in computing, it is not only the most rapidly increasing AI application but has also attracted the most interest (Chui et al., 2018). ML involves the use of algorithms aimed at instructing a system how to attain its goals and how to improve its skills over time (Ma & Sun, 2020). ML algorithms are suitable for multiple applications and uses, ranging from the automatic planning of search engine optimization to product recommendation systems. As a specific ML sub-form, deep learning (DL) is a powerful AI technology that uses deeper layers of artificial neuron networks, enabling ML to process huge amounts of unstructured data in non-linear ways (Ma & Sun, 2020; Syam & Sharma, 2018). Virtual agents (VAs) also form part of the technology set that falls under the AI rubric and range from instant messaging aps, through voice assistants like Amazon's Alexa, to more advanced intelligent assistants like IBM's Watson. Arguably, VAs are the most pervasive form of AI used in the business realm, especially to perform basic customer care tasks like placing and tracing orders or answering FAQs.

A final set of technologies which has been widely affected by recent AI development includes virtual reality (VR) and augmented reality (AR) (Syam & Sharma, 2018). VR comprises those applications aimed at recreating real or virtual environments. VR accelerated notably over the past years, especially as a result of the availability of more affordable and user-friendly immersive devices like goggles and helmets. AR comprises those computer-based technologies aimed at

*Table 12.1* A taxonomy of AI: key functionalities and use cases

| AI | Definition | Key functionalities | Use cases |
| --- | --- | --- | --- |
| Computer vision (CV) | Set of artificial applications and processes able to automate tasks performed by the human visual system | Entity recognition and motion analysis: it extracts, classifies, and analyses data from images and videos. Navigation: it rebuilds a 3D representation of the environment from a 2D image to drive an artificial agent. | Clarifai: it leverages AI to improve the customer experience across the shopping journey (www.clarifai.com). Cubix: it discovers the right media, quickly and easily – through cost effective metadata enhancement and semantic searching through AI/ML based service (www.ortana.tv/Home/cubix). |
| Natural language processing (NLP) and natural language generation (NLG) | Programs and applications that enable machines to understand human language (NLP) or to generate human-like language outputs (NLG) | Speech and text recognition: it extracts and analyses data from spoken to written natural language. Speech and text generation: it replicates spoken and written natural language. | Talkwalker: it performs AI powered analysis and provides real time insights of all social channels and online media, across 187 languages (www.talkwalker.com). Automated insights: it uses AI to transforms data into clear, human-sounding narratives – for any industry and application (www.automatedinsights.com). |
| Machine learning (ML) and deep learning (DL) | Field of study that gives computers the ability to learn without being explicitly programmed | ML: it learns from data for classification or prediction purposes. DL: it enhances the effectiveness of ML through the use of deeper layers of Artificial Neuron Networks. | Episerver: it uses ML algorithms optimized for commerce to deliver personalized real-time product recommendations (www.episerver.com). Node: it predicts volume, sales and leads, forecasts pivotal objectives and provides dynamic roadmaps (www.node.io). |
| Virtual agents (VA) | Digital assistants powered by AI components, including virtual chatbots, voice assistants, virtual agents | Virtual assistance: it provides responsive real-time assistance. | Drift: AI-powered chatbots that engage and qualify every single site visitor, automatically placing and tracing orders, answering FAQs 24/7, pulling availabilities, and sending emails (www.drift.com). |
| Immersive technologies (AR and VR) | Computer-based simulations aimed at recreating real or fancy environments (VR) or combining real and virtual elements to augment the real-time experiences in the real world (AR) | They provide novel, interactive virtual (VR) or mixed (AR) experiences in real time at low cost. | Bodyswaps: it leverages VR visors to show how products and services will look like before purchase (www.bodyswaps.co). |

augmenting real-world experiences by combining real and virtual objects within the same environment. AR applications are attracting more attention from both academics and practitioners (Hinsch et al., 2020) and are proven enhancers of consumer-brand relationships, consumer experiences, and brand perceptions (Barhorst et al., 2021; Javornik, 2016; Rauschnabel et al., 2019; Scholz & Smith, 2016; Scholz & Duffy, 2018).

Since AI includes a wide range of technologies and potential uses, a thorough review of all the benefits of AI-powered technologies and applications for brands is beyond this chapter's scope. Although both academics and practitioners frequently invoke these benefits (e.g., Chui et al., 2018; Puntoni et al., 2021), there is a paucity of literature providing a systematic and comprehensive overview of the relationship of marketing and AI (Davenport et al., 2020). In particular, a thorough analysis of the extant literature reveals a paucity of studies covering the impact of AI and its benefits for the brand management practice in general, and the brand experience in particular. The next section provides a brief overview of the state of knowledge in these untapped fields.

## 4. The application of AI to brand management practice

Despite the shortage of literature, the practical application of AI in brand management has the potential to support and augment brand experience, as it allows companies to more efficiently and effectively deliver on their promises to target audiences, thereby producing positive spillover effects on brand value (West et al., 2018). Recent literature contends that specific AI-powered technologies and applications are well suited to maximize the effectiveness of advertising along the consumer journey (Kietzman et al., 2018) and to facilitate the sales management process (Chintagunta et al., 2016; Kaartemo & Helkkula, 2018; Martínez-López & Casillas, 2013; Syam & Sharma, 2018). Scholars have also emphasized the superior prediction capabilities and greater accuracy of ML and DL algorithms, compared to traditional statistical techniques, to forecast marketplace changes and to predict sales variations to the benefit of brands (Jalal et al., 2016). NLP has already been used to great effect by brands to continuously, systematically, and in real time monitor target audiences – to gain a first-hand understanding and knowledge of their opinions – by applying mining techniques to easily accessible and retrievable user-generated content (UGC) like reviews, social media posts, and similar online reactions (Liu et al., 2017, 2021). AI-powered service robots are also recognized as reliable frontline service employees, allowing brands to serve and follow up consumers with increasing human-like interaction (Van Doorn et al., 2017).

At a time when brand-consumer relationships are highly interactive and span multiple touch points, the scant available literature suggests that AI's core contribution to brand management practice can be summarized in terms of four intertwined benefits (Davenport et al., 2020; De Bruyn et al., 2020; Ma & Sun, 2020). First, AI allows access to superior and more accurate consumer insights by orchestrating the myriad of unstructured data, produced by brands' touch points, within a unified knowledge source (Balducci & Marinova, 2018). Second, AI fosters the development of consumer-brand relationships to reach new horizons. Due to its ability to reach high levels of personalization, AI enables brands to resonate more quickly with the consumer. Third, AI can support those marketing operations that are increasingly channelled to the domain of machines, like programmatic advertising and real-time bidding, which are regarded as important vehicles to foster brand experiences in full force (Shanahan et al., 2019). Lastly, AI undoubtedly facilitates scaled-up marketing and branding strategies to attain a higher level of efficiency. Since automation requires little, if any, human intervention and can be flexibly scaled depending on the need, it dramatically reduces (human) biases and therefore enables brands to achieve higher levels of consistency regarding the way in which they are delivered to consumers (Chan & Tung, 2019).

But does AI actually improve, or merely affect, the co-creation of brand experience? AI technologies, as they are designed and built, seem to have all the required hallmarks to foster value co-creation processes, such as *active interaction* or the presence of an *interactive platform* (Ballantyne, 2004), as well as the sharing of knowledge through *ongoing communication* (Vargo & Lusch, 2004). For example, merely think of 'simple' and widely used AI-powered automatic chatbots or virtual assistants like Apple's Siri, which are designed to be dialogic, interactive, and responsive. Not only are they activated by human-to-machine communication, but their *raison d'être* is communication, as all the data they are fed with, and taught by, stem from an ongoing and ceaseless two-way, human-technology dialogue. What makes AI potentially disruptive for brand management is its *own* unique capacities for interaction with other entities and its ability to allow these entities to express their own roles in interaction (Novak & Hoffman, 2018). In an increasing technology-mediated context, the co-creation process stems from the exchange of platformed interactions among different agents, artifacts, processes, and interfaces belonging to a network system, and from the interactions between different network systems (Ramaswamy & Ozcan, 2018). Technologies are no longer tools and applications that improve and smooth consumer-brand interactions and make value co-creation more effective. By contrast, they are active actors in interactions that transform the dyadic consumer-brand relationship into a triadic consumer-brand-technology interaction. This revised conceptualization of actors and their role in the (value) co-creation process is based on a revised definition of agency. Accordingly, agency is no longer considered the exclusive prerequisite of human agents, but also as a domain of non-human technologies with an ability to learn and to adapt their behaviour by taking context into account. It follows that value changes from an idea of *value-in-use* to one of *value-in-interactional-creation* (Ramaswamy & Ozcan, 2018).

Besides the acknowledgement of its agentic role in consumer-brand relationships, it is also necessary to recognize the role of AI in the making of experiences. Puntoni et al. (2021) recently focused on the experiential side of AI and produced a typology of the experiences that consumers attain through AI. The typology includes (1) *data capture* experience, (2) *classification* experience, (3) *delegation* experience, and (4) *social* experience. In brief, *data capture* experience refers to AI's ability to provide consumers with the experience of endowing their personal data directly to algorithms, to the point where they feel better served by the latter. Successful examples of data capture are provided by the many fitness tracking apps like FitBit and Under Armour's Record, which integrate AI to create and deliver personalized training and nutrition plans to users based on their data. *Classification* experience happens when consumers perceive AI-enabled, personalized predictions to be the result of themselves being classified as a certain type of consumer. Examples of classification experience are Netflix's and Spotify's AI-powered recommendation systems, which are not only based on individuals' past viewing and listening histories, but also on contextual information such as the day of the week, the time of the day, the device, and its location. *Delegation* experiences are those in which consumers involve AI-powered technology in performing tasks on their behalf. For example, a daily-enacted delegation is performed every time Siri is asked to fix a schedule on your agenda, or every time a car driver asks the car assistant to find a location without removing their hands from the steering wheel. Finally, *social* experience refers to 'AI's capability for engaging in reciprocal communication' (Puntoni et al., 2021, p. 13). Social experiences can assume two different forms: the first is when consumers are aware that they are interacting with a technological agent, for example when using voice; the second is when consumers interact with an AI without initially knowing that it is nonhuman, for example when receiving customer service from an automated chatbot.

Where does this reasoning lead to, from a brand management perspective? How are brand management research and practices affected by the acknowledgment that AI-powered technologies and applications are actant agents capable of shaping and reshaping the way in which consumers and brands are involved in the value co-creation process? We argue that the implications of the aforesaid theoretical elaboration cannot be limited to the theoretical realm, since they undoubtedly are more substantial. Because of its unique technical characteristics and its multiple forms, AI can be used with great effect to make the most of the multiple interactions taking place in the value and experience co-creation network that is fostered or created by AI. For instance, specific forms of AI like VR and AR are already being applied to allow consumer access to new imaginative realities (Scholz & Smith, 2016). These immersive technologies – and the contexts they create – enable customers to fantasize and increase their feeling of engagement, and to develop new and untapped value co-creation scenarios that exist only insofar as the technologies are purposefully applied in pursuit of novel contexts of actions (Javornik, 2016). Therefore, apart from enabling technologies to become more *interactive*, AI facilitates the transformation of these technologies into *experiential* platforms which transform the way in which brand experiences are created and provide new lifeblood to the corporate brand. The luxury fashion brand Gucci for example has recently embraced the technological transformation of AI by partnering with the AR provider Wanna. The collaboration resulted in the launch of an in-app virtual shoes try-on which allows customers to wear Gucci's sneakers by simply pointing their smartphones' camera at their feet and then sharing their 'catwalk' experience on social media. This move not only enhanced in-store conversion and customer engagement with the brand, but it also allowed the rejuvenation of the brand and enabled it to gain differentiation in the conservative field of luxury (Liu et al., 2019). However, transforming an AI-powered technology or application into an experiential tool is not risk free if viewed from the viewpoint of the brand. Experience should not be built to benefit the company but should emanate from the customer to allow both the brand and the consumer to enjoy mutual benefits in a win-win manner. Similarly, a technology-powered experience should be designed in a genuine customer-centric way (Puntoni et al., 2021) and, to be effectively deployed, must be built on a deep knowledge of consumers' attitudes, perceptions, needs, wants, and behavioural patterns. This assumption is corroborated by Novak and Hoffman (2018) who contend that AI can, to all intent and purposes, support experiential platforms for value co-creation, as long as an object-oriented ontology, i.e., one in which consumers and technologies are viewed as being capable of playing communal and/or agentic interactive roles, is adopted (Novak & Hoffman, 2018).

However, the depiction of AI as an absolute source of positive brand experiences distorts reality as AI has a 'dark side' which must not be underestimated. The rapid pace at which these technologies become available goes hand-in-hand with the social concern that these technological advancements are not flawless (De Bruyn et al., 2020; Du & Xie, 2020). Beyond issues like ethical design and algorithmic bias (Lambrecht & Tucker, 2019), unemployment (McClure, 2018), physical and mental harm (van den Eijnden et al., 2016), and privacy and cybersecurity (Martin & Murphy, 2017), AI paradoxically limits the consumers' role in the process of co-creating experiences to a finite number of alternatives (Andrè et al., 2018; Puntoni et al , 2021). The main sources of consumer value disappear if the choice is completely outsourced and delegated in full to an artificial agent (Puntoni et al., 2021). In other words, a more passive role on the part of consumers in AI-powered contexts poses challenges to brand experience co-creation processes, the interactive and experiential essence of which is impoverished if consumer behaviour can be fully predicted (or influenced) *a priori*.

How can we reconcile these opposites? The next section outlines theoretical answers to these questions, drawing on ANT (Callon, 1999; Latour, 1992, 2005). Being concerned about investigating the social and the technical in combination (Walsham, 1997), ANT offers an appropriate theory to understand how the wide-ranging set of technologies that fall under the AI rubric changes the way in which consumers are involved in the process of co-creating brand experiences.

## 5. An ANT perspective of brand experience co-creation at the time of AI

As previously argued, in the AI age we realize that brand experience co-creation is at the mercy of two antagonistic forces. The first is the beneficial augmentation of AI power that accompanies the promise of endless opportunities like one-to-one customization and real-time customer support. The second is the concurrent risk of a perilous reversal of roles, where the machines' agency can undermine human supremacy, by confining the consumers to mere passive receptors of *a priori*-defined and imposed experiences which are not jointly and contextually co-created. This emerging paradox is also inherent to, and well-acknowledged in, the co-creation literature stream, which states that despite co-creation being 'the consequence of the emergence of a gifted, competent, skilled, active consumer' (Cochoy, 2015, p. 2), this does not imply that the consumers' (active) role is always and necessarily purposeful, mindfully enacted, and desired in reality.

Starting from this apparently unsolvable paradox, we propose a theoretical solution to this co-creational puzzle by merging the co-creation literature with the empirical and situated approach of ANT; a theory that shifts the attention from the process through which social phenomena (such as co-creation) manifests itself, to the objective and contextual features of the occurrence of these phenomena (Latour, 2005; Law, 2009; Callon, 1999). Stated differently, we contend that the resolution of the paradox inevitably created by AI use in brand experience co-creation requires a shift toward a new ontology. This rewarding ontological shift is possible if filtered through the lens of ANT which can be successfully combined with SDL to resolve the aforesaid co-creational brand-experience paradox. As Andreini et al. (2018) argued, the use of the SDL approach to study brand experience co-creation dynamics requires a redirection of attention to the co-creation context.

Brand experience emerges when marketers set up certain brand cues and consumers actively interact with them. Since the way in which consumers interact with these cues cannot be determined and defined *a priori*, brand experiences are equally unpredictable and hard to foresee (Chandler & Vargo, 2011; Akaka & Vargo, 2015). The same actors co-create and live through different brand experiences in different contexts, to the extent that the context becomes a vital part of the co-creation process.

The SDL approach's sensitivity to a contextual view of brand experience makes it well suited to complement ANT, as the two approaches share conceptual overlaps. As the SDL approach transcends a mere dyadic view of value co-creation and delineates a clear distinction between *operand* and *operant* resources, ANT similarly advocates an ontological migration from a Cartesian subject-object view to ontological indeterminacy (Bettany, 2007). Indeed, according to the principle of symmetry and ontological openness (Latour, 2005), the phenomenological reality of experiences is enacted in heterogenous ways by a multiplicity of human and nonhuman actors, who are theoretically and empirically approached with no prepended anthropocentric privileging of subject over object, semiotic over material, content over context, or technical over cultural. Similar to SDL's *operant* resources, ANT postulates that nonhuman actors, such as any form of artifacts can express agency so as to influence, encourage, impede, or enable the action of others in an action network (Latour, 2005). Therefore, nonhumans are not merely 'placeholders' or 'intermediaries' of the actions of others (Callon, 1999); they are capable of making a difference in the network (Bajde, 2013). Despite their partial overlap and compared to the SDL, ANT allows stepping beyond the nonhuman side of action. SDL is naturally inclined to view technologies as exogenous, i.e., context-embedded tools used to improve or smooth demand-supply interactions. Differently, as ANT strives at overcoming the dichotomous opposition of subject(s) and object(s), it enlarges the way in which technologies are framed beyond their 'utility' or their contextual nature, toward a new ontology where humans (e.g., consumers) and nonhumans (e.g., AI) are neither equated nor implicitly assumed to have privileged positions of domination of the one over the other (Amsterdamska, 1990; Khong, 2003). Overcoming this dichotomy implies that the subject-object relationship is not intended to denote a combination of separate entities. Rather, object and subject become a 'hybrid' entity as defined by Latour (2005). In other words, ANT does not separate object and subject but considers them as a new autonomous entity. A man brandishing a weapon is not simply an agent holding a passive object, but an entirely new *hybrid* entity (Latour, 2005). Similarly, a consumer interacting with a technology capable of agency, like AI, should not be simply seen as a subject 'consuming a service' or an agent that is aided by a technological tool, but as a new *assemblage* capable of actions that cannot be performed by the agent on its own (e.g., fast computation, prediction, anomaly detection) and that are uniquely human and highly idiosyncratic because they are tailored around and personalized through the human data that consumers endow to AI. Using a similar ontological perspective, Kotliar (2020) studied choice-inducing algorithms and posited that agency neither resides in the humans who eventually choose, nor only in their interaction with the algorithms that assist or guide their choices, but in a diverse agentic swarm of human and nonhuman agents who operate within specific social and cultural contexts. As such, AI overcomes the taken-for-granted paradigm in terms of which consumption is an act performed by a consuming actant subject over a consumed passive object, and conflates the consumer and the consumed by tracing entirely new paths of consumption and value creation. To some extent, it is possible to affirm that while consumers 'consume' AI, they are also simultaneously 'consumed' by AI, as the latter requires the former to exist and work. Indeed, while we watch Netflix, listen to a song on Spotify, choose the next bestseller to read, or search for our next potential love interest, we are simultaneously watched, heard, tested, and monitored by the same AI algorithms. The result is that these algorithms make use of previous cognitive and behavioural patterns to become more intelligent, and to refine their functioning more and more. In this regard, it is important to recall that technology's ability to meet our expectations, i.e., to provide us with the song we want to listen to or with the love interest we have been waiting for all along, mainly depends on the particular way of using these services. No wonder that erratically skipping from a particular movie to another or providing incomplete or erroneous personal data will inevitably result in the poor performance of a recommendation system, thus leading to an unsatisfactory experience with the used technology. A skilled consumer interacting with a high-performance AI will permit the materialization of a collaboratively co-created set of choices that benefits all involved parties. For example, through AI, firms can gain a better knowledge of users' behaviour, the users can gain continuous access to content that meets their expectations; and the technologies that keep on being fed with unbiased, first-hand consumer inputs can improve their ability to predict future behaviour and choice patterns. Eventually, this can lead to the materialization of a positive brand experience that is by nature unique and idiosyncratic, unless other consumers have identical tastes and preferences, identical skills, and symmetrical interaction interfaces. This is a brand experience that, we emphasize, is not produced by the brand, is not created by the consumer, and is not co-created by using technological aids. Rather, it is a brand experience that is uniquely created by a *hybrid* entity in which subjective agency and objective agency are conflated to the extent that they are inseparable. The hybrid experiential assemblage that emerges from the encounter of AI, brands and consumers is not simply socially constructed, but socio-materially constructed (Bajde, 2014). For this reason, the socio-materiality that constitutes existing brand experiences created by AI-powered technologies or applications requires an approach that assigns equal importance to both subject and object and that has an implicit tendency to avoid the attribution of supremacy to the former over the latter and vice versa (Bajde, 2013). In practical terms, this implies approaching brand experiences phenomenologically, equipped with context sensitivity, and interpreting each brand experience as the outcome of a unique and non-repeatable *hybrid* entity that results from the combination of the brand, the consumer, and the technology.

This ANT-based perspective not only provides a new theoretical understanding of this specific form of co-creation that takes into account the unique features of AI, but also – and foremost – has significant theoretical and practical implications as it allows an open approach to the phenomenon of brand experience co-creation, equipped with a greater sensitivity for the role played by the latest technological advancements in these co-creating dynamics.

The most important research and practical implications stemming from the aforesaid theoretical elaboration are briefly indicated and explained in the next section.

## 6. Theoretical and practical implications

How does the theoretical elaboration provided here make more sense of the brand experience dynamics at the time of AI? More specifically, how does the reported theoretical position stimulate empirical research in the field? While we believe that the use of a combined SDL-ANT-informed view of co-creation is *per se* useful and valuable, the theoretical puzzle that we address in this chapter is particularly useful as it reveals and opens up new empirical research possibilities. In accordance with the ontological posture we propose, not only the technology in general or the generic subject-object interaction that the technology enables is of interest, but also the triadic brand-consumer-technology combination through which a brand experience is co-created deserves particular attention. Therefore, researchers should be keen to use methods that simultaneously take the phenomenology of subjective experience and the role played by the context into account. As Bueger and Mireanu (2014) state, ANT calls for ethnographic methods, especially if the research is aimed at shedding light on objects, contexts, and interactions patterns, or on more general phenomena that currently require an understanding (Bueger & Bethke, 2014). For example, ethnographic enquiries focus on how and to what extent AI brings about new or different forms of brand experience and allows a deeper understanding and 'thicker' knowledge of how consumers interact with the specific technology, as well as how the specific technology adapts itself to the specific user, up to a point where it modifies the user's behavioural patterns. In general, the conceptualization of brand experience, of brand experience co-creation, and of the role assigned to AI in co-creation require scholars to turn to non-positivist epistemologies and related research methods, and to look at brand experience beyond a stimuli-reaction paradigm that tends to 'objectify' the chain of effects between brand stimuli and brand experience (Hatch, 2012). Longitudinal methods seem to be well suited to capture the occurrence of subject-object interactive dynamics, as well as to keep track of changes in these interactions over time. If it is assumed that AI-powered technologies and applications have the ability to learn and that learning requires their use over time, the way in which these technologies develop and the kind of experiences they provide to consumers require the researcher to keep track of changes over time.

What is especially important is the primary role that ANT bestows on nonhuman actors. Thus, research approaching AI through the lenses we indicated in this chapter should always begin by (critically) exploring and unravelling how human and nonhuman agents interact and how much agency is deployed by the nonhuman actant. This can be done via ethnography but also through a deep and detailed description of the context, specifically using secondary data (such as big data) that allow the observer to equally understand the type and amount of agency of the nonhuman actant. In this regard, case studies undoubtedly present a potent research methodology to provide details on how AI is applied to the brand experiences co-creation process in specific settings. The market is already crowded with firms using AI to improve experiences, or to make them more effective or more memorable. This provides fertile ground to be investigated for the sake of gaining a better understanding of how AI functions in material terms, as well as to serve the purpose of theory building (Eisenhardt & Graebner. 2007).

In addition to opening new avenues of researching brand experience co-creation dynamics, this theoretical exposition also has implications for practitioners. First, due to AI's agentic nature, we caution brand managers to synergistically collaborate with information and computer scientists, as well as with sociologists and psychologists. This collaboration is required to align the marketing and the technology perspectives (Puntoni et al., 2021), and to ensure that the principles of the latter, namely accuracy and efficiency, are not pursued to its detriment, e.g., to the detriment of sales, brand equity, and customer satisfaction.

As previously argued, the outcomes stemming from the use of AI should not be taken for granted, as if they were inherently true and immutable. Actually, AI-algorithms are more human than we believe them to be, to the point where they can be conceived as a 'coded manifestation of specifically positioned human subjects' (Kotliar, 2020, p. 11). As Kotliar (2020) incisively notes, highly automated algorithms are a by-product of human action and are, for this reason, not free of errors. We recommend that brand managers approach the process of creating brand experiences through or assisted by AI 'from the cradle to the grave' and continuously monitor the extent to which the sense of pleasure experienced by consumers gives way to a sense of frustration implicit in the reduced sense of autonomy they experience when using AI. As experience is co-produced by interaction, it is necessary to continuously monitor how consumers use and relate to AI in order to determine whether discrepancies emerge, to assess whether these discrepancies are imputable to consumers' misbehaviour or to technological flaws, and to intervene by instituting the necessary correctives, such us training and educational activities that target the consumer or by releasing bias-free versions of the AI application (Puntoni et al., 2021).

## 7. Conclusion

The emergence and diffusion of AI represent what is arguably one of the most disrupting technological revolutions in recent human history. However, despite the renewed interest and conceptual enlargement of brand experience embracing more consumer-centric, socially-constructed, and context-sensitive approaches (Andreini et al., 2018), recent research hardly addresses the current role that AI technologies play in the creation of new and different forms of brand experience. In this chapter, at a theoretical level, we explored this *terra incognita* by constructing an updated framework of brand experience co-creation that combines recent theoretical refinements of the brand experience concept (Andreini et al., 2018). This is done within a unique conceptual framework that in a rewarding manner merges the SDL of markets (Vargo & Lusch, 2004, 2008, 2011) and ANT (e.g., Callon, 1999; Latour, 1992, 2005). After fine-tuning the concept of brand experience co-creation in terms of the SDL perspective and providing a more acceptable definition of the overarching AI concept, we postulate that, in AI-mediated contexts, brand experience co-creation processes are contested by two antagonistic forces, represented by the countless prospects of AI and by the dangerous confinement of consumers to the role of passive receptors of *a priori*-imposed experiences, respectively. We contend that going beyond a mere subject-object dichotomy is not sufficient to reconcile this co-creational paradox. We therefore claim that by being interactive, adaptive, context- and user-sensitive, AI is a real actant resource component of the inseparable brand-consumer-technology triad, of a new hybrid entity capable of socio-materially constructing totally new brand experiences.

This new theoretical understanding of AI-powered, brand experience co-creation processes and networks opens entirely new landscapes for both scholars and practitioners of brand management. Whilst we posit that scholars should turn to non-positivist epistemologies and empirical-situated research methods to effectively extend our knowledge of this complex phenomenon, the practitioners should abandon the technology-focused perspective, which is typical of AI domains, acknowledge the limitations of this technological actor, and create an ongoing AI-mediated process that includes continuous monitoring and (re)adaptation.

## References

Akaka, M. A., & Vargo, S. L. (2015). Extending the context of service: From encounters to ecosystems. *Journal of Services Marketing, 29*(6/7), 453–462.

Akaka, M. A., Vargo, S. L., & Lusch, R. F. (2012). An exploration of networks in value cocreation: A service-ecosystems view. In S. L. Vargo & R. F. Lusch (Eds.), *Review of marketing research: Special issue – Toward a better understanding of the role of value in markets and marketing* (pp. 13–50). Bingley: Emerald Group Publishing.

Amsterdamska, O. (1990). Surely you are joking, Monsieur Latour! *Science, Technology, & Human Values, 15*(4), 495–504.

André, Q., Carmon, Z., Wertenbroch, K., Crum, A., Frank, D., Goldstein, W., Huber, J., van Boven, L., Weber, B., & Yang, H. (2018). Consumer choice and autonomy in the age of artificial intelligence and big data. *Customer Needs and Solutions, 5*, 28–37.

Andreini, D., Pedeliento, G., Zarantonello, L., & Solerio, C. (2018). A renaissance of brand experience: Advancing the concept through a multi-perspective analysis. *Journal of Business Research, 91*, 123–133.

Bajde, D. (2013). Consumer culture theory (re) visits actor – Network theory: Flattening consumption studies. *Marketing Theory, 13*(2), 227–242.

Bajde, D. (2014). Consumer culture theory: Ideology, mythology and meaning in technology consumption. *International Journal of Actor-Network Theory and Technological Innovation, 6*(2), 10–25.

Balducci, B., & Marinova, D. (2018). Unstructured data in marketing. *Journal of the Academy of Marketing Science, 46*(4), 557–590.

Ballantyne, D. (2004). Dialogue and its role in the development of relationship specific knowledge. *Journal of Business & Industrial Marketing, 19*(2), 114–123.

Bandura, A. (1977). Self-efficacy: Toward a unifying theory of behavioral change. *Psychological Review, 84*(2), 191–215.

Barhorst, J. B., McLean, G., Shah, E., & Mack, R. (2021). Blending the real world and the virtual world: Exploring the role of flow in augmented reality experiences. *Journal of Business Research, 122*, 423–436.

Bettany, S. (2007). The material semiotics of consumption or where (and what) are the objects in consumer culture theory? In R. W. Belk & J. F. Sherry (Eds.), *Consumer culture theory* (Research in Consumer Behavior, Vol. 11, pp. 41–46). Bingley: Emerald Group Publishing.

Brakus, J. J., Schmitt, B. H., & Zarantonello, L. (2009). Brand experience: What is it? How is it measured? Does it affect loyalty? *Journal of Marketing, 73*(3), 52–68.

Brodie, R. J. (2017). Commentary on "Working consumers: Co-creation of brand identity, consumer identity, and brand community identity". *Journal of Business Research, 70*(1), 430–431.

Brodie, R. J., Glynn, M. S., & Little, V. (2006). The service brand and the service-dominant logic: Missing fundamental premise or the need for stronger theory? *Marketing Theory, 6*(3), 363–379.

Bueger, C., & Bethke, F. (2014). Actor-networking the 'failed state' – An enquiry into the life of concepts. *Journal of International Relations and Development, 17*(1), 30–60.

Bueger, C., & Mireanu, M. (2014). Proximity. In C. Aradau, J. Huysmans, A. Neal, and N. Voelkner (Eds.), *Critical security methods: New frameworks for analysis* (pp. 134–157). London: Routledge. https://www.routledge.com/Critical-Security-Methods-New-frameworks-for-analysis/Aradau-Huysmans-Neal-Voelkner/p/book/9780415712958

Callon, M. (1999). Actor-network theory-the market test. *The Sociological Review, 47*(1), 181–195.

Chan, A. P. H., & Tung, V. W. S. (2019). Examining the effects of robotic service on brand experience: The moderating role of hotel segment. *Journal of Travel & Tourism Marketing, 36*(4), 458–468.

Chandler, J. D., & Vargo, S. L. (2011). Contextualization and value-in-context: How context frames exchange. *Marketing Theory, 11*(1), 35–49.

Chintagunta, P., Hanssens, D. M., & Hauser, J. R. (2016). Marketing science and big data. *Marketing Science*, *35*(3), 341–342.

Chui, M., Manyika, J., Miremadi, M., Henke, N., Chung, R., Nel, P., & Malhotra, S. (2018, April). *Notes from the AI frontier: Applications and value of deep learning* (McKinsey global institute discussion paper). Retrieved August 28, 2020 from www.mckinsey.com/featured-insights/artificial intelligence/notes-from-the-aifrontier-applications-and-value-of-deep-learning

Cochoy, F. (2015). Consumers at work, or curiosity at play? Revisiting the prosumption/value cocreation debate with smartphones and two-dimensional bar codes. *Marketing Theory*, *15*(2), 133–153.

Davenport, T., Guha, A., Grewal, D., & Bressgott, T. (2020). How artificial intelligence will change the future of marketing. *Journal of the Academy of Marketing Science*, *48*(1), 24–42.

De Bruyn, A., Viswanathan, V., Beh, Y. S., Brock, J. K. U., & von Wangenheim, F. (2020). Artificial intelligence and marketing: Pitfalls and opportunities. *Journal of Interactive Marketing*, *51*, 91–105.

Du, S., & Xie, C. (2020). Paradoxes of artificial intelligence in consumer markets: Ethical challenges and opportunities. *Journal of Business Research*, *129*, 961–974.

Edvardsson, B., Tronvoll, B., & Gruber, T. (2011). Expanding understanding of service exchange and value co-creation: A social construction approach. *Journal of the Academy of Marketing Science*, *39*(2), 327–339.

Eisenhardt, K. M., & Graebner, M. E. (2007). Theory building from cases: Opportunities and challenges. *Academy of Management Journal*, *50*(1), 25–32.

Gidhagen, M., Helkkula, A., Löbler, H., & Jonas, J. (2017). Human-to-nonhuman value cocreation and resource integration: Parasocial actors in a service ecosystem in *Service Dominant Logic, Network and Systems Theory and Service Science: Integrating three Perspectives for a New Service Agenda*. Proceedings of the 2017 Naples Forum on Service.

Gummerus, J. (2013). Value creation processes and value outcomes in marketing theory: Strangers or siblings? *Marketing Theory*, *13*(1), 19–46.

Halliday, S. V. (2016). User-generated content about brands: Understanding its creators and consumers. *Journal of Business Research*, *69*(1), 137–144.

Hatch, M. J. (2012). The pragmatics of branding: An application of Dewey's theory of aesthetic expression. *European Journal of Marketing*, *46*(7/8), 885–899.

Hatch, M. J., & Schultz, M. (2010). Toward a theory of brand co-creation with implications for brand governance. *Journal of Brand Management*, *17*(8), 590–604.

Helkkula, A. (2011). Characterising the concept of service experience. *Journal of Service Management*, *22*(3), 367–389.

Hinsch, C., Felix, R., & Rauschnabel, P. A. (2020). Nostalgia beats the wow-effect: Inspiration, awe and meaningful associations in augmented reality marketing. *Journal of Retailing and Consumer Services*, *53*, 101987.

Huang, M., & Rust, R. T. (2018). Artificial intelligence in service. *Journal of Service Research*, *21*(2), 155–172.

Huang, T., & Vandoni, C. E. (1996). Computer vision: Evolution and promise. *19th CERN School of Computing, Geneva, CERN*, 21–25.

Iglesias, O., Ind, N., & Alfaro, M. (2013). The organic view of the brand: A brand value co-creation model. *Journal of Brand Management*, *20*(8), 670–688.

Iglesias, O., Markovic, S., & Rialp, J. (2019). How does sensory brand experience influence brand equity? Considering the roles of customer satisfaction, customer affective commitment, and employee empathy. *Journal of Business Research*, *96*, 343–354.

Ind, N., Iglesias, O., & Schultz, M. (2013). Building brands together. *California Management Review*, *55*(3), 5–26.

Jaakkola, E., Helkkula, A., Aarikka-Stenroos, L., Akaka, M. A., Vargo, S. L., & Schau, H. J. (2015). The context of experience. *Journal of Service Management*, *26*(2), 206–223.

Jalal, M. E., Hosseini, M., & Karlsson, S. (2016). Forecasting incoming call volumes in call centers with recurrent neural networks. *Journal of Business Research*, *69*(11), 4811–4814.

Javornik, A. (2016). Augmented reality: Research agenda for studying the impact of its media characteristics on consumer behaviour. *Journal of Retailing and Consumer Services*, *30*, 252–261.

Jurafsky, D., & Martin, J. H. (2000). *Speech and language processing: An introduction to natural language processing, computational linguistics, and speech recognition*. Upper Sadder River, NJ: Prentice Hall.

Kaartemo, V., & Helkkula, A. (2018). A systematic review of artificial intelligence and robots in value co-creation: Current status and future research avenues. *Journal of Creating Value*, *4*(2), 211–228.

Khong, L. (2003). Actants and enframing: Heidegger and Latour on technology. *Studies in History and Philosophy of Science Part A*, *34*(4), 693–704.

Kietzmann, J., Paschen, J., & Treen, E. (2018). Artificial intelligence in advertising: How marketers can leverage artificial intelligence along the consumer journey. *Journal of Advertising Research, 58*(3), 263–267.

Kotliar, D. M. (2020). Who gets to choose? On the socio-algorithmic construction of choice. *Science, Technology, & Human Values, 46*(2), 346–375.

Lambrecht, A., & Tucker, C. (2019). Algorithmic bias? An empirical study of apparent gender-based discrimination in the display of STEM career ads. *Management Science, 65*(7), 2966–2981.

Latour, B. (1992). Where are the missing masses? The sociology of a few mundane artefacts. In W. E. Bijker & J. Law (Eds.), *Shaping technology/building society*. Cambridge, MA: MIT Press.

Latour, B. (2005). *Reassembling the social: An introduction to actor – Network theory*. Oxford: Oxford University Press.

Law, J. (2009). Actor – Network theory and material semiotics. In B. S. Turner (Ed.), *The new blackwell companion to social theory*. Oxford: Wiley-Blackwell.

Liu, S., Perry, P., & Gadzinski, G. (2019). The implications of digital marketing on WeChat for luxury fashion brands in China. *Journal of Brand Management, 26*(4), 395–409.

Liu, X., Burns, A. C., & Hou, Y. (2017). An investigation of brand-related user-generated content on Twitter. *Journal of Advertising, 46*(2), 236–247.

Liu, X., Shin, H., & Burns, A. C. (2021). Examining the impact of luxury brand's social media marketing on customer engagement: Using big data analytics and natural language processing. *Journal of Business Research, 125*, 815–826.

Ma, L., & Sun, B. (2020). Machine learning and AI in marketing – Connecting computing power to human insights. *International Journal of Research in Marketing, 37*(3), 481–504.

Martin, K. D., & Murphy, P. E. (2017). The role of data privacy in marketing. *Journal of the Academy of Marketing Science, 45*(2), 135–155.

Martínez-López, F., & Casillas, J. (2013). Artificial intelligence-based systems applied in industrial marketing: An historical overview, current and future insights. *Industrial Marketing Management, 42*(4), 489–495.

McAlexander, J. H., Schouten, J. W., & Koenig, H. F. (2002). Building brand community. *Journal of Marketing, 66*, 38–54.

McCarthy, J., & Hayes, P. J. (1981). Some philosophical problems from the standpoint of artificial intelligence. In B. L. Webber & N. J. Nilsson (Eds.), *Readings in artificial intelligence* (pp. 431–450). Burlington: Morgan Kaufmann Publishers.

McClure, P. K. (2018), "You're fired," says the robot: The rise of automation in the workplace, technophobes, and fears of unemployment. *Social Science Computer Review, 36*(2), 139–156.

McColl-Kennedy, J. R., Vargo, S. L., Dagger, T. S., Sweeney, J. C., & Kasteren, Y. V. (2012). Health care customer value cocreation practice styles. *Journal of Service Research, 15*(4), 370–389.

Merrilees, B. (2016). Interactive brand experience pathways to customer-brand engagement and value co-creation. *Journal of Product & Brand Management, 25*(5), 402–408.

Merz, M. A., He, Y., & Vargo, S. L. (2009). The evolving brand logic: A service-dominant logic perspective. *Journal of the Academy of Marketing Science, 37*(3), 328–344.

Mohd-Any, A. A., Winklhofer, H., & Ennew, C. (2015). Measuring users' value experience on a travel website (e-value) what value is cocreated by the user? *Journal of Travel Research, 54*(4), 496–510.

Novak, T., & Hoffman, D. L. (2018). Relationship journeys in the internet of things: A new framework for understanding interactions between consumers and smart objects. *Journal of the Academy of Marketing Science, 47*(2), 216–237.

Payne, A., Storbacka, K., Frow, P., & Knox, S. (2009). Co-creating brands: Diagnosing and designing the relationship experience. *Journal of Business Research, 62*(3), 379–389.

Pine, J. B., & Gilmore, J. H. (1999). *The experience economy*. Boston, MA: Harvard Business Press.

Puntoni, S., Reczek, R. W., Giesler, M., & Botti, S. (2021). Consumers and artificial intelligence: An experiential perspective. *Journal of Marketing, 85*(1), 131–151.

Ramaswamy, V., & Ozcan, K. (2018). What is co-creation? An interactional creation framework and its implications for value creation. *Journal of Business Research, 84*, 196–205.

Rauschnabel, P. A., Felix, R., & Hinsch, C. (2019). Augmented reality marketing: How mobile AR-apps can improve brands through inspiration. *Journal of Retailing and Consumer Services, 49*, 43–53.

Russell, S. J., & Norvig, P. (2016). *Artificial intelligence: A modern approach*. Englewood Cliffs, NJ: Prentice Hall.

Salomonson, N., Åberg, A., & Allwood, J. (2012). Communicative skills that support value creation: A study of B2B interactions between customers and customer service representatives. *Industrial Marketing Management, 41*(1), 145–155.

Schau, H. J., Muñiz Jr, A. M., & Arnould, E. J. (2009). How brand community practices create value. *Journal of Marketing, 73*(5), 30–51.

Schembri, S. (2009). Reframing brand experience: The experiential meaning of Harley – Davidson. *Journal of Business Research, 61*(12), 1299–1310.

Schmitt, B. (1999). Experiential marketing. *Journal of Marketing Management, 15*(1–3), 53–67.

Scholz, J., & Duffy, K. (2018). We are at home: How augmented reality reshapes mobile marketing and consumer-brand relationships. *Journal of Retailing and Consumer Services, 44*, 11–23.

Scholz, J., & Smith, A. N. (2016). Augmented reality: Designing immersive experiences that maximize consumer engagement. *Business Horizons, 59*(2), 149–161.

Shanahan, T., Tran, T. P., & Taylor, E. C. (2019). Getting to know you: Social media personalization as a means of enhancing brand loyalty and perceived quality. *Journal of Retailing and Consumer Services, 47*, 57–65.

Syam, N., & Sharma, A. (2018). Waiting for a sales renaissance in the fourth industrial revolution: Machine learning and artificial intelligence in sales research and practice, *Industrial Marketing Management, 69*, 135–146.

Turing, A. (1950). Computing machinery and intelligence. *Mind, 59*(236), 433–460.

Vallaster, C., & Von Wallpach, S. (2013). An online discursive inquiry into the social dynamics of multi-stakeholder brand meaning co-creation. *Journal of Business Research, 66*(9), 1505–1515.

Van den Eijnden, R. J., Lemmens, J. S., & Valkenburg, P. M. (2016). The social media disorder scale. *Computers in Human Behavior, 61*, 478–487.

Van Doorn, J., Mende, M., Noble, S. M., Hulland, J., Ostrom, A. L., Grewal, D., & Petersen, J. A. (2017). Domo arigato Mr. Roboto: Emergence of automated social presence in organizational frontlines and customers' service experiences. *Journal of Service Research, 20*(1), 43–58.

Vargo, S. L., & Lusch, R. F. (2004). Evolving to a new dominant logic for marketing. *Journal of Marketing, 68*(1), 1–17.

Vargo, S. L., & Lusch, R. F. (2008). Service-dominant logic: Continuing the evolution. *Journal of the Academy of Marketing Science, 36*(1), 1–10.

Vargo, S. L., & Lusch, R. F. (2011). It's all B2B . . . and beyond: Toward a systems perspective of the market. *Industrial Marketing Management, 40*(2), 181–187.

Vargo, S. L., Maglio, P. P., & Akaka, M. A. (2008). On value and value co-creation: A service systems and service logic perspective. *European Management Journal, 26*(3), 145–152.

Walsham, G. (1997). Actor-network theory and is research: Current status and future prospects. In A. S. Lee, J. Liebenau, & J. I. DeGross. (Eds.), *Information systems and qualitative research. IFIP – The international federation for information processing* (pp. 466–480). Boston, MA: Springer.

West, A., Clifford, J., & Atkinson, D. (2018). "Alexa, build me a brand" an investigation into the impact of artificial intelligence on branding. *The Business & Management Review, 9*(3), 321–330.

Wirth, N. (2018). Hello marketing, what can artificial intelligence help you with? *International Journal of Market Research, 60*(5), 438–453.

# 13
# HONEY OR CONDENSED MILK? IMPROVING RELATIVE BRAND ATTRACTIVENESS THROUGH COMMERCIAL AND SOCIAL INNOVATIONS

*Seidali Kurtmollaiev, Line Lervik-Olsen, and Tor W. Andreassen*

And when Rabbit said, 'Honey or condensed milk with your bread?' he was so excited that he said, 'Both,' and then, so as not to seem greedy, he added, 'But don't bother about the bread, please.'

– A. A. Milne, *Winnie-the-Pooh*

## 1. Introduction

On the one hand, corporate brands face daily market demands on innovation, especially in light of intensified competition. Consumers want novel and unique experiences, and letting competitors offer them that without a fight is the surest way out of the market for a brand. On the other hand, worsening social and environmental problems obligate all market players to actively take care of people and the planet.

In the first stage of the COVID-19 pandemic, many firms made radical changes in their market offerings and refocused their corporate brands to contribute to the common battle against the virus. For example, fashion brands like Louis Vuitton and Prada fabricated face masks and medical gowns, while alcohol and perfume brands like Pernod Ricard, Old Fourth Distillery, and Guerlain converted their production lines to produce hand sanitisers. In addition to helping local communities, such brands found an opportunity to efficiently counteract plummeting returns early in the pandemic. Another example of social responsiveness is many brands' support for Black Lives Matter, the social movement against racially motivated violence. Major market players such as Apple, Netflix, Twitter, Nike, and Citigroup took a clear stand on the issue, with Nike releasing a socially conscious message 'For once, don't do it,' which was reposted by other brands, including Converse and Nike's main competitor, Adidas. Although most corporate brands eventually return to their core value propositions, such activities reflect managers' increased understanding of the importance of socially responsible behaviour and its positive ripple effects. This demonstrates the long way modern companies have come since the first corporations, such as the Dutch East India Company and East India Company, which were actively involved in the slave trade, armed conflicts, corruption, and looting of resources.

Taking a stand may not be easy, especially when it concerns controversial issues (Schmidt et al., 2021). The negative responses that Gillette received for the campaign 'We Believe in the Best in Men' or Stormberg for its support of the World Wide Fund for Nature's 'Save Our Wolves' campaign in Norway are reminders of how complex and uncontrollable societal debates can be. They demonstrate that brand-associated social and environmental practices engage both consumers and non-consumers, which contrasts with more traditional relations between brands and individual consumers founded on sales and product usage. Moreover, society's growing expectations for socially responsible business practices leave little doubt that merely taking a stand or running a campaign is not enough. Traditional corporate and social responsibility in the form of philanthropy or reactive attempts to address negative externalities caused by the firm's activities are also insufficient. Instead, society requires that sustainability be deeply ingrained in all business aspects, from operations to offerings. The notion of the 'triple bottom line,' coined in 1997 by John Elkington, seems to have finally left the realm of wishful thinking to instead reflect real-world practices.

Having a distinct, relevant, and desirable corporate brand is the keystone to a firm's survival as the whole purpose of branding is to attract consumers' attention by increasing the salience of corporate characteristics and forming corporate associations (Brown & Dacin, 1997; Keller, 1998). With approximately 300,000 and 700,000 trademarks registered every year in the United States and Europe, respectively (according to World Intellectual Property Organization), having a brand that is attractive to consumers is essential. An attractive brand engages consumers who may not only like the brand but even identify with it (Marin & de Maya, 2013; So et al., 2017). Consumers also tend to remain loyal to brands they are attracted to and downplay negative information about them, forgiving mistakes (Elbedweihy et al., 2016). In turn, consumers switching to another brand indicates that the original brand is failing to meet their expectations, which anticipates the firm's loss of income and market share (Al-Kwifi & Zafar, 2015).

Many studies have attempted to uncover the factors that make brands attractive. Evidence suggests that corporate brand attractiveness may increase when an organization explicitly constructs and communicates distinctive brand characteristics as if they were human personality traits – the so-called 'brand personality' – with the focus on expertise and competence (Brown & Dacin, 1997; Sophonsiri & Polyorat, 2009). For example, when a brand's target audience is homogeneous, a targeted way to improve brand attractiveness is to express brand personality and values congruent with the particular customer segment (Elbedweihy et al., 2016). In this chapter, we discuss how firms can build attractive corporate brands by expressing actual innovativeness and social and environmental responsibility. We introduce the notion of relative brand attractiveness, arguing that brand success is better explained when brand attractiveness is conceptualized in relative rather than absolute terms. We present three studies on relative brand attractiveness using empirical data from the Norwegian Innovation Index (NII) – the world's first customer-based ranking of innovative firms, which has been adopted in the United States (since 2018), Sweden (2019), Finland (2020), and Denmark (2021). Following a carefully designed procedure, the NII captures firms' innovations and customers' perceptions of changes in value co-creation resulting from these innovations. The main informants are a nationally representative sample of the Norwegian population aged 15 years or older. Through a professional bureau, our research team has collected more than 23,000 responses annually from customers of approximately 80 corporate brands in 20 industries since 2016. The publicly available result is the annual rating and ranking of major corporate brands in Norway across various sectors based on innovativeness, relative attractiveness, and customer loyalty. Although the NII builds upon the assertion that the customer is the final judge of innovations, it also acknowledges that innovations are launched by firms. To capture firms' actual launches, the NII team annually conducts an additional qualitative study in which the marketing directors of firms on the ranking list present concrete changes they made in the previous year. Customers participating in the main quantitative study also have an opportunity to share their thoughts on companies' activities in a text field, allowing direct comparison of managers' and customers' perspectives on innovation based on the actors' own reflections and vocabulary.

In the first study, based on quantitative data, we show that innovative corporate brands are more attractive than their competitors and that sustainability initiatives increase the brand's chances of being perceived as innovative. In the second study, also based on quantitative data, we find that social innovations generally have a stronger relationship with perceived innovativeness than digital innovations, but that digital innovations have a positive impact on social innovations. In the third study, based on qualitative data, we explain why innovations that managers believe will be interesting and relevant for consumers are often not viewed as such by the consumers. Finally, we discuss the sustainable approach to building an innovative corporate brand and the role of shared understanding in this process.

## 2. Building relative brand attractiveness: being first or doing right?

### 2.1. Defining relative brand attractiveness

Brand attractiveness refers to consumers' positive evaluation of a brand's distinctive and relatively enduring characteristics (Bhattacharya & Sen, 2003; Currás-Pérez et al., 2009). According to Bhattacharya and Sen (2003), consumers are likely to perceive a brand as attractive when it satisfies one of their self-definitional needs – that is, self-continuity (maintaining a stable and consistent sense of self), self-distinctiveness (distinguishing the self from others in social contexts), and self-enhancement (seeing the self in a positive light). The authors suggest that managers can make a brand attractive by ensuring its similarity to consumers' identities, its distinctiveness in characteristics valuable to consumers and its prestige. Firms with appealing brands can charge premium prices, achieve higher profitability and better access to investments, and attract stronger job applicants (Fombrun & Shanley, 1990). Consumers are also typically more satisfied with such brands and tend to trust and praise them (Walsh & Beatty, 2007). As a result, it has traditionally been assumed that by creating an attractive brand and ensuring consumer satisfaction, firms can reduce incentives for brand switching and gain more loyal consumers (Bhattacharya & Sen, 2003; Johnson et al., 2001).

Although this assumption seems intuitive, it omits the fact that the market includes multiple players and that consumers form associations and derive experiences based on their interactions with many firms on the market. A brand can be attractive in itself, but consumers will be less loyal if competing brands are equally or more attractive (Sirohi et al., 1998). Therefore, instead of thinking about brand attractiveness in absolute terms, it is crucial to focus on the brand's relative superiority with respect to its competitors (Andreassen & Lervik, 1999). As the literature suggests, relative brand attractiveness may play a major role in resisting brand-switching behaviour (Al-Kwifi & Zafar, 2015) and be more efficient in securing the firm's market share and share of wallet than product usage and customer satisfaction (Shukla, 2004; Keiningham et al., 2015).

We define relative brand attractiveness as the extent of consumers' positive evaluation of the brand's distinctive and relatively enduring characteristics in relation to competing brands. As a subjective, perception-based measure, this concept describes a consumer attitude that is holistic and not necessarily in accordance with specific objective data. For example, consumers may evaluate a brand as more attractive even when competing offerings have lower prices, higher quality, or more stylish designs because the focal brand has a better congruence with the consumers' beliefs or context of use. As Vargo and Lusch (2016) state, 'value is always uniquely and phenomenologically determined by the beneficiary' (p. 8).

## 2.2. Innovation as a way to increase brand attractiveness

Innovation is the principal motor behind the creation and maintenance of the most distinctive brand characteristics, and the association between brand distinctiveness and innovativeness tends to be empirically strong (e.g., Wong & Merrilees, 2008; Corkindale & Belder, 2009). Essentially, brands provide strategic focus to the development of new solutions and support the introduction and adoption of innovations, while innovations influence brand perception and attitude (Brexendorf et al., 2015). As an enduring characteristic, corporate brand innovativeness does not build upon specific and singular product launches or product attributes but upon regular innovation activities over time (Kunz et al., 2011), reflecting the firm's reputation in reliably developing and introducing creative solutions (Brexendorf & Keller, 2017). For corporate brands, being perceived as innovative often equates to being modern and up-to-date (Gürhan-Canli & Batra, 2004; Henard & Dacin, 2010). An innovative brand signals characteristics such as energy, leadership, success, and a pioneering nature, which are typically attractive and desirable to consumers (Aaker, 2007). Innovativeness also signals higher utility and various positive emotions, including excitement, astonishment, adventurousness, happiness, delight, and satisfaction, that consumers may experience when they interact with the brand (Kunz et al., 2011; Lowe & Alpert, 2015; Thompson et al., 2005). Moreover, an innovative brand engages its consumers, who start to identify with it, feel passionate about it, and actively participate in its community (Yen et al., 2020). They may even forgive or positively view the brand's deviations from category norms and regard these deviations as a positive sign of innovation efforts (Barone & Jewell, 2013).

Many corporate brands explicitly try to position themselves as innovative to increase customer loyalty (Henard & Dacin, 2010). Yet when a brand regularly introduces new offerings, consumers assess them against competing alternatives. If the novel characteristics are more valuable than what is on the market, consumers may see the brand as more attractive than its competitors (Andreassen & Lervik, 1999). Conversely, when competing brands launch successful innovations, the focal brand becomes less attractive (Dotzel et al., 2013). Existing theory suggests, therefore, that corporate brand innovativeness may play a key role in building and maintaining relative brand attractiveness.

In addition to having expectations about innovation, consumers are becoming conscious of the negative effects of the products they buy and use. They want to contribute to responsible production and consumption and, as evidence suggests, are increasingly attracted to brands that are socially responsible (e.g., Marin & Ruiz, 2007; Currás-Pérez et al., 2009). Some consumers use ethical values to construct their identities, associating themselves with an ethical consumption community and avoiding brands that embody the values of consumerist society (Papaoikonomou et al., 2016). Accordingly, Kay (2006) has suggested that a corporate brand's first step to becoming strong, attractive, and connected to consumer values should be creating a link to social responsibility. Many businesses already recognize that they must become more sustainable to avoid being ignored or outright rejected by their stakeholders. According to the Global Sustainable Investment Alliance, in 2019, the sustainable investment market reached USD 30.7 trillion in developed countries alone (68% increase since 2012), indicating the attractiveness of sustainable brands to not only customers but also investors.

## 2.3. Innovation vs. social responsibility

Neither innovation nor social responsibility comes for free, and a firm with limited resources may find it challenging to decide which of these areas to prioritize in resource allocation. To test which investment strategy focus – innovation or social responsibility – is the most effective in increasing brand attractiveness, we used structural equation modelling on the 2016–2017 NII data from 2,612 respondents. The respondents answered questions about their perceptions of the 15 largest Norwegian brands in five consumer-facing industries (banking, telecommunication, retail, online shopping, and postal services). To measure perceived brand innovativeness and social and environmental responsibility, we used items from Kunz et al. (2011) and Walsh and Beatty (2007), respectively. For relative brand attractiveness, we relied on Andreassen and Lervik-Olsen (2008), asking respondents to compare the brand of interest to competing brands and indicate the extent to which it offered better-value and higher-quality products and services, had a stronger reputation, and was more attractive.

Our finding is that the *direct* effect of perceived innovativeness on relative brand attractiveness is much stronger than that of perceived social responsibility, with standardized beta $b = .62$ (standard error S.E. $= .09$) and $b = .17$ (S.E. $= .04$), respectively. Innovative brands are simply more attractive. However, this does not mean that innovativeness trumps social responsibility. Although the modest effect size of perceived social responsibility aligns with previous findings on the relationship between brand ethicality and brand equity (Iglesias et al., 2019), our result comes with a twist. While the direct effect of brand social responsibility on relative brand attractiveness is not remarkably high, the *total effect* is about three times larger because, as our data show, consumers tend to perceive socially responsible brands as more innovative ($b = .57$, S.E. $= .06$). In other words, perceived innovativeness partially mediates the effect of perceived social responsibility on relative brand attractiveness. Although prioritizing innovation in general may seem to be a good strategy, firms that prioritize investments in *responsible innovation* may achieve higher yields due to the combined effects of being perceived as both socially responsible and innovative.

This finding raises another question: can firms strategically aim for this effect by focusing on the areas in which consumers are best able to discern responsible innovation? When firms innovate for consumers, they introduce significant changes in their market offerings, which, in turn, primarily affect consumer perceptions of brand innovativeness, social responsibility, and attractiveness. To test these effects in our study, we concentrated on two major areas in which consumers could experience changes directly – value proposition and interaction space. Value proposition – the promise of benefits that a brand offers to satisfy consumer needs or, from the customer perspective, the promise of an experience that consumers will receive from engaging with the brand (Payne et al., 2017) – is the cornerstone of the relationship between brand and consumer. Examples of such benefits and experiences are eventual knowledge and employment in the case of educational institutions, positive emotions, and memories in the case of amusement parks or a low-cost, environmentally friendly transfer between locations in the case of public transportation. We use the term *interaction space* to describe all physical and digital touchpoints that contribute to the brand experience, such as physical surroundings and products, equipment, webpages, and mobile applications.

According to our analysis, changes in value proposition have positive effects on both perceived brand innovativeness ($b = .20$, S.E. $= .03$) and social responsibility ($b = .27$, S.E. $= .04$), with the latter effect being larger. This suggests that changes in value proposition do not have to be about the environment or society to prompt perceptions of brand innovativeness (and, hence, attractiveness). If they are, however, the total effect is considerably larger. Moreover, changes in interaction space do not have a significant direct effect on innovativeness, but they positively affect the perception of social responsibility ($b = .22$, S.E. $= .04$), indirectly influencing perceived innovativeness. This means that firms have a better chance of succeeding if they, for example, change the design of their brand-related physical and digital environment for environmental or social reasons rather than for purely aesthetic ones. The latter type of change may have no noticeable effect on brand attractiveness.

Overall, responsible innovation seems to be a winning strategy for increasing brand attractiveness in relation to competing brands.

## 3. Bits and bytes or people and rights?

### 3.1. Digital innovation

Building a brand's innovative image is not easy. 'Innovativeness' as a brand characteristic is intangible and hard to evaluate, and as a notion, it has multiple interpretations. The most straightforward and reliable way to influence consumers' perceptions of a brand's innovativeness is to regularly launch innovations that consumers can experience. As we have shown, prioritizing socially responsible innovation may be a good choice for corporate brand strategy, which may not come as a surprise as society increasingly expects and demands companies to invest in social innovation. However, recent years have also witnessed an unprecedented increase in the scope and scale of digital transformation, which has prompted society's expectations and demands regarding the use of digital technologies and solutions. The COVID-19 pandemic has demonstrated that the general population has matured regarding the use of digital solutions, whether to order items online for home delivery, run professional meetings and social events, or visit museums. In addition to solving consumer problems and enabling new brand experiences, digitalization offers opportunities for cost-cutting and efficiency improvement, mainly due to the steadily decreasing costs of digital components and broad diffusion of digital devices (Fichman et al., 2014). In fact, digital innovation is becoming the primary driver of business innovation, and a number of companies have strategically stated that they are prioritizing digitalization to achieve their business goals (Nylen & Holmström, 2015). Could focusing on digital innovation rather than social innovation be a better choice when building the image of an innovative corporate brand?

In a broad sense, digital innovation involves a new product, process, or business model embodied in or enabled by information technology (Fichman et al., 2014). This embodying or enabling can take various forms, with information technology playing a facilitating role (e.g., enabling access to information and communication or simplifying transactions), serving as the context (e.g., e-commerce) or being a product or service itself (e.g., software, cloud services) (Huang & Rust, 2013). Most firms pursue digital innovation to optimize their operations and/or improve brand experience, which makes the firm's production and sales the focus areas for digital innovation. Firms that embrace social innovation have a broader focus on various stakeholders and even non-stakeholders, including actors who are outside the target audience of the brand's value proposition, non-human animals and natural environments.

Although both digital and social innovation are important, the discrepancy between the amount of digital innovations and the amount of social innovations, the tremendous success of digital players (e.g., Google, Amazon, Facebook, Uber) and the popularization of terms such as *digitalization, digital transformation, digital revolution,* and *industry 4.0* demonstrate where business priorities currently lie. Even a simple Google Images search with the keyword *innovations* results in images that represent digital, not social, advances. From the traditional managerial perspective, it may seem easy to decide between investing limited resources in something with clear economic benefits (e.g., cost reduction, product improvement, the creation of new revenue streams) and something that may have only a potential social or environmental impact and no apparent economic returns. The decision becomes easier when managers consider a reporting timeframe: the impact of digital innovations is likely to be visible much sooner. In the eye of the profit-oriented manager, digital innovations are simply a better choice. In some cases, they have even become a requirement, for example, due to government regulations or industry standards.

Digital innovation has had a tremendous impact on consumers as well, and it is hard to find a single aspect of their everyday lives that it has left untouched. Easy access, low switching costs, and countless alternatives are some reasons why digital innovations have prompted a new type of consumption – the 'liquid consumption' (Bardhi & Eckhardt, 2017). In contrast to the more traditional, 'solid' consumption, with its focus on owning brands with a stable performance, liquid consumption relies on renting and sharing, and it favours accessibility over stability. Examples include consumers choosing online music streaming platforms over CD and MP3 players or bicycle-sharing and carsharing systems over owned vehicles.

Despite the omnipresence of digital innovations, little is known about how they affect brand associations. Digital environments can be conducive for cultivating relationships between consumers and brands as well as among consumers considering the numerous possibilities for establishing and maintaining one-to-one, one-to-many, and many-to-many communication patterns. Nowadays, having a webpage that allows consumer feedback (e.g., comments, ratings) or engaging with consumers through community fora is commonplace. Yet the same environment can also be destructive for brand relationships given the burgeoning variety of alternatives 'just one click away,' the virality of electronic word-of-mouth and little incentive to remain loyal to online brands (Olsen, 2018). In this context, ensuring high relative brand attractiveness through innovation becomes crucial not only to entice new consumers but also to retain existing ones. By regularly launching new digital solutions, brands have the chance to keep pace with a changing market and stay innovative in the eyes of the consumer. It is also reasonable to assume that consumers who perceive their current brand of choice to be innovative and at the forefront of technological development will have less feeling of 'the grass being greener on the other side.'

### 3.2. Digital innovation vs. social innovation

By nature, digital innovation differs from social innovation in how it influences brand positioning. As new digital solutions primarily provide functional gains (e.g., timesaving, cost-cutting, increased ease of use, seamlessness), by engaging in digitalization, firms essentially secure and strengthen the *functional* positioning of their brands. Digital innovations may also contribute to the elaboration of brands with *experiential* concepts. Social innovations, however, can offer little, if any, functional or experiential benefits to individual consumers directly. For example, a typical household in the United States using Unilever products may see no personal benefit in Unilever and Acumen's joint initiative 'Social Innovation Challenge on Plastics,' which focuses on lifting waste pickers in other countries out of poverty. Similarly, Patagonia's free reparation of damaged clothing to promote environmental protection may bother some consumers because of logistical inconveniences, waiting time or the fact of having to wear repaired clothes. Instead of individual consumers' needs, social innovations target broader social, cultural, economic, and environmental conditions, producing positive outcomes predominantly at the aggregate level (Pol & Ville, 2009). Such positive outcomes include improved education and environmental quality, longer life expectancy, greater gender equality, community development, and poverty alleviation. Consequently, instead of functional benefits or direct personal gains, individual consumers typically associate social innovations with the common good and emotional benefits (e.g., warm-glowing), which creates a foundation for *symbolic* and *emotional* brand positioning (Bhat & Reddy, 1998; Hartmann et al., 2005).

It has long been assumed that brand management should focus on a specific concept (e.g., functional or symbolic) and rely on a corresponding positioning strategy and marketing mix (Park et al., 1986). For example, it has been regarded as inappropriate to apply a brand positioning strategy suitable for managing a brand with a functional concept to managing a brand with a symbolic concept or to combine several concepts because such inconsistent branding could lead to consumer confusion and poor differentiation from competitors. Empirical evidence on this issue remains inconclusive, with some studies favouring a focused approach (e.g., Esmaeilpour, 2015; Delgado-Ballester & Sabiote, 2015) and others finding a combination of several strategies more advantageous (Hartmann et al., 2005).

To test how positioning brands as regularly introducing digital or social innovations affects brand innovativeness and relative brand attractiveness, we used structural equation modelling on the 2019 NII data, consisting of 10,836 responses to 79 corporate brands in 19 industries. We measured associations related to digital innovations with items that indicated the extent to which the firm's product and services could be described as digital, the extent to which the respondents applied digital technology when they bought and used the firm's offerings, the extent to which digital solutions were used in the communication between the respondent and the firm, and the extent to which the respondent associated the firm with advanced digital technologies. To capture associations related to social innovation, we relied on items that described the degree to which corporate brands provided solutions positive for the environment and society, prioritized doing good for the environment and society and regularly presents new solutions to social and environmental problems. To measure perceived brand innovativeness and relative brand attractiveness, we used Kunz et al. (2011) and Andreassen and Lervik-Olsen (2008).

The analysis confirmed our previous finding that perceived brand innovativeness is a critical success factor for relative brand attractiveness ($b = .78$, S.E. $= .01$). We also find that, in line with existing theory, both digital and social innovations positively affect perceived brand innovativeness. We were, however, surprised to find that, concerning brand innovativeness, the effect size for social innovations is more than five times larger than the effect size for digital innovations: the standardized coefficients are .73 (S.E. $= .03$) and 0.14 (S.E. $= .02$), respectively. With minor variability, this finding holds across various industries and consumer age groups, providing evidence for social innovations as a highly effective focus of corporate brand strategy.

Does this mean that corporate brands should abandon focusing on digital innovation in favour of social innovation? Our analysis indicates that the answer is 'no' because digital innovation significantly and positively impacts social innovation ($b = .58$, S.E. $= .01$). In other words, digital innovation can increase the chances of succeeding with social innovation, and using digital innovation to generate and diffuse social innovations is a much better strategy than either implementing digital solutions for merely operational and commercial reasons or prioritizing social innovation alone. Mediated by social innovation, the indirect effect of digital innovation on perceived brand innovativeness ($b = .42$, S.E. $= .02$) is three times higher than its direct effect. Corporate brands that have the best of both worlds treat digital and social innovations not as mutually exclusive but as complementary.

## 4. Getting it right

### 4.1. Juxtaposing manager and consumer views on innovativeness

A history of successful innovations is a prerequisite for a corporate brand to develop an innovative reputation. While managers do not introduce innovations with the objective of making them fail, up to 70–90% of new fast-moving consumer goods disappear from the market within one year after launch (Gourville, 2006). For most corporate brands, any innovation flop risks inducing a storm of negative reactions and significant losses, including reputational damage (Barone & Jewell, 2013). Although managers tend to justify innovation failures by blaming consumers for demonstrating low demand for new products and services (Eurostat, n.d.), we see the actual reason for the mismatch between how managers and consumers interpret innovation.

Innovation practice and research have traditionally prioritized the managerial perspective, but there have long been calls to cover both external and internal stakeholders' perceptions in the analysis of corporate brands (Morsing & Kristensen, 2001). These calls have led to the emergence of a stakeholder-driven perspective that rejects the old-fashioned view of managers as having full control over brand identity and instead considers corporate brand meanings as co-created by multiple stakeholders (Iglesias et al., 2020). Consumers in particular have received a more central place, being recognized as active brand value co-creators (Merz et al., 2009). Often, consumers perceive different values in the same brand (Michel, 2017) and construct their own contexts in both physical and digital spaces in ways that brand managers may have not even considered (Ramaswamy & Ozcan, 2016).

To analyse how consumers and managers construct meanings about brand innovativeness, we conducted a qualitative study using the 2016 and 2017 NII data (Kurtmollaiev et al., 2018). We examined nine main players in three different industries in Norway: the airline industry (Scandinavian Airlines, Norwegian, Widerøe), banking industry (DNB, Nordea, Sbanken), and retail industry (Meny, Rema 1000, Coop Extra). For each corporate brand, we compared qualitative interviews with marketing directors with the qualitative part of the NII survey of consumers. We interviewed the directors about what kind of innovations they launched in their corporate brands and when, while consumers provided descriptions of their experiences with the brands and commented on observed changes. In total, we analysed comments from 1,255 airline passengers, 1,229 bank consumers, 1,683 retailing consumers, as well as one marketing director from each market player. In addition to value proposition and interaction space, we also considered two further dimensions of value co-creation – value realization and relationship experience. Value realization refers to the co-creation of value through the resource integration process, which includes how products and services are delivered and how consumers use them. For a bank, examples of value realization would be the various processes it uses to deliver its services to consumers through online banking, ATM or front office, as well efforts that consumers make, including the use of various devices and self-service solutions. Relationship experience reflects the extent to which consumers feel taken care of and how a corporate brand communicates with its consumers. For a retail store, examples of relationship experience include loyalty programs, employees' behaviour towards consumers, and the company's communication strategy (e.g., tone of voice). Table 13.1 summarizes the study examples of the companies' innovations and the consumers' perceptions of the changes in the respective dimensions of value co-creation.

## 4.2. What managers do is not what consumers see

As we find, the way consumers recognize and perceive innovations is neither one-sided nor straightforward. Although consumers notice changes, they may not register them as separate innovations but associate them with changes in either the total brand experience or parts of it. More importantly, the perception of changes can vary significantly between not only consumers and managers but also consumers. This is largely because consumers see changes in a particular context that includes social and natural surroundings, the consumers' backgrounds, and the consequences of the changes. In this context, consumers may develop such strong attitudes and emotional reactions that they start engaging for or against changes. Although this engagement tends to decrease gradually over time, it can have a considerable impact on the corporate brand reputation, as well as the firm's financial results and even survival.

Table 13.1 The comparison of the firm's innovation activities and the consumers' perceptions of innovations

| Dimensions of value co-creation | Industry | Firm's innovations | Consumers' perceptions of firm's innovations |
|---|---|---|---|
| Value proposition | Bank | Upgrade of stock trade | 'The bank's new solution for buying and selling stocks was very bad in the beginning. Now it is better.'<br>'Stock trading has become too difficult on a tablet.' |
| | Retail | Change in the assortment of products | 'Richer selection of vegetarian and healthy food.'<br>'Vegan selection.'<br>'They have expanded the selection of vegetarian and vegan food considerably.' |
| | Airline | New destinations | 'They have started new routes.'<br>'New routes, but also shutdown of some of the existing routes.'<br>'They have destinations that I want to travel to. It is possible that I will adjust my travel plans based on where they fly directly to.' |
| Value realization | Bank | Update and streamlining of processes, the removal of several manual processes, efficiency improvements | 'They are faceless to me, and we do most of the work ourselves.'<br>'Services go by themselves.' |
| | Retail | Online ordering system, home delivery, self-checkouts | 'New self-checkouts. Online store.'<br>'Have started to shop a lot in the online store.'<br>'They have a self-service solution for payments. It means they are going to reduce the number of employees. Many young people have got jobs and work experience through working in stores. I would rather pay a few kroners extra than to allow store jobs to be removed for the younger generation.' |
| | Airline | Digitalization, automatization, more self-service online, and the efficiency improvements in the complaint process | 'Little progress in online solutions. Poor feedback in the complaint process.'<br>'Easier and more intuitive online solutions.'<br>'Better and faster solution on expense refunds for cancellations.' |
| Relationships experience | Bank | New customer segmentation ('from younger to older, from those with significant money to those with less money'), changed service delivery in physical branches | 'I shall go away from this bank who is not interested in having me as a customer.'<br>'The client managers did not take care of me as a VERY loyal customer.'<br>'They have introduced "office hours," which irritates me terribly. After all, without their consumers, the bank can just forget it all!'<br>'Closed doors and booking of appointments to get into the bank.' |
| | Retail | Change of the existing communication form, bonus solutions for users, more active online interaction | 'Discounts in the app.'<br>'Coupons, the app's discounts.'<br>'Over-polite staff that says 'bye' before I have even packed my purchase.' |

(Continued)

Table 13.1 (Continued)

| Dimensions of value co-creation | Industry | Firm's innovations | Consumers' perceptions of firm's innovations |
|---|---|---|---|
| Interaction space | Airline | Transition to a consolidated operational customer relationship management for all sellers, support and customer service | 'The fantastic chat-function that is available 24/7 from everywhere in the world.' 'Service and safety, good communication with customers and with other airline companies.' |
| | Bank | Reduction in the number of physical branches | 'Shutdowns of local branches.' 'They have moved out of the city centre.' 'They close down local branches in excess.' 'Closed offices, and, therefore, they are bankrupt in my eyes.' |
| | Retail | New design of the app, the continuous refurbishment of the stores | 'The store is very changed, and the app is updated.' |
| | Airline | webpage has received new design and better and smarter solutions | 'The dreadful, ugly and useless new webpage.' 'They have got a CONSIDERABLY worse webpage and online solutions!' 'The webpage. They are totally tragic. Went from bad to worse!' |

## *The perception of the distinctiveness of change*

Unless a change occurs in the whole business model, innovations normally take the form of a specific outcome, such as the removal of a manual process, change of the assortment, introduction of a new loyalty programme, or launch of new webpage. In some cases, novel solutions replace existing ones, whereas in other cases, the old and the new elements coexist. Regardless of the form, managers retain a clear distinction between the 'old' and 'new' in their products, services, processes, programmes, and facilities. However, although consumers notice changes (and may even mention specific examples), they do not see innovations 'in a vacuum.' Instead, they evaluate how their experience with the brand changes as a result of those innovations. For example, they evaluate a new webpage based on how much faster and easier it is to obtain information or place orders, a new stock trade system as more or less complicated, and updated processes as allowing slower or faster problem-solving. Overall, customers assess the change based on the extent to which they perceive that the execution of a 'job-to-be-done' (Christensen et al., 2016) is better or worse than before. This evaluation is crucial for consumers' perceptions of a corporate brand as creative and innovative.

## *Consumers' emotional reactions to change*

In most cases, consumers not only notice innovations cognitively but also experience emotional reactions, which are sometimes strong. What is interesting from both theoretical and practical perspectives is that consumers may have similar perceptions of the type and extent of change, but their emotional responses to it can be very diverse. For example, most consumers notice when a firm increases its degree of self-service. Some consumers respond positively to the change, feeling that it gives them more control and causes less interaction with the firm's employees. However, for the same reasons, other consumers may perceive the change as negative: they lose the opportunity to interact with people, making the corporate brand faceless in their eyes. Differences in interpretations invoke an entire spectrum of emotions. For example, some consumers react calmly to changes in their bank service, perceiving the changes as a natural and logical development and banks as everyday things 'like milk and bread' to which they 'have no emotional relations.' Other consumers can be so 'terribly irritated' that they describe their banks using strong vocabulary and eventually end their customer relationship.

## Duration of the effect of a change on consumers' emotional reactions and perceptions

When we analyse consumers' reactions over time (since we collect our data on a rolling basis), we observe that the intensity of emotions decreases and subdues after a while. For example, when the Norwegian grocery chain REMA 1000 launched its mobile app Æ in January 2017, it had a considerable impact on our respondents. In a pre-launch campaign, the brand tried to build suspense in an Apple-like manner but failed to deliver a unique value proposition. This led to a stream of negative reactions from users, despite the fact that the app was of good quality. Almost all respondents reacted with dissatisfaction and anger after the launch. Yet our data indicate that the number of Æ-related comments gradually decreased during the year, being replaced with comments about the firm's offerings, physical surroundings in the stores, price, and customer service. The app has remained part of the REMA 1000 shopping experience. A similar example is Scandinavian Airlines' launch of a new webpage in spring 2017. Consumers initially described the new webpage in a negative manner, but after several months, they started to focus on other aspects of the company's service.

## Differences in interpretations of change between consumers and managers

Our data show that managers and consumers can interpret (and frame) changes very differently. Usually, managers see their innovations in a positive light, but consumers' views are more varied. For example, managers typically communicate automatization and digitalization as optimization, whereas consumers interpret them as cost-cutting, using consumers as a free labour force, and as a sign of organizational greed. Managers may present segmentation as the opening of a new market, whereas consumers may interpret it as discrimination and neglect. In addition to such qualitative differences in interpretations, we observe differences in the perceptions of the extent and amount of changes. While managers often claim that they introduce numerous innovations, consumers assert that there are too few change attempts in corporate brands.

## The role of context in perceiving changes

These differences are the result of a bigger phenomenon: the impact of context on the perception of changes. For managers, the innovations that they launch are mainly related to one context – their operations and sales – which also defines employees' beliefs, attitudes, and interpretations. Consumers, however, find themselves in different situations and use the same products and services from different starting points, with their situations, backgrounds, and relationships having a critical effect on their perception of changes. When consumers evaluate brand innovativeness, they tend to merge the evaluation of the change with its consequences. This holistic evaluation depends on consumers' backgrounds and social relations. Consumers may associate changes in value position (for example, the introduction of new food products by grocery chains or new destinations by airlines) with either disregard or support for local environments and communities. They may interpret changes in value realization (for example, the introduction of self-service solutions) based on labour market situations and unemployment rates. They may see changes in relationship experience (for example, new communication forms) in light of common assumptions about corporate strategy and managers' intentions and evaluate changes in interaction space (for example, new webpage design) with respect to contemporary aesthetic standards and expectations of functionality.

What do these differences in managers' and consumers' perceptions mean for corporate branding? A corporate brand that engages in numerous innovation initiatives is not necessarily viewed as innovative by its consumers. In some cases, the intended effect does not reach consumers simply because corporate brands poorly communicate their innovations. For example, in many cases, consumers need not only information about new offerings but also 'training' in how and when to use new solutions. The main reason for weaker brand innovativeness, however, is that consumers find meaning not in innovation initiatives per se but in their results in a context. Hence, corporate brands that are able to introduce changes that improve the total brand experience are perceived as more innovative. To achieve this, managers need to recognize consumers' beliefs, preferences, and emotions in a wider social context and learn how to communicate using consumers' own language, which implies taking an 'outside-in' perspective. Conversely, innovating without regard to the customer perspective may have damaging effects on customers' perceptions of brand innovativeness.

When managers plan to introduce an innovation, they need to evaluate what effect it will have on the total brand experience. As with any other change, innovations can provoke strong emotional reactions, which can vary along both positive-negative and active-passive dimensions. There is a difference between a dissatisfied customer and an angry customer, as well as between a satisfied customer and an excited customer. These variations often have a strong impact on brand reputation and a firm's financial results. Even cautious consumers can become excited when they see and understand the benefits of innovations. Yet this strategy works only if consumers' and managers' perceptions of innovations align. If consumers and managers have conflicting views about changes, excited consumers can easily become angry consumers, which usually has a negative impact on the corporate brand. This effect can aggravate if managers intentionally create excitement around the launch, but the extent and relevance of the innovation is low from the customers' perspective, as happened in the case of REMA 1000's shopping app.

Although it might seem that managers can influence consumers' perceptions of changes relatively easily through marketing communication, this alone is not sufficient. Often, the change is defined not only by the choice of words and communication form but also by the consumers' own interpretations of the change in light of various contexts. This implies that the success of innovation depends on a deep understanding of individual and social circumstances. Managers can develop such an understanding through direct observations and interviews with consumers in particular contexts, which also require an open mind-set and empathy (Leonard & Rayport, 1997; Brown, 2008). By recognizing the uniqueness of each customer's interpretation and building a conversational space in which individual customers and the organization come together, managers can strategically capitalize on the multiplicity of views, suggestions, and ideas (Iglesias et al., 2013). In cases where the managers have insufficient knowledge about consumer contexts, it may be wise to reduce innovation visibility or introduce changes gradually.

## 5. Conclusions: finding balance in brand innovativeness

Few, if any, now believe that an economy in which we extract resources from the planet and process them in factories to create goods that we throw away after use is sustainable. Yet that is what we have done and still do. Today's mass production of cheap consumer goods produces substantial waste – more than ever – and the quantities are growing. According to the World Bank, the total amount of waste in 2016 was approximately two billion tons and is estimated to be 3.4 billion tons in 2050. Of this, only 16% is recycled. No less disturbing is the slow progress in solving social challenges. About 10% of the world's population lives in poverty and is undernourished, and 30% is without safely managed drinking water. Income inequality within and between countries, violence, political instability, and armed conflicts are on the rise, whereas access to quality education and job opportunities remains very limited.

In this context, innovation is a somewhat double-edged sword. It has, in many ways, contributed to the development of an unequal, 'throw-away' society worldwide by multiplying offerings, triggering consumer wants and needs and affecting income distribution (e.g., Aghion et al., 2019). At the same time, innovation is also the best available tool to improve our lives and eradicate social and environmental challenges. These two sides – commercial and social – are nearly impossible to separate, and our analysis indicates that there is little to gain in trying to do so. Commercial and social innovations are like Winnie-the-Pooh's honey and condensed milk, with consumers preferring to have both.

As Figure 13.1 illustrates, focusing on either commercial (including digital) or social innovation is myopic, whereas engaging in neither suggests stagnation. A sustainable strategy is to balance commercial and social innovations: after all, economic viability, social equity, and environmental protection are the three pillars of sustainability. The balanced approach can take the form of using knowledge, experience, and resources gained from commercial innovation in social innovation initiatives. It may also involve initiating only commercial innovation projects that have clearly defined positive outcomes for society and the environment. From the corporate branding perspective, this approach clearly pays off because the most innovative brands, in the eye of the consumer, are those with a sustainable innovation strategy. Consumers consider such brands more attractive than competing brands. Hence, brands that regularly launch both commercial and social innovations have a higher chance of becoming the consumer's first choice and enjoying high customer loyalty.

It is important, however, to remember that managers and consumers may have different understandings of innovation. A commercial innovation that managers see as unanimously and universally positive may provoke anger and frustration in consumers looking at it through their

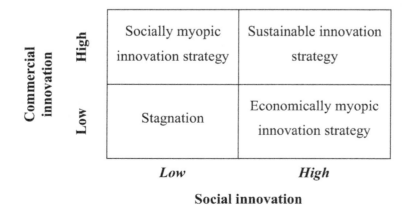

*Figure 13.1* Innovation strategies depending on innovation type

social lenses. A social innovation that managers may dismiss because it does not promise immediate pecuniary results could secure consumers' loyalty in the long run. Realizing the importance of social innovations but unwilling to fully embrace them, many brands resort to deceptive communication as an easy fix: so as not to seem greedy, they try to appear innovative and concerned about the environment or society. A typical example is 'colourwashing' (e.g., greenwashing, pinkwashing, brownwashing) – that is, the practice of communicating unsubstantiated values in activities, products, and services to become more attractive to socially and environmentally aware consumers. Such practices grossly underestimate consumers. As our analysis shows, consumers are relatively good at perceiving innovations, even those related to the corporate backstage, and are not only able to detect fraudulent communication but also much better at contextualizing innovations than managers. This means that managers have to be genuine and more diligent in embracing a conscientious approach to addressing market needs, desires, and feedback (Iglesias & Ind, 2020). Instead of maintaining the illusion of having full control over the development of innovation and brand meanings, managers should aim to effectively facilitate the co-creation of meaning through multiple stakeholders (Iglesias & Bonet, 2012). This can be done by strategically using conversational spaces specifically designed to promote collaborative interactions among stakeholders. As previous evidence suggests, stakeholders often gladly engage in co-creation because it provides them with an opportunity to find fulfilment, create shared meaning and socialize (Ind et al., 2013). By closely cooperating throughout all stages of the innovation process, cultivating multiple forms of communication and diligently evaluating social and environmental outcomes of innovation together with various stakeholders, managers can significantly improve their corporate brands' positioning and odds of market success (Ind et al., 2017). More importantly, such cooperation can genuinely contribute to creating a better future for all.

## References

Aaker, D. (2007). Innovation: Brand it or lose it. *California Management Review, 50*(1), 8–24.
Aghion, P., Akcigit, U., Bergeaud, A., Blundell, R., & Hémous, D. (2019). Innovation and top income inequality. *The Review of Economic Studies, 86*, 1–45.
Al-Kwifi, S., & Zafar, A. (2015). An intellectual journey into the historical evolution of marketing research in brand switching behavior – Past, present and future. *Journal of Management History, 21*, 172–193.
Andreassen, T. W., & Lervik, L. (1999). Perceived relative attractiveness today and tomorrow as predictors of future repurchase intention. *Journal of Service Research, 2*, 164–72.
Andreassen, T. W., & Lervik-Olsen, L. (2008). The impact of customers' perception of varying degrees of customer service on commitment and perceived relative attractiveness. *Managing Service Quality, 8*, 300–328.
Bardhi, F., & Eckhardt, G. (2017). Liquid consumption. *Journal of Consumer Research, 44*(3), 582–597.
Barone, M. J., & Jewell, R. (2013). The innovator's license: A latitude to deviate from category norms. *Journal of Marketing, 77*(1), 120–134.
Bhat, S., & Reddy, S. (1998). Symbolic and functional positioning of brands. *Journal of Consumer Marketing, 15*, 32–43.
Bhattacharya, C. B., & Sen, S. (2003). Consumer – Company identification: A framework for understanding consumers' relationships with companies. *Journal of Marketing, 67*(2), 76–88.
Brexendorf, T. O., Bayus, B., & Keller, K. L. (2015). Understanding the interplay between brand and innovation management: Findings and future research directions. *Journal of the Academy of Marketing Science, 43*, 548–557.
Brexendorf, T., & Keller, K. (2017). Leveraging the corporate brand: The importance of corporate brand innovativeness and brand architecture. *European Journal of Marketing, 51*, 1530–1551.
Brown, T. (2008). Design thinking. *Harvard Business Review, 86*(6), 84–92.
Brown, T. J., & Dacin, P. (1997). The company and the product: Corporate associations and consumer product responses. *Journal of Marketing, 61*(1), 68–84.

Christensen, C., Hall, T., Dillon, K., & Duncan, D. (2016). Know your customers' jobs to be done. *Harvard Business Review*, *94*, 54–62.

Corkindale, D., & Belder, M. (2009). Corporate brand reputation and the adoption of innovations. *Journal of Product & Brand Management*, *18*, 242–250.

Currás-Pérez, R., Bigné-Alcañiz, E., & Alvarado-Herrera, A. (2009). The role of self-definitional principles in consumer identification with a socially responsible company. *Journal of Business Ethics*, *89*, 547–564.

Delgado-Ballester, E., & Sabiote, E. F. (2015). Brand experimental value versus brand functional value: Which matters more for the brand? *European Journal of Marketing*, *49*, 1857–1879.

Dotzel, T., Shankar, V., & Berry, L. L. (2013). Service innovativeness and firm value. *Journal of Marketing Research*, *50*(2), 259–76.

Elbedweihy, A., Jayawardhena, C., Elsharnouby, M. H., & Elsharnouby, T. H. (2016). Customer relationship building: The role of brand attractiveness and consumer-brand identification. *Journal of Business Research*, *69*(8), 2901–2910.

Elkington, J. (1997). *Cannibals with forks – Triple bottom line of 21st century business.* Stoney Creek: New Society Publishers.

Esmaeilpour, F. (2015). The role of functional and symbolic brand associations on brand loyalty. *Journal of Fashion Marketing and Management*, *19*, 467–484.

Eurostat. (n.d.). Community innovation survey. Retrieved from https://ec.europa.eu/eurostat/web/science-technology-innovation/data/database?node_code=inn

Fichman, R. G., Santos, B., & Zheng, Z. (2014). Digital innovation as a fundamental and powerful concept in the information systems curriculum. *MIS Quarterly*, *38*, 329–343.

Fombrun, C., & Shanley, M. (1990). What's in a name? Reputation building and corporate strategy. *Academy of Management Journal*, *33*(2), 233–258.

Gourville, J. T. (2006). Eager sellers and stony buyers: Understanding the psychology of new-product adoption. *Harvard Business Review*, *84*(6): 98–106. https://hbr.org/2006/06/eager-sellers-and-stony-buyers-understanding-the-psychology-of-new-product-adoption

Gürhan-Canli, Z., & Batra, R. (2004). When corporate image affects product evaluations: The moderating role of perceived risk. *Journal of Marketing Research*, *41*(2), 197–205.

Hartmann, P., Ibáñez, V., & Saínz, F. J. (2005). Green branding effects on attitude: Functional versus emotional positioning strategies. *Marketing Intelligence & Planning*, *23*, 9–29.

Henard, D. H., & Dacin, P. A. (2010). Reputation for product innovation: Its impact on consumers. *Journal of Product Innovation Management*, *27*(3), 321–335.

Huang, M.-H., & Rust, R. T. (2013). IT-related service: A multidisciplinary perspective. *Journal of Service Research*, *16*(3), 251–258.

Iglesias, O., & Bonet, E. (2012). Persuasive brand management. *Journal of Organizational Change Management*, *25*(2), 251–264.

Iglesias, O., & Ind, N. (2020). Towards a theory of conscientious corporate brand co-creation: The next key challenge in brand management. *Journal of Brand Management*, *27*, 710–720.

Iglesias, O., Ind, N., & Alfaro, M. (2013). The organic view of the brand: A brand value co-creation model. *Journal of Brand Management*, *20*, 670–688.

Iglesias, O., Landgraf, P., Ind, N., Markovic, S., Koporcic, N. (2020). Corporate brand identity co-creation in business-to-business contexts. *Industrial Marketing Management*, *85*, 32–43.

Iglesias, O., Markovic, S., Singh, J. J. et al. (2019). Do Customer perceptions of corporate services brand ethicality improve brand equity? Considering the roles of brand heritage, brand image, and recognition benefits. *Journal of Business Ethics*, *154*, 441–459.

Ind, N., Iglesias, O., & Markovic, S. (2017). The co-creation continuum: From tactical market research tool to strategic collaborative innovation method. *Journal of Brand Management*, *24*, 310–321.

Ind, N., Iglesias, O., & Schultz, M. (2013). Building brands together: emergence and outcomes of co-creation. *California Management Review*, *55*(3), 5–26.

Johnson, M. D., Gustafsson, A., Andreassen, T. W., Lervik, L., & Cha, J. (2001). The evolution and future of national customer satisfaction index models. *Journal of Economic Psychology*, *22*(2), 217–245.

Kay, M. J. (2006). Strong brands and corporate brands. *European Journal of Marketing*, *40*(7–8), 742–760.

Keiningham, T., Aksoy, L., & Williams, L. (2015). *The wallet allocation rule: Winning the battle for share.* Hoboken, NJ: John Wiley and Sons.

Keller, K. L. (1998). *Strategic brand management building, measuring, and managing brand equity.* Upper Saddle River, NJ: Prentice Hall.

Kunz, W., Schmitt, B., & Meyer, A. (2011). How does perceived firm innovativeness affect the consumer? *Journal of Business Research, 64*(8), 816–822.

Kurtmollaiev, S., Lervik-Olsen, L., & Andreassen, T. (2018). Innovasjon: Det du gjør er ikke det de ser. *Magma*, 21–28.

Leonard, D., & Rayport, J. F. (1997). Spark innovation through empathic design. *Harvard Business Review, 75*, 102–115.

Lowe, B., & Alpert, F. (2015). Forecasting consumer perception of innovativeness. *Technovation, 45–46*, 1–14.

Marin, L., & de Maya, S. R. (2013). The role of affiliation, attractiveness and personal connection in consumer-company identification. *European Journal of Marketing, 47*, 655–673.

Marin, L., & Ruiz, S. (2007). "I Need You Too!" corporate identity attractiveness for consumers and the role of social responsibility. *Journal of Business Ethics, 71*, 245–260.

Merz, M. A., He, Y., & Vargo, S. L. (2009). The evolving brand logic: A service-dominant logic perspective. *Journal of the Academy of Marketing Science, 37*, 328–344.

Michel, G. (2017). From brand identity to polysemous brands: Commentary on "Performing identities: Processes of brand and stakeholder identity co-construction". *Journal of Business Research, 70*, 453–455.

Morsing, M., & Kristensen, J. (2001). The question of coherency in corporate branding – Over time and across stakeholders. *Journal of Communication Management, 6*(1), 24–40.

Nylen, D., & Holmström, J. (2015). Digital innovation strategy: A framework for diagnosing and improving digital product and service innovation. *Business Horizons, 58*(1), 57–67.

Olsen, L. (2018). Future of branding in the digital age. In A. Sasson (Ed.), *At the forefront, looking ahead*. Oslo: Universitetsforlaget.

Papaoikonomou, E., Cascón-Pereira, R., & Ryan, G. (2016). Constructing and communicating an ethical consumer identity: A Social Identity Approach. *Journal of Consumer Culture, 16*, 209–231.

Park, C. W., Jaworski, B. J., & Macinnis, D. (1986). Strategic brand concept-image management. *Journal of Marketing, 50*, 135–145.

Payne, A., Frow, P., & Eggert, A. (2017). The customer value proposition: Evolution, development, and application in marketing. *Journal of the Academy of Marketing Science, 45*, 467–489.

Pol, E., & Ville, S. (2009). Social innovation: Buzz word or enduring term? *Journal of Socio-economics, 38*, 878–885.

Ramaswamy, V., & Ozcan, K. (2016). Brand value co-creation in a digitalized world: An integrative framework and research implications. *International Journal of Research in Marketing, 33*(1), 93–106.

Schmidt, H. J., Ind, N., Guzmán, F. and Kennedy, E. (2021). Sociopolitical activist brands. *Journal of Product & Brand Management*. http://doi.org/10.1108/JPBM-03-2020-2805

Shukla, P. (2004). Effect of product usage, satisfaction and involvement on brand switching behavior. *Asia Pacific Journal of Marketing and Logistics, 16*(4), 82–104.

Sirohi, N., McLaughlin, E. W., & Wittink, D. R. (1998). A model of consumer perceptions and store loyalty intentions for a supermarket retailer. *Journal of Retailing, 74*(2), 223–245.

So, K. K. F., King, C., Hudson, S., & Meng, F. (2017). The missing link in building customer brand identification: The role of brand attractiveness. *Tourism Management, 59*, 640–651.

Sophonsiri, S., & Polyorat, K. (2009). The impact of brand personality dimensions on brand association and brand attractiveness: The case study of KFC in Thailand. *Journal of Global Business and Technology, 5*, 51–62.

Thompson, D., Hamilton, R., & Rust, R. (2005). Feature fatigue: When product capabilities become too much of a good thing. *Journal of Marketing Research, 42*(4), 431–442.

Vargo, S. L., & Lusch, R. F. (2016). Institutions and axioms: An extension and update of service-dominant logic. *Journal of the Academy of Marketing Science, 44*, 5–23.

Walsh, G., & Beatty, S. E. (2007). Customer-based corporate reputation of a service firm: Scale development and validation. *Journal of the Academy of Marketing Science, 35*(1), 127–143.

Wong, H., & Merrilees, B. (2008). The performance benefits of being brand-orientated. *Journal of Product & Brand Management, 17*, 372–383.

Yen, C. H., Teng, H. Y., & Tzeng, J. C. (2020). Innovativeness and customer value co-creation behaviors: Mediating role of customer engagement. *International Journal of Hospitality Management, 88*. http://doi.org/10.1016/j.ijhm.2020.102514.

# 14
# A SYSTEMATIC LITERATURE REVIEW OF SUSTAINABILITY IN CORPORATE SERVICES BRANDING

Identifying dimensions, drivers, outcomes, and future research opportunities

*Stefan Markovic, Yuqian Qiu, Cristina Sancha, and Nikolina Koporcic*

## 1. Introduction

In an ever more competitive and interconnected business environment, it has become relevant for brands to show their commitment to sustainability at a corporate level (Balmer, 2001; Ind, 1997; Sierra et al., 2017). Sustainability can be defined as the 'ability of an organization to favorably drive its actions towards concerns and welfare of people, planet and profits in a way that the company will be able to empower itself to meet its own and its customers' current and future requirements successfully' (Gupta et al., 2013, p. 288). To operationalize the concept of sustainability, the Triple Bottom Line (TBL) approach is often adopted, which highlights three main dimensions of sustainability: economic, environmental, and social (Elkington, 1994, 2018; Goh et al., 2020; Svensson et al., 2016). First, the economic dimension surpasses the traditional idea of corporate capital gains, and relates to the broader impact a company has on its economic environment (Ho & Taylor, 2007). For instance, the economic dimension is concerned with how the company helps its local economy or the survival of its suppliers. Second, the environmental dimension has to do with the amount of resources (e.g., energy, water) a company employs and the waste it generates during its operations (Hubbard, 2009). The environmental dimension, therefore, deals with the footprint that corporate activities leave on the natural environment (OECD, 2001). Third, the social dimension relates to the impact a company has on its communities (Hubbard, 2009), and thus is concerned with the wellbeing of employees and other internal and external stakeholders (Gimenez et al., 2012).

Previous research has shown that sustainability can help corporate brands achieve a plethora of organizational advantages, including customer affective commitment and customer loyalty (Fan, 2005; Markovic et al., 2018). Accordingly, an increasing number of corporate brands have started to consider sustainability as a strategic factor in their business models and go-to-market strategies (McKinsey, 2011). Whilst the quest for sustainability has traditionally been related to corporate product brands, corporate services brands are increasingly acknowledging its importance and embracing sustainability as a strategic tool to boost their reputation (Markovic et al., 2018).

In fact, building reputable corporate brands is perceived to be even more relevant in services contexts than in the field of goods, due to the different nature of services (Dall'Olmo Riley & de Chernatony, 2000; Iglesias et al., 2020). Unlike goods, services have an intangible, heterogeneous, inseparable, and perishable nature (Markovic et al., 2018; Zeithaml et al., 1985). In that sense, while corporate product brands can offer tangible offerings with homogeneous levels of quality, the distinct nature of services makes it difficult to standardize service quality (Berry, 1980; Booms & Bitner, 1981; Markovic et al., 2018). Moreover, services contexts are generally richer in customer-brand touchpoints than the field of goods (Gronroos, 2006), which further emphasizes the importance of building reputable corporate services brands. An increasingly popular way to do so consists of portraying their commitment to sustainability, ideally during every customer-brand interaction and touchpoint (Iglesias et al., 2020).

However, not all service businesses commit to sustainability in the same way (Lozano & Huisingh, 2011). Whilst some corporate services brands embrace sustainability by only considering its environmental dimension, others focus on the social and/or economic dimensions (Blake et al., 2019; Di Bella & Al-Fayoumi, 2016; Luu, 2017). This raises concerns about what dimension of sustainability corporate services brands primarily focus on. Thus, this chapter aims to systematically review the existing literature on sustainability and corporate services brands in order to identify what dimensions of sustainability are mainly used in the field of corporate services branding, as well as their key drivers and outcomes. In addition, this chapter intends to identify the future research opportunities that emerge from this body of literature.

## 2. Method

To achieve these research objectives, this chapter adopts the systematic literature review method (Pittaway et al., 2004; Tranfield et al., 2003). This method enables an in-depth understanding of the previous body of literature that is relevant to address specific research objectives. It also enables the detection of key themes from previous studies and to outline the challenges and future research directions in a specific context (Burgess et al., 2006). Furthermore, it provides research rigour and mitigates the bias in the selection of papers (Tranfield et al., 2003), leading to the detection of high-quality publications.

To conduct the systematic literature review, we embodied an explicit procedure of database search and implemented a set of pre-defined protocols (Crossan & Apaydin, 2010). These are the steps that we followed to screen the previous publications:

i   Web of Science was selected as the search platform due to its broad and multidisciplinary scope (Clarivate Analytics, 2020).
ii  For the search string, we included '(corporate brand* OR corporate service* brand*) AND (service*) AND (sustainab*)' in title, or abstract, or keywords. The combination of these key terms was considered relevant for capturing a sufficiently broad list of studies that are related to our research objectives.
iii Timeframe was not delimited, and we decided to only include peer-reviewed management/business journals and book chapters to ensure the use of high-quality papers.

This search resulted in a total of 25 papers. Then, a deletion of duplicates and items that could not be accessed was performed, resulting in a total of 23 papers. In addition, two papers not published in English were excluded, so 21 papers remained. Subsequently, an abstract analysis was performed to keep only those papers that focus on sustainability in corporate services contexts. This resulted in a total of 13 papers. This step was performed by two independent researchers to enhance reliability. If any discrepancy emerged in the selection of papers, a discussion between the two researchers was held to reach an agreement. A full paper analysis was then conducted, in which we verified that the selected papers could address our research objectives. No papers were excluded at this stage, and a total of 13 papers were finally included in our analysis (see Table 14.1 for a list of references and their abstracts).

## 3. Analysis and findings

Each paper was coded and then examined by two independent researchers to minimize bias. The selected papers were then systematically categorized to facilitate their synthesis according to the following variables: year of publication; methodology (i.e., qualitative, quantitative, or mixed); study context; journal/book publisher; dimensions of sustainability dealt with; and core findings.

### 3.1 Descriptive analysis and findings

The selected 13 papers were descriptively analysed in this section, with regard to the year of publication, methodology, study context, and journal/book publisher. The aim was to identify the trends in the emerging body of literature and to establish a future trajectory.

As shown in Figure 14.1, the selected papers were published between 2011 and 2020. However, it can be concluded that, although the topic has received academic visibility since 2011, it only achieved exposure after 2015. From 2016 onwards, the research on the topic gradually increased, as nine papers were published since then. Despite a sharp decline in 2018, there was then a rebound of research on the topic from 2019 onwards.

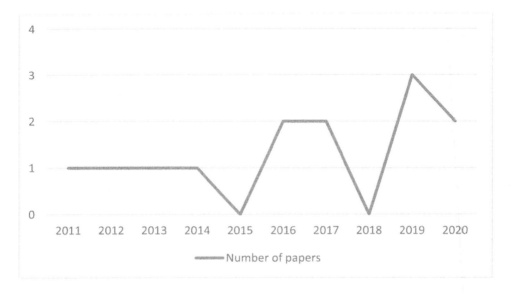

*Figure 14.1* Evolution of publications

Table 14.1 Papers included in the analysis

| Authors | Title | Abstract |
|---|---|---|
| Blake et al. (2019) | The relationship between sports sponsorships and corporate financial returns in South Africa | '**Purpose** Sponsorship is a major contributor to income in the South African sports arena, and is a critical component allowing sports unions to remain financially viable and sustainable. Sports sponsoring companies, however, have long questioned the financial returns generated from these ventures. The purpose of this paper is to understand whether financial returns of companies with sports sponsorship in South Africa are significantly different to those without. This research was conducted on Johannesburg Stock Exchange (JSE) listed companies that sponsored sport consistently between 2000 and 2015 for a period of two years. A quantitative methodology was employed whereby share price, revenue, and earnings growth were analysed, comparing firms that did not adopt strategies involving sports sponsorships to those that did. **Design/methodology/approach** A quantitative methodology was employed, whereby share price, revenue and earnings growth were analysed, comparing firms that did not adopt strategies involving sports sponsorships to those that did. South Africa is an emerging market and a member of the BRICS Forum ranked 14th in the sport sponsorship market globally (Sport Marketing Frontiers, 2011), becoming increasingly dominant in the global sports industry (Goldman, 2011). The population consisted of JSE-listed Main Board and alternative exchange companies that participated in any form of consistent sports sponsorship in the given time frame: 2000–2015, where the company's share price, revenue and earnings per share (EPS) data for the period were available from the INET BFA database. The JSE is ranked 17th in terms of market capitalisation (over $1 trillion) in the world, being the largest stock exchange on the African continent with over $30bn being traded on average monthly. Multiple journals today publish research done on the JSE, for example the *International Journal of Sports Marketing and Sponsorship*, *Investment Analysts Journal*, and the *South African Journal of Accounting Research*. This stock exchange is 125 years old and has over 400 listed companies of which 358 are domestic (Kruger et al., 2014). **Findings** Results show that companies involved in sports sponsorship during the period analysed did not experience enhanced share price or revenue growth in excess of those companies not involved in sports sponsorship. As a whole, sports sponsoring companies did however experience greater income growth (EPS) than those companies not involved in sports sponsorship. Enhanced revenue growth was found in the consumer services sector, indicating that sport sponsorship in this sector drives brand image and recall resulting in enhanced revenues. These results though indicate that a multitude of differing objectives may exist for companies engaging with sports sponsorship, with increased sales not the singular objective. In general it is concluded that sports sponsorship is considered to achieve a broad spectrum of outcomes that are likely to contribute to increased profitability. **Research limitations/implications** The relatively small size of 40 firms on the JSE in the South African sports sponsorship market is a limitation for this research. The purely quantitative approach limited the ability to gain the required level of |

(*Continued*)

Table 14.1 (Continued)

| Authors | Title | Abstract |
|---|---|---|
| | | insight into those sectors with small samples, which a qualitative study would reveal. SABMiller as example could not be analysed against its sector peers, given that it is one of the most prominent and consistent sports sponsors in South Africa across all major sporting codes. The telecommunications sector was represented entirely by companies that were involved in sports sponsorship and, hence, no in-depth comparison could be conducted within this sector. Vodacom, a major sponsor of sport in South Africa, could not be compared with its peers utilising purely financial and statistical methods. Cell C is one of the most prominent sponsors of rugby in South Africa, through its title sponsorship of the Cell C Sharks, and was not included in this study as it is not listed on the JSE. It is suggested that such companies should be included in a qualitative study approach.<br>**Practical implications** The results of the Mann–Whitney U test for the consumer services and financial sectors confirm no significant difference in EPS growth for companies utilising consistent sports sponsorship as part of their marketing mix to those that do not. The consumer services sector has seen above-average revenue growth from sports sponsorship compared with its sector peers; however, the sector was unable to convert this increased revenue growth into increased profits, suggesting that the cost of sponsoring, as well as the operating costs associated with sports sponsorship, counteract any growth in revenue.<br>**Social implications** The sample of sports-sponsoring companies experienced a larger annual mean EPS growth rate of 30.6 per cent compared to the remaining JSE Main Board companies which grew EPS annually at 27.4 per cent. The results of the Mann–Whitney U test confirm a significant difference in EPS growth for companies utilising consistent sports sponsorship as part of their marketing mix. From a practical interpretive perspective, this result reveals that those companies in South Africa involved in sports sponsorship consistently attain greater than market-related profit growth. This poses some interesting points for discussion, given that revenue growth was not statistically different, which suggests that many sponsors are utilising the sponsorships for purposes other than sales growths that result in a profitable outcome. The potential range of options is large but would likely comprise the creation of stronger supplier relationships, resulting in optimised business inputs. Sponsors might be utilising sponsorships to improve corporate social status, which assists them in creating regulatory compliance, in some instances. Additionally, these sponsorships may be utilised to maintain key client relationships that provide the highest levels of profitability, and whilst this might not grow revenue through new business acquisition, it may result in higher profitability as a result of a loyal and stable customer base.<br>**Originality/value** Much of the available research focusses on the sponsorship of specific sporting events and the share price impact thereof at specific occasions like the announcement, renewal, and termination. Where research is conducted across a multitude of sporting events and codes, this predominantly focusses on share price performance only, with varying and somewhat inconclusive results. There is little research focussing on wider, more comprehensive sets of sponsored events |

(Continued)

Table 14.1 (Continued)

| Authors | Title | Abstract |
|---|---|---|
| | | and sporting codes, and that seeks to provide an understanding of financial returns for sponsoring properties. In a study of more than 50 US-based corporations it was found that, as a group, corporations which consistently invested in sports sponsorships outperformed market averages, and that those with higher sponsorship spend achieved higher returns (Jensen & Hsu, 2011). The study utilised descriptive statistics. More analysis, utilising detailed statistical analysis, is required to better understand the effects of sponsorship on the wider set of variables analysed. In this case, a five-year compound annual growth rate was calculated for stock price appreciation, total revenue, net income and EPS, and analysed descriptively with only means and standard deviation. Measurement of such variables assists with an understanding of the materialized results of sponsorship as opposed to much of the work in this field, which analyses market reactions to sponsorship announcements.' (pp. 2–3) |
| Cheng and Lunn (2015) | Training and qualification: Employee training at Galaxy Entertainment Group | 'What do companies do with employee training when their financial chips are down? The knee-jerk reaction is usually to cut the training budget, as training is often seen as an expense rather than an investment in the company's future. This chapter focuses on the case of a leading casino company in Macau and how its ongoing employee training efforts have not lost their momentum despite the recent downturn in gaming revenue. The sustainability of its training agenda rests on its unwavering focus on the service culture that is branded World Class, Asian Heart. The Galaxy Entertainment Group (GEG) attempts to differentiate itself in the intensely competitive gaming environment through strengthening this WCAH identity. It has tweaked its training programs, consolidating hundreds of disparate packages for different employees to a more systematic and comprehensive training of all employees in the critical corporate culture while separating skills training for different groups organized by function. In the tougher financial climate, the company will face further challenges to achieve its training objectives in the most cost-effective manner.' (pp. 1–2) |
| Di Bella and Al-Fayoumi (2016) | Perception of stakeholders on corporate social responsibility of Islamic Banks in Jordan | '**Purpose** The purpose of this paper is to explore the various perceptions of stakeholders on corporate social responsibility (CSR) of Islamic Banks in Jordan.<br>**Design/methodology/approach** The data are collected from multiple stakeholder groups of two Islamic Banks in particular: Jordan Islamic Bank for Finance and Investment and Islamic International Arab Bank. The methods adopted to examine the data are the descriptive analysis and analysis of variance. With regard to the purpose of this research, the concept of Islamic CSR and its dimensions have been considered as: rooted in the Islamic ethical system, represented through the profit and loss arrangements, embedded within the principles behind financial services provided by Islamic Banks, and benchmarked by the Accounting and Auditing Organization of Islamic Financial Institutions' (AAOIFI) corporate governance standard.<br>**Findings** The results indicate that stakeholders have expressed a positive attitude toward the concept of CSR. Proving that the issue of CSR is an important factor in Islamic banking and to the perception of various stakeholders' groups, the focus |

(Continued)

Table 14.1 (Continued)

| Authors | Title | Abstract |
|---|---|---|
| | | shifted into identifying the dimensions which shape the Islamic CSR. In reference to previous research results, the Islamic banking sector in Jordan has an in-built dimension that promotes social responsibility.<br>**Practical implications** The study recommends that Islamic Banks improve CSR activities in order to better exploit this commitment with a cultural identity yet again. This identity has a direct influence on the branding of Islamic finance in local markets. The structure of offered products reflects regional beliefs and provides a suite of services. In terms of services, the services provided are geared toward specific market segments within local communities. This as a result directs a number of strategic decisions made by Islamic Banks, which are based on the structure of their offerings, brand identity and customer service levels.<br>**Originality/value** In Jordan, studies about the perception of stakeholders on CSR from an Islamic perspective are almost non-existent. Thus, providing solutions for study questions and presenting empirical evidence regarding CSR issues will certainly add a new dimension to the literature. Moreover, the conclusions and recommendations may help regulators and decision makers in enhancing the competitiveness and the sustainability of the Islamic banking sector in Jordan.' (p. 30) |
| Edvardsson and Enquist (2011) | The service excellence and innovation model: lessons from IKEA and other service frontiers | 'The objective of this paper is to achieve a better understanding of the role of ethical values in forming and directing a strategy for service excellence, service innovation, and value-in-context. The paper argues that sustainability and corporate social responsibility are the key drivers of value resonance and service excellence. A case-study approach is used in the context of retail service providers, and the main case is the furniture company IKEA. Key values of our case are identified, analysed, and compared with values in other companies. The findings suggest that the innovation management of these firms has been characterised by: (1) business platforms (such as physical and web-based experience rooms) that facilitate their customers' service experiences; (2) service brand and marketing communication based on values resonance among the norms and ethical values of customers, the company, and the wider society; and (3) sharing of corporate values among leaders and employees to provide energy and direction for excellence and sustainable business development. A new framework known as "The business model of service excellence and innovation – known as the service excellence and innovation (SEIB) model" is developed. The new framework focuses on how to create and manage resource configurations that enable, support, and direct customers in value co-creation and service exchange.' (p. 535) |
| Hanson et al. (2019) | Society or the environment? Understanding | 'This research examines how and why consumers evaluate brand messages about corporate social responsibility (CSR) activities differently. Insights from secondary data suggest that brands may prioritize environmental activities over social activities, and vice versa, depending on the type of company. Using a field experiment and surveys, we explore whether consumers' attitudes toward these brand decisions follow company priorities. We find that consumers perceive brands that |

*(Continued)*

Table 14.1 (Continued)

| Authors | Title | Abstract |
|---|---|---|
| | how consumers evaluate brand messages about corporate social responsibility activities | sell goods and communicate messages about environmental sustainability activities more positively than services companies, while consumers perceive brands that provide services and communicate messages about social sustainability activities more positively than goods companies. We show that the tangibility of the brand's offering also impacts brand attitudes in a similar way. These findings have important implications for brand managers as they communicate CSR activities and attempt to maximize sustainability investments across various causes.' (p. 21) |
| Ishaq (2020) | Multidimensional green brand equity: a cross-cultural scale development and validation study | 'A plethora of studies indicate that brand equity is an intangible asset that played a vital role in increasing overall performance and customer preferences. The next logical questions would be the following: How can a firm offer eco-friendly brands? and How can one measure green brand equity? The purpose of this research is to propose an original, unique, and validated scale to measure multidimensional green brand equity for both products and services in a cross-cultural context. This study used a multistep scale development research design, and collected data from 980 consumers of telecommunication and home appliances industries in Pakistan and Italy. The six-dimensional green brand equity scale consists of social influence, sustainability, perceived quality, brand awareness, brand association, and brand leadership. As the green brand equity scale was invariant across Pakistan and Italy, researchers can test this scale both conceptually in the research and theoretically in the corporate environment.' (p. 1) |
| Luu (2017) | CSR and organizational citizenship behaviour for the environment in hotel industry; the moderating roles of corporate entrepreneurship and employee attachment style | '**Purpose** The aim of this study is to investigate how corporate social responsibility (CSR) contributes to organizational citizenship behavior for the environment (OCBE) among employees in hotel industry. Corporate green brand should be built not only from the provision of green products or services but also from green behavior among employees in their daily activities. This study also seeks the understanding of the moderating effects of corporate entrepreneurship (CE) and employees' attachment styles on the relationship between CSR and OCBE.<br>**Design/methodology/approach** The data for testing the study model were harvested from respondents in the hotel industry in Vietnam business context.<br>**Findings** The research results unveiled the positive effect of CSR on OCBE and the roles of CE and employee attachment styles in moderating this effect.<br>**Research limitations/implications** Hospitality organizations should integrate CSR initiatives into their sustainable strategy to shape employee OCBE. Entrepreneurial values should also be cultivated among employees to drive them to further respond to CSR initiatives and engage in OCBE.<br>**Originality/value** – This study expands CSR and green research streams by identifying the effect of CSR on OCBE among hotel employees as well as moderation mechanisms of CE and employee attachment styles for such an effect.' (p. 2867) |

(Continued)

Table 14.1 (Continued)

| Authors | Title | Abstract |
|---|---|---|
| Pratihari and Uzma (2019) | A survey on bankers' perception of corporate social responsibility in India | **'Purpose** The purpose of this paper is to understand the perception of the bankers towards an integrated approach to corporate social responsibility (CSR) initiatives in a strategic way of achieving sustainable growth of the banking sector. The paper additionally provides insights into different CSR initiatives and their implementation process in the context of scheduled commercial banks (SCB) of India.<br>**Design/methodology/approach** The study is exploratory and endorses the qualitative approach of primary research methodology by adopting a non-random stratified sampling method. The localist approach of the face-to-face interview has been applied to collect the data from 26 elite class respondents from 13 SCBs. The interview method was semi-structured and open-ended. The conformity, trustworthiness, credibility, transferability, dependability test of the study have ensured the quality of the data.<br>**Findings** The study reveals that the bankers perceive CSR as a moral obligation for the benefit of the society, beyond the regular banking operations. Further, the study comprehends that the CSR initiatives play a vital role in establishing the bank's image, brand and reputation, as well as, building a strong bond of trust among the employees and the bank management. Besides, CSR activities facilitate to cultivate a better culture by improvising in the quality of customer service for achieving competitive advantages.<br>**Research limitations/implications** The findings of the study represent a significant contribution to CSR theory from the interface of banking and society. Significantly, the results confirm that CSR initiatives play a vital role in building trust and minimise the gap between the employees and the management of the bank. The banks can increase its acceptance in the society and achieve competitive advantage by integrating CSR objectives with the business objectives to strengthen the corporate personality and brand.<br>**Practical implications** The study will help practitioners to develop the social identity of their firm to achieve competitive advantages in long-run. The bankers can channelise their limited resources while planning, designing and the implementation of different CSR activities with the overall goal of the bank in a cost-effective way. The study is confined only to public and private SCBs and limited to the geographical scope of one state in India. Therefore, further exploration may be carried out by considering other banks and geographic regions in India and different cross-cultural settings.<br>**Originality/value** The originality of the study lies with the in-depth analysis and quality check of the data. The results can contribute significant value to the qualitative method of conducting research.' (p. 225) |
| Singh and Malla (2017) | Does corporate social responsibility | 'Triple bottom line is making businesses increasingly conscious about the people, planet and profit. On one side where earning profits are crucial for organizations, the concept of sustainable corporate social responsibility (CSR) is also |

(Continued)

Table 14.1 (Continued)

| Authors | Title | Abstract |
|---|---|---|
| | matter in buying behaviour? A study of Indian consumers | emerging as a major concern for the corporate strategy. How to strike a balance between the two is one of the major challenges ahead for organizations. Moreover, Indian consumers are also nowadays becoming more aware about the responsibilities that a firm should possess. They are not ignorant as they were earlier; media is more vigilant and companies have now started knowing about the escalating negative effects of neglecting society, dynamism, building brand reputation by incorporating CSR and increased competition in the marketing environment for being socially responsible. Therefore, this article is an endeavour to measure the extent to which Indian consumers are aware about CSR and whether CSR has any impact on Indian consumers' actual buying behaviour. Data were collected from 232 respondents via a questionnaire. The results showed a significant positive effect of independent variables called intensity, intended loyalty and influence of socially responsible firms on dependent variables which is consumers' actual buying behaviour. Regression analysis was carried out to arrive at the result. In addition to this, the study also found that Indian consumers are aware about the CSR activities of the organizations. The result also indicated that CSR is one of the determining factors while purchasing any product or services.' (p. 781) |
| Vallaster and Lindgreen (2013) | The role of social interactions in building internal corporate brands: implications for sustainability | 'This article examines internal brand building, which is defined as the alignment of a corporation and employees around a brand. The notion of social interactions may provide a valuable perspective on brand-related interactive space, in which top management communicates brand-related information to employees and employees share brand-related information. Depth interviews, observations, and documentary analysis reveal how a social interaction-based, internal, brand-building process influences employees' actions and perceptions of the branded environment. Social interactions might generate brand commitment and shared brand beliefs in certain conditions. These findings have key implications for sustainability.' (p. 279) |
| Ward (2012) | Dirtgirl world: corporate social responsibility and ethical consumption in the world of children's television programming | 'Discussions in the field of ethical consumption usually refer to the mainstreaming of ethical and environmental concerns that impact on consumer behaviour in the consumption of food and material goods, and in some cases to television programs (especially lifestyle and makeover programs) that acknowledge the environmentally concerned viewer by encouraging the consumption of goods and services that minimise environmental impact. These studies recognise the field of commodity consumption as an important site for thinking about practices of identity-formation and the construction of the self as a responsible, environmentally and ethically concerned citizen who makes politically based decisions in everyday practice. But rarely is a TV program itself presented as a green commodity produced with the intention to be ecologically and ethically sound in its branded identity. This article showcases the production and distribution of the preschool television program dirtgirlworld as a response by ecologically minded individuals to engage with the challenges of today's environmental crises. This is a case study that connects ethical consumption and corporate social responsibility with screen production and distribution. The central thrust of this article is to posit the example of dirtgirlworld as part of a global social movement towards a more ecologically |

(*Continued*)

Table 14.1 (Continued)

| Authors | Title | Abstract |
|---|---|---|
| Xu (2014) | Understanding CSR from the perspective of Chinese diners: the case of McDonald's | sustainable existence. However, the suggestion here is that this case study also lends itself to much-needed conversation about how media studies can engage with our current ecological crises beyond the practice of eco-criticism.' (p. 29)<br><br>'**Purpose** The study aims to explore the expectations and perceptions of corporate social responsibility (CSR) strategies among Chinese fast-food diners, and to investigate the relationships among CSR strategies, consumer satisfaction and customer loyalty behaviors. Chinese diners' knowledge about a real world brand's CSR activities was also investigated. **Design/methodology/approach** Setting the research context on the fast food industry in China and selecting McDonald's as the subject brand, a survey study was conducted in a Southern Chinese mid-scale city. A convenience sample of 320 was withdrawn, and the data were analyzed with SPSS 18.0.<br>**Findings** Results from the study show that the Chinese fast food diners expect restaurant companies to attach more importance to (product) nutrition and well-being (of customers) and environment sustainability to be considered socially responsible. CSR performance was found to be the most influential factor in the consumers' loyalty behaviors compared to customer satisfaction with service, product and the total visit experience. The study also found that many of McDonald's CSR activities were unknown to the Chinese respondents.<br>**Originality/value** China is an attractive market to most global companies including fast food chain companies. Understanding Chinese diners' expectations and perceptions toward companies' CSR strategies will contribute to the success rate of companies operating in China. In addition, by using a real-world brands as the research context, the study tries to avoid perception bias of respondents due to the different interpretations of CSR in different organizations and industries.' (p. 1002) |
| Zhang et al. (2020) | Does one bad apple ruin a firm's green brand image? Examining frontline service employees' environmentally irresponsible behaviors | '**Purpose** Drawing on the branded service encounters perspective, the purpose of this study is to investigate how frontline service employees' environmentally irresponsible behaviors affect customers' brand evaluations.<br>**Design/methodology/approach** The research conducted two experiments. The first experiment explored the effect of frontline service employees' environmentally irresponsible behaviors on customers' brand evaluations via corporate hypocrisy. The second experiment explored the moderation effect of employees' prototypicality and the importance of corporate social responsibility (CSR) among customers.<br>**Findings** Experiment 1 indicates that for firms with a green brand image, frontline employees' environmentally irresponsible behaviors result in customers' perception that the firm is hypocritical, thus reducing their brand evaluations. Experiment 2 shows that employee prototypicality and CSR importance to the customer enhance the negative impact of frontline employees' environmentally irresponsible behaviors on customers' brand evaluations through customers' perception of corporate hypocrisy. |

(*Continued*)

Table 14.1 (Continued)

| Authors | Title | Abstract |
|---------|-------|----------|
|  |  | **Research limitations/implications** This study is one of the first efforts to explore how frontline service employees' environmentally irresponsible behaviors affect customers' responses. It helps understand the impact of frontline employees' counter-productive sustainable behaviors on customers' brand perception, as well as the relationship between CSR and employees.<br>Practical implications This study suggests that firms' green brand image does not always lead to positive customer response. When frontline employees' behaviors are inconsistent with firms' green brand image, it can trigger customers' perceptions of corporate hypocrisy and thus influence their brand evaluations. Therefore, firms should train frontline service employees to make their behaviors align with the firms' green brand image.<br>**Originality/value** This study is one of the first efforts to explore how frontline service employees' environmentally irresponsible behaviors affect customers' responses. It helps understand the impact of frontline employees' counter-productive sustainable behaviors on customers' brand perception, as well as the relationship between CSR and employee.'<br>(pp. 2501–2502) |

As illustrated in Figures 14.2 and 14.3, various research methods were applied in the selected papers: seven papers use quantitative methods; five papers are qualitative; and one paper employs mixed methods. Of note, all papers are empirical, with no theoretical pieces developed yet.

Regarding study context, various services contexts are covered. As shown in Table 14.2, study contexts include food and beverage, hotel, telecommunications, TV programmes, financial services/banking, casino, and general services industries that are not specified. Notably, three of the selected papers focus on the banking industry.

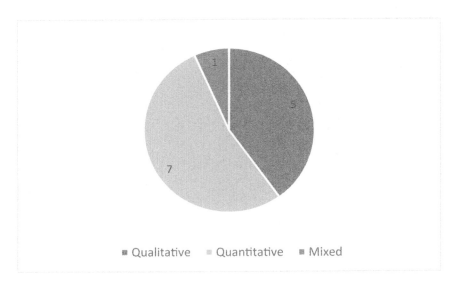

*Figure 14.2* Analysis of papers based on research methodology

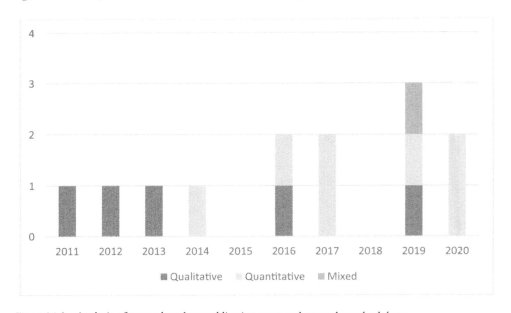

*Figure 14.3* Analysis of papers based on publication years and research methodology

*A systematic literature review*

Table 14.2 Study contexts of papers

| Study context | Reference |
|---|---|
| Food and beverage | Xu (2014); Zhang et al. (2020) |
| Hotel | Luu (2017) |
| Telecommunications | Ishaq (2020) |
| TV programs | Ward (2012) |
| Financial services/banking | Blake et al. (2019); Di Bella and Al-Fayoumi (2016); Pratihari and Uzma (2019) |
| Casino | Cheng and Lunn (2015) |
| General services industries | Edvardsson and Enquist (2011); Hanson et al. (2019); Singh and Malla (2017); Vallaster and Lindgreen (2013) |

Table 14.3 Journals and book publishers

| | |
|---|---|
| Journals (12) | *International Journal of Contemporary Hospitality Management* (2 papers) |
| | *Journal of World Business* |
| | *European Journal of Marketing* |
| | *Total Quality Management & Business Excellence* |
| | *Journal of Brand Management* |
| | *International Journal of Market Research* |
| | *Euromed Journal of Business* |
| | *International Journal of Sports Marketing & Sponsorship* |
| | *Social Responsibility Journal* |
| | *Global Business Review* |
| | *Media International Australia* |
| Book Publishers (1) | Springer |

As presented in Table 14.3, one study was published in a book (Springer), while 12 papers were published in academic journals. Among the 12 journal papers, two were published in *International Journal of Contemporary Hospitality Management* (Luu, 2017; Xu, 2014), whilst the remaining 10 papers appeared in the different journals listed in Table 14.3.

### 3.2 Content analysis and findings

The content analysis of the selected papers aimed to identify what dimensions of sustainability are mainly used in the field of corporate services branding, which are their drivers and outcomes, and what are the future research opportunities that emerge in this body of literature (presented in Section 4).

#### 3.2.1 Dimensions of sustainability

As shown in Table 14.4, different dimensions of sustainability were explored in the selected papers. The analysis of the selected 13 papers revealed that eight papers studied only one dimension of sustainability, providing a partial view of the phenomenon and neglecting interrelations,

*Table 14.4* Dimensions of sustainability studied in the selected papers

| Dimensions of sustainability | Papers |
| --- | --- |
| Environmental | Luu (2017); Ward (2012); Xu (2014); Zhang et al. (2020) |
| Social | Cheng and Lunn (2015); Di Bella and Al-Fayoumi (2016); Singh and Malla (2017) |
| Economic | Blake et al. (2019) |
| Mixed | Environmental and social: Hanson et al. (2019) |
| | Social and economic: Vallaster and Lindgreen (2013) |
| All dimensions | Edvardsson and Enquist (2011); Ishaq (2020); Pratihari and Uzma (2019) |

trade-offs, and synergies with the rest of dimensions. Among these eight papers, four papers focused on the environmental dimension, three on the social dimension, and one on the economic dimension. The remaining five papers covered at least two dimensions of sustainability. Among these five papers, three papers covered all dimensions, and two papers had a mixed focus – one focusing on the social and environmental dimensions and the other, on the social and economic dimensions. Nevertheless, as shown in Table 14.4, in total, there are five papers that studied the economic dimension of sustainability; eight papers that examined the environmental dimension; and eight papers that studied the social dimension. Overall, there remains a limited number of papers adopting a holistic view of sustainability (i.e., looking into the social, environmental and economic dimensions simultaneously).

When it comes to the environmental dimension of sustainability, it is important to note that 'environmentally sustainable' is often also referred to as 'environmentally friendly' or 'pro-environmental' (Han et al., 2009). In addition, we found that the papers that studied the environmental dimension of sustainability in the corporate services branding context tend to focus on the environmentally sustainable behaviour of employees. This is often linked to organizational citizenship behaviour for the environment (OCBE), which refers to employee behaviour oriented towards environmental improvement within the organization that is not necessarily rewarded or required as such (Daily et al., 2009). In the context of corporate services branding, the selected papers investigated relevant drivers and consequences of OCBE-related practices. For example, Luu (2017) highlighted the growing importance of environmentally responsible management in the hospitality context, especially concerning employee behaviour. This explains that, when employees perceive their organization as socially responsible, they are likely to engage in pro-environmental actions. Furthermore, Zhang et al. (2020) studied the environmentally irresponsible behaviours of frontline service employees in the beverage industry. They found that when employees behave in an environmentally irresponsible manner in service encounters, customers tend to evaluate the brand in a less favourable way. Moreover, they found that employees' environmentally irresponsible behaviour might trigger corporate hypocrisy, which refers to the assumption that a brand claims something that it never is, or never does (Wagner et al., 2009). Corporate hypocrisy can then negatively influence customer perceptions of the brand and purchase intentions (Zhang et al., 2020).

The social dimension of sustainability, in isolation, appeared in three papers (Cheng & Lunn, 2015; Di Bella & Al-Fayoumi, 2016; Singh & Malla, 2017). Di Bella and Al-Fayoumi (2016) found that, in the context of Islamic banks, the social dimension of sustainability is positively perceived by stakeholders. They further argued that the Islamic banking system has an intrinsic framework (i.e., ethics in the *Holy Quran*) that promotes social sustainability, so the fair treatment of employees and avoidance of evil practices such as fraud. Overall, they proposed that, under the guidance of Islamic ethics and principles, banks are likely to improve their social sustainability activities and enhance society's awareness on social sustainability. Singh and Malla (2017) found that, in services contexts, brands that implement social sustainability are likely to boost customer purchase behaviour. They further stressed that customers tend to look for the social dimension of sustainability while choosing service provider. Cheng and Lunn (2015) suggested that, in the casino context, employee training is crucial for developing the social dimension of sustainability. They explained that the casino brand can communicate and express their mission, vision and values through different training programmes. Therefore, employees are likely to assimilate the brand's culture and engage in behaviours that are aligned with the brand values, such as exceptional service delivery and respectful behaviours. These employee behaviours can have a positive influence on the community and strengthen the social dimension of the brand's sustainability.

One paper examined the economic dimension of sustainability in isolation (Blake et al., 2019). Namely, in the services sector, Blake et al. (2019) showed that brands that are engaged in sports sponsorship are likely to improve their image and economic sustainability. They further found that brands that sponsor sports receive more financial gains than those that do not engage in any sports sponsorship. Moreover, they argued that sports sponsorship behaviours are likely to support the survival of the sports industry and have a positive impact on the economic environment.

Two papers studied mixed dimensions of sustainability (Hanson et al., 2019; Vallaster & Lindgreen, 2013). Hanson et al. (2019) focused on the environmental and social dimensions. Their findings indicated that customers tend to perceive more positively product brands that communicate their environmental sustainability initiatives than services brands that do the same. However, they argued that customers are likely to better perceive services brands that communicate their social sustainability activities than product brands that also do so. Vallaster and Lindgreen (2013) suggested that employees are crucial for building the social and economic dimensions of sustainability. They proposed that by building identification with the brand, employees are likely to engage in behaviours that support the brand and promote the social and economic aspects of the brand's sustainability.

Finally, there are three papers that covered all three dimensions of sustainability (Edvardsson & Enquist, 2011; Ishaq, 2020; Pratihari & Uzma, 2019). These papers concentrated on the great value of sustainability in the corporate services branding context. Specifically, in the context of services brands like IKEA and Starbucks, Edvardsson and Enquist (2011) found that sustainability is a key driver of service excellence and service innovation. They further highlighted the important role of sustainability in providing the right mix of knowledge, culture, and structure in order to support and deliver service excellence. For example, the service innovation in Starbucks aims to create personalized customer experiences and motivate employees to secure customer loyalty. This process was found to be driven by both the original values of Starbucks and sustainability values (Edvardsson & Enquist, 2009). In line with this, Ishaq (2020, p. 3) found that sustainability is a key dimension of green brand equity, which refers to 'a set of brand assets and liabilities about environmental, social, and economic concerns . . . that boost or decline the value offered by the brand.' Similarly, in the banking sector, Pratihari and Uzma (2019) found that the brand's sustainability activities positively influence the brand's image and reputation, and strengthen the employee-brand relationship.

Based on this analysis, the three dimensions of sustainability are represented in our selected papers. However, there remains a limited number of papers that focus on the interrelationship among the three dimensions. Accordingly, several scholars have called for further research on such interrelationship, since focusing on a single dimension may provide an incomplete view of the phenomenon and could result in omitting relevant ethical and moral aspects related to sustainability (e.g., Richardson, 2009).

### 3.2.2 Drivers and outcomes of (the dimensions of) sustainability

The majority of the papers presented here focus on the antecedents and consequences of (different dimensions of) sustainability, and some papers address the crucial role of (different dimensions of) sustainability in the context of corporate services branding.

More specifically, four papers have dealt with the antecedents or drivers of (the dimensions of) sustainability (Anitsal et al., 2019; Blake et al., 2019; Cheng & Lunn, 2015; Edvardsson & Enquist, 2011; Vallaster & Lindgreen, 2013) (see Table 14.5). Anitsal et al. (2019) proposed that service co-creation contributes to sustainability in the airline context. Blake et al. (2019) found that sports sponsorship can lead to a wide range of outcomes that are likely to boost economic sustainability. Cheng and Lunn (2015) suggested that, in the casino industry, employee training is crucial to establish social sustainability. Studying services brands, Edvardsson and Enquist (2011) found that sharing corporate values among the leaders and employees is likely to improve the brand's sustainability. Finally, Vallaster and Lindgreen (2013) proposed that employee identification with the brand is likely to promote employee-brand supportive behaviours and improve the brand's sustainability.

Five papers studied the consequences or outcomes of (the dimensions of) sustainability (Di Bella & Al-Fayoumi, 2016; Edvardsson & Enquist, 2011; Pratihari & Uzma, 2019; Singh & Malla, 2017; Zhang et al., 2020) (see Table 14.6). In the banking industry, Di Bella and Al-Fayoumi (2016) found that brands tend to generate more positive stakeholder perceptions by engaging in socially responsible activities. Pratihari and Uzma (2019) proposed that sustainability has a positive influence on brand image and reputation. Zhang et al. (2020) found that frontline service employees' environmentally irresponsible behaviour is likely to increase customer perceived corporate hypocrisy and negatively affect customers' overall brand evaluation. Moreover, in the context of services brands, Edvardsson and Enquist (2011) found that sustainability is a key driver of service excellence and service innovation. Finally, Singh and Malla (2017) showed that, in services contexts, socially responsible brands are likely to foster customer purchase behaviour.

*Table 14.5* Papers studying the drivers of (dimensions of) sustainability

| Papers | Drivers |
| --- | --- |
| Blake et al. (2019) | Sports sponsorship |
| Cheng and Lunn (2015) | Employee training |
| Edvardsson and Enquist (2011) | Sharing corporate values among leaders and employees |
| Vallaster and Lindgreen (2013) | Employee identification with the brand |

*Table 14.6* Papers studying the outcomes of (dimensions of) sustainability

| Papers | Outcomes |
| --- | --- |
| Di Bella and Al-Fayoumi (2016) | Positive stakeholder perceptions |
| Edvardsson and Enquist (2011) | Service excellence and service innovation |
| Pratihari and Uzma (2019) | Brand image and reputation |
| Singh and Malla (2017) | Customer purchase behaviour |
| Zhang et al. (2020) | Corporate hypocrisy and negative customer brand perception (outcomes of environmental irresponsibility) |

## 4. Future research opportunities

Following these descriptive and content analyses, we propose some future research directions within the realm of sustainability and corporate services branding. These directions aim to serve as a guide for researchers to position their studies, enabling the development of new research streams.

### 4.1 Key drivers of sustainability in the field of corporate services branding

In light of this analysis, four papers studied the drivers of sustainability (see Table 14.5), including sports sponsorship, employee training, sharing corporate values among leaders and employees, and employee identification with the brand. Although these factors play a fundamental role in driving sustainability, they tend to have a spotlight on employees. Employees are crucial for establishing sustainability in the corporate services branding context. This is because important service attributes have to be co-created by employees and organizational outsiders. For example, in services contexts, Cheng and Lunn (2015) highlighted that employee identification with the brand's values through training programmes is crucial to establish social sustainability. However, and although it is recognized that employees are crucial for establishing sustainability in corporate services brands, we encourage that future research examines how other stakeholders' behaviours can influence sustainability.

When addressing the drivers of sustainability, out of the four papers, only Edvardsson and Enquist (2011) studied the key drivers of the environmental dimension of sustainability. Therefore, future studies could further delve into this dimension and investigate its key drivers. Considering this analysis, it would be relevant to conduct such future studies in services contexts other than financial services and casinos. In addition, future studies may investigate how sustainability is influenced by the same variable across different services contexts. If the influence yielded by a specific variable is the same across contexts, it would be relevant to look for potential synergies between sustainability practices across such contexts.

### 4.2 Key outcomes of sustainability in the field of corporate services branding

Our analysis shows that sustainability in corporate services branding has several positive outcomes (see Table 14.6), including positive stakeholder perceptions, service excellence and service innovation, brand image and reputation, customer trust and satisfaction, customer purchase behaviour, and reduced level of corporate hypocrisy. However, a few studies in other contexts have found that sustainability does not always have positive consequences (e.g., Luchs et al., 2010). For example, in the product branding context, Luchs et al. (2010) proposed that sustainability may not always have a positive influence on customer preferences. Therefore, future research could explore potential negative or less favourable consequences of sustainability practices in services contexts. Similarly, the study by Hanson et al. (2019) suggested that customers tend to perceive more positively services brands that communicate their social sustainability activities, in comparison with product brands that do the same. Therefore, future research could explore similarities and differences in sustainability outcomes between corporate services and product brands.

In addition, considering our analysis, we encourage that future studies focus on the outcomes of the economic and environmental dimensions of sustainability, and do so in services contexts other than financial services, and the food and beverage industry. It would also be relevant that future research examines and compares the outcomes of sustainability across different services contexts, uncovering the reasons for potential similarities and differences.

Finally, and regardless of the antecedents and consequences, there is still a need to conduct qualitative studies to investigate the process of sustainability implementation in corporate services branding. To this end, future studies should consider analysing different cases where sustainability is successfully or unsuccessfully implemented. Future studies could also explore both internal and external factors that influence a successful sustainability implementation.

## References

Anitsal, M. M., Anitsal, I., & Anitsal, S. (2019). Is your business sustainable? A sentiment analysis of air passengers of top 10 US-based airlines. *Journal of Global Scholars of Marketing Science*, 29(1), 25–41.

Balmer, J. M. T. (2001). The three virtues and seven deadly sins of corporate brand management. *Journal of General Management*, 27(1), 1–17. https://doi.org/10.1177/030630700102700101

Berry, L. L. (1980). Services marketing is different. *Business*, 30(3), 24–29.

Blake, J., Fourie, S., & Goldman, M. (2019). The relationship between sports sponsorships and corporate financial returns in South Africa. *International Journal of Sports Marketing and Sponsorship*, 20(1), 2–25. https://doi.org/10.1108/IJSMS-12-2016-0088

Booms, B. H., & Bitner, M. J. (1981). Marketing strategies and organization structures for service firms. *Marketing of Services*, 25(3), 47–52.

Burgess, K., Singh, P. J., & Koroglu, R. (2006). Supply chain management: A structured literature review and implications for future research. *International Journal of Operations & Production Management*, 26(7), 703–729. https://doi.org/10.1108/01443570610672202

Cheng, S. M., & Lunn, S. (2015). Training and qualification: Employee training at galaxy entertainment group. In M. Zeuch (Ed.), *Handbook of human resources management* (pp. 1–13). Springer. https://doi.org/10.1007/978-3-642-40933-2_8-1

Clarivate Analytics. (2020, December 20). *Web of science core collection*. Retrieved from https://clarivate.com/products/web-of-science/web-science-form/web-science-core-collection/

Crossan, M. M., & Apaydin, M. (2010). A multi-dimensional framework of organizational innovation: A systematic review of the literature. *Journal of Management Studies*, 47(6), 1154–1191. https://doi.org/10.1111/j.1467-6486.2009.00880.x

Daily, B. F., Bishop, J. W., & Govindarajulu, N. (2009). A conceptual model for organizational citizenship behavior directed toward the environment. *Business & Society*, 48(2), 243–256. https://doi.org/10.1177/0007650308315439

Dall'Olmo Riley, F., & de Chernatony, L. (2000). The service brand as relationships builder. *British Journal of Management*, 11(2), 137–150. https://doi.org/10.1111/1467-8551.t01-1-00156

Di Bella, V., & Al-Fayoumi, N. (2016). Perception of stakeholders on corporate social responsibility of Islamic Banks in Jordan. *EuroMed Journal of Business*, 11(1), 30–56. https://doi.org/10.1108/EMJB-01-2015-0003

Edvardsson, B., & Enquist, B. (2009). *Values-based service for sustainable business: Lessons from IKEA*. London: Routledge.

Edvardsson, B., & Enquist, B. (2011). The service excellence and innovation model: Lessons from IKEA and other service frontiers. *Total Quality Management & Business Excellence*, 22(5), 535–551. https://doi.org/10.1080/14783363.2011.568242

Elkington, J. (1994). Towards the sustainable corporation win-win-win business strategies for sustainable development. *California Management Review*, 36, 90–100. https://doi.org/10.2307/41165746

Elkington, J. (2018). 25 years ago I coined the phrase "triple bottom line." Here's why it's time to rethink it. *Harvard Business Review*, 25, 2–5. Retrieved from https://hbr.org/2018/06/25-years-ago-i-coined-the-phrase-triple-bottom-line-heres-why-im-giving-up-on-it

Fan, Y. (2005). Ethical branding and corporate reputation. *Corporate Communications: An International Journal*, 10(4), 341–350. https://doi.org/10.1108/13563280510630133

Gimenez, C., Sierra, V., Rodon, J. (2012). Sustainable operations: Their impact on the triple bottom line. *International Journal of Production Economics*, 140(1), 149–159. https://doi.org/10.1016/j.ijpe.2012.01.035

Goh, C. S., Chong, H. Y., Jack, L., & Faris, A. F. M. (2020). Revisiting triple bottom line within the context of sustainable construction: A systematic review. *Journal of Cleaner Production, 252*, 119884. https://doi.org/10.1016/j.jclepro.2019.119884

Goldman, M. M. (2011). Post-crisis sports marketing business model shifts. *Managing Global Transitions, 9*(2), 171–184.

Gronroos, C. (2006). Adopting a service logic for marketing. *Marketing Theory, 6*(3), 317–333. https://doi.org/10.1177/1470593106066794

Gupta, S., Czinkota, M., & Melewar, T. C. (2013). Embedding knowledge and value of a brand into sustainability for differentiation. *Journal of World Business, 48*(3), 287–296.

Han, H., Hsu, L. T. J., & Lee, J. S. (2009). Empirical investigation of the roles of attitudes toward green behaviors, overall image, gender, and age in hotel customers' eco-friendly decision-making process. *International Journal of Hospitality Management, 28*(4), 519–528. https://doi.org/10.1016/j.ijhm.2009.02.004

Hanson, S., Jiang, L., Ye, J., & Murthy, N. (2019). Society or the environment? Understanding how consumers evaluate brand messages about corporate social responsibility activities. *Journal of Brand Management, 26*(1), 21–34. https://doi.org/10.1057/s41262-018-0110-8

Ho, L. C. J., & Taylor, M. E. (2007). An empirical analysis of triple bottom-line reporting and its determinants: Evidence from the United States and Japan. *Journal of International Financial Management & Accounting, 18*(2), 123–150. https://doi.org/10.1111/j.1467-646X.2007.01010.x

Hubbard, G. (2009). Measuring organizational performance: Beyond the triple bottom line. *Business Strategy and the Environment, 18*(3), 177–191.

Iglesias, O., Markovic, S., Bagherzadeh, M., & Singh, J. J. (2020). Co-creation: A key link between corporate social responsibility, customer trust, and customer loyalty. *Journal of Business Ethics, 163*, 151–166. https://doi.org/10.1007/s10551-018-4015-y

Ind, N. (1997). *The corporate brand*. Oxford: Macmillan.

Ishaq, M. I. (2020). Multidimensional green brand equity: A cross-cultural scale development and validation study. *International Journal of Market Research*. https://doi.org/10.1177/1470785320932040

Jensen, J. A., & Hsu, A. (2011). Does sponsorship pay off? An examination of the relationship between investment in sponsorship and business performance. *International Journal of Sports Marketing and Sponsorship, 12*(4), 72–84.

Kruger, T. S., Goldman, M., & Ward, M. (2014). The impact of new, renewal and termination sponsorship announcements on share price returns. *International Journal of Sports Marketing and Sponsorship, 15*(4), 10–25.

Lozano, R., & Huisingh, D. (2011). Inter-linking issues and dimensions in sustainability reporting. *Journal of Cleaner Production, 19*(2–3), 99–107. https://doi.org/10.1016/j.jclepro.2010.01.004

Luchs, M. G., Naylor, R. W., Irwin, J. R., & Raghunathan, R. (2010). The sustainability liability: Potential negative effects of ethicality on product preference. *Journal of Marketing, 74*(5), 18–31. https://doi.org/10.1509/jmkg.74.5.018

Luu, T. T. (2017). CSR and organizational citizenship behavior for the environment in hotel industry. *International Journal of Contemporary Hospitality Management, 29*(11), 2867–2900. https://doi.org/10.1108/IJCHM-02-2016-0080

Markovic, S., Iglesias, O., Singh, J. J., & Sierra, V. (2018). How does the perceived ethicality of corporate services brands influence loyalty and positive word-of-mouth? Analyzing the roles of empathy, affective commitment, and perceived quality. *Journal of Business Ethics, 148*(4), 721–740. https://doi.org/10.1007/s10551-015-2985-6

McKinsey. (2011). *The business of sustainability. McKinsey global survey results*. Retrieved from www.mckinsey.com/business-functions/sustainability/our-insights/the-business-of-sustainability-mckinsey-global-survey-results

Organisation for Economic Cooperation and Development. (2001). *Sustainable development: Critical issues*. Retrieved from www.oecd.org/greengrowth/sustainabledevelopmentcriticalissues-freeoverviewofthereport.htm

Pittaway, L., Robertson, M., Munir, K., Denyer, D., & Neely, A. (2004). Networking and innovation: A systematic review of the evidence. *International Journal of Management Reviews, 5*(3–4), 137–168. https://doi.org/10.1111/j.1460-8545.2004.00101.x

Pratihari, S. K., & Uzma, S. H. (2019). A survey on bankers' perception of corporate social responsibility in India. *Social Responsibility Journal, 16*(2), 225–253. https://doi.org/10.1108/SRJ-11-2016-0198

Richardson, B. J. (2009). Keeping ethical investment ethical: Regulatory issues for investing for sustainability. *Journal of Business Ethics, 87*(4), 555–572. https://doi.org/10.1007/s10551-008-9958-y

Sierra, V., Iglesias, O., Markovic, S., & Singh, J. J. (2017). Does ethical image build equity in corporate services brands? The influence of customer perceived ethicality on affect, perceived quality, and equity. *Journal of Business Ethics, 144*(3), 661–676. https://doi.org/10.1007/s10551-015-2855-2

Singh, R., & Malla, S. S. (2017). Does corporate social responsibility matter in buying behaviour? – A study of Indian consumers. *Global Business Review, 18*(3), 781–794. https://doi.org/10.1177/0972150917692206

Sport Marketing Frontiers. (2011). *Report: Country by ranking.* Retrieved from http://frontiers.sportbusiness.com

Svensson, G., Høgevold, N., Ferro, C., Varela, J. C. S., Padin, C., & Wagner, B. (2016). A triple bottom line dominant logic for business sustainability: Framework and empirical findings. *Journal of Business-to-Business Marketing, 23*(2), 153–188. https://doi.org/10.1080/1051712X.2016.1169119

Tranfield, D., Denyer, D., & Smart, P. (2003). Towards a methodology for developing evidence-informed management knowledge by means of systematic review. *British Journal of Management, 14*(3), 207–222. https://doi.org/10.1111/1467-8551.00375

Vallaster, C., & Lindgreen, A. (2013). The role of social interactions in building internal corporate brands: Implications for sustainability. *Journal of World Business, 48*(3), 297–310. https://doi.org/10.1016/j.jwb.2012.07.014

Wagner, T., Lutz, R. J., & Weitz, B. A. (2009). Corporate hypocrisy: Overcoming the threat of inconsistent corporate social responsibility perceptions. *Journal of Marketing, 73*(6), 77–91. https://doi.org/10.1509/jmkg.73.6.77

Ward, S. (2012). Dirtgirlworld: Corporate social responsibility and ethical consumption in the world of children's television programming. *Media International Australia, 145*(1), 29–38. https://doi.org/10.1177/1329878X1214500105

Xu, Y. (2014). Understanding CSR from the perspective of Chinese diners: The case of McDonald's. *International Journal of Contemporary Hospitality Management, 26*(6), 1002–1020. https://doi.org/10.1108/IJCHM-01-2013-0051

Zeithaml, V. A., Parasuraman, A., & Berry, L. L. (1985). Problems and strategies in services marketing. *The Journal of Marketing, 49*(2), 33–46. https://doi.org/10.1177/002224298504900203

Zhang, L., Wu, J., Chen, H., & Nguyen, B. (2020). Does one bad apple ruin a firm's green brand image? Examining frontline service employees' environmentally irresponsible behaviors. *European Journal of Marketing, 54*(10), 2501–2521. https://doi.org/10.1108/EJM-11-2019-0844

# 15
# BUILDING STRONG CORPORATE BRANDS
Towards valuable and sustainable experiences

*Nicholas Ind*

**A commentary**

This section of the book has a broad theme and consequently the chapters themselves are quite diverse, although they do have links with each other. They also break the bounds of the section and provide interesting connections with other chapters. For example, Frederico Mangiò, Giuseppe Pedeliento, and Daniela Andreini's chapter on the role of artificial intelligence in delivering brand experience connects with Venkat Ramaswamy's chapter (B6) on the nature of experience ecosystems – although they have interestingly divergent views on service dominant logic. Similarly, Carsten Baumgarth's chapter on the B★Canvas 2.0, which describes a tool for the management of corporate brands, can be linked to Line Schmeltz and Anna Karina Kjeldsen's chapter on polyphony (D17) and Alessandra Zamparini, Francesco Lurati, and Luca M. Visconti's chapter on polysemy (D18). The polyphonic and polysemic perspectives interestingly challenge some of the core assumptions about managing corporate brands by showing the challenges of coherency in a multi-voiced world. If this were an authored book, the reader might be wondering about the lack of a consistent authorial voice, but with an edited collection of chapters, these contradictions and divergences make the field of corporate brand management richer and create the opportunity to reflect on the changes that are taking place and how we might approach them, not by rejection but by accepting heterogeneity.

The heading of this section, 'Building strong corporate brands' sounds like a punchy title, not least because it is reminiscent of the title of David Aaker's 1995 book 'Building Strong Brands.' The enduring appeal of Aaker's book is that it provides managers with a clear means of building brand equity. In Chapter 11, Carsten Baumgarth takes us on a guided tour of the B★Canvas 2.0 model, which is a managerial perspective on managing corporate brands – and has as its end goal, enhancing brand equity. So, what's new here? The corporate brand orientation with its variety of stakeholders is, but it would also be true to say that traditional models of brand building tend to over-egg the marketing communication aspect of brand building and give insufficient emphasis to the role of other influences, especially employees as brand deliverers. Once you move beyond the idea that corporate branding = communication, then it becomes more complex and creates a challenge of giving coherence to the diversity of experiences by being attentive to corporate culture and internal brand management. In an apposite metaphor, Baumgarth, references this bringing together of elements as like the 'cogs in a good mechanical watch' and he then shows us those entrained cogs working coherently in the example of the German company, Werkhaus. Like a good horologist, the brand manager here should have the ability to both analyse the workings and from this observation, develop a plan that can deliver superior performance. As well as illustrating the value of the model with well-established companies, Baumgarth also reminds us the value it can deliver for start-ups, where issues of corporate branding are not always front of mind, but the desire for speed is. He argues that one benefit of the model is its flexibility and ability to incorporate unforeseen developments, that are typical of the start-up world. Whether applied to mature or new corporate brands, Baumgarth argues that the B★Canvas 2.0 model brings together three key elements in brand foundations, brand touchpoints, and brand performance that are rooted in practice and make explicit the links between the roots of the corporate brand, its points of interactions with stakeholders, and the resulting equity for the public and customers. This view of equity then encompasses what Baumgarth calls final performance, which encompasses the organizational purpose and economic and social impacts.

If Baumgarth's chapter focuses perhaps more on the first part of this section header, Mangiò, Pedeliento, and Andreini's chapter orients itself towards the second: 'towards valuable and sustainable experiences.' In doing so, they remind us of the importance of stakeholder centricity and the increasingly powerful role that artificial intelligence (AI) plays in brand building and the delivery of the brand experience. The failing of academic research here is that it has hardly kept pace with practice. Companies, such as Philips, Microsoft, and John Deere (see Venkat Ramaswamy's chapter for the story of John Deere) are using AI to an ever-greater degree in creating brand aligned touchpoints to deliver, together with partners, experience ecosystems that integrate human and non-human interactions, but as the chapter notes 'recent research hardly addresses the current role that AI technologies play in the creation of new and different forms of brand experience.' The interesting challenge that the chapter writers pinpoint is that alongside the opportunities AI provides for enhancing experiences it also can treat stakeholders as passive recipients of preconceived ideas as to what those experiences should be, rather than as active co-creators. Ironically this suggests the importance of a human-centric, context-specific perspective, that is 'capable of sociomaterially constructing totally new brand experiences.' The persuasive argument here is that AI is evolving rapidly and has the potential to realize new and relevant customer-brand-technology interactions, but it also has the possibility to be dominated by the technology and to give too much emphasis to organizational efficiency. The implication is that brand owners need to think through their motivations, to monitor the impacts, and to adapt to changing needs.

While AI may be a way to deliver new experiences, we might pause and think, how do consumers perceive these brand innovations? Is an innovative corporate brand more attractive than a less innovative one? In their chapter, with the quirky title, 'Honey or Condensed Milk?', Seidali Kurtmollaiev, Line Lervik-Olsen, and Tor W. Andreassen provide the answer. Drawing on research over several years from the Innovation Index they constructed, they use the data to show that consumers find those brands that combine innovation and sustainability, the most attractive. The combination of the two is fascinating, because the temptation is to see commercial innovation as one thing and social and environmental innovation as something else. The research shows that corporate brands can have it both ways either by transferring knowledge from one sphere to the other or by integrating social and economic innovation and commercial innovation. They note that 'brands that regularly launch both commercial and social innovations have a higher chance to become the consumer's first choice and enjoy high customer loyalty.' From this finding it would seem clear that corporate brands need to use their purpose to ensure a stakeholder perspective that recognizes the need to meet their different responsibilities and to create relevant value. This in turn requires brands to be close to their stakeholders. Yet, Kurtmollaiev, Lervik-Olsen, and Andreassen note that there is often a dissonance here. By marrying consumer insights together with research into the attitudes of corporate brand managers, they observe that innovation is understood differently. A commercially led innovation may provoke anger among consumers if it is seen as socially irresponsible, while a social innovation can be seen negatively if it fails to confer immediate benefits. Brands are sometimes swayed by the opportunity of socially responsible innovation to make unsubstantiated claims, but consumers are good at sniffing out these manipulations. The writers note of consumers, that 'they are not only able to detect fraudulent communication, but also much better in contextualizing innovations than managers.' The prescription then is to unify innovation so that it delivers value and to cooperate with stakeholders through all the stages of the innovation process.

If an integrated approach to sustainability innovation is an essential ingredient in consumer perceptions of brand attractiveness, we might expect to find academic research pursuing the implications. Yet, as Stefan Markovic, Yuqian Qiu, Cristina Sancha, and Nikolina Koporcic show in their analysis of the research into corporate service brands, there is a clear gap. The focus in this chapter is on the concept of sustainability and its integral dimensions of economic, environmental, and social (which relate to the Triple Bottom Line of People, Planet, and Profit). What they uncover in this meta-analysis is that the number of published papers on this area of corporate branding is quite limited and also fragmented in that most do not address the mutuality of the dimensions, but rather give emphasis to one of them. As one the premises of the Triple Bottom Line is a holistic approach, the tendency to ignore the links is limiting. Here we ought to urge the research community to investigate further a connected approach to the economic, environmental, and social dimensions of corporate brands. In spite of the research gap, Markovic et al. echo in their analysis, the positive findings of Kurtmollaiev et al., in noting,

> Our analysis shows that sustainability in corporate services branding has several positive outcomes . . . including positive stakeholder perceptions, service excellence and service innovation, brand image and reputation, customer trust and satisfaction, customer purchase behaviour, and reduced level of corporate hypocrisy.

## The future of corporate brand building

The four chapters of this section describe some of the current practices and research agendas connected to building strong corporate brands and they also hint at a future that encompasses opportunities and challenges connected to the co-creation of corporate brands, the role of technology in the delivery of brand experiences, the importance of innovation, and the value of integrating sustainability into the core of the corporate brand. In this section of the commentary, we will use these signals to look at how these opportunities and challenges might play out, by placing the consumer – corporate brand relationship at the centre. When this relationship goes awry, as Kurtmollaiev et al., point out, then what corporate brands intend and what consumers experience becomes misaligned. On the other hand, when brands are close to consumers and other stakeholders, they are more likely to be attuned to each other. This idea is borne out by Interbrand's Best Global Brands study, which analyses, among other things, the source of corporate brand strength. Looking at the brand strength scores between 2014–2019 of the top 20 fastest growing brands, two key dimensions emerge: relevance (the brand's ability to anticipate and address customers' needs) and responsiveness (the brand's ability to change internally to meet those needs by evolving and renewing itself) (Interbrand, 2019).

The dimension of relevance requires an empathy with an organization's stakeholders. As Satya Nadella, CEO of Microsoft (one of those fast-growing brands) writes, 'At the core of our business must be the curiosity and desire to meet a customer's unarticulated and unmet needs with great technology. There is no way to do that unless we absorb with deeper insight and empathy what they need' (Nadella, 2017, p. 101). Nadella's point concerns the need to move beyond traditional market research methods towards an intimacy with customers. This requires a human-centric approach, a willingness to get close to customers, and the use of data as a means of acquiring insight into what people do – as well as what they say they do. There is an obvious connection here to Mangiò et al.'s chapter in the way that AI can be used both as an insight method and as a means of continuously delivering, and learning about, customer experiences. However, AI can be a blunt tool without the sensitivity to interpret the 'why' of customer behaviour. Alongside the use of technology as a brand-customer relationship enabler, there is also a requirement for a shift in philosophy. This concerns one of the core themes of this book, which is about a co-creative approach to corporate brand management.

The classical view of corporate brand management sees the corporate brand as a managerial creation. Managers may listen to their stakeholders, but it is the internal experts who shape the brand identity. In this view the temptation is to see stakeholders as passive recipients of whatever the corporate brand does. However, in a co-creative perspective the psychological distance between the corporate brand and the stakeholder is compressed, and both become active in influencing each other as well as internal and external stakeholders. This shifts the idea of the corporate brand from being something fixed into a dynamic entity that is always evolving and adapting. It also changes the nature of leadership away from controlling the brand towards one of orchestration, where managers are conductors (Michel, 2017) – or maybe even more appropriately towards one of jazz improvisation, which involves listening to each other and adapting within an agreed structure (Hatch, 1999). This may make the idea of the corporate brand discordant and certainly, as Schmeltz and Kjeldsen write in this book, it can become cacophonous, but in most cases the core of the corporate brand remains fairly constant over time, even if there are some elements that are more mutable as the brand transitions through a set of interrelated performances (Iglesias et al., 2020). This means that the brand has a rhythm punctuated by syncopation, which can enrich its meaning, until at a certain point it loses its coherence. The implication is that managers need to set the tempo, but they cannot control the meaning of the corporate brand, which extends beyond the purview of the organization: 'We'd argue that co-creation is not a choice for organizations. Rather it is the reality of how brands are connected to all their different stakeholders through networks of interest' (Ind & Schmidt, 2019).

One of the results of listening and opening up the organization to the influence of stakeholders is the recognition of the growing demands to be aware of environmental and social issues. As Kurtmollaiev et al., and Markovic et al., indicate in their chapters, issues connected to sustainable thinking and practices have become central in building strong brands. Sustainability is no longer an optional extra. Corporate brand relevance requires organizations to absorb societal concerns and to become issue fluent. Highly rated sustainable brands, such as Unilever and Patagonia (Globescan/SustainAbility, 2020), are adept at listening to the changing expectations of stakeholders and using corporate purpose to define their actions – especially within the context of a deep environmental commitment, but also in the case of some Unilever brands (e.g., Dove and self-esteem, Knorr and nutrition, Lifebuoy and hygiene) in relevant social issues. As the importance of environmental and social issues is likely to continue to grow in importance for key stakeholders, so the need of corporate brands to respond will become ever more urgent. As ESG measures (environmental, social, and governance) become more coherent and widespread, so will organizations not only need to deliver profitable growth, they will also need to demonstrate how they deliver on People and Planet.

The other vital element of brand strength – responsiveness – is of course also connected to relevance, in that it is concerned with the ability of the corporate brand to respond to societal and market changes, challenges, and opportunities. This concerns the culture of the organization, its leadership, and its agility. This point links us to Carsten Baumgarth's chapter in that his B★Canvas 2.0 model reminds of the importance of analysis and planning. Corporate brands do have agency that is determined by their histories and their expectations of the future. However, writing this book in the year of COVID-19, also reminds that plans can easily be upended by contact with reality. As former heavyweight boxing champion, Mike Tyson said in preparation for a fight with rival Evander Holyfield, 'Everyone has a plan 'till they get punched in the mouth' (Freedman, 2013, p. ix). Looking to the future and to a world of increasing volatility and uncertainty, a corporate brand needs to have a clarity of purpose that enables it to be agile and to adapt as new contexts and challenges emerge (Gast et al., 2020; Younger et al., 2020). This requires self-knowledge as to why the corporate brand exists, an intimate understanding of the relevant issues in the world and an open, co-creative approach that enables the brand to work together with partners.

This does not suggest that a corporate brand should be changing direction all the time, flip-flopping without clear intent. There is little value in a corporate brand purpose, if it is not used to actually connect the organization's capabilities to its strategic decision-making. This indicates that the purpose itself should draw on the brand's roots and then be lived in day-to-day choices about what to do and what not to do. When the purpose moves beyond words into actions, it enables the organization to respond at speed. During COVID-19, which required rapid adjustments, companies such as Verizon, SAP, and Philips were able to contribute effectively, together with their partners, because they had clarity about purpose and could bring relevant capabilities into play. For example, wireless carrier, Verizon Communications has a purpose that is concerned with realizing the promise of the digital world to enhance the ability of humans, businesses, and society to do new things and do good. It thus gives emphasis to a broad responsibility to all stakeholders. When COVID-19 hit, the company avoided furloughing its 135,000 employees and enhanced compensation for engineers and other staff performing essential services. Verizon also pledged not to end contracts for customers who couldn't pay. *Forbes*, which rated Verizon number 1 in its list of the 100 largest employers among U.S. public companies in terms of response to the public health crisis, noted, 'The largest U.S. wireless carrier by subscribers has instituted one of the most expansive sick leave policies of big employers. It also scored top marks for backup dependent care and efforts to help surrounding communities' (Minaya, 2020). Amidst the easy talk of environmental and social claims – which Kurtmollaiev et al., connect to colourwashing (greenwashing, pinkwashing and brownwashing) – companies such as Verizon are notable for making specific and measurable commitments in terms of carbon neutrality, digital inclusion, community building, and small business development.

## Future research agendas

If we were to travel back in time, we'd find that in the past corporate brand strength was predicated on current performance and expectations of future cash flows, derived from brand awareness, judgements, feelings, and resonance that was built around core brand attributes (Keller, 1993). Ideas such as sustainability and responsibility would have been tangential or for the odd niche brand, like Patagonia, that had built its positioning around meeting the challenge of the environmental crisis. Now, under pressure from government, employees, media, partners, financiers, and customers, mainstream corporate brands are incorporating sustainability into their strategies. This is about realizing the benefits of being a first mover in sustainability, ameliorating risk, and enhancing desirability, and for some, a belief in the importance of doing the right thing; of corporate brands taking on a central role in addressing the fundamental problems that confront the world (Golob et al., 2020). However, whatever the motivations, corporate brands need also to deliver financially. In doing so, tensions can emerge. Decisions to embrace more sustainable packaging for example, might at least in the short-term, imply greater costs, while better wages for those in a supply chain might impinge on margins. Yet there is no inherent contradiction between doing the right thing and performance, because good choices connected to sustainability and purpose also contribute to corporate brand equity, by making organizations more appealing places to work, safer places to invest in, and more reliable partners to work with and by having more trustworthy brands that meet consumer needs (Gast et al., 2020).

As the chapters in this section demonstrate, the way strong corporate brands are built is changing due to technology, societal pressures, and the imperatives of thinking and acting sustainably. This is an issue for managers and the way they work together with their stakeholders to co-create new and sustainable experiences, but it should also be a concern for the academic community and the conducting of research. How to plan and execute brand strategies, the role of artificial intelligence and approaches to innovation and sustainability all need to be better understood. As Kurtmollaiev et al. show, these are interconnected issues. They note that while digital innovation may secure and strengthen the functional positioning of a brand and may contribute to the elaboration of brands with experiential concepts, on its own, it does not significantly impact perceived brand innovativeness. Rather, it is social innovation, which has a more emotional appeal that fosters perceptions of innovation (five times as much). Yet, this is not an argument for ignoring digital because they go on to observe that digital innovation can increase the chances of succeeding with social innovation and 'using digital innovation to generate and diffuse social innovations is a much better strategy than either implementing digital solutions for merely operational and commercial reasons or prioritising social innovation alone.'

Overall, the temptation to compartmentalize different aspects of corporate brand building should be rejected in favour of emphasizing the flows that link them. The connections outlined in this commentary on these chapters provide rich food for thought (honey and condensed milk) and suggest opportunities for researchers to further explore these themes by looking at:

- How corporate brand planning and brand models can adapt to a volatile and uncertain world, where brand managers hold less influence
- How artificial intelligence can be used in an ethical way to build brands
- How artificial intelligence can help build better human-centric insights
- The uses of artificial intelligence in managing customer relationships and strengthening brand equity – especially in the creation of emotional benefits
- The relationship between commercial and sustainable innovation and how this can best be managed to deliver positive experiences
- Whether consumers and other stakeholders can be effective in co-creating innovations in sustainability
- How to measure the impact of sustainability investments on different stakeholders
- The impacts of an integrated triple bottom line approach on corporate brand equity

# References

Freedman, L. (2013). *Strategy: A history*. Oxford: Oxford University Press.
Gast, A., Illanes, P., Probst, N., Schaninger, B., & Simpson, B. (2020, April 22). Purpose: Shifting from why to how. *McKinsey Quarterly*. Retrieved from https://www.mckinsey.com/%7E/media/McKinsey/Business%20Functions/Organization/Our%20Insights/Purpose%20Shifting%20from%20why%20to%20how/Purpose-Shifting-from-why-to-how-v3.pdf

Globescan. (2020, August 12). *The 2020 globescan/sustainability leaders survey*. Retrieved from https://globescan.com/2020-sustainability-leaders-report/

Golob, U., Davies, M. A. P., Kernstock, J., & Powell, S. M. (2020). Trending topics plus future challenges and opportunities in brand management. *Journal of Brand Management, 27*, 123–129.

Hatch, M. J. (1999). Exploring the empty spaces of organizing: How improvisational jazz helps redescribe organizational structure. *Organization Studies, 20*(1), 75–100.

Iglesias, O., Landgraf, P., Ind, N., Markovic, S., & Koporcic, N. (2020). Corporate brand identity co-creation in business-to-business contexts. *Industrial Marketing Management, 85*, 32–43.

Keller, K. L. (1993). Conceptualizing, measuring, and managing customer-based brand equity. *Journal of Marketing*, 1–22.

Michel, G. (2017). From brand identity to polysemous brands: Commentary on "Performing identities: Processes of brand and stakeholder identity co-construction". *Journal of Business Research, 70*, 453–455.

Minaya, E. (2020, May 26). *The forbes corporate responders. New ranking of nation's top employers' responses to pandemic*. Retrieved from www.forbes.com

Nadella, S. (2017). Hit refresh. The quest to rediscover Microsoft's soul and imagine a better future for everyone. London: William Collins.

Younger, R., Mayer, C., & Eccles, R. (2020). *Enacting purpose within the modern corporation: A framework for boards of directors*. Oxford: EPI.

# D

# Polysemic corporate brand narratives

Connecting internal and external communities

# 16
# INTEGRATING MULTIPLE VOICES WHEN CRAFTING A CORPORATE BRAND NARRATIVE

*Paul A. Argenti*

## 1. Introduction

As of 2020, there were 4.57 billion active internet users, and the average internet user spent 6 hours and 43 minutes a day online.[1] Compare this with only 50 years ago, when the internet was just an idea. While people are online today, they are not just passively ingesting content; they are writing and engaging with each other. This reality has changed the way that companies must interact with the outside world. In a hyperconnected world, incorporating a variety of voices into company narratives, brands, and communication strategies has become ever more important. This hyperconnected world has changed how people form expectations and opinions of companies and products.[2] As such, companies and brands need to match this changed reality with an updated strategy.

Therefore, the way we communicate about the corporate brand in the 21st century is through messages built in collaboration with our key constituencies, including customers, employees, investors, and communities. Gone are the days when brand identity creation and control laid exclusively in the hands of the marketing executives and those in the C-suite; rather, co-creation is now the name of the game. At Airbnb, for example, customers are both those who offer their homes and those who travel. Their story of 'belong anywhere' relies on Airbnb's interaction with both customer types.[3] They've launched their customer stories pages so that when potential customers think 'Airbnb,' they think of local stories, waiting to be told.[4] The Danish company, LEGO is another example. Their reinvention[5] was based on a concept they refer to as 'camping with customers.' Anne Flemmert Jensen, senior director of the company's Global Insights group, has a team that spent all of its time travelling around the world, speaking with children and families, and participating in their daily lives. Even sports teams have learned the power of such co creation as we can see in Manchester City FCs 'co-creation' site.[6],[7] This developed together with a new club badge and in conjunction with supporters through focus groups, surveys, and user testing.

These changes, moreover, have forced companies to confront the long-held notion that a monolithic communications strategy is best. Rather, while alignment is imperative on foundational issues such as core values and basic strategy, companies now must become more comfortable with the notion of a polysemous brand,[8] one in which the brand can evolve to fit the needs of its various constituencies and is expressed in various flavours. Thus, 'brand consistency' takes on new meaning in today's world. A company and its leadership serve as wellsprings for foundational mission, but brand identity is amorphous thanks to the contributions of a much wider world.

This chapter will propose that the way to develop a resonant message is by engaging constituencies directly and that direct engagement and strong messaging will lead to a stronger brand image and, ultimately, a stronger bottom line.[9],[10],[11] We will start with a look at the frameworks, or building blocks, that underpin our thinking about corporate brand. Next, we will look at hyperconnected brands, process benefits, insights-based benefits, consumer engagement techniques, employee and community engagement, and, finally, measurement.

## 2. The frameworks: understanding the building blocks

Before examining the how and why of creating narratives, we first must be clear on *how* to think strategically about communication. The Corporate Communication Strategy framework is iterative and centred around who the firm hopes will receive the message.[12] While communication starts with the firm, messages should be informed by what constituencies a firm is communicating with. After constituencies receive the message, they respond back to the corporation. The corporation receives this response and updates their next message based on the response.

We will use this Corporate Communication Strategy Framework to structure our approach to building an effective, resonant narrative and communication strategy (Table 16.1). The framework starts with organization character. This is internally created, and is perceived by customers, communities, investors, and employees who all communicate among each other. Company reputation is the aggregate of those perceptions (Figure 16.1):[13]

*Company character* refers to those aspects of brand that the company is able to directly control or create; these include tangible artifacts, from logos to messages to websites to buildings. An organization's character is best communicated through stories and narratives. They engender emotions from those on the receiving end and stick with the audience. Companies further develop these artifacts with feedback from core constituencies and continually iterate on them in a cycle of feedback.

Just as a company analyses how constituencies respond to a message, they can analyse how constituencies respond to and further develop artifacts. Are the artifacts that we are releasing resonating in the way we would expect? Are our constituencies responding positively to our character? Does our representation of ourselves match what constituencies perceive to be the truth? Federal Express' change to FedEx is a great example of this point. Similar to the Corporate Communication Strategy Framework itself, this iterative process ensures that there is alignment between what a corporation says or does and how customers understand it.

### *Narrative*

One of the most effective ways to communicate who you are as a company is through your narrative. Stories are sticky. They engender emotions. They develop connections. If you were writing a novel, you develop the character, in this case your company, and weave together a plausible and persuasive story about how it fits into your broader context: your competitors, your customers, and their experience. Moreover, research shows that our brains think of companies as people, with personalities and emotions. Companies must create a narrative for a company that harnesses that power.[14] People have feelings about the character, and they resonate with the character as you would in a movie. These examples help to illustrate this point:

*Integrating multiple voices*

*Table 16.1* Key definitions for understanding the building blocks of corporate communication

| Term | Definition | Question[17] |
|---|---|---|
| Company character and identity | Consists of a company's defining attributes such as its people, products, and services | Who are you? |
| Corporate brand | A brand that spans an entire company; conveys an organization's character; conveys expectations of what the company will deliver in terms of products, services, and customer experience; can be aspirational | What do you say you are and want to be? |
| Narrative | The story an organization creates to describe its reason for being and how it fits into its broader context | What is your story, and how does it connect to your message and corporate brand? |
| Image | A reflection of an organization's identity and its corporate brand; the organization as seen from the viewpoint of *one constituency*; depending on which constituency is involved, an organization can have many different images | What do constituencies think of you and who you tell them you are? |
| Reputation | The collective representation of multiple constituencies' images of a company, built up over time and based on a company's identity programs, its performance, and how constituencies have perceived its behaviour; earned by the company | What do all constituencies think of who you tell them you are and what you've done? |

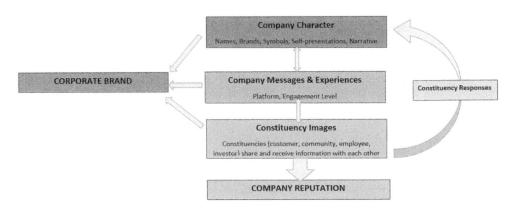

*Figure 16.1* The ongoing exchange of ideas and information that builds company brand, character, and reputation

- Warby Parker, a direct-to-consumer eyewear company, has a textbook narrative.
    o *It frames a problem*: Glasses are too expensive. Warby's narrative goes into as much detail as describing one of the founders losing their glasses on a backpacking trip and forgoing them for a semester of graduate school because of the expense. We can all imagine ourselves there. We immediately have empathy for the character and the situation.

- o  *It then describes the villain*: The eyewear industry dominated by one company that 'keeps prices artificially high while reaping huge profits from consumers who have no other options.'[15]
- o  *It presents our heroes*: the founders of Warby Parker
- o  *It delivers a solution*: An easy, fun way to shop for affordable stylish eyewear

- Innocent Juice, a UK-based drink company, distils its narrative down to 109 words: 'We started innocent in 1999 after selling our smoothies at a music festival. We put up a big sign asking people if they thought we should give up our jobs to make smoothies, and put a bin saying "Yes" and a bin saying "No" in front of the stall. Then we got people to vote with their empties. At the end of the weekend, the "Yes" bin was full, so we resigned from our jobs the next day and got cracking. Since then we've started making coconut water, juice and kids' stuff, in our quest to make natural, delicious, healthy drinks that help people live well and die old.'[16] In those short words, we have a sense for who the heroes are and what they want to achieve through the company.

*Corporate brand* spans the entire company and conveys expectations of what the company will deliver. A corporate brand can be aspirational. It should answer the question 'Who do you say you are and want to be?' In many ways, a corporate brand is a type of shortcut, or mental heuristic. The goal is to activate a set of accurate and positive associations when a constituency thinks of a brand; a company engages in corporate branding when it markets the company itself as a brand.

*Image*, on the other hand, is how individual constituencies perceive and experience a company's artifacts, brand, narrative, and self-presentations. A company has a vast array of constituencies: customers, communities, employees, shareholders, suppliers, etc. Within those constituencies, there are further cleavages. Customers, for example, might be segmented based on their identity and needs. Gen-Zers with pocket change from their parents will react differently to a message than young professionals with disposable income.

Inevitably, the differences between how various constituencies perceive these artifacts can vary.

For example, shareholders and the community might perceive a piece of information or message differently based on their context. These images do not exist in isolation. Images between constituencies interact. How employees, for example, perceive an organization's character can affect how customers perceive an organization's character. This is because perceived image does not just come from artifacts released by an organization. Incorporating constituencies' perspectives in messaging produces a more resonant image.

*Reputation* is an aggregate of images across consistencies. While companies create a brand, they earn a reputation. A brand is directly crafted by a company, whether through a logo, message, or set of artifacts. Companies have direct control over their brand. Reputation, while affected by a company's actions, is not a direct reflection of any one message or one artifact that a company has released. It is the collective perceptions of a vast and diverse set of constituencies. While companies can hope that what they release to the universe will lead to a specific reputation, it is ultimately largely out of their hands. A firm thus has control over its actions and representations, but it does not have control over other organizations' actions that affect constituencies images or how constituencies perceive a firm's actions.

While complete alignment between a company's self-presentations, constituents' perception, and reality is not always possible, companies benefit from tracking the extent to which its brand identity fluctuates between different settings and should aim to ensure that its core values and missions are not lost in the various ways in which brand can represent itself. Homogeneity in brand representation is certainly not the aim, but consistency around core concepts creates more positive brand awareness and associations. This is critical in cultivating the highest levels of awareness and most favourable associations. Such cohesiveness of brand image supports consumer recall of brands, and consequently, builds brand awareness and positive associations.[18]

In fact, the point of the conversation with different constituencies is ensuring alignment between what is in various constituencies' heads and how an organization represents itself. It creates a type of cognitive dissonance without it. This discomfort translates to less trust and less positive brand associations. The most effective companies with enduring brands build memory structures within consumers' heads. Given the limited capacity of consumers to remember, memory structures are fragile. Building strong memory structures requires consistency, persistence, and reputation.[19] Moreover, strong brands capitalize on their heritage too, as research from Bain describes, 'avoid eroding memory structures.' Take for example Coca-Cola. It's Spencerian script logo was developed in 1886, the contoured bottle from 1916, and distinct red colour from 1920. Coca-Cola has leveraged its history to be an enduring brand in customers' psyches.[20]

Today, however, consistency becomes more challenging given how many companies are organized. Marketing is siloed from communications which is siloed from product. This produces chinks in the armour of what should be consistent communication from one company.

This silo mentality is certainly not intentional – it stems from reporting structure.

Given the size and complexity of organizations, it is therefore critical to develop a one-company culture. At its core, a one-company culture is one where all employees are aligned to act in the organization's best interest. A simple test is whether everyone in an organization – from the CEO to the fresh out of school assistant – can answer the question 'What is our strategy?' Developing a one-company culture is the most effective way to ensure consistency across an organization's communications.[21]

In each framework, arrows are all bi-directional, indicating that not only does information flow both ways, but it must in order to ensure that companies and brands are responding to what they hear from constituencies. Social media and new online technologies have amplified the importance of these arrows. What was once a more purposeful exchange has become second nature, particularly for digital natives. As a result, companies must ensure that they are harnessing the power of social media and online technologies as they craft their brand and communicate with constituencies. The question for companies today is how to apply this foundational framework to an increasingly online and connected world. Companies and their constituents are increasingly online; brands must be there too.

## 3. Hyperconnected brands

We are living in a hyperconnected world and firms must engage as such. As a result, bringing voices into brand narratives is critical. We can all conjure up the images from the hit American television program *Mad Men* – an executive sitting in a smoky room drinking rye whiskey and attempting to craft a company's brand. In the middle of the 20th century, crafting a brand was left to experts. Today, successful brands are crafted iteratively and with the help of constituents.

Take for example make-up company Glossier. Launched in 2014, it is now valued at more than 1.2 billion USD.[22] This company started as a blog *Into the Gloss* with 1.5 million passionate readers, focused on accessible products with authentic reviews. From there, founder Emily Weiss launched a customer-centric make up and skincare brand. Products were developed based on what she and her team had heard on their website and tested using their core group of followers.

Glossier took customer voice so seriously that early on, it developed a Slack channel where its top 100 customers could interact with each other and company representatives, they invited New York-based customers to its offices for pizza and rosé,[23] and crowdsourced ideas for attributes of its new facewash.[24]

It is easier to create a brand *with* stakeholders through online channels. Why? Because a brand lives outside of an organization once it is released online. With the increased connectivity, we not only see our conception of a brand broaden, but also lines around ownership and creation blur.[25] The risk in creating a brand image divorced from constituent perspectives is inconsistency. One small mistake can quickly become magnified on the internet; there is no putting the genie back in the bottle.

Branding has thus become blurred. Companies cannot fully control a message or narrative because so much branded content lives beside constituent-generated content.[26] It can even be hijacked by consumers and firm partners.[27] Historically, brands provided consumers with expectations around what the company would deliver. Image comes from constituency impressions of a company's behaviour, and reputation is the aggregate of those perceptions.

Now, brands continue to create expectations, *but so do constituents* (Figure 16.2). 'A brand is no longer what we tell the consumer it is – it is what consumers tell each other it is,' according to Scott Cook of Intuit, a global financial technology company known for such products as Turbo Tax and QuickBooks.

Authority has thus shifted. The centre of control and influence has changed from institutions to communities of individuals.

As a result, communications today is about *collaborating with* rather than *controlling* constituencies. Individuals are no longer primarily getting their information from companies; they are getting it from those around them and online.

As customers access more information on brands, expectations, on average, rise.

In a study of American and Indian consumers, researchers found that high involvement customers, or customers who accessed more electronic word-of-mouth about two categories of products, hotel services and cell phones, had higher expectations about the brands. In other words, the more electronic word-of-mouth a customer accesses, the higher the expectations around a brand. This indicates that what stakeholders hear from each other about brands certainly affects how stakeholders perceive brands.[28] Online sentiment and constituency perspectives become increasingly important to manage given who customers trust.

For example, customers are more likely to trust peers. Eighty-three percent of consumers said that they completely trust the recommendation of a friend or family member. Two thirds say they trust online reviews.[29] This means that companies *must* engage thoughtfully with constituencies online.

Constituencies are talking about brands and shaping narratives in public, online spaces. The question is not *does* it happen, but will firms passively stand by, or become active partners.

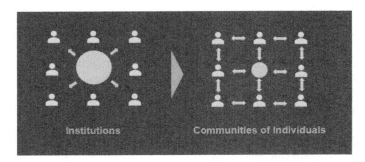

*Figure 16.2* The number of constituencies with which an institution must engage and the authority they exert of them has shifted considerably

Firms have the opportunity and imperative to shape the process by which constituents engage online. Companies set up guardrails and structures that support the narrative and overall goals of the brand. Rather than aiming for full control over constituencies, research suggests that an authentic dialogue is more effective for customers[30] and the objective should move from control to influence. Establishing a structure makes it more likely that the process moves in a positive way for firms.

## 4. Benefits of engagement

### 4.1 Process benefits

Establishing dialogues and engaging constituencies in the conversation about your brand has benefits beyond improved consistency. Simply the process of engaging constituencies has benefits to the firm. For example, engaging with constituents improves the relationship between the brand and the individual. Research has shown that social media interaction with a brand, through a Facebook page, for example, generates a more positive relationship between brands and consumers. This effect is particularly pronounced when the brand takes on human-like qualities. M&Ms, for example, have created human-like cartoon characters to represent the M&Ms brand. These human-like qualities engender more interest from consumers and make consumers feel closer to a brand.[31] This could look like consumers perceiving brands as 'warm,' 'kind,' and 'silly' or as 'cold' or 'snobby.'

Engaging in a dialogue with consumers is part of building customer relationships. Customer relationships, separate from any insights that these relationships might bring, are valuable. Some would argue that these customer relationships could even be viewed as more valuable than brands themselves. A study of M&A transactions showed that assessed brand value was declining, while the value of customer relationships was increasing. This is not to say that brands are not valuable or important; the strongest brands will leverage their strong customer relationships to increase their brand equity. 'Customers still value strong brands, but what constitutes a strong brand is more dependent on customers' direct experience with an offering, and their relationship with the firm producing it.'[32] Getting customers to engage verbally with brands can build loyalty. Starbucks, for example, manipulated attitudes about the brand using language.[33]

Kevin Lane Keller, expert on brands and brand value, articulates four stages of brand development: identity, meaning, response, and relationships. By fostering engagement between brands and constituents, relationships are formed. These relationships encourage brand resonance, a critical component of building brand value.[34]

Brand resonance itself has four components: behavioural loyalty, attitudinal attachment, sense of community, and active engagement. Engagement, through the form of conversations, supports the latter two components. Improved relationships with brands increases loyalty, customer retention, and ultimately, customer lifetime value.

Relationships between brand and consumers can also serve as a buffer against negative narratives that customers might encounter. If a customer has a strong relationship with a brand, they are less likely to heed or be affected by negative messages (i.e., negative reviews) of the brand. This means that establishing strong relationships helps protect companies from outside messages that could work against their desired brand narrative.[35,36]

### 4.2 Insights-based benefits

Beyond process-based benefits, engaging with constituencies produces direct, tangible benefits. Simply put, engagement increases sales. Numerous studies have tracked that high electronic word-of-mouth correlates with sales increases. If you can get people talking about your product and brand, you see higher sales.[37] Companies have already leveraged social media to drive sales. Increasingly, firms are spending more and more on social media. In 2019, Facebook ad revenue approached 70 billion dollars.[38]

Not all online engagement, however, is created equal. Researchers found that higher level customer engagement, like shares or comments on platforms like Facebook, contributed to higher brand equity and value, compared to low engagement activities, such as likes or loves.[39] Beyond sales, companies can use online platforms to engage in 'social listening.' Companies that can successfully aggregate social media and online content can harness it into incredible insights.[40]

Monitoring and aggregating online stakeholder responses can provide insight on product design.

Johnsonville sausage's social media team noticed in their online monitoring that customers were posting about the Keto diet and sausage. Users noted that sausage is great for Keto, but when the Johnsonville team reviewed their own content, they found that their online recipes included bread or pasta. Johnsonville turned to user-generated content to find keto-friendly recipes, asked for permission to share them and created a keto section of their online recipe bank.[41,42]

Online data also allows for the identification of pain points. Many organizations, including large, not-for-profit organizations, use social listening to improve their operations. USPS's intelligence group comes out with a daily report that summarizes all conversations relevant to USPS. From there, the report is distributed out to management departments, who use that to get early insights into potential problems.[43] A McKinsey study argues that shifting customer service interactions online, a more overt application of social listening principles, offers substantial opportunity for savings by shifting customers away from costly call centres.[44]

Monitoring social media channels allows for increased personalization of customer experience. Kimpton Hotels, for example, created a 24/7 'social listening desk' where employees monitor what customers are saying at and about Kimpton hotels. When one guest tweeted that she was feeling under the weather, the desk routed the tweet to the local hotel's front desk, whose employees sent soup to her room. Kimpton has utilized social media effectively to create what they describe as a 'ridiculously personal' experience to bolster its reputation.[45,46]

## 5. Consumer engagement techniques

Companies, knowing that engaging with constituents to develop their communications and narratives not only increases the consistency of their message, but improves their bottom line, are left to determine *how* to best engage with and influence their constituencies. The most effective ways to engage with constituents depends on what aligns with a firm's character and the amount of control a firm wants to exert. Companies should select a portfolio of high, medium, and low-control engagement methods based on their goals.

### 5.1 High-control opportunities

*High-control opportunities to engage* include brand-owned platforms/communities and online events. Brand communities are not new with the advent of the internet; we have seen offline communities thrive and inform how stakeholders engage with brands. For example, look at John Deere's offline communities. It shows how brands take on a life of their own.

Also, look at the seemingly ubiquitous Make America Great Again (MAGA) hat. Five years after the first red hat appeared, the MAGA hat has a life and meaning of its own, beyond simply representing US President Donald Trump. It was even named 'symbol of the year' by Stanford

University's Symbolic Systems group.[47] What started as a symbol of Trump's campaign has become a symbol tied to but not reliant on him. The red hat has now become an international symbol for a culture, set of ideals, and lifestyle. MAGA hats are now worn by those on the far right in other countries. This has grown to represent a staunch and often racialized nationalism in foreign countries.[48] While the Trump campaign might support these usages of the red MAGA hat, the Trump campaign did not originate these representations. Rather, the MAGA hat exists, connected to but with a meaning distinct from Donald Trump's own identity.

Offline communities take on a life of their own, much like online communities. Online communities, however, can be easier to monitor (as long as firms know where to look) because they are accessible to the firm. Online brand communities are increasingly becoming core aspects of not just digitally native, but online firms' strategies, and when well-constructed, can pay dividends.

*My Starbucks Idea*: This is a ten-year online community where customers were invited to submit ideas, have moderated conversations with each other and partners, and ultimately led to offline changes/offerings. Cake pops, splash sticks, and free Wi-Fi all originated through My Starbucks Idea. This platform created opportunities to engage not only with the brand, but also with other constituents, including employees.[49] Beyond actionable changes, My Starbucks Idea as a platform reinforces Starbucks' customer-centric narrative of being a third place for consumers.

*American Express:* 'Established in 1850, American Express has been the most valuable credit card brand for a number of years now. In an effort to grow its business with small and medium-sized enterprises (SMEs), the company recently set out to create a win-win partnership with these customers. By helping independent retailers attract more shoppers, Amex would benefit from the increase in transaction volume. To make it happen, the company initiated the Open Forum, a virtual platform for small business owners to connect with Amex and one another. Open Forum works as a catalyst that helps small businesses become more successful. The platform features various educational resources and tools. As a result, a growing community of SMEs has come to appreciate Amex not just as a credit card company, but as an advisor. The culmination of this effort is Small Business Saturday, an annual event held the weekend after Thanksgiving to help small businesses claim their share of the US holiday rush. The Small Business Saturday Facebook page attracted more than one million followers in less than three weeks, now totaling at well over three million. Even President Obama tweeted about the event repeatedly, encouraging fellow Americans to "shop small."'[50]

Brand-owned online brand communities (OBCs) are engagement opportunities where brands are able to engage, learn, and grow with their core customers. Brands establish the architecture of the community. Who gets to participate? How do they engage? What is the feedback mechanism?

What is the impact: targeted, high quality feedback on a largely brand-defined set of topics? Engagement is driven by image and brand congruity. OBCs that have high levels of perceived fit with customer self-image and values have higher levels of engagement.[51]

A well-run OBC comes with many benefits to firms such as:

- Reduced customer support costs – 49% of businesses with online communities report cost savings of 10% to 25% annually.[52]
- Boosted brand exposure and credibility, making it easier to sell without selling.[53]
- 67% of businesses use their communities for insights on new products or services and features.[54]
- Heightened engagement and better customer retention.[55]
- Customers spend more when they engage in an OBC.[56]

But how can you get it right? Marketing scholar Susan Fournier writes, 'Executing community requires an organization-wide commitment and a willingness to work across functional boundaries. It takes the boldness to reexamine everything from company values to organizational design. And it takes the fortitude to meet people on their own terms, cede control, and accept conflict as part of the package.'[57] In short, it's really challenging. Companies need to create an environment where consumers are motivated and excited to share, while also ensuring that they feel heard. This requires thoughtful planning and a long-term strategy with an eye on how the OBC creates value not just for the company, but also for the customer.

## 5.2 *Medium control opportunities*

In developing high-performing OBCs, companies should do extensive research to ensure fit and find ways to bring in high levels of personalization. Medium control opportunities to engage are characterized as brands having moderate, but not full control over engagement methods. To examine this, we will look at ambassadors and influencers posting either to social media or blogs.

Brands today can choose to engage with brand ambassadors or influencers who occupy the space between a firm and the customer. Brand ambassadors or influencers post on online spaces, sharing their experience with a brand. Ambassadors and influencers are often a personification of the narrative and image a company has worked to produce. For example, when Patagonia's founder Yvon Chouinard announced two new Patagonia ambassadors, he said 'they personify Patagonia's core values by reflecting the soul of their sport, leading an uncommon lifestyle, providing insight for innovative product designs and being activists for the environment,' underscoring that ambassadors and influencers are opportunities to tell constituents who companies are.[58]

Ambassadors are influencers selected by companies based on alignment, goals, target audience, and budget. Some of these include micro-influencers – influencers with a follower base between 1,000 and 10,000 – which hold more credibility and authenticity for millennials.[59] It is critical for there to be fit between influencer and the brand.[60] Tressie Lieberman, Vice President, Digital Marketing and Off-Premise at Chipotle, highlights that key to their influencer strategy is 'finding the real fans of the brand' who love the product *first*, and who are influencers *second*.[61] David Dobrick (described as Gen Z's Jimmy Fallon),[62] one influencer Chipotle partners with, has more than 17 million YouTube subscribers, and has partnered in several integrated marketing campaigns with the goal of increasing authentic engagement with the brand. She highlights how critical it is that you find influencers who will display authenticity to find content and messaging that resonates with the public.[63]

Influencers and brand ambassadors have become increasingly present in the past decade, and traction appears to be growing. In a report from Klear:[64]

- Sponsored posts demonstrated a 48% increase of Instagram influencer activity in 2019, a 9% increase from 2018 growth figures.
- Fifty-four percent of all influencer content was created by Millennials aged 25–34.
- Ninety percent of all branded partnerships were with micro-influencers, who have a fanbase of 5,000 to 30,000 followers.

Influencers and brand ambassadors offer firms a moderate level of control. Firms can develop guidance or write into contracts explicit posting and content schedules. This could look like, for a food company, a blogger posting once about using the product, developing and posting two recipes that feature the product, and cross-posting the content on each of their social media channels. It is critical to give influencers flexibility so that they can maintain authenticity. This supercharges the importance of brand congruence with influencers.[65]

Influencers and brand ambassadors, however, represent a medium control avenue because they are people with their own lives and histories, some of which may not be fully congruent with a brand's desired image. We originally defined organizational character as answering the question 'Who are you?' An influencer or brand ambassador answers that question with a human representation of who that brand could be.

Take for example the at-home fitness company Peloton. Peloton considers its instructors to be not just employees but also brand ambassadors. When new instructors are hired, they are introduced to the Peloton community through a series of interviews, shout outs, and endorsements from fellow instructors. They are introduced with a personal story and as a part of Peloton's broader company narrative. Peloton customers engage with instructors beyond through simply streaming their fitness classes. They post on instructors' personal Instagram and Facebook accounts. Peloton supports this by helping instructors craft their brands on and off the screen. Peloton views its relationships with its instructors as synergistic and almost as sub-brands under the larger Peloton umbrella.[66],[67]

This has lots of impact: Customers perceive increased corporate credibility and more positive attitude towards brand-owned posts when they are first exposed to an influencer with product/brand rather than product-only conditions.[68] Campaign effectiveness varies depending on the platform and match.[69] Ambassadors and influencers offer opportunities for companies to build richer and more consistent and resonant brand narratives.

## 5.3 Low-control opportunities

*Low-control opportunities to engage* include reviews and posts on third-party platforms and social media brand advocates. These lower-control opportunities to engage are double-edged swords – they are frequently the most authentic, but also the most challenging to manage. Examples include platforms like Facebook, Twitter, TripAdvisor, or Reddit. Firms can be tagged on social media, and conversations stemmed by brand advocates. Where some of the richest engagement can come because it is conversations directly with customers. It also comes with the highest stakes because it happens on an online public setting where all potential future customers, stakeholders, investors, employees can see it.

Brand advocates are critical in influencing others – they see substantially higher levels of trust from others and are intrinsically motivated to share about a brand or product.[70] Companies can work to cultivate brand advocates through building brand trust and brand identification.[71] Strong brand advocates can have an outsized impact on the brand because of how responsive customers are to e-WOM, positive reviews, and referrals. Cultivating brand love seems to be the most direct route to garnering brand advocates. Brand love is built through customer satisfaction, customer value, and relationship marketing.[72]

One example of executing a brand love strategy is Brooklinen, referred to as 'the internet's favourite sheets.' Early on, Brooklinen's founders dropped off sets of sheets and handwritten notes to influencers, inviting them to try their sheets.[73] Brooklinen continued its influencer strategy in 2017 when it used dog influencers for a campaign.[74] Brooklinen's strategy has yielded dividends; it has over 50,000 five-star reviews[75] and has grown its revenue to over $100 million in 2019, with 40% coming from repeat customers.[76]

Online platforms should be viewed as a dialogue rather than a microphone. Customers quickly lose interest if they do not feel like they have the opportunity to engage with brands.[77] Carolyn Tisch Blodgett, SVP of Brand and SVP for Global Marketing at Peloton from

2016–2020, says explicitly that people want to have two-way relationships with brands. They do not want to just be spoken to – they want to speak back.[78] Thus, if companies are using customer engagement as a way to develop consistent and resonant messages, they will engage in a dialogue. The danger is viewing social media as 'free marketing,' rather than an opportunity to deeply engage with constituents.

Deciding when to engage on social media can be challenging. John Deere Director of Strategic Public Relations, and architect of Deere's social media strategy, Jen Hartmann likens online conversations to conversations that happen in coffee shops. If you walk into a coffee shop and hear someone complaining about your company or product, you wouldn't step into the conversation and problem-solve. Similarly, she recommends that firms wait to become directly engaged until they are tagged.[79]

The rules shift when a customer is posting a review on your or a third-party website. Best practice is to respond directly to negative reviews with a customer service orientation and offer to bring the conversation offline (you should *not* attempt to refute the review or engage in a drawn-out back and forth).[80] For positive reviews, there is no impact in posting a response. If a firm wants it to be part of their strategy, wait until the review is on the second page. Company responses to positive reviews can negatively affect perceptions of a company or brand. Research supports that excessive involvement can be detrimental.[81,82]

These principals particularly apply when there is a risk that the complaint goes viral, as it did for United Airlines after they damaged a musicians' guitar. The musician wrote a song titled 'United Breaks Guitars' and accumulated 1.5 million views in three days. Researchers found that the most effective way to mitigate the risk of the post going viral is to offer to take the complaint offline, whereas some responses, for example, offering compensation, had the opposite effect.[83] Firms should manage low control avenues by maximizing consistency, listening to customers, and treating online posting as a way to have a conversation, rather than broadcast a message. Brands with strong online narratives and congruence between social media pages and corporate websites are more likely to have consistent e-WOM postings.

Regardless of the portfolio of strategies a firm deploys, engaging consistently and authentically with consumers is key. A recent BCG customer survey shows that customers are looking for more authentic engagement with brands and are put off by sales pitches. This authentic engagement with constituents not only builds awareness and image but also serves as a way for brands to gather information to create a consistent, resonant narrative.[84]

As firms plan messaging and communications strategies, they should come back to the strategic communications framework, and ask:[85]

o   Who are we attempting to reach?
   - Given that, what is the best communication channel?
   - What is the best way to structure the message?
o   What do we want them to do?
o   How have they responded?
o   How must we adjust our message?

## 6. Employee and community engagement

Pushing beyond a consumer lens, firms can and should also engage employees and communities as they develop their narrative and communication strategies. Connectivity creates more opportunity for constituencies to communicate with each other, amplifying the importance of congruent messages and positive relationships. Given how online all constituencies are, it is easier for them to communicate with each other. This sideways communication creates both new and different expectations, and provides more data points for stakeholders to evaluate the brand relative to its original brand promise. Experiences with and from employees create, amplify, or defy narratives that customers and other constituencies have about a brand. And employees are the most trusted group regarding a firm across a variety of topics (Figure 16.3).[86] Firms should leverage this to enhance narratives about their brands.

Beyond cultivating the narrative, employees are closest to consumers, and they have insight into what works. Some of the highest-performing brands have developed explicit processes to ensure that employee perspectives are considered. Alibaba formalized a co-creation process with its employees, where at regular intervals, employees are invited to engage in co-creation. They ideate based on what they are hearing from customers. This not only involves employees in decision-making, but bolsters its reputation as being customer-centric.[87]

Increased levels of news dispersion also make firm treatment of employees and communities a part of a brand. The public is increasingly engaged in following the news. Compared to 2018, 22% more consumers are news consumers and amplifiers, now up to 62%.[88] In an Edelman Trust Barometer survey, 78% of those surveyed said that 'how a company treats its employees is one of the best indicators of its level of trustworthiness,' indicating that the employee narrative is critical to maintaining positive narratives and reputation.[89]

This created trouble for Amazon when, during the COVID-19 crisis, it faced heat for sub-par safety standards. When workers from one warehouse protested, Amazon fired one of the protest leaders. As a result, Amazon faced public criticism[90] and is embroiled in a lawsuit.[91] That

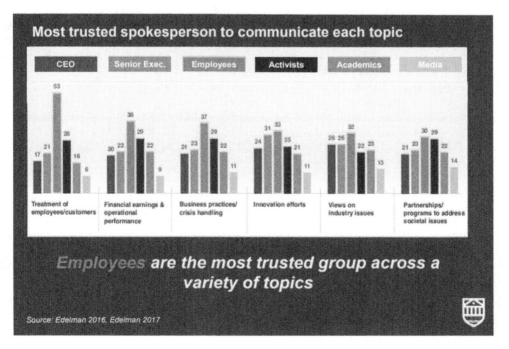

*Figure 16.3* Employees are consistently viewed as the most trustworthy group to speak to a variety of topics

criticism extended to shareholders. At a shareholder call in 2020, shareholders pressed management on employee treatment.[92]

Companies must also ensure that images, messages, and representations align with the community in which the company operates. This ranges from ensuring images used in promotion are consistent with the community, to ensuring that partnerships or placement is in line with a firm's overall image and message. In terms of promotional images, they should represent target constituencies and customers.

Partnerships, images, and messaging represent various artifacts of the firm that help define the character – the images a firm uses, the partnerships it forms, the places it advertises. As such, it is critical for these all to be aligned with the desired brand image for that community.

## 7. Risks and mitigation

Engaging online produces new risks for firms that demand mitigation. One aspect of this is lost control of the conversation: user participation risk. This presents an opportunity for someone to take your brand/product out of its intended context. Someone who may be loosely associated with your brand via online platform is tied to you – how does that impact how others perceive you?

TIKI torches, a 60-year-old company in the US, found itself in trouble when white nationalists marched through the streets in Charlottesville, VA carrying Tiki Torches.[93]

TIKI customers responded (Figure 16.4):[94]

TIKI responded quickly, saying, 'TIKI Brand is not associated in any way with the events that took place in Charlottesville and are deeply saddened and disappointed. We do not support their message or the use of our products in this way. Our products are designed to enhance backyard gatherings and to help family and friends connect with each other at home in their yard,' but for many, TIKI torches continue to be associated with white nationalists. Headlines in Charlottesville have continued to refer to them as 'torch marchers.'[95]

Beyond external factors, some companies launch ill-designed campaigns that provide the opportunity for the public to trash their brands. Take #McDstories,[96] as an example (Figure 16.5, clockwise starting in upper left corner).[97],[98],[99]

There is a higher risk that employees share confidential or compromising information:

o   18% of companies investigated the exposure of confidential, sensitive, or private information posted to a social media sharing site;[100]
o   34% of employers report having reprimanded or fired an employee for something shared online.[101]

*Figure 16.4*   TIKI customers were quick to call out the company after viewing their use during the violence in Charlottesville

*Integrating multiple voices*

*Figure 16.5* Customers tagging #McDstories on Twitter drew attention to times where the company fell far short of its standards

Amazon has attempted to mitigate this risk by developing a tight external communications policy, but it also faced backlash from employees; more than 350 posted a public statement denouncing the policy, along with Amazon's treatment of the environment.[102]

As a result, we see higher expectations around reciprocal engagement. As companies engage more deeply with people online, customers have higher expectations around how much and how companies engage back.[103] And Jen Hartmann cites expectations around reciprocal engagement when John Deere decided to speak out against hatred and discrimination during the Black Lives Matters protests in the US.[104]

This responsiveness is critical to maintain eWOM. Companies should immediately respond to negative tweets, posts, reviews. They build positive affinities when they do so, and have the opportunity to hurt the brand's reputation if they don't.[105] The key, however, is for online engagement to feel authentic. Posting too much has a neutral to negative impact on ROI.[106]

There are also higher expectations around speaking out on values.[107] Millennials have higher expectations around hearing about companies' stances. Stances from CEOs can become tied to the brand. For example, 75% of Millennials report that if a customer base includes millennials, companies should speak out.[108] Increased transparency and expectations around authenticity between brands and constituencies makes this challenging. Speaking out can add or detract from brand value, depending on whether: (1) the issue aligns with the company strategy, (2) a company's ability to meaningfully influence the issue, and (3) the expected stakeholder response.[109]

As companies become increasingly reliant on online conversations for feedback and research, there is a risk that those who are most vocal online are not representative of all customers and stakeholders. Specific personality types are more likely to be active in online conversation. Research has supported that those who are extraverted, open to experiences, or altruistic are more likely to engage online.[110] This indicates that a loud online response is not always indicative of broader constituent sentiment.

Dick's Sporting Goods[111] tightened its gun sale policies and stopped selling assault weapons after the Parkland shooting in 2018. While this spurred a highly negative online response, Dick's stock price increased 20% the following quarter with only a mild negative impact on sales.

Nordstrom and Ivanka Trump[112] offer another example. In 2017, US President Donald Trump blasted Seattle-based retailer Nordstrom for dropping his daughter Ivanka Trump's clothing line.

His tweet produced a 1700% increase in mentions on Twitter and other social media sites, and the valance of tweets shifted from positive to negative. Offline conversation sentiment, as measured by surveys, stayed positive. Ultimately, Nordstrom saw a 2.5% sales increase for the holiday season compared to the previous year

**As companies engage in online communication, mitigating these risks is critical.** First and foremost, the best way to mitigate risk is to ensure that companies put out high quality content.[113] Content should be congruent with the brand and other representations of the company both online and offline. It needs to be well thought-through and executed, and tested among different constituency groups.

- Plan for predictable surprises. While some surprises are truly surprising, many can be expected.[114]
    - *Risk analysis*
        - Risk analysis assembles a team of experts to evaluate potential outcomes of an action or campaign. These experts assign likelihoods and potential impacts of each outcome. This should guide decisions about whether to move forward with an action and how to prepare for potential constituent responses;
        - In 2019, Adidas UK launched a campaign where Twitter users could generate jerseys with their Twitter handle on the back to promote a soon-to-be released Arsenal jersey. Twitter trolls quickly created racist jerseys that flooded Twitter, and Adidas retweeted them. This was eminently predictable – in 2014, the New England Patriots launched a similar effort that produced a similar outcome, as did Microsoft's 2016 Twitter chatbot;[115],[116]
        - The threat of a message hijack should have been recognized, particularly given that this had occurred several times before.
    - *Scenario planning*[117]
        - Scenario planning entails bringing together a creative and knowledgeable group of people to review company strategies, external trends, and potential flashpoints. This group designs potential plausible scenarios, and the broader organization uses these to design preventative or preparatory plans.

Both strategies highlight the need for marketing and communications departments to think critically about a range of potential responses to guide decision-making and planning.

In addition to anticipating predictable surprises, companies can train employees on what to look for and empower them to elevate issues. Unlike an Andon chord, there's no 'stopping' a viral negative campaign. Companies should train employees to proactively respond. Train employees on what communication is consistent with a firm's brand; empower them to take those actions.[118] Firms that have developed a one-company culture are best positioned to have employees who instinctively understand how and when to respond. They develop well-defined guardrails for online engagement with constituents. John Deere credits a robust governance policy for how it has avoided and responded quickly to social media missteps.[119]

## 8. Measurement

Finally, firms are left with determining whether their work is moving the needle. To best evaluate this, they should use both leading and lagging indicators to evaluate their success.

## 8.1 Leading indicators

**Leading indicators** tell the story of work in real-time and focus on process-based metrics. This includes measuring the perceptions that each of the constituencies have with the brand and determining whether they are consistent with what images the firm wants. Qualitatively, this entails such tools as focus groups. For example, when international cosmetics company Coty relaunched Clairol, it relied heavily on focus groups, along with social listening, to design its well-received 'Colour of Confidence' campaign.[120] On the quantitative front, surveys and net promotor scores offer means of tracking sentiment and success. A company like Costco, for example, has an incredibly high NPS, whereas internet providers tend to have low NPSs.[121]

Many tools require some amount of time to pass before impact can be measured. In addition to more advanced tools, firms should use an array of metrics that provide real-time feedback. Donna Hoffman et al. offer a framework for quantifying the impact of social media engagement by analysing each channel's prospective metrics across different goals. They highlight three: brand awareness, brand engagement, and word of mouth. Metrics should look different depending on the platform.[122]

Larger firms may choose to engage with companies that specialize in sentiment tracking and reputation analysis such as Morning Consult or RepTrak. Regardless of the tool, however, firms should ask themselves whether their messages are aligned and consistent with their meanings and representations of the brands.

## 8.2 Lagging indicators

**Lagging indicators** give us a full picture of results, namely how efforts affect overall brand and company value. Increased online presence produces more awareness and consistency, which in turn increases the value of the brand. A McKinsey study confirms that strong digital capabilities and engagement leads to higher conversion rates and higher sales.[123]

Companies also track the financial value of brands, which gives us a lens with which to view the potential upside and impact of conversations with consumers about brands. For example, Interbrand, one of the most popular brand valuation websites, turns to such metrics as role of brand index (RBI) and brand strength,[124] which measures the percentage of the purchase due to a brand, as determined by market research, benchmarking, and 'expert assessment.' Such an approach assists companies in translating that more abstract concept of brand value into bottom-line impact.

## 9. Conclusion

In an increasingly connected world, whether to engage with constituents is no longer the question. Instead, companies must ask how they will engage with constituencies and how they will contend with the challenge of moving from control of constituencies to co-creation with constituencies. By continually engaging with constituents, companies are better primed to enter the iterative process of communication and co-creation, allowing them to keep a finger on the pulse of constituencies' perceptions of the company and the extent to which their own contributions to brand creation are perhaps straying too far from the core mission or values of what a company seeks to achieve. Ultimately, this additional level of engagement positions a company well for today's new age of the democratized brand, an age in which all constituencies hold the potential for some level of brand co-creation and an age that is here for the long hall.

## Notes

1. Clement, J. (2020, June 4). *Digital users worldwide 2020*. Retrieved from www.statista.com/statistics/617136/digital-population-worldwide/#:~:text=Worldwide%20digital%20population%20as%20of%20April%202020&text=Almost%204.57%20billion%20people%20were,percent%20of%20the%20global%20population
2. Swaminathan, V., et al. (2020, March). Branding in a hyperconnected world: Refocusing theories and rethinking boundaries. *Journal of Marketing, 84*(2), 24–46.
3. Airbnb. (2014). *Belong anywhere*. Retrieved from https://blog.atairbnb.com/belong-anywhere/
4. Airbnb community stories. Airbnb Website. Retrieved from www.airbnb.com/community-stories
5. Davis, J. (2017, June 4). How Lego clicked: The super brand that reinvented itself. *The Guardian*. Retrieved from www.theguardian.com/lifeandstyle/2017/jun/04/how-lego-clicked-the-super-brand-that-reinvented-itself
   Co-creation: 5 examples of brands driving consumer-centric innovation. *Vision Critical*. 2016. Retrieved from www.visioncritical.com/blog/5-examples-how-brands-are-using-co-creation
7. Glenday, J. (2016, July 5). It's all about the fans for Manchester City FC's all-new 'co-creation' site. *The Drum*. Retrieved from www.thedrum.com/news/2016/07/05/it-s-all-about-fans-manchester-city-fcs-all-new-co-creation-site
8. https://www-sciencedirect-com.dartmouth.idm.oclc.org/science/article/pii/S0148296316305410
9. Business branding: Bringing strategy to life." *McKinsey Quarterly*, March 2013. Retrieved from www.mckinsey.com/~/media/McKinsey/Business%20Functions/Marketing%20and%20Sales/Our%20Insights/B2B%20Business%20branding/1-McKinsey-Business-Branding-Bringing-Strategy-to-Life_0.pdf
10. Lehmann, S., et al. (2020, May 27). The future of brand strategy: It's time to 'go electric'. *McKinsey*. Retrieved from www.mckinsey.com/business-functions/marketing-and-sales/our-insights/the-future-of-brand-strategy-its-time-to-go-electric
11. Rego, L. L., et al. (2009, November). Consumer-based brand equity and firm risk. *Journal of Marketing, 73*, 47–60.
12. Argenti, P. A. (2016). *Corporate Communication* (7th ed.). McGraw Hill. Print.
13. Argenti, P., & Druckenmiller, B. (2004). Reputation and the corporate brand. *Corporate Reputation Review, 6*, 368–374.
14. Bonchek, M. (2016, March 25). How to build a strategic narrative. *Harvard Business Review*. Retrieved from https://hbr.org/2016/03/how-to-build-a-strategic-narrative
15. Warby, P. *History*. Retrieved from www.warbyparker.com/history
16. Innocent Drinks. *Our story*. Retrieved from www.innocentdrinks.co.uk/us/our-story#
17. Argenti and Druckenmiller (2004).
18. Keller, K. L. (2008). *Strategic brand management: Building, measuring, and managing brand equity* (3rd ed.). Pearson. Print.
19. Brusselmans, G., et al. (2014, March 19). The biggest contributor to brand growth. *Bain and Company*. Retrieved from www.bain.com/insights/the-biggest-contributor-to-brand-growth/
20. Coca-Cola. *125 years of sharing happiness*. Retrieved from www.coca-colacompany.com/content/dam/journey/us/en/our-company/history/coca-cola-a-short-hisotry-125-years-booklet.pdf
21. Argenti, P. (2016, September). Creating a one-company culture: internal strategy for external success. *The European Business Review*. Retrieved from http://amp.tuck.dartmouth.edu/assets/ee/files/Creating_a_One-Company_Culture.pdf
22. www.inc.com/emily-canal/glossier-makeup-skincare-emily-weiss-unicorn-valuation.html
23. Avery, J. (2019, October 22). Glossier: Co-creating a cult brand with a digital community. *Harvard Business School*.
24. Glossier Instagram. (2020, January 29). Retrieved from www.instagram.com/p/B76PgymBV34/
25. Swaminathan (2020).
26. Ibid.
27. Fournier, S., & Avery, J. J. (2010, October 1). *The uninvited brand*. Boston University School of Management Research Paper No. 2010–32. Retrieved from https://ssrn.com/abstract=1963055
28. Krishnamurthy, A., & Kumar, R. (2018). Electronic word-of-mouth and brand image: Exploring the moderating role of involvement through a consumer expectations lens. *Journal of Retailing and Consumer Services, 43*, 149–156.
29. Nielsen. (2015, September). *Global trust in advertising*. Retrieved from www.nielsen.com/wp-content/uploads/sites/3/2019/04/global-trust-in-advertising-report-sept-2015-1.pdf

30  Shao, W., et al. (2015). Brandscapes: Contrasting corporate-generated versus consumer-generated media in the creation of brand meaning. *Marketing Intelligence and Planning, 33*(3), 414–443.
31  Hudson, S., et al. (2016). The influence of social media interactions on consumer-brand relationships: A three-country study of brand perceptions and marketing behaviors. *International Journal of Research Marketing, 33*, 27–41.
32  Binder, C., & Hanssens, D. (2015, April 14). Why strong customer relationships trump powerful brands. *Harvard Business Review*. Retrieved from https://hbr.org/2015/04/why-strong-customer-relationships-trump-powerful-brands
33  Waters, M. (2020, July 12). Why we speak Starbucks. *The Economist*. Retrieved from www.economist.com/1843/2020/07/22/why-we-speak-starbucks
34  Keller (2008).
35  Chang, A., et al. (2013). Online brand community response to negative brand events: The role of group eWOM. *Internet Research, 23*(4), 486–506.
36  Chiou, J., et al. (2013). How negative online information affects consumers' brand evaluation. *Online Information Review, 37*(6), 910–926.
37  Babić Rosario A., et al. (2016, June). The effect of electronic word of mouth on sales: A meta-analytic review of platform, product, and metric factors. *Journal of Marketing Research, 53*(3), 297–318.
38  Clemet, J. (2020, February). Facebook: advertising revenue worldwide 2009–2019. *Statista*. Retrieved from www.statista.com/statistics/271258/facebooks-advertising-revenue-worldwide/
39  Shay, R., & Van Der Horst, M. (2019, March 20). Using brand equity to model ROI for social media marketing. *International Journal on Media Management, 21*(1), 24–44.
40  Yip, P., & Blaclard, V. (2019, December 23). Social listening is revolutionizing new product development. *MIT Sloan Management Review*. Retrieved from https://sloanreview.mit.edu/article/social-listening-is-revolutionizing-new-product-development/
41  How Johnsonville makes the social media sausage. *Convince and Convert Social Pros Podcast*. Retrieved from www.convinceandconvert.com/podcasts/episodes/how-johnsonville-makes-the-social-media-sausage/
42  Johnsonville. *Johnsonville Keto-friendly recipes*. Retrieved from www.johnsonville.com/recipes/healthy-living/keto-friendly.html
43  How the USPS built a social media program that combines content and customer service. *Convince and Covert Social Pros Podcast*. Retrieved from www.convinceandconvert.com/podcasts/episodes/how-the-usps-built-a-social-media-program-that-combines-content-and-customer-service/
44  BenMark, G. (2014, January 1). Why the COO should lead social media customer service. *McKinsey Quarterly*. Retrieved from www.mckinsey.com/business-functions/marketing-and-sales/our-insights/why-the-coo-should-lead-social-media-customer-service
45  Cardona, M. Kimpton's CCO has no reservations about 'Ridiculously Personal' Experiences. *CMO by Adobe*. Retrieved from https://cmo.adobe.com/articles/2017/2/the-cmocom-interview-kathleen-reidenbach-chief-commercial-officer-kimpton-hotels--restaurants.html#gs.atqi2k
46  Sinha, J. (2015, August 3). The risks and rewards of brand personification using social media. *MIT Sloan Management Review*. Retrieved from https://sloanreview.mit.edu/article/the-risks-and-rewards-of-brand-personification-using-social-media/
47  Make America great again hat wins symbolic systems' symbol of the year for 2016. *Stanford News*. January 9, 2017. Retrieved from https://news.stanford.edu/thedish/2017/01/09/make-america-great-again-hat-wins-symbolic-systems-symbol-of-the-year-for-2016/
48  Robins-Early, N. (2019, June 4). How far-right extremists abroad adopted trump's symbols as their own. *Huffington Post*. Retrieved from www.huffpost.com/entry/trump-extremism-maga-hat_n_5ca5075be4b082d775dfca37
49  Fournier, A. (2019, March 20). My Starbucks idea: An open innovation case study. *Braineet*. Retrieved from www.braineet.com/blog/my-starbucks-idea-case-study/
50  Business Branding.
51  Islam, J., et al. (2018). Consumer engagement in online brand communities: A solicitation of congruity theory. *Internet Research, 28*(1), 23–45.
52  Brenner, M. (2019, March 9). 5 examples of brilliant online brand communities. *Content Marketing*. Retrieved from https://marketinginsidergroup.com/content-marketing/5-examples-brilliant-brand-communities-shaping-online-world/
53  Ibid.
54  Ibid.

55. Ibid.
56. DeGroat, B. (2012, February 2). Firms' own social networks better for business than Facebook. *University of Michigan*. Retrieved from https://news.umich.edu/firms-own-social-networks-better-for-business-than-facebook/
57. Fournier, S., & Lee, L. (2009, April). Getting brand communities right. *Harvard Business Review*. Retrieved from https://hbr.org/2009/04/getting-brand-communities-right
58. Hart, L. (2006, June 30). Dane, Emily Jackson join dad as Patagonia Ambassadors. *Outdoor Industry*. Retrieved from https://outdoorindustry.org/press-release/dane-emily-jackson-join-dad-as-patagonia-ambassadors/
59. Sinha, J., & Fung, T. (2018, April 24). The right way to market to millennials. *MIT Sloan Management Review*. Retrieved from https://sloanreview.mit.edu/article/the-right-way-to-market-to-millennials/
60. Breves, P. L., et al. (2019, December 1). The perceived fit between Instagram influencers and the endorsed brand. *Journal of Advertising*. Retrieved from www.journalofadvertisingresearch.com/content/59/4/440.article-info
61. How chipotle got 1 billion views on a single TikTok promotion. *Convince and Convert Social Pros Podcast*. Retrieved from www.convinceandconvert.com/podcasts/episodes/how-chipotle-got-1-billion-views-on-a-single-tiktok-promotion/
62. Tanzer, M. (2020, March 12). Meet David Dobrik, Gen Z's Jimmy Fallon. *WSJ Magazine*. Retrieved from www.wsj.com/articles/david-dobrik-interview-youtube-liza-fallon-vlog-11584028115
63. How chipotle got 1 billion views on a single TikTok promotion.
64. Steimer, S. (2019, December 12). 2019 data and statistics roundup. *American Marketing Association*. Retrieved from www.ama.org/marketing-news/2019-data-and-statistics-roundup/
65. Oriola, S. (2019, August 20). Where influencer marketing goes wrong (and how to fix it). *MIT Sloan Management Review*. Retrieved from https://sloanreview.mit.edu/article/where-influencer-marketing-goes-wrong-and-how-to-fix-it/
66. Wegert, T. (2016, November 10). How content made Peloton the fastest-growing company in New York. *The Content Strategist*. Retrieved from https://contently.com/2016/11/10/peloton-fastest-growing-company/
67. Hart, A. (2017, April 12). For Peloton head marketer Carolyn Tisch Blodgett, it's all about people loving the bike. *Marketing Today Podcast*. Retrieved from www.marketingtodaypodcast.com/41-for-peloton-head-marketer-carolyn-tisch-blodgett-its-all-about-people-loving-the-bike/
68. Jin, V., & Muqaddam, A. (2019). Product placement 2.0: Do brands need influencers, or do influencers need brands? *Journal of Brand Management, 26*(5), 522–537.
69. Hughes, C., et al. (2019, September). Driving brand engagement through online social influencers: An empirical investigation of sponsored blogging campaigns. *Journal of Marketing, 83*(5), 78–96.
70. Argenti, P., & Barnes, C. (2009). Digital strategies for powerful corporate communications, 47–73.
71. Becerra, E., & Badrinarayanan, V. (2013). The influence of brand trust and brand identification on brand evangelism. *Journal of Product & Brand Management*, 271–383.
72. Schreane, T. (2020, February 13). Creating a culture of brand love. *American Marketing Association*. Retrieved from www.ama.org/marketing-news/creating-a-culture-of-brand-love/#:~:text=Brand%20love%20is%20a%20marketing,customer%20value%20and%20relationship%20marketing
73. Best direct-to-consumer social media campaigns. *TalkWalker*. 20 March 2020. Retrieved from www.talkwalker.com/blog/best-direct-to-consumer-dtc-social-media-campaigns
74. Main, S. (2017, September 1). Bedding startup Brooklinen used crowd-sourced images from pet influencers for its new campaign. *Adweek*. Retrieved from www.adweek.com/brand-marketing/bedding-startup-brooklinen-used-crowd-sourced-images-from-pet-influencers-for-its-new-campaign/
75. www.brooklinen.com/
76. LeSavage, H. (2020, March 4). Brooklinen secures $50 million in funding to take its bedding international. *Retail Brew*. Retrieved from www.morningbrew.com/retail/stories/2020/03/04/brooklinen-secures-50-million-funding-take-bedding-international.html
77. Shao (2014).
78. Hart (2017).
79. How a 180-year-old brand made a huge social media pivot. *Convince and Convert Social Pros Podcast*. Retrieved from www.convinceandconvert.com/podcasts/episodes/how-a-180-year-old-brand-made-a-huge-social-media-pivot/
80. Dunn, L., et al. (2020, May 27). Making the best of bad reviews. *Harvard Business Review*. Retrieved from https://hbr.org/2020/05/making-the-best-of-bad-reviews

81  Shay (2019).
82  Manis, K. T., et al. (2020, May). 5 principles for responding to customer reviews. *Harvard Business Review*. Retrieved from https://hbr.org/2020/05/5-principles-for-responding-to-customer-reviews
83  Bower, T. (2020, May). How to keep complaints from spreading. *Harvard Business* Review. Retrieved from https://hbr.org/2020/05/how-to-keep-complaints-from-spreading
84  Zuckerman, N., et al. (2015, July 30). Branded content: Growth for marketers and media companies. *Boston Consulting Group*. Retrieved from www.bcg.com/publications/2015/media-entertainment-branded-content-growth-for-marketers-and-media-companies.aspx
85  Argenti (2016).
86  Edelman. Trust barometer global results. Retrieved from www.slideshare.net/EdelmanInsights/2017-edelman-trust-barometer-global-results-71035413 slide 47
87  Reeves, M., et al. (2015, June). The self tuning enterprise. *Harvard Business Review*. Retrieved from https://hbr.org/2015/06/the-self-tuning-enterprise
88  Edelman. *Trust barometer global report*. Retrieved from www.edelman.com/sites/g/files/aatuss191/files/2019-02/2019_Edelman_Trust_Barometer_Global_Report.pdf slide 17
89  Roach, C. (2019, May 8). Trust and the new employee contract. *Edelman*. Retrieved from www.edelman.com/research/trust-and-new-employee-employer-contract
90  Conger, K. (2020, May 11). Senators want to know if Amazon retaliated against whistle-blowers. *The New York Times*. Retrieved from www.nytimes.com/2020/05/07/technology/amazon-coronavirus-whistleblowers.html?searchResultPosition=18
91  Amazon warehouse employees sue over virus brought home from work. *Bloomberg News*. Retrieved from www.bloomberg.com/news/articles/2020-06-03/amazon-warehouse-employees-sue-over-virus-brought-home-from-work
92  Yohn, D. L. (2020, June 2). Amazon faces a crucible moment with employees. *Forbes*. Retrieved from www.forbes.com/sites/deniselyohn/2020/06/02/amazon-faces-a-crucible-moment-with-employees/#26f1c83f3822
93  Schonbrun, Z. (2017, August 20). Tarnished by Charlottesville, Tiki Torch company tries to move on. *The New York Times*. Retrieved from www.nytimes.com/2017/08/20/business/media/charlottesville-tiki-torch-company.html
94  Verlander, B. (2017, August 12). *Twitter Tweet*. Retrieved from https://twitter.com/Verly32/status/896416816108638209?ref_src=twsrc%5Etfw%7Ctwcamp%5Etweetembed%7Ctwterm%5E896416816108638209%7Ctwgr%5E&ref_url=https%3A%2F%2Fwww.nytimes.com%2F2017%2F08%2F20%2Fbusiness%2Fmedia%2Fcharlottesville-tiki-torch-company.html
95  Coughlin, A. (2019, September 11). Burning questions: Why hasn't the county prosecuted the torch marchers? *C-Ville*. www.c-ville.com/burning-questions-why-county-prosecute-torch-marchers/
96  Hill, K. (2012, January 24). #McDStories: When a hashtag becomes a bashtag. *Forbes*. Retrieved from www.forbes.com/sites/kashmirhill/2012/01/24/mcdstories-when-a-hashtag-becomes-a-bashtag/#10c071caed25
97  Curry, C. (2012, January 24). 'McDialysis? I'm loving it! McDonald's Twitter promo fair. *ABC News*. Retrieved from https://abcnews.go.com/blogs/headlines/2012/01/mcdialysis-im-loving-it-mcdonalds-twitter-promo-fail
98  First Post Staff. (2012, January 26). McDonalds demonstrates how not to use twitter. *First Post*. Retrieved from www.firstpost.com/tech/news-analysis/mcdonalds-demonstrates-how-not-to-use-twitter-2-3593999.html
99  https://twitter.com/healthy_food/status/161974803174146049
100  Goodchild, J. (2010, September 20). Fear of data loss, social media security risks rising. *Computerworld*. Retrieved from www.computerworld.com/article/2749274/fear-of-data-loss--social-media-security-risks-rising.amp.html
101  CareerBuilder Press Release. August 9, 2018. Retrieved from http://press.careerbuilder.com/2018-08-09-More-Than-Half-of-Employers-Have-Found-Content-on-Social-Media-That-Caused-Them-NOT-to-Hire-a-Candidate-According-to-Recent-CareerBuilder-Survey
102  Matsakis, L. (2020, January 27). Defying company policy, over 300 Amazon employees speak put. *Wired*. Retrieved from www.wired.com/story/amazon-employees-protest-communications-policy/
103  Ind, N., et al. (2013, May). Building brands together: Emergence and outcomes of co-creation. *California Management Review*, 55(3), 5–26. doi:10.1525/cmr.2013.55.3.5.
104  Hartmann, J. (2020, June 12). Personal Interview.
105  Chung, S., et al. (2020, March). Financial returns to firms' communication actions on firm-initiated social media: Evidence from Facebook business pages. *Information Systems Research*.

106 Shay (2019).
107 Argenti, P. (2020). When to speak out. Retrieved from https://hbr.org/2020/10/when-should-your-company-speak-up-about-a-social-issue
108 Rogers, J. (2018, November 6). Millennials, your company's response to issues makes every day election day for your brand. *Fleishman Hillard*. Retrieved from https://fleishmanhillard.com/2018/11/reputation-management/companys-response-issues-makes-every-day-election-day-brand/
109 Argenti (2020).
110 Marbach, J., et al. (2019). Customer engagement in online brand communities: The moderating role of personal values. *European Journal of Marketing*, 53(9), 1671–1700.
111 Fay, B., et al. (2019). Deriving value from conversations about your brand. *MIT Sloan Management Review*, Winter.
112 Ibid.
113 Argenti (2020).
114 Watkins, M., & Bazerman, M. (2003, March). Predictable surprises: The disasters you should have seen coming. *Harvard Business Review*.
115 Steinbuch, Y. (2019, July 2). Adidas social media campaign for new Arsenal jersey hijacked by Twitter trolls. *New York Post*. Retrieved from https://nypost.com/2019/07/02/adidas-social-media-campaign-for-new-arsenal-jersey-hijacked-by-twitter-trolls/
116 Manson, P. (2016, March 29). The racist hijacking of Microsoft's chatbot shows how the internet teems with hate. *The Guardian*. Retrieved from www.theguardian.com/world/2016/mar/29/microsoft-tay-tweets-antisemitic-racism
117 Watkins (2003).
118 Keller (2008)
119 Hartmann (2020).
120 Schiffer, J. (2018, March 26). Inside Coty's relaunch of Clairol. *RGA News*. Retrieved from www.rga.com/news/articles/inside-coty-s-relaunch-of-clairol
121 Amaresan, S. (2019, October 2). What is a good net promoter score. *Hubspot*. Retrieved from https://blog.hubspot.com/service/what-is-a-good-net-promoter-score
122 Hoffman, D., & Fodor, M. (2010, October 1). Can you measure the ROI of your social media marketing? *MIT Sloan Management Review*. Retrieved from https://sloanreview.mit.edu/article/can-you-measure-the-roi-of-your-social-media-marketing/
123 Bughin, J. (2015, February 1). Brand success in an era of Digital Darwinusm. *McKinsey Quarterly*. Retrieved from www.mckinsey.com/industries/technology-media-and-telecommunications/our-insights/brand-success-in-an-era-of-digital-darwinism
124 Interbrand Best Global Brands. Methodology. Retrieved from www.interbrand.com/best-brands/best-global-brands/methodology/#:~:text=Interbrand's%20brand%20valuation%20methodology%20seeks,delivering%20even%20further%20growth%20tomorrow

# 17
# CORPORATE BRAND MANAGEMENT AND MULTIPLE VOICES
## Polyphony or cacophony?

*Line Schmeltz and Anna Karina Kjeldsen*

### 1. Introduction

This chapter introduces the notion of (multiple) brand voices and demonstrates how this idea can be utilized in brand management to counter the complexity and multiplicity that brands face today. The overall argument of the chapter is that multiple voices as metaphor, which has until now been applied primarily in organizational theory, offers both a theoretical and practical framework through which today's brand managers can understand and navigate the context, situation, and communication of their brand. The metaphor offers a more dynamic and organic approach to managing brands because it focuses on embracing and orchestrating diverse brand voices. This connects to the more recent approaches to brand management and developments such as co-creation and continuous strategic negotiation of the brand. Thus, this chapter argues that brands which follow this approach should no longer pursue the traditional aims of alignment, control, and stringent 'mono-vocality,' but rather utilize the potential of multivocality in the pursuit of creating brand polyphony.

The chapter further focuses on the *internal* voices of the brand. They are scarcely addressed in current brand management literature, and on the rare occasions that they are, they are most often treated as one, homogenous voice. In organizational studies, on the other hand, the notion of polyphony as a strategic means to hear and negotiate between internal voices from a management perspective is well-known. The idea presented here, then, is that we can transfer the notion of internal polyphony known from organizational studies to the brand management field, and thereby develop and understand brand management in a way that better matches developments and challenges for brand managers of today. Internal stakeholders are just as diverse as are external stakeholders, and, moreover, they are crucial in the overall orchestration of the brand, as they constitute central touchpoints where the brand is communicated and negotiated every day with a wide range of external stakeholders. Through the illustrative case of the National Gallery of Denmark, the chapter will demonstrate why the internal voices need to be approached as diverse and resonant of many and not necessarily matching agendas, and, consequently, how orchestrating them will become key in future brand management.

Finally, the chapter will point out the challenges and opportunities in embracing the notion of branding as orchestration of multiple voices, especially how to reach polyphonic balance, with the ever-present danger of multivocality turning into cacophony.

## 1.1. What is voice?

In order to apply the metaphor of polyphony, a definition of the constituting element of *voice* is necessary. Here, voice is understood as the stakeholders, internal as well as external, who can actively and explicitly express ideas, thoughts, and evaluations by taking part in brand conversations which in turn become part of the construction of the brand. Needless to say, this is a very dynamic process, unstable and inconstant, and in many ways a process like this can be perceived as the opposite or contradiction to the traditional perception of corporate identity and branding with its focus on stringent, ordered and aligned processes. The chapter therefore starts by outlining the historic developments in brand management, which have paved the way for this new approach to brand management.

## 2. Brand management – moving from the Industrial Age to the New Age paradigm

Back in the day, branding was about making sure that farmers could identify which cattle belonged to which farmer (Keller, 2008), so the brand was a very simple way of marking ownership. Ownership, and differentiation, was also absolutely key in the early years of branding as we know it (cf. Heding et al., 2020; Johansen, 2018), but the context in which branding takes place today is in many ways much more complex, dynamic, and contradictory, and simultaneously characterized by multiple stakeholder expectations (cf. Hatch & Schultz, 2010; Ind & Schmidt, 2019; Schmeltz & Kjeldsen, 2016).

Over the last decades, we have consequently witnessed a development in both academia and practice, where the traditional well-known Industrial Age paradigm of corporate branding has been further developed – and even left behind by some (Christodoulides, 2007; Ind, 2015; Schmeltz & Kjeldsen, 2019A). The Industrial Age paradigm focuses on a planned, company-centric, inside-out approach to brand management, where building, maintaining, and communicating a stable brand is pivotal. Communication is understood as transmission of messages strictly aligned with one another so as to create one, corporate brand voice. In many ways, this no longer matches the reality and context in which corporate branding operates. Conversely, in the new age paradigm of corporate branding (Christodoulides, 2007), the focus has changed so that brand management is now seen as ongoing and emergent in both practices and strategies. Branding is network-based and constructivist, and the brand meaning is continuously negotiated between the inside and the outside of the organization. This allows for more stakeholders to take part in the brand process, in other words making room for many diverse voices to become part of the brand (Christodoulides, 2007: Ind, 2015; Schmeltz & Kjeldsen, 2019A). Part of the move from the Industrial Age paradigm to the New Age paradigm of branding is a greater attention to, and recognition of, the importance of relationships in branding rather than repeated, identical brand messages. As noted by Christodoulides (2007, p. 292), 'new age branding is fast moving from a predominant emphasis on marketing communications to primary emphasis on relationships.' The new approach to branding carries considerable implications: companies need to let go of the idea that they can control the brand singlehandedly. It requires more from companies to work with this approach, where they are, admittedly, still responsible for outlining and shaping the identity of the brand, but where they must 'also be willing to accept that brand meaning is constantly negotiated with many other stakeholders' (Iglesias et al., 2013, p. 671). In turn, this leads us back to the importance of creating relationships through branding – or even as the prerequisite for branding – and how a focus on relationship building and support completely changes the role of brand managers. In this new setting, 'communication professionals must manage not only the brand, but more so the relationships forming and shaping the brand' (Schmeltz & Kjeldsen, 2019A: 305).

## 2.1. Brand management – from one voice to multiple voices

The very short explanation of the development of brand management is that we have moved from an understanding of the brand as being of a static nature to that of being of a very dynamic, or perhaps even organic, nature (Iglesias et al., 2013). In other words, we can see the different approaches to corporate branding as being positioned on a continuum covering three positions – from static to dynamic to an organic, networked position. The positions can be understood as both theoretical positionings, but also as indicative of a historically generated development, illustrating that brand management was originally rooted in an economic, functionalistic paradigm based on positivist and rational logics (Esmann Andersen & Antorini, 2013; Johansen, 2018) and that it has later moved into a humanistic, interpretive paradigm, based on constructionist, emotional logics (Johansen, 2018) (although never completely leaving the economic paradigm behind). Moreover, this also reflects how our understanding of communication per se has developed from being a purely transmission-based understanding to allowing for a more interaction- and relation-based understanding, or perhaps even a collaborative perspective, of what communication is (cf. Heath & Bryant, 1992; Putnam & Cheney, 1985). If we follow the rather simple continuum running from static to dynamic and organic, this further ties in with many of the dominant descriptions of corporate branding development as, for example, *waves* (cf. Hatch & Schultz, 2008; Schultz et al., 2005), with the idea of *schools of brand management* (cf. Ind & Schmidt, 2019; Schmidt & Redler, 2018), with *brand approaches as linked to theoretical underpinnings* (see e.g., Heding et al., 2020) with perspectives on branding or *brand metaphors* (see e.g., Esmann Andersen & Antorini, 2013) and with *brand eras* (Merz et al., 2009). Figure 17.1 illustrates how the development of the categorizations and conceptualizations of brand management can be compared and connected across theoretical contributions to the notions of static,

| Represented by: | Static | | Dynamic | | | Organic & networked |
|---|---|---|---|---|---|---|
| Schultz, Antorini & Csaba, 2005; Hatch & Schultz, 2008 | First wave of branding (marketing mind-set) | | Second wave of branding (corporate mind-set) | | | Third wave of branding (enterprise mind-set) |
| Ind & Schmidt, 2019; Schmidt & Redler, 2018 | The image school | The behavioral school | The identity school | | The strategic school | The co-creative school |
| Heding, Knudtzen & Bjerre, 2009 | The economic approach | The identity approach | The consumer-based approach | The personality-based approach | The relationship based approach | The community approach | The cultural approach |
| Esmann Andersen & Antorini, 2013 | Marketing-driven | | Relationship driven | | | Open source driven |
| Merz, He & Vargo, 2009 | Brand as identifiers The individual | Brand as functional images Brand as symbolic images | Brand as knowledge Brand as relationship partners Brand as promise | | | Brand as dynamic and social processes |
| | Goods-focus brand era | Value-focus brand era | Relationship-focus brand era | | | Stakeholder-focus brand era |
| Esmann Andersen & Antorini, 2013 | Brand monologue | | Brand dialogue | | | Brand conversations |
| Orientation | Sender-oriented approaches | | Receiver-oriented approaches | | | Network/context-oriented approaches |
| Voice | One voice → Two voices → | | Many voices → | | | Multiple voices → Polyphonic branding |

*Figure 17.1* Brand perspectives related to voice

dynamic, and organic and networked. The latter is said to lean towards enterprise or co-created branding (cf. Gregory, 2007; Hatch & Schultz, 2010; Iglesias et al., 2013; Ind, 2015; Ind et al., 2013; Johansen & Esmann Andersen, 2012; Karmark, 2013)

Figure 17.1 further adds the idea of voices or multivocality to the generally accepted descriptions of how branding has evolved over time, and it can be seen how the metaphor supports and adds a new layer to the descriptions. In the very static, transmission-based view on branding, there is only one acceptable and allowed voice (defined, controlled, and expressed by the organization behind the brand), whereas the more we move towards the dynamic view and the organic, networked view, where communication tends to have a more interactive and collaborative nature, the more voices we need to consider, accept, listen to, and potentially integrate into the brand. Further, it is worth noticing that towards this end of the continuum, voices both inside and outside of the organization are included in the branding process. Thus, the dynamic view, with its focus on constructing and maintaining relationships with stakeholders, calls for more voices to be heard and their opinions to be integrated into brand management and messaging. Ultimately, it can be argued that including multiple voices is an embedded precondition for truly managing a co-created, organic brand. This development marks the relevance of adopting the metaphor of voice and polyphony from organizational studies into brand management, vis-à-vis polyphonic branding which will be discussed and unfolded in this chapter.

## 2.2. Brand co-creation and the metaphor of voice

It is important to note that the metaphor of voice is not new within the field of corporate branding. Over the last decades we have discussed the necessity of alignment in messaging and communication about who the company is, what the company says, and how the company is perceived in order to build and maintain a favourable image or change and repair an unfavourable one (cf. Hatch & Schultz, 2008, 2009). In this connection, speaking with one, consistent corporate brand voice has been seen as a way to strengthen the brand, following the underlying reasoning that the more companies repeat the same messages and demonstrate concord and agreement, the more they solidify and strengthen their corporate brand. But by broadening and extending the metaphor of voice to more voices and polyphony, we can gain a more nuanced understanding of what happens, especially with a co-creative approach to brand management.

The metaphor of voice is thus of particular relevance to the most recent approaches to brand management. Specifically, companies working with branding from a co-creation perspective could potentially benefit from understanding and strategically managing branding as a fusion or an orchestration of voices. Co-creation, originating from scholarly fields such as service science, innovation, and technology management (Galvagno & Dalli, 2014), has gained a solid footing in the fields of both strategic communication in general, where dialogic processes between organization and stakeholders continuously create and develop new shared meanings (Aggerholm, 2018, p. 2) and the field of corporate branding which is of particular interest to this book. As mentioned, the co-creative approach to branding requires that 'organizations to a large extent involve both external and internal stakeholders in an ongoing dynamic process of creating and developing the corporate brand' (Schmeltz & Kjeldsen, 2019A, p. 304). In consequence of understanding and approaching branding in this manner, more than one voice must evidently be taken into consideration and accepted as co-constructing the brand because the goal is for all stakeholders to continuously engage in creating, negotiating, and further developing the corporate brand (Schmeltz & Kjeldsen, 2019A). At times, co-creation can even supersede the initial strategic aims which brand managers had set forth (Iglesias et al., 2013).

## Study as illustrative case, Part 1: how the Danish National Gallery started co-creating, and thus opened up their brand to their external audiences

In 2011, the Danish National Gallery embarked on a branding process, which they called 'From Institution to Brancasttx1d.' The process included changing its name from the Danish National Gallery/Statens Museum for Kunst to the abbreviation SMK. The name change marked a big shift in the Gallery's brand identity and consequently brand communication reflecting the wish of the Gallery to change its image among current visitors, but also, and perhaps more importantly, among non-visitors. The Gallery's communication department had conducted extensive research and carried out several brand and customer analyses revealing that the Gallery was perceived as being old, fusty, and somewhat boring. On top of that, the market research also revealed that the museum presumably failed in connecting with all the stakeholders that it wanted to – the traditional museum visitor was catered for, but as a public museum, the Gallery has an obligation to cater for all members of Danish society, and it became clear that this was not the case. The head of communication was greatly inspired by recent developments within corporate branding and its move away from the very planned, sender-oriented communication to focusing on the receiver and even letting the receivers take part in, and actually co-construct, brand messages. This new approach served as the starting point for a new way of communicating about the corporate brand – a move from transmission to dialogue, interaction, and co-creation.

The first step in the museum's brand co-creation process was to invite both users and non-users of the museum to co-create the meaning of the Gallery's new name, the acronym SMK. For this purpose, the campaign 'What is SMK to you?' was launched, where both regular visitors and non-visitors could offer their own interpretation of what the acronym SMK meant to them and submit their suggestions. All suggestions were displayed as part of an exhibition at the museum towards the end of the campaign. Suggestions as to what SMK meant to people included everything from *Spreading Fine Art* to *Dust, Mould and Sculls* (translated from Danish where the words obviously matched the acronym of SMK) revealing quite diverse perceptions of the Gallery. The campaign itself was, however, highly successful and marked a turn in the museums' communication with its stakeholders: the external stakeholders were given the opportunity to have a brand voice – and they took it.

Based on the learning and input generated through the campaign, SMK continued working on developing their brand through co-creation with stakeholders, external as well as internal. It soon turned out, however, that co-creating with internal stakeholders and giving them a brand voice was much more complicated than initially expected.

*Source: The illustrative case is based on Schmeltz & Kjeldsen, 2019A, 2019B.*

### 3. The origin of the metaphor of voice and polyphony

The term *polyphony* derives from Greek and means 'many sounds.' Polyphony originally relates to music and orchestration, meaning the co-existence and sound of several different tones, melody lines, or voices – all coming together in polyphonic harmony. The term *polyphony* first appeared as a metaphor in the work of literary critic and philosopher Mikhail Bakhtin who, in his study of Dostoyevsky's novels, suggested that they consisted of, and included, many different voices each having its own world view and point of departure, and that they were voices 'that combine, but do not merge, into the unity of an event' (Bakhtin, 1984, p. 208). The notion of polyphony has later been adopted by, and applied in, organizational studies for example by Hazen (1993), who further developed the notion so as to include the many voices and their different discourses that together constitute an organization. Further, as stated by Kornberger et al. (2006), applying the metaphor of polyphony as a way of understanding organizations allows us to also include the silent voices in our organizational analyses, as the metaphor implies that polyphony is always present in an organization even though, in some cases, we can only hear one, dominant voice or discourse. An important point in polyphony studies is, then, that even though the polyphony may be nearly drowned out by the dominant voice, the other voices, will still be present, even if they are quiet (Carter et al., 2003). The transfer of the metaphor from the literary world to organizational studies seems quite straightforward (albeit some scholars do not see the transfer as being overly successful, cf. Letiche, 2010), as it aligns with other dominant thoughts on the role of, and relationship between, organization, language, and discourse in organizational studies, as for example *discourse* as represented by Foucault (1972) and Weick's *sensemaking in organizations* (1995). The latter explains how collective sensemaking plays out in groups who 'interactively create social reality, which subsequently becomes, for example, the organizational reality' (Aggerholm, 2018, p. 1). The notion of collective sensemaking in itself suggests that multiple voices are present in the organization, and Shotter (2008) has also noted that polyphony can be used as a way of 'organizing our thinking in organizational theorizing' (Shotter, 2008, p. 1). Moreover, in her seminal piece, Belova (2010) has further argued that the metaphor is especially applicable to organizational studies when studying the complexity, multiplicity, and ambivalence in relation to identity. Finally, Aggerholm and Thomsen (2015) also see polyphony as a useful framework for studying strategic communication in organizations, and they further underline that polyphony as a design and analytic process can both uncover the many diverse voices of the organization and also the hidden interaction constituting organizations (Aggerholm & Thomsen 2020, p. 174), which managers need to discover, recognize, and navigate.

### 3.1. Transferring polyphony from organizational studies to corporate brand management

Drawing on the original understanding of polyphony as a plurality of voices in novels as presented by Bakhtin, Shotter (2008) argues that the metaphor can move us from a referential-representational perspective on language towards a more relational and processual perspective. Drawing a parallel with corporate brand management, much the same development in perspectives can be detected as illustrated in Figure 17.1. We move from the brand as one voice, i.e., rational, transmission-based branding focusing on representing the brand in the same ways continuously, to the brand as having multiple voices, i.e., relational branding focusing on establishing and strengthening relationships between brand and stakeholders (e.g., as presented by Fournier, 1998) and co-creative branding (cf. Iglesias et al., 2013; Ind, 2015) focusing on the process and on accepting that 'the brand is always becoming' (Ind, 2019).

According to Belova et al. (2008), Bakhtin's notion of polyphony is widely applied in organizational studies in the following two ways: as a textual strategy which relates specifically to research writing, and – more importantly for the field of corporate branding – as an analytical tool or lens through which we can seek to understand organizational practice as a 'multi-centred, non-linear, and intersubjective activity' (Belova et al., 2008, p. 494). Recently, we have also started to see scholars within strategic communication adopting and applying the metaphor of polyphony to their field of research as well. In the *Routledge Handbook of Strategic Communication*, Aggerholm and Thomsen (2015) explain how the general linguistic turn in social sciences and the consequently increasing interest in discursive-oriented studies have helped us understand concepts, traditionally perceived as being purely linguistic concepts, as also being applicable and useful when studying strategic communication. They argue that polyphony constitutes a concept that can be transferred to the field of strategic communication, and as part of that field, we argue it can also be applied to corporate brand management. Parallel to our previous description of the move towards brand co-creation, Aggerholm and Thomsen (2015, p. 175) also note that when applying polyphony to the field of strategic communication, the communication understanding or model changes from the simple transmission model to a more complex, non-linear, processual model characterized by interaction and negotiation between multiple voices.

Table 17.1 demonstrates how a transfer of the metaphor of polyphony from organizational studies to a corporate branding setting seems immediately obvious. The metaphor can be the basis on which to develop a textual strategy for communicating the brand in which polyphony can be used to incorporate and combine the different worldviews represented by different relevant stakeholders. Likewise, polyphony as a metaphor or lens through which to see, analyse and understand the organizational world as 'discursive spaces where heterogeneous and multiple voices engage in a contest for audibility and power' (Belova et al., 2008, p. 493) can also be transferred to the setting of corporate branding. Thereby, we can see, analyse, and understand how the corporate brand is made up of many different voices – also within the organization. Further, the power and potential of the multivocal approach thus lies in connecting multiple internal voices (employees representing different positions in the organization) with multiple external stakeholders (asking different things of the organization). Consequently, by adopting and applying the polyphony metaphor from organizational studies in corporate branding studies and practice, we can allow and make room for more ownership, engagement, and co-creation (strategically) by stakeholders, and thereby create the sought after, 'true' stakeholder dialogue. The metaphor of polyphony is thus considered a metaphor which can help corporate branding connect internal and external audiences strategically, which has proven particularly difficult in a co-creation approach to corporate branding.

As in most other areas of life, easy solutions are hard to find, and this also applies to brand co-creation. Even though the concept sounds very appealing and immediately transferable and applicable to a modern understanding of how communication processes work, there are still a number of potential obstacles when working with this approach. Table 17.2 provides an overview of the pros and cons of working with brand co-creation

## 3.2. The potential of polyphony

Just as Belova et al. (2008) suggest that organizational sensemaking of events is a polyphonic process, this chapter argues that sensemaking of corporate brands is also a polyphonic process vis-à-vis other collective organizational sensemaking processes (Maitlis & Christianson, 2014; Sandberg & Tsoukas, 2015). Consequently, we need to accept and strategically work towards allowing for different voices to be heard and acknowledge that these different voices affect one another, negotiate with one another, and thus continually change, or alter, at least parts of the corporate brand in this collective process where they make sense of the brand. In more detail, polyphony as a component in a co-creative branding strategy can aid brand managers in developing and executing corporate brand messaging that can give voice to and connect internal and external stakeholders by allowing for more than one (brand) voice to be heard.

Table 17.1 Transferring and translating polyphony from organizational studies to corporate branding

| Using polyphony in organizational studies | Using polyphony in corporate branding studies |
| --- | --- |
| Voices and their different discourses constitute the organization. | Voices and their different discourses constitute the brand. |
| Multiple voices are present in the organization. | Multiple voices are present in the brand |
| Silent voices are included in organizational analysis – even when quiet they still play a role in the organization. | Silent voices can be included in brand analysis – even when quiet they still play a role in the brand. |
| Polyphony as design and analytic process can uncover the many diverse voices of the organization. | Polyphony as design and analytic process can uncover the many diverse voices in the brand. |
| Polyphony can be applied as a way of studying complexity, multiplicity, and ambivalence in relation to identity. | Polyphony can be applied as a way of studying complexity, multiplicity, and ambivalence in relation to brand identity. |
| Polyphony as design and analytic process can also uncover the hidden interactions constituting the organization. | Polyphony as design and analytic process can also uncover the hidden interactions constituting the brand. |
| As an analytical tool, polyphony can help us understand organizational practices as multi-centred, intersubjective, non-linear activities. | As an analytical tool, polyphony can help us understand branding as more than simple transmission, but rather as non-linear, processual, complex, and characterized by interaction and negotiation between voices. |
| Polyphony as a metaphor can move us from a referential-representational perspective on language towards a more relational and processual perspective. | Polyphony as a metaphor can move us from a rational, transmission-based understanding of branding with focus on continuously representing the brand in the same way to a more relational, co-creative understanding of branding in which focus is on establishing and strengthening relationships between brand and stakeholders. |
| Polyphony can be applied as a textual strategy specifically related to research writing. | Polyphony can be applied as a textual/rhetorical strategy specifically related to communicating the brand by way of incorporating multiple worldviews represented by stakeholders. |
| The metaphor of polyphony illustrates how the organizational world consists of discursive spaces where many voices compete for being heard and for power. | The metaphor of polyphony illustrates how the brand lives through discursive spaces, vis-à-vis touchpoints, where many voices compete for being heard and for power. |

Table 17.2 Pros and cons of brand co-creation (based on Schmeltz & Kjeldsen, 2019a)

| Pros of co-creation | Cons of co-creation |
| --- | --- |
| Increasing organizational transparency | Lack of involvement |
| Creating stakeholder engagement and loyalty | Loss of ownership and control |
| True stakeholder dialogue | Disharmony in brand identity |
| Connection between all stakeholders – internal as well external | Resistance towards allowing others to be part of and define the brand |

By permitting a multiplicity of voices to play an active part in the continuous negotiations of the corporate brand, the organization supports and embraces the many various perceptions and uses of the brand which exist among different stakeholders. The challenge of combining and balancing multiple voices is of course considerable, as the organization must try to avoid any of the voices dominating the brand or countering one another to an extent where they conflict. Furthermore, and in opposition to prior approaches to brand management, taking a polyphonic approach to branding, might, *in extremis*, mean that the notion of *one* brand identity or *one* brand core, as something stable and central to the brand initially defined by the organization, becomes inapt. In its most radical consequence, the polyphonic approach to branding entails letting go of control and ownership of what the brand is and can become.

From organizational studies (Belova et al., 2008), we can further learn that polyphony as a metaphor can explain and help us understand and make sense of 'organizations as discursive spaces' where there is no 'universally agreed central voice' (Belova et al., 2008, p. 495). Again, corporate brand managers can adopt the metaphor and apply it in the setting of the corporate branding process in which recent approaches suggest that we take a more emergent, less controlled approach in which there is room for different interpretations and understandings of what the brand is, and what it stands for. Just as the organization is a complex arena in which sensemaking unfolds in several different places and between several people simultaneously, so is branding.

Further, polyphony as an approach to brand management offers a way to address the often-conflicting diversity of interests that each brand faces today and the challenge of speaking with several voices at the same time. This has been described as brand *ambidexterity* (Melewar & Nguyen, 2015) or organizational, *strategic ambiguity* (Eisenberg, 1984). By applying the metaphor of polyphony, these diverse interests move from being an outside pressure and expectation placed on the brand and organization to potentially becoming an integral and strategic approach to branding. Again, we find suggestions of the same development and recommendations if we look to organization studies, where Brunsson (1989) has coined such a strategic explication and acceptance of divergent interests as *organizational hypocrisy*. Thus, polyphony enables the brand to embrace conflicting interest vis-à-vis voices, not necessarily to align or bring them to agreement, but to encompass diverse interests which is a challenge that all brands face today.

What further supports the suggestion of applying the polyphony metaphor to corporate brand management is that the metaphor helps us move beyond the notion that it is simply a question of accepting and acknowledging that many different voices can play a vital part in the process (the question of who participates in the process). We can push this even further, as these voices can even play a role on the tactical level as we can adopt their tone of voice, choice of words, etc. (how they speak in the process). This point is also accentuated by Sullivan and McCarthy (2008) in their work on polyphony and organizational truths.

Summing up, the polyphonic view of the organization that we know from organizational studies can be a valuable contribution to the field of brand management. But following this approach, it becomes evident that the role of the brand manager changes considerably when a multivocal approach to branding is applied. This will be discussed in more detail in the next section.

## 4. The role of the brand manager in the polyphonic brand approach

According to Carter et al. (2003, p. 295), polyphony constitutes a basic premise for the organization, and it is a process which the managers will have to accept and manage. If, once again, we transfer the metaphor of polyphony to a corporate branding context, this has several implications for the brand manager and brand management in the organization.

Within organizational theory, when trying to conceptualize the management of voices, the idea of translation has been introduced. Translation is, however, not to be understood in the instrumental manner where focus is on translating correctly from one language to another, but rather on the functional, interpretive approach to translation where the focus is on understanding each other (Kornberger et al., 2006). In a corporate brand management setting, the functional translation would entail that the voices reach consensus and agreement, whereas the interpretive approach would allow that different interpretations, by way of voices, could co-exist. In other words, expecting voices to speak the same language or find a common language may not be achievable, but we can strive towards interpretations that can support a shared realm of understanding between voices, so as to create productive harmony rather than dysfunctional cacophony.

Kornberger et al. (2006) suggest that managers must take upon themselves the role of interpreting and translating between the different voices audible in the organization. They further state that polyphony can be used not only for describing organizational life but also for understanding the management of different voices in the organization. Navigation by translating between voices ensures that diversity in voices is upheld, which is said to enrich organizational life. In other words, 'the role of managers in managing polyphony is to translate these heterogenous discourses by conveying the message with its context and underlying meanings without having to unify or erase differences that enrich organizational life' (Aggerholm & Thomsen, 2015, p. 176). Again, if we transfer this idea to corporate branding, it can help us explain the new role of communication professionals (and brand managers) which is subject to considerable change (Figure 17.2).

The traditional role of the communication professional as the initiator and facilitator of communication (and consequently relationship building) is changing. Notably in companies working with brand co-creation, the role of communication professionals moves towards that of being mediators and negotiators between brand voices – particularly inside the company (Schmeltz & Kjeldsen, 2019a, 2019b). Here, brand managers will face the challenge of managing disagreement, clashes and power struggles between internal voices in a strategically productive way, so as to give room for and orchestrate diversity while at the same time avoiding that the process becomes dysfunctional. Further, it could be argued that the internal orchestration of diverse voices enables a stronger connection with a wider array of external voices. This connection of internal and external voices may have even better chances of succeeding if organizations attempt to recruit employees that represent many different voices. By securing great diversity between internal voices, a better reflection of the diversity of external voices can be realized. Supporting and ensuring internal diversity, by way of different organizational members, may therefore also be a future task of the organization's communication professionals.

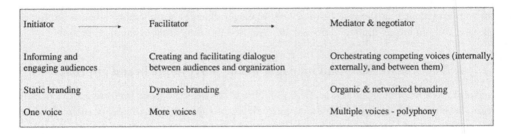

*Figure 17.2* The new role of the communication professionals

## 5. Internal co-creation and polyphony

As argued, we wish to draw particular attention to the internal stakeholders and their voices as constituents of every brand. In most literature on the role that employees and other internal stakeholders play in branding, we see a dominant understanding of internal stakeholders as being more controllable, often even as an instrument which the organization can use to communicate the brand more forcefully and consistently (as we see it within the fields of for example employer branding and employee advocacy). However, as the SMK case in this chapter illustrates, this is perhaps not the most realistic or fruitful presentation of the role that internal stakeholders play in building the brand. Brand co-creation is as much an internal as internal-external process and exchange (Iglesias & Ind, 2020; Schmeltz & Kjeldsen, 2019a) and furthermore, internal stakeholders have just as many and diverse positions as to what the brand is, and could be, as external stakeholders. It follows, that internal stakeholders also represent, not one, but multiple brand voices – and in most organizations, polyphony would arguably already exist, even if we only focused on listening to internal stakeholders alone. Thus, it could be argued that the brand is already internally co-created by the many internal voices, meaning that different internal stakeholder groups negotiate and communicate the brand, vis-à-vis their own positions. In organizational studies, the fact that organizations encompass internal voices of different worldviews and positions has been argued to be a positive or even a prerequisite for healthy development, innovation, and for driving creativity and change (Amabile, 1996; Van Dijk et al., 2012). However, when we look to brand management-theory, this point has largely been ignored and deserves further attention and academic scrutiny.

Allowing for the internal voices to express the diverse views or versions of the brand may not only create more internal development, innovation, etc. By letting the diverse internal voices of the brand be heard, the organization is better prepared for meeting and embracing the diversity of voices outside of the brand. Internal polyphony thus acts as a mirror of the external polyphony, and from a communication point of view, this would enhance and support the exchange and understanding between internal and external stakeholders in the co-creation of the brand.

## 6. Implications of working with polyphonic branding

The metaphor of polyphony clearly has high explanatory power in terms of describing the processes taking place between company, brand, and stakeholders through various branding touchpoints. However, the metaphor also aids us in understanding aspects in relation to the many examples of corporate branding that do not play out as expected. Importantly, polyphony can also take the shape of cacophony, for example in the event that critical voices also take part in the brand discussion. Critical voices should be understood not only as voices that are critical toward the brand *per se*, but perhaps more importantly voices belonging to prominent stakeholders who are not in agreement as to what the brand is. But cacophony could also arise if the many voices communicating the brand move in directions that are either too far from one another, or in conflict, in which case the balance and necessary harmony of the many diverse voices is threatened. In other words, we need to pay attention to what happens when voices collide. When focusing specifically on internal stakeholders, we learn, as already mentioned, that they are much more complex than just one, homogenous group. Moreover, to employees multivocality may be seen as giving them power, but this can, arguably, also make them feel overwhelmed by the associated responsibility. Having a voice also adds expectations that you use it.

In the following, a number of other, potential implications of the multivocal approach to brand management identified in the literature will be discussed, still with a particular focus on the internal stakeholders.

## 6.1. Lack of interplay and dialogue between voices

It is important to note that even though we acknowledge that many different voices take part and play a role in organizational and branding processes, the metaphor cannot help us predict or determine whether these voices actually enter into dialogue with one another. Sometimes they do, sometimes they do not. When entering into dialogue and reaching consensus, which could be desirable in both organizational and branding processes, we could see polyphony as displaying harmony. Likewise, in the event that voices do not enter into dialogue or do not agree, i.e., are disharmonious, polyphony could potentially lead to cacophony where the corporate brand comes across as being every which way and perhaps even self-contradictory. However, it should be noted that even though dialogue and a resulting consensus between voices might seem immediately attractive, it is perhaps also quite unrealistic to achieve just that. Perhaps we need to recognize that voices will always discuss, negotiate, and thus continuously change brand meaning if the brand is to stay alive and relevant to many.

## 6.2. Orchestration by harmonizing or balancing voices

An interesting discussion that naturally follows from allowing and accepting numerous stakeholders as brand authors or voices of the brand is the question of *how much* polyphony a brand can accommodate. In other words: how much polyphony should a company allow for in their brand expression before they risk creating a cacophony of fragmented, and potentially even conflicting, sounds? First, this could be perceived as a matter of harmonizing, i.e., keeping the multiple voices within a shared chord, as argued by van Ruler (2005). Here the solution is to maintain polyphonic harmony, while still allowing for improvisation, organic co-development and brand challenge, by making sure that the voices still build on, or refer to, so-called compatible zones of meaning. Second, it could be seen as a matter of balancing, where the company behind the brand will always hold more power through its voices than the other, external voices. Accepting the proposition that the company will always be representative of the strongest voices, would for some mean that polyphony can never really play out and unfold its strategic potential. However, we see polyphony as allowing for more voices to be heard, but not necessarily distributing power equally between voices, as this depends on how much power the organization is willing to relinquish. The polyphonic brand may then be managed through strategically balancing the array of diverse voices in relation to the ever-changing situation and context of the brand.

## 6.3. Strategic listening becomes even more important

In terms of translation between voices, Kornberger et al. (2006) further underline the importance of the skill of listening. In a brand management setting, listening is also critical, especially when opening up for more voices to participate in brand communication: brand communities, brand tribes, etc., are just a few examples of sites where voices loudly express their interpretation of the brand and actively and explicitly engage in discussion and negotiation about what the brand is. An important task for the brand manager here is also to attempt to understand the 'language' of other voices and to find a way to navigate, sometimes conflicting, voices in a manner that does not necessarily unify voices, but which reconciles or incorporates them.

## 6.4. The risk of territorializing

As we are zooming in on the internal stakeholders, specifically the notion of *territorializing* (Ind & Bjerke, 2007) must be considered. The term covers how battles for power and domain show themselves through the different internal voices, as these voices come from people who hold, or can be trying to gain, legitimacy and power in the organization. In other words, they try to renegotiate power and positioning in the organization by way of using their brand voices (Schmeltz & Kjeldsen, 2019A). Adopting the multivocal approach can both be used as a reason to address this and find common ground (positively), but it may also set fire to ongoing, hidden, or unsurfaced conflicts (with negative effects).

## 6.5. Strategizing together

A final point to be addressed is the challenge of following a fluid, ever-changing brand strategy. When organizations allow for all stakeholders to have a voice and let those voices be part of the brand voice, it inevitably becomes quite challenging for companies to pursue a set strategy, as most traditional business models often strongly prescribe. The question thus is who controls the strategy. Co-creative and polyphonic branding definitely calls for an approach to strategizing which sees the strategy not as a set document containing rigidly designed goals to pursue (Mintzberg, 1994; Weick et al., 2005), but rather as a more emergent and organic process which constantly changes in reflection of both internal and external stakeholders' expectations, preferences, and inputs through their voices. Co-creation inevitably leads to co-controlling. And along those lines, managing a brand instead becomes a matter of continuous branding.

## 7. Voices in action: brand touchpoints

As intriguing as a conceptualization of how to transfer a concept from one theoretical field to another is, it still needs to be further explored how, in this case the metaphor of voices, can be not only theoretically applied, but also how the metaphor can have practical implications and relevance as well. Figure 17.3 sums up the implications of implementing polyphonic branding applying an internal, an in-between, and an external management focus, respectively.

The concept of multivocality and its underlying metaphor of many voices and polyphony can be operationalized in connection with co-creation through so-called brand touchpoints (Batey, 2008; Iglesias & Bonet, 2012). Brand touchpoints can be defined as the decisive points

*Figure 17.3* Implications of polyphony on brand management

| *Internal management focus* | *Co-creational/in-between focus* | *External management focus* |
| --- | --- | --- |
| Listening to, embracing, and translating diverse internal voices, i.e., internal co-creation | Orchestrating: harmonizing or balancing voices | Listening to, embracing, and translating diverse external voices, i.e., external co-creation |
| | Connecting internal and external voices | |
| Recruiting for polyphony | Strategically casting of employees for meeting/mirroring diverse external voices | Locating diverse voices and networks of voices co-creating the brand |
| | Touchpoints as spaces for co-creation | |
| | Incorporating and combining different worldviews represented by different stakeholders in brand messaging | |

of co-creation where 'the external stakeholders are in contact with, and also interact with, the brand, either directly or indirectly' (Schmeltz & Kjeldsen, 2019A, p. 308), and examples include advertising, marketing, online communication, frontline employees, etc. The general idea so far has been that the touchpoints which the company can be said to control should preferably be based on a shared understanding of the brand among internal stakeholders (Thelander & Säwe, 2015), or that as a very minimum the internal voices must communicate by way of compatible zones of meaning (Schmeltz & Kjeldsen, 2019a; van Ruler, 2005). Through the metaphor of polyphony, the ideal of complete consensus among internal stakeholders is no longer as prevalent, as polyphony and including many voices, who may or may not agree on brand meaning, to a greater extent (at best) produces compatible zones of meaning. If such compatible zones of meaning are established, then brand managers subsequently need to consider how to actually manage, or orchestrate, these kinds of touchpoints. Establishing compatible zones of meaning is evidently a daunting task for brand managers working strategically with brand co-creation and polyphony, and, once again, we need to pay special attention to internal stakeholders who can have just as much difficulty establishing those zones as can external stakeholders. The second part of the case of the Danish National Gallery illustrates this in more detail.

## Study as illustrative case, Part 2: the many internal voices in the Danish National Gallery – the delicate balance between polyphony and cacophony

From a theoretical point of view, a public sector organization such as the Danish National Gallery lends itself particularly well to brand co-creation processes. First of all, a public sector organization can benefit from the co-creation approach to building its brand, as a public sector organization, by definition, is owned by everybody in society. In this case, every citizen in Denmark has a stake in the Gallery. Moreover, being owned by everybody also means that the organization has a strong potential for creating close connections with these stakeholders, and the direct engagement with citizens is further supported by the organization's democratically driven responsibilities. The other side of the coin is that public organizations, such as SMK, are often also characterized by more restrictions, rules, and regulations than private sector organizations (Fredriksson & Pallas, 2016). They do not have the same degree of freedom, and what is unquestionably most important for the illustrative case in this chapter, they are often comprised of very diverse employee groups, which can lead to complex power relations and power struggles. Through Part 2 of the case of SMK, we will now illustrate how such structures may carry over into brand co-creation processes where the aim is to hear all the voices of the organization.

Following the immediate success of the rebranding campaign of the Danish National Gallery as SMK among external stakeholders, the museum found, much to its own surprise, that working with and engaging internal stakeholders actually turned out be much more of a challenge than external stakeholders. At first, one should think that it would be relatively easy to engage internal stakeholders as they should be interested in having a voice and a say in what their organization is and should be. The challenge turned out to be, however, that the internal stakeholders were so diverse and represented so many different communicational practices that were far from seeing eye-to-eye as to what SMK is, or should be. So, even though the many communicative actors (curators, researchers, educators, artists, management, communication professionals, etc.) all had communicational areas of practice (knowledge communication, pedagogical communication, management communication, marketing communication, corporate communication) the result of hearing and allowing for internal voices to be present in the brand resulted in what could be termed cacophony rather than polyphony.

In more detail, a qualitative analysis of the Gallery's communication identified no less than six different internal voices, and hence six different perceived identities, which could potentially be reflective of how identity was constantly negotiated – perhaps even battled – and expressed in different ways by different organizational members. These six voices, *the organizational voice, the corporate voice, the marketing voice, the user voice, the institutional voice*, and *the expert voice* were distinctly different both in their choice of communicational style, terminology, and in their tone of voice.

The very interesting point here is that all voices were actually communicating to the same external audiences. The great challenge for the Gallery, then, was how to unite all these voices in a manner that would create polyphony instead of cacophony. When entering into discussions about how this could be done, it soon became clear that the many different voices were informed or created not only by organizational members' different perceptions of their own organization, but to a great extent also by underlying, internal power struggles. The polyphony of voices thus revealed not only a willingness from organizational members to contribute with their story as to who their organization was, but that they also used their voices to negotiate about the SMK identity internally, to territorialize, and to fight unresolved battles between departments and professional areas of communicative practices. In other words, many internal stakeholders used brand communication aimed at external audiences to solidify their own position in the organization and re-negotiate power with other internal stakeholders.

The case illustrates how, in practice, the promises and the potential of having multiple voices expressing a much more nuanced, accurate, and interesting picture of what the organizational brand is can turn out to be quite challenging. Applying the metaphor of multiple voices to brand management, in particular brand co-creation, on the one hand holds great potential, but on the other hand, it also requires a lot from the organization and its members. The power balance may shift inside the organization when all internal stakeholders are invited to be an active part of the brand voice. Moreover, multivocal corporate branding may also lead to internal stakeholders being asked to share their power and control, sometimes change their work processes and perhaps even re-evaluate how they see their own profession and its role in the organization. This can be seen as a both healthy and productive exercise for the organization, which can ultimately strengthen the corporate brand. But it does require a lot from the organization and its members, and it seems fair to assume that in order for an organization to succeed with multivocal corporate branding, it requires that internal members can reach at least a certain level of consensus or compatibility between brand perceptions in order to achieve polyphony rather than cacophony.

*Source: The illustrative case is based on Schmeltz & Kjeldsen, 2019A, 2019B.*

*Figure 17.4 The brand polyphony continuum*

| Brand polyphony continuum | |
|---|---|
| Low degree of polyphony | High degree of polyphony |
| Brand is managed. | Brand is negotiated. |
| Organization behind brand in some control (company-centric) | Organization behind brand in collaboration (networked, multi-centred, non-linear, and intersubjective) |
| Ideal: Harmony/compatible zones of meaning | Ideal: Absolute polyphony i.e., unrestrained organic development |
| Stable/static brand core + fluid/open conversations of brand in touchpoints | Fluid brand core(s) + and fluid/open conversations of brand in touchpoints |
| Touchpoints are where brand is negotiated. | Touchpoints are local, temporary manifestations of the brand. |
| Most relevant management ability; keeping voices in harmony | Most relevant management ability; listening to, interpreting, and translating voices |
| Danger: Pseudo-polyphony | Danger: Cacophony |

## 8. Polyphonic brand voices: harmony or cacophony?

In order to summarize the theoretical discussion of the metaphor of voices and connect it to the findings of the empirical case study, the chapter concludes by presenting a model illustrating the different modes of voices (from monophony over polyphony to cacophony) combined with the related challenges and opportunities to each of the types, respectively.

Figure 17.4 illustrates that polyphonic branding can take many shapes and thus covers a large scale of variations or degrees of polyphony. Variations run from including a few voices, monophony, between which it is relatively easy to create harmony, but simultaneously the risk of creating pseudo-polyphony increases. At the other end of the spectrum, the high degree of polyphony increases chances of reaping the benefits of co-creation in terms of, for example, creating true stakeholder dialogue and high engagement, but at the same time it carries the risk of creating cacophony, rather than polyphony and harmony between voices. A central task for future co-creative brand managers then is to master the art of orchestrating voices. The brand managers of tomorrow should therefore focus on listening to, interpreting, and translating between voices in order to balance or harmonize – i.e., orchestrate polyphonic harmony.

## References

Aggerholm, H. K. (2018). Cocreation of meaning. In R. L. Heath & W. Johansen (Eds.), *The international encyclopedia of strategic communication* (pp. 1–5). New York: Wiley & Sons. https://doi.org/10.1002/9781119010722.iesc0022

Aggerholm, H. K., & Thomsen, C. (2015). Strategic communication: The role of polyphony in management team meetings. In D. Holzhausen & A. Zerfass (Eds.), *The Routledge handbook of strategic communication* (pp. 172–189). London: Routledge.

Aggerholm, H. K., & Thomsen, C. (2020). Change management and communication in public sector organizations. The Gordian knot of complexity, accountability and legitimacy. In V. Luoma-aho & M. Canel (Eds.), *The handbook of public sector communication* (pp. 197–213). Hoboken, NJ: John Wiley & Sons Inc.

Amabile, T. M. (1996). *Creativity in context: Update to the social psychology of creativity*. London: Routledge.

Bakhtin, M. M. (1984). *Problems of Dostoevsky's poetics.* Minneapolis, MN: University of Minnesota Press. https://doi.org/10.5749/j.ctt22727z1

Batey, M. (2008). *Brand meaning.* London: Routledge.

Belova, O. (2010). Polyphony and the sense of self in flexible organizations. *Scandinavian Journal of Management, 26*(1), 67–76. https://doi.org/10.1016/j.scaman.2009.11.009.

Belova, O., King, I., & Sliwa, M. (2008). Introduction: Polyphony and organization studies: Mikhail Bakhtin and beyond. *Organization Studies, 29*(4), 493–500. https://doi.org/10.1177%2F0170840608088696

Brunsson, N. (1989). *The organization of hypocrisy. Talk, decisions and actions in organizations.* New York: Wiley.

Carter, C., Clegg, S. Hogan, J., & Kornberger, M. (2003). The polyphonic spree: The case of the Liverpool Dockers. *Industrial Relations Journal, 34*(4), 290–304. https://doi.org/10.1111/1468-2338.00276

Christodoulides, G. (2007). Breaking free from the industrial age paradigm of branding. *Journal of Brand Management, 15*(4), 291–293. https://doi.org/10.1057/palgrave.bm.2550134.

Eisenberg, E. M. (1984). Ambiguity as strategy in organizational communication. *Communication Monographs, 51*(3), 227–242. https://doi.org/10.1080/03637758409390197

Esmann Andersen, S., & Antorini, Y. M. (2013). Brand management: Teoretisk introduktion. In K. Eiberg, S. Nørholm Just, E. K. Karlsholt, & S. Møberg Torp (Eds.), *Markedskommunikation i praksis* (pp. 77–91). Frederiksberg: Samfundslitteratur.

Foucault, M. (1972). *The archeology of knowledge and the discourse on language.* New York: Pantheon Books.

Fournier, S. (1998). Consumers and their brands: Developing relationship theory in consumer research. *Journal of Consumer Research, 24*(4), 343–373. https://doi.org/10.1086/209515

Fredriksson, M., & Pallas, J. (2016). Characteristics of public sectors and their consequences for strategic communication. *International Journal of Strategic Communication, 10*(3), 149–152. https://doi.org/10.1080/1553118X.2016.1176572

Galvagno, M., & Dalli, D. (2014). Theory of value co-creation: A systematic literature review. *Managing Service Quality, 24*(6), 643–683. https://doi.org/10.1108/MSQ-09-2013-0187.

Gregory, A. (2007). Involving stakeholders in developing corporate brands: The communication dimension. *Journal of Marketing Management, 23*(1–2), 59–73. https://doi.org/10.1362/026725707X178558

Hatch, M. J., & Schultz, M. (2008). *Taking brand initiative: How companies can align strategy, culture, and identity through corporate branding.* San Francisco, CA: Jossey-Bass.

Hatch, M. J., & Schultz, M. (2009). Of bricks and brands: From corporate to enterprise branding. *Organizational Dynamics, 38*(2), 117–130. https://doi.org/10.1016/j.orgdyn.2009.02.008

Hatch, M. J., & Schultz, M. (2010). Toward a theory of brand co-creation with implications for brand governance. *Journal of Brand Management, 17*(8), 590–604. https://doi.org/10.1057/bm.2010.14.

Hazen, M. A. (1993). Towards polyphonic organization. *Journal of Organizational Change Management, 6*(5), 15–26. https://doi.org/10.1108/09534819310072747.

Heath, R. L., & Bryant, J. (1992). *Human communication theory and research: Concepts, contexts, and challenges.* London: Routledge.

Heding, T., Knudtzen, C., & Bjerre, M. (2020). *Brand management: Mastering research, theory and practice* (3rd ed.). London: Routledge.

Iglesias, O., & Bonet, E. (2012). Persuasive brand management: How managers can influence brand meaning when they are losing control over it. *Journal of Organizational Change Management, 25*(2), 251–264. https://doi.org/10.1108/09534811211213937

Iglesias, O., & Ind, N. (2020). Towards a theory of conscientious corporate brand co-creation: The next key challenge in brand management. *Journal of Brand Management, 27*(6), 710–720. https://doi.org/10.1057/s41262-020-00205-7

Iglesias, O., Ind, N., & Alfaro, M. (2013). The organic view of the brand: A brand value co-creation model. *Journal of Brand Management, 20*(8), 670–688. https://doi.org/10.1057/BM.2013.8

Ind, N. (2019). *Whose brand is it anyways?* Retrieved from http://cocreatingbrands.org/wp-content/uploads/2019/11/Whoise-brand-is-it.pdf

Ind, N. (2015). How participation is changing the practice of managing brands. *Journal of Brand Management, 21*(9), 734–742. https://doi.org/10.1057/bm.2014.35

Ind, N., & Bjerke, R. (2007). *Branding governance: A participatory approach to the brand building process.* New York: Wiley.

Ind, N., Iglesias, O, & Schultz, M. (2013). Building brands together: Emergence and outcomes of co-creation. *California Management Review, 55*(3), 5–26. https://doi.org/10.1525/cmr.2013.55.3.5

Ind, N., & Schmidt, H. J. (2019). *Co-creating brands. Brand management from a co-creative perspective*. London: Bloomsbury.

Johansen, T. S. (2018). Branding/brand management. In R. L. Heath & W. Johansen (Eds.), *The international encyclopedia of strategic communication* (pp. 1–15). New York: Wiley & Sons. https://doi.org/10.1002/9781119010722.iesc0013

Johansen, T. S., & Esmann Andersen, S. (2012). Co-creating ONE: Rethinking integration within communication. *Corporate Communication: An International Journal*, *17*(3), 272–288. https://doi.org/10.1108/13563281211253520

Karmark, E. (2013). Corporate branding and corporate reputation. In C. E. Carroll (ed.). *The handbook of communication and corporate reputation* (pp. 446–459). Chichester: Wiley-Blackwell. https://doi.org/10.1002/9781118335529.ch36

Keller, K. L. (2008). *Strategic brand management: Building, measuring, and managing brand equity* (3rd ed.). Old Tappan: Pearson Education.

Kornberger, M., Clegg, S. R., & Carter, C. (2006). Rethinking polyphonic organization: Managing as discursive practice. *Scandinavian Journal of Management*, *22*(1), 3–30. https://doi.org/10.1016/j.scaman.2005.05.004

Letiche, H. (2010). Polyphony and its other. *Organization Studies*, *31*(3), 261–277. https://doi.org/10.1177%2F0170840609357386

Maitlis, S., & Christianson, M. (2014). Sensemaking in organizations: Taking stock and moving forward. *Academy of Management Annals*, *8*(1), 57–125. http://dx.doi.org/10.1080/19416520.2014.873177

Melewar, T. C., & Nguyen, B. (2015). Five areas to advance branding theory and practice. *Journal of Brand Management*, *21*(9), 758–769. https://doi.org/10.1057/bm.2014.31

Merz, M. A., He, Y., & Vargo, S. L. (2009). The evolving brand logic: A service-dominant logic perspective. *Journal of the Academy of Marketing Science*, *37*, 328–344. https://doi.org/10.1007/s11747-009-0143-3

Mintzberg, H. (1994). The fall and rise of strategic planning. *Harvard Business Review*, *72*(1). 107–114. https://hbr.org/1994/01/the-fall-and-rise-of-strategic-planning

Putnam, L. L., & Cheney, G. (1985). Organizational communication: Historical development and future directions. In T. W. Denson (Ed.), *Speech communication in the twentieth century* (pp. 13–56). Carbondale, IL: Southern Illinois University Press.

Sandberg, J., & Tsoukas, H. (2015). Making sense of the sensemaking perspective: Its constituents, limitations, and opportunities for further development. *Journal of Organizational Behavior*, *36*(1), 6–32. https://doi.org/10.1002/job.1937

Schmeltz, L., & Kjeldsen, A. K. (2016). Naming as strategic communication: Understanding corporate name change through an integrative framework encompassing branding, identity and institutional theory. *International Journal of Strategic Communication*, *10*(4), 309–331. https://doi.org/10.1080/1553118X.2016.1179194

Schmeltz, L., & Kjeldsen, A. K. (2019a). Co-creating polyphony or cacophony? A case study of a public organization's brand co-creation process and the challenge of orchestrating multiple internal voices. *Journal of Brand Management*, *26*(3), 304–316. https://doi.org/10.1057/s41262-018-0124-2

Schmeltz, L., & Kjeldsen, A. K. (2019b). The case of SMK – Co-creation in the context of the Danish National Gallery. In N. Ind & H. J. Schmidt (Eds.), *Co-creating brands. Brand management from a co-creative perspective* (pp. 257–263). London: Bloomsbury.

Schmidt, H. J., & Redler, J. (2018). How diverse is corporate brand management research? Comparing schools of corporate brand management with approaches to corporate strategy. *Journal of Product and Brand Management*, *27*(2), 185–202. https://doi.org/10.1108/JPBM-05-2017-1473

Schultz, M., Antorini, Y. M., & Csaba, F. F. (2005). *Corporate branding, purpose/people/process: Towards the second wave of corporate branding*. Copenhagen: Copenhagen Business School Press.

Shotter, J. (2008). Dialogism and polyphony in organizing theorizing in organization studies: Action guiding anticipations and the continuous creation of novelty. *Organization Studies*, *29*(4), 501–524. https://doi.org/10.1177%2F0170840608088701

Sullivan, P., & McCarthy, J. (2008). Managing the polyphonic sounds of organizational truths. *Organization Studies*, *29*(4), 525–541. https://doi.org/10.1177%2F0170840608088702

Thelander, Å., & Säwe, F. (2015). The challenge of internal stakeholder support for co-creational branding strategy. *Public Relations Inquiry*, *4*(3), 323–341. https://doi.org/10.1177/2046147X15573882

Van Dijk, H., Van Engen, M. L., & Van Knippenberg, D. (2012). Defying conventional wisdom: A meta-analytical examination of the differences between demographic and job-related diversity relationships with performance. *Organizational Behavior and Human Decision Processes, 119*(1), 38–53. https://doi.org/10.1016/j.obhdp.2012.06.003

Van Ruler, B. (2005). Co-creation of meaning theory. In R. L. Heath (Ed.), *Encyclopaedia of public relations* (pp. 135–138). Los Angeles: Sage.

Weick, K. E. (1995). *Sensemaking in organizations*. Los Angeles, CA: Sage.

Weick, K. E., Sutcliffe, K. M., & Obstfeld, D. (2005). Organizing and the process of sensemaking. *Organization Science, 16*(4), 409–421. https://doi.org/10.1287/orsc.1050.0133

# 18
# POLYSEMIC CORPORATE BRANDING
## Managing the idea

*Alessandra Zamparini, Luca M. Visconti, and Francesco Lurati*

This study was supported by Swiss National Science Foundation (SNSF) under grant number 100018_162733

### 1. Introduction

> The Locarno Film Festival may appear to be a schizophrenic event . . . with many schizophrenic interpretations, because clearly it is an event . . . that has more keys to interpretation. It is an international event for journalists, cultural operators and members of the film industry. It's a national event in terms of big events and showcases the Piazza Grande and happy, festive streets. The fact that Edward Norton and Andy Garcia have walked the red carpet here is of interest to locals and local newspapers, but the *New York Times* doesn't give a damn about that because they have Andy Garcia at home, so they are interested in the quality of the films, new discoveries and so on. . . . With its national economic dimension and national media, it is clearly a national event, but it takes place in Ticino, so the regional aspect is also very important. You can't completely separate all these aspects.
>
> *(Locarno Film Festival marketing employee, interview)*

*Polysemy* refers to the multiple possible meanings a sign conveys which stratify over time, increasing said sign's semantic richness (Vicente & Falkum, 2017). Brands are intrinsically and inescapably polysemic, as their meanings derive from the cumulation of numerous actions and the involvement of varied actants. Brands may intentionally pursue polysemy when they rely upon ambiguity and ambivalence, often embedded in the collective discourses and 'social contradictions' that brands may tackle (Holt, 2004; Holt & Cameron, 2010). Brands may also originate and evolve based on encoders' layered meanings, receivers' agentic interpretations, media's fragmentation, and the plurality of stakeholders concurring to their construction. Over time, multiple voices or authors can contribute in reading and building different brand meanings – a concept often referred to as polyphony (Kjeldsen & Schmeltz, 2022), which links to brand polysemy, as we discuss later in the chapter. However, whatever the source, brand polysemy consists of the very semantic richness of brands (Brown, 2014), resulting from the assemblage of meanings delivered to and/or co-produced with stakeholders (Diamond et al., 2009; Michel,

2017), which 'take their own meanings from and project their own feelings onto the offer' (Brown, 2014, p. 100).

The very word *brand* is polysemic and not univocally understood in different domains, as much as the function of brands may range from ownership being expressed of something (e.g., cattle, patented products) or someone (e.g., slaves, members of brand community; Levy, 2015) to self-identification with a brand (Stokburger-Sauer et al., 2012). Brands are now best understood as complex, multifaceted organic systems (Iglesias & Ind, 2020), and managers often struggle to understand the boundaries of the object they are supposed to manage. People, for their part, often use the word *brand* to define objects they consume and companies they love or hate and even to label their personal identities or social links (Muñiz & O'Guinn, 2001).

Acknowledging that brand polysemy exists is paramount in contemporary brand management for a number of reasons. Consumers and other stakeholders increasingly expect to play an agentic role in brand-meaning construction, which inevitably leads to fractured interpretations of the brand – less a crystallized vehicle of coherent univocal meanings delivered by brand custodians (Kapferer, 2012) and more a emergent result of interactions, dialogue, and co-creational activities between brand managers and stakeholders, as well as within stakeholder communities (Essamri et al., 2019; von Wallpach et al., 2017). Opportunity, as well as the additional need for polysemy, also derives from the fast multiplication of touchpoints, each with its specific affordances and limits in communicating or enabling the construction of the brand (Yoganathan et al., 2019). Finally, brand meanings are susceptible to different interpretations depending on different moments in the brand life cycle and contexts. For most brands, their presence on more globalized markets raises the chance of resonating differently in countries with very different economic, social, and cultural rhythms (Eckhardt, 2015; Ger, 1999), making managers act like 'anthropologists who either seek out the curiosities of the exotic places or who orient to their aspects of common humanity' (Levy, 2015, p. 188).

These reasons also explain why polysemy prominently entered the branding debate, breaking with linear brand models dominated by the 'brand mantra' (Keller, 1999, p. 44) of consistent and coherent brand identity (Balmer & Soenen, 1999), unambiguous personality, and crisp unique selling propositions (Joachimsthaler & Aaker, 2009). Once marketers and corporate storytellers accepted that the meaning of brands was outside their strict control (Csaba & Bengtsson, 2006; Hatch & Schultz, 2009), the 'monoglot' or 'monosphere' of branding (Brown, 2006, p. 64) started to be, at least partially, affected by a rising conscience of instability, de-structuration, and multiplicity in both brand environments and consumer identities (Diamond et al., 2009).

Although 'the monosphere [is] still going strong' (Brown, 2006, p. 64) in corporate brand management – as the resistant notions of brand identity, brand promise, and brand personality confirm – the winds of 'co-creation' led corporate brand managers to start questioning how they could relax the wheel on brand-meaning control and rather benefit from polysemy. With the rise of social media, in line with an increasing visibility and pressure from consumers' interpretations of brands (Muniz & O'Guinn, 2001), corporate brand management models became more open, organic, and co-creational. Corporate brands are now increasingly conceptualized as social processes, whereby brand meanings are created in the conversational space between organizations and their stakeholders (Iglesias & Ind, 2020). Brand identity and brand purpose remain central in this view. However, brand identity is no longer seen as something crystallized (Csaba & Bengtsson, 2006; Michel, 2017; Vallaster & von Wallpach, 2013; von Wallpach et al., 2017) that provides the roots for an enduring monosemic promise or covenant (Balmer, 2012; Kapferer, 2012). Brand identities are instead 'a continually evolving constellation of meanings, constructed through a dialectical process among a multitude of stakeholders in relation to their individual and collective identities' (Essamri et al., 2019, p. 366).

The managerial challenges polysemy prompts are still significant. What is the role of brand managers in polysemic meaning making? Within the scholarly discourse, their role is said to have shifted from 'custodians' (Kapferer, 2012) to 'facilitators' and 'conductors' (Michel, 2017). However, in daily managerial action they still have to harmonize, legitimate, negotiate, and balance the meanings emerging from the multiple interpretations of the brand (Essamri et al., 2019). Literature on co-creation in particular emphasizes the need for managers to relax control and embrace the diversity of brand meanings owned by stakeholders, (Ind et al., 2013) while simultaneously maintaining strategic direction in the dynamic conversations developing with internal and external stakeholders (Hatch & Schultz, 2009). The rationale behind such a conflicting expectation is that the brand's purpose is still to provide an inspirational guide in orchestrating multiple meanings and avoiding disruption (Iglesias et al., 2013). Within the consumer literature, considerable empirical attention has been given to brand communities and members' production of brand meanings (Brown, 2014; Diamond et al., 2009). Yet corporate brand management literature falls shorter in accounting for how brand direction work interacts with stakeholders' meaning appropriation and the production of the brand's semantic building blocks (Essamri et al., 2019; Iglesias & Bonet, 2012). Whether polysemy is a 'source of complexity or richness' (Michel, 2017, p. 454) and how powerful polysemic brands should be managed are still unanswered questions.

In this chapter, it is not our ambition to provide a historical reconstruction or to advance conceptualizations of brand polysemy. Rather, our aim is to disentangle the elements at play and the practical challenges polysemy poses when managing corporate brands. First, we elaborate on what it takes to manage a corporate brand dealing with polysemy; we support our illustration with the visual metaphor of a colour wheel. Second, we provide an example of the challenges polysemy poses to managers through the case of the Locarno Film Festival (LFF) corporate brand. We conclude by discussing the concrete thoughts and managerial trade-offs inherent in polysemic corporate brand management.

## 2. Dealing with polysemy in corporate brand management

In order to discuss how polysemy plays out in corporate brand management today, we need to split the ontological from the phenomenological level. First, the ontological level allows us to capture how managers continue to envision the essence of their brands. In a still large number of cases, managers design for, and propose brands to, stakeholders as monosemic symbols of coherent corporate identities. This approach to branding relies upon a scientific, positivist understanding of brands and brand management that emphasizes consistency and the absence of logical contradictions (Visconti et al., 2020). Market-wise, consumer research on decision-making (Payne et al., 1991) and the elaboration likelihood model (Petty & Cacioppo, 1986) paved the way for understanding that the complexity of 'work' consumers and audiences are likely to undertake diminishes with decreasing involvement and perceived risks. As such, simpler brand messages may better resonate with mass-market products/services and low-involvement contexts. It is no surprise, then, that iconic brands such as Coca Cola or McDonald's are also still privileging monosemy in the way they reach out to target markets and audiences. From an ontological viewpoint, we conclude that brand polysemy remains relatively circumscribed.

Second, the phenomenological level allows us to inspect how each individual stakeholder lives and interprets the brand. Therefore, from the phenomenological viewpoint, we must acknowledge that polysemy exists even for those brands conceptualized and managed under the coherency and stability paradigm. Brands are polysemous because every individual attaches his or her own meanings to the brand. Individual stakeholders may prefer to interpret brands linearly and establish rather passive interactions with brands, elaborating around the clear and

## Polysemic corporate branding

monosemic meanings guided by brands' gatekeepers. Other stakeholders may instead prefer to engage more actively with brands and the co-creational practices of brand meanings. Active brand counterparts are more likely to generate polysemic meanings on their own as their stronger involvement may result in a deeper inspection of the various facets of a brand.

In light of these clarifications, our focus in this chapter is twofold. First, we privilege brand stakeholders' phenomenological, experiential perspective. This choice derives from the simple, yet firm, conviction that what stakeholders eventually understand of, and do with, brands is what really determines a corporate brand's performance. Second, considering that brand stakeholders may have lower/higher interest in playing an active role in brand-meaning manipulation, we especially focus on how corporate brand managers can simultaneously manage brand monosemy (for rather passive stakeholders) and polysemy (for active, participative audiences). In doing so, we dedicate particular treatment to the managerial aspects of the problem, which to date have remained more underexplored.

For this endeavour, we use the visual metaphor of a colour wheel (Figure 18.1) to represent the semantic richness of brand polysemy. A colour wheel is a circular figure portraying different colour hues in a circular shape, generally including primary, secondary, and tertiary colours. Originally invented by Isaac Newton for his experiments in the physics of light, various developments of the wheel are still commonly used in visual arts and design as a tool to shade and combine colours. A number of the wheel's characteristics suggest that it could serve as a useful visualization for the universe of different meanings originating in stakeholder experiences that constitute a brand's polysemy.

First, multiple colours are not sharply divided, with colour hues shading into each other, just as brand meanings do. Meanings associated with the brand weave into each other for the accumulated experience of each stakeholder in time, but also because of the different occasions or

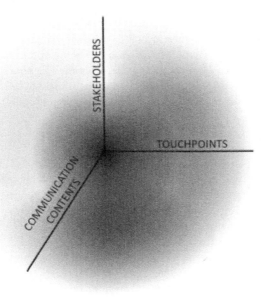

*Figure 18.1* The colour wheel and axes

touchpoints in which a stakeholder connects with the brand. Luxury wine brands provide a typical example. The brand Petrus Pomerol changes meaning throughout a wine lover's lifetime and across consumer segments. For young wine consumers, it is often an unattainable desired wine, but then it becomes the wine of special occasions (e.g., graduation, marriage). For some segments, it is the ultimate in wine expression; for others, it is a symbol of ostentation or social status. Lastly, meanings blur into each other because of the continuous interactions among stakeholders.

Second, some fixed colour combinations are conventionally deemed more harmonious, but they are by no means the only possible ones; contrasting compositions are almost as equally appreciated as harmonious ones. Therefore, the colour wheel suggests that brand meanings originating in stakeholders' polysemic experiences are interpretable as a meaning repertoire, which a brand manager can use as a palette to design brand communications with different degrees of similarity, complementarity, or even contrast.

Third, different hues also show different degrees of intensity in the colour wheel. Even if in most representations hues are less intense in the centre compared to the circumference, if we shift direction (as we do in our figure), we suggest that more intense colours visualize meanings that are close to the original brand purpose, whereas milder colours stand for peripheral meanings. These attached meanings are probably less controlled by brand managers, but – once generated – are subject to incorporation into, and mixing with, other meanings created by other stakeholders or by each stakeholder through different interactions with the brand. They are indeed available for brand managers for original and unusual combinations with more core brand meanings, 'short-term and flexible propositions' allowing for stakeholders' 'constant reinterpretations of meaning and experience' (Iglesias et al., 2013, p. 682).

In sum, the colour wheel figure helps visualize three descriptive aspects of brand polysemy: (1) the multiplicity of meanings associated with the brand; (2) their interweaving, combinations and contrasts; and (3) their closeness to the brand purpose. How do we cope with this complexity when communicating the brand? How can brand managers navigate between direction and stakeholder ownership of multifaceted brand meanings? In order to disentangle some of the challenges involved in this task, we can represent the visual metaphor of the colour wheel not as a flat palette of given multiple meanings, but as a dynamic three-dimensional space. We posit that this space, wherein brand corporate communication takes shape, has no clear boundaries and that polysemy originates and evolves around three main axes: (1) stakeholders, (2) communication contents, and (3) touchpoints. The representation in Figure 18.1 is an artificial freeze frame of a section of the three-dimensional space – a device to facilitate the management of the brand and navigate polysemy without getting lost in it. We now elaborate further on each axis.

## 2.1 Stakeholders

Stakeholders are essential in the origination of a polysemic meaning space for the brand. Indeed, their experience creates additional brand meanings. The propensity to live and co-produce brand polysemy varies across stakeholders, and some stakeholder groups are more prone to accept and produce polysemy compared to others. Consumer culture theorists (Arnould & Thompson, 2005) were the first to call attention to brand polysemy. Consumers are actors in socio-cultural processes of meaning production, in which brands are symbolic inspirations – and cultural tools – for individual and collective identity projects (Arnould & Thompson, 2015; Diamond et al., 2009; Visconti et al., 2020) in both analogic (Belk, 1988) and digital (Belk, 2013) settings. Employees often engage in comparable processes, and organizational studies have increasingly addressed the power of corporate brands as cultural resources for a neo-normative, self-construction of the ideal worker (Müller, 2017). Other stakeholder groups seem, by definition, more reluctant to engage with polysemy, such as investors or regulators, for whom ambiguity is often perceived as a sign of brand weakness.

Individuals simultaneously belonging to different stakeholder groups are frequently more prone to seek polysemy and play with it than individuals clearly belonging to just one stakeholder group. For instance, employees are often also consumers of the brand; therefore, their experience is far richer and multifaceted compared to external consumers. However, it would be misleading to think about propensity to polysemy based exclusively on membership to clear stakeholder groups. The propensity to live the polysemy of the brand may differ according to individuals' personal characteristics or life experiences. In addition, propensity to engage with polysemy is not a dichotomous state; individuals can engage with polysemy to almost infinite degrees – from not at all to a few meanings to the entire semantic richness. Moreover, stakeholders may move in their degree of openness to polysemy over time for various circumstances.

## 2.2 Communication contents

Brand managers and corporate storytellers use the meanings circulating in the wheel to produce different kinds of communication contents (Holt & Cameron, 2010), including some targeted to specific stakeholders (e.g., brand equity values) and some aimed at a more general audience (e.g., corporate identity narratives). Whereas a traditional approach to the brand suggests that communicators seek coherence and alignment in all communication contents (Kapferer, 2012) – for instance, communicating the same identity traits, core tenets, and values across all corporate messages – the co-creational approach suggests that communicators are more like mediators and conductors of user-generated contents (Michel, 2017) than authors. Brand communicators likely need to be authors and facilitators at the same time.

Polysemy can be embraced in certain communication contents – for example, in our metaphor multiple colours can be used and mixed together – in order to provide the brand semantic richness certain stakeholders request (Brown, 2014; Diamond et al., 2009). Thus, through their active experience of the brand, they can appropriate, recombine, and perhaps transform the meanings conveyed through communication contents and input new brand nuances in the polysemy wheel. In other words, brand communicators can control the direction of their work by nurturing polysemy with polysemy.

Yet meanings can also be leveraged to create communication contents that favour a more coherent reading of the brand. Scholars have warned against the risk of lacking consistency when pursuing brand extensions (Broniarczyk & Alba, 1994; Park et al., 1991) and alliances (Lanseng & Olsen, 2012) or in managing brands across channels (Lee & Jeong, 2014; Payne et al., 2017) and geographic markets (Bengtsson et al., 2010; Matthiesen & Phau, 2005). For instance, certain communication contents may focus only on central meanings – the ones closest to the core – to continue reassurances about the brand purpose and its heritage. Other communication contents may instead build heavily on a few new and specific peripheral meanings attached to the brand. We think of communications specifically targeted to particular stakeholder segments and emphasizing innovative brand meanings that may be brought about by new stakeholders or pushed by brand renovation projects and brand extensions engineered by the company. Whether leveraged meanings are core or peripheral, this type of communication content aims at favouring monosemic experiences of the brands, even if only for certain stakeholders at a certain point in time.

## 2.3 Touchpoints

Touchpoints are the third axis organizing and stimulating corporate brand polysemy. We have a few observations about touchpoints that, albeit simple, complement our reasoning about stakeholders and communication contents. First, the multiplication of touchpoints, in principle, may not translate into higher brand polysemy if all touchpoints concur in providing an aligned brand image. However, in practice, touchpoints differ in nature (online, offline, and blended), rate of control (owned, earned, and paid), relational richness (one-to-one, one-to-many, and many-to-many), and objectives (e.g., reach, engagement, and control), which makes achieving brand monosemy more challenging. In addition, if brand touchpoints need to be agile and flexible in order to co-construct solutions (Walsh, 2018), brand polysemy becomes inevitable as co-construction fragments meanings. That being said, the number of touchpoints *per se* does not contribute much in understanding how to deal with polysemy. In fact, although we could assume that stakeholders may develop multiple brand associations while coming into contact with more touchpoints, we could also hypothesize that, after having experienced many meanings attached to the brand across multiple touchpoints, a stakeholder may choose his or her favourite set of brand meanings, thereby becoming a more passive 'consumer' of the brand.

Second, from a practical perspective, it is more relevant to unveil what types of touchpoints are more suitable to convey the semantic richness of the brand, which are more likely to welcome and valorize stakeholders' generated meanings and which tend to satisfy simpler readings of the brand. On the one hand, some touchpoints are immersive and co-creative in their nature, thereby inviting stakeholders' additional meanings. Digital co-creative platforms (Ind et al., 2013) and memorable shopping experiences (Diamond et al., 2009) both provide, and welcome, an extremely rich and varied set of meanings related to the brand (Moisio & Arnould, 2005). On the other hand, other touchpoints are less open to incorporate stakeholder meanings, but they can be extremely effective in providing semantic richness to be appropriated by stakeholders (Iglesias & Bonet, 2012; Müller, 2017). Examples are brand storytelling and brand visual symbols. These kinds of touchpoints remain an important part of the overall brand strategy and, combined with the right content and target stakeholder, may play a useful role in the whole picture.

To summarize, our visual metaphor illustrates three very concrete axes that brand managers need to consider in their dynamic relationships to understand and cope with the polysemic meaning space that forms around the brand. Despite the simplicity with which we tried to illustrate the three axes and their implications, managing brand polysemy is anything but easy. In the following section, we illustrate this complexity using the Locarno Film Festival (LFF) as an example, with a particular focus on the challenges that managers need to overcome when handling such a rich corporate brand.

## 3. Locarno Film Festival case

The Locarno Film Festival is among the oldest film festivals in Europe. It was first held in 1946, and as of 2001, LFF has been awarded the A category by the International Federation of Film Producers Association (FIAPF), ratifying its position in the circuit of the ten most prestigious competitive festivals in the world. It is also a member of the Top Swiss Events, along with events like the Montreux Jazz Festival and Art Basel. Often referred to as 'the smallest among big ones,' it is characterized by a thought-provoking selection of auteur filmmaking and by its vocation to discovery, as testified by the many young directors – including, among others, Stanley Kubrick and Spike Lee – whose careers took off after passing through Locarno. Locarno is also well-known for the informal experience it provides to both artists and festivalgoers, which favours close contact among directors, actors, and the public in a cosy summer night environment. The participatory nature of the LFF festivalscape (Lee et al., 2008) is also due to the lack of permanent festival structures and the distributed presence of LFF around the small city, with screening places borrowed from private and public theatres along with open-air projections and lounges. Among these is the iconic Piazza Grande mega screen, creating a magical atmosphere that 8,000 spectators share with directors presenting their work.

---

**Box 18.1. The festival's DNA (LFF document – courtesy of Locarno Film Festival)**

*The festival's DNA*

- Very well established traditional Swiss Top Event characterized by an optimal balance of culture and glamour
- High cultural reputation, both national and international
- Piazza Grande screening experience: state of the art projections in an outstanding location with special guests every night
- Diversity – from newcomers to global cinema icons
- A festival for the audience and for professionals
- Variety of film selections and categories, and multiple side events
- One of the oldest film festivals worldwide, with a strong tradition of talent discovery
- International educational platform

---

LFF was born as a temporary precarious organization but, like many other festivals in the last decades, eventually developed a managerial structure to organize the event, manage finances and human resources and, last but not least, manage its brand, especially in the relationship with sponsoring partners (Getz, 2010). LFF is now a non-profit association governed by a General Assembly and a Board of Governors. At the executive level, the artistic director and the chief operations officer (COO) report directly to a Board of Directors chaired by the president of the association. The artistic director closely supervises all artistic programming activities together with a distributed team of international collaborators. All activities dedicated to industry professionals (Locarno Pro) and educational activities (Locarno Academy) fall under the artistic director's ultimate responsibility. The COO manages all other departments, including the Branding and Marketing Department. The only function for which the two executives share responsibility is communication.

The LFF brand has been professionally managed since the early 2000s, and a rebranding effort took place in 2006 in order to re-align the disordered visual elements and touchpoints of the brand. In particular, more or less legitimately, various stakeholders and companies had appropriated the leopard print, which constituted one of the festival's visual identity codes, after the statuette shape featuring a leopard. As such, management needed to work carefully on its corporate brand's visual identity in order to protect the brand and the association with sponsoring partners. If the visual brand identity is very defined and highly controlled by LFF management, brand meanings are much more complex. Such complexity stems from the LFF's long history, with multiple brand meanings accumulating over time as well as the personal visions of succeeding artistic directors, and from the incredible growth of the festival itself and its activity domains, attracting an increasingly large number and variety of stakeholders.

Our illustrative case of the LFF brand polysemy builds on a close ethnographic case study (Visconti, 2010) of engagement with the festival, developed in the last five years in the context of a larger study. We interviewed festival managers, employees, and festivalgoers (37 semi-structured interviews) and conducted both non-participant and participant observations of managerial meetings, festival days, and festival public events during the rest of the year (e.g., general assemblies, press conferences, and local ceremonies). This larger study led to several informal interactions with LFF brand managers while our ethnographic experience of the festival enabled us to engage in close contact with a large variety of stakeholders living the LFF brand – not to mention record our own experiences. Finally, we accessed a large number of internal documents (strategic plans, marketing research, presentations to partners) and public messages (press kits, online communication, annual reports).

In the next sections, we provide a brief, yet as detailed as possible, representation of the rich polysemy of the LFF brand. Next, we provide a few examples of how brand managers navigate this complexity when working with communication contents targeted to various stakeholders and through different touchpoints. Our aim with this illustration is not to give a best practice example, but rather to highlight, through the revelatory case of an extremely complex brand, the tensions and challenges at play when addressing a brand's polysemy.

### 3.1 LFF brand polysemy

In our conversations with LFF top management and close collaborators, they summarized the LFF as a space for the creation of 'other collective imaginations.' This purpose originates in the festival's longstanding focus on discovering new talents on the global scene, who will be 'the *grand auteurs* of future cinema' (internal document) and contribute to a novel understanding of the seventh art and, more broadly, of society. The brand purpose is sustained by the longstanding tradition of artistic quality, international orientation, and openness. The vocation for the 'new cinema' is rooted in the origins of the festival that, as the current president often repeats in public speeches, was 'the only place in which you could see movies of the Italian Neorealism and Soviet movies in the fifties.' It is an event described by its historians as a place aiming to evoke 'the true international character of cinema, not imposing a unique artistic model . . . and an anonymous generalist taste' (Volonterio, 1997, p. 63).

As the artistic reputation and the number of festivalgoers continually grew over time, so did the complexity of the event, which is in line with the requirements of the festival sector (Getz, 2010; Troisi et al., 2019). The variety of activities that are an important corollary to the main film competition dramatically increased in number (see Figures 18.2 and 18.3), with reference to events both strictly related to cinema and in other domains:

> Today, the LFF has become an increasingly complex organism, which has grown under the pressure of an increasingly broad spectrum of needs to be met. [These include] not only the basic ones related to the value of films and screenings, but also those related to professionals in the film industry ('Locarno Pro'), education ('Locarno Academy') or childhood ('Locarno Kids'), without forgetting the commercial development activities (Food & Beverage of the Festival), which are essential to provide a comfortable situation for spectators during the event.
>
> (LFF internal strategy document)

*Figure 18.2* LFF activity domains
*Source:* LFF presentation – courtesy of Locarno Film Festival

*Figure 18.3* LFF official sections
*Source:* LFF presentation – courtesy of Locarno Film Festival

Each domain of activity brought new stakeholders to interact with the LFF management and the artistic direction. Each of them contributed new meanings to the LFF brand, as one marketing manager effectively summarized in an interview:

The whole Locarno becomes a festival, it becomes a celebration moment, and so even those who don't necessarily follow the festival, those who follow it even marginally have a way . . . they meet here and they add something.

### 3.2 Managing the LFF brand between ownership and direction

Given the extreme polysemic richness of the LFF brand and the complexity of stakeholder groups, communication contents and touchpoints with which managers must cope, we offer a few examples to illustrate the challenges facing LFF brand communicators. In the interest of depth and brevity, our illustration revolves around one stakeholder group only (i.e., festivalgoers) to help navigate polysemy between festivalgoers' meaning ownership and managerial direction work.

Festivalgoers are the heart of festivals. Some festivals exist only thanks to festivalgoers' creative communitarian practices, as in the traditional folkloristic roots of carnivalesque parades (Cohen, 1982) and their contemporary reinterpretations. Examples like the Edinburgh Fringe Festival and Burning Man clearly show that the very purpose of the events emerges in the micro participative actions of each festivalgoer, who not only attends a spectacle, but actively contributes to creating it (Kozinets, 2002; Munro & Jordan, 2013). Even for more mannered festivals, where organizers actually propose a spectacle to participants, festivalgoers contribute a great deal to the purpose of the event. This is the case for LFF, which – as widely agreed – is not simply 'an open-air cinema' (marketing manager, interview) but a 'space for dialogue and exchange,' a space where 'everyone can express freely' (LFF internal document). This chorality is foundational to the LFF corporate brand identity and has emerged over time from the experience of frequent and *cinéphile* festivalgoers. Said participants not only watch movies, but also bring their own emotional reactions to every film performance and do so powerfully: by crying, laughing, applauding, and harshly booing during film screenings. To them, LFF is the experience of 'travelling to an exotic place to experience a different self from the rest of the year' (artistic collaborator and former frequent festivalgoer, interview). When addressing these stakeholders, LFF brand managers can easily play with all the core meanings gravitating around the brand purpose and accumulating in the festival's mythological narratives over time. These meanings are truly co-created and easy to leverage by most corporate storytellers, who have been passionate festivalgoers themselves and can use narratives of their own experience to communicate the brand. A very recent example is the speech of the newly appointed artistic director, Giona Nazzaro. At the occasion of his first meeting with the press and the public, he reminded them of his past as an LFF *aficionado* – how he felt while watching Kiarostami's movies in Piazza Grande, how he raced from one theatre and another to see all the films, and the festive atmosphere of a critical but loving community of film lovers.

Both the growth of the festival and the development of the festival industry as a leisure tourist experience led LFF managers to start communicating with a diverse community of festivalgoers. Beyond the *cinéphile*, other typical *personae* representing frequent festivalgoers are general local publics, industry professionals, and institutional guests. We take here the example of young locals to highlight the extreme difference of meanings they attach to and expect from the LFF brand. As one young festivalgoer told us:

> [During festival days] there's a lot of people. And you can live Locarno in a different way. Places like la Rotonda [the Festival Village] offer youthful entertainment. And yes, I used to go there with my friends, but we avoided completely places such as Piazza Grande, where people go to see very boring movies.

Music, beer, and ethnic food are core parts of the festival experience for many *non-cinéphile* audiences. Brand managers are conscious of the slippery slope they face when involving stakeholders so far from the brand core meanings. However, they are also aware that nightlife, fun, and entertainment are an indispensable part of contemporary festivals. 'We cannot deny the party-like aspect of the LFF;' it is 'an entry door for young local audiences' and it 'provides additional value to our sponsoring partners' (marketing manager, interview). In addition, coordinators of creative sections acknowledge that:

> During parties, you figure out who people actually are. And not necessarily in their best light, in fact (laughs). . . . But . . . this dimension and contradictions, even if sometimes I find them a little depressing, but overall, they fit, just because the festival is complex. It brings together different audiences, different imageries: from Piazza Grande to the most *cinéphile* sections of the competition there is no point of contact, never really anyone. Just as from the festival at la Rotonda to certain targeted off festival cultural events, there is no correspondence there either.

Such examples illuminate that brand communicators are aware of the complex polysemy surrounding the festival, even within the core group of festivalgoers. They are also aware that, in order to survive, they need to cope with this richness, avoiding overly risky divergences in brand communications while still letting some contradictions coexist. Our understanding is that they try to navigate this complexity in two ways.

First, they use segmentation and targeting so as to direct distinct brand meanings to different audiences within the festivalgoer stakeholder group. By drawing from the polysemic LFF brand repertoire, they convey said distinct meanings through different touchpoints capable of segmenting the different festivalgoer groups. For example, artistic directors and managers of the Locarno Pro and Locarno Academy sections mainly leverage artistic meanings offered by works in the competition as well as from workshops and masterclasses with guest film directors. They do so during the event, in the formal speeches and interviews and through informal interactions targeting artists and film lovers. They do it by keeping the high standing of LFF's core product – the films selected for the international competition – 'because it is around these 20, 25 movies that we build all our international credibility' (marketing manager, interview). Some additional touchpoints they use to reach out to *cinéphiles* include personal involvement in the international festival circuit and the various artistic and educational projects in which they are involved, such as the Locarno in Los Angeles initiative (a three-day screening of movies shown in Locarno) or year-round consultancies for film productions in less developed film industries within the Open Doors section. Some other touchpoints that proved excellent in segmenting passionate festivalgoers include the different programme-oriented touchpoints actionable during the event (i.e., the festival catalogue, *Pardo Live* magazine, and Locarno Live TV). LFF's cross-media communications often include narratives, pictures, and videos capturing emotional climaxes during films – more so in summer, when the festival is approaching (Figure 18.4).

Meanings related to the 'Locarno Experience' are instead targeted to a more general public of festivalgoers and conveyed through local and national advertising, posters on the way to Locarno in the weeks before the event and the communication co-developed with sponsoring partners, which include merchandising, advertising, and teasers on trains, PostBus, and SWISS in-flight information. Locarno nightlife and VIP lounges – which serve to reinforce the hype and glamour of the festival for audiences especially passionate about the social side of the event – are also promoted in collaboration with the Ascona-Locarno tourist office. In this way LFF communicators clearly target stakeholders looking for a reassuring but not overly complex reading of the LFF brand.

*Figure 18.4* Photo mobilizing *cinéphile* emotional experience on the LFF website
Source: courtesy of Locarno Film Festival

Second, this segmentation and targeting strategy is complemented by the contrary attempt to transport and expose each segment of festivalgoers to different facets of the LFF brand. For example, brand communicators try to involve young local audiences, who experience LFF as a form of summer fun, by sharing some more accessible audio-visual-related meanings of the LFF brand (e.g., film teasers before music concerts; virtual reality experience). In addition, brand managers continually develop new touchpoints to expand bridges between the various LFF domains and favour the creation of brand new LFF narratives across its domains. In this regard, the work that they have developed over the last few years has been exemplary as it targets a new generation of curious festivalgoers looking for artistic discovery and social critique beyond the traditional *auteur* cinema format. Known as BaseCamp, this initiative is an immersive experience in which young creatives from different disciplines (ranging from photography to science) live together in former barracks while attending the festival. They enjoy affordable access to the festival's core activities and create a niche community within the larger festivalgoer community by organizing live music sessions, collective symposia, and arts exhibitions. Figure 18.5 represents the barracks and a poster of the BaseCamp daily programme, where festival-led *cinéphile* meanings are coupled with participants' activity proposals (e.g., underground rock music concert). We posit that the exposure of the same segment to a richer polysemy of the LFF brand serves two alternative purposes. First, it helps migrate some of the social- and fun-driven festivalgoers to more central segments by means of progressive familiarization and education. Second, it enriches each segment's experience of and with the LFF brand, even when festivalgoers are not likely to move from one segment to another.

The examples presented thus far illustrate LFF brand managers' strategic use of monosemy and polysemy for distinct festivalgoer segments. However, a certain interaction of meanings, and thus a certain degree of polysemy, naturally occurs during the event itself. As a physical space, Locarno is at the same time split into somewhat clear-cut areas, each hosting distinct events for specific festivalgoer segments, while being small enough as a whole to facilitate natural

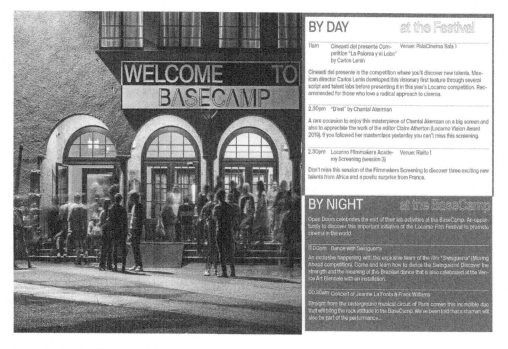

*Figure 18.5* BaseCamp activities
Source: combination of photos published on LFF website – courtesy of Locarno Film Festival

interactions across segments. Therefore, beyond brand managers' strategic actions, different festivalgoers enter in contact with a great variety of LFF touchpoints and communication content as much as with a number of different types of festivalgoers (alternative intellectuals, national politicians, film directors, and students). For example, Piazza Grande serves as a melting pot for said different meanings and segments.

Given this complexity, the risk that natural contradictions result in open gaps is always present and leaves the LFF brand (and its managers) under constant pressure. If we stick to the festivalgoers' example, this risk manifests mostly in relation to the traditional *cinéphile* profile, consisting of brand identity guardians, generally 50+ years old, who have remained affectively attached to their then-experience of a non-professionalized, precarious, and socially critical festival. The following quote clearly pinpoints such feelings:

> I remember, in the seventies, the audience was clearly much less. . . . Back then, if a film wasn't good, the audience would clearly make its voice heard. Now, they also applaud films I consider unworthy. . . . Today, LFF is a bulimic festival. There is too much, . . . movies and more. It is impossible to seriously engage with all the proposed contents.
> (local cinephile festivalgoer, interview)

In conclusion, we have focused the LFF case on the stakeholder group of festivalgoers to illustrate the strategic use, as much as the inevitable coexistence of monosemy and polysemy for a corporate brand. We hope the case helps unveil the complexity of managing a polysemic brand, even when addressing one stakeholder group at a time. In the interest of concision, we do not analyse similar challenges for other stakeholder groups, but our empirical data confirm that this subtle equilibrium between monosemy and polysemy concerns all of them. For example, for financing partners, we can roughly distinguish between institutional funders and private sponsors. If the former prefer a relatively bold, monosemic interpretation of the LFF, which to their eyes facilitates the brand's cultural promotion and financial stability, the latter are keen on LFF brand polysemy, which accounts for the brand's cultural richness, trendiness, and broader marketability. In our presentation of the LFF corporate brand, we favoured a stakeholder-centred approach (here, festivalgoers). However, by focusing on a specific touchpoint, open to the different stakeholder groups that may interact with that touchpoint, we may narrate similar challenges. Thus, tensions between monosemy and polysemy appear at the level of each stakeholder and each touchpoint.

In the final section of this chapter, we draw on the LFF revelatory case to discuss the managerial trade-offs that polysemy poses for corporate brand management.

## 4. Brand polysemy and its managerial trade-offs

The visual metaphor we used to represent the semantic richness of brand polysemy and the axes around which polysemy originates and is manageable are a practical translation of what Diamond et al. (2009) would address as brand gestalt. This notion effectively captures our perspective, as it conveys an understanding of corporate brands as both the product of a complex system and a structure providing unity across meaning complexity, which different stakeholders can recognize as part of the same brand. Through the notion of gestalt, Diamond et al. (2009, p. 119) emphasize that handling polysemy entails much more than a plain combination of a 'matrix' or 'manifold' of possibilities (Berthon et al., 2007; Urde, 2022). Rather, it requires navigating a system 'within which the brand resides or from which it emerges' and in which elements 'are in continuous interaction with one another.' As such, knowing the distinct meanings of the same corporate brand and understanding their interactions in the system enable corporations and individuals to manage powerful brands (Diamond et al., 2009).

In this chapter, we have suggested that brand polysemy could be better conceptualized and managed by looking into the three areas/axes of (1) stakeholders, (2) communication contents, and (3) brand touchpoints. Of course, polysemy emerges not only within each of these areas, but also in the (re)combinations of stakeholders, contents, and touchpoints. In this section, we wish to direct attention to four managerial tensions that polysemy creates for corporate brands. Although we acknowledge that polysemy is not limited to corporate brand managers' control, we adopt their perspective on these tensions in line with the chapter's managerial ethos. Finally, being against the normative assumption of the one-size-fits-all approach to managerial decisions, we prefer to raise a number of questions that may help managers frame challenges related to polysemic corporate branding.

### *4.1 Harmony versus dissonance*

Co-creational and organic views of the brand relax the notion of brand-meaning coherence, and even brand identity is considered plastic (Michel, 2017). Said perspectives posit that brand polysemy arises from both the multiple, phenomenological interpretations of the different stakeholders (Essamri et al., 2019) and the multiple identities comprising each stakeholder due to the dynamic interactions with the brand (von Wallpach et al., 2017). As a result, brand meanings emerge that may favour competing views of the brand. Semantically rich brands are particularly subject to phenomenological competing views and, thus, to polysemy. These competing views, in their turn, may constitute the very essence of a complex, successful corporate brand.

The LFF corporate brand is one such case, with a number of meaning tensions characterizing its unique essence. Our case illustrates a few of them, such as its perceived international versus local orientation, its discovery and provocation ethos versus its ability to provide comfortable entertainment, the *cinéphile* versus the pop culture grounding, and its artsy versus market nature. Interdisciplinary scholarly research on festivals has concluded that the very concept of a corporate brand is paradoxical for festivals (Toraldo & Islam, 2019) because it tries to harness the chaotic and disruptive sociological experience that festivals intrinsically imply (Cohen, 1982; Rao & Dutta, 2012). A number of festivals have indeed powerful brands, most of them sharing the recurrent identity tension between communitarian aspirations and the commodification of experience (Kozinets, 2002; Munro & Jordan, 2013). With due differences, such essential dissonances may arise, also in more conventional organizations. Today's largely felt tension between profit and sustainability is an example. When corporate brands have strong polysemic tensions pervading their narratives, narrative persuasion (Iglesias & Bonet, 2012; Van Laer et al., 2014) or any other systematic attempt to counterbalance these tensions is unlikely to succeed. Rather, said brands are more likely to live with, and profit from, contradictory and even conflicting interpretations of the brand narrative which organize and nurture the polysemic richness of these corporate brands. When harmony, here defined as the absence of polysemy and tensions, is replaced by brand dissonance, some relevant questions emerge. How can managers prevent dissonance from transforming into complete noise? To what extent can a strong brand purpose provide an adequate centredness to brands pursuing, or being exposed to, severe polysemy deriving from diverse stakeholders' brand-meaning co-creation? Is targeting communicated meanings to different stakeholders and in different situations enough? As brands need a rich polysemy for some of their stakeholders, how can brand managers filter out excessively rich and confusing meanings for those stakeholders expecting more harmonic brand narratives?

## 4.2 Polyphony versus polysemy

The corporate brand literature increasingly discusses the relevance of polyphony, defined as the coexistence of the voices of multiple stakeholder groups interpreting the same sign – in this case, a corporate brand or one of its expressions (e.g., events, social media accounts, websites). Engaging in multilogues – that is, in the 'discursive process involving multiple interdependent stakeholders who simultaneously interact with each other' (Vallaster & von Wallpach, 2013, p. 1513) – is by now a well-established recommendation for brand managers (Berthon et al., 2007; Michel, 2017). Yet this same literature acknowledges that polyphony may also cause cacophony in brand interpretations, thereby requiring some form of direction (Kjeldsen & Schmeltz, 2022). A polysemic approach instead relates to the semantic richness of that sign (here, the brand or one of its expressions). As such, it refers to the multiple meanings that a sign may hold, either for the same interpreter or for different interpreters confronted with said sign. Thus, polysemy does not necessarily entail polyphony, as polysemy may in fact occur within the same interpreter. Our case documents that the presence of divergent meanings for the same stakeholder may sometimes derive from some distinct roles this person has played over time at the festival (e.g., some initially passionate festivalgoers later becoming festival collaborators). Often polyphony and polysemy emerge jointly, as the same sign is typically available for the interpretation of different actors. Furthermore, the more polysemous a sign, the higher the likelihood for it to stimulate polyphonic responses.

Our case also illustrates that various stakeholders – for example, young artists – may in fact attribute diverse meanings to the LFF brand (e.g., creativity, discovery, but also entertainment and fun). Conversely, our data show that, at other times, stakeholders may move from a polysemic to a more monosemic experience with the brand. This means that corporate brand managers need to constantly question the extent to which each stakeholder aspires to a more or less polysemic engagement with the brand, recognizing that his or her preference can vary over time. It also means that corporate brand managers need to attentively monitor the number and type of stakeholder groups involved in the discourse of their corporate brand in order to monitor polyphony and understand to what extent a brand's polysemy stimulates divergent interpretations in such multilogues. Our conclusion warns against traditional stakeholder segmentation models and the interrelated risk of overlooking important differences within each stakeholder group. In light of the distinction we have made between polyphony and polysemy, which stakeholders (or touchpoints) are best suited to polyphony versus polysemy? When engaging stakeholders, what are the cultural and discursive resources each person or group brings with them? How can we map not only people entering in contact with the brand, but also the meanings they bring into the brand through the various touchpoints?

### 4.3 Preservation versus transformation

The preservation of brand heritage is a common theme in corporate brand management. Today, corporate brand managers are confronted with ambivalent expectations. They are expected to act as guardians of a brand's heritage (i.e., serving a preservation function) while also continually innovating to keep the brand relevant for the times (for customers and external stakeholders) and 'cool' (for internal stakeholders interested in the 'cashability' of the brand). Notably, as respect for brand heritage seems to become less obsessive in a number of organizations, some external stakeholders are in fact turning into real paladins of brand heritage. Traditional *cinéphiles* turning their noses up to the more popular and glamorous activities of the LFF provide a good illustration in this regard. In a completely different market, the recent example of the #jesuisspeculoos protest in Belgium consisted of a number of brand customers reacting negatively to the change of name of the Speculoos biscuit, which was interpreted as the profanation of a long-existing and much-cherished Belgian tradition (McHugh, 2020). Indeed, heritage and the preservation of historical meanings remain important elements in polysemy (Burghausen, 2022). Hence, how can brand managers, or other stakeholders involved in the co-construction of the brand, preserve heritage as new meanings constantly migrate onto the brand? In addition, are novel meanings and transformation necessarily enemies of a corporate brand's heritage? The literature on organizational and brand identity demonstrates that past textual and material memory of a brand are in fact possible enablers of – rather than constraints to – change processes and future-oriented imaginations (Hatch & Schultz, 2017; Schultz & Hernes, 2013). When new and distinctive identity narratives are created from a repertoire of narrative commons, they contribute to preserving, not destroying, the commons which each actor maintains alive in the brand storytelling (Illia & Zamparini, 2016), which can be a challenging endeavour for brand managers. How can they maintain a repertoire of traditional meanings looked after by certain stakeholders (e.g., brand paladins) while not censoring new authentic assemblages of polysemic brand experiences?

### 4.4 Internal versus external focus

Polysemy may also provide fresh energy to the foundational dilemma on the internal versus external focus of the brand (Hatch & Schultz, 2009). The debate is at the same time both classic and contemporary in corporate brand management research, if we look into recent scholarly calls to (re)consider internal stakeholders as key actors in a brand's co-creation (Iglesias et al., 2013; Kjeldsen & Schmeltz, 2022). An excellent case is made for employees, who in fact may act as internal brand stewards and thus have a powerful voice in brand-meaning creation and communication. The LFF case is problematic in setting clear-cut boundaries between internal versus external stakeholders. For example, most collaborators are freelancers, meaning they are to some extent internals, yet they also professionally participate in a number of external, distinct organizations, which may be more or less closely related to cinema. Within the group of stable employees, most acquired their role following years of collaboration with the festival and are today qualifiable as internal. Although perhaps extreme in some ways, the LFF case is nonetheless revelatory of boundary-crossing dynamics that, albeit less extremely, increasingly play out in more traditional companies as well (Kornberger et al., 2006). The porosity between the internal and external boundaries of a corporate brand leads to the democratization of authorship on the brand's meanings, as traditional internal brand gatekeepers enter the conversation with other, partially legitimate decision-makers having 'a step' in the organization. This is even more likely in those companies engaging in practices of cultural cultivation (Harrison & Corley, 2011, p. 391) – that is, 'practices that contribute to the intermingling of organizational and societal cultures' – whereby elements of broader cultures are also imported and translated into the company by bringing representatives of that culture into the company. With all due adaptations, the case of LEGO, probably the most researched case of co-creation (Hatch & Schultz, 2010; Ind et al., 2013; von Wallpach et al., 2017), also shows similar dynamics. More broadly, in line with the trend launched by tech firms, we see that an increasing number of companies work closely with business partners in large ecosystems (Ramaswamy, 2022; Ramaswamy & Ozcan, 2018). In this evolved landscape, how can managers distinguish internal versus external focus in polysemic brand management? How can they manage polysemic brands as platforms of meaning construction crossing the organizational boundaries?

In conclusion, we are aware that we provide more questions than answers in this chapter. We also acknowledge that the case we have used to inspire and illustrate our theorizing is distinctive in that it is an event corporate brand with a strong experiential nature. Whatever the specificities of our case or of corporate brands more generally, the multiplication of touchpoints, multimodal communication contents, and stakeholders' participation in corporate brands' co-construction concur in questioning when polysemy can help a brand flourish rather than dilute its value. By means of a visual metaphor, this chapter modestly contributes by identifying (1) three main axes that corporate brand managers can inspect or use to manage brand polysemy (stakeholders, communication contents, and touchpoints) and (2) four critical areas of decisions that corporate brand managers face when managing polysemy. For each of these areas, we proposed some questions that we hope will help managers make more conscious and context-sensitive decisions.

## References

Arnould, E. J., & Thompson, C. J. (2005). Consumer culture theory (CCT): Twenty years of research. *Journal of Consumer Research*, *31*(4), 868–882. https://doi.org/10.1086/426626

Arnould, E. J., & Thompson, C. J. (2015). Introduction: Consumer culture theory: Ten years gone (and beyond). In E. J. Arnould & C. J. Thompson (Eds.), *Consumer culture theory* (pp. 1–21). Bingley: Emerald Group Publishing Limited. https://doi.org/10.1108/S0885-211120150000017001

Balmer, J. M. (2012). Strategic corporate brand alignment: Perspectives from identity based views of corporate brands. *European Journal of Marketing*, *46*(7–8), 1064–1092. https://doi.org/10.1108/03090561211230205

Balmer, J. M., & Soenen, G. B. (1999). The acid test of corporate identity management™. *Journal of Marketing Management*, *15*(1–3), 69–92. https://doi.org/10.1362/026725799784870441

Belk, R. W. (1988). Possessions and the extended self. *Journal of Consumer Research*, *15*(2), 139–168. https://doi.org/10.1086/209154

Belk, R. W. (2013). Extended self in a digital world. *Journal of Consumer Research*, 40(3), 477–500. https://doi.org/10.1086/671052

Bengtsson, A., Bardhi, F., & Venkatraman, M. (2010). How global brands travel with consumers: An examination of the relationship between brand consistency and meaning across national boundaries. *International Marketing Review*, 27(5), 519–540. https://doi.org/10.1108/02651331011076572

Berthon, P., Holbrook, M. B., Hulbert, J. M., & Pitt, L. (2007). Viewing brands in multiple dimensions. *MIT Sloan Management Review*, 48(2), 37–43.

Broniarczyk, S. M., & Alba, J. W. (1994). The importance of the brand in brand extension. *Journal of Marketing Research*, 31(2), 214–228. https://doi.org/10.1177/002224379403100206

Brown, S. (2006). Ambi-brand culture. In J. Schroeder & M. S. Morling (Eds.), *Brand culture* (pp. 16–26). London: Routledge. https://doi.org/10.4324/9780203002445

Brown, S. (2014). She was fine when she left here: Polysemy, patriarchy, and personification in brand titanic's birthplace. *Psychology & Marketing*, 31(1), 93–102. https://doi.org/10.1002/mar.20678

Burghausen, M. (2022). Toward a co-creational perspective on corporate heritage and corporate heritage brands. In O. Iglesias, N. Ind, & M. Schultz (Eds.), *The Routledge companion to corporate branding*. London: Routledge.

Cohen, A. (1982). A polyethnic London carnival as a contested cultural performance. *Ethnic and Racial Studies*, 5(1), 23–41. https://doi.org/10.1080/01419870.1982.9993358

Csaba, F. F., & Bengtsson, A. (2006). Rethinking identity in brand management. In J. Schroeder & M. S. Morling (Eds.), *Brand culture* (pp. 118–135). London: Routledge. https://doi.org/10.4324/9780203002445

Diamond, N., Sherry Jr., J. F., Muñiz Jr., A. M., McGrath, M. A., Kozinets, R. V., & Borghini, S. (2009). American girl and the brand gestalt: Closing the loop on sociocultural branding research. *Journal of Marketing*, 73(3), 118–134. https://doi.org/10.1509/jmkg.73.3.118

Eckhardt, G. M. (2015). Commentary: The cultural approach to branding. In J. E. Schroeder (Ed.), *Brands: Interdisciplinary perspectives* (pp. 107–115). London: Routledge.

Essamri, A., McKechnie, S., & Winklhofer, H. (2019). Co-creating corporate brand identity with online brand communities: A managerial perspective. *Journal of Business Research*, 96, 366–375. https://doi.org/10.1016/j.jbusres.2018.07.015

Ger, G. (1999). Localizing in the global village: Local firms competing in global markets. *California Management Review*, 41(4), 64–83. https://doi.org/10.2307/41166010

Getz, D. (2010). The nature and scope of festival studies. *International Journal of Event Management Research*, 5(1), 1–47.

Harrison, S. H., & Corley, K. G. (2011). Clean climbing, carabiners, and cultural cultivation: Developing an open-systems perspective of culture. *Organization Science*, 22(2), 391–412. https://doi.org/10.1287/orsc.1100.0538

Hatch, M. J., & Schultz, M. (2009). From corporate to enterprise branding. *Organizational Dynamics*, 38(2), 117–130. https://doi.org/10.1016/j.orgdyn.2009.02.008

Hatch, M. J., & Schultz, M. (2010). Toward a theory of brand co-creation with implications for brand governance. *Journal of Brand Management*, 17(8), 590–604. https://doi.org/10.1057/bm.2010.14

Hatch, M. J., & Schultz, M. (2017). Toward a theory of using history authentically: Historicizing in the Carlsberg Group. *Administrative Science Quarterly*, 62(4), 657–697. https://doi.org/10.1177/0001839217692535

Holt, D. B. (2004). *How brands become icons: The principles of cultural branding*. Boston, MA: Harvard Business Press.

Holt, D., & Cameron, D. (2010). *Cultural strategy: Using innovative ideologies to build breakthrough brands*. Oxford: Oxford University Press.

Iglesias, O., & Bonet, E. (2012). Persuasive brand management: How managers can influence brand meaning when they are losing control over it. *Journal of Organizational Change Management*, 25(2), 251–264. https://doi.org/10.1108/09534811211213937

Iglesias, O., & Ind, N. (2020). Towards a theory of conscientious corporate brand co-creation: The next key challenge in brand management. *Journal of Brand Management*, 27(6), 710–720. https://doi.org/10.1057/s41262-020-00205-7

Iglesias, O., Ind, N., & Alfaro, M. (2013). The organic view of the brand: A brand value co-creation model. *Journal of Brand Management*, 20(8), 670–688. https://doi.org/10.1057/978-1-352-00008-5_9

Illia, L., & Zamparini, A. (2016). Legitimate distinctiveness, historical bricolage, and the fortune of the commons. *Journal of Management Inquiry*, 25(4), 397–414. https://doi.org/10.1177/1056492616637917

Ind, N., Iglesias, O., & Schultz, M. (2013). Building brands together: Emergence and outcomes of co-creation. *California Management Review*, 55(3), 5–26. https://doi.org/10.1525/cmr.2013.55.3.5

Joachimsthaler, E., & Aaker, D. A. (2009). *Brand leadership: Building assets in an information economy*. New York: Simon and Schuster.

Kapferer, J. N. (2012). *The new strategic brand management: Advanced insights and strategic thinking*. London: Kogan Page.

Keller, K. L. (1999). Brand mantras: Rationale, criteria and examples. *Journal of Marketing Management*, 15(1–3), 43–51. https://doi.org/10.1362/026725799784870513

Kjeldsen, A. K., & Schmeltz, L. (2022). Corporate brand management and multiple voices: Polyphony or cacophony? In O. Iglesias, N. Ind, & M. Schultz (Eds.), *The Routledge companion to corporate branding*. London: Routledge.

Kornberger, M., Clegg, S. R., & Carter, C. (2006). Rethinking the polyphonic organization: Managing as discursive practice. *Scandinavian Journal of Management*, 22(1), 3–30. https://doi.org/10.1016/j.scaman.2005.05.004

Kozinets, R. V. (2002). Can consumers escape the market? Emancipatory illuminations from Burning Man. *Journal of Consumer Research*, 29(1), 20–38. https://doi.org/10.1086/339919

Lanseng, E. J., & Olsen, L. E. (2012). Brand alliances: The role of brand concept consistency. *European Journal of Marketing*, 46(12), 1108–1126. https://doi.org/10.1108/03090561211247874

Lee, S. A., & Jeong, M. (2014). Enhancing online brand experiences: An application of congruity theory. *International Journal of Hospitality Management*, 40, 49–58. https://doi.org/10.1016/j.ijhm.2014.03.008

Lee, Y. K., Lee, C. K., Lee, S. K., & Babin, B. J. (2008). Festivalscapes and patrons' emotions, satisfaction, and loyalty. *Journal of Business Research*, 61(1), 56–64. https://doi.org/10.1016/j.jbusres.2006.05.009

Levy, S. (2015). The technology of branding. In J. E. Schroeder (Ed.), *Brands: Interdisciplinary perspectives* (pp. 187–192). London: Routledge.

Matthiesen, I., & Phau, I. (2005). The 'HUGO BOSS' connection: Achieving global brand consistency across countries. *Journal of Brand Management*, 12(5), 325–338. https://doi.org/10.1057/palgrave.bm.2540229

McHugh, K. (2020, November 10). Spéculoos: How Belgium's beloved biscuit is unifying a divided nation. *Euronews*. Retrieved from www.euronews.com/2020/11/10/speculoos-how-belgium-s-beloved-biscuit-is-unifying-a-divided-nation

Michel, G. (2017). From brand identity to polysemous brands: Commentary on "Performing identities: Processes of brand and stakeholder identity co-construction." *Journal of Business Research*, 70, 453–455. https://doi.org/10.1016/j.jbusres.2016.06.022

Moisio, R., & Arnould, E. J. (2005). Extending the dramaturgical framework in marketing: Drama structure, drama interaction and drama content in shopping experiences. *Journal of Consumer Behaviour*, 4(4), 246–256. https://doi.org/10.1002/cb.10

Müller, M. (2017). 'Brand-centred control': A study of internal branding and normative control. *Organization Studies*, 38(7), 895–915. https://doi.org/10.1177/0170840616663238

Muniz, A. M., & O'Guinn, T. C. (2001). Brand community. *Journal of Consumer Research*, 27(4), 412–432. https://doi.org/10.1086/319618

Munro, I., & Jordan, S. (2013). 'Living Space' at the Edinburgh Festival Fringe: Spatial tactics and the politics of smooth space. *Human Relations*, 66(11), 1497–1525. https://doi.org/10.1177/0018726713480411

Park, C. W., Milberg, S., & Lawson, R. (1991). Evaluation of brand extensions: The role of product feature similarity and brand concept consistency. *Journal of Consumer Research*, 18(2), 185–193. https://doi.org/10.1086/209251

Payne, E. M., Peltier, J. W., & Barger, V. A. (2017). Omni-channel marketing, integrated marketing communications and consumer engagement. *Journal of Research in Interactive Marketing*, 11(2), 185–197. https://doi.org/10.1108/JRIM-08-2016-0091

Payne, J., Bettman, J. R., & Johnson, E. J. (1991). Consumer decision making. *Handbook of Consumer Behaviour*, 50–84.

Petty, R. E., & Cacioppo, J. T. (1986). The elaboration likelihood model of persuasion. In: *Communication and persuasion. Springer series in social psychology* (pp. 1–24). Heidelberg: Springer. https://doi.org/10.1007/978-1-4612-4964-1_1

Ramaswamy, V. (2022). Embracing a co-creation paradigm of experience value creation. In O. Iglesias, N. Ind, & M. Schultz (Eds.), *The Routledge companion to corporate branding*. London: Routledge.

Ramaswamy, V., & Ozcan, K. (2018). Offerings as digitalized interactive platforms: A conceptual framework and implications. *Journal of Marketing*, 82(4), 19–31. https://doi.org/10.1509/jm.15.0365

Rao, H., & Dutta, S. (2012). Free spaces as organizational weapons of the weak: Religious festivals and regimental mutinies in the 1857 Bengal Native Army. *Administrative Science Quarterly*, 57(4), 625–668. https://doi.org/10.1177/0001839212467744

Schultz, M., & Hernes, T. (2013). A temporal perspective on organizational identity. *Organization Science*, *24*(1), 1–21. https://doi.org/10.1177/0001839212467744

Stokburger-Sauer, N., Ratneshwar, S., & Sen, S. (2012). Drivers of consumer – Brand identification. *International Journal of Research in Marketing*, *29*(4), 406–418. https://doi.org/10.1016/j.ijresmar.2012.06.001

Toraldo, M. L., & Islam, G. (2019). Festival and organization studies. *Organization Studies*, *40*(3), 309–322. https://doi.org/10.1177/0170840617727785

Troisi, O., Santovito, S., Carrubbo, L., & Sarno, D. (2019). Evaluating festival attributes adopting SD logic: The mediating role of visitor experience and visitor satisfaction. *Marketing Theory*, *19*(1), 85–102. https://doi.org/10.1177/1470593118772207

Urde, M. (2022). What does your corporate brand stand for? In O. Iglesias, N. Ind, & M. Schultz (Eds.), *The Routledge companion to corporate branding*. London: Routledge.

Vallaster, C., & von Wallpach, S. (2013). An online discursive inquiry into the social dynamics of multi-stakeholder brand meaning co-creation. *Journal of Business Research*, *66*(9), 1505–1515. https://doi.org/10.1016/j.jbusres.2012.09.012

Van Laer, T., De Ruyter, K., Visconti, L. M., & Wetzels, M. (2014). The extended transportation-imagery model: A meta-analysis of the antecedents and consequences of consumers' narrative transportation. *Journal of Consumer Research*, *40*(5), 797–817. https://doi.org/10.1086/673383

Vicente, A., & Falkum, I. (2017). Polysemy. *Oxford Research Encyclopedia of Linguistics*. Retrieved from https://oxfordre.com/linguistics/view/10.1093/acrefore/9780199384655.001.0001/acrefore-9780199384655-e-325

Visconti, L. M. (2010). Ethnographic case study (ECS): Abductive modeling of ethnography and improving the relevance in business marketing research. *Industrial Marketing Management*, *39*(1), 25–39. https://doi.org/10.1016/j.indmarman.2008.04.019

Visconti, L. M., Peñaloza, L., & Toulouse, N. (Eds.). (2020). *Marketing management: A cultural perspective*. London: Routledge.

Volonterio, G. (1997). *Dalle suggestioni del parco alla grande festa del cinema*. Venezia: Marsilio.

von Wallpach, S., Hemetsberger, A., & Espersen, P. (2017). Performing identities: Processes of brand and stakeholder identity co-construction. *Journal of Business Research*, *70*, 443–452. https://doi.org/10.1016/j.jbusres.2016.06.021

Walsh, D. (2018). A new paradigm for brand touchpoints. In A. Sundar (Ed.), *Brand touchpoints* (pp. 3–18). Nova.

Yoganathan, V., Osburg, V. S., & Akhtar, P. (2019). Sensory stimulation for sensible consumption: Multi-sensory marketing for e-tailing of ethical brands. *Journal of Business Research*, *96*, 386–396. https://doi.org/10.1016/j.jbusres.2018.06.005

# 19
# VISITORS' DESTINATION BRAND ENGAGEMENT'S EFFECT ON CO-CREATION

An empirical study

*Raouf Ahmad Rather, Linda Hollebeek, Dale L.G. Smith, Jana Kukk, and Mojtaba Ghasemi*

## 1. Introduction

As a growing global phenomenon (Narangajavana et al., 2017), social media sees important effects in tourism, particularly regarding the way tourists use or access information (Ebrahimi et al., 2019; Harrigan et al., 2018). In other words, social media have impacted the tourism ecosystem by shifting visitor behaviour (e.g., Booking.com, Trivago, TripAdvisor; Alalwan et al., 2017), including by fostering consumer/brand relationships (Iglesias et al., 2013; Ebrahimi et al., 2019; So et al., 2014, 2020; Wang & Kim, 2019). Correspondingly, the tourism-based social media literature has garnered significant academic interest (Harrigan et al., 2018; Li et al., 2020; Narangajavana et al., 2017).

The engagement concept has been adopted in domains including marketing, organizational behaviour, psychology, and hospitality, to name a few (Kumar & Pansari, 2016; Itani et al., 2019; Rather & Camilleri, 2019a). In marketing, customer engagement (CE) is the most commonly adopted engagement form (e.g., Kumar et al., 2019; Hollebeek et al., 2019a), whichtypically transpires with a brand (e.g., So et al., 2014; Ahn & Back, 2018). CE, which has been defined asa customer's 'motivationally driven, volitional investment of focal operant resources (including cognitive, emotional, behavioral, and social knowledge/kills), and operand resources (e.g., equipment) in [their] brand interactions' (Hollebeek et al., 2019b, p.166), has been shown to generate a host of favourable tourism customer and firm outcomes, including enhanced sales, word-of-mouth, and cocreation (e.g., Harrigan et al., 2018; Rather et al., 2019). However, empirically derived understanding of CBE in the tourism-based *social media* context remains scarce (Harrigan et al., 2018; Li et al., 2020; So et al., 2020), thus revealing an important gap.

Specifically, despite literature-based advances, few studies have addressed the role of specific consumer-based pre-conditions to CBE, including psychological factors (e.g., customer-brand identification, social identity; Prentice et al., 2018, 2019; Van Doorn et al., 2010). In response to this gap, we investigate visitors' uses and gratifications (U&G)-informed social media involvement as a crucial CBE driver (Malthouse et al., 2013; Hollebeek et al., 2016). The U&G perspective elucidates consumers' motivations for using specific media and show how this gratification fulfils their needs (Ko et al., 2005; Smock et al., 2011). We further investigate CBE's impact on brand-based co-creation and brand loyalty, thereby exposing CBE a mediating factor in the relationship of brand identification and social media involvement on the one hand, and brand co-creation and loyalty on the other.

Given CBE's motivational nature (Hollebeek et al., 2014, 2019b), brand identification and social media involvement were chosen as key CBE antecedents (Hollebeek & Chen, 2014; Prentice et al., 2019). The uses-and-gratifications perspective delineates consumer motivations for selecting specific media, including functional and/or social-identity motives (Lam et al., 2010; Rather, 2018, 2019), which we deem important in the tourism-based social media context.

This research makes the following contributions. First, irrespective of the growing understanding of CBE in tourism marketing, little remains known about the effect of consumer-perceived brand identification and social media involvement on CBE, as therefore empirically examined in this study. Second, we find visitors' destination brand engagement to positively affect the development of their brand co-creation and loyalty, highlighting engagement's pivotal role in managing tourism brands. Third, we ascertain destination brand loyalty's favourable impact on brand co-creation, revealing important managerial insight.

The chapter unfolds as follows. The next section reviews the related literature and defined hypotheses and relationships, from where conceptual framework is proposed (Figure 19.1). The method deployed to test these hypotheses is outlined, followed by a description of the results. Finally, important implications are presented, followed by a discussion of research limitations and future research.

## 2. Theoretical background

### 2.1 The uses-and-gratifications perspective

The uses-and-gratifications (U&G) perspective addresses how/why people utilize media to fulfil their needs (Katz & Foulkes, 1962; Ko et al., 2005). This perspective advocates that consumers actively search for, may identify with, and use media to satisfy their specific (e.g., informational, hedonic) needs (Hollebeek et al., 2016; Ku et al., 2013).

Recently, the U&G perspective has been employed to predict consumers' social media-related behaviours (Choi et al., 2016). In social media marketing, a brand's objective is to attract an audience (e.g., customer/guest) by offering the individual gratification or value through its content (Malthouse et al., 2013). Therefore, content should be designed in such a way that it generates

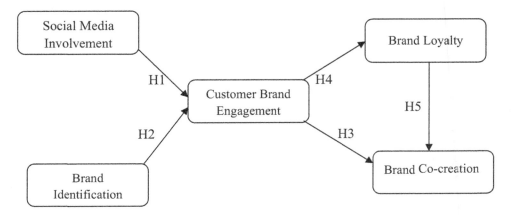

*Figure 19.1* Conceptual framework

value for consumers, igniting their desire to develop value-laden engagement and relationships with the brand (Hollebeek & Macky, 2019; Malthouse et al., 2013). The U&G perspective analyses consumers' motivations for engaging with social media and addresses how these gratifications satisfy their needs, resulting in heightened engagement and long-term relationships.

However, research into the U&G-based role of social media involvement in driving CBE for destination brands remains limited (Choi et al., 2016; Islam & Rahman, 2017). Thus, we investigate the impact of U&G-driven social media involvement on customer motivation to engage with tourism brands (Kaur et al., 2020; Lim & Kumar, 2019). We next review important literature on CBE.

## 2.2. Customer (brand) engagement

CE has gained extensive attention in marketing from the mid- to late-1990s (Brodie et al., 2011, 2013; Hollebeek, 2011a, 2011b; Hollebeeket al., 2019b; Rather et al., 2019; Rather & Hollebeek, 2020). Reflecting its growing importance, the Marketing Science Institute (MSI) has continuously listed the undertaking of further CE research in their Research Priorities since 2010 (e.g., MSI, 2020). In line with the growing attention devoted to CE, a number of CE-based sub-concepts have emerged, as outlined, including customer brand engagement (CBE), as first coined by Hollebeek, 2011a, 2011b. Given that CE's most common engagement object (i.e., that which the customer engages *with*) is the brand, CE and CBE exhibit high theoretical similarity. The key difference is that CBE (vs. CE) makes the engagement object of the brand explicit (whereas this remains implicit in CE). Following Hollebeek et al. (2014) and Harrigan et al. (2018), we employ the CBE concept, given its explicit *brand* focus, as applied here to the tourism context (e.g., Rather et al., 2018; Rather & Sharma, 2018, 2019).

Despite the debate surrounding CBE's conceptualization, most scholars agree regarding the concept's two-way, interactive nature (Groeger et al., 2016; Mollen & Wilson, 2010; Rather, 2020). That is, CE centres on the customer's (brand) interactions. For example, Hollebeek et al. (2014, p.154) define CBE as 'a consumer's positively valenced brand-related cognitive, emotional, and behavioral activity during or related to focal consumer/brand interactions,' revealing the concept's interactive nature and fitting with the U&G-informed perspective's *proactive* view of the customer (e.g., Hollebeek & Macky, 2019; Li et al., 2020). Second, modifying Hollebeek et al.'s (2019b) definition, Hollebeek et al. (2018, 2020c) recognize CBE as a *boundedly* (vs. fully) *volitional* concept, given its potential limitations imposed by a range of factors, including institutional arrangements, institutions, and/or other actors (Vargo & Lusch, 2016).

Third, most conceptualizations consider CBE as a multidimensional concept that is generally viewed to comprise emotional, cognitive, and behavioural dimensions, as deployed in this study (Hollebeek et al., 2014; Islam et al., 2019, 2020; Mollen & Wilson, 2010). Some authors extend CE/CBE to a four-dimensional model by including a social aspect (Brodie et al., 2013; Vivek et al., 2014), which is important in the social media-based tourism context. By contrast, other scholars view CE as a unidimensional concept, typically by highlighting *engagement behaviours* (e.g., Groeger et al., 2016; Van Doorn et al., 2010).

Based on this synthetic review, we define CBE as 'the intensity of an individual's participation in and connection with an organization's [brand] offerings and/or [brand-related] activities, which either the customer or the organization initiates' (Vivek et al., 2012, p.133). This connection, in turn, is conducive to fostering a tourism customer's cognitive, affective, and behavioural brand-related activities in- or outside of purchase situations (Hollebeek et al., 2014; So et al., 2014). We view CBE as a reflective second-order construct involving enthused participation, conscious attention, and social connection (So et al., 2020; Vivek et al., 2014), thus fitting with the social media-based tourism context that is typified by customer/brand connection and exchange. As tourists tend to spend considerable time on tourism-based social media platforms (e.g., TripAdvisor, AirBnB), examining their engagement in this context is key (Baldus et al., 2015; Li et al., 2020).

In line with the rise of social media, a growing scholarly and practitioner focus on social media-based CBE is observed (e.g., Brodie et al., 2013; Hollebeek et al., 2014; Li et al., 2020; Touni et al., 2020). Social media channels offer users an interactive means to engage with brands and generate value (e.g., by liking or sharing brand-related content; Gummerus et al., 2012), which may also invite other users' contributions. Consequently, social media-based CBE may facilitate consumers' influencing of others (e.g., by sharing their personal brand experience; Brodie et al., 2013). Correspondingly, these authors refer to social media-based CBE as a highly interactive process based on 'learning, sharing, advocating, socializing, and co-developing' (p.112). We next review important literature on brand co-creation.

### 2.3. Brand co-creation

In this section, we discuss key brand cocreation literature. First, as observed for CBE, debate also surrounds co-creation's definition. For example, Prahalad and Ramaswamy (2004, p.8) define co-creation as 'joint creation of value by the company and the customer, allowing the customer to co-construct the service experience to suit her context.' However, Vargo and Lusch (2016, p.9) define co-creation as 'the actions of multiple actors, often unaware of each other, that contribute to each other's wellbeing.' Despite their differences, these definitions share co-creation's interactively generated, value-creating (or -destroying) nature (Hollebeek et al., 2019b). Therefore, in line with the U&G perspective, brand co-creation assumes consumers to be active (vs. passive) actors in their own value-creating processes (Prahalad & Ramaswamy, 2000; Vargo & Lusch, 2004). By engaging users, social media-based tourism communications are conducive to cocreating value (Grissemann & Stokburger-Sauer, 2012; Ind et al., 2017).

Second, cocreation is typically considered a multidimensional concept. For example, Ranjan and Read (2016) suggest the following cocreation dimensions: (i) consumer-perceived *value-in-use*, which reflects the consumer's experience in utilizing an offering (Prebensen et al., 2015), and (ii) *coproduction*, which covers the consumer's 'shared production, shared inventiveness, or co-design' (e.g., by offering feedback, co-innovating new services/products).

Third, service-dominant (S-D) logic-based advances highlight co-creation's systemic nature (Merz et al., 2009; Vargo & Lusch, 2016). A *service system* is 'a value co-production configuration of people, technology, other internal and external service systems, and shared information (such as language, processes, metrics, prices, policies, and laws)' (Spohrer et al., 2007, p.2). Examples of service systems include destinations, sites, attractions, or cities, thus revealing high applicability to the tourism context. Moreover, tourism-based service systems include configurations of people, resources, and technology that facilitate brand co-creation (Blazquez-Resino et al., 2015). We next review the concept of destination branding.

### 2.4. Destination brands vs. corporate brands

The literature reveals extensive support for destination (place) branding, with various commentators having acknowledged these brands' similarities (vs. corporate brands; Hankinson, 2007; Kavaratzis & Hatch, 2013; Skinner, 2008). Therefore, corporate branding acumen has paved the way for the development of insight into place (destination) branding (Hankinson, 2007; Skinner, 2008). For example, Riel et al. (1997) define brands as 'an ethos, aims, and values that create a sense of individuality, which differentiates a brand' (Hatch & Schultz, 2001).

Ritchie and Ritchie (1998, p.103) define a *destination brand* as a name, symbol, logo, word or other graphic that both identifies and differentiates the destination, [that] . . . conveys the promise of a memorable travel experience that is uniquely associated with the destination. It also serves to consolidate and reinforce the recollection of pleasurable memories of [an individual's] destination experience.

We next introduce our model and hypothesis development.

## 3. Research model and hypotheses

### 3.1. Social media involvement's impact on CBE

*Social media involvement* can be defined as a consumer's perceived level of interest in or personal relevance of social media-based brand communications (see Hollebeek et al., 2014; Zaichkowsky, 1985; Mittal & Lee, 1989). Though the interface of social media and involvement and their respective effect on CBE has been studied in prior research, existing research has typically investigated consumers' involvement with particular brands (vs. social media content). Therefore, in this research, we explore the effect of consumers' social media involvement on CBE (Hajli et al., 2017; Li et al., 2020; Rather & Hollebeek, 2021). Specifically, we posit that a tourism consumer's innate interest in particular brand-related social media content (e.g., a tourism deal) will be conducive to their investment in it (e.g., by spending time liking, sharing, or commenting on it). As shown in Figure 19.1, we propose:

H1:  Social media involvement positively impacts a visitor's destination brand engagement.

### 3.2. Brand identification's impact on CBE

Consumers' brand identification can be defined as the extent to which they view the brand as part of their identity (Kaur et al., 2020; Rather, 2017; Rather et al., 2018, 2020). Therefore, visitors who identify with the destination brand will tend to develop an affective sense of belonging to the brand (Rather & Hollebeek, 2019; Tajfel & Turner, 1979), which is expected to in turn benefit their ensuing brand-related (e.g., purchase) behaviours. Based on this notion, we posit that the more a consumer identifies with a tourism brand, the greater their expected investment in interacting with the brand (Rather & Hollebeek, 2020). We propose:

H2:  Brand identification positively impacts a visitor's destination brand engagement.

### 3.3. CBE's impact on brand co-creation

In this and the next section, we address CBE's proposed consequences, as shown in Figure 19.1. *Co-creation* refers to 'a customer's perceived value arising from interactive, joint, collaborative or personalized brand-related activities for or with stakeholders in service systems' (Hollebeek et al., 2019b, p.170). As advanced in S-D logic (e.g., Vargo & Lusch, 2004, 2016), value is not just co-created by firms, but it may be co-created by *any* actor ensemble (e.g., Hollebeek et al., 2019b, 2020c; Iglesias & Ind, 2020; Zhang et al., 2017), including visitors, brands, and/ or fellow customers (Binkhorst & Dekker, 2009; Clark et al., 2020; Im & Qu 2017). As CE develops, consumers become increasingly likely to share their personal information/experience with others (Chen et al., 2018; Pansari & Kumar, 2017; Prebensen et al., 2014). Though the

CBE/brand co-creation-interface has been previously explored (e.g., Chathoth et al., 2014, 2016; Hollebeek et al., 2019b; Ind et al., 2013; Zhang et al., 2017), little remains known about the dynamics typifying this linkage for destination brands. We therefore posit:

H3: Visitors' destination brand engagement positively impacts brand co-creation.

### 3.4. Customer brand engagement's effect on brand loyalty

*Brand loyalty* refers to 'a deeply held commitment to rebuy or re-patronize a preferred product/service consistently in the future, despite other situational and marketing factors that have the potential to induce switching behavior' (Oliver, 1999, p.34). CBE has been found to represent an important vehicle for fostering brand loyalty (Harrigan et al., 2018; Iglesias et al., 2011; Hollebeek et al., 2014), though empirical exploration into this relationship in the tourism context remains relatively sparse (Rather, 2021a; So et al., 2020). Through tourism brand-related social media content, tourism firms may engage consumers, in turn sparking their loyalty intent (e.g., through the development of affective brand-related ties; Rather, 2021a; So et al., 2020; De Vries & Carlson, 2014; Harrigan et al., 2018). We thus posit that visitors' brand loyalty can be reinforced by engaging them in brand-related social media interactions (De Valck et al., 2009; Hollebeek et al., 2020a). Therefore,

H4: Visitors' destination brand engagement positively impacts brand loyalty.

### 3.5. Brand loyalty's effect on co-creation

Brand management has largely shifted its focus from a product focus (e.g., Aaker, 1996) to a service focus (e.g., Berry, 2000; Hollebeek et al., 2014). Thus, brands are increasingly viewed as emerging and social in nature (Gensler et al., 2013; Ind et al., 2013), in line with relationship marketing research, which suggests that high-quality customer/firm relationships are likely to stimulate value-laden interactions and elevated brand loyalty (Fournier, 1998; Palmatier et al., 2006). Consumers exhibiting high brand loyalty will be more likely to make brand-related contributions, leading us to posit:

H5: Brand loyalty positively impacts brand co-creation with tourism brands.

## 4. Methodology

### 4.1. Research design and data collection

Tourism companies, including airlines or hotels, tend to actively promote themselves on social media (e.g., Trivago, TripAdvisor; Li et al., 2020; So et al., 2020). The popularity of these platforms can, in part, be ascribed to consumers' ability to engage in two-way (vs. traditional one-way) communications with brands (Narangajavana et al., 2017; Parrey et al., 2019; Sasser et al., 2014), as outlined. In this study, we use a questionnaire to gauge the modelled constructs. First, we screened the respondents by only allowing those who had (a) utilized social media to search for travel information, and (b) had travelled to major destination or attraction sites in India (e.g., Phalgam, Kokernag).

The paper-and-pencil questionnaires were completed from November 2019 to January 2020. Of 500 distributed surveys, we received 418 valid responses, representing a 83.6% response rate. Soper's (2014) sample size calculator implied the adequacy of our sample size (i.e., the minimal sample recommended for SEM with 5 latent factors, 26 observed variables (p<0.05), and a projected effect size of 0.03, is 113). We also verified the sample size in relation to the questionnaire items. Hair et al. (2016) advocate that 5–10 responses per item are sufficient. As the study encompassed 26 items, a sample of 418 respondents suffices. Descriptive analysis showed that 53% of the respondents were male (47% female). Moreover, 32% were 18–28 years of age, 30% were 29–39, 25% were aged 40–50, and 13% were 51 years of age or over.

### 4.2. Variables and measurement

*Social media involvement* was gauged by employing Ebrahimi et al.'s (2019) four-item scale. To measure *CBE*, we adopted Vivek et al.'s (2014) ten-item, three-dimensional scale that incorporates conscious attention (three items), enthused participation (four items), and social connection (three items; see also Hollebeek et al., 2014). *Brand co-creation* was gauged by using Grissemann and Stokburger-Sauer's (2012) four-item scale, which comprises co-production and value-in-use dimensions (Ranjan & Read, 2016). *Brand identification* was measured by using Rather and Hollebeek's (2019) four-item scale. Finally, *brand loyalty* was measured by adopting Harrigan et al.'s (2017) four-item instrument. All the items were collected on seven-point scales ranging from *strongly disagree* (1) to *strongly agree* (7), as outlined in the Appendix.

## 5. Results

### 5.1. Measurement model-, reliability-, and validity testing results

Prior to testing the measurement properties, we examined skewness and kurtosis values to examine whether our data satisfied the normality assumption (Kim, 2013). The attained kurtosis values ranged from -0.07 to 0.62, with skewness values ranging from -0.33 to -0.05 (i.e., below the cut-off value of 2), thus satisfying the normality assumption. Next, confirmatory factor analysis (CFA) using maximum likelihood estimation was conducted to evaluate scale reliability and validity (Byrne, 2013; Raza et al., 2020). The model fit results were satisfactory: $\chi^2$ = (291.57), df = (134), $\chi^2$/df (2.17); CFI (0.95); NFI (0.96); GFI (0.92); RMSEA (0.063), and SRMR (0.026).

Each construct's Cronbach's alpha was between 0.89 and 0.95, thus above the threshold value of 0.7 (Hair et al., 2016; Shams et al., 2020b; Rather & Shakir, 2018), representing adequate reliability. All of the constructs' standardized factor loadings (SFLs) ranged from 0.74–0.92 (i.e., significant). The composite reliability (CR) ranged from 0.83–0.92, thus exceeding the value of 0.6 (Hair et al., 2016). Further, the average variance extracted (AVE) of each factor ranged from 0.61 to 0.77 (i.e., over 0.5), thus evidencing convergent validity (see Table 19.1). Finally, adopting Fornell and Larcker (1981), the square root of the AVE for each construct surpassed the correlation between the constructs, revealing discriminant validity (see Table 19.1). We next address our hypothesis testing results.

### 5.2. Hypothesis testing results

We used structural equation modelling (SEM) with AMOS20 software to test the hypothesized relationships. The results revealed an acceptable model fit: $\chi^2$ = (310.25), df = (137), $\chi^2$/df (2.26); CFI (0.94); NFI (0.95); GFI (0.90); RMSEA (0.064) and SRMR (0.028).

The results indicate that social media involvement positively and significantly affects CBE ($\beta$ = 0.55, p < .001), supporting H1. Relatedly, brand identification significantly impacts CBE

Table 19.1 Reliability, correlations, and discriminant validity

| Construct | α | CR | AVE | SMI | CA | EP | SC | BID | BCO | BLY |
|---|---|---|---|---|---|---|---|---|---|---|
| SMI | .95 | .85 | .77 | **.84** | | | | | | |
| CA | .92 | .92 | .63 | .51 | **.81** | | | | | |
| EP | .93 | .88 | .72 | .60 | .54 | **.82** | | | | |
| SC | .94 | .83 | .61 | .63 | .55 | .56 | **.80** | | | |
| BID | .89 | .86 | .70 | .59 | .57 | .57 | .52 | **.82** | | |
| BCO | .93 | .84 | .67 | .53 | .52 | .55 | .61 | .58 | **.81** | |
| BLY | .91 | .89 | .69 | .51 | .54 | .50 | .53 | .52 | .59 | **.83** |

*Notes:* α = Cronbach's alpha, CR = composite reliability, AVE = average variance extracted, SMI = social media involvement, CA = conscious attention, EP= enthused participation, SC = social connection, BID = brand identification, BCO = brand co-creation, BLY = brand loyalty. The off diagonal factors are the correlations amongst the study constructs. The bold diagonal factors are the square root of the variance shared amongst the factors and its measures.

Table 19.2 Structural model results

| | Relationship | $R^2$ | β | t-value | Result |
|---|---|---|---|---|---|
| H1 | SMI → CBE | 0.63*** | 0.55 | 9.55 | Supported |
| H2 | BID → CBE | 0.63*** | 0.53 | 7.13 | Supported |
| H3 | CBE → BCO | 0.65*** | 0.56 | 10.32 | Supported |
| H4 | CBE → BLY | 0.67*** | 0.59 | 12.01 | Supported |
| H5 | BLY → BCO | 0.63*** | 0.54 | 8.43 | Supported |

*Note:*** Significant for p < 0.001

(β = 0.53, p < .001), hence supporting H2. Collectively, both predictors (i.e., SMI, BI) explain 63% of the observed variance in CBE. Second, as proposed in H3, CBE strongly effects brand co-creation (β= 0.56, p<.001). CBE explains 65% of the observed variance in brand co-creation. Third, as hypothesized in H4, CBE highly impacts brand loyalty (β= 0.59, p< .001). CBE explains 67% of the observed variance in brand loyalty. Finally, as postulated in H5, brand loyalty strongly impacts brand co-creation (β= 0.54, p<. 001), which explains 63% of the observed variance in brand co-creation. A summary of the hypothesis testing results is provided in Table 19.2.

## 6. Discussion

### 6.1. Theoretical implications

By integrating social media involvement, brand identification, CBE, brand co-creation, and brand loyalty in our proposed model, this study contributes to the tourism-, social media-, and CBE literature. First, we provide insight into the role of visitors' social media-based brand engagement and its effect on co-creation and loyalty. While extant research has established a positive impact of brand identification on CE (e.g., Kaur et al., 2020; Rather et al., 2021; Wang & Kim, 2019), empirical insight into this association in the tourism-based social media context remains sparse (e.g., MSI, 2020), as therefore explored in this chapter. That is, our empirical results corroborate that the more consumers identify with a brand (e.g., in terms of its values), the more they are expected to engage with it on social media. In the destination marketing context, this means that raising consumers' destination brand identification is instrumental in building their engagement with destination brands (see also Kumar & Kaushik, 2020; Rather & Hollebeek, 2019). Consequently, our results suggest that appealing or linking to consumers' identification-driving (e.g., integrity, corporate social responsibility) values is critical in fostering not only brand engagement, but also positive downstream behavioural outcomes, including destination brand co-creation and loyalty.

Second, while category or brand involvement has also been previously deployed as a CBE antecedent, the dynamics characterizing the role of tourists' involvement with specific tourism-related social media *content* and its effect on CBE remain nebulous, as therefore explored in this chapter. Specifically, our empirical results indicate that the more involved consumers are with destination brand-related social media content, the higher their ensuing destination brand engagement will be. Based on this finding, we deduce a critical role of social media content design and creation in cultivating consumers' destination brand engagement (see also Hollebeek & Macky, 2019). Linking this finding to our preceding result, we expect consumers to optimally engage with social media content that appeals to their values (e.g., respectful service provision that is high in integrity, creativity in content execution, elevated procedural, distributive, and interactional justice in service provision; Ambrose & Schminke, 2003), thus offering important novel insight. Overall, our results suggest a pivotal role of consumers' social media involvement and brand identification in cultivating CBE, exposing their strategic importance. Third, based on our results, we derive specific implications for further tourism, social media, and CBE research, as discussed further in Section 6.3.

## *6.2. Practical implications*

This research also provides insight for tourism (marketing) practitioners. Contemporary tourism brands should know the value of CBE, particularly in the social media context, which is expected to generate enhanced returns. Our results confirm that firms' social media investments can generate significant benefit. We therefore recommend tourism marketers to underscore CBE's critical role (e.g., by regularly posting interesting brand-related content; Hollebeek & Macky, 2019). Relatedly, this research uncovered consumers' tourism-based brand identification as a significant driver of CBE, brand loyalty, and brand co-creation, suggesting the importance of consumers' emotional connection to the brand (Hollebeek et al., 2014). One way to stimulate visitors' brand identification is by aligning tourism brands with consumer values (e.g., social responsibility), which is conducive to CBE.

To cater to prospective tourists, managers are advised to develop multiple Web 2.0-based platforms (Ebrahimi et al., 2019; Hollebeek, 2019; Rather, 2021a, 2021b), including mobile apps, e-commerce websites, virtual reality-based touch-points, and brand communities (Hollebeek et al., 2020a, 2020b; Viswanathan et al., 2017), which are expected to be effective in raising CBE. Further, managerial monitoring of users' activities on specific platforms is anticipated to be useful for optimal content design.

Moreover, given the positive, significant association of CBE and brand loyalty, we recommend the deployment of relational visitor tactics, including loyalty programs (Melnyk & Bijmolt, 2015; Hollebeek et al., 2021a, 2021b). These programs will tend to progressively reward more engaged visitors (e.g., with freebies, reward points), thus unlocking firms' capacity to develop and capitalize on more engaged users' brand knowledge or influencer value (Pansari & Kumar, 2017).

## 6.3. Limitations and future research

This study yields significant opportunity for further research. For example, it serves as a springboard for further tourism-based CBE research. For example, to what extent does (prospective) tourists' elevated CBE as displayed online (e.g., on tourism platforms, such as TripAdvisor) foster their high engagement with specific tourism services (e.g., attraction sites, hotel accommodation) and elevated purchase behaviour? What can online tourism platforms do to facilitate this conversion process?

In addition, this study has several limitations which yield further opportunities for further study. First, we used cross-sectional data, which was collected at a particular point in time, thus potentially limiting its applicability at other times. Therefore, longitudinal research would offer more generalizable results (e.g., Viswanathan et al., 2017). Second, we collected our data from Facebook, Instagram, Booking.com, and Trivago users, thus excluding users of other common social media platforms, including Twitter, Telegram, Pinterest, and so on (Hollebeek, 2019; Hollebeek et al., 2018). Thus, future researchers may wish to explore our model in other social media or related brand community contexts.

Third, our model is limited to our assessment of the modelled relationships. Therefore, future research is advised to investigate other pertinent CBE-based nomological associations, which may include consumer perceived value (congruity), brand image, brand associations, and so on, to impart new insight (MacInnis, 2011; Rather & Camilleri, 2019b; Shams et al., 2020a). Fourth, this chapter investigates two key CBE consequences, including brand loyalty and -co-creation. Therefore, additional dependent variables may be used, such as brand trust/satisfaction, brand commitment, brand love, or brand attachment (Hollebeek & Rather, 2019; Hollebeek et al., 2019a; Rather & Hollebeek, 2020; Shams et al., 2020b). Moreover, the addition of relevant moderating factors may offer further insight (e.g., customer age; Rather & Hollebeek, 2021; Rather et al., 2021). Finally, as the tourism sector is currently suffering severe consequences from COVID-19 (Hollebeek et al., 2020c; Itani & Hollebeek, 2021; Rather, 2021b), some of our modelled constructs may not currently exist at consumers' top of mind (e.g., as they navigate the required social distancing/isolation, and other challenges). Therefore, reconducting this study *post*-COVID-19 is recommended, enabling further researchers to compare and contrast their findings (vs. ours).

## References

Aaker, D. A. (1996). Should you take your brand to where the action is? *Harvard Business Review, 75*(5), 135–142.

Ahn, J., & Back, K.-J. (2018, September). Antecedents and consequences of customer brand engagement in integrated resorts. *International Journal of Hospitality Management, 75*, 144–152.

Alalwan, A. A., Rana, N. P., Dwivedi, Y. K., & Algharabat, R. (2017). Social media in marketing: A review and analysis of the existing literature. *Telematics and Informatics, 34*(7), 1177–1190.

Ambrose, M., & Schminke, M. (2003). Organization structure as a moderator of the relationship between procedural justice, interactional justice, perceived organizational support, and supervisory trust. *Journal of Applied Psychology, 88*(2), 295–305.

Baldus, B. J., Clay, V., & Roger, C. (2015). Online brand community engagement: Scale development and validation. *Journal of Business Research, 68*(5), 978–985.

Berry, L. L. (2000). Cultivating service brand equity. *Journal of Academy of Marketing Science, 28*(1), 128–137.

Binkhorst, E., & Dekker, T. D. (2009). Agenda for co-creation tourism experience research. *Journal of Hospitality Marketing & Management, 18*(2–3), 311–327.

Blazquez-Resino, J. J., Molina, A., & Esteban-Talaya, A. (2015). Service-dominant logic in tourism: The way to loyalty. *Current Issues in Tourism, 18*(8), 706–724.

Brodie, R. J., Hollebeek, L. D., Juric, B., & Ilic, A. (2011). Customer engagement: Conceptual domain, fundamental propositions, and implications for research. *Journal of Service Research, 14*(3), 252–271.

Brodie, R. J., Ilic, A., Juric, B., & Hollebeek, L. (2013). Consumer engagement in a virtual brand community: An exploratory analysis. *Journal of Business Research, 66*(1), 105–114.

Byrne, B. M. (2013). *Structural equation modeling with AMOS.* London: Routledge.

Chathoth, P. K., Ungson, G. R., Altinay, L., Chan, E. S. W., Harrington, R., & Okumus, F (2014). Barriers affecting organisational adoption of higher order customer engagement in tourism service interactions. *Tourism Management, 42,* 181–193.

Chathoth, P. K., Ungson, G. R., Harrington, R. J., & Chan, E. S. W. (2016). Co-creation and higher order customer engagement in hospitality and tourism services. *International Journal of Contemporary Hospitality Management, 28*(2), 222–245.

Chen, T., Drennan, J., Andrews, L., & Hollebeek, L. (2018). User experience sharing: Understanding customer initiation of value co-creation in online communities. *European Journal of Marketing, 52*(5–6), 1154–1184.

Choi, E.-K. (Cindy), Fowler, D., Goh, B., & Yuan, J. (Jessica). (2016). Social media marketing: Applying the uses and gratifications theory in the hotel industry. *Journal of Hospitality Marketing & Management, 25*(7), 771–796.

Clark, M., Lages, C., & Hollebeek, L. (2020). Friend or foe? Customer engagement's value-based effects on fellow customers and the firm. *Journal of Business Research, 121,* 549–556.

De Valck, K., van Bruggen, G. H., & Wierenga, B. (2009). Virtual communities: A marketing perspective. *Decision Support Systems, 47*(3), 185–203.

De Vries, N. J., & Carlson, J. (2014). Examining the drivers and brand performance implications of customer engagement with brands in the social media environment. *Journal of Brand Management, 21*(6), 495–515.

Ebrahimi, P., Hajmohammadi, A., & Khajeheian, D. (2019). Place branding and moderating role of social media. *Current Issues in Tourism, 23*(14), 1723–1731.

Fornell, C., & Larcker, D. F. (1981). Evaluating structural equation models with unobservable variables and measurement error. *Journal of Marketing Research, 18*(1), 39–50.

Fournier, S. (1998). Consumers and their brands: Developing relationship theory in consumer research. *Journal of Consumer Research, 24*(4), 343–373.

Gensler, S., Völckner, F., Liu-Thompkins, Y., & Wiertz, C. (2013). Managing brands in the social media environment. *Journal of Interactive Marketing, 27*(4), 242–256.

Grissemann, U. S., & Stokburger-Sauer, N. E. (2012). Customer co-creation of travel services: The role of company support and customer satisfaction with the co-creation performance. *Tourism Management, 33*(6), 1483–1492.

Groeger, L., Moroko, L., & Hollebeek, L. D. (2016). Capturing value from non-paying consumers' engagement behaviours: Field evidence and development of a theoretical model. *Journal of Strategic Marketing, 24*(3–4), 190–209.

Gummerus, J., Liljander, V., Weman, E., & Pihlström, M. (2012). Customer engagement in a facebook brand community. *Management Research Review, 35*(9), 857–877.

Hair, J. F., Tomas, G., Hult, M., Ringle, C. M., & Sarstedt, M. (2016). *A primer on partial least squares structural equation modeling (PLS-SEM).* Thousand Oaks, CA: SAGE.

Hajli, N., Shanmugam, M., Papagiannidis, S., Zahay, D., & Richard, M.-O. (2017). Branding co-creation with members of online brand communities. *Journal of Business Research, 70,* 136–144.

Hankinson, G. (2007). The management of destination brands: Five guiding principles based on recent developments in corporate branding theory. *Journal of Brand Management, 14*(3), 240–254.

Harrigan, P., Evers, U., Miles, M. O., & Daly, T. (2017). Customer engagement with tourism social media brands. *Tourism Management, 59,* 597–609.

Harrigan, P., Evers, U., Miles, M. O., & Daly, T. (2018). Customer engagement and the relationship between involvement, engagement, self-brand connection and brand usage intent. *Journal of Business Research, 88,* 388–396.

Hatch, M. J., & Schultz, M. (2001). Are the strategic stars aligned for your corporate brand? *Harvard Business Review,* 128–134.

Hollebeek, L. D. (2011a). Exploring customer brand engagement: Definition & themes. *Journal of Strategic Marketing, 19*(7), 555–573.

Hollebeek, L. D. (2011b). Demystifying customer brand engagement: Exploring the loyalty nexus. *Journal of Marketing Management, 27*(7–8), 785–807.

Hollebeek, L. D. (2019). Developing business customer engagement through social media engagement-platforms: An integrative SD logic/RBV-informed model. *Industrial Marketing Management, 81,* 89–98.

Hollebeek, L. D., Andreassen, T. W., Smith, D. L. G., Grönquist, D., Karahasanović, A., & Marquez, A. (2018). Epilogue – Service innovation actor engagement: An integrative model. *Journal of Services Marketing, 32*(1), 95–100.

Hollebeek, L. D., & Chen, T. (2014). Exploring positively-versus negatively-valenced brand engagement: A conceptual model. *Journal of Product & Brand Management, 23*(1), 62–74.

Hollebeek, L. D., Clark, M., Andreassen, T., Sigurdsson, V., & Smith, D. (2020a). Virtual reality through the customer journey: Framework and propositions. *Journal of Retailing & Consumer Services, 55*. https://doi.org/10.1016/j.jretconser.2020.102056

Hollebeek, L. D., Das, K., & Shukla, Y. (2021a, December). Game on! How gamified loyalty programs boost customer engagement value. *International Journal of Information Management, 61*, 102308. https://doi.org/10.1016/j.ijinfomgt.2021.102308

Hollebeek, L. D., Glynn, M. S., & Brodie, R. (2014). Consumer brand engagement in social media: Conceptualization, scale development and validation. *Journal of Interactive Marketing, 28*(2), 149–165.

Hollebeek, L. D., Kumar, V., & Srivastava, R. K. (2020b). From customer-, to actor-, to stakeholder engagement: Taking stock, conceptualization, and future directions. *Journal of Service Research*, 1–16. https://doi.org/10.1177/1094670520977680. https://journals.sagepub.com/doi/10.1177/1094670520977680

Hollebeek, L. D., & Macky, K. (2019). Digital content marketing's role in fostering consumer engagement, trust, and value: Framework, fundamental propositions, and implications. *Journal of Interactive Marketing, 45*(1), 27–41.

Hollebeek, L. D., Malthouse, E. C., & Block, M. P. (2016). Sounds of music: Exploring consumers' musical engagement. *Journal of Consumer Marketing, 33*(6), 417–427.

Hollebeek, L. D., & Rather, R. A. (2019). Service innovativeness and tourism customer outcomes. *International Journal of Contemporary Hospitality Management, 31*(11), 4227–4246.

Hollebeek, L. D., Smith, D. L. G., Kasabov, E., Hammedi, W., Warlow, A., & Clark, M. K. (2020c). Customer brand engagement during service lockdown. *Journal of Services Marketing, 35*(2), 201–209.

Hollebeek, L. D., Sprott, D. E., Andreassen, T. W., Costley, C., Klaus, P., Kuppelwieser, V., Karahasanovic, A., Taguchi, T., Ul Islam, J., & Rather, R. A. (2019a). Customer engagement in evolving technological environments: Synopsis and guiding propositions. *European Journal of Marketing, 53*(9), 2018–2023.

Hollebeek, L. D., Sprott, D., & Brady, M. (2021b). Rise of the machines? Customer engagement in automated service interactions. *Journal of Service Research, 24*(1), 3–8.

Hollebeek, L. D., Srivastava, R. K., & Chen, T. (2019b). SD logic – Informed customer engagement: Integrative framework, revised fundamental propositions, and application to CRM. *Journal of the Academy of Marketing Science, 47*(1), 161–185.

Iglesias, O., & Ind, N. (2020). Towards a theory of conscientious corporate brand co-creation: The next key challenge in brand management. *Journal of Brand Management*, 1–11. https://doi.org/10.1057/s41262-020-00205-7.

Iglesias, O., Ind, N., & Alfaro, M. (2013). The organic view of the brand: A brand value co-creation model. *Journal of Brand Management, 20*, 670–688.

Iglesias, O., Singh, J. J., & Batista-Foguet, J. M. (2011). The role of brand experience and affective commitment in determining brand loyalty. *Journal of Brand Management, 18*(8), 570–582.

Im, J., & Qu, H. (2017). Drivers and resources of customer co-creation: A scenario-based case in the restaurant industry. *International Journal of Hospitality Management, 64*, 31–40.

Ind, N., Iglesias, O., & Markovic, S. (2017). The co-creation continuum: From tactical market research tool to strategic collaborative innovation method. *Journal of Brand Management, 24*(4), 310–321.

Ind, N., Iglesias, O., & Schultz, M. (2013). Building brands together: Emergence and outcomes of co-creation. *California Management Review, 55*(3), 5–26.

Islam, J. U., Hollebeek, L. D., Rahman, Z., Khan, I., & Rasool, A. (2019). Customer engagement in the service context: An empirical investigation of the construct, its antecedents and consequences. *Journal of Retailing and Consumer Services, 50*, 277–285.

Islam, J. U., & Rahman, Z. (2017). The impact of online brand community characteristics on customer engagement: An application of stimulus-organism-response paradigm. *Telematics and Informatics, 34*(4), 96–109.

Islam, J. U., Shahid, S., Rasool, A., Rahman, Z., Khan, I., & Rather, R. A. (2020). Impact of website attributes on customer engagement in banking: A solicitation of stimulus-organism-response theory. *International Journal of Bank Marketing, 38*(6), 1279–1303.

Itani, O. S., & Hollebeek, L. (2021). Light at the end of the tunnel: Visitors' virtual reality (versus in-person) attraction site tour-related behavioral intentions during and post-COVID-19. *Tourism Management, 84*, 104290.

Itani, O. S., Kassar, A.-N., & Loureiro, S. M. C. (2019). Value get, value give: The relationships among perceived value, relationship quality, customer engagement, and value consciousness. *International Journal of Hospitality Management, 80*, 78–90.

Kamboj, S., Sarmah, B., Gupta, S., & Dwivedi, Y. (2018). Examining branding co-creation in brand communities on social media: Applying the paradigm of stimulus-organism-response. *International Journal of Information Management, 39*, 169–185.

Katz, E., & Foulkes, D. (1962). On the use of the mass media as escape: Clarification of a concept. *Public Opinion Quarterly, 26*(3), 377–388.

Kaur, H., Paruthi, M., Islam, J. U., & Hollebeek, L. D. (2020). The role of brand community identification and reward on consumer brand engagement and brand loyalty in virtual brand communities. *Telematics and Informatics, 46*. https://doi.org/10.1016/j.tele.2019.101321.

Kavaratzis, M., & Hatch, M. J. (2013). The dynamics of place brands: An identity-based approach to place branding theory. *Marketing Theory, 13*(1), 69–86.

Kim, H.-Y. (2013). Statistics notes for clinical researchers: Assessing normal distribution using skewness and kurtosis. *Restorative Dentistry & Endodontics, 38*(1), 52–54.

Ko, H., Cho, C.-H., & Roberts, M. S. (2005). Internet uses and gratifications: A structural equation model of interactive advertising. *Journal of Advertising, 3*(2), 57–70.

Ku, Y.-C., Chu, T.-H., & Tseng, C.-H. (2013). Gratifications for using CMC technologies: A comparison among SNS, IM, and e-mail. *Computers in Human Behavior, 29*(1), 226–234.

Kumar, V., & Kaushik, A. (2020). Does experience affect engagement? Role of destination brand engagement in developing brand advocacy and revisit intentions. *Journal of Travel & Tourism Marketing, 37*(3), 332–346.

Kumar, V., & Pansari, A. (2016). Competitive advantage through engagement. *Journal of Marketing Research, 53*, 497–514.

Kumar, V., Rajan, B., Gupta, S., & Pozza, I. D. (2019). Customer engagement in service. *Journal of the Academy of Marketing Science, 47*(1), 138–160.

Lam, S. K., Ahearne, M., Hu, Y., & Schillewaert, N. (2010), Resistance to brand switching when a radically new brand is introduced: A social identity theory perspective. *Journal of Marketing, 74*(6), 128–146.

Li, F., Larimo, J., & Leonidou, L. C. (2020). Social media marketing strategy: Definition, conceptualization, taxonomy, validation, and future agenda. *Journal of the Academy of Marketing Science*, 1–20.

Lim, H., & Kumar, A. (2019). Variations in consumers' use of brand online social networking: A uses and gratifications approach. *Journal of Retailing and Consumer Services, 51*, 450–457.

MacInnis, D. (2011, July). A framework for conceptual contributions in marketing. *Journal of Marketing, 75*, 136–154.

Malthouse, E. C., Haenlein, M., Skiera, B., Wege, E., & Zhang, M. (2013). Managing customer relationships in the social media era: Introducing the social CRM house. *Journal of Interactive Marketing, 27*(4), 270–280.

Marketing Science Institute (MSI). (2020). *Research priorities 2020–2022*. Retrieved from www.msi.org/wp-content/uploads/2020/06/MSI_RP20-22.pdf

Melnyk, V., & Bijmolt, T. (2015). The effects of introducing and terminating loyalty programs. *European Journal of Marketing, 9*(3), 398–419.

Merz, M. A., He, Y., & Vargo, S. L. (2009). The evolving brand logic: A service-dominant logic perspective. *Journal of Academy of Marketing Science, 37*(3), 328–344.

Mittal, B., & Lee, M.-S. (1989). A causal model of consumer involvement. *Journal of Economic Psychology, 10*(3), 363–389.

Mollen, A. H. W. (2010). Engagement, telepresence and interactivity in online consumer experience: Reconciling scholastic and managerial perspectives. *Journal of Business Research, 63*(9–10), 919–925.

Narangajavana, Y., Fiol, L. J. C., Tena, M. A. M., Artola, R. M. R., & García, J. S. (2017). The influence of social media in creating expectations. An empirical study for a tourist destination. *Annals of Tourism Research, 65*, 60–70.

Oliver, R. L. (1999). Whence consumer loyalty? *Journal of Marketing, 63*(1), 33–44.

Palmatier, R. W., Dant, R. P., Grewal, D., & Evans, K. R. (2006). Factors influencing the effectiveness of relationship marketing: A meta-analysis. *Journal of Marketing, 70*(4), 136–153.

Pansari, A., & Kumar, V. (2017). Customer engagement: The construct, antecedents, and consequences. *Journal of the Academy of Marketing Science, 45*(3), 294–311.

Parrey, S. H., Hakim, I. A., & Rather, R. A. (2019). Mediating role of government initiatives and media influence between perceived risks and destination image: A study of conflict zone. *International Journal of Tourism Cities, 5*(1), 90–106.

Prahalad, C. K., & Ramaswamy, V. (2000). Co-opting customer competence. *Harvard Business Review, 78*(1), 79–90.

Prahalad, C. K., & Ramaswamy, V. (2004). Co-creation experiences: The next practice in value creation. *Journal of Interactive Marketing, 18*(2), 5–14.

Prebensen, N. K., Kim, H., & Uysal, M. (2015). Cocreation as moderator between the experience value and satisfaction relationship. *Journal of Travel Research, 55*(7), 934–945.

Prebensen, N. K., Woo, E., & Uysal, M. S. (2014). Experience value: Antecedents and consequences. *Current Issues in Tourism, 17*(10), 910–928.

Prentice, C., Han, X. Y., Hua, L.-L., & Hu, L. (2019). The influence of identity-driven customer engagement on purchase intention. *Journal of Retailing and Consumer Services, 47*, 339–347.

Prentice, C., Wang, X., & Lin, X. (2018). An organic approach to customer engagement and loyalty. *Journal of Computer Information Systems*. https://doi.org/10.1080/08874417.2018.1485528.

Ranjan, K. R., & Read, S. (2016). Value co-creation: Concept and measurement. *Journal of the Academy of Marketing Science, 44*, 290–315.

Rather, R. A. (2017). Investigating the impact of customer brand identification on hospitality brand loyalty: A social identity perspective. *Journal of Hospitality Marketing and Management, 27*(5), 487–513.

Rather, R. A. (2018). Exploring customers' attitudes towards the hospitality brands in India: A social identity perspective. In M. A. Camileri (Ed.), *The branding of tourist destinations: Theoretical and empirical insights* (pp. 207–231). Bingley: Emerald Publishing.

Rather, R. A. (2019). Consequences of consumer engagement in service marketing: An empirical exploration, *Journal of Global Marketing, 32*(2), 116–135.

Rather, R. A. (2020). Customer experience and engagement in tourism destinations: The experiential marketing perspective. *Journal of Travel & Tourism Marketing, 37*(1), 15–32.

Rather, R. A. (2021a). Monitoring the impacts of tourism-based social media, risk perception and fear on tourists' attitude and revisiting behaviour in the wake of COVID-19 pandemic. *Current Issues in Tourism, 24*(23), 1–9.

Rather, R. A. (2021b). Demystifying the effects of perceived risk and fear on customer engagement, co-creation and revisit intention during COVID-19: A protection motivation theory approach. *Journal of Destination Marketing & Management, 20,* June 2021, 100564. https://doi.org/10.1016/j.jdmm.2021.100564

Rather, R. A., & Camilleri, M. A. (2019a). The effects of service quality and consumer-brand value congruity on hospitality brand loyalty. *Anatolia, 30*(4), 547–559.

Rather, R. A., & Camilleri, M. A. (2019b). The customers' brand identification with luxury hotels: A social identity perspective. In *Academy of Marketing Science World Marketing Congress* (pp. 429–443). Cham: Springer.

Rather, R. A., & Hollebeek, L. D. (2019). Exploring and validating social identification and social exchange-based drivers of hospitality customer loyalty. *International Journal of Contemporary Hospitality Management, 31*(3), 1432–1451.

Rather, R. A., & Hollebeek, L. D. (2020). Experiential marketing for tourism destinations. In S. K. Dixit (Ed.), *The Routledge handbook of tourism experience management and marketing*. London: Routledge.

Rather, R. A., & Hollebeek, L. D. (2021). Customers' service-related engagement, experience, and behavioral intent: Moderating role of age. *Journal of Retailing & Consumer Services, 60*, May 2021, 102453. https://doi.org/10.1016/j.jretconser.2021.102453

Rather, R. A., Hollebeek, L. D., & Islam, J. U. (2019). Tourism-based customer engagement: The construct, antecedents, and consequences. *The Service Industries Journal, 39*(7–8), 519–540.

Rather, R. A., Hollebeek, L. D., & Rasoolimanesh, S. M. (2021). First-time versus repeat tourism customer engagement, experience, and value cocreation: An empirical investigation. *Journal of Travel Research*. Online first. https://doi.org/10.1177/0047287521997572

Rather, R. A., Najar, A. H., & Jaziri, D. (2020). Destination branding in tourism: Insights from social identification, attachment and experience theories. *Anatolia, 31*(2), 29–43.

Rather, R. A., & Parray, S. H. (2018). Customer engagement in increasing affective commitment within hospitality sector. *Journal of Hospitality Application and Research, 13*(1), 72–91.

Rather, R. A., & Sharma, J. (2018). Customer engagement for evaluating customer relationships in hotel industry. *European Journal of Tourism, Hospitality and Recreation*, 8(1), 1–13.

Rather, R. A., & Sharma, J. (2019). Dimensionality and consequences of customer engagement: A social exchanges perspective. *Vision*, 23(3), 255–266.

Rather, R. A., Tehseen, S., & Parrey, S. H. (2018). Promoting customer brand engagement and brand loyalty through customer brand identification and value congruity. *Spanish Journal of Marketing*, 1, 23–32.

Raza, A., Rather, R. A., Iqbal, M. K., & Bhutta, U. S. (2020). An assessment of corporate social responsibility on customer company identification and loyalty in banking industry: A PLS-SEM analysis. *Management Research Review*, 43(11), 1337–1370.

Riel, C. B. M., & Balmer, J. M. T. (1997). Corporate identity: The concept, its measurement and management. *European Journal of Marketing*, 31, 340–355.

Ritchie, J. R. B., & Ritchie, R. J. B. (1998). The branding of tourism destinations. In *Annual congress of international association of scientific experts in tourism* (pp. 1–31), Marrakech, Morocco.

Sasser, S., Kilgour, M., & Hollebeek, L. D. (2014). Marketing in an interactive world: The evolving nature of communication processes using social media. In A. Ayanso & K. Lertwachara (Eds.), *Harnessing the power of social media and web analytics* (pp. 29–52). Hershey: IGI Global.

Shams, G., Rather, R. A., Rehman, M. A., & Lodhi, R. N. (2020b). Hospitality-based service recovery, outcome favourability, satisfaction with service recovery and consequent customer loyalty: An empirical analysis. *International Journal of Culture, Tourism and Hospitality Research*, 15(2), 266–284.

Shams, G., Rehman, M. A., Samad, S., & Rather, R. A. (2020a). The impact of the magnitude of service failure and complaint handling on satisfaction and brand credibility in the banking industry. *Journal of Financial Services Marketing*, 25, 25–34.

Skinner, H. (2008). The emergence and development of place marketing's confused identity. *Journal of Marketing Management*, 24(9–10), 915–928.

Smock, A. D., Ellison, N. B., Lampe, C., & Wohn, D. Y. (2011). Facebook as a toolkit: A uses and gratification approach to unbundling feature use. *Computers in Human Behavior*, 27(6) 2322–2329.

So, K. K. F., King, C., & Sparks, B. (2014). Customer engagement with tourism brands: Scale development and validation. *Journal of Tourism Research & Hospitality*, 38(3), 304–329.

So, K. K. F., Wei, W., & Martin, D. (2020). Understanding customer engagement and social media activities in tourism: A latent profile analysis and cross-validation. *Journal of Business Research*.

Soper, D. S. (2014). *A-priori sample size calculator for structural equation models [software]*. Retrieved from www.danielsoper.com/statcalc/calculator.aspx?id=89.

Spohrer, J., Maglio, P. P., Bailey, J., & Gruhl, D. (2007). Steps toward a science of service systems. *IEEE Computer*, 40(1), 71–77.

Tajfel, H., & Turner, J. (1979). The social identity theory of intergroup behavior. In S. Worchel & W. G. Austin (Eds.), *Psychology of intergroup relations Nelson-hall* (pp. 33–47). Chicago, IL: Chicago University Press.

Touni, R., Kim, W. G., & Ali, M. A. (2020). Antecedents and an outcome of customer engagement with hotel brand community on Facebook. *Journal of Hospitality & Tourism Research*, 44(2), 278–299.

Van Doorn, J., Lemon, K. N., Mittal, V., Nass, S., Pick, D., Pirner, P., & Verhoef, P. C. (2010). Customer engagement behavior: Theoretical foundations and research directions. *Journal of Service Research*, 13(3), 253–266.

Vargo, S. L., & Lusch, R. F. (2004). Evolving to a new dominant logic for marketing. *Journal of Marketing*, 68(1), 1–17.

Vargo, S. L., & Lusch, R. F. (2016). Institutions and axioms: An extension and update of service-dominant logic. *Journal of the Academy of Marketing Science*, 44, 5–23.

Viswanathan, V., Hollebeek, L., Malthouse, E., Maslowska, E., Kim, S. J., & Xie, W. (2017). The dynamics of consumer engagement with mobile technologies. *Service Science*, 9(1), 36–49.

Vivek, S. D., Beatty, S. E., Dalela, V., & Morgan, R. M. (2014). A generalized multidimensional scale for measuring customer engagement. *Journal of Marketing Theory and Practice*, 22(4), 401–420.

Vivek, S. D., Beatty, S. E., & Morgan, R. M. (2012). Customer engagement: Exploring customer relationships beyond purchase. *Journal of Marketing Theory and Practice*, 20(2), 122–146.

Wang, Z., & Kim, H. G. (2019). Can social media marketing improve customer relationship capabilities and firm performance? Dynamic capability perspective. *Journal of Interactive Marketing*, 39, 15–26.

Zaichkowsky, J. L. (1985). Measuring the involvement construct. *Journal of Consumer Research*, 12(3), 341–352.

Zhang, M., Guo, L., Hu, M., & Liu, W. (2017). Influence of customer engagement with company social networks on stickiness: Mediating effect of customer value creation. *International Journal of Information Management*, 37(3), 229–240.

# Appendix

## Social Media Involvement (SMI)

SMI1: The photos of this tourism destination in Facebook/Instagram made me interested to travel.
SMI2: Attractiveness of tours to this tourism destination shared in Facebook/Instagram made me interested to travel.
SMI3: The memories that people of this tourism destination shared in Facebook/Instagram made me interested to travel.
SMI4: Comments in Facebook/Instagram posts encouraged me to travel to this tourism destination.

## Customer Brand Engagement (CBE)

### CONSCIOUS ATTENTION (CA)

CA1: Anything related to this tourism destination grabs my attention.
CA2: I pay a lot of attention to anything about this tourism destination.
CA3: I like to learn more about this tourism destination.

### Enthused Participation (EP)

EP1: I spend a lot of my discretionary time in this tourism destination.
EP2: I am passionate about this tourism destination.
EP3: My days would not be the same without this tourism destination.
EP4: I am heavily into this tourism destination.

### Social Connection (SC)

SC1: I enjoy this tourism destination more when I am with others.
SC2: I love this tourism destination with the company of my friends.
SC3: This tourism destination offers more fun when other people around me do it too.

## Brand Identification (BID)

BID1: I identify strongly with this tourism destination.
BID2: When someone criticizes tourism destination, it feels like a personal insult.
BID3: When I talk about tourism destination, I usually say 'we' rather than 'they.'
BID4: When someone praises tourism destination, it feels like a personal compliment.

## Brand Co-creation (BCO)

BCO1: I am interested in participating in this co-creation experience.
BCO2: I intend to be actively involved or participate in this co-creation experience.
BCO3: I have used my experience from previous visits in order to arrange this trip.
BCO4: I have the intention to discuss this co-creation experience with the service provider.

## Brand Loyalty (BLY)

BLY1: I would recommend this tourism destination to someone who seeks my advice.
BLY2: I would say positive things about this tourism destination site to other people.
BLY3: I would encourage friends and relatives to do business with this tourism destination.
BLY4: I will do more business with tourism destination in the next few years.

# 20
# CORPORATE BRAND NARRATIVES
## Polysemy, voice, and purpose

*Joep Cornelissen*

In this brief commentary, I will reflect on the contributions in this section of the handbook. All four contributions are thoughtful and informative studies that elaborate on the role of consumers and other stakeholders in the co-creation of a corporate or product brand. These chapters make a considered case for conceiving of brands as a created between an organization and its stakeholders, rather than seeing brand management more 'monolithically' as in the control of organizations and their brand managers. When taken together as a section, they also complement each other well; one chapter (Argenti) provides a general strategic communication framework for thinking about the process through which brands are co-created; two chapters (Schmeltz and Kjeldsen (2022) and Zamparini et al. [2022]) dive deep into the role of multiple voices and stakeholders within this co-creation process; and the final chapter in the set (Rather et al., 2022) offers empirical evidence on the link between stakeholder engagement and co-creation. Three of the four chapters also share a focus on service settings ranging from a museum and a festival to destination branding. In this way, the chapters nicely complement and strengthen each other conceptually, in moving from a broader to more specific focus, and from general case illustrations and qualitative studies to empirical based survey-evidence. Building on the rich insights of these chapters, my aim in this brief commentary is to add a few reflections and offer some thoughts on the topic and on possibilities for further research.

## Corporate brand narratives and co-creation

Across the four chapters in this section, there is a clear conviction that brands are relational constructs, essentially signifiers and intangible associations that exist *in between* organizations and their customers and other stakeholders. They are 'held' as images, ideas, and interpretations by both 'internal' members of the organization as well as by 'external' stakeholders alike. Whilst brands may represent an economic value to an organization who owns them, the actual intangible meanings associated with the brand are co-created and co-constituted with stakeholders inside and outside of the organization. This foundational idea, which is embraced by all four chapters, rests on a contrast with more traditional ideas of brand management in which the meaning of a brand was controlled by a brand manager in the organization through design and communications. The criticism of this traditional view, and of the principles associated with it (such as brand portfolio management, positioning, strategic messaging), rests to a large extent, as these chapters suggest, on a fundamental shift in the media that are used by organizations to communicate with stakeholders.

Argenti (2022) sketches the broad technological, market, and media developments that have affected organizations and their brand management. He singles out the role of social media which (with an emphasis on interactivity) has heralded a new era in which brands and reputations are not 'managed' but created in interplay with an organization's stakeholders. Argenti offers a useful strategy framework and some illustrative case examples for brand managers to help them think through the details and ramifications of such a co-creation approach, one in which they nudge and seed content in conversations but also leave ample freedom to stakeholder to share and create their own impressions.

In this co-creation view, a (corporate) brand and the reputation a company has is not simply given, as a position to be taken up or protected by brand managers, but is an intangible asset that is established in relationships and thus co-constructed with stakeholders. Brand managers who adopt this co-creation frame realize that in a social media environment a reputation is shaped by the organization as well as by the community of stakeholders it embraces. They see the opportunities that social media provide to foster goodwill for their organizations and believe that a reputation is not theirs to claim but is constantly being established and re-established in interactions with their stakeholders, both on- and off-line.

Schmeltz and Kjeldsen (2022) take this co-creation view as their point of departure and aim to analyse more deeply when and how the multiplicity of 'internal' and 'external' stakeholders involved in the process may lead to a single, collectively shared brand narrative or whether rather it may evolve into a 'cacophony' of voices. They conceptualize this process through the idea of voice and of how different voices may be expressed and may harmoniously coalesce, or not. Introducing the voice metaphor allows them to add a further layer to the branding process, one that recognizes it as a dialogic, conversational process in which different voices are expressed and may reveal the image or reputation that the brand enjoys at a particular point in time. Schmeltz and Kjeldsen (2022) draw on Bakhtin's work on voice and dialogue and make the case for focusing as much on different 'internal' voices besides ones 'external' to the organization.

The voice metaphor is instructive, not least as it captures the idea that the organization can itself as part of this conversational co-creation process make its own voice heard. An organization can think of finding its own 'voice'; that is, an engaging and natural style of communicating and one that 'reflects' its core identity or character (Argenti, 2022). When there is a genuine experience of such a 'human' corporate voice through Twitter feeds, blogs, and social networking sites, it translates into positive feelings, a favourable image, and strong stakeholder relationships.

In their chapter, Zamparini et al. (2022) extend this line of thinking. Whilst they accept many of the same premises around brands as being co-created, they suggest that beyond the idea of voice it is important to capture better how different stakeholders interpret the brand. They coin with a nod to semiotics the idea of brand polysemy, the different meanings that a brand may have in the minds of different individuals. What is useful here, compared to the first two chapters, is that they focus on meanings and interpretations as being important and as effectively co-creating brands regardless of whether individuals actively 'voice' their opinions on- or off-line. Zamparini and colleagues offer a visual metaphor of colour as a heuristic to capture differences in interpretations as different hues or colour combinations. The key take-away of this metaphor is that co-creation is about collective constructed meanings, which adds an additional layer beyond the idea that the brand is a reflection of those who have taken the effort to voice their views.

The final chapter in this set by Rather et al. (2022) offers an empirical study of the drivers of co-creation in the context of tourism. They study a range of antecedents and effects of co-creation and find among other things that customers' brand engagement on a destination positively affects brand co-creation and loyalty. This insight is a pivotal addition to the other chapters in this section, in that it recognizes that brand engagement is an important enabler for co-creation. In other words, organizations need to create conditions for dialogue and involvement for co-creation to take place. This may seem obvious at one level, but it is important to establish this point empirically. The contribution of Rather and colleagues also brings this section full circle, in that it underscores empirically the importance of using (social) media to foster and enable co-creation.

Indeed, these chapters together provide in my view nothing short of a coherent research programme, a coherent and sustained area of research that is focused on establishing the tenets of brand co-creation. These authors do so by coining different concepts and frameworks and by using different methods (desk research, qualitative and quantitative methods), but they all work off the same base assumptions and all are geared towards better interpreting and explaining how brand co-creation works. In the remainder of this short commentary, I will add some thoughts to this endeavour in the hope that this may contribute to the excellent effort that is already underway.

## *Developing theory as part of this research programme*

A first suggestion is to think of the forms of theorizing that may help drive and further develop this research programme on brand co-creation and the role of brand narratives in this context. Three of the chapters suggest particular metaphors as a heuristic for thinking about these subjects; as essentially useful vehicles to think about these topics and make some headway. Argenti offers a schematic framework built around the idea of a company revealing its 'character' through its 'artifacts' (products, buildings communications, etc.) when such artifacts are embraced and interpreted by stakeholders. Schmeltz and Kjeldsen draw similarly on a metaphor, but this time of voice. They draw on theoretical writings on dialogue and voice at an inter-personal level and cast brand dynamics involving organizations as similarly based on a conversation involving different voices. And Zamparini and colleagues coin a visual metaphor, but in their case not as a direct representation of co-creation but as a way of thinking *about* differences in stakeholder interpretations of a brand. In their case, the metaphor does not directly feature in the theorizing but is more of a shorthand for thinking about semiotic differences.

In all these instances, these metaphors play important roles in pinpointing aspects of reasoning, and as in the case of Argenti and Schmeltz and Kjeldsen in a very direct and fundamental way. Indeed, both sets of authors reason by analogy (Ketokivi et al., 2017) when they represent co-creation dynamics, through a metaphor of 'revealing oneself' as an organization (Argenti, 2022) in interactions with stakeholders, or as a process of singular voices adding up into a meta-narrative of the brand (Schmeltz & Kjeldsen, 2022). In both instances, the analogy, or metaphor, provides the core base of the subsequent argumentation. Indeed, thinking about both these chapters, there may be value as a field in reflecting on these base assumptions; between both chapters there is for example a difference, however slight perhaps, between whether the organization is accorded a privileged position in the co-creation process or less so. This difference may be partly about different theoretical presuppositions, but it can also be brought out and made part of subsequent theorizing. For example, are there some instances where the co-creation process is more asymmetrical, with the organization still having a more decisive voice than other stakeholders. And if so, how is this manifested in specific interactions and in the brand meanings and narratives that ensue (Michel, 2017)? There is also the related issue here of what vantage point we take in our research; interestingly enough, only the chapter by Rather et al. (2022) takes decidedly a consumer point of view, whereas the three other chapters, whilst embracing a co-creation view, are still interested in how from the organization's view (and the view of the brand manager) a process of co-creation can be understood, fostered as well as 'managed.'

Reflecting on these differences in vantage points and assumptions, there may be value in systematically elaborating, theoretically and empirically, the contours and boundary conditions of the co-creation view. The chapters in this section effectively already do this; but moving forward it may be helpful to reflect beyond individual studies and contributions on the development of the research programme as a whole (Ketokivi et al., 2017). What I am advocating here is not only one form of theorizing (e.g., whether that is more interpretive as in Schmeltz and Kjeldsen [2022] and in Zamparini et al. [2022]), but a joint effort to add and extend theorizing and to develop richer and more nuanced insights on differences in co-creation processes and how these foster a joint understanding, or narrative, of a brand. Besides studying the dynamics of co-creation, such an effort could then also reflect on the idea of a brand narrative. Whilst the chapters here offer a rich set of sources to think about this concept, there is also room it seems for a more sustained effort to unpack this concept as well. For example, the writings here suggest quite a coherently packaged set of meanings, but what about ante-narratives, or meanings that have not yet been configured into a narrative form (that is, into a sequence that positions the organization in relation to an outcome or goal or the brand in relation to a particular purpose or benefit)? Are such meanings less important compared to a clearly crystalized brand narrative? And what about instances where multiple narratives vie for attention? These and other questions of course do not exist separate from the co-creation view, and these would thus also be useful to address as part of the current research programme. Similarly here the idea would not be to challenge the presupposition about narratives being important, but to interrogate their role, uses, and the variable form that they might take (and alongside other concepts perhaps such as frames or cognitive mental models (see Rather et al., 2022) – thus making it an object for further research.

## *Character, purpose, and brand narratives*

One further point that seems opportune to reflect on is, as mentioned, the specific role of organizations in the co-creation process. Co-creation may, as mentioned earlier, be a dialogic process particularly in service settings such as the ones covered by the chapters in this section. But at the same time co-creation may not always be a 'true' open and multi-party conversation, where whatever transpires as an outcome (that is, the constructed meaning of a brand) is the result of a mutual co-construction process by 'internal' and 'external' stakeholders. Argenti (2022) makes the point that organizations, and the brand managers working for them, not only have a clear stake but also have interests and motives to portray their brand in a particular way. One important area where this strategic, interest-driven motive is clear is in the current discussions around purpose-led organizations and conscious or conscientious brands (Iglesias & Ind, 2020). Purpose-led organizations pursue a particular set of ideals or values for their organizations and for their brands, such as addressing social ills, health, and well-being, or environmental issues through their products and services. In such instances, organizations are intrinsically motivated to pursue, as Argenti notes, a set of ideals and values that reflect their own sense of character – that is, their own sense of what values and commitments the company stands for. In fact, if we take this idea of character seriously as a concept (and not just as the equivalent of identity (cf. Argenti, 2022)), it gives the idea that organizations may still engage in processes of co-creation and be open to influences and interpretations from external stakeholders. Yet, at the same time, an organization's character, rooted as it is in its own values, places comparatively greater emphasis on personal autonomy than on being accountable to the views of others, even if this involves powerful groups such as customers or shareholders. Consider, for example, purpose-led companies such as Danone or Unilever who, in line with their pledged purposes, have a strong character and value-based commitments around their brands and need to find ways to both mitigate and overcome the institutional pressures from shareholders who want to see greater prospects of growth and more significant financial returns in the short term. There is of course a risk for such companies that if they give way to the growth narratives of the financial markets (and to shareholder capitalism in general) they lose a sense of their character and of the purpose trajectory that they have been on altogether. Indeed, such organizations may recognize specific demands or voices, but equally may feel that their own value-based ethos transcends the clamour of such voices. The recent case of Danone is a good example of such a position, with the company repeatedly trying to brand itself as a company built for long-term sustainable value, but where major shareholders construed a different narrative around a company that had lagging behind its direct competitors and with a complex governance structure that made it less poised for growth. These different narratives led in this instance to a stand-off, which ultimately led to the dismissal of the CEO of Danone. As in this case, there is value I believe in comparing different scenarios of co-creation, including scenarios that do not just involve customers but also other primary stakeholders such as shareholders and employees. It would then in turn be interesting to explore processes of actual co-creation, where parties come together and collectively shape the brand, versus contexts where such alignment is harder to achieve, and with alternative narratives competing for attention. The context of conscious brands and purpose-led organizations offers a particularly interesting setting for such questions, I believe, in that corporate organizations in such instances engage in conversations but are also motivated to hold onto their own values and thus to their preferred meanings for their brands.

*Concluding comments.* The excellent chapters in this section are all coherently connected and together make a lot of progress on the question of how brands are collectively construed and how this may take the form of a brand narrative. I have been selective in picking up two points for reflection, which build on but in some ways also go beyond these chapters. The emerging research area of brand co-creation is rich, and these chapters have given us many detailed insights and points to think about as research in this field moves forward.

## References

Argenti, P. A. (2022). Integrating multiple voices when crafting a corporate brand narrative. In O. Iglesias, N. Ind, & M. Schultz (Eds.), *The Routledge companion to corporate branding*. London: Routledge.

Iglesias, O., & Ind, N. (2020). Towards a theory of conscientious corporate brand co-creation: the next key challenge in brand management. *Journal of Brand Management, 27*, 710–720.

Ketokivi, M., Mantere, S., & Cornelissen, J. (2017). Reasoning by analogy and the progress of theory. *Academy of Management Review, 42*, 637–658.

Michel, G. (2017). From brand identity to polysemous brands: Commentary on 'Performing identities: Processes of brand and stakeholder identity co-construction'. *Journal of Business Research, 70*, 453–455.

Rather, R. A., Hollebeek, L., Smith, D. L. G., Kukk, J., & Ghasemi, M. (2022). Visitors' destination brand engagement's effect on co-creation: An empirical study. In O. Iglesias, N. Ind, & M. Schultz (Eds.), *The Routledge companion to corporate branding*. London: Routledge.

Schmeltz, L., & Kjeldsen, A. K. (2022). Corporate brand management and multiple voices: Polyphony or cacophony? In O. Iglesias, N. Ind, & M. Schultz (Eds.), *The Routledge companion to corporate branding*. London: Routledge.

Zamparini, A., Visconti, L. M., & Lurati, F. (2022). Polysemic corporate branding: Managing the idea. In O. Iglesias, N. Ind, & M. Schultz (Eds.), *The Routledge companion to corporate branding*. London: Routledge.

# E

# The temporality of corporate branding

Balancing the past and future

# 21
# TOWARDS A CO-CREATIONAL PERSPECTIVE ON CORPORATE HERITAGE BRANDING

*Mario Burghausen*

## 1. Introduction

This chapter seeks to link the field of *corporate heritage branding* scholarship (see Balmer, 2017 for an overview) with the emerging *co-creation perspective* and approach to corporate branding (Iglesias et al., A1). Both research areas have grown in popularity within marketing in recent years but have not yet been discussed in conjunction specifically. This is surprising because corporate heritage branding researchers stress the important role of stakeholders – stakeholders of the past, present, and future – for corporate heritage brands and identities (Balmer, 2017; Lee & Davies, 2019) while corporate branding scholars adopting a co-creational perspective highlight the role of history and the past, for example (Iglesias et al., 2020).

By adopting a co-creational perspective, I argue in this chapter that corporate heritage and corporate heritage brands are always also predicated on the temporal agency of multiple stakeholders (internal and external) and not only marketers or managers alone. *Temporal agency* broadly refers to the ability of stakeholders to shape and influence, produce and reproduce temporal relations that have constitutive import for their own subjectivities as well as the organizational, social, and cultural contexts they inhabit (Emirbayer & Mische, 1998). This implies that the relevance of corporate heritage and corporate heritage brands is dependent on the specific socio-historical context and situation in which some aspects of an organization's and/or brand's past are turned into heritage through the active involvement of stakeholders too. They are not simply passive perceivers of corporate heritage (brands) but through their temporal agency stakeholders actively establish meaningful links between past, present, and future that are constitutive for corporate heritage and the strategic efficacy of corporate heritage brands. In other words, what constitutes corporate heritage and its relevance and consequence for the organization and its stakeholders is always negotiated and co-created (Balmer & Burghausen, 2019) as much as corporate brands are co-created in terms of their value, meaning, etc.

First, the general background and wider context of this chapter's focus on corporate heritage branding is outlined providing a concise overview of this emerging field of scholarship. The subsequent parts establish and discuss conceptual aporias and implications of the notion of corporate heritage and corporate heritage brands from the paradigmatic position of co-creation in a dynamic socio-cultural and multi-stakeholder context.

## 2. Background and context of corporate heritage branding

The research area of *corporate heritage branding* has seen growing scholarly support since its formal inception 15 years ago (Balmer et al., 2006, Urde et al., 2007). In recent years, marketing researchers have garnered a body of empirical evidence and conceptual works (see Balmer, 2017) that has established the concept of heritage and with it the problem of temporality – broadly understood here as the relation(s) between past, present, and future – as an important contemporary marketing and branding topic in its own right. This concern goes beyond and is different from the traditional interest in the history of marketing as a discipline and practice or the use of the historical method in marketing (Balmer & Burghausen, 2019; cf. Jones & Tadajewski, 2016).

### *2.1 Heritage and other temporal concepts in marketing and beyond*

The growing interest in corporate heritage branding specifically originated with the work of John Balmer, Stephen Greyser, and Mats Urde, who formally introduced the concepts of corporate heritage and corporate heritage brands to marketing and branding in two foundational articles (Balmer et al., 2006; Urde et al., 2007). Of course, the term *heritage* is being used in the branding and marketing literature by others and had been so before 2006 already. However, these contributions frequently do not focus on heritage as the main concept of interest (e.g., Brown et al., 2003) or use it very loosely as a generic label in lieu of other concepts or issues of primary concern. For example, various contributions use the term for simply denoting temporal progression, change, or accrual over time (Berthon et al., 2003); longevity, maturity, and age of an organization or its brand (Aaker, 1996); or historical references and temporal associations vis-à-vis a (corporate) brand (Keller & Lehman, 2006). Mostly, though, the term *heritage* has been and is often still being used in marketing and branding scholarship as a mere synonym for various other temporal modes – most prominently standing for history or the past per se – without further specification, elaboration, or a dedicated adoption of the concept of heritage itself (Burghausen & Balmer, 2014a; Balmer & Burghausen, 2015a).

Further, there is a parallel and related stream of scholarly work in marketing that is concerned with the notion of *brand heritage* and *heritage brands* (Wiedmann et al., 2011; Rose et al., 2016). This research area is interested in the effects of brand heritage for product and service branding vis-à-vis consumers (Orth et al., 2019; Pecot et al., 2019; Mencarelli et al., 2020) but not corporate heritage branding as such (but cf. Santos et al., 2016; Pecot & de Barnier, 2018). Because of the great overlap and interdependence between product, service, and corporate branding, both fields of brand scholarship have productively influenced each other and have jointly contributed to the growing interest in heritage and related temporal concepts within marketing in general (see Pecot, E22). Due to the focus of this volume on corporate brands and this chapter's concern with the contributions and relevance of corporate heritage branding scholarship, though, I do not elaborate on this stream.

Concurrently, marketing has seen a lasting intertest in consumer nostalgia (Holbrook & Schindler, 2003) and nostalgia advertising (Muehling & Sprott, 2004), retro-branding (Brown et al., 2003), history marketing (Schug, 2003), and other forms of marketing and consumption for which temporal relations between past, present, and future are of importance (de Groot, 2009). The same goes for the various topical and timely strands of research on history, memory, and temporality in management and organization studies. Various research streams of management research have been stablished with potential relevance for corporate heritage and corporate branding scholarship. These include but are not limited to questions of the various 'uses of the past' (Wadhwani et al., 2018) and the role of history (Hatch & Schultz, 2017; Suddaby et al., 2019), memory (Anteby & Molnar, 2012), and temporality (Hernes & Schultz, 2020) in instrumental, conceptual, and methodological terms (Bucheli & Wadhwani, 2013) including apropos organizational identities and identification (Schultz & Hernes, 2013; Ravasi et al., 2019). At the same time the concept of heritage as it has been developed and discussed within marketing could be highly relevant for the above debates too (see Balmer and Burghausen, 2015b; Andersen, 2020). Yet, there has been to date little or no dialogue between organization theory and management research on the one hand and corporate heritage and brand heritage scholarship on the other. This dialogue is overdue but again beyond the scope of this chapter.

More generally, these developments indicate a fundamental reorientation within business and management studies as well as marketing witnessing a new or better renewed interest in history (Maclean et al., 2020), the past (Balmer & Burghausen, 2019), and temporality (Dawson & Sykes, 2016) akin to a 'historic turn' (Clark & Rowlinson, 2004). Similar 'turns' have been suggested for the social sciences and humanities (Adam, 1995; Tamm & Olivier, 2019), and fundamental temporal shifts in the relation between past, present, and future have been observed within current societies more widely (Assmann, 2013; Hartog, 2015; Landwehr, 2016). The same goes for the scholarly interest in and quotidian popularity of heritage and other temporal concepts such as memory as social and cultural phenomena (Lowenthal, 1998; Zerubavel, 2004). The interest in corporate heritage branding can be seen as a contribution to these debates and a manifestation of these wider trends and shifts.

## 2.2 Foundations of corporate heritage branding

More specifically, *corporate heritage branding* scholars have suggested and shown that certain organizations and/or their corporate brands exhibit and can be characterized by particular traits that qualify as a kind of 'institutional heritage' (Balmer et al., 2006), which is in simplified terms 'the heritage of an organization' that is distinct from the organization's past or history per se (Urde et al., 2007; Burghausen & Balmer, 2014a).

Some organizations, it has been shown, successfully leverage this 'institutional heritage' for corporate marketing and/or branding purposes as *corporate heritage*. Heritage in that sense is about meaningful and relevant organizational and/or brand traits that are valued by and valuable for internal and external stakeholders in the present not only because of a retrospective link to the past but concurrently due to a prospective link to an envisioned future (Burghausen & Balmer, 2014a). Thus, it is not only about an actual or perceived inheritance from the past (cf. Pecot & de Barnier, 2017) but always also about a bequest to the future (Burghausen, 2013) that turns some aspect of the past into heritage and not mere history, for example. Drawing on these insights, *corporate heritage* is defined as:

> all the traits and aspects of an organisation [and/or corporate brand] that link its past, present, and future in a meaningful and relevant way. Thus, it refers to some aspect of an organisation's [and/or corporate brand's] past that is still deemed by current internal and/or external stakeholders to be relevant and meaningful for contemporary concerns and purposes but concurrently perceived as worth to be maintained and nurtured for future generations; it is the selectively appropriated and valorised past . . . or 'all that is (still) relevant' in the light of contemporary concerns and purposes.
> (Burghausen & Balmer, 2014a, p. 394–395)

This definition clearly already identifies and stresses the importance of all stakeholders (including consumers) and their pivotal role in constituting corporate heritage.

Apart from leveraging *corporate heritage* for corporate marketing purposes more generally (e.g., corporate websites, advertising, anniversaries, museums), it has been suggested that certain organizations utilize it for corporate branding specifically (Urde et al., 2007).

Thus, a distinction has been made between *corporate heritage brands* proper and corporate brands with a heritage (Urde et al., 2007). The former are corporate brands with a dedicated brand identity and positioning based on and derived from the corporate heritage while the latter do not utilize the corporate heritage for that purpose specifically (Urde et al., 2007). For example, while department stores Selfridges and Fortnum & Mason in London both boast a rich and meaningful corporate heritage, only the latter of the pair would qualify as a corporate heritage brand in the above sense. The activation and utilization of corporate heritage as a branding asset is contingent and thus a strategic decision (Urde et al., 2007; Balmer, 2011b). Similarly, while all organizations evolve some form of identity – corporate and/or organizational – (Hatch & Schultz, 2000) not every organization requires a corporate brand (Balmer & Gray, 2003). The latter is a strategic decision too.

The same group of scholars also argued from the beginning that corporate heritage potentially affords these organizations a competitive advantage if used, managed, and maintained as a strategic resource and asset underpinning their corporate brand identity and positioning (Urde et al., 2007). However, they also cautioned that the usefulness and effectiveness of heritage-based corporate branding is not a given or universally feasible per se. It requires strategic deliberation (of internal and external circumstance and context) and ongoing, careful, and dedicated management stewardship of the corporate heritage and, if applicable, the corporate heritage brand (Balmer et al., 2006; Urde et al., 2007).

The notion of corporate heritage brand stewardship outlines fundamental management requirements of said brands (Urde et al., 2007; Balmer, 2011b), which was later empirically substantiated and developed into a coherent management framework (see Burghausen & Balmer, 2014b; Burghausen & Balmer, 2015). These management imperatives refer to the uncovering, validating, articulating, activating, relating, adopting, and finally protecting of the corporate heritage of an organization and/or its corporate brand (Urde et al., 2007; Burghausen & Balmer, 2014b; cf. Iglesias et al., 2020). These imperatives (and activities) are based on – at once – retrospective brand exploration as well as prospective brand strategizing in order to maintain the relevance of the corporate heritage for current and future purposes (Balmer, 2011b; Moussa & de Barnier, 2020). This concurrence of retrospection and prospection may lead managers to uncover or rediscover some aspect of the past as a latent corporate (brand) heritage that can be activated for current marketing purposes and a future-oriented strategic renewal and innovation too (Cooper et al., 2015; Santos et al., 2016; Sammour et al., 2020).

More broadly, the scholarly domain of *corporate heritage branding* is concerned with certain organizational and marketing phenomena – such as corporate heritage (Balmer et al., 2006) and corporate heritage brands (Urde et al., 2007) – that are characterized inter alia by a specific temporal relation between past, present, and future, *viz. omni-temporality* (Balmer, 2013).

Conceptually, *omni-temporality* sets corporate heritage apart from other temporal modes such as corporate history, memory, tradition, nostalgia, etc. (Burghausen & Balmer, 2014a; Balmer & Burghausen, 2019). It is a defining feature of corporate heritage brands too (Balmer, 2013). This quality manifests as a corporate heritage brand's perceived 'timelessness' (Urde et al., 2007) or 'relative invariance' (Balmer, 2011a, 2013), based on an actual and/or perceived intergenerational continuity (Balmer, 2013), despite substantive and/or symbolic changes over time (Balmer, 2011a, 2013; also see Brunninge & Hartmann, 2019). In other words, corporate heritage and corporate heritage brands are paradoxical as they seem to stay the same while nonetheless changing over time (Balmer, 2011a, 2013; Cooper et al., 2020).

Finally, the power of corporate heritage brands rests on the interplay between a perceived or ascribed authenticity of the corporate heritage brand qua corporate heritage (Balmer, 2011b; Hudson & Balmer, 2013). Mutual trust and affinity of stakeholders with the corporate brand and its heritage across generations are co-constitutive too (Balmer, 2011b). Thus, the status of the corporate heritage brand itself and its wider socio-cultural import and appeal for stakeholders as mentioned earlier are requirements for the mutual and reciprocal *authenticity, trust, and affinity* of corporate heritage brands with stakeholders and vice versa (Balmer, 2011b, Burghausen, 2013; cf. Hatch & Schultz, 2017). This notion of reciprocity implies active stakeholder involvement and engagement and already augurs to some extent a co-creation approach to corporate heritage brands.

Since 2006, the field of corporate heritage branding has blossomed in conceptual and empirical terms. Subsequent research and publications have considerably substantiated, broadened, and advanced the area. The stream of conceptual and empirical research has successfully employed corporate heritage and related concepts as a theoretical lens and shown their descriptive and explanatory efficacy in relation to corporate heritage branding in varied contexts and beyond (see Balmer & Burghausen, 2015a; Balmer, 2017 for overviews).

## 2.3 Key constitutive processes of corporate heritage branding

The corporate heritage branding literature has so far identified a number of constitutive processes that underpin the constitution and gestation of corporate heritage and corporate heritage brands. From the extant literature five interdependent and ongoing *transformations of the past into corporate heritage* (Burghausen, forthcoming; also see Balmer, 2017; Balmer & Burghausen, 2019) can be discerned, which are predicated on activities and practices that frequently involve stakeholders and are thus highly pertinent for this chapter. They are:

- *Valorizing* the past in the present and for the future: This is the selective investment of the past as heritage vis-à-vis an organization and/or its brand with value in the present and concurrently(!) with an assumed value for the future by and for stakeholders (Urde et al., 2007; Burghausen & Balmer, 2014a).
- *(Re)interpreting* the past in the present and for the future: This is the imbuing with symbolic relevance of a selected past as heritage vis-à-vis an organization and/or its brand that is temporally extended beyond the past itself. It is being given a new or expanded meaning by and for stakeholders in the present and for the future, which is different from the meaning of the past per se (Balmer, 2011a; Burghausen & Balmer, 2014a; Brunninge & Hartmann, 2019; cf. Hatch & Schultz, 2017).
- *Appropriating* the past in the present and for the future: This is the active acceptance and adoption (i.e., 'taking ownership') of a selected past as heritage vis-à-vis an organization and/or its brand by managers, consumers and/or other stakeholders. It becomes to them concurrently(!) 'our inheritance' in the present and 'our bequest' made to the future, which affords opportunities and responsibilities but may also be a constraint or burden as well as a source for contestation and resistance (Balmer, 2013; Burghausen and Balmer 2014b; Brunninge & Hartmann, 2019; cf. Iglesias et al., 2020).
- *Augmenting* the past in the present and for the future: This is the ascription of socially and culturally relevant identity roles and affiliations of the organization and/or its brand qua heritage by and for stakeholders, which goes beyond the organization and/or corporate brand itself. It is predicated on a substantive and/or symbolic (direct or vicarious) link between the past, present, and future of the organization and/or its brand vis-à-vis a wider socio-cultural context (Balmer, 2013; Balmer & Chen, 2017).

- *Manifesting* the past in the present and for the future: This is the substantive actualization and affective experience of the past as heritage vis-à-vis an organization and/or its brand through meaningful cultural artefacts and social practices by and for stakeholders (Hudson, 2011; Santos et al., 2016; Burghausen, forthcoming).

These transformations are interdependent processes, which implies that the ongoing translation of some aspect of the past into heritage is co-dependent on an all five processes that can be depicted as a continuous cycle of constitutive activities and practices (Figure 21.1).

To illustrate this, the past of an organization and/or brand becomes heritage because it (still) adds some form of value for the organization and its stakeholders in the present and for an envisaged future. It is not simply a past that stakeholders commemorate (in a corporate brand museum, for example) but a past that (still) has instrumental and/or symbolic relevance and import (e.g., the use of archival materials for product and process innovations, the legacy of a founder's ethos shaping the current corporate culture; a sense of familiarity and stability derived from the continuity of the organization and its brand). Yet, by investing the past with additional value in the present and for the future its meaning also changes (it is not mere history or memory that informs the present). As such, valorization always also requires (re)interpretation, and by reinterpreting the meaning of the past it acquires additional symbolic value as heritage in the

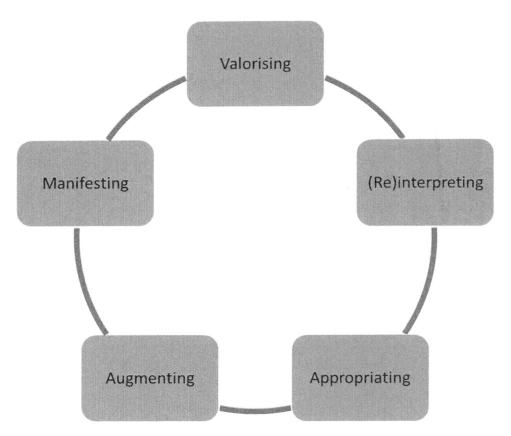

*Figure 21.1* Transforming the past into corporate heritage

present and for the future too. Even further, the past is valuable to us as heritage only insofar it is or becomes 'our heritage' through the process of appropriation, taking ownership of the past, which in turn again requires a changed meaning through (re)interpretation.

Likewise, the wider socio-cultural relevance of a corporate heritage (brand) is based on an augmentation of its role and affiliations beyond the organization or its brand. This in turn necessitates the (re)interpretation of the temporal relations not only between the past, present, and future of the organization or its brand but also relation with the past, present, and future of other social and cultural entities such as a community, nation, industry, and so on. Yet, it is often this wider socio-cultural relevance of the corporate heritage (brand) which adds value in the present and for a future. For instance, the status and appeal of Shepherd Neame (a UK brewery based in Faversham, Kent) as a corporate heritage brand is not only predicated on its own omni-temporality, its inter-generational continuity over time as 'Britain's Oldest Brewer' (Burghausen, 2013), but concurrently rests on a substantive and symbolic link with the past, present, and future of Faversham (communal), Kent (regional), the UK (national), as well as the industrial heritage of brewing and hop growing in these geographies and so on (Burghausen, 2013). Recently, Spielmann at al. (2019) have shown a similar dynamic for wineries across cultural contexts while Balmer and Chen (2015) show the wider socio-cultural relevance of the Chinese brand Tong Ren Tang as a corporate heritage brand.

Finally, the past as corporate heritage needs to be given some substantive and affective form in the present through cultural artifacts and social practices in order to have a continued value for the organization and its stakeholders. It is not merely a 'dead past' but a 'living past' that is very much present as heritage. The past can become part of the present as heritage through product and service design (Hudson, 2011; Santos et al., 2016); corporate architecture (Bargenda, 2015) but also corporate events (Burghausen, 2013), for example. By being very much present in the sense that it can be experienced as heritage the past still adds value, has meaning, and can be made into our own, often with an appeal far beyond the organization and its brand alone.

Thus, these are also expansive processes that potentially anchors the past as heritage in the present and for the future, beyond the focal organization and corporate brand, within the wider socio-cultural context of shared cultural meanings, value, and identities. As such, corporate heritage brands can acquire a relevance akin to cultural heritage for certain groups, a community, or a place (see Balmer & Chen, 2015, 2017). Take for example the strong and vociferous reactions to the closure of Whitechapel Bell Foundry in London – until 2017 the oldest ongoing manufacturing company in Britain that had cast inter alia the Liberty Bell in Philadelphia as well as Big Ben in London – and the community campaign to save it and its corporate heritage (O'Brien, 2021). This expanded relevance of the past as corporate heritage beyond the organization itself is always also a shared relevance, a relevance related to shared value, meaning, identity, and experience for now and in the future that requires the active involvement of stakeholders to be of instrumental efficacy and constitutive import.

## 3. Corporate heritage (brand) co-creation

The so far presented foundations, conceptual traits and constitutive processes derived from the extant corporate heritage branding literature already indicate an active role of internal and external stakeholders. Thus, apart from managerial stewardship, these transformations always also imply and require stakeholders actively shaping the temporal relations between past, present, and future, viz. *temporal agency*. By exercising their temporal agency through the valorization, (re)interpretation, appropriation, augmentation, and manifestation of the past in the present and for the future, stakeholders transform aspects of the past into corporate heritage. Moreover, the contemporary bearing of a corporate heritage brand itself and its wider sociocultural relevance and appeal are likewise actively negotiated with multiple stakeholders. For this notion to be conceptually, empirically, and pragmatically relevant and efficacious adopting a co-creation approach to corporate heritage branding is warranted and timely.

Yet, the original contributions by Balmer and colleagues and most subsequent contributions too are very much still steeped in a more traditional instrumental reading of corporate heritage branding. So far, the main body of research on corporate heritage and corporate heritage brands has largely adopted a managerial approach (but cf. Brunninge & Hartmann, 2019; Balmer & Burghausen, 2019) but not yet a decidedly co-creational perspective. As such, the question of how stakeholders, other than marketers and managers, are actively involved in the constitution and also contestation of corporate heritage and corporate heritage brands remains obscured and requires further conceptual and empirical work. The co-creation approach to corporate branding offers a perspective that has the potential to clarify and specify, lifting the veil of obscurity that still muffles corporate heritage branding in this respect.

### 3.1 Corporate brand co-creation and stakeholder agency

The *co-creation approach to corporate brand management* is the logical next step in the development of our field (Hatch & Schultz, 2010; Ind et al., 2013). It takes seriously the original notion of stakeholder orientation as suggested by the earliest contributions (Balmer, 1995; Ind, 1997) as well as subsequent elaborations of corporate branding (Hatch & Schultz, 2001; Balmer & Gray, 2003; Knox & Bickerton, 2003).

However, this new perspective acknowledges more explicitly the active involvement and engagement of stakeholders in the creation of value (Iglesias et al., 2013), meanings (Vallaster & von Wallpach, 2013), identities (von Wallpach et al., 2017; Iglesias et al., 2020), and experiences (Stach, 2019), to name just few important dimensions and aspects of co-creation (see Ind & Coates, 2013).

It addresses, inter alia, the challenges posed by shifting, blurring, and dissolving boundaries of organizations, within and between their internal and external spheres (Hatch & Schultz, 1997, Hatch & Schultz, 2009). This perspective strives to come to terms with the fluid, dynamic, and less-stable articulations of corporate (brand) identities (da Silveira et al., 2013), which are negotiated (Gregory, 2007) through constant interaction and dialogue with stakeholders (Johansen & Nielsen, 2011; Cornelissen et al., 2012). The co-creation perspective also addresses the embedded nature of corporate brands as they are constituted in fragmented, polyvocal, and often contradictory organizational and institutional environments of acting and activist stakeholder groups (Handelman, 2006; Palazzo & Basu, 2007; Kornum et al., 2017).

It represents an extension of the 'shared ownership' (Balmer, 2006, 2010) and corporate brand covenant perspective (Balmer & Greyser, 2003), coming to term with the more widely 'shared control' (Hatch & Schultz, 2009, 2010) of corporate brands, sometimes akin to a perceived or actual loss of managerial control over them (Fisher & Smith, 2011; Iglesias & Bonet, 2012). From a co-creational point of view the substance and relevance of corporate brands – their value, identity, and meaning – cannot be decided by management alone.

I see this development towards a co-creational perspective as a timely and warranted evolution rather than revolution in our thinking about corporate brands that ought to influence theorizing and practice in the future more directly. It raises important and challenging questions about participation, conscientiousness, ethicality, and sustainability regarding corporate brands vis-à-vis multiple active stakeholders and their interests (Iglesias et al., A1). There is no monolithic public; there are no passive audiences and no accepting constituents anymore, if there ever were in the first place.

The challenge of genuine participatory and reciprocal corporate brand co-creation is not only a question of by whom, where, and when value creation takes place or how that value is eventually shared between firm and stakeholders. It is also a question of 'shared control' over the corporate brand (Hatch & Schultz, 2009, 2010), its value, identity, and meaning(s) that potentially and actually reduces managerial control and alters managerial agency (Fisher & Smith, 2011; Iglesias & Bonet, 2012; Ind, 2014).

Sharing control requires continuous negotiation (Gregory, 2007) and dynamic alignment (Balmer, 2012) as well as constant interaction and dialogue with stakeholders (Johansen & Nielsen, 2011; Cornelissen et al., 2012). This also raises the question of how feasible are an assumed stability, coherence, and specificity of a corporate (brand) identity (Moingeon, B. & Ramanantsoa, 1997) and its meaning(s) more generally under the precepts and conditions of co-creation (da Silveira et al., 2013; Iglesias et al., 2013).

Consequently, there has been a shift in our focus from enduring to evolving traits (Balmer, 2010) on towards an emergentist, constructionist, and relational perspective on the constitution and gestation of corporate brands (Iglesias et al., 2013; Biraghi & Gambetti, 2015).

In addition, shared control implies fluidity, fragmentation, and polyvocality (Schmeltz & Kjeldsen, 2019) in terms of corporate brand co-creation if a multitude of stakeholders are actively involved (Kornum et al., 2017; von Wallpach et al., 2017), potentially leading to tension, conflict, and contestation in a multi-stakeholder environment too (Handelman, 2006; Palazzo & Basu, 2007).

As such, the conceptual and practical question of corporate brand co-creation is not only a question of individual or collective stakeholder agency vis-à-vis the corporate brands but also a question of multiplicity and the continuous alignment, negotiation, accommodation, and sometimes conciliation of multiple interests, meanings, voices, identities, etc. within a wider socio-cultural context that is co-created too.

Drawing on this, at a more abstract level we can discern at least four main generic dimensions of co-creation that have been discussed or alluded to in the extant and fast-growing literature on corporate brand co-creation. These four dimensions of corporate brand co-creation, to me, each imply different general forms of stakeholder agency:

- The dimension of *value co-creation* implies pragmatic, including utilitarian and functional, agency of multiple stakeholders vis-à-vis corporate brands.
- The dimension of *meaning co-creation* implies symbolic, including hermeneutic and semiotic, agency of multiple stakeholders vis-à-vis corporate brands.
- The dimension of *identity co-creation* implies individual (self-identity), collective (group-identity), and institutional (entity-identity) agency of multiple stakeholders vis-à-vis corporate brands.
- The dimension of *experience co-creation* implies aesthetic, including emotive and performative, agency of multiple stakeholders vis-à-vis corporate brands.

Of course, these generic dimensions of co-creation and their associated abstract types of stakeholder agency are not mutually exclusive but often overlap and are jointly constitutive for co-created corporate brands. For example, the question of identity co-creation at the level of the individual, group, or institution in relation to a corporate brand always also implies questions of meaning, value, and experience co-creation; while co-created experiences are meaningful and valuable to stakeholders for their individual, collective, or institutional identity projects vis-à-vis the corporate brand too.

### 3.2 Temporal co-creation and temporal agency

In addition to these generic co-creation dimensions and their associated types of stakeholder agency, I suggest here a fifth dimension of co-creation (Figure 21.2), which so far has rarely been addressed directly in the corporate marketing literature outside corporate heritage scholarship (see Balmer & Burghausen, 2019) and a few other recent exceptions, for example (see Hatch & Schultz, 2017; Iglesias et al., 2020).

I suggest labelling this additional dimension of co-creation *temporal co-creation*, tentatively defined as the co-creation of specific temporal relations between past, present, and future that are constitutive for corporate brands predicated on stakeholders' *temporal agency*. To reiterate, temporal agency broadly refers to the ability of stakeholders to shape and influence, produce, and reproduce temporal relations that have constitutive import for their own subjectivities as well as the organizational, social, and cultural contexts they inhabit (Emirbayer & Mische, 1998).

This additional dimension of corporate brand co-creation suggests that stakeholders are not just passively experiencing or perceiving temporality as a specific link between past, present, and future as given, for example, but are individually and collectively shaping temporal relations and structures too. In this view, time, memory, history, and heritage are ongoing – individual and collective – socio-cultural accomplishments rather than natural constants or ontic essences. These temporal relations and structures are foundational for corporate brand co-creation too, the corporate brand and its ascribed and perceived relevance, import, legitimacy, and authenticity vis-à-vis stakeholders. In other words, these co-created temporal relations, which may manifest as history, memory, and indeed heritage, are co-constitutive for the co-creation of the meaning, value, identity, and experience of a corporate brand.

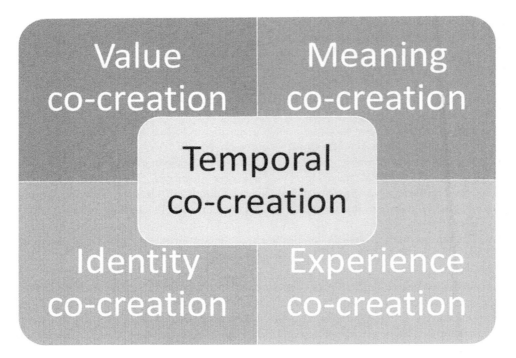

*Figure 21.2* The five co-creation dimensions

In that sense, organizations and their corporate brands are always also temporal entities and constitute a nexus of multiple temporal relations (Adams, 1995; Landwehr, 2016). These include inter alia, durations, tempos, rhythms, orientations, directions, periodizations, or punctuations of time (Adam, 1995; Zerubavel, 2004) but also the narrations and manifestations of past, present, and future and the link and direction between these timeframes (Ricoeur, 1990; Polkinghorne, 1998) that are locally specific to an organization and its corporate brand. To put it differently, the corporate brand is co-created by stakeholders in time, through time, and as time as well as in history, through history, and as history. Thus, history (memory, tradition, etc.) and indeed heritage, their wider instrumental effects, and cultural and social relevance in the present (and for the future) are themselves contingent on a socio-historic context of widely shared and accepted temporal mentalities, practices, and so on, which themselves are temporally dynamic and situationally specific (i.e., evolving and emerging).

As such, *temporal agency* by stakeholders is exercised through temporal practices, discourses, interactions, performances, etc. and gives rise to emergent temporal processes, forms (e.g., artefacts, habits, narratives, and individual orientations or shared mentalities), and institutions, which constitute multiple temporal relations vis-à-vis a corporate brand and other stakeholders as well as the perceived historicity of the corporate brand itself.

### 3.3 Co-creation and corporate heritage branding

This raises a couple of related questions for corporate heritage branding scholarship. First, in what form and to what effect are multiple stakeholders (in addition to marketers and managers) involved in the temporal co-creation of corporate heritage per se and corporate heritage brands in particular? Second, and more fundamentally, what is their role and how are they involved in the constitution of the temporal relations between past, present, and future that are characteristic for corporate heritage and corporate heritage brands (i.e., omni-temporality)?

Adopting a co-creation perspective, the emerging insights generated by corporate heritage branding scholars outlined in this chapter so far suggest that internal and external stakeholders (additional to management and marketers) exercise their *temporal agency* and co-create a corporate heritage (brand) inter alia through actively and continuously engaging in the valorization, (re)interpretation, appropriation, augmentation, and manifestation of a corporate brand's and/or organization's past as corporate heritage in the present and for the future.

First, conceptually this means that the co-creation of a corporate heritage (brand) happens by stakeholders actively engaging in these transformative processes turning some aspect of the past into heritage by exercising temporal agency. Yet, these transformations, at a more fundamental level, are predicated on and are more specific manifestations of this temporal agency exercised in conjunction with other forms of agency characteristic of multiple forms of corporate brand co-creation as outlined previously (i.e., value, meaning, identity, and experience). As such, the temporal relations between past, present, and future characteristic for corporate heritage (brands) as they are co-created by stakeholders are not constituted in isolation but conflate with other types of co-creation. Thus, temporal agency and the temporal co-creation of a corporate heritage (brand) involves the four other dimensions of co-creation and their associated types of stakeholder agency too.

We can say that corporate heritage (brand) co-creation by stakeholders is predicated on temporal co-creation conflated with other forms of stakeholder co-creation that underpin the transformations of the past into heritage and are co-constitutive for shaping the specific temporal relations that characterize a corporate heritage (brand). Temporal agency vis-à-vis corporate heritage brands is conflated agency, so to speak.

By way of description and example, the valorization of the past into heritage as a form of temporal co-creation by stakeholders is predicated on value co-creation but also implicates other forms of co-creation such as meaning (as symbolic value), experience (as affective value), and identity (as affinity value). Likewise, the (re)interpretation of the past as heritage is surely linked to meaning co-creation, which may also entail a form of value co-creation (symbolic value), may be linked to issues of identity and identification (identity co-creation) and so on. The way the past manifests in the present as heritage first links to experience co-creation, surely, but experiences also carry meaning (meaning co-creation), may perform identities (identity co-creation) and constitute a value too (value cocreation).

The appropriation of the past as 'our heritage' implicates questions of identity and identification (identity co-creation) and affective appeal (experience co-creation), which may acquire value for us and others (value co-creation) and necessitates interpretive efforts (meaning co-creation). Finally, the augmentation of the past as heritage beyond the corporate heritage requires identity co-creation but concurrently involves other forms of co-creation too so that the corporate heritage (brand) acquires a wider socio-cultural meaning that has value and can be positively experienced by different groups.

Second, the relevance and import of co-created corporate heritage brands in the present and for the future – as a nexus of multiple temporal relations – is predicated on and embedded in a wider, equally co-created and evolving, temporal and historical context (Assmann, 2013; Hartog, 2015). In other words, corporate heritage (brand) co-creation as described here plays out not only vis-à-vis the organization or its corporate brand but stakeholders also shapes the dominant temporal relations that enable or inhibit the social or cultural relevance and strategic efficacy of corporate heritage branding as an approach to corporate branding in a particular time and place but not others. For example, changes in the temporal fabric of modernity (Assmann, 2013; Hartog, 2015), of which the growing concern for and interest in heritage are just indicators (Lowenthal, 1998), provide the contemporary contextual conditions that make a corporate heritage branding strategy viable and efficacious. Yet, taking the notion of co-creation seriously suggests that these contextual and situational conditions are also dynamic and predicated on social and temporal relations brought about by the (collective) agency of stakeholders.

We can say that the strategic efficacy and socio-cultural relevance of co-created corporate heritage (brands) is predicated on temporal co-creation conflated with other forms of stakeholder co-creation that are co-constitutive for shaping the specific temporal relations that characterize the contextual and situational conditions for corporate heritage branding. Temporal agency vis-à-vis corporate heritage brands is temporally embedded agency, so to speak.

Figure 21.3 visually integrates and depicts these conceptual points and links developed in this chapter in graphical form.

By way of a brief illustrative example, Britain's oldest brewer Shepherd Neame (SN) is actively being valorized as corporate heritage brand by stakeholders as an integral part of the local and regional community and their collective identity and history. Beyond the instrumental value of still provisioning good beers and pubs as well as employment, for example, the brand has symbolic value as it is taken by stakeholders to represent the community and region, while through the firm's long-standing involvement in local festivities and shared traditions it has affective value for them too (Burghausen, 2013). Likewise, going to 'Sheps' is part of the experience of growing up and living in Kent and has been for generations. Something would be amiss if SN was not there anymore. Yet, maybe 40 or 50 years ago, SN was one of many regional breweries in the UK and was not positioned as a corporate heritage brand at all (Burghausen, 2013). It was only with the demise of many local breweries and a growing concentration in the industry, together with more importantly a shift in the general temporal sentiment in the UK and beyond, that the firm was able to exploit its increasingly unique position as a regional brewer with a long history; even laying claim to being 'Britain's Oldest Brewer' from the 1990s

*Towards a co-creational perspective*

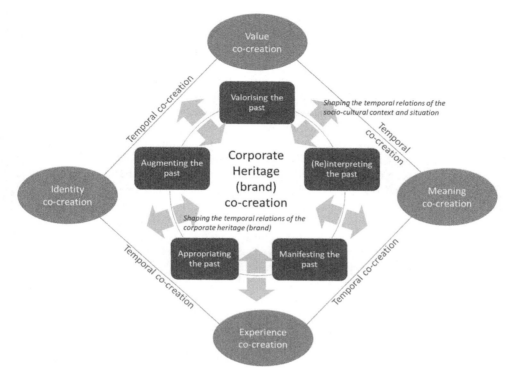

*Figure 21.3* A corporate heritage (brand) co-creation framework

onwards. Yet, this was only possible because stakeholders started to care for its status as a corporate heritage brand investing it with additional meaning, value and so on. This of course, required the active and joint reinterpretation of the past and its meaning in the present as heritage, not only by the firm but stakeholders too (Burghausen, 2013). As such, stakeholders shape the value, meaning, identity, and experience of SN as a corporate heritage brand as much as the temporal context within which such a branding strategy can be successful for SN.

## 4. Towards corporate heritage branding co-creation

What are the implications of a co-creational perspective then? The following points are noteworthy in light of extant debates within corporate heritage branding to date but by no means exhaustive.

Regarding corporate heritage (brand) co-creation we can broadly say that the material and ideational remnants of the past that are being turned jointly into corporate heritage by stakeholders afford certain usages in the present and for the future and not others. Yet, there are always substantive limits, not yet well specified, on how far the past and what aspects of the past can be valorized, (re)interpreted, appropriated, etc. as corporate heritage. Yet, despite this observation the agency of stakeholders is never completely determined by that state of affairs, but these past remnants and more importantly the temporal relations between past, present, and future that manifest through them can be more fundamentally altered, rendering them into corporate heritage through these interdependent transformations that underpin corporate heritage (brand) co-creation.

For example, both managers and stakeholders may at first adopt the past (their own or 'borrowed' from elsewhere; Burghausen & Balmer, 2014a; see Brunninge & Hartmann, 2019) in the present and for the future for various reasons and purposes such as the co-creation of a corporate brand. Yet, through their adoption managers and stakeholders not merely 'represent' or 'use' the past (as found) in the present and for the future, again, for the purpose of corporate brand co-creation, for example. Instead, they actively constitute and refashion that past as corporate heritage through the multiple transformations (i.e., valorization, (re)interpretation, appropriation, augmentation, and manifestation) in accordance with present objectives and purposes and anticipated future concerns. Thus, through these transformations stakeholders exercise their temporal agency and co-create corporate heritage (brands) in the first place.

Further, the active constitution of the past in the present and for the future as corporate heritage has the positive implication that the past as heritage is not fixed but malleable and flexible (see Burghausen & Balmer, 2014a; Balmer & Burghausen, 2019; Brunninge & Hartmann, 2019) to be adapted in light of changing organizational or societal concerns. However, it also implies the potential for contestation if the version of corporate heritage espoused by the corporate heritage brand conflicts with the lived experiences, shared meanings, or current concerns of stakeholders and wider society. Thus, from a co-creation perspective a unified version and singular purpose of the past as heritage cannot be assumed. It suggests temporal multiplicity too. Multiple temporal relations constituted by various stakeholders require active negotiation between the corporate brand (or better its management) and its various stakeholders (as individual and as a group). Consequently, the negotiation of multiple temporal relations between corporate heritage brand and stakeholders is not necessarily a harmonious affair. Temporal tensions, contradictions, and contestations may ensue. These can be productive and destructive, because the temporal dimension of linking past present and future and turning the past into heritage is always conflated with the value, meaning, identity, and experience of the corporate brand itself and beyond (as suggested earlier).

For corporate heritage (brand) co-creation, the notion of multiple temporal relations indicates that the relevance and import of corporate heritage and corporate heritage brands is predicated on a specific constellation of these multiple temporal relations within and without the organization and vis-à-vis the corporate brand in the present and for the future that are evolving over time. This renders corporate heritage branding either fruitful or futile during certain periods and not others. In other words, the symbolic and instrumental relevance of corporate heritage is waxing and waning over time. Yet, more importantly these multiple temporal relations determine what management and stakeholders collectively agree to be a relevant and meaningful corporate heritage in the first place. Thus, the material and ideational substance and content of corporate heritage is contingent itself and needs to be renewed and validated by each new generation of stakeholders which requires their active engagement in co-creation.

In that sense, the omni-temporality of corporate heritage (brands) is co-created through continuous cultural transmission over time and validation in the present and for an anticipated future. Again, this is and needs to be negotiated with multiple stakeholders and their sometimes conflicting priorities and interests and cannot be deduced from some inherent immutable traits nor unilaterally decreed by the corporate brand (and its managers) once and for all. Likewise, omni-temporality requires intergenerational continuity and relevance of corporate heritage (brands). In other words, temporal relations do not only coexist and require negotiation in the present but across time and between generations of stakeholders too. This is specifically pertinent for corporate heritage (brands) due to their omni-temporal nature as they conflate and cut across the temporal strata of past, present, and future. Corporate heritage brands cannot ignore historical corporate responsibilities or valorize something into heritage for purely nostalgic reasons without endangering the present and future relevance and import of the corporate heritage (brand) for their various stakeholders, who themselves are active temporal agents dealing with multiple temporalities and often temporal contradictions themselves.

## 5. Conclusion

The suggested integrative framework (Figure 21.3) derived from my reading of the corporate heritage branding and corporate brand co-creation literatures presented in this chapter ought to help interested readers in exploring the co-creation of corporate heritage (brands) further. The framework is not meant to be conclusive nor dogmatic but intended as guidance and an inspiration for future debate only.

Future research could explore in more detail the different dimensions of the framework and how they interact and manifest in practice with a focus on how, when, and why stakeholders maintain or transform, accept or contest certain temporal relations – their value, meaning, and so on – vis-à-vis corporate heritage brands but not others? Research into the dynamics between corporate heritage brands and their co-created temporal context would be a worthwhile endeavour too. Finally, the integrative perspective presented here asks future researchers to look into links between temporal co-creation and other forms of co-creation and vice versa.

This chapter has tentatively outlined a co-creation perspective on corporate heritage branding. I hope that my preliminary theoretical musings encourage and maybe even inspire other colleagues to explore and engage with the, to me, fascinating but also complex questions of time, temporality, historicity in marketing more generally, as well as temporal agency and multiplicity vis-à-vis corporate branding more specifically. To me, these questions are not just pertinent for corporate heritage scholarship but for the growing community of corporate brand co-creation scholars too.

This realization might very well reflect our current Zeitgeist and the challenges of our times, which can catch up with us again from the past and already greet us from the future. *Time matters*, as do futures and pasts, whether as history, memory, utopias, etc. and indeed as heritage too!

## References

Aaker, D. A. (1996). *Building strong brands*. New York: The Free Press.
Adam, B. (1995). *Timewatch*. Cambridge: Polity Press.
Andersen, M. A. (2020). Times are changing: The role of heritage identity on employee identification in a Danish family-owned company. *Corporate Communications: An International Journal*, 25(3), 477–494. https://doi.org/10.1108/CCIJ-04-2020-0076
Anteby, M., & Molnar, V. (2012). Collective memory meets organizational identity: Remembering to forget in a firm's rhetorical history. *Academy of Management Journal*, 55(3), 515–540. https://doi.org/10.5465/amj.2010.0245
Assmann, A. (2013). *Ist die Zeit aus den Fugen?* München (Munich): Hanser.
Balmer, J. M. T. (1995). Corporate branding and connoisseurship. *Journal of General Management*, 21(1), 351–373. https://doi.org/10.1177/030630709502100102
Balmer, J. M. T. (2010). Explicating corporate brands and their management: Reflections and directions from 1995. *Journal of Brand Management*, 18(3), 180–196. https://doi.org/10.1057/bm.2010.46
Balmer, J. M. T. (2011a). Corporate heritage identities, corporate heritage brands and the multiple heritage identities of the British Monarchy. *European Journal of Marketing*, 45(9–10), 1380–1398. https://doi.org/10.1108/03090561111151817
Balmer, J. M. T. (2011b). Corporate heritage brands and the precepts of corporate heritage brand management. *Journal of Brand Management*, 18(8), 517–544. https://doi.org/10.1057/bm.2011.21
Balmer, J. M. T. (2012). Strategic corporate brand alignment: Perspectives from identity based views of corporate brands. *European Journal of Marketing*, 46(7–8), 1064–1092. https://doi.org/10.1108/03090561211230205

Balmer, J. M. T. (2013). Corporate heritage, corporate heritage marketing, and total corporate heritage communications. *Corporate Communications: An International Journal, 18*(3), 290–326. https://doi.org/10.1108/CCIJ-05-2013-0031

Balmer, J. M. T. (Ed.). (2017). *Foundations of corporate heritage*. London: Routledge.

Balmer, J. M. T., & Burghausen, M. (2015a). Explicating corporate heritage, corporate heritage brands and organisational heritage. *Journal of Brand Management, 22*(5), 364–384. https://doi.org/10.1057/bm.2015.26

Balmer, J. M. T., & Burghausen, M. (2015b). Introducing organisational heritage: Linking corporate heritage, organisational identity and organisational memory. *Journal of Brand Management, 22*(5), 385–411. https://doi.org/10.1057/bm.2015.25

Balmer, J. M. T., & Burghausen, M. (2019). Marketing, the past and corporate heritage. *Marketing Theory, 19*(2), 217–227. https://doi.org/10.1177/1470593118790636

Balmer, J. M. T., & Chen, W. (2015). Corporate heritage brands in China. Consumer engagement with China's most celebrated corporate heritage brand – Tong Ren Tang: 同仁堂. *Journal of Brand Management, 22*(3), 194–210. https://doi.org/10.1057/bm.2015.14

Balmer, J. M. T., & Chen, W. (2017). Corporate heritage brands, augmented role identity and customer satisfaction. *European Journal of Marketing, 51*(9–10), 1510–1521. https://doi.org/10.1108/EJM-07-2017-0449

Balmer, J. M. T., & Gray, E. R. (2003). Corporate brands: What are they? What of them? *European Journal of Marketing, 37*(7–8), 972–997. https://doi.org/10.1108/03090560310477627

Balmer, J. M. T., & Greyser, S. A. (Eds.). (2003). *Revealing the corporation. An anthology*. London: Routledge.

Balmer, J. M. T., Greyser, S. A., & Urde, M. (2006). The crown as a corporate brand: Insights from monarchies. *Journal of Brand Management, 14*(1–2), 137–161. https://doi.org/10.1057/palgrave.bm.2550031

Bargenda, A. (2015). Corporate heritage brands in the financial sector: The role of corporate architecture. *Journal of Brand Management, 22*(5), 431–447. https://doi.org/10.1057/bm.2015.16

Berthon, P., Holbrook, M. B., & Hulbert, J. M. (2003). Understanding and managing the brand space. *Sloan Management Review, 41*(1), 49–54.

Biraghi, S., & Gambetti, R. C. (2015). Corporate branding: Where are we? A systematic communication-based inquiry. *Journal of Marketing Communications, 21*(4), 260–283. https://doi.org/10.1080/13527266.2013.768535

Brown, S., Kozinets, R. V., & Sherry, J. F. (2003). Teaching old brands new tricks: Retro Branding and the revival of brand meaning. *Journal of Marketing, 67*(3), 19–33. https://doi.org/10.1509/jmkg.67.3.19.18657

Brunninge, O., & Hartmann, B. J. (2019). Inventing a past: Corporate heritage as dialectical relationships of past and present. *Marketing Theory, 19*(2), 229–234. https://doi.org/10.1177/1470593118790625

Bucheli, M., & Wadhwani, R. D. (Eds.). (2013). *Organizations in time*. Oxford: Oxford University Press.

Burghausen, M. (2013). *Explicating corporate heritage identity stewardship theory from a corporate marketing perspective: A qualitative case study of Great Britain's oldest brewer* [Doctoral dissertation, Brunel University]. BURA. Retrieved from http://bura.brunel.ac.uk/handle/2438/13067

Burghausen, M. (forthcoming). The presence of the omni-temporal: Theoretical foundations of (corporate) brand heritage design. *Journal of Brand Management*.

Burghausen, M., & Balmer, J. M. T. (2014a). Repertoires of the corporate past: Explanation and framework. Introducing an integrated and dynamic perspective. *Corporate Communications: An International Journal, 19*(4), 384–402. https://doi.org/10.1108/CCIJ-05-2013-0032

Burghausen, M., & Balmer, J. M. T. (2014b). Corporate heritage identity management and the multi-modal implementation of a corporate heritage identity. *Journal of Business Research, 67*(11), 2311–2323. https://doi.org/10.1016/j.jbusres.2014.06.019

Burghausen, M., & Balmer, J. M. T. (2015). Corporate heritage identity stewardship: A corporate marketing perspective. *European Journal of Marketing, 49*(1–2), 22–61. https://doi.org/10.1108/EJM-03-2013-0169

Clark, P., & Rowlinson, M. (2004). The treatment of history in organisation studies: Towards an 'historic turn'? *Business History, 46*(3), 331–352. doi:10.1080/0007679042000219175

Cooper, H., Merrilees, B., & Miller, D. (2015). Corporate heritage brand management: Corporate heritage brands versus contemporary corporate brands. *Journal of Brand Management, 22*(5), 412–430. https://doi.org/10.1057/bm.2015.17

Cooper, H., Merrilees, B., & Miller, D. (2020). The corporate heritage brand paradox: Managing the tension between continuity and change in luxury brands. *Australasian Marketing Journal, 6*(1). https://doi.org/10.1016/j.ausmj.2020.08.003

Cornelissen, J. P., Christensen, L. T., & Kinuthia, K. (2012). Corporate brands and identity: Developing stronger theory and a call for shifting the debate. *European Journal of Marketing, 46*(7–8), 1093–1102. doi:10.1108/03090561211230214

Dawson, P., & Sykes, C. S. (2016). *Organizational change and temporality*. London: Routledge.

Emirbayer, M., & Mische, A. (1998). What is agency? *American Journal of Sociology, 103*(4), 962–1023. https://doi.org/10.1086/231294

Fisher, D., & Smith, S. (2011). Cocreation is chaotic: What it means for marketing when no one has control. *Marketing Theory, 11*(3), 325–350. https://doi.org/10.1177/1470593111408179

Gregory, A. (2007). Involving stakeholders in developing corporate brands: The communication dimension. *Journal of Marketing Management, 23*(1–2), 59–73. https://doi.org/10.1362/026725707X178558

Groot, J. (2009). *Consuming history*. London: Routledge.

Handelman, J. M. (2006). Corporate identity and the societal constituent. *Journal of the Academy of Marketing Science, 34*(2), 107–114. https://doi.org/10.1177/0092070305284970

Hartog, F. (2015). *Regimes of historicity: Presentism and experiences of time*. New York: Columbia University Press.

Hatch, M. J., & Schultz, M. (1997). Relations between organizational culture, identity and image. *European Journal of Marketing, 31*(5), 356–365. https://doi.org/10.1108/03090569710167583

Hatch, M. J., & Schultz, M. (2000). Scaling the tower of babel. In M. Schultz, M. J. Hatch, & M. Holten Larsen (Eds.), *The expressive organization* (pp. 11–35). Oxford: Oxford University Press.

Hatch, M. J., & Schultz, M. (2001). Are the strategic stars aligned for your corporate brand? *Harvard Business Review, 79*(2), 128–134.

Hatch, M. J., & Schultz, M. (2009). Of bricks and brands. *Organizational Dynamics, 38*(2), 117–130. https://doi.org/10.1016/j.orgdyn.2009.02.008

Hatch, M. J., & Schultz, M. (2010). Toward a theory of brand co-creation with implications for brand governance. *Journal of Brand Management, 17*(8), 590–604. doi:10.1057/bm.2010.14

Hatch, M. J., & Schultz, M. (2017). Toward a theory of using history authentically. *Administrative Science Quarterly, 29*. https://doi.org/10.1177/0001839217692535

Hernes, T., & Schultz, M. (2020). Translating the distant into the present: How actors address distant past and future events through situated activity. *Organization Theory, 1*(1). https://doi.org/10.1177/2631787719900999

Holbrook, M. B., & Schindler, R. M. (2003). Nostalgic bonding: Exploring the role of nostalgia in the consumption experience. *Journal of Consumer Behaviour, 3*(2), 107–127. https://doi.org/10.1002/cb.127

Hudson, B. T. (2011). Brand heritage and the renaissance of Cunard. *European Journal of Marketing, 45*(9–10), 1538–1556. doi:10.1108/03090561111151880

Hudson, B. T., & Balmer, J. M. T. (2013). Corporate heritage brands: Mead's theory of the past. *Corporate Communications: An International Journal, 18*(3), 347–361. https://doi.org/10.1108/CCIJ-Apr-2012-0027

Iglesias, O., & Bonet, E. (2012). Persuasive brand management: How managers can influence brand meaning when they are losing control over it. *Journal of Organizational Change Management, 25*(2), 251–264. https://doi.org/10.1108/09534811211213937

Iglesias, O., Ind, N., & Alfaro, M. (2013). The organic view of the brand: A brand value co-creation model. *Journal of Brand Management, 20*(8), 670–688. https://doi.org/10.1057/bm.2013.8

Iglesias, O., Ind, N., & Schultz, M. (2020). History matters: The role of history in corporate brand strategy. *Business Horizons, 63*(1), 51–60. https://doi.org/10.1016/j.bushor.2019.09.005

Iglesias, O., Landgraf, P., Ind, N., Markovic, S., & Koporcic, N. (2020). Corporate brand identity co-creation in business-to-business contexts. *Industrial Marketing Management, 85*, 32–43. https://doi.org/10.1016/j.indmarman.2019.09.008

Ind, N. (1997). *The corporate brand*. London: Palgrave Macmillan.

Ind, N. (2014). How participation is changing the practice of managing brands. *Journal of Brand Management, 21*(9), 734–742. https://doi.org/10.1057/bm.2014.35

Ind, N., & Coates, N. (2013). The meanings of co-creation. *European Business Review, 25*(1), 86–95. https://doi.org/10.1108/09555341311287754

Ind, N., Iglesias, O., & Schultz, M. (2013). Building brands together: Emergence and outcomes of co-creation. *California Management Review, 55*(3), 5–26. https://doi.org/10.1525/cmr.2013.55.3.5

Johansen, T. S., & Nielsen, A. E. (2011). Strategic stakeholder dialogues: A discursive perspective on relationship building. *Corporate Communications: An International Journal, 16*(3), 204–217. https://doi.org/10.1108/13563281111156871

Jones, D. G. B., & Tadajewski, M. (Eds.). (2016). *The Routledge companion to marketing history*. London: Routledge.

Keller, K. L., & Lehmann, D. R. (2006). Brands and branding: Research findings and future priorities. *Marketing Science*, 25(6), 740–759. https://doi.org/10.1287/mksc.1050.0153

Knox, S., & Bickerton, D. (2003). The six conventions of corporate branding. *European Journal of Marketing*, 37(7–8), 998–1016. https://doi.org/10.1108/03090560310477636

Kornum, N., Gyrd-Jones, R., Al Zagir, N., & Brandis, K. A. (2017). Interplay between intended brand identity and identities in a Nike related brand community: Co-existing synergies and tensions in a nested system. *Journal of Business Research*, 70, 432–440. https://doi.org/10.1016/j.jbusres.2016.06.019

Landwehr, A. (2016). *Die anwesende Abwesenheit der Vergangenheit*. Frankfurt a. M.: S. Fischer.

Lee, Z., & Davies, I. (2019). Navigating relative invariance: Perspectives on corporate heritage identity and organizational heritage identity in an evolving nonprofit institution. *Journal of Business Research*. https://doi.org/10.1016/j.jbusres.2019.05.038

Lowenthal, D. (1998). *The heritage crusade and the spoils of history*. Cambridge: Cambridge University Press.

Maclean, M., Clegg, S., & Suddaby, R. (Eds.). (2020). *Historical organization studies: Theory and applications*. Abingdon, Oxon: Routledge.

Mencarelli, R., Chaney, D., & Pulh, M. (2020). Consumers' brand heritage experience: Between acceptance and resistance. *Journal of Marketing Management*, 36(1–2), 30–50. https://doi.org/10.1080/0267257X.2019.1692057

Moingeon, B., & Ramanantsoa, B. (1997). Understanding corporate identity: The French school of thought. *European Journal of Marketing*, 31(5–6), 383–395. https://doi.org/10.1108/eb060638

Moussa, A., & de Barnier, V. (2020). How can corporate heritage identity stewardship lead to brand ambidexterity? *Journal of Strategic Marketing*, 27(4), 1–16. https://doi.org/10.1080/0965254X.2020.1786845

Muehling, D. D., & Sprott, D. E. (2004). The power of reflection: An empirical examination of nostalgia advertising effects. *Journal of Advertising*, 33(3), 25–35. https://doi.org/10.2307/4189264

O'Brien, H. (2021, May 11). The bells vs the boutique hotel: The battle to save Britain's oldest factory. *The Guardian*. Retrieved from www.theguardian.com/news/2021/may/11/whitechapel-bell-foundry-battle-save-britains-oldest-factory.

Orth, U. R., Rose, G. M., & Merchant, A. (2019). Preservation, rejuvenation, or confusion?: Changing package designs for heritage brands. *Psychology & Marketing*, 36(9), 831–843. https://doi.org/10.1002/mar.21215

Palazzo, G., & Basu, K. (2007). The ethical backlash of corporate branding. *Journal of Business Ethics*, 73(4), 333–346. https://doi.org/10.1007/s10551-006-9210-6

Pecot, F., & de Barnier, V. (2017). Corporate heritage or corporate inheritance: A French perspective. In J. M. T. Balmer (Ed.), *Foundations of corporate heritage* (pp. 302–314). London: Routledge.

Pecot, F., & de Barnier, V. (2018). Brands using historical references: A consumers' perspective. *Journal of Brand Management*, 25(2), 171–184. https://doi.org/10.1057/s41262-017-0076-y.

Pecot, F., Valette-Florence, P., & de Barnier, V. (2019). Brand heritage as a temporal perception: Conceptualisation, measure and consequences. *Journal of Marketing Management*, 108(1), 1–20. https://doi.org/10.1080/0267257X.2019.1667414

Polkinghorne, D. E. (1998). Narrative Psychologie und Geschichtsbewusstsein: Beziehungen und Perpektiven. In J. Straub (Ed.), *Erzählung, Identität und historisches Bewusstsein* (pp. 12–45). Frankfurt a. M.: Suhrkamp.

Ravasi, D., Rindova, V., & Stigliani, I. (2019). The stuff of legend: History, memory, and the temporality of organizational identity construction. *Academy of Management Journal*, 62(5), 1523–1555. https://doi.org/10.5465/amj.2016.0505

Ricoeur, P. (1990). *Time and narrative, volume 3*. Chicago, IL: University of Chicago Press.

Rose, G. M., Merchant, A., Orth, U. R., & Horstmann, F. (2016). Emphasizing brand heritage: Does it work? And how? *Journal of Business Research*, 69(2), 936–943. https://doi.org/10.1016/j.jbusres.2015.06.021

Sammour, A., Chen, W., Balmer, J. M. T., Botchie, D., & Faraday, J. (2020). Crafting the forever now: Corporate heritage brand innovation at John Lewis Partnership. *Strategic Change*, 29(1), 115–126. https://doi.org/10.1002/jsc.2315

Santos, F. P., Burghausen, M., & Balmer, J. M. T. (2016). Heritage branding orientation: The case of Ach. Brito and the dynamics between corporate and product heritage brands. *Journal of Brand Management*, 23(1), 67–88. https://doi.org/10.1057/bm.2015.48

Schmeltz, L., & Kjeldsen, A. K. (2019). Co-creating polyphony or cacophony? A case study of a public organization's brand co-creation process and the challenge of orchestrating multiple internal voices. *Journal of Brand Management, 26*(3), 304–316. https://doi.org/10.1057/s41262-018-0124-2

Schug, A. (2003). *History marketing.* Bielefeld: Transcript.

Schultz, M., & Hernes, T. (2013). A Temporal perspective on organizational identity. *Organization Science, 24*(1), 1–21. https://doi.org/10.1287/orsc.1110.0731

Silveira, C. da, Lages, C., & Simões, C. (2013). Reconceptualizing brand identity in a dynamic environment. *Journal of Business Research, 66*(1), 28–36. https://doi.org/10.1016/j.jbusres.2011.07.020

Spielmann, N., Discua Cruz, A., Tyler, B. B., & Beukel, K. (2019). Place as a nexus for corporate heritage identity: An international study of family-owned wineries. *Journal of Business Research.* https://doi.org/10.1016/j.jbusres.2019.05.024

Stach, J. (2019). Meaningful experiences: An embodied cognition perspective on brand meaning co-creation. *Journal of Brand Management, 26*(3), 317–331. https://doi.org/10.1057/s41262-018-0133-1

Suddaby, R., Coraiola, D., Harvey, C., & Foster, W. (2019). History and the micro-foundations of dynamic capabilities. *Strategic Management Journal, 1*(2), 131. https://doi.org/10.1002/smj.3058

Tamm, M., & Olivier, L. (Eds.). (2019). *Rethinking historical time.* London: Bloomsbury.

Urde, M., Greyser, S. A., & Balmer, J. M. T. (2007). Corporate brands with a heritage. *Journal of Brand Management, 15*(1), 4–19. https://doi.org/10.1057/palgrave.bm.2550106

Vallaster, C., & von Wallpach, S. (2013). An online discursive inquiry into the social dynamics of multi-stakeholder brand meaning co-creation. *Journal of Business Research, 66*(9), 1505–1515. https://doi.org/10.1016/j.jbusres.2012.09.012

Wadhwani, R. D., Suddaby, R., Mordhorst, M., & Popp, A. (2018). History as organizing: Uses of the past in organization studies. *Organization Studies, 39*(12), 1663–1683. https://doi.org/10.1177/0170840618814867

Wallpach, S. von, Hemetsberger, A., & Espersen, P. (2017). Performing identities: Processes of brand and stakeholder identity co-construction. *Journal of Business Research, 70*, 443–452. https://doi.org/10.1016/j.jbusres.2016.06.021

Wiedmann, K.-P., Hennigs, N., Schmidt, S., & Wuestefeld, T. (2011). The importance of brand heritage as a key performance driver in marketing management. *Journal of Brand Management, 19*(3), 182–194. https://doi.org/10.1057/bm.2011.36

Zerubavel, E. (2004). *Time maps.* Chicago, IL: University of Chicago Press.

# 22
# CROSS-FERTILIZATION OF HERITAGE BETWEEN PRODUCT AND CORPORATE BRANDING

*Fabien Pecot, PhD, Associate Professor in Marketing at TBS Barcelona*

## 1. Introduction

If we believe the famous aphorism from Jorge Santayana to be true –'those who cannot remember the past are condemned to repeat it' – there can only be true innovation through a good knowledge of the past. Very few brand managers really start a project from scratch. Marketing work continuously involves adapting elements of the past to concerns of the present, with the intention of securing future growth. When brand managers think about this balance, they can engage with the concept of heritage that is understood as an evocation and use of the past for the future, in the present. Considering a brand's heritage triggers many questions. What did we receive from our predecessors in the company? What would we like to transmit to future managers? What is the heritage of our company and of our brands? Do we make the most of it? Does it have value for our stakeholders? Does it connect with our future plans?

For scholars – and particularly scholars in the discipline of marketing – these questions relate to the concept of *brand heritage* if they focus on the product or service brand level, or to the concept of *corporate heritage* if they focus on the corporate brand level. That is because they would find two different streams of literature. One ('brand heritage') engages with product brands, marketing mix activities, and consumer perceptions; this stream typically defines heritage as a set of brand associations that can be made more or less salient in the mix (Aaker, 1996). Another ('corporate heritage') engages with corporate brands, strategic activities, and other stakeholders. This second stream defines heritage as a dimension of corporate identity, and some scholars view heritage companies as a distinct category (Balmer & Burghausen, 2019; Urde et al., 2007). My own trajectory as a researcher has led me to live at the border of both streams. From this ambiguous position, I contemplate in this chapter the missed opportunities for cross-fertilization with respect to the importance of heritage in corporate and product brand management. While significant work has been achieved, the following review will highlight opportunities to quantify corporate heritage and engage with external stakeholders that are not consumers, and also focus on the need to look at the co-creation processes in brand heritage research.

The first section of the chapter reviews the product brand literature and the second section focuses on corporate branding literature. Both sets of literature look at the way that brand heritage is discussed in these two streams and both follow the same structure: the definition of brand heritage, its management, and its effects. In the third section, I suggest that both streams are interested in the broader question of permanence in brand management. I propose that a cross-fertilization of both streams can generate new research about the external validation and quantification of corporate brand heritage principles and move towards a finer-grain approach of the co-creation processes at play in product brand heritage research. I conclude with a call for more collaborations between the scholars of both streams of research, for the greater good of brand management.

## 2. Brand heritage in product branding

Marketing researchers have always seen brand heritage cues in advertising, on packaging, and in the way some stores are designed. Referring to the company's founder, maintaining the same logo, showcasing iconic products . . . these practices are anything but new. And indeed, researchers interested in consumer behaviour and brand management have been interested in this phenomena long before we started to discuss corporate heritage (Urde et al., 2007). We can think about nostalgia (Holbrook, 1993), retro-branding and brand revivals (Brown et al., 2003), and authenticity (Grayson & Martinec, 2004). This literature at the product brand level does not necessarily use the conceptual lens of 'brand heritage,' but it also looks at the representation of, or the reference to, the past in marketing material. Heritage has later been coined at the corporate brand level, but a comprehensive review needs to build on these contributions too (i.e., on nostalgia, retro-branding, and authenticity).

### 2.1. Definition

Several definitions of brand heritage co-exist in product brand literature. There are only a few mentions of it before the 1990s, and most papers cite Aaker's 'Building strong brands' (Aaker, 1996) and/or the *Journal of Brand Management* article by Urde and colleagues (Urde et al., 2007) as key references. Aaker defines brand heritage as one dimension of the brand's identity, under the brand symbols of storied legacy and historical connections. Brand heritage is here conceptualized as a symbol or a set of symbols, intangible attributes that marketers can use to generate value (Keller & Lehmann, 2006). Marketing scholars interested in product branding tend to rely on this definition as a set of associations that is emphasized at the product brand level.

Others cite Urde and colleagues' definition, which isolates five dimensions assessing the presence of heritage in the organization. This definition stems from qualitative field work on the way corporate brands are managed. Hakala et al. (2011) discuss the relevance of these dimensions in product brand heritage. They conclude that consumers mostly engage with products and symbols in order to assess whether a product brand has heritage or not. These symbols communicate consistency and continuity, in addition to the longevity of the brand. In a way, the symbols on the products are the visible part of the heritage quotient defined by Urde et al. (2007).

Building on Aaker and on Urde, Greyser, and Balmer, I have suggested my own definition as 'a dynamic construct based on an inherited or borrowed past, with a view to supporting brand identity and being transmitted' (Pecot & De Barnier, 2017, p. 72). This definition distinguishes the managerial concerns for transmission and support to the product brand identity from the content of what is constructed and eventually made available to the consumers. It considers brand heritage as a construction negotiated internally and externally. This construction is made visible through a set of visual and textual symbols.

## 2.2. Management

The literature on the management of brand heritage can be organized into four sections. The first is the positioning, the second focuses on packaging and labels, the third on retail, and the fourth on communication tools. There is no specific research on the role of brand heritage on the pricing strategies, although some scholars have looked at the effect of brand heritage salience on price premium, as I discuss later.

Research looking at the role of brand heritage in the positioning is usually interested in the strategic use of brand heritage (Dion & Mazzalovo, 2016; Hudson, 2011; Pecot & de Barnier, 2018; Santos et al., 2016). Hudson (2011) looks at the case of Carnival's acquisition of Cunard. He explains how the new owners engaged in the (re)construction of Cunard's brand heritage in order to reposition the brand. The topic of repositioning is particularly salient for brand resurrections, that is when a company or an entrepreneur brings back to life a brand that had been famous once but had disappeared. Dion and Mazzalovo (2016) provide a typology for the reactivation of sleeping beauty brands depending on the link they seek with the past: revitalization (little emphasis on the past), retro-branding (relating the present with the past), and copying (the past is at the core of the value proposition). In both papers, the description of the processes does not make much space for co-creation and rather describes an omnipotent manager. On the contrary, an in-depth analysis of the revitalization of a traditional Finnish house slipper brand highlights the role of consumers in the adoption and diffusion of the new designs, through online communities (Närvänen & Goulding, 2016). Similarly, Santos et al. (2016), as well as Pecot and De Barnier (2018), consider the role of other stakeholders in the use of brand heritage at the product brand level. Santos et al. (2016) look at the synergies between the product and the corporate levels: e.g., the use of corporate heritage traits in product development. They show that the use of heritage artefacts helps in getting internal stakeholders on board with the product brand heritage and with the new positioning strategy. Pecot and De Barnier (2018) find that consumers exposed to brand heritage packaging perceive two different positionings: one that is more familiar and proximate, and another that is more aristocratic and distant. We also highlight the role of materiality to prove the genuineness of the heritage claim.

When it comes to the more operational marketing mix, the research on brand heritage in product and packaging is the least developed, but there is more if we extend our remit to research on heritage-related topics. There are some insights from the literature on food, showing how visual cues signifying traditions were used by Tesco to fabricate their 'farm' range (Barnes, 2017), or how old photographs can help position a brand that is effectively new as nostalgic (Wagner, 2018). There are in-depth case studies of breweries reproducing symbols relating to local history on their packaging (Ikäheimo, 2021), or naming a new product line from a motto (Hatch & Schultz, 2017). More generally, the literature on design shows how brands can adopt a heritage look through a neo-retro graphic design (Celhay et al., 2020). We can also learn from the literature on brand stories, and particularly the role of very short stories, which often build on the origin of the brand (Solja et al., 2018). All of them prove the role of brand heritage in making the packaging an efficient communication tool for the brand positioning. However, they do not engage directly with the concept of brand heritage, as Orth et al. do (2019). They focus on the change of packaging for heritage brands and show how consistency in the design reduces confusion and enhances the perception of brand heritage. They also evidence the role of the brand mascot as a key element to mitigate the negative effect of the change of packaging (Orth et al., 2019). The roles of graphic designers and external agencies as co-creators of the packaging is sometimes referred to but not directly discussed.

The most in-depth analysis of brand heritage display in retail stems from luxury (Dion & Borraz, 2015). The authors consider heritage stores: locations such as Chanel's Rue Cambon store, lying at the core of a brand's identity. They show how the implementation of mythical narratives, ritual practices, and symbolic boundaries tend to make the store sacred. The brand heritage obviously plays an important role in this strategy, providing stories and artefacts to nurture the sacralization process. While Dion and Borraz investigated the case of actual heritage brands, the design of retail spaces can also be used to construct and to reinforce a 'faux' heritage, as exemplified by Ralph Lauren (Joy et al., 2014).

Research on brand museums has considered FMCG brands (Chaney et al., 2017; Mencarelli et al., 2019). Such research shows how brands use techniques borrowed from museums to transform the brand and its artefacts into pieces of art, and thus form part of the local heritage (Chaney et al., 2017). A second paper explores consumers' reactions, between acceptance and resistance. To each intended objective of displaying heritage corresponds a form of consumer resistance: suspicion of the scientific, criticism of the authentic, and denial of the aesthetic (Mencarelli et al., 2019). This gives an example of how the heritage aspect of the brand is the result of a negotiation with the consumers, and beyond – with any museum visitor. As we discussed earlier, artefacts play a role, as pieces of evidence of the heritage claim (Pecot & de Barnier, 2018). Joy et al. (2014) mention consumers' interpretation as part of the co-creation process. However, none of the other papers report on the additional inputs of external stakeholders, particularly those involved in the creation of the stores or the museums, such as architects, design agencies, or interior designers, whereas it is quite often not the marketing managers or the brand artistic directors themselves who design the locations.

Finally, some research looks at the use of brand heritage in product brand communications (Carvajal Pérez et al., 2020; Martino & Lovari, 2016; Rose et al., 2017; Youn & Jin, 2017). Considering the use of brand heritage from a public relations perspective, Martino and Lovari (2016) propose a list of 13 actions involving brand heritage; some are common to most communication mixes, some are specific to heritage brands (e.g., historical collections, anniversaries, and ceremonies). Several pieces of research manipulate brand heritage in advertising (Merchant & Rose, 2013; Rose et al., 2017), either through visual or textual elements such as a claim, the use of a founding date, or of ornaments. However, there is no reported investigation of how heritage brand advertisements are constructed. Rose et al. (2017) show that university advertisements using brand heritage are more efficient than those not using it. The difference appears stronger when the heritage advertisement has a connection to the present. Recent work also looks at the use of old advertisements to engage customers on social media (Youn & Jin, 2017), and Carvajal-Pérez et al. (2020) consider the design of communication tools (digital applications, videos, and architectural space) that need to refer to the tradition of the brand while being innovative. Again, most of this work eludes the inputs of external or internal stakeholders. Martino and Lovari (2016) report the implication of media, partners, or local authorities in the activations around brand museums or anniversaries, but not in the position of co-creators or negotiators of the way brand heritage is construed or displayed.

## 2.3. Effects

When brand heritage researchers use qualitative methods at the product brand level, it is mostly observations and interviews with consumers or, on less frequent occasions, with managers (Chaney et al., 2017; Dion & Borraz, 2015; Halwani, 2020; Hudson, 2011; Pecot & de Barnier, 2018). There are many articles using quantitative methods to measure how much consumers perceive a brand to have heritage (Merchant & Rose, 2013; Pecot et al., 2018, 2019; Rose et al., 2016, 2017). These papers use measurement scales that have been developed in different contexts, but they all aim to capture consumers' perception of brand heritage salience: that is, how much people consider a brand to make use of its heritage.

The development of such tools allows the quantitative assessment of an effect on consumers' attitudes and behaviours. Brand heritage is shown to have a variety of positive effects on attitudes towards advertisements (Rose et al., 2017), attitudes towards the brand (Pizzi & Scarpi, 2019), purchase intention (Rose et al., 2016), and price premium (Pecot et al., 2018). We can distinguish four different explanations of why brand heritage increases perceived value: economic, functional, affective, and social (Wuestefeld et al., 2012). These are listed thus:

- Economic value: the longevity of the brand commands a price premium (Baumert & de Obesso, 2021). This can be explained by signalling theory (Pecot et al., 2018).
- Functional value: brand heritage claims positively influence credibility and perceived quality (Pecot et al., 2018), trust (Rose et al., 2016), but also perceptions of authenticity (Fritz et al., 2017; Pecot et al., 2019).
- Affective value: there is a positive effect on brand attachment (Merchant & Rose, 2013), personal nostalgia (Pecot et al., 2019), and positive emotions (Rose et al., 2016).
- Social value: heritage luxury brands are used to gain the respect of family members, or to bestow prestige on their owners (Halwani, 2020). They are also considered as being part of a future transmission within the family (Kessous et al., 2017).

Quantitative studies also include consumer-based moderators. These inform about the characteristics at the stakeholder level that influence the effect of brand heritage. For instance, being more familiar or past-oriented with the brand increases the effect of brand heritage on the perception of brand credibility (Pecot et al., 2018). People with prevention focus (as opposed to a promotion focus) are also more likely to transform brand heritage into purchase intention (G. Rose et al., 2016).

To summarise this first section, brand heritage is defined as a construction that is made visible through a set of visual and textual symbols. These symbols are used in the positioning strategy as well as in the marketing mix. Most of the research on brand heritage has focused on the salience of these symbols in facets of the mix, and on the quantification of their subsequent effect on consumers in terms of economic and functional and affective value, and to a lesser extent in terms of social value. We now turn to corporate branding literature in order to appreciate the similarities and differences.

## 3. Brand heritage in corporate branding

After brand heritage emerged in Aaker's model of brand identity, it was used with different meanings: e.g., as an ambivalent legacy (something of the past only), as opposed to retro and revival (Brown et al., 2003), as a synonym of brand essence (Leigh et al., 2006), or in close relation with the country of origin (Simms & Trott, 2006). It is fair to say that brand heritage was not truly conceptualised until it was introduced at the corporate level through the study of European Monarchies as corporate brands (Balmer et al., 2006), and extended to more mainstream forms of organizations (Urde et al., 2007).

In this corporate approach, heritage serves to define a distinct category of corporate brands requiring to be managed in a specific way (Balmer, 2011). There is some recent exploration of its effects on perceived value, but it remains arguably scarce compared to the overall volume of contributions.

### 3.1. Definition

This first stream of literature aims at defining corporate brand heritage as a dimension of the brand's identity (Urde et al., 2007), and at marshalling the category of corporate heritage brands as a specific kind of corporate brand (Balmer, 2011). Corporate brand heritage is defined here as a set of criteria: 'track records, longevity, core values, use of symbols, and particularly in an organizational belief that its history is important' (Urde et al., 2007, p. 4). 'Corporate heritage brand' designates an organization highlighting its heritage in its corporate identity and making it central to its positioning strategy (Urde et al., 2007). Researchers have further refined three fundamental characteristics: omni-temporality (i.e., the coalescence of the past, present, and future in a single timeframe), inter-generational continuity (i.e., the transmission of corporate traits between generations of managers and stakeholders), and augmented role identities (i.e., those organizations that also play a role in their territory, culture, or society) (Balmer & Burghausen, 2019). These characteristics have been found in multiple case studies focusing on the internal level of analysis, but their perception by external stakeholders has not been studied (e.g., Burghausen & Balmer, 2014; Spielmann et al., 2019).

In addition, there are investigations of specific sources of corporate heritage. As past images shape present images, consumers' past images – or image heritage – represent another side of corporate heritage (Rindell et al., 2015). The appropriations from cultural heritage is another source, as depicted in the study of recent luxury Chinese brands tapping into a rich national culture (Schroeder et al., 2015). These contributions highlight two external inputs to the definition of corporate heritage, from a consumer and from a cultural perspective. They also show that a corporate heritage is constructed and is different from what might have really happened, to the extent of cases of invented heritage and infused authenticity (Brunninge & Hartmann, 2019).

## 3.2. Management

The second stream of research on corporate heritage looks at the specific management of these corporate brands. The idea of stewardship as a particular managerial mindset is central to this model (Burghausen & Balmer, 2015). This mindset is found in an organizational awareness (of the sociohistorical position of the company, of its heritage, and of one's duties and obligations towards the company) and related dispositions (e.g., a sense of continuance and of responsibility). Such stewardship characterises the managers of corporate heritage brands and makes these companies different. Corporate brand heritage identities are implemented through specific practices: stories (narrating), visual design (visualizing), the enactment of rituals and tradition (performing), but they also have a material translation into the objects that managers use and display, or into the architecture (embodying) (Burghausen & Balmer, 2014).

A series of investigations extend our knowledge of corporate brand heritage management by looking at specific corporate heritage identity traits, or at more specific contexts. They consider the dynamic cases of corporate heritage recovery after a crisis (Cooper et al., 2015) or the tensions arising from the negotiations and shaping of corporate heritage identity over time (Lee & Davies, 2019). Others look at the management of corporate heritage in specific brand architectures such as the network (Urde & Greyser, 2015), in relation to product branding strategies (Santos et al., 2016), or at the role of the place and its own cultural heritage in the management of a territorial corporate heritage brand (Spielmann et al., 2019). They mention debates, conflicts, discussions, and other social interactions taking place around the definition and implementation of corporate heritage internally. Corporate brand heritage appears to be negotiated by various stakeholders, rather than being the result of one group's will. These findings resonate with the literature on co-creation of the corporate brand: a dynamic construction that is in constant negotiation with internal and external stakeholders (Hatch & Schultz, 2010; Iglesias et al., 2013, 2019; Vallaster & von Wallpach, 2013). Although it is not directly mentioned in corporate heritage literature, corporate brand heritage is co-created (Iglesias et al.,

2013). Its construction implies negotiations and discussions (Vallaster & von Wallpach, 2013) with prior generations of managers and with internal stakeholders (e.g., archivists, owners, marketing managers) (Burghausen & Balmer, 2014; Lee & Davies, 2019).

Some researchers engage with the communication of corporate heritage to external audiences as the nexus between corporate identity and its effects on stakeholders (Balmer, 2013). They suggest that the use of historical references in corporate communications provides reliability (Blombäck & Brunninge, 2009). They show that linking corporate heritage to CSR increases the perception of a responsible brand image (Blombäck & Scandelius, 2013), and more generally that the effective tools to communicate corporate heritage externally are symbols (Sammour et al., 2020). However, there is very little investigation of the communication to external stakeholders if we compare it to the literature on product brand heritage.

### 3.3. Effects

A third stream of research on corporate heritage is interested in capturing its value. A conceptual piece based on Mead's theory of the past suggests that corporate heritage conveys four kinds of value propositions: authenticity, reliability, personal nostalgia, and historical nostalgia (Hudson & Balmer, 2013). Recent efforts have tried to measure corporate heritage equity, or added value, either through a survey of customers of a traditional Chinese corporate brand, showing the positive effect of corporate heritage on customer satisfaction (Balmer & Chen, 2017), or through a regression of the heritage-value of corporate brand on the firm's financial value (Paek et al., 2020). In order to capture perceived corporate heritage or heritage-value, both papers move from the categorical definition of corporate brand heritage (based on organizational characteristics) to a definition based on the salience of particular associations. Unfortunately, they do not engage in a scale development process. An original contribution of corporate heritage research to the question of value is the empirical exploration of the negative equity of corporate heritage. There are some suggestions of negative organizational traits in Balmer (2013), and a historical approach shows how the same suggestions of corporate heritage traits can become a liability as the context changes (Sørensen & Heller, 2018).

To summarise this second section, corporate brand research on brand heritage has made a significant contribution to marketing scholarship by focusing on the concept of heritage and on its applicability to brand management. Prior research had mentioned brand heritage without really making it the focal point of their investigations. Then, because of its interest for the corporate level, most researchers have looked at the characteristics of companies that make corporate heritage a central tenet of their identity. Through case studies, they show how these companies operate, how they manage and implement their corporate heritage. Compared to research on product brand heritage, there is less engagement with external communication and with its effects on stakeholders. Now that we have reviewed both streams of research, the third and last section discusses opportunities for more dialogue between these two streams.

## 4. Cross-fertilization between brand heritage and corporate heritage research

From this review, it appears that brand heritage and corporate heritage research look at a similar phenomenon, but with different priorities and with a different methodological focus. Both are concerned with the broader question of permanence in brand management. While marketing as a discipline is rather future-looking and concerned with novelty and change (Nevett, 1989), brand heritage and corporate heritage investigate situations where managers and consumers

*Table 22.1* Key similarities and differences between brand heritage and corporate heritage literature

|  | *Product Brand Heritage* | *Both Levels* | *Corporate Brand Heritage* |
|---|---|---|---|
| Definition | Focus on brand associations and their salience. | Heritage is made of multiple sources and constructed. | Focus on the characteristics of the category. |
| Management | Focus on consumers (e.g., use of brand heritage in adverts). | External communication through symbols. | Focus on internal stakeholders (e.g., the implementation of the identity). |
| Effects | Mostly quantitative. Specific scales and detailed positive effects. Considers moderators. | Heritage adds value to consumers. | Few conceptual and quantitative papers. Considers negative equity. |

look for a balance between the past and the future, between change and continuity. They agree on the fact that a corporate or a brand heritage is constructed from multiple sources (Pecot & De Barnier, 2017; Rindell et al., 2015; Schroeder et al., 2015), that symbols are key to consider the communication of a product or corporate brand's heritage (Hakala et al., 2011; Sammour et al., 2020), and that it adds value to external stakeholders (Paek et al., 2020; Pecot et al., 2018).

However, we can see that there are significant differences too (Table 22.1). Corporate heritage research has mostly focused on internal matters, on understanding what characterises corporate heritage brands, but also how they are managed and how the identity is implemented. To do that, the research often analyses the relationships between different internal stakeholders, but does not engage with marketing mix activities or their effects on external stakeholders. There are exceptions around engaging with external stakeholders, but without quantification (Rindell et al., 2015; Santos et al., 2016), or without engaging with other stakeholders rather than consumers (Balmer & Chen, 2017; Paek et al., 2020).

Brand heritage research, on the other side, focuses either on how the heritage is used at the strategic level and through different facets of the mix, or on the effect that this salience has on consumer perception. The main unit of analysis is external, and it does not engage with internal stakeholders. Again, there are exceptions, but these are only conceptual (Pecot & De Barnier, 2017), or do not question the internal negotiations at stake when formalizing the brand heritage (Hudson, 2011; Pecot & de Barnier, 2018). We now suggest opportunities for cross-fertilization of both streams.

## 4.1. What brand heritage research can bring to corporate heritage research

Research on brand heritage can make three contributions to corporate brand heritage: 1) through the quantification of the phenomenon; 2) in validating some of the key principles through an external viewpoint; and 3) in considering stakeholder-based characteristics moderating the effects of brand heritage.

First, many brand heritage projects have adopted an hypothetico-deductive approach, stemming from consumer behaviour scholarship. This approach complements the more exploratory and qualitative focus taken from corporate heritage literature. While trying to measure the perception that one stakeholder group (consumers) has of brand heritage salience, the literature on brand heritage paves the way for replication to apply to other stakeholders. For instance, we saw that corporate heritage scholarship is interested in isolating corporate heritage identity traits, and that there are discussions around their number and relative importance. John

Balmer suggested a list of corporate heritage identity traits in 2011; this list was later refined in a co-authored reflective paper with Mario Burghausen (Balmer, 2011; Balmer & Burghausen, 2019). These traits are defined qualitatively and are being used in case study research, but we do not know which ones are the most relevant for external stakeholders. Based on the brand heritage research, an extension of this research could be a quantitative validation of these traits. The respondents would not be the consumers, but people who have a deep knowledge of the companies: employees, shareholders, media, B2B customers, regulators... Following a standard scale development process, corporate heritage researchers could build a scale that measures how salient are the corporate identity traits at the corporate level. Such a scale would be an interesting tool to produce industry ranking and to monitor the effectiveness of a new strategy. We can also imagine comparisons of perceived salience of corporate heritage between internal and external stakeholders in order to assess the solidity of the claim.

A corollary contribution is the validation of corporate heritage principles through an external viewpoint. We can take the example of relative invariance suggested by Balmer (2011). These principles were often assessed qualitatively through case studies, from the internal perspective: that means papers which show that relative invariance exists in the way managers care to handle the organization (Lee & Davies, 2019). Literature on brand heritage adds to this the proof that part of the value that an external stakeholder places on a heritage brand precisely depends on a mix of stability and adaptability (Pecot et al., 2019). It shows the validity of the principle beyond the intention of the organization. Although there is no discussion that corporate heritage research shows the validity of its findings through the accumulation of qualitative evidence, a quantitative take on the phenomenon will help in broadening the scope of our academic audience to more mainstream journals, conferences, and doctoral programmes.

A third contribution is the consideration of stakeholder-based characteristics that moderate the influence of brand heritage. Existing research has shown that brand familiarity, time orientation, and regulatory focus influence these effects for consumers (Pecot et al., 2018; G. Rose et al., 2016). Further research using a quantitative approach could explore whether these still stand with other stakeholders. But most importantly, different moderators that make sense for other stakeholders should be considered. For instance, in the case of a supplier or a B2B customer, they might perceive a firm's corporate heritage differently if they are themselves a corporate heritage brand.

## 4.2. Contributions of corporate heritage literature to the research on brand heritage at the product level

Research on corporate heritage can contribute to the research on brand heritage through the principles of co-creation. Whereas brand heritage researchers tend to take heritage as a static element that is made by the managers and pushed on the consumers, corporate researchers offer a more nuanced approach, particularly if we add inputs from co-creation. This encourages further research in three directions: 1) by putting the consumer in a more active role; 2) by exploring internal tensions; and 3) by looking at negotiations with external providers.

First, further research on product brand heritage creation and on its effects on consumer behaviour could benefit from putting consumers in a more active role. While research on revitalization positions consumers as co-creators of the brand meaning (Brown et al., 2003; Närvänen & Goulding, 2016), brand heritage research tends to depict a consumer that receives rather passively. The acceptance of the discourse displayed in the brand museum appears in qualitative research (Mencarelli et al., 2019) but not in quantitative studies. Moderators are considered, which accounts for the contribution of a consumer trait to the co-creation of brand heritage effect on attitudes or behaviours. However, there is no discussion of a co-creation of the brand heritage itself; our conceptual piece from 2017 acknowledges this (Pecot & De Barnier, 2017). Further research could look into acceptance as a moderator, and what leads to more or less acceptance, because it might operate as an important boundary condition. We also know that image heritage is an important source of meaning (Rindell et al., 2015), but there have not been estimations of their differential effects on known downstream variables. Finally, many museums or campaigns invite consumers to share their stories or memories with the brand, which is an input to the brand's heritage if it becomes appropriated or used to sustain the positioning. These are all avenues for further research that brand heritage scholars could consider.

The second avenue for further research concerns the internal tensions around the creation of brand heritage and its salience on marketing materials. The role of internal stakeholders is crucial in co-creation (see, for instance, Merrilees et al. (2021). Most product brand heritage research takes packaging, logos, and advertisements as stimuli without considering the context in which they were produced. Co-creation literature supposes the existence of various stakeholders with various views and resources (Vallaster & von Wallpach, 2013). Internal stakeholders' views compete and can be in conflict. Each stakeholder use its resources to achieve the best outcome. For instance, conflicts around the construction of the brand's heritage can arise between historians or archivists and the department of marketing, or the engineers in charge of new product development. From a marketing-as-practice perspective (Skålén & Hackley, 2011), it would be very interesting to look at these conflicts to better understand how brand heritage is formalised, and how it ends up being used. Building on the idea of corporate brand stewardship (Burghausen & Balmer, 2015), product brand heritage scholars could consider the role and mindset of brand managers, archivists, sales representatives, designers, etc.

The third avenue for further research relates to the second but shifts the focus to the external stakeholders, and their involvement in the way brand heritage is made salient on marketing material. The literature on corporate co-creation emphasises the role of external stakeholders, such as individual consumers (Minkiewicz et al., 2014), online communities (Ind et al., 2013), but also regulators or media (Vallaster & von Wallpach, 2013). We are well aware that many marketing operations are put in place in collaboration with external stakeholders (e.g., agencies, providers, designers etc.). For instance, it seems crucial to consider the role of advertising agencies in the definition and operationalization of brand heritage (Phillips et al., 2014). The same occurs in new product development, where design agencies play a very important role (Hemonnet-Goujot et al., 2019). Adidas is a great case to use to highlight the role of outsiders in the revelation and the curation of the available historical resources, but also of external designers in adapting the heritage (Iglesias et al., 2019). Organizing an anniversary, opening a museum or launching an advertising campaign involves collaborations with agencies, designers, architects, etc. Even if the description of the brand heritage is part of the brief and remains out of the discussion, its salience in the event or material is often the result of negotiations. Also, heritage brands are often very deeply rooted in their local environment, so the role of local authorities would need to be explored, as well as the interaction of effects with the country of origin.

## 5. Conclusion

This chapter offers an updated overview of the existing research around the concept of brand heritage and corporate heritage, as well as a dialogue between both. The result is the identification of several avenues for further research that students and scholars can select in order to expand both fields. We can see that corporate heritage and brand heritage have evolved in parallel. Corporate heritage scholarship tends to focus on the managerial level of analysis and brand heritage tends to engage with both the managerial and consumer levels of analysis, but rarely considers co-creation. This chapter is a call for more dialogue between both scholarships. On the one hand, corporate heritage researchers could benefit from engaging more with brand heritage research in order to deepen their exploration of the other stakeholders, in a similar way that brand heritage scholars have explored consumers. They could also benefit from the methodological arsenal developed by consumer researchers interested in brand heritage (measurement scales, experimental designs) to help them to study relations between corporate brands and their stakeholders. On the other hand, brand heritage researchers can build extended literature on corporate heritage in order to reconsider the role of the consumers beyond the mere reception of brand heritage material. They should also question the process of construction of brand heritage and of marketing materials based on brand heritage. These are too often taken for granted; they are often the results of conflicts and negotiations, internally and externally. If, instead of indulging in their methodological and epistemological differences, scholars from both streams could see their differences as complementary, it is the entire scholarship interested in the broader role of the past in brand management that could progress.

# References

Aaker, D. (1996). *Building strong brands*. New York: The Free Press.

Balmer, J. M. T. (2011). Corporate heritage identities, corporate heritage brands and the multiple heritage identities of the British Monarchy. *European Journal of Marketing*, 45(9–10), 1380–1398. https://doi.org/10.1108/03090561111151817

Balmer, J. M. T. (2013). Corporate heritage, corporate heritage marketing, and total corporate heritage communications: What are they? What of them? *Corporate Communications: An International Journal*, 18(3), 290–326. https://doi.org/10.1108/CCIJ-05-2013-0031

Balmer, J. M. T., & Burghausen, M. (2019). Marketing, the past and corporate heritage. *Marketing Theory*, 19(2), 217–227. https://doi.org/10.1177/1470593118790636

Balmer, J. M. T., & Chen, W. (2017). Corporate heritage brands, augmented role identity and customer satisfaction. *European Journal of Marketing*, 51(9–10), 1510–1521. https://doi.org/10.1108/EJM-07-2017-0449

Balmer, J. M. T., Greyser, S., & Urde, M. (2006). The crown as a corporate brand: Insights from monarchies. *Journal of Brand Management*, 14(1–2), 137–161. https://doi.org/10.1057/palgrave.bm.2550031

Barnes, A. (2017). Telling stories: The role of graphic design and branding in the creation of 'authenticity' within food packaging. *International Journal of Food Design*, 2(2), 183–202. https://doi.org/10.1386/ijfd.2.2.183_1

Baumert, T., de Obesso, M., & de las, M. (2021). Brand antiquity and value perception: Are customers willing to pay higher prices for older brands? *Journal of Business Research*, 123, 241–254. https://doi.org/10.1016/j.jbusres.2020.09.060

Blombäck, A., & Brunninge, O. (2009). Corporate identity manifested through historical references. *Corporate Communications: An International Journal*, 14(4), 404–419. https://doi.org/10.1108/13563280910998754

Blombäck, A., & Scandelius, C. (2013). Corporate heritage in CSR communication: A means to responsible brand image? *Corporate Communications: An International Journal*, 18(3), 362–382.

Brown, S., Kozinets, R. V., & Sherry, J. F. (2003). Teaching old brands new tricks: Retro branding and the revival of brand meaning. *Journal of Marketing*, 67(3), 19–33. https://doi.org/10.1509/jmkg.67.3.19.18657

Brunninge, O., & Hartmann, B. J. (2019). Inventing a past: Corporate heritage as dialectical relationships of past and present. *Marketing Theory*. https://doi.org/10.1177/1470593118790625

Burghausen, M., & Balmer, J. M. T. (2014). Corporate heritage identity management and the multimodal implementation of a corporate heritage identity. *Journal of Business Research*, 67(11), 2311–2323. https://doi.org/10.1016/j.jbusres.2014.06.019

Burghausen, M., & Balmer, J. M. T. (2015). Corporate heritage identity stewardship: A corporate marketing perspective. *European Journal of Marketing*, 49(1–2), 22–61. https://doi.org/10.1108/EL-01-2014-0022

Carvajal Pérez, D., Masson, P. Le, Araud, A., Chaperon, V., & Weil, B. (2020). Creative heritage : Overcoming tensions between innovation and tradition in the luxury industry identity. *Creativity and Innovation Management*, 1–12. https://doi.org/10.1111/caim.12378

Celhay, F., Magnier, L., & Schoormans, J. (2020). Hip and authentic. Defining neo-retro style in package design. *International Journal of Design*, *13*(3), 1–29.

Chaney, D., Pulh, M., & Mencarelli, R. (2017). When the arts inspire businesses: Museums as a heritage redefinition tool of brands. *Journal of Business Research*. https://doi.org/10.1016/j.jbusres.2017.10.023

Cooper, H., Miller, D., & Merrilees, B. (2015). Restoring luxury corporate heritage brands: From crisis to ascendency. *Journal of Brand Management*, *22*(5), 448–466. https://doi.org/10.1057/bm.2015.9

Dion, D., & Borraz, S. (2015). Managing heritage brands: A study of the sacralization of heritage stores in the luxury industry. *Journal of Retailing and Consumer Services*, *22*, 77–84. https://doi.org/10.1016/j.jretconser.2014.09.005

Dion, D., & Mazzalovo, G. (2016). Reviving sleeping beauty brands by rearticulating brand heritage. *Journal of Business Research*, *69*(12), 5894–5900. https://doi.org/10.1016/j.jbusres.2016.04.105

Fritz, K., Schoenmueller, V., & Bruhn, M. (2017). Authenticity in branding – Exploring antecedents and consequences of brand authenticity. *European Journal of Marketing*, *51*(2), 324–348. https://doi.org/10.1108/EJM-10-2014-0633

Grayson, K., & Martinec, R. (2004). Consumer perceptions of iconicity and indexicality and their influence on assessments of authentic market offerings. *Journal of Consumer Research*, *31*(2), 296–312. https://doi.org/10.1086/422109

Hakala, U., Lätti, S., & Sandberg, B. (2011). Operationalising brand heritage and cultural heritage. *Journal of Product & Brand Management*, *20*(6), 447–456. https://doi.org/10.1108/10610421111166595

Halwani, L. (2020). Heritage luxury brands: Insight into consumer motivations across different age groups. *Qualitative Market Research: An International Journal*. https://doi.org/10.13140/RG.2.2.30269.90089

Hatch, M. J., & Schultz, M. (2010). Toward a theory of brand co-creation with implications for brand governance. *Journal of Brand Management*, *17*(8), 590–604. https://doi.org/10.1057/bm.2010.14

Hatch, M. J., & Schultz, M. (2017). Toward a theory of using history authentically: historicizing in the Carlsberg group. *Administrative Science Quarterly*, *62*(4). https://doi.org/10.1177/0001839217692535

Hemonnet-Goujot, A., Manceau, D., & Abecassis-Moedas, C. (2019). Drivers and pathways of NPD success in the marketing – External design relationship. *Journal of Product Innovation Management*, *36*(2), 196–223. https://doi.org/10.1111/jpim.12472

Holbrook, M. B. (1993). Nostalgia and consumption preferences: Some emerging patterns of consumer tastes. *Journal of Consumer Research*, *20*(2), 245. https://doi.org/10.1086/209346

Hudson, B. T. (2011). Brand heritage and the renaissance of Cunard. *European Journal of Marketing*, *45*(9–10), 1538–1556. https://doi.org/10.1108/03090561111151880

Hudson, B. T., & Balmer, J. M. T. (2013). Corporate heritage brands: Mead's theory of the past. *Corporate Communications: An International Journal*, *18*(3), 347–361. https://doi.org/10.1108/CCIJ-Apr-2012-0027

Iglesias, O., Ind, N., & Alfaro, M. (2013). The organic view of the brand: A brand value co-creation model. *Journal of Brand Management*, *20*(8), 670–688. https://doi.org/10.1057/bm.2013.8

Iglesias, O., Ind, N., & Schultz, M. (2019). History matters: The role of history in corporate brand strategy. *Business Horizons*, *63*(1), 51–60. https://doi.org/10.1016/j.bushor.2019.09.005

Ikäheimo, J. P. (2021). Arctic narratives : Brewing a brand with neolocalism. *Journal of Brand Management*. https://doi.org/10.1057/s41262-021-00232-y

Ind, N., Iglesias, O., & Schultz, M. (2013). Building brands together. *California Management Review*, *55*(3), 5–27. Retrieved from www.majkenschultz.com/wp-content/uploads/Academic Publications/Building Brands Together.2013.pdf

Joy, A., Wang, J. J., Chan, T. S., Sherry, J. F., & Cui, G. (2014). M(Art)worlds: Consumer perceptions of how luxury brand stores become art institutions. *Journal of Retailing*, *90*(3), 347–364. https://doi.org/10.1016/j.jretai.2014.01.002

Keller, K. L. & Lehmann, D. R. (2006). Brand and branding: Research findings and future priorities. *Marketing Science*, *25*(6), 740–759. https://doi.org/10.1287/mksc.l050.0153

Kessous, A., Valette-Florence, P., & De Barnier, V. (2017). Luxury watch possession and dispossession from father to son: A poisoned gift? *Journal of Business Research*, *77*, 212–222. https://doi.org/10.1016/j.jbusres.2016.12.006

Lee, Z., & Davies, I. (2019). Navigating relative invariance: Perspectives on corporate heritage identity and organizational heritage identity in an evolving nonprofit institution. *Journal of Business Research*. https://doi.org/10.1016/j.jbusres.2019.05.038

Leigh, T. W., Peters, C., & Shelton, J. (2006). The consumer quest for authenticity: The multiplicity of meanings within the MG subculture of consumption. *Journal of the Academy of Marketing Science*, *34*(4), 481–493. https://doi.org/10.1177/0092070306288403

Martino, V., & Lovari, A. (2016). When the past makes news: Cultivating media relations through brand heritage. *Public Relations Review*, *42*(4), 539–547. https://doi.org/10.1016/j.pubrev.2016.03.009

Mencarelli, R., Chaney, D., & Pulh, M. (2019). Consumers' brand heritage experience : Between acceptance and resistance. *Journal of Marketing Management*, 1–21. https://doi.org/10.1080/0267257X.2019.1692057

Merchant, A., & Rose, G. M. (2013). Effects of advertising-evoked vicarious nostalgia on brand heritage. *Journal of Business Research*, *66*(12), 2619–2625. https://doi.org/10.1016/j.jbusres.2012.05.021

Merrilees, B., Miller, D., & Yakimova, R. (2021, December). Building brands through internal stakeholder engagement and co-creation. *Journal of Product and Brand Management*. https://doi.org/10.1108/JPBM-03-2020-2784

Minkiewicz, J., Evans, J., & Bridson, K. (2014). How do consumers co-create their experiences? An exploration in the heritage sector. *Journal of Marketing Management*, *30*(1–2). https://doi.org/10.1080/0267257X.2013.800899

Närvänen, E., & Goulding, C. (2016). Sociocultural brand revitalization: The role of consumer collectives in bringing brands back to life. *European Journal of Marketing*, *50*(7–8), 1521–1546. https://doi.org/10.1108/02656710210415703

Nevett, T. (1989). The uses of history in marketing education. *Journal of Marketing Education*, *11*(2), 48–53. https://doi.org/10.1177/027347538901100208

Orth, U. R., Rose, G. M., & Merchant, A. (2019). Preservation, rejuvenation, or confusion? Changing package designs for heritage brands. *Psychology & Marketing*. https://doi.org/10.1002/mar.21215

Paek, W., Ryu, H., & Jun, S. (2020). Heritage-based value of a corporate brand: Antecedents and effects on the firm's financial value. *Journal of Product and Brand Management*. https://doi.org/10.1108/JPBM-06-2019-2431

Pecot, F., & de Barnier, V. (2018). Brands using historical references: A consumers' perspective. *Journal of Brand Management*, *25*(1), 171–184. https://doi.org/10.1057/s41262-017-0076-y

Pecot, F., & De Barnier, V. (2017). Brand heritage: The past in the service of brand management. *Recherche et Applications En Marketing*, *32*(4), 72–90. https://doi.org/10.1177/2051570717699376

Pecot, F., Merchant, A., Valette-Florence, P., & De Barnier, V. (2018). Cognitive outcomes of brand heritage: A signaling perspective. *Journal of Business Research*, *85*, 304–316. https://doi.org/10.1016/j.jbusres.2018.01.016

Pecot, F., Valette-Florence, P., & de Barnier, V. (2019). Brand heritage as a temporal perception: Conceptualisation, measure and consequences. *Journal of Marketing Management*, 1–20. https://doi.org/10.1080/0267257X.2019.1667414

Phillips, B. J., McQuarrie, E. F., & Griffin, W. G. (2014). The face of the brand: How art directors understand visual brand identity. *Journal of Advertising*, *43*(4), 318–332. https://doi.org/10.1080/00913367.2013.867824

Pizzi, G., & Scarpi, D. (2019). The year of establishment effect on brand heritage and attitudes. *Journal of Consumer Marketing*. https://doi.org/10.1108/JCM-05-2018-2665

Rindell, A., Santos, F. P., & De Lima, A. P. (2015). Two sides of a coin: Connecting corporate brand heritage to consumers' corporate image heritage. *Journal of Brand Management*, *22*(5), 467–484. https://doi.org/10.1057/bm.2015.20

Rose, G., Merchant, A., Orth, U. R., & Horstmann, F. (2016). Emphasizing brand heritage: Does it work? And how? *Journal of Business Research*, *69*(2), 936–943. https://doi.org/10.1016/j.jbusres.2015.06.021

Rose, M., Rose, G. M., & Merchant, A. (2017). Is old gold? How heritage "sells" the university to prospective students: The impact of a measure of brand heritage on attitudes toward the university. *Journal of Advertising Research*, *57*(3), 335–351. https://doi.org/10.2501/JAR-2017-038

Sammour, A. A., Chen, W., & Balmer, J. M. T. (2020). Corporate heritage brand traits and corporate heritage brand identity: The case study of John Lewis. *Qualitative Market Research*, *23*(3), 447–470. https://doi.org/10.1108/QMR-03-2018-0039

Santos, F. P., Burghausen, M., & Balmer, J. M. T. (2016). Heritage branding orientation: The case of Ach. Brito and the dynamics between corporate and product heritage brands. *Journal of Brand Management*, *23*(1), 67–88. https://doi.org/10.1057/bm.2015.48

Schroeder, J., Borgerson, J., & Wu, Z. (2015). A brand culture approach to Chinese cultural heritage brands. *Journal of Brand Management*, *22*(3), 261–279. https://doi.org/10.1057/bm.2015.12

Simms, C. D., & Trott, P. (2006). The perceptions of the BMW Mini brand: The importance of historical associations and the development of a model. *Journal of Product & Brand Management*, *15*(4), 228–238. https://doi.org/10.1108/10610420610679593

Skålén, P., & Hackley, C. (2011). Marketing-as-practice. Introduction to the special issue. *Scandinavian Journal of Management*, 27(2), 189–195. https://doi.org/10.1016/j.scaman.2011.03.004

Solja, E., Liljander, V., & Söderlund, M. (2018). Short brand stories on packaging: An examination of consumer responses. *Psychology & Marketing*, 35(4), 294–306. https://doi.org/10.1002/mar.21087

Sørensen, A. R., & Heller, M. (2018). A bittersweet past: The negative equity of corporate heritage brands. *Journal of Consumer Culture*. https://doi.org/10.1177/1469540518773803

Spielmann, N., Discua, A., Tyler, B. B., & Beukel, K. (2019). Place as a nexus for corporate heritage identity : An international study of family-owned wineries. *Journal of Business Research*, 1–12. https://doi.org/10.1016/j.jbusres.2019.05.024

Urde, M., & Greyser, S. A. (2015). The Nobel Prize: The identity of a corporate heritage brand. *Journal of Product and Brand Management*, 24(4), 318–332. https://doi.org/10.1108/JPBM-11-2014-0749

Urde, M., Greyser, S. A., & Balmer, J. M. T. (2007). Corporate brands with a heritage. *Journal of Brand Management*, 15(1), 4–19. https://doi.org/10.1057/palgrave.bm.2550106

Vallaster, C., & von Wallpach, S. (2013). An online discursive inquiry into the social dynamics of multi-stakeholder brand meaning co-creation. *Journal of Business Research*, 66(9), 1505–1515. https://doi.org/10.1016/j.jbusres.2012.09.012

Wagner, K. (2018). Nostalgic photographs in the contemporary image ecology: The example of Tyrrells crisp packaging. *Journal of Aesthetics and Culture*, 10(1). https://doi.org/10.1080/20004214.2017.1421375

Wuestefeld, T., Hennigs, N., Schmidt, S., & Wiedmann, K.-P. (2012). The impact of brand heritage on customer perceived value. *Der Markt*, 51(2–3), 51–61. https://doi.org/10.1007/s12642-012-0074-2

Youn, S., & Jin, S. V. (2017). Reconnecting with the past in social media: The moderating role of social influence in nostalgia marketing on Pinterest. *Journal of Consumer Behaviour*, 16(6), 565–576. https://doi.org/10.1002/cb.1655

# 23
# CLOSING CORPORATE BRANDING GAPS THROUGH AUTHENTIC INTERNAL BRAND STRATEGIES

*Michael B. Beverland and Pınar Cankurtaran*

## 1. Introduction

An enduring ideal in Western philosophical thought (Newman, 2019), authenticity has crossed over into the marketplace with consumers, employees and brands all seeking or projecting a sense of 'the real, genuine, and true' (Beverland & Farrelly, 2010). In the past two decades, the emergence of cultural branding models, subcultures of consumption, doppelgänger branding, co-creation, brand storytelling and brand purpose, among many others have all been framed in issues of authenticity (Beverland, 2009; Fournier & Eckhardt, 2019; Giesler, 2012; Holt, 2004; Kates, 2004; Rose & Wood, 2005; Thompson et al., 2006). Practitioners speak of being more authentic in their communications, in their social media strategies, and in the delivery of high-order brand purpose, while simultaneously warning of the dangers of being perceived as inauthentic by various stakeholders. Brand rating agencies such as Interbrand now include authenticity in their measures of financial brand value (Interbrand, 2019), while researchers suggest authenticity is central to co-creation and modern marketing (Beverland, 2021; Ind & Schmidt, 2019). However, authenticity has yet to be explicitly examined in relation to corporate branding, and in the context of this chapter, as a way of achieving alignment between the intended corporate identity, image with external stakeholders, and firm culture (i.e., internal branding).

A central contribution of the corporate branding literature is the focus on alignment between the firm's intended identity, the image of that firm among stakeholders, and the firm's culture (Hatch & Schultz, 2008). In contrast to marketing's traditional focus on product-level branding, which emphasized the external cues necessary to ensure brand identity and image alignment with targeted consumers (Keller, 2003), the corporate branding approach drew inspiration from organization studies, alerting us to how failure to attend to the internal firm aspects of branding could create the very problems marketers were trying to avoid (Balmer et al., 2009). In corporate brand models, alignment between identity and image must take into account organizational culture, in particular employees' brand understanding and engagement (Chung & Byrom, 2021; Merrilees et al., 2020; Saleem & Iglesias, 2016; Urde, 2003). Therefore, it is necessary to complement externally facing brand marketing with internal brand building programs (Brodie, 2009; de Chernatony & Segal-Horn, 2003; Ind, 2014). Internal branding is defined as follows:

[T]he process through which organizations make a company-wide effort within a supportive culture to integrate brand ideologies, leadership, HRM, internal brand communications and internal brand communities as a strategy to enable employees to consistently cocreate brand value with multiple stakeholders.

(Saleem & Iglesias, 2016, p. 50)

Authenticity offers a useful lens for examining strategic alignment gaps between identity, image, and culture for a number of reasons. First, if employees can see themselves in the brand's identity, then they are more likely to embrace market-oriented change, ensuring the brand's equity is sustained (Ravasi & Phillips, 2011). Second, investing in internal branding ensures that employees genuinely 'live the brand,' giving rise to customer experiences of brand authenticity that are difficult to replicate (Ind, 2014; Miles & Mangold, 2005). Third, Arnould and Price (2000) argue that, in the context of consumption, self-authentication requires engaging in collective authoritative performances that reconnect individuals to the group. Actions that enable consumers to achieve their desired authentic self are always bound by collective norms. In the context of internal branding, this means that any attempts at self-authentication by the brand should avoid undermining the collective identity of its employees (Balmer et al., 2009). Fourth, cultural examinations of brand strategy suggest that authenticity is central to legitimacy with valuable sources of brand symbolism such as subcultures, communities, and tribes (Kates, 2004). Brands strive to come across as authentic cultural insiders who embody the ideology of the subculture that they draw value from, and also to ensure the renewal of that relationship through cultural innovation (Holt, 2004). This is particularly important given the need to achieve stakeholder alignment between brand image and identity in corporate branding, which can ultimately be undermined by inauthentic expressions of brand values by employees (in part driven by corporate policies) (Merrilees et al., 2020). Avoiding inauthentic expressions of brand values is particularly critical when firms seek to engage in 'brand activism' or 'brand purpose' whereby they embrace a higher order narrative that seeks to align the brand with a particular social movement or ideology (Vredenburg et al., 2020). Finally, we believe that the narrative transportation so essential for authentic brand storytelling (van Laer et al., 2014; see also Rose & Wood, 2005) is also essential for greater internal brand engagement (Hatch & Schultz, 2013, 2017).

Researchers have drawn from a range of theoretical traditions to examine the paradoxical nature of marketplace authenticity, the strategic benefits and challenges of having an authentic position in the marketplace, consumer judgements of authenticity, and the value of authenticity to brands (among many others) (Becker et al., 2019; Beverland & Farrelly, 2010; Grayson & Martinec, 2004; Rose & Wood, 2005). Findings indicate that brands that enhance their authenticity enjoy stronger consumer relationships, enhanced consumer sentiment, improved financial outcomes, and easier expansion into new categories (Morhart et al., 2015; Napoli et al., 2014; Spiggle et al., 2012). Although much has been done on how brands and organizations communicate authenticity externally, less attention has been paid to how firms organize for authenticity. This is curious given the profound role of stakeholders in shaping perceptions of authenticity within particular industries (Beverland, 2005) and the historic emphasis in brand management research on the role of employees in building brands from the inside out (Miles & Mangold, 2005). Given that in many sectors, employees are critical performers of brand values (Hochschild, 1983), examining the role of authenticity in internal branding gives greater prominence to this neglected stakeholder in corporate brand research.

In this chapter, we seek to connect research on corporate branding, with its focus on aligning the front and back stage of the brand, with work on authenticity. In particular we focus on (1) strategies for enhancing the internal authenticity of the brand and (2) internal branding approaches to build authenticity from the inside out. To address these questions, we will draw on a recent systematic review of the nature of authenticity (Lehman et al., 2019). With debates still raging over the very nature of authenticity, Lehman et al.'s (2019) review organized a fragmented literature into three perspectives: authenticity as *consistency*, authenticity as *conformity*, authenticity as *connection*. In this chapter we will use these three perspectives to explore avenues for internal brand authenticity. The rest of the chapter is structured as follows: first we conduct a short review on the nature of marketplace authenticity; second, we explore the three perspectives on authenticity and their implications for internal branding; third, we discuss implications for practice and future research, before concluding the chapter. We draw on examples from our own research and consulting practice throughout.

## 2. Authenticity and corporate branding

The value of authenticity to buyers and sellers can be traced back to early history, when sellers sought to assure distant buyers that the goods were the genuine article (Bastos & Levy, 2012; Moore & Reid, 2008). This objective view of authenticity, which focused on a direct connection between the object and its originator, defined the practice of marketplace authenticity for centuries. However, the emergence of the symbolic approach to branding in 1950s (Levy, 1959) paved the way for authenticity to take on more stylized connotations that went beyond the objective interpretation. Examinations of corporate identity identified that specialist firms would deploy elements of authenticity such as continuation of historic tradition, craft production, passion and sincerity in order to distinguish themselves from larger, generalist producers (Carroll & Swaminathan, 2000). Subsequent examinations identified that what was claimed as 'real, genuine and true' (Beverland & Farrelly, 2010) was often down to careful impression management, involving the balance of tradition with modernity, craft production and industrialization, and commercial motives with claims of sincerity (Beverland, 2005).

Ultimately, judgements of firms' authenticity claims involves beliefs about what 'ought to be' rather than what might be factually true (Grayson & Martinec, 2004). Studies of consumers indicate that objective or indexical authenticity is less valued than iconic claims which may be approximate, stylized, or even invented (Beverland et al., 2008). Studies of organizational claims also support the approximate or even high stylized and fictional nature of many accounts of corporate authenticity (Jones et al., 2005; Peterson, 2005). This stylized nature of authenticity partly arises from the need for change in the marketplace, while simultaneously sustaining fealty to category norms (Lehman et al., 2019) and social consensus (Newman, 2019). Thus, while many claims of authenticity emphasize an indexical or continued connection to heritage, the demands for relevance in the present require careful impression management to connect everything that is new to an enduring ethos or identity, both for consumers (Beverland & Farrelly, 2010) and employees (Ravasi & Phillips, 2011). This often leads organizations to downplay certain aspects of their operations that do not fit with the socially constructed nature of authenticity (Beverland, 2005).

Why is this so? Although authors agree that authenticity is subjectively experienced and reinforces previously existing expectations (Beverland & Farrelly, 2010), assessments of authenticity are also structured by social expectations. For example, the origin of the term 'authentic' suggests it stems from deep within us, and is an expression unconcerned with instrumental goals or societal conventions (Umbach & Humphrey, 2017). This results in authenticity being attributed to artists and iconoclasts for example, but not to commercial entities (Peterson, 2005). When artists become perceived as too commercially minded, they lose authenticity, and the value of their works often declines (Fine, 2003). Likewise, if organizations step away from their heritage, such as when orchestras adopt more popular formats (Glynn & Lounsbury, 2005), brand museums embrace populism at the expense of the firm's accepted heritage (Carù et al., 2017) or employees of a firm renowned for its superior quality, technology and design are told that market relevance requires them to step away from these pursuits (Ravasi & Phillips, 2011), the disconnection from the past can undermine the veracity of authenticity claims, resulting in critical backlash and distrust in strategic direction.

On the flipside, organizations that leverage authenticity, such as through connecting past and present, can build legitimacy for their initiatives (Jones & Smith, 2005). For example, controversial decisions over the hiring of high-profile employees, such as designers, can be rendered legitimate if the employee's skillset can be tied to a tradition or ethos that fits the organization (Delbridge & Edwards, 2008). New market-driven initiatives that seem at odds with the firm's present identity can be embraced by employees if they can be tied to the firm's past, even if the tradition itself has been broken for some time (Hatch & Schultz, 2017). Market motivated shifts in the firm's internal logic also need to be authenticated in terms of the historical, collective identity shared by employees if they are to be embraced (Ravasi & Phillips, 2011). Finally, the authenticity of a firm's claims (i.e., connecting identity and image; Hatch & Schultz, 2008) can be enhanced if employees have a sense of shared tradition with the community of practice to which they seek to appeal (Harrison & Corley, 2011). Thus, we contend that carefully managed impressions of authenticity can enhance corporate brand initiatives and therefore are of relevance to the theorizing and practice of internal branding.

However, internal branding requires attention to what we call 'authenticity work.' Gilmore and Pine (2007) identify that although brands may be objectively inauthentic (because they are commercial creations and therefore tainted by commercial motives), they can be rendered authentic through the right performance. This, by its very nature, requires a focus on employees, who in many industries are carriers of corporate identity (Brodie, 2009; de Chernatony & Segal-Horn, 2003). Although there is substantial research on the external communication of authenticity, there is much less insight into the behind-the-scenes internal branding practices necessary to enable co-creation to occur (beyond classic accounts of the experiences of authenticity and emotional labour in service industries – see for example, Hochschild (1983)). This oversight is important for a number of reasons. First, corporate branding research identifies the importance of linking the brand's front stage or identity with its backstage or culture (Hatch & Schultz, 2001, 2008). Second, research on corporate identity revitalization shows that employees need to see themselves in the new brand (i.e., to be able to place themselves in the employer brand narrative) (Hatch & Schultz, 2017; Ravasi & Phillips, 2011). Third, recent co-creation branding models suggest that organizations should mirror the cultural environment from which they draw their identity (and resources) (Holt, 2004).

To identify and explore tensions and challenges in authenticity and internal branding, we draw upon a recent synthesis of the literature on authenticity (Lehman et al., 2019). Lehman and colleagues integrated firm and consumer studies on authenticity, providing much needed conceptual clarity to the domain. As such, we believe their three perspectives on authenticity provide a valuable basis for exploring the role of authenticity in the context of internal corporate branding initiatives. The three forms of authenticity identified by Lehman et al. (2019) are described below and form the basis for the rest of this chapter.

1. Authenticity as consistency: a more 'objective' form of authenticity whereby the brand delivers on its promises, often reflected in claims of 'living the brand' or 'building the brand from the inside out.'
2. Authenticity as conformity: rooted in social constructionism, brands are deemed authentic to the extent they conform to relevant norms that exist within society, communities of practice, categories, and in the case of internal branding, firms.
3. Authenticity as connection: indexical or iconic links between the brand and a sense of heritage (time, place, and culture), including links between the brand's founder, their ethos, and other aspects of identity.

In drawing on these three perspectives on authenticity, we seek to identify new insights for internal branding researchers, including avenues for further inquiry. We do so with reference to relevant theoretical and empirical research as well as examples from our own research and practice.

## 2.1. Authenticity as consistency

This form of authenticity concerns alignment between the firm's brand identity and its image. In essence, authenticity as consistency focuses on whether the brand 'walks the walk' (Beverland, 2009). In brand management research, this form of authenticity has received the most attention, particularly with the recognition of the power of employer branding and the need to 'build brands from the inside out' (Ind, 2014; Miles & Mangold, 2005). Brand models, whether rooted in the customer-based brand equity framework or in corporate branding, focus on ensuring one can deliver on promises. This involves (among many others) fostering interaction between staff and stakeholders, strengthening employee engagement, using tools such as stakeholder surveys and customer journey analysis, and executing formal internal branding programs to align the brand's 'back stage' to its 'front stage' (Beverland, 2021).

Corporate branding research for example has focused on achieving alignment between intended brand identity, brand image, and firm culture (Greyser & Urde, 2019; Hatch & Schultz, 2008). Often rooted in the branding of services (Brodie, 2009), these models seek to build consistency between the brand, external stakeholders, and employees (Balmer et al., 2009). By closing the gaps between these domains, the brand's promises are delivered and experienced consistently (Hatch & Schultz, 2001). Internal branding is needed to not only ensure staff understand the brand's identity, but also equip them to deliver on the promises made (de Chernatony & Segal-Horn, 2003; Iglesias & Saleem, 2015; Kraak & Holmqvist, 2017). Attention to the wider context in which employees operate is also essential, in order to create alignment between rewards systems for example, and brand-driven behaviours (Iglesias & Saleem, 2015).

For example, in the fallout following Kraft's Australia marketing team decision to name its extension of the iconic Vegemite brand iSnack 2.0, marketing director Simon Talbot was struck by how disappointed staff were at the choice. Although the negativity was in part due to the poor choice of name, the real reason for the backlash ran deeper. Charged with turning around the declining sales of the iconic breakfast condiment, Talbot had engaged directly with customers to uncover the meaning of Vegemite in their daily lives through the celebrated 'How do you love your Vegemite?' campaign. The aim was to turn the company into a customer-centric organization and return the brand to its cocreated heritage (the brand's name had been developed through a public competition in the 1930s and had long embedded itself in day-to-day Australian life), thereby revitalizing the brand's historic truths and realigning the brand's culture with the desired new identity. The campaign was a success, yet the decision to ignore customer input on the name in favour of a quirky, Apple inspired name ran counter to the brand's desired identity and more importantly made a mockery of the internal branding program, leaving staff wondering why they had worked so hard over many months to return the brand to local icon status. This backlash among staff, more so than customers who were buying the product nonetheless, led Talbot to capitulate and return the naming decision to public vote (Keinan et al., 2012).

Authenticity as consistency is also captured in the focus on alignment in corporate branding research. Hatch and Schultz (2001) identify three gaps that a corporate branding strategy must bridge: identity-image, image-culture, and identity-culture. The first gap concerns the classic breakdown between intended and received brand identity. This may of course be driven by behind-the-scenes problems that result in promises being rendered inauthentic, but may also be driven by shifts in the wider meso and macro context surrounding the brand that have little to do with internal factors (Preece et al., 2019). The other two gaps are issues that concern us here. Gaps between identity and culture have been covered above in the discussion of the staff backlash to the iSnack 2.0 naming, whereas gaps between image and culture may result in the lack of interaction between users and employees.

Returning to the earlier Vegemite example, a combination of risk aversion (expressed as 'never change the brand') and an aging staff base led employees to view the brand very differently to a new generation of adopters – typically new immigrants who did not use the brand at breakfast, but instead used it as a base for soups and other south East Asian dishes (Keinan et al., 2012). Similarly, staff at ailing Kodak could not connect to a revitalization plan that stressed the brand's new found cool with younger consumers. The gap only closed when Kodak staff were exposed to employees and customers of retro-brand Lomography. The result was greater engagement with a strategy focused on leveraging 'cool,' and a series of relaunches of legendary branded product-lines such as Ektachrome (Keinan et al., 2018). Similarly, in highly siloed Yamaha, a one-brand strategy had to overcome divisional resistance. The guitar division for example believed that their buyers would not tolerate the same brand expression as those for concert pianos. However, research conducted by the organization's senior marketing officer to address divisional concerns showed that all customers were attracted to Yamaha for its reputation across instrumental categories (i.e., what attracted guitar buyers to Yamaha was its reputation for pianos, and vice versa), and provided the impetus for staff to see themselves as part of a larger, single-branded, whole (Beverland, 2021).

Authenticity through consistency difficulties in arise predominantly from the way employees experience the perceived truth of the brand. That is, should the brand's desired identity be inconsistent with the lived reality of employees or the firm's backstage practices, employees are likely to view any corporate brand identity as insincere. Consistency also draws our attention to the opportunity, indeed the requirement, to co-create identity with employees, often through exposing them to stakeholders' views of the brand, or ensuring that employees can see themselves in the intended brand identity.

### *2.2. Authenticity as conformity*

On the face of it, conformity seems to be the opposite of authenticity since it suggests one follows rules at the expense of one's true self (Newman, 2019). However, a significant stream of research indicates that, for a brand to be a typical representation of a product/service category or consumer subculture, it must conform to its written and unwritten norms (Beverland et al., 2010; Holt, 2002). This involves communicating through the correct 'cultural codes' or the:

> Symbols and systems of meaning that are relevant to members of a particular culture (or subculture). These codes can be utilized to facilitate communication within the "inside group" and also to obscure the meaning to "outside groups."
>
> (Hyatt & Simons, 1999, p. 23)

These codes are learned through immersion in context and practice, and therefore are demonstrated in embodied practice. That is, one does not say one is authentic, one demonstrates it through action (in fact, saying one is an authentic member of a category or subculture would be perceived as 'trying too hard' and therefore insincere). Arguably, this form of authenticity is more difficult to manage, because the difference between real and fake or sincere and trying too hard involves shades of grey (Potter, 2011) and because the standards for such judgements can shift, requiring active and ongoing engagement with the context and its consumers (Beverland, 2005; Kates, 2004).

Within the branding literature, two types of authenticity as conformity stand out: typicity and cultural embeddedness. In regard to the first, in order to be judged an authentic representation of a certain class, the brand must conform to certain rules. For example, fine wine brands downplay commercial intent, reference connections to place, and engage in strategic ambiguity (Dickinson-Delaporte et al., 2010) in order to communicate their authenticity. Ambiguity is needed in order to balance or juggle different tensions facing the brand, including the need for relevance vs. consistency, modernity vs. heritage, and sincerity vs. commercial reality (Beverland, 2005). In regards to the second, conformity allows the brand to speak as a subcultural insider, thereby enhancing its legitimacy and cultural authority (Arsel & Thompson, 2011; Holt, 2004; Kates, 2004).

Conformity via typicity is closely aligned to both connection and consistency, but involves loose coupling or even decoupling between the brand's front and back stages. For example, rather than overtly responding to contemporary trends, luxury wine brands downplay the reality of their marketing and technical prowess in their storytelling, while giving prominence to traditions, heritage, and accidental discoveries (Beverland, 2005). This helps reinforce their image as artisans focused on maintaining cultural traditions; rather than market leaders focused on exploiting their position (Beverland, 2009). They do this because they must conform to two competing goals: maintaining a market leadership position in terms of quality and sensory appeal while also appearing above short-term fashions in order to maintain a sense of timelessness among all their stakeholders. Similar concerns occurred in cultural organizations such as orchestras when new management attempted to move them to a more commercial orientation (Glynn & Lounsbury, 2005). Balancing cultural and commercial concerns involves a careful performance to ensure that the brand does not appear insincere, the key standard of judgement in relation to conformity.

Conformity via cultural embeddedness has its roots in consumer culture theory (CCT) (Arnould & Thompson, 2005) and the cultural branding model of Douglas Holt (2004). Here, the brand's value derives from its ability to be relevant through connecting to users' individual and collective identity goals (Arnould & Price, 2000), and the challenge for internal branding involves ensuring the brand speaks and acts as a cultural insider or what Holt (2002) calls a 'citizen artist.' For example, in his extended examination of Budweiser, Holt (2004) identifies how the brand's ability to represent masculinity came from the cultural authority that it accrued through morphing its message and identity to reflect shifting views of masculinity in relation to role identity and the deeper cultural anxieties accompanying this shift (Holt & Thompson, 2004). Likewise, Kates' (2004) examination of the North American LGBT market identified how some brands' ongoing alignment with subcultural concerns meant they became seen as 'gay friendly,' securing them insider status (or cultural-cognitive legitimacy, where the brand becomes a taken for granted part of the cultural landscape).

While to the best of our knowledge, no studies have examined how conformity can be achieved in internal branding, the CCT literature offers some guidance. First, firms must somehow mirror the language, rituals, practices and norms of their target communities (Arsel & Thompson, 2011; Holt, 2004). Second, they must understand the ways in which value is cocreated in these communities, and focus on ways to strengthen value-adding practices (Schau et al., 2009). Third, community engagement must not be siloed into marketing communications but be treated as a strategic priority. Exploring the celebrated case of the Harley Owners Groups (HOG), Fournier and Lee (2009) show how that Harley-Davidson leveraged its brand community as a significant driver of brand strategy rather than treating it simply as marketing communications. Finally, continued engagement enables firms to adapt to shifts in community values and concerns, thereby enhancing the brand's legitimacy (Kates, 2004).

Beverland (2009) identifies that firms building authenticity become immersed in their markets, a strategy that involves enduring day-to-day involvement in the context in which users (and other stakeholders) operate. Immersion is aimed at avoiding charges of cultural appropriation or co-optation of consumer generated material (Holt, 2002), which under conditions of co-creation, is critical to maintaining legitimacy and ultimately authenticity (Beverland, 2021). Immersion is one practice by which employees can become 'citizen artists' (Holt, 2004), as ongoing engagement with stakeholders lived realities can provide the basis for more legitimate brand activities. In this sense, immersion can create employees who are able to speak and act as cultural insiders, and who therefore take more of a stewardship role towards various stakeholder groups. This often results in more sensitive marketing approaches (e.g., Beverland & Ewing, 2005), that then see the brand embedded more tightly within a community because staff are seen as fellow community members and the brand is imbued with sincerity.

Deploying employees to act as de facto ethnographers in their respective communities or categories is one way brands immerse themselves in the context. Some forms of immersion can be obvious and direct, such as involvement at fan days or events, meet the customer days, exposure of senior managers to frontline experience, and direct engagement by employees in the focal activities of target communities (Beverland, 2009). Lovehoney for example employs members of the LGBT community to ensure its marketing communications are on point (Cankurtaran & Beverland, 2019). Other forms of immersion are less direct, and occur through embodied practice. For example, staff at the Morgan Motor Company are encouraged to take part in amateur vintage car racing events in order to connect the specialist craft brand with an enduring tradition of racing, but also to provide the basis for further innovations. How? These events, with strict rules and budget limitations mean the staff become masters of extracting performance from old technology with low-cost solutions, enabling the firm to make further enhancements to their vehicles without undermining their authenticity in the eyes of owners.

Authenticity as conformity also relates to strategic repositioning. Studies of brands engaged in a turnaround or seeking to extend their range of operations into other categories highlight the importance of gaining staff consent. Staff at Carlsberg for example were sceptical of the beer behemoth's attempts to move into the high-quality craft segment with a new product range. Claims that the new range involved the brand going right back to its founding roots needed to be authenticated with historical evidence. Furthermore, senior management failed to understand the conformity requirements of the category (external-conformity) and expectations among staff that the new brand would be a departure from the firm's mass market tradition. Following the unsuccessful initial launch, a relaunch (involving more staff input) saw a more restricted approach to distribution and a different set of channel partners (up-market *horeca*), which enabled staff to engage with the program (Hatch & Schultz, 2017). Failure to conform to the identity needs of staff saw British Airways much touted multi-cultural livery get withdrawn (Balmer et al., 2009).

These examples suggest that internal brand authenticity and internal brand engagement is also cocreated, and require the development of strategies that enable staff to continue to see themselves in the brand story. The emergence of commercial storytelling has given rise to practitioner and academic interest in crafting brand stories that engage and persuade consumers. One particularly promising strategy to achieve this is narrative transportation, whereby the reader (i.e., the consumer) empathizes with the story's characters and feels like they are part of the plot, suspending disbelief in the process (Van Laer et al., 2014). In their study of reality television, Rose and Wood (2005) demonstrate how connecting one's identity with the brand story via narrative transportation is critical to authenticity. We propose that what applies for consumers also applies to employees, such as the Bang & Olufsen staff who, in line with the firm's revitalization objectives, had to engage (and get on board) with the idea of a more customer centric organization. Rather than just adopt a mass market stance, internal debate focused on how the firm's craft tradition and emphasis on a particular aesthetic sensibility and design language could be married to logic that required the firm to respond to quality and performance challenges from mass market brands (Ravasi & Phillips, 2011). Similarly, Yamaha's *Make Waves* campaign was borne out of the firm's long held passion for natural sound, with the campaign launch highlighting this connection across all of the products produced by the firm. This, plus targeted research on specific product markets, helped encourage internal buy-in, turning some of the most sceptical opponents of the one brand initiative into its greatest advocates (Beverland, 2021).

Authenticity as conformity relates primarily to issues of sincerity – is the brand being genuine in intent vis-à-vis a target community or category? This issue arises when two brand-identity-image gaps occur (Hatch & Schultz, 2008): (1) gaps between the brand-image and brand-culture, and (2) gaps between brand-identity and brand-culture. The first gap arises because the firm is disconnected to its core user base or misunderstands the contexts in which it operates. The second gap occurs because the firm fails to engage with employees' identity concerns, and results in a backlash against the imposition of the brand program that employees cannot relate to. Addressing both gaps involve co-creation, the first focused outward, the second inward. The policies which encourage greater engagement by employees with both the external context in which brand stakeholders draw their identity and the brand itself, remain under-researched, an issue we will address below.

## 2.3. Authenticity as connection

The third form of authenticity relates to a sense of connection to time, place and culture (Lehman et al., 2019). Although these connections have been modelled in terms of their indexical truth or iconic approximation (Grayson & Martinec, 2004), empirical work suggests these are best imagined as two ends of a continuum (Beverland et al., 2008). Brands need to oscillate between both, depending on the objective they want to achieve and indeed the criticism or challenge they are facing from external stakeholders. Although it is tempting to view connection in terms of objective authenticity, this is too narrow a reading. Brands must not just be from somewhere, they must be carriers of place, time and/or culture, giving rise to the need for the connection to be felt and experienced. These can be objective, indexical or more iconic, symbolic connections to time, place and culture.

To date, research has primarily focused on the power of more indexical, objective connections, such as unbroken connections to place, or cultural traditions, or regional practices. In these instances, firms engage in a range of practices to maintain traditions, such as through multi-generational teams that new employees are encultured into firm traditions and ensure that the firm's products and design language evolves slowly, over decades or centuries (Beverland,

2009). However, research on the internal branding aspects of maintaining connections to place, time and culture mains scarce. Traditions are by their nature invented and subject to revision (Hobsbawn & Ranger, 1983), and even the notion of place changes over time (for example, the physical boundary of wine producing regions is often subject to change for a variety of reasons, such as commercial pressures demanding more production; Beverland, 2005).

For new brands, or revitalized old brands, the decision to reference place for example can be fraught with danger. Brands such as Shinola Detroit attempt to push back against globalization by reinvesting in the origin of American manufacturing prowess. Opened for business in 2011, Shinola Detroit aimed to draw on the manufacturing heritage of Detroit, historic home to American's 'Big Three' automakers. Rock City (as Detroit is known) had been torn by racial division for much of its history, and seen its population and tax base decline with loss of manufacturing due to the North American Free Trade Agreement and a desire to move to non-unionized right to work states. In 2013, Detroit declared bankruptcy. However, a 'Detroit revival' movement had sprung up in the 2000s, with many firms taking advantage of tax breaks and low-cost building space to leverage the city's heritage of making. Although this development connected with the desire of many to buy local after the fall out of the 2008 global financial crisis, among the city's residents, the arrival of a largely white group of venture capitalists and start-ups, generated a mixed response. For many, the new firms did little for the people who lived in Detroit, and added little to the city's tax base which provided the services people desperately needed (Marotta, 2021).

Shinola took over the former General Motors innovation laboratory in downtown Detroit and used these associations to promote their luxury brand of locally made watches, leather goods, bicycles and other items reflecting a rugged American past (Avery et al., 2020). The brand stressed its localness through its prominently displayed Made in Detroit tagline, and through a range of advertisements celebrating the life of the city. However, this glocalization or reterritorialization strategy (Sharifonnasabi et al., 2020) runs the risk of being seen as insincere on many fronts, and Shinola's claims to be of Detroit were subjected to immediate critique. First, the Federal Trade Commission ruled that Shinola's Made in Detroit (and even Made in the USA) claim was misleading, given that its watch manufacturing largely involved the assembly of parts from Hong Kong and Switzerland (Avery et al., 2020).

The racial history of Detroit and its subsequent financial decline also gave rise to resentment against 'white saviour' carpet-baggers such as Shinola who leverage the 'New Detroit' in their branding (Marotta, 2021). This critique reflects a different connection challenge to that represented by a lack of local manufacturing content; here stakeholders question the sincerity of a firm's connection to the city, seeing brands such as Shinola as seeking to profit from the symbolism of Detroit (as America's historic manufacturing engine room) without truly understanding the nature of place. A particularly extensive critique came from the RETHINK Shinola Project (RSP), an art project questioning Shinola's relationship to place and race. Identifying that the brand name was drawn from a shoe polish that used explicit racist imagery, RSP attacked the brand's claims to connection, suggesting it was one of several white saviours who were profiting from the misery of the city and its downtown residents (Avery et al., 2020). This critique is less about objective connections and more about sincerity of connection to place.

To rebuild more sincere connections Shinola did a number of things. First, they directed investment into the heart of Detroit, primarily through a hotel that celebrates the city's aesthetic and manufacturing prowess. This did little to counter the criticism however, as the clientele was predominantly the new wave of white start-up capitalists taking advantage of cheap land and buildings in the city. Shinola then turned to their employees, who are overwhelmingly African American, and featured them in their communications, while realigning their 'of Detroit' strategy to focus on the long-term residents (mostly non-white) who were part of the city's comeback narrative (such as small urban farmers, local craftspeople and so on, who they also featured in their downtown hotel's retail space). A new range of mid-priced watches featured connections to local sports teams and their historic rivals to help place the brand in the collective memory of the city. In doing so, Shinola, through leveraging employer stories, outreach, and their external identity, sought a more sincere connection with time, place, and culture.

Authenticity as connection may at first appear like a derivation of conformity. Certainly, there are overlaps between all three forms of authenticity, but whereas conformity is more about speaking as an insider, connection involves reterritorialization as a means of counter-acting the place-lessness of globalization. In authenticity terms, connection is about rebuilding collective bonds by demonstrating that something *essential* of particular places, times, or cultures lies at the heart of the brand's identity. Therefore, for the brand, it involves both authenticating acts and authoritative performances (Arnould & Price, 2000). An authenticating act is the brand's individual identity and reflects a statement of intent (such as Shinola's desire to leverage Detroit's heritage). Authenticating acts are important but they will be judged as insincere unless brands engage in authoritative performances by forging deep and real connections to time, place, and culture (such as Shinola's subsequent city-focused strategy). Telling employees stories (of which they are also part) and getting them involved in the local community are two ways to do this.

Corporate brand research has uncovered the power of connection strategies For example, Hatch and Schultz (2013) identify how allowing employees to experience the lived traditions of the company resulted in greater engagement with the brand and helped activate the brand identity internally. Initially, staff at Carlsberg's information technology division (CIT) found it difficult to embrace the firm's brand strategy that was primarily focused on beer craft and production, a discourse that seemed to exclude them. Encouraged to engage in brewing process, CIT staff were able to experience the brand promise and see how their own functional discipline was in fact embedded to the very essence of the firm. Carlsberg is one example of a firm that has used connections to its enduring history to reinvigorate its external brand. They have leveraged these connections also in their conformity strategy discussed previously, where they undertook a historical examination to uncover their true craft heritage traditions as a means of ensuring employee buy-in to a new product line, and provided seemingly excluded employees with direct experience of traditions to drive greater brand engagement (Hatch & Schultz, 2017).

Another example involves the reorganization of Yamaha Music's fragmented brand portfolio under one corporate brand identity and logic. Here, the internal branding work focused specifically on overcoming resistance among divisional staff to the idea of a single brand. The brand slogan 'Make Waves' drew on interviews from Yamaha sponsored musicians from the full range of genres served by the music giant. Uniting these musicians was a passion for creativity, both in terms of personal expression and the impact of their music on an audience. This strategy was embedded in the firm's history through the construction of an innovation roadmap that located the firms enduring passion for two values: 'perfect sound' and 'musician to the front.' This roadmap demonstrated the connection between the brand's inspirational founder Tarakusu Yamaha, and the innovation and design philosophy since 1887. The resulting connection between customers, staff, and the firm's heritage generated significant internal engagement behind the single brand idea, and is attributed to the recent rise in the brand's external equity (Beverland, 2021).

In summary, authenticity as connection is a reterritorialized approach to brand identity that poses challenges for placeless global brands. As we see in the case of Shinola for example, attempting to appear from somewhere without forging real and meaningful connections results in a backlash from stakeholders who cannot abide by the brand's insincerity. In essence, attempting to connect to somewhere while operating as if from everywhere (i.e., as a globalized brand), triggers claims of insincerity, resulting in lost authenticity and legitimacy. The challenge of connection involves placing the brand in the enduring collective memory of place or culture, forging links with like-minded stakeholders, investing directly in place, drawing on time-honoured traditions, and telling local stories, including those of the staff behind the brand.

## 3. Implications and conclusions

In this section we discuss the implications of the above review for future research in internal branding. To the best of our knowledge, scholars have not formally examined issues of authenticity in the context of internal branding (although authenticity concerns do arise in studies of emotional labour among service employees, primarily in relation to the authentic self). Close attention to internal branding and authenticity is needed given the prevailing view that brands are built from the inside out (Miles & Mangold, 2005), and critically, the breach of individual and collective consumer-brand relationship norms are often attributable to failures of organizational culture (Hietanen & Rokka, 2015). Although partially addressed in the focus on consistency between identity, image and culture in corporate branding research (Hatch & Schultz, 2008; 2013), the emphasis on authenticity in more recent models of branding and co-creation (Beverland, 2021; Ind & Schmidt, 2019) suggest authenticity is an important strategic issue, not only for delivering on promises but also for ensuring internal engagement with the brand.

We model our discussion around an adaptation to Hatch and Schultz's (2008) corporate brand model. In Figure 23.1, we describe how authenticity in internal branding is reinforced and activated to connect brand culture, brand identity, and brand image (since the focus of this chapter is on internal branding, we have restricted our attention to the relationship between culture and identity, and culture and image). The arrow leading from brand identity to brand culture identifies how brand identity can be made real through instilling employees with a sense of purpose. Purpose-based strategies focus on higher order ideals (Aaker, 2018) and, as demonstrated by Hatch and Schultz (2013) and the examples above, can help employees find

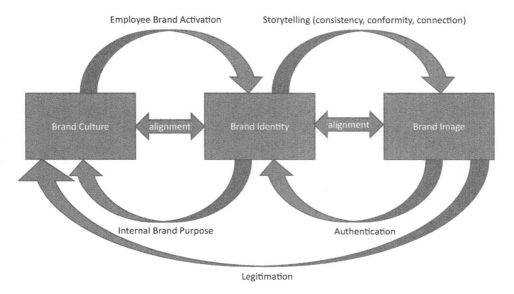

*Figure 23.1* Closing authenticity gaps in internal branding

themselves in the brand's identity and enduring narrative. Once this is achieved, we propose that this will generate greater engagement and help with activation (bringing the brand to life), and enhance the authenticity (consistency, conformity, and/or connection) of the brand's storytelling. We also emphasize the importance of engaging employees more closely with the source of brand image, to help them understand the expectations that drive consistency, the rules framing conformity, and the notions of sincerity that drives connection. Thus, we identify a further feedback loop from image to culture based on the immersion strategies discussed above. This helps ensure further alignment between culture-identity-image as employees get to experience the lived reality of the stakeholders who authenticate the firm's identity claims. This approach is in line with co-creation whereby the legitimacy of identity claims is ultimately bestowed upon firms (as opposed to being a resource to manage top down) by their external stakeholders (Deephouse & Carter, 2005).

The review in this chapter opens up a number of avenues for future research. First, examining issues of authenticity in the context of internal branding offers much in terms of theoretical and practical insights. For example, existing scales of brand authenticity (Morhart et al., 2015; Napoli et al., 2014) could be modified to examine the authenticity of the employer brand. This would allow the testing of hypotheses involving unique contributions of internal brand authenticity to key employer brand outcomes, helping unpack the value the construct and its practical gains. Potential outcome variables include employee and potential employee sentiment, self-identification, engagement, and preferred employer choice. Other tools used in the consumer arena, such as narrative transportation (Van Laer et al., 2014) could be deployed to identify the ways in which employees can place themselves in the employer brand. What mechanisms of internal branding enable employees to connect to the organization's intended identity, engage more with identity programs and even enable people to embrace brand-driven change?

Research could also be conducted on the internal branding value of authenticating cues such as brand museums, immersive activities, brand purpose, founder values, and heritage. Can these cues be leveraged to enhance the authenticity of the brand internally and externally, therefore closing key corporate brand gaps between culture, image and identity? In relation to culture-image gaps, what policies and practices are needed for the brand (and organization) to be seen as a legitimate insider at the subcultural or category level? How does the use of employees in external branding campaigns (aimed at reinforcing authenticity as connection) help or hinder consumer and stakeholder authenticity judgements? To what extent does the use of a stewardship logic help employees engage with the brand (Hernandez, 2012), but more importantly connect with the communal context that provides the basis for authenticity through conformity?

Finally, are there downsides to internal brand authenticity? For example, could concerns for authenticity create a similar brand iron cage (Holt, 2004) that hinders the ability to change? Holt's cultural brand model suggests that firms should be prepared to radically reshape their identity when societal changes render the old irrelevant. However, the ability of firms to be this agile around identity is subject to question. How might firms reinvent or reinterpret their authenticity strategies to align with a new social reality, and what role will employees play in this? It is likely that such shifts may trigger sensemaking challenges for employees, creating a backlash, which may ultimately undermine any identity change program. Furthermore, to what extent can firms manage the challenges posed by the stewardship logic employees are expected to engage in? What happens for example when employees believe brand-driven programs fail tests of conformity or connection with stakeholders? And, to what extent can brand ambidexterity (which balances consistency and relevance; Beverland et al., 2015) create a more dynamic type of internal brand authenticity that addresses these dangers?

Practically, managing for authenticity requires brand managers to address issues of consistency, conformity, and connection, although the emphasis on each may change over the life of the brand and in response to shifts in external and internal environment. This chapter highlighted that internal brand authenticity involves two strategic considerations: alignment between the external and internal environments and employee (current and prospective) engagement with the brand. Greater employee engagement with the brand may help achieve greater consistency, and also ensure that commitment is sustained over time. It may also help trigger the sense of ownership necessary for staff to engage with the context and users, learn the unwritten rules of conformity, or enact the 'citizen-artist' practices central to cultural brand co-creation. These communal co-creation practices are all critical given the increased emphasis on brand purpose and its power to motivate employees (Jones, 2017). The use of employees as the face of the company may help reinforce engagement, as it invests employees with a sense of pride and connects the self with the employer brand.

# References

Aaker, D. (2018). *Creating signature stories: Strategic messaging that energies, persuades and inspires.* New York: Morgan James Publishing.

Arnould, E. J., & Thompson, C. J. (2005). Consumer culture theory (CCT): Twenty years of research. *Journal of Consumer Research, 31*(4), 868–882. https://doi.org/10.1086/426626

Arnould, E. J., & Price, L. L. (2000). Authenticating acts and authoritative performances: Questing for self and community. In S. Ratneshwar, D. G. Mick, & C. Huffman (Eds.), *The why of consumption: Contemporary perspectives on consumer motives, goals, and desires* (pp. 140–163). London: Routledge.

Arsel, Z., & Thompson, C. J. (2011). Demythologizing consumption practices: How consumers protect their field-dependent identity investments from devaluing marketplace myths. *Journal of Consumer Research, 37*(5), 791–806. https://doi.org/10.1086/656389

Avery, J., Eckhardt, G. M., & Beverland, M. B. (2020). *Brand storytelling at Shinola* (Case N-520-102). Boston, MA: Harvard Business School Publishing.

Balmer, J. M. T., Stuart, H., & Greyser, S. A. (2009). Aligning identity and strategy: Corporate branding at British Airways in the late 20th century. *California Management Review, 51*(3), 6–23. https://doi.org/10.2307/41166491

Bastos, W., & Levy, S. J. (2012). A history of the concept of branding: Practice and theory. *Journal of Historical Research in Marketing, 4*(3), 347–368. https://doi.org/10.1108/17557501211252934

Becker, M., Wiegand, N., & Reinartz, W. J. (2019). Does it pay to be real? Understanding authenticity in TV advertising. *Journal of Marketing, 83*(1), 24–50. https://doi.org/10.1177/0022242918815880

Beverland, M. B. (2005). Crafting brand authenticity: The case of luxury wines. *Journal of Management Studies, 42*(5), 1003–1029. https://doi.org/10.1111/j.1467-6486.2005.00530.x

Beverland, M. B. (2009). *Building brand authenticity: 7 habits of iconic brands.* London: Palgrave Macmillan.

Beverland, M. B. (2021). *Brand management: Co-creating brand meaning* (2nd ed.). Los Angeles, CA: SAGE.

Beverland, M. B., & Farrelly, F. J. (2010). The quest for authenticity in consumption: Consumers' purposive choice of authentic cues to shape experienced outcomes. *Journal of Consumer Research, 36*(5), 838–856. https://doi.org/10.1086/615047

Beverland, M. B., Farrelly, F. J., & Quester, P. G. (2010). Authentic subcultural membership: Antecedents and consequences of authenticating acts and authoritative performances. *Psychology & Marketing, 27*(7), 698–716. https://doi.org/10.1002/mar.20352

Beverland, M. B., Lindgreen, A., & Vink, M. (2008). Projecting authenticity through advertising: Consumer judgments of advertisers' claims. *Journal of Advertising, 37*(1), 5–15. https://doi.org/10.2753/JOA0091-3367370101

Beverland, M. B., Wilner, S. J., & Micheli, P. (2015). Reconciling the tension between consistency and relevance: Design thinking as a mechanism for brand ambidexterity. *Journal of the Academy of Marketing Science, 43*(5), 589–609. https://doi.org/10.1007/s11747-015-0443-8

Beverland, M. B., & Ewing, M. T. (2005, September–October). Slowing the adoption and diffusion process to enhance brand repositioning: The consumer driven repositioning of Dunlop Volley. *Business Horizons, 48*, 385–391. https://doi.org/10.1016/j.bushor.2005.01.001

Brodie, R. J. (2009). From goods to service branding: An integrative perspective. *Journal of Service Research*, 9(1), 107–111. https://doi.org/10.1177/1470593108100064

Beverland, M. B. & Cankurtaran, P. (2019). *Lovehoney: Selling sexual wellness in the USA* (p. 24). Case Centre 519-0156-1. TU Delft Research Portal.

Carroll, G. R., & Swaminathan, A. (2000). Why the microbrewery movement? Organizational dynamics of resource partitioning in the US brewing industry. *American Journal of Sociology*, 106(3), 715–762. https://doi.org/10.1086/318962

Carù, A., Ostillio, M. C., & Leone, G. (2017). Corporate museums to enhance brand authenticity in luxury goods companies: The case of Salvatore Ferragamo. *International Journal of Arts Management*, 19(2), 32–45.

Chung, S. Y. A., & Byrom, J. (2021). Co-creating consistent brand identity with employees in the hotel industry. *Journal of Product & Brand Management*, 30(1), 74–89. https://doi.org/10.1108/JPBM-08-2019-2544

De Chernatony, L., & Segal-Horn, S. (2003). The criteria for successful services brands. *European Journal of Marketing*, 37(7–8), 1095–1118. https://doi.org/10.1108/03090560310477681

Deephouse, D. L., & Carter, S. M. (2005). An examination of differences between organizational legitimacy and organizational reputation. *Journal of Management Studies*, 42, 329–360. https://doi.org/10.1111/j.1467-6486.2005.00499.x

Delbridge, R., & Edwards, T. (2008). Challenging conventions: Roles and processes during non-isomorphic institutional change. *Human Relations*, 61(3), 299–325. https://doi.org/10.1177/0018726708088996

Dickinson-Delaporte, S., Beverland, M. B., & Lindgreen, A. (2010). Building corporate reputation with stakeholders: Exploring the role of message ambiguity for social marketers. *European Journal of Marketing*, 44(11–12), 1856–1874. https://doi.org/10.1108/03090561011079918

Fine, G. A. (2003). Crafting authenticity: The validation of identity in self-taught art. *Theory and Society*, 32(2), 153–180. https://doi.org/10.1023/A:1023943503531

Fournier, S., & Eckhardt, G. M. (2019). Putting the person back into person-brands: Understanding and managing the two-bodied brand. *Journal of Marketing Research*, 56(4), 602–619. https://doi.org/10.1177/0022243719830654

Fournier, S., & Lee, L. (2009). Getting brand communities right. *Harvard Business Review*, 87(4), 105–111.

Giesler, M. (2012). How doppelgänger brand images influence the market creation process: Longitudinal insights from the rise of Botox cosmetic. *Journal of Marketing*, 76(6), 55–68. https://doi.org/10.1509/jm.10.0406

Gilmore, J. H., & Pine, B. J. (2007). *Authenticity: What consumers really want*. Boston, MA: Harvard Business School Press.

Glynn, M. A., & Lounsbury, M. (2005). From the critics' corner: Logic blending, discursive change and authenticity in a cultural production system. *Journal of Management Studies*, 42(5), 1031–1055. https://doi.org/10.1111/j.1467-6486.2005.00531.x

Grayson, K., & Martinec, R. (2004). Consumer perceptions of iconicity and indexicality and their influence on assessments of authentic market offerings. *Journal of Consumer Research*, 31(2), 296–312. https://doi.org/10.1086/422109

Greyser, S. A., & Urde, M. (2019, January–February). What does your corporate brand stand for? *Harvard Business Review*, 80–88.

Harrison, S. H., & Corley, K. G. (2011). Clean climbing, carabiners, and cultural cultivation: Developing an open-systems perspective of culture. *Organization Science*, 22(2), 391–412. https://doi.org/10.1287/orsc.1100.0538

Hatch, M. J., & Schultz, M. (2013). The dynamics of corporate brand charisma: Routinization and activation at Carlsberg IT. *Scandinavian Journal of Management*, 29(2), 147–162. https://doi.org/10.1016/j.scaman.2013.03.005

Hatch, M. J., & Schultz, M. (2001, February). Are the strategic stars aligned for your corporate brand? *Harvard Business Review*, 79, 128–134.

Hatch, M. J., & Schultz, M. (2008). *Taking brand initiative: How companies can align strategy, culture, and identity through corporate branding*. New York: John Wiley & Sons.

Hatch, M. J., & Schultz, M. (2017). Toward a theory of using history authentically: Historicizing in the Carlsberg Group. *Administrative Science Quarterly*, 62(4), 657–697. https://doi.org/10.1177/0001839217692535

Hernandez, M. (2012). Toward an understanding of the psychology of stewardship. *Academy of Management Review*, 37(2), 172–193. https://doi.org/10.5465/amr.2010.0363

Hietanen, J., & Rokka, J. (2015). Market practices in countercultural market emergence. *European Journal of Marketing*, *49*(9–10), 1563–1588. https://doi.org/10.1108/EJM-02-2014-0066

Hobsbawn, E., & Ranger, T. (1983). *The invention of tradition*. Cambridge: Cambridge University Press.

Hochschild, A. R. (1983). *The managed heart: Commercialization of human feeling*. Berkeley, CA: University of California Press.

Holt, D. B. (2002). Why do brands cause trouble? A dialectical theory of consumer culture and branding. *Journal of Consumer Research*, *29*(1), 70–90. https://doi.org/10.1086/339922

Holt, D. B. (2004). *How brands become icons: The principles of cultural branding*. Boston, MA: Harvard Business School Press.

Holt, D. B., & Thompson, C. J. (2004). Man-of-action heroes: The pursuit of heroic masculinity in everyday consumption. *Journal of Consumer Research*, *31*(2), 425–440. https://doi.org/10.1086/422120

Hyatt, J., & Simons, H. (1999). Cultural codes – Who holds the key? The concept and conduct of evaluation in Central and Eastern Europe. *Evaluation*, *5*(1), 23–41. https://doi.org/10.1177/13563899922208805

Iglesias, O., & Saleem, F. Z. (2015). How to support consumer-brand relationships: The role of corporate culture and human resources policies and practices. *Marketing Intelligence & Planning*, *33*(2), 216–234. https://doi.org/10.1108/MIP-10-2014-0196

Ind, N. (2014). Living the brand. In K. Kompella (Ed.), *The definitive book on branding* (pp. 199–218). London: SAGE.

Ind, N., & Schmidt, H. J. (2019). *Co-creating brands: Brand management from a co-creation perspective*. London: Bloomsbury.

Interbrand. (2019). *Best global brands ranking 2019*. Retrieved September 29, 2020 from www.interbrand.com/best-brands/best-global-brands/2019/ranking/

Jones, C., Anand, N., & Alvarez, J. L. (2005). Guest editors' introduction: Manufactured authenticity and creative voice in cultural industries. *Journal of Management Studies*, *42*(5), 893–899. https://doi.org/10.1111/j.1467-6486.2005.00525.x

Jones, D., & Smith, K. (2005). Middle-earth meets New Zealand: Authenticity and location in the making of The Lord of the Rings. *Journal of Management Studies*, *42*(5), 923–945. https://doi.org/10.1111/j.1467-6486.2005.00527.x

Jones, R. (2017). *Branding: A short introduction*. Oxford: Oxford University Press.

Kates, S. M. (2004). The dynamics of brand legitimacy: An interpretive study in the gay men's community. *Journal of Consumer Research*, *31*(2), 455–464. https://doi.org/10.1086/422122

Keinan, A., Eckhardt, G. M., & Beverland, M. B. (2018). *Kodak: The rebirth of an iconic brand* (Case 9–519–051). Boston, MA: Harvard Business School Publishing.

Keinan, A., Farrelly, F. J., & Beverland, M. B. (2012). *Introducing iSnack2.0: The new Vegemite* (Case 9–512–020). Boston, MA: Harvard Business School Publishing.

Keller, K. L. (2003). *Strategic brand management* (2nd ed.). Old Tappan, NJ: Pearson Education.

Kraak, J. M., & Holmqvist, J. (2017). The authentic service employee: Service employees' language use for authentic service experiences. *Journal of Business Research*, *72*(3), 199–209. https://doi.org/10.1016/j.jbusres.2016.04.182

Lehman, D. W., O'Connor, K., Kovács, B., & Newman, G. E. (2019). Authenticity. *Academy of Management Annals*, *13*(1), 1–42. https://doi.org/10.5465/annals.2017.0047

Levy, S. J. (1959, July–August). Symbols for sale. *Harvard Business Review*, 117–124.

Marotta, S. (2021). Old Detroit, new Detroit: "Makers" and the impasse of place change. *Cultural Geographies*, *28*(2), 377–391. https://doi.org/10.1177%2F1474474020978481

Merrilees, B., Miller, D., & Yakimova, R. (2020). Building brands through internal stakeholder engagement and co-creation. *Journal of Product & Brand Management*. https://doi.org/10.1108/JPBM-03-2020-2784

Miles, S. J., & Mangold, W. G. (2005). Positioning Southwest Airlines through employee branding. *Business Horizons*, *48*(6), 535–545. https://doi.org/10.1016/j.bushor.2005.04.010

Moore, K., & Reid, S. (2008). The birth of the brand: 4000 years of branding. *Business History*, *50*(4), 419–432. https://doi.org/10.1080/00076790802106299

Morhart, F., Malär, L., Guèvremont, A., Girardin, F., & Grohmann, B. (2015). Brand authenticity: An integrative framework and measurement scale. *Journal of Consumer Psychology*, *25*(2), 200–218. https://doi.org/10.1016/j.jcps.2014.11.006

Napoli, J., Dickinson-Delaporte, S., Beverland, M. B., & Farrelly, F. J. (2014). Measuring consumer-based brand authenticity. *Journal of Business Research*, *67*(6), 1090–1098. https://doi.org/10.1016/j.jbusres.2013.06.001

Newman, G. E. (2019). The psychology of authenticity. *Review of General Psychology*, *23*(1), 8–18. https://doi.org/10.1037/gpr0000158

Peterson, R. A. (2005). In search of authenticity. *Journal of Management Studies*, *42*(5), 1083–1098. https://doi.org/10.1111/j.1467-6486.2005.00533.x

Potter, A. (2011). *The authenticity hoax: Why the "real" things we seek don't make us happy.* New York: Harper Perennial.

Preece, C., Kerrigan, F., & O'Reilly, D. (2019). License to assemble: Theorizing brand longevity. *Journal of Consumer Research*, *46*(2), 330–350. https://doi.org/10.1093/jcr/ucy076

Ravasi, D., & Phillips, N. (2011). Strategies of alignment: Organizational identity management and strategic change at Bang & Olufsen. *Strategic Organization*, *9*(2), 103–135. https://doi.org/10.1177/1476127011403453

Rose, R. L., & Wood, S. L. (2005). Paradox and the consumption of authenticity through reality television. *Journal of Consumer Research*, *32*(2), 284–296. https://doi.org/10.1086/432238

Saleem, F. Z., & Iglesias, O. (2016). Mapping the domain of the fragmented field of internal branding. *Journal of Product & Brand Management*, *25*(1), 43–57. https://doi.org/10.1108/JPBM-11-2014-0751

Schau, H. J., Muñiz, A. M. Jr., & Arnould, E. J. (2009). How brand community practices create value. *Journal of Marketing*, *73*(5), 30–51. https://doi.org/10.1509/jmkg.73.5.30

Sharifonnasabi, Z., Bardhi, F., & Luedicke. M K. (2020). How globalization affects consumers: Insights from 30 years of CCT globalization research. *Marketing Theory*, *20*(3), 273–298. https://doi.org/10.1177/1470593119887469

Spiggle, S., Nguyen, H. T., & Caravella, M. (2012). More than fit: Brand extension authenticity. *Journal of Marketing Research*, *49*(6), 967–983. https://doi.org/10.1509/jmr.11.0015

Thompson, C. J., Rindfleisch, A., & Arsel, Z. (2006). Emotional branding and the strategic value of the doppelgänger brand image. *Journal of Marketing*, *70*(1), 50–64. https://doi.org/10.1509/jmkg.70.1.050.qxd

Umbach, M., & Humphrey, M. (2017). *Authenticity: The cultural history of a political concept.* London: Palgrave Macmillan.

Urde, M. (2003). Core value-based corporate brand building. *European Journal of Marketing*, *37*(7–8), 1017–1040. https://doi.org/10.1108/03090560310477645

Van Laer, T., De Ruyter, K., Visconti, L. M., & Wetzels, M. (2014). The extended transportation-imagery model: A meta-analysis of the antecedents and consequences of consumers' narrative transportation. *Journal of Consumer Research*, *40*(5), 797–817. https://doi.org/10.1086/673383

Vredenburg, J., Kapitan, S., Spry, A., & Kemper, J. A. (2020). Brands taking a stand: Authentic brand activism or woke washing? *Journal of Public Policy & Marketing*, *39*(4), 444–460. https://doi.org/10.1177/0743915620947359

# 24
# WHEN HISTORY INSPIRES BRAND STRATEGY

## Lessons for place brands and corporate brands

*Mihalis Kavaratzis*

## 1. Introduction

Within place management and marketing, the past has a particular appeal as a source of identity elements (e.g., Govers & Go, 2009) and image associations and, as this chapter will explicate, is often called to play a role as a resource for place brand strategy (e.g., Braun, 2011; Ashworth & Kavaratzis, 2011). In different ways and to different extents, this is also true for corporate branding. A brand's history has been suggested as a significant anchor and inspiration for brand strategy (e.g., Hatch & Schultz, 2017) and brand heritage is shown to enhance brand credibility (Pecot et al., 2019) and create a sense of stability (Rose et al., 2016).

This reliance on history is related to a wider turn towards cultural understandings of brands and what has been termed a 'brand culture perspective' (Schroeder, 2009). Within such an approach, it is thought that culture in general and history specifically provide a useful context in which we need to understand consumer interaction with brands. Therefore, cultural issues need to be included in brand research and brand management, along with purely managerial considerations (Holt, 2004). As Schroeder (2009, p. 124) puts it, 'the brand culture perspective acknowledges brands' representational and rhetorical power both as cultural artifacts and as engaging bearers of meaning, reflecting broad societal, cultural and ideological codes.' A brand based on history can be seen as the archetype of a brand with representational and rhetorical power to both showcase the past (i.e., the brand as cultural artifact) and to engage stakeholders in a dialogue over the place's present and future directions (i.e., the brand as bearer of meaning). Transforming the past into a brand resource, however, requires a complicated process, which is the subject of this chapter's scrutiny.

The starting point of the argumentation developed here is that both place brands and corporate brands are co-created by stakeholders, who have a sense of the brand's history and heritage that helps them understand its identity and relate to it. The chapter opens with a discussion of the reasons why places and corporations use their history in their branding efforts. It goes on to examine practices of how history is used in corporate branding through the lens of the framework proposed by Iglesias et al. (2020) of 'uncovering, remembering, curating, and embedding' history in the corporate brand. The examination then turns to the use of history within place branding. Drawing on examples from practice, the chapter accounts for the several ways in which historical events and personalities, along with the marks they have left on the physical and social mosaic of places, are highlighted by place branding strategies and tactics.

This examination shows that history is important for both place and corporate branding. However, while it can be beneficial to rely on history, it can also lead to significant tensions. A major such tension is that the role of history in brand strategy is caught in a dualism between path dependency and path creation. On the one hand, the use of history creates path dependency (Ericson, 2006; Braun, 2011), which might be seen to lead to more authentic place brands, as they are based on the place's history, and to more engaging place brands, particularly for local communities who are likely to feel attachment to that history. On the other hand, this path dependency raises two important complications that are elucidated in the chapter. First, history needs to be turned into heritage and the process through which this happens is neither straightforward nor devoid of conflict. Secondly, path dependency can have the reverse effect of acting as a 'cage that inhibits strategic choice by limiting the range of options' (Iglesias et al., 2020, p. 53, citing Ericson, 2006). As Garud and Karnøe (2001) have shown in relation to entrepreneurship, path dependency highlights the role played by history but 'falls short of conceptualizing the roles of actors in creating history in real time' (p. 28). The same authors offer the idea of path creation as a contrast to path dependency, highlighting the agency of various actors in making choices that deviate from pre-scribed paths.

To minimise the risk of limiting strategic options due to path dependency and failing to understand the possibilities of path creation, it helps if we take a look at the flow between past, present, and future. That is precisely what the chapter goes on to do, accounting for how the past (history) is used in the present (heritage) and how it links to a potential future (strategy). Finally, some useful lessons for both place branding and corporate branding are drawn that deepen and expand our understanding around the use of history in branding.

## 2. Why use history in place vs. corporate branding?

The relationship between place branding and corporate branding has been examined in relative detail. A lot of the support for place branding in its early attempts of conceptualisation was found within the corporate branding literature (Hankinson, 2007). There are, of course, significant inherent differences between places and commercial organizations for which branding was initially developed (see also Anholt, 2007). A first difference relates to the lack of control that place brand steerers have over the entity they are branding (i.e., the place) and the fact that place brand development requires a wider combination of knowledge and expertise. For instance, the implementation of a place branding strategy might require the participation of planners, architects, community leaders, politicians, in addition to that of managers, marketers, and communications experts. Another difference relates to the multiplicity of a place's stakeholders and, therefore, 'creators,' which is greater than for corporate brands. To complicate things further, due to the political nature of place branding, these stakeholders often have conflicting interests and demands from the same place, stemming from a place's different uses (e.g., residence, visitation, leisure, investment, etc.). An additional difference is that a place is made of a complex set of interactions between the physical place (what is known as the place's materiality) and its psychological and emotional extensions, based on various representations, institutional activities, as well as everyday practices (Kavaratzis & Kalandides, 2015). Arguably, these are not entirely unfamiliar to corporate brand steerers, and perhaps global brands are indeed entities of similar complexity to cities or other places. However, it is certainly true that importing approaches and methods from the commercial world to the world of place development is not straightforward (Braun, 2011; Campelo et al., 2014). While it is clear that place branding can only be considered as a distinct form of branding applicable to places, the links between the two are many, including a particular attention to brand co-creation and, importantly for this chapter, a reliance on (or, at least, a significant role of) history in brand development.

A brief overview of the variety of reasons that render history a useful resource for both place branding and corporate branding is necessary. Starting with places, the significance of their historical development is fundamental for any attempt to support place development and the past is very often used in place branding efforts. A first, economic – usually linked to tourism – reason is obvious in that 'the conserved, enhanced or recreated events, personalities, associations, surviving objects and structures are treated as resources supporting the existence of a heritage industry' (Ashworth, 2012, p. 22), most obviously linked to the attraction of cultural tourists. Socio-political reasons are also very important because history signifies in appealing ways a continuity between past and present. On the one hand, this is a useful socialization tool that 'educates' new generations and outsiders alike in society's norms. On the other hand, a more critical view sees this as instrumental for a legitimation process in which 'the events of the past are narrated to the present . . . so that the currently dominant political ideologies and groups can justify their dominance' (Ashworth, 2012).

This appealing connection between past and present satisfies also psychological needs for individuals 'so that the comfort of the past may anchor the excitement of the future' (Lynch, 1972). This is essential in conceptualising a collective identity and instilling a feeling of community at various spatial scales. It is not surprising then that place branding utilizes history. The place brand needs to be based on and reinforce such feelings of shared identities and promote them to outsiders and it is exactly an 'excitement of the future' that it is supposed to foster in local populations and communicate to outside audiences. Ashworth and Kavaratzis (2011) also add that, as a construction of the creative imagination (something we will come back to later) the past can be used to convey various desirable attributes linked to the place's brand. This makes the past an obvious (perhaps deceptively so) source of content for place branding activities.

The usefulness of the brand's history for corporate branding has been noted repeatedly (e.g., Hatch & Schultz, 2017; Iglesias et al., 2020). Hatch and Schultz (2017) note that the intentional use of history serves purposes that include 'legitimation and sensemaking, driven respectively by power and organizational identity' (p. 686) to which they add authenticity as another driver. Within the process of managing organizations and their brands, the importance of the past lies mainly in its power to shape identities and, thereby, help form communities. For example, Holt (2004) emphasizes the role of the brand's heritage in the projection of powerful myths that help brands such as Coca Cola and Harley Davidson achieve iconic status. History is influential because it contextualizes several other organizational phenomena (Brunninge, 2009), such as the processes of strategy-making, inertia, or strategic change. It has been noted that studies dealing with history in organizations either examine how top managers use history strategically or how a wider range of stakeholders engage with history to make sense of the identity of organizations (Hatch & Schultz, 2017). According to Iglesias et al. (2020), four reasons support the use of history for strategic brand development: history enriches the understanding of organizations as located in time; history inspires future strategy and corporate brand identity by drawing on those historical elements and resources that are relevant to current concerns; history can make the case for change, motivate people to overcome challenges, and help them enact strategies; history can promote authenticity and legitimate strategy by bringing out the unique and distinctive attributes that encourage employee and stakeholder identification.

While some similarities become evident, arguably, the arguments for the use of history in corporate branding are more straightforward and less political than those in place branding. Corporations might be in a position to make their history beneficial for brand strategy in ways that places cannot. However, it is also clear that history is a more fundamental consideration in place branding, and it provides more obvious resources, in the sense that more people can relate to a place's history and more easily. More similarities can be identified by reversing the question of 'Why do we use history?' into 'What happens when history is forgotten?' Iglesias et al. (2020) argue that companies might go through periods when they forget or reject their history and during these periods, they typically lose their strategic focus, they pursue multiple brand extensions and various unstructured innovations, and there is diminished employee engagement. It is plausible to argue that place branding initiatives that forget or neglect the place's history show the same or very similar characteristics. They tend to be fragmented with no strategic focus, they are often disconnected to the place's cultural and social reality, they call upon 'innovation' or 'creativity' without substantial demonstration and they lack stakeholder engagement, particularly showing an absence of resident involvement. For example, as Kavaratzis and Ashworth (2015) have shown, the common branding claim by cities to be 'cities of culture' is very often disconnected from their historical cultural production, leading to an unsuitable and 'out of place' claim that, in turn, leads to dissatisfaction of the residents with the strategy and a lack of brand buy-in.

## 3. Making history instrumental

In what ways does history become instrumental for branding, and how is this demonstrated? A detailed case study of Adidas leads Iglesias et al. (2020) to propose that history can help corporate brand strategy through a process of uncovering, remembering, curating, and embedding history. As the authors explain, *uncovering* includes searching for insights in the company's history and looking back to the value of the brand's history as a strategic resource. *Remembering* relates to the creation of mechanisms to record the lessons of the past (document archives, photos, campaigns, tributes to the founder, etc.). *Curating* indicates that events and ideas need to not only be recorded passively, but managers need to actively involve them in new projects (for instance by involving those entrusted with the role of history management in the company) and ensuring the lessons of history are relevant to the contemporary context. Finally, *embedding* describes the way in which the curated history is embedded into corporate practices both in terms of external brand expressions and in the internal corporate culture. This section uses this framework to examine examples within place branding that relate to these four processes.

### 3.1 Uncovering history

Uncovering history is, arguably, more straightforward in places rather than corporations, not because it is easier or simpler but because it is performed by a range of professions and institutions. Historians, archaeologists, and experts in other disciplines regularly uncover historical links in places. Not only are the uncovered links to history of paramount importance for place branding, but also the instances of uncovering the place's history generate momentum for the place and its brand, attract press attention, can attract investment, and can put places 'on the map.' Uncovering a place's history and making it part of the place's brand narrative can happen in three different modes as the next paragraphs will explicate: directly, organically, and strategically.

On occasion, uncovering might be inflicted very *directly* by fortuitous events, as with the discovery of the remains of King Richard III (1452–1485) in Leicester, UK. The then King of England lost his life at the Battle of Bosworth (1485) and was buried in nearby Leicester. A few years later, his tomb was destroyed and his remains were lost (many believed they were thrown in a nearby river). In 2012, excavations in a car park in the centre of Leicester brought to the surface a skeleton, which through DNA examination was confirmed as belonging to Richard III. This discovery attracted an unprecedented (not only for the city's standards) amount of press attention nationally but also worldwide and drastically increased awareness of Leicester.

Richard's remains were transferred ceremonially to Leicester's Cathedral where his was given a fitting re-burial. The story of the discovery is the main element of the city's promotion ever since and Leicester Cathedral has become the city's main tourist attraction.

Uncovering might also happen more *organically* by various stakeholders. An extreme example would be Chernobyl and its nearby town of Pripyat, Ukraine. Due to a well-known tragic event (an accident in a nuclear factory) in 1986, Chernobyl was trapped into a persistent, world-wide notoriety, which in any strategic sense was undesirable, although it did not matter much because the place was anyway abandoned. However, certain groups of stakeholders became interested in this particular history – and, therefore, the place – and started visiting Chernobyl. Through their agency, they indeed uncovered a history that otherwise would remain latent, as clearly demonstrated by the official proclamation of Chernobyl as a tourist attraction in 2011.

Closer to the corporate setting, uncovering may also happen as a result of purposeful *strategy-making*. Exceptionally successful, for instance, is Barcelona's use of the eccentric architect Antoni Gaudí (1852–1926) since the 1980s as part of a wider strategy to re-brand the city from 'city of industry' to 'city of culture.' Along with various 'Gaudi tours' that are on offer and the images of his buildings that feature heavily in promotional material and postcards, two of the most popular souvenirs from the city are his mosaic lizard 'El Drac' (which he designed in Park Güell together with his collaborator Josep Maria Jujol) as well as the 'Sagrada Familia.'

## 3.3 Remembering history

Remembering the place's history is in essence very similar to remembering in corporate terms, but in a different scale, as it often affects whole populations, the physical appearance of places, and it can also feed political tensions. It is not only a matter of purposefully erecting monuments or statues to celebrate and remember the past, but also a matter of allowing the relics of the past to remain visible in the physical environment. Museums are by definition there precisely to remember and to remind a place's history, public archives also, as well as several other historical sources. Places are scattered with monuments and statues and many other markers of the past and of our remembering the past. Amongst the countless examples, perhaps a telling one is the former Headquarters of the Hungarian secret police in Budapest (1945–1956), which has been transformed into the House of Terror, a very popular museum exhibiting the crimes and atrocities committed by the fascist and communist regimes in the country, including those committed in the building itself. It is not only links to historical events that are remembered but links to personalities as well. An illustrative example is the town of Stratford-upon-Avon in the UK, the birthplace and gravesite of William Shakespeare (1564–1616), which attracts approximately 2.5 million visitors each year. The whole historic centre of the town is a celebration of the famous playwright, his life, and works. The past offers itself for a rather liberal use as demonstrated by the example of Ulm, Germany, birthplace of Albert Einstein (1879–1955), which is dotted with statues and monuments to the scientist, although Einstein spent there only a little more than the first year of his life and he himself declined the honour-citizenship presented to him by the city at his 70th birthday. Places that have actively exploited their historical connections to musicians or styles of music as part of their brand include diverse examples from Salzburg (Mozart) to Liverpool (the Beatles) or New Orleans (traditional jazz). Furthermore, history occasionally bestows places with mythological characters to be 'remembered' and used to the benefit of the place's brand. Robin Hood (Nottingham, UK) is an illustrative example, as is Santa Claus, whose most known residence is Rovaniemi in Finland, although it is also claimed by various places in the Nordic Countries as well as Canada and the US state of Alaska. Pasts and places can be linked so compellingly that the two sometimes become inextricable and, in many cases, the where becomes part of the what (Ashworth & Kavaratzis, 2011). The examples of Mecca or Bethlehem are illustrative, as is the example of Chernobyl mentioned earlier.

## 3.4 Curating history

Curating the place's history is the process of choosing what to remember and showcase. That is not only a fundamental choice for the development of the place brand, but also one of the place brand's core functions. All place brands attempt to create a narrative of the place (Lichrou et al., 2014). Choosing elements of the past that reinforce and illustrate that narrative is not only necessary in order to develop the narrative itself, but the other way around, the chosen narrative also dictates what parts of the past fit well and can be chosen (and what elements cannot). The relationship between history and the brand is similar to the wider relationship between brands and culture characterized by an 'on-going iteration between contributing to culture and drawing from it' (Maclaran, 2009, p. 74). In this sense, curating the past is both prerequisite and consequence of the place branding strategy. What to remember and how is, of course, contested. For example, the *Palace of Culture*, in Warsaw (1955) originally a gift by the Soviet Union and known as 'Joseph Stalin's Palace of Culture and Science' has now been transformed into a combination of theatres, cultural exhibition centres, a multiplex cinema, and various offices. In several other occasions, relict buildings and signature structures associated with certain historical periods were deemed undesirable. On occasion, the policy selected for dealing with such structures has been simple demolition. On the other hand, some places that have experienced repeated ideological change have pursued cycles of creation/demolition/recreation. An example highlighted by Ashworth and Kavaratzis (2011) is the Prussian/Imperial *Stadtschloss* (built 1702–1706) in Berlin Mitte, which was demolished by the DDR in 1950, later replaced by the socialist *Palast der Republik* in 1973, which in turn was demolished in 2008 to be replaced by a replica of the original *Stadtschloss* in 2012.

## 3.5 Embedding history

Embedding the place's history is very similar to the organizational setting. Most often, embedding happens in the physical environment, through events and festivals, as well as through the place brand's external communications. Regarding the physical environment, the past is often embedded purposefully in the mosaic of cities and other locations. This is related to a wider effort to use noticeable buildings and signature structures in order to convey messages about the place's identity and uniqueness – in other words, its brand reputation – as well as, of course, about the aspirations of the place's government. Such embedding very often leads to a different function of history pointing to what Hatch and Schultz (2017) call 'renewing,' with restored premises and revitalized functions for old structures. A former power station is thus transformed into a modern art gallery (*Tate Modern*, London) or an old railway station into a museum (*Musee d'Orsay*, Paris) making through both form and function statements about the city's past and future simultaneously. The personality associations discussed earlier, can also be physically embedded in the city, such as the works of Gaudí in Barcelona (mentioned earlier), or those of Hundertwasser (1928–2000) in Vienna, Austria, or Mackintosh (1868–1928) in Glasgow, Scotland. Embedding can also happen in the form of events and festivals. On occasion, festivals celebrate the city's history directly. For example, founded in January 1323, Vilnius, the capital of Lithuania, is planning a series of events to celebrate its 700th birthday in 2023. In the run-up to the milestone 700th birthday, the Vilnius Festival of Light started in 2019 and takes place every January in order to celebrate the city's birthday and prepare residents and visitors alike for the bigger-scale festival of 2023. Often, festivals celebrate the place's famous children and their historical contributions, particularly convenient when they are celebrated musicians. A simple example is the festival devoted to the great classical composer Franz Liszt (1811–1886) in his birthplace, the small town of Raiding, Austria (Doborjan, Hungary during Liszt's life). In terms of embedding the past in a place's promotional activities and external brand communications, there are literally countless examples in place branding practice across the world. Examples include merchandizing in the shape of a place's historical monuments (for example, the Eifel Tower or the Big Ben) sold as souvenirs, or in the shape of historical figures such as Einstein's head sold in the city of Ulm, his birthplace as already mentioned. Naturally, leading the trend are countries and tourism destinations whose historical sites attract a large number of tourists. For instance, Greece, a country reliant on tourism for its economic viability, has focused on its ancient history and mythology in many promotional campaigns. The examples range from early place-promotional attempts with drawings of historical sites such as Delphi and Knosos in the 1950s, to posters showcasing the Acropolis of Athens in the 1980s, to the slogans used by the Greek National Tourism Organisation in more recent campaigns such as 'Greece Chosen by the Gods' or 'Live your Myth in Greece.'

## 4. Looking back to move forward

The previous sections have shown that history is often an inspiration and resource for brand strategy. That is valid for both corporate and place branding and it is often practiced. There seems to be an effective process that makes history (the past) valuable for current concerns (the present) and transforms it into a strategy (the future). However, in order to validate this transformation process, both its parts (that is, past-to-present and present-to-future) need further scrutiny. Two considerations are important here. First, it is not history as such that is used, but history's commodification into heritage, in other words, a selective interpretation of history, packaged and commodified into heritage. Second, if brand strategy relates to the future, then heritage is called to play a mediating role between past, present, and future, something that requires an appreciation of time. These two considerations are examined in what follows, focusing first on places and then making parallels with organizations.

### *4.1 From history to heritage*

As already stated, it is not history (or the past) that is used in branding but, rather, heritage, which is a highly selective and packaged version of the past (Ashworth & Kavaratzis, 2011). Heritage expresses shared memories and includes tangible and intangible elements (Yagi & Frenzel, 2020). Heritage is a major concern within urban development studies, as well as a quite substantial industry in its own right. Ashworth (2012) explains that, as a concept, heritage grew from an interest in the preservation of the remains of the past (for instance, preserving the form of important and/or beautiful buildings) and evolved towards conservation, which expanded that interest to wider areas and, therefore, involved the area's contemporary function. This also 'brought the planner and manager into the process along with the architect and historian' (Ashworth, 2012, p. 15). More recently, the role of the manager and, especially, the marketer have been accentuated due to a market orientation that attempts to select certain relics of the past and package them into a product, following consumer demand and other market criteria. So, whereas history is the past as recorded in our memory, heritage is a commodity, specifically produced in order to be consumed. In selecting the relics of the past that will be 'packaged,' heritage is also used as a marker of value (Yagi & Frenzel, 2020) as it is also a process of assessing which traditions, objects, and spaces are valuable enough to become objects of consumption. Therefore, to understand the creation of heritage, it is important to examine the political and communicative process (Ingram, 2016) that allows value judgements to be made over what will become heritage, the outcome of which is contested, meaning that 'heritage is never a given, but constantly made, remade and potentially un-made' (Yagi & Frenzel, 2020, p. 87). In other words, what matters in heritage is not how this heritage is defined; what matters is how this heritage is made to matter and by whom.

This constant remaking happens through interpretation or, as Brunninge (2009) notes about organizational history, '[it] can only be known through interpretation' (p. 11). It is this interpretation that gives form to the heritage product, so, literally, what is sold and bought is this interpretation and not the resource (Ashworth, 2012). In its simple form, and as an example, interpretation happens through representation. As Hall (1997, p. 3) argues, we give meaning to things 'by our use of things, and what we say, think and feel about them – how we represent them.' Branding acquires much of its role and significance by providing a central aim and direction for this interpretation and representation. The resources used in it are the varied events, personalities, memories, associations, and physical relics that were examined in the previous section. The critical element is the conversion of these resources into products through interpretation, which involves resource selection and 'packaging' on the side of an assumed producer, as well as 'unpackaging' on the side of an assumed consumer. In other words, interpretation is required in order to produce the heritage product (so, from the producer's point of view), and this producer's interpretation is the produced outcome that is 'sold.' However, interpretation is also required in order to consume the heritage product (so, from the consumer's point of view), and it is this consumer's interpretation that is actually 'bought.' Thus, there are two inherent discrepancies in this process of commodification, representation, and interpretation.

The first obvious discrepancy relates to the agents who initiate and direct the process of selection and packaging. The scale of potential resources to be used and the need to select them invariably raises the question: whose past will be deemed adequately valuable to be represented? And that instantly raises its reverse question: whose will not? Heritage is never all-inclusive; on the contrary, all heritage disinherits through the very process of its creation (Ashworth & Kavaratzis, 2011). So, whose interpretations and representations of the past are chosen to become heritage is a matter of framing the past (or parts of it) to fit the present. That means including as much as excluding, highlighting as much as making disappear, helping to remember as much as helping to forget. This is, of course, inextricably linked to power. As we have already seen, a major reason for the use of history within both place and corporate branding is in order to legitimize the actions of managers and other powerful groups. Or as Brunninge (2009) highlights, managers often draw upon the heritage of the organization to legitimize the changes they eventually initiate. So, whoever gets the power to do so interprets and represents their selected version of the past 'packaged' and promoted into heritage. In fact, like all strategies, brand strategy also legitimizes the actions of strategists and provides them with 'enormous freedom to conduct their business of framing the conversations backstage, unseen by and unaccountable to the public' (Kornberger, 2012, p. 98). That is a highly contentious and politically charged matter, especially within place branding.

This is not the only discrepancy, though. There is another, perhaps more implicit, potential discrepancy between the interpretations and representations of the producer and those of the consumer. In other words, the heritage sold and the heritage bought are not necessarily the same. As the classic analysis of the *Circuit of Culture* (Du Gay et al., 1997) describes, culture and cultural artefacts are not created through simple production steps but through the 'articulation of a number of distinct processes whose interaction can and does lead to variable and contingent outcomes' (Du Gay et al., 1997, p. 3). Heritage users (in the case of places, local residents, or visitors) are not passive recipients of the represented past, but they actively interpret the heritage product in their own ways, which can be different from the intentions of the producers. As Nayak and Jeffrey (2011, p. 103) argue, 'people are not empty vessels who absorb past cultures uncritically . . . but are creative and critical disseminators who may in turn rearticulate these habits to produce new meanings.'

The events that took place in Bristol, UK in 2020 are perhaps illustrative of the tensions discussed here. On June 7, 2020, during protests related to the Black Lives Matter movement, the statue of Bristol-born merchant Edward Colston (1636–1721) was toppled by the crowd, carried to the port of the city, and thrown into the sea. The statue had been erected in 1895 as memorial to the merchant whose philanthropic work had benefited his birth city significantly. However, Colston's reputation had come under intense scrutiny as it was proven that he was widely involved in the Transatlantic Slave Trade, particularly through his activities within the Royal African Company, which is known to have transferred several thousands of slaves from West Africa to the Americas. The statue commemorating him became a subject of controversy and criticism already in the 1990s but had remained in place. During the protest in June 2020, the crowd's reaction was to topple, deface, and dispose of it. The city council removed the statue from the sea and put it in safe storage. The events caused intense debates across the country as to the value of memorial monuments as well as the controversies and intricacies of contemporary evaluations of historical events. This is only one example of re-evaluations and re-interpretations of historical events and personalities not only by authorities and formal institutions (as has happened across the former Eastern European countries extensively) but also by communities, social groups, and the society at large.

Indicative of what Miles (2007) calls 'displaced narratives' (p. 152), these examples show that there are multiple interpretations of history and heritage in circulation. In a branding sense, this is where the co-creation approach to brands becomes relevant. A more traditional approach to brands as communication sees consumers as rather passive in the process of meaning creation, whereas a brand-culture (as mentioned earlier) or brand co-creation perspective sees consumers as active meaning-makers. Ind and Holm (2012) describe how the traditional model has broken down and how attention has turned to increased interactivity and more transparent relationships between organizations and consumers. 'Increasingly branding is concerned with enabling dialog as the brand evolves in interaction with its stakeholders' (Ind & Holm, 2012, p. 46). It is, therefore, particularly important to note the suggestion that contemporary brands are offered not as 'cultural blueprints' but as 'cultural resources' for people to use (Holt, 2004).

## 4.2 From heritage to strategy

As we have seen in the previous section, the past represented by heritage can be seen from the perspective of defining the events, personalities, and communities that have left their stamp, but this is not the only perspective and it is not necessarily what matters. The creation of heritage through interpretations of the past does not only happen for the needs of the present but also aiming at a desired future. '[H]eritage is that part of the past which we select in the present for contemporary purposes . . . and choose to bequeath to the future' (Ashworth & Graham, 2016, p. 7). The brand based on heritage is a brand that is capable of providing a sense of continuity and at the same time convey a promising future. As Hatch and Schultz (2017, p. 691) describe:

> using history involves the present-centred immediacy of bringing history into consciousness and consciously contextualizing activity using historical material when

creating the future. . . . through historicizing in the present, actors distribute the past in both space and time in ways that enact the future.

These references to the future are very important and bring heritage as strategy into the discussion. Indeed, strategy is a future-oriented endeavour. In the words of Kornberger (2012, p. 87), 'strategy can be conceived as an organisationally sanctioned and societally institutionalised mode of creating legitimate futures.' Strategy-making engages with problems and obligations that are imposed by the future and our wish to influence this future in desirable ways. Strategy has been described as an exercise that reduces anxiety by providing answers to future questions (Ourousoff, 2010). In this sense, strategy makes it possible to consume the future in the present, precisely as heritage makes it possible to consume the past in the present. Thus, the future as we imagine it gives us the reason to act in the present and the interpreted past becomes the resource for this action again in the present. This raises queries about the linearity of time.

Going against linear narratives that connect past present and future in unbroken trajectories, it is possible to argue that the past does not necessarily flow smoothly into the future but the two are linked in more unorganised and circular ways. Neither the past nor the future exists independently of the present and the transition from the one to other does not necessarily have to be considered irrevocable, at least in terms of brand strategy. The conception of time has indeed been challenged (e.g., Brunninge, 2009). For instance, Ericson (2006) talks about the past as a communicative partner of the present that makes its appearances in windows of opportunity within the strategy process. On the one hand, that relates to the malleability of both past and future. For example, research demonstrates that memory-making is indeed a social endeavour, and memory is a collective achievement that does not remain stable but evolves over time (e.g., Van Assche et al., 2009). Therefore, historical tradition as a communicative partner of the present, actually belongs to the future (Ericson, 2006). That reinforces the proposition by Hatch and Schultz (2017, p. 686) that studies can fruitfully focus on 'memories of particular aspects of history and track how they ebb and flow through time.' On the other hand, it also relates to the desire to bring both past and future into the present and points to how that might be the only important idea about both past and future. The brand is a strategic plan and, like all strategies, it deliberately attempts to confront the uncertainty of the future proposing a course of action that will take us to a desirable future position. Although it might sound counterintuitive, this planned future position is not what really matters; rather, what matters can be found in the present: it is the way in which the plan brings together contemporary forces that will work to make that future position come true. A plan that works is not a plan that predicts future states of the world; it is a plan that engages allies in the present (Kornberger & Klegg, 2011). That is how heritage causes people to act in certain ways, and that is how the heritage-based brand also has an impact: by making both the past and the future a little more 'visible' in the present. An indicative proposition is that by Hatch and Schultz (2017) who add the prefix 're' and talk about rediscovering, recontextualizing, reclaiming, renewing, and re-embedding history in their analysis of the use of history in organizations. As the authors say, 'when they retell history, narrators distribute its artifacts and meanings spatially (throughout the organization and/or to external audiences) and temporally (into the future), both of which imply renewal' (Hatch & Schultz, 2017, p 687).

## 5. Heritage as always emergent

Ultimately, it is then plausible to draw parallels between corporate and place branding in the ways that both look back at the past to move forward towards the future. Ashworth (2012) describes four preconditions of heritage management that relate to the processes described by

Iglesias et al. (2020) in many ways: (a) accepting the necessity for intervention (which to an extent relates to 'uncovering'); (b) accepting the process of heritage planning (which largely relates to 'remembering'); (c) selecting the heritage product (which is the same as 'curating'); and (d) organizing and implementing successful intervention (which is 'embedding').

Regarding *uncovering/intervening*, the question is what should be uncovered as part of brand strategy and what not. The degree to which this is a legitimate question, and who has the right to answer it, is arguably more straightforward in corporate branding. It is not really the right of place brand steerers (local authorities and politicians or consultants and strategists) to simply 'pick and mix.' In *remembering/planning*, the creation of a heritage place product and its marketing for specific economic or political purposes implies new valuations of the past and its surviving artefacts, and thus a new philosophy for their management. Regarding *curating/selecting the heritage product*, the shaping of any heritage product inevitably excludes several groups (social, ethnic, etc.) that are disinherited, having their own historical experience discounted. As Ashworth (2012, p. 28) puts it, 'all heritage involves choice from a wide range of pasts, many of which will not be selected.' Regarding *embedding/implementing successful interventions*, things are probably clearer, but an additional difficulty for places is that the heritage product that will become part of the brand strategy is not produced and managed by a single organization. Rather, many different organizations are responsible for each part of the heritage creation process, and often they have quite different motives.

As we have seen, a further lesson from places that might be useful for corporate brands is that a process of re-interpretation is always likely, as history is read and re-read from different perspectives. This points to the potential reactions of consumers to corporate brand history not only now, but also in the future. The contested nature of heritage and the always likely re-interpretations of history can have a powerful impact on brand resonance. In the place context, this is well exemplified by the Colston Statue example discussed previously. In the organizational context, the reactions might not be as dramatic as that, but this effect is still an important consideration for brand management. Therefore, it might be a useful suggestion to add to the four processes of uncovering, remembering, curating, and embedding suggested by Iglesias et al. (2020) an additional process of *re-evaluating* history. This re-evaluating needs to happen proactively and be the initiative of the brand rather than re-actively after consumers have already expressed their dissatisfaction.

This chapter has examined how both the past and the future are brought into the present and are transformed into objects for intervention and consumption through strategy-making. It becomes clear that a heritage-based brand (both corporate and place) is made of layer upon layer of historical meanings that have become important over time; it is sourced in various meaning-making elements; it calls for active pursuit of co-creation; and it needs to evoke authenticity. First, then, this chapter makes it clear that all this is obviously dependent on a rigorous engagement with stakeholders. As Ind and Todd (2011, p. 47) note, '[b]rands are no longer made by organizations. Rather, they are constructed in a space in which organizations are influencers and listeners.' For effective branding, there is a clear need to involve a wide range of brand stakeholders in the branding process, both managers and consumers, both 'insiders' and 'outsiders.' Making history relevant to the present and future through the processes examined in this chapter 'is a delicate balance and requires management teams that mix insiders and outsiders' (Iglesias et al., 2020, p. 59). Kavaratzis and Hatch (2021) have used this understanding to propose a place branding process that allows for stakeholder engagement in all its stages. Second, this chapter highlights the necessity for branding to embrace the ambiguity of heritage: like all identity propositions, brands are made, remade, and unmade following their inherent contradictions and ambiguities. This might mean that such contradictions and ambiguities should be accepted and even embraced rather than rejected, in which case, there might be no need for consensus on the meaning of the brand. As Ind and Todd (2011, p. 59) argue, 'the richness of a city's identity can only be conveyed when place brand managers have the courage to generate new ways of thinking and doing and are willing to reject some traditional mantras of brand thinking.' Instead of searching for the final, all-inclusive brand statement that will unite all involved, branding might welcome the conflicting propositions and facilitate their co-existence. This creates rather elusive brands (Kavaratzis & Hatch, 2021) that are much less controllable by managers but much more effective in relating to people.

Borrowing from identity studies, perhaps a helpful idea is the distinction between inherited and emergent views of identity within organizational studies as identified by Czarniawska (2000). As Czarniawska (2000) explains, inherited identity is based on the acceptance that a true self is in existence, a self that has an authentic, deep identity. Emergent identity is based on the acceptance that true self is under construction, a self that has a contingent, constantly performed identity. This can be usefully transferred to heritage as part of identity and as part of the brand. Viewing heritage as 'inherited' (thus staying loyal to the term's etymology) assumes that the meaning of heritage is determined by the past and its marks on the present. Viewing heritage as 'emergent' (thus going against the term's etymology) assumes that the meaning of heritage is in ongoing construction and determined by interpretation and negotiation. It is obvious that if heritage is to be infiltered with the future orientation that is necessary for it to form the basis of strategy, it is the emergent view that is more useful. In other words, the inherited view advocates: *'this is who we were – therefore this is who we are,'* whereas the emergent view advocates: *'this is who we have been – therefore this is who we can be.'* The heritage-based brand is caught in the middle of these tensions, which are resolved when we consider what we – as marketers – need from it and what we should expect: contemporary relevance and engagement. Therefore, the best way to understand the contribution of heritage to branding is to look at the ways in which heritage engages audiences beyond the past and before the future: in the here and now. In other words, the past has a strong potential to act as an 'enrolment' tool for branding and can entice people to engage with the brand. However, the fundamental questions always need to be answered: which emergent heritage is used and for what negotiated future purposes? Answering those is the prerogative of a wide range of brand stakeholders who need to be involved in the branding process.

# References

Anholt, S. (2007). *Competitive identity, the new brand management for countries, regions and cities*. London: Palgrave Macmillan.

Ashworth, G. J. (2012). From history to heritage, from heritage to identity: In search of concepts and models. In G. J. Ashworth & P. Larkham (Eds.), *Building a new heritage: Tourism, culture and identity in the New Europe* (pp. 13–30). London: Routledge.

Ashworth, G. J., & Graham, B. (2016). Senses of place, senses of time and heritage. In G. J. Ashworth & B. Graham (Eds.), *Senses of place: Senses of time* (pp. 3–14). London: Routledge.

Ashworth, G. J., & Kavaratzis, M. (2011). Why brand the future with the past? The role of heritage in the construction and promotion of place brand reputations. In F. Go & R. Govers (Eds.), *International place branding yearbook 2011* (pp. 25–46). London: Palgrave Macmillan.

Braun, E. (2011). History matters: The path dependency of place brands. In F. Go & R. Govers (Eds.), *International place branding yearbook 2011*. London: Palgrave Macmillan.

Brunninge, O. (2009). Using history in organizations how managers make purposeful reference to history in strategy processes. *Journal of Organizational Change Management*, 22(1), 8–26.

Campelo, A., Aitken, R., Thyne, M., & Gnoth, J. (2014). Sense of place: The importance for destination branding. *Journal of Travel Research*, 53(2), 154–166.

Czarniawska, B. (2000). Identity lost or identity found? Celebration and lamentation over the postmodern view of identity in social science and fiction. In M. Schultz, M. J. Hatch & M. H. Larsen (Eds.), *The expressive organization: Linking identity, reputation and the corporate brand* (pp. 271–283). Oxford: Oxford University Press.

Du Gay, P., Hall, S., Jones, L., Mackay, H., & Negus, K. (1997). *Doing cultural studies: The history of the Sony Walkman*. Los Angeles, CA: SAGE.

Ericson, M. (2006). Exploring the future, exploiting the past. *Journal of Management History*, 12(2), 121–36.

Garud, R., & Karnøe, P. (2001). Path creation as a process of mindful deviation. In R. Garud & P. Karnøe (Eds.), *Path dependence and creation* (pp. 1–39). New York: Lawrence Earlbaum Associates.

Govers, R., & Go, F. (2009). *Place branding: Glocal, virtual and physical identities, constructed imagined and experienced*. Basingstoke: Palgrave MacMillan.

Hall, S. (1997). *Representation: Cultural representations and signifying practices*. London: Sage.

Hankinson, G. (2007). The management of destination brands: five guiding principles based on recent developments in corporate branding Theory. *Journal of Brand Management*, 14(3), 240–254.

Hatch, M. J., & Schultz, M. (2017). Toward a theory of using history authentically: Historicizing in the Carlsberg Group. *Administrative Science Quarterly*, 62(4), 657–697.

Holt, D. (2004). *How brands become icons: The principles of cultural branding*. Cambridge, MA: Harvard University Press.

Iglesias, O., Ind, N., & Schultz, M. (2020). History matters: The role of history in corporate brand strategy. *Business Horizons*, 63, 51–60.

Ind, N., & Holm, E. (2012). Beyond place branding. In F. Go & R. Govers (Eds.), *International place branding yearbook 2012* (pp. 45–55). London: Palgrave Macmillan.

Ind N., & Todd L. (2011). Beyond the fringe: Creativity and the city. In F. Go & R. Govers (Eds.), *International place branding yearbook 2011* (pp. 47–59). London: Palgrave Macmillan.

Ingram, M. (2016). Emplacement and the politics of heritage in low-income neighbourhoods of Marseille. *International Journal of Heritage Studies*, 22(2), 117–130,

Kavaratzis, M., & Ashworth, G. J. (2015). Hijacking culture: The disconnection between place culture and place brands. *Town Planning Review*, 86(2), 155–176.

Kavaratzis, M., & Hatch, M. J. (2021). The elusive destination brand and the ATLAS wheel of place brand management. *Journal of Travel Research*, 60(1), 3–15.

Kavaratzis, M., & Kalandides, A. (2015). Rethinking the place brand: The interactional formation of place brands and the role of participatory place branding. *Environment and Planning A*, 47, 1368–1382.

Kornberger, M. (2012). Governing the city: From planning to urban strategy. *Theory, Culture & Society*, 29(2), 84–106.

Kornberger, M., & Klegg, S. R. (2011). Strategy as performative practice: The case of Sydney 2030. *Strategic Organization*, 9(2), 136–162.

Lichrou, M., O'Malley, L., & Patterson. M. (2014). On the marketing implications of place narratives. *Journal of Marketing Management*, 30(9–10), 832–856.

Lynch, K. (1972). *What time is this place?* Cambridge, MA: MIT Press.

Maclaran, P. (2009). Building brand cultures. In E. Parsons & P. Maclaran (Eds.), *Contemporary issues in marketing and consumer behaviour* (pp. 73–88). Amsterdam: Elsevier.

Miles, M. (2007). *Cities and culture*. London: Routledge.

Nayak, A., & Jeffrey, A. (2011). *Geographical thought: An introduction to ideas in human geography*. London: Routledge.

Pecot, F., Velette-Florence, P., & de Barnier, V. (2019). Brand heritage as a temporal perception: conceptualisation, measure and consequences. *Journal of Marketing Management*, 35(17–18), 1624–43.

Rose, G. M., Merchant, A., Orth, U. R., & Horstmann, F. (2016). Emphasizing brand heritage: Does it work? And how? *Journal of Business Research*, 69(2), 936–943.

Schroeder, J. E. (2009). The cultural codes of branding. *Marketing Theory*, 9(1), 123–126.

Ourousoff, A. (2010). *Wall street at war: The secret struggle for the global economy*. Cambridge, UK: Polity Press.

Van Assche, K., Devlieger, P., Teampau, P., & Verschraegen, G. (2009). Forgetting and remembering in the margins: Constructing past and future in the Romanian Danube Delta. *Memory Studies*, 2(2), 211–234.

Yagi, T., & Frenzel, F. (2020, June 25–26). *Heritage slum: Tour guides and the production of cultural value* [Conference presentation]. International Seminar Series of Tourism and Place Making (TAPLAM) Group, Leicester, UK.

# 25
# BALANCING THE PAST AND FUTURE IN CORPORATE BRANDING

*Majken Schultz*

## 1. Introduction

One of the most compelling developments in current theorizing is how scholars' interest in temporality has moved from philosophy and sociology to a broad range of social sciences (Adam, 2004; Ancona et al., 2001; Emirbayer & Mische, 1998; Hernes, 2014; Mead, 1932). This interest has defined a new research agenda and has prompted increasing reflection on the temporal embedding of phenomena that we take for granted. While some classic concepts of temporality have assumed a linear development from the past, to the present and to the future, more-recent discussions question how actors construct and connect the past and future while being in the present. In some ways, temporality has underpinned corporate branding from the outset, in that concepts of brand identity and brand culture invariably concern the origin and evolution of corporate brands. By the same token, corporate brand strategies concern future trajectories of what the brand might become. For example, some scholars have addressed how localized pasts influence cultural foundations for branding (e.g., Holt, 2004; Schroeder, 2009; Schroeder & Salzer-Mörling, 2006), while others have discussed the challenges of creating alignment between a future-oriented brand vision and more-past-oriented culture(s) and image(s) (Hatch & Schultz, 2008). However, none of these conceptions of corporate branding has taken an explicit temporal view.

The more explicit development of temporality in corporate branding reflects a duality in that temporality influences both the concept itself and corporate branding as an empirical phenomenon. First, stronger recognition of the importance of history and heritage and how they may become a resource in strategizing for the future has advanced the temporal conceptualization of corporate branding (e.g., Aaker, 2004; Balmer, 2009, 2011; Brunninge, 2009; Hatch & Schultz, 2017; Iglesias et al., 2020; see also Burghausen and Pecot, this volume). As the section chapters demonstrate, scholars have extended the temporal conceptualization of corporate branding to include how multiple temporalities influence the co-creation of corporate brands, along with increasing focus on the agency involved in balancing the past and future. Second, we are witnessing increased temporal awakening in companies' corporate brands, including the use of the past to create legitimacy and authenticity, to a more proactive stance toward the distant future, for example in the 'greening' of brand purpose. Multiple stakeholders have also embraced this temporal awakening, as it invites them to reconnect with their local brand

*Balancing the past and future*

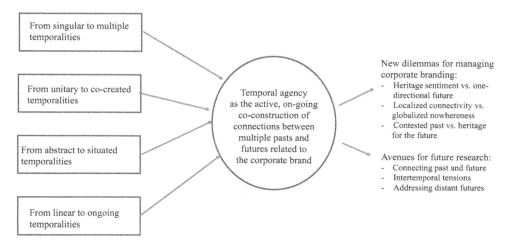

*Figure 25.1* Developments in views on temporality in corporate branding

histories (see Kavaratzis, this volume). For example, the enthusiasm for local micro-breweries illustrates this. Other stakeholders have raised critical voices regarding how the past has been misused and/or misinterpreted for political purposes, as Beverland discusses in this volume. Together, these developments present new opportunities and dilemmas for corporate branding, for example, as heritage becomes an increasingly valuable but also malleable and contested resource in strategizing for the future.

This commentary first pinpoints how temporality has been conceptualized in four recent developments relevant to corporate branding: (1) from singular to multiple temporalities, (2) from unitary to co-created temporalities, (3) from abstract to situated temporalities, and (4) from linear to ongoing temporalities. Together, these developments prompt greater concern with how temporal agency is created and enacted. Second, the commentary discusses how these developments raise new dilemmas for corporate branding in balancing the past and future, as the past and future are becoming both more desired and contested by stakeholders. Finally, the commentary concludes with reflections for future research on corporate branding. Figure 25.1 illustrates the commentary's overall argument by summarizing the four developments in temporality and their implications for brand management and future research.

## 2. Developments in temporality

While several developments in the conceptualization of temporality in the social sciences have emerged, this commentary focuses on those most relevant to corporate branding. The chapters of the section reflect these developments and discuss the key concepts in more depth.

### *2.1 From singular to multiple temporalities*

Early works on corporate branding have tended to consider actors within singular temporal trajectories. For example, scholars have assumed that historical events yield similar impacts for the whole corporate brand and convey the same meaning to different stakeholders. Yet, a growing body of literature acknowledges that corporate brands are sites of encounters for stakeholders with different temporalities both across time and in time. Temporal multiplicity *across time* refers to how the meaning of a corporate brand may change with shifting generations and trends in society, as Kavaratzis illustrates in how the meaning of branded places changes with shifting political sentiments. A related issue concerns whether corporate brands can maintain intergenerational continuity and relevance, as Burghausen discusses in this section. Temporal multiplicity *in time* refers to differences in temporal orientations held by different stakeholders. As strategy and organization studies suggest, such multiplicity entails both differences in orientation toward the past and future and in temporal distancing from the present (e.g., Bluedorn & Standifer, 2006; Schultz & Hernes, 2020). For example, corporate heritage brands are defined by their orientation toward the distant past, carefully orchestrated by their management and communication units, as Burghausen discusses. However, the distant past may also be evoked in relation to a possible new future. This is illustrated by recent discussions in the British monarchy (see also Balmer, 2009, 2011) caused, among others, by changes in the status of members of the royal family.

## 2.2 From unitary to co-created temporalities

Even though corporate branding may include stakeholders holding different temporal orientations, corporate branding also concerns how stakeholders are involved in the construction of the brand's temporality. While early works often assumed that a unitary actor in the upper echelons defined the corporate brand's temporal orientation, recent developments have stressed multiple stakeholders' co-creation of corporate branding, as also argued in the introduction to this volume (see also, Ind et al., 2013, 2017; Ramaswamy & Ozcan, 2016). The emergence of cocreation is relevant to numerous areas of corporate branding (as Section B in this volume demonstrates) and has influenced the co-creation of temporality. For example, Burghausen proposes six questions to future research on corporate heritage branding from a combined 'co-creational and temporal perspective,' such as 'How, when, and why do different types of stakeholder agency intersect and interact?' In his chapter, Beverland shows the relevance of co-creation to various forms of authenticity, arguing that both internal and external stakeholders may bring a sense of time and place to corporate branding through co-creation. Kavaratzis discusses how co-creation entails active meaning-making among stakeholders seeking to evoke authenticity. Finally, Pecot demonstrates how insights from co-creation of corporate brand heritage may enrich research on product brands. While all chapters in the section demonstrate that emphasis on temporality expands the scope of co-creation in corporate branding, they also suggest that issues of transparency and the cultural embedding of stakeholders (e.g., Hatch & Schultz, 2010) become even more important with the emergence of co-created temporalities.

## 2.3 From abstract to situated temporalities

The move from abstract, timeless, and often global temporality to a more situated temporality localized in time and space also reflects temporal developments in corporate branding. In the theoretical realm, stronger focus on how actors perform corporate branding enhances this development. Corporate brands are not timeless abstractions or pure cognitive undertakings but are composed of numerous specific practices performed by actors localized in time and space (see also Orlikowski & Yates, 2002). Hernes and Schultz (2020) elaborate this situated view, demonstrating how temporal structures localize ongoing activity but also how actors may go beyond, and potentially transform, those temporal structures by addressing distant events. These authors focus on the transformative power of temporal distancing in a corporate landscape dominated by short-termism. In relation to corporate branding, the move to situated temporality may involve actors going beyond abstract and timeless corporate brands and pursuing a more localized connectivity, such as the inclusion of local or specific events beyond the brand's dominant temporality. In his elaboration of a connected form of authenticity in corporate branding, Beverland argues that it has become increasingly challenging for corporate brands to be from 'nowhere.' This, in turn, transforms the creation of authenticity into a 'connection [that] involves reterritorialization as a means of counter-acting the place-lessness of globalization.'

Such authentic connectivity also entails reconquering a sense of time, as corporate branding becomes more sensitized to its localized pasts and futures. This is significant, for example, in the brewing industry, where the place-less global corporate brands have become much more concerned with the origin and potentiality of their localized brands, responding to consumer preferences for 'our local beer.' In addition, growing research in 'place branding,' as Kavaratzis elaborates (this section), reflects how stakeholders are increasingly sensitized to how local histories are materialized and inscribed in local symbols and artifacts. Sometimes, specific places may transform into corporate brands themselves, for example, as the place itself becomes a symbol of a specific history, or time period.

### 2.4 From linear to ongoing temporalities

Finally, the conceptualization of corporate branding entails a shift from a unidirectional, linear temporal trajectory from the past to the present, to the future, and toward a more dynamic and ongoing balancing of the intersections between the past and future. An ongoing view of temporality originates strongly in philosophy and sociology, and assumes that actors are located in the present, from which they construct and reconstruct the past and future (Mead, 1932; Emirbayer & Mische, 1998). The concept of the ongoing construction of time focuses on how actors construct and reconnect distant and near-past and -future events in an ever-shifting present (e.g., Schultz & Hernes, 2013; Hernes, 2014; Hatch & Schultz, 2017; Suddaby et al., 2010). In the conceptualization of corporate branding, the ongoing and multidirectional construction of connections between the past, present, and future may transform the meaning and enactment of corporate brands. A shift in expectations for the emerging future may bring new aspects of the past to the forefront, just as renegotiations of the meaning of past heritage may point to new future directions for the brand. Karavatzis states that corporate brand heritage is an 'ongoing construction and determined by interpretation and negotiation.' He argues that such construction processes also involve the corporate brand's future orientation, suggesting a novel trajectory for what a corporate brand might become.

By the same token, Burghausen stresses the processual and ongoing nature of how stakeholders engage a corporate brand. He argues that 'history and heritage etc. are continuous, individual and collective, socio-cultural accomplishments rather than natural constants/ontic essences.' In that sense, the temporality of corporate branding is embedded in the ongoing accomplishments of actors, as they continuously adjust the meaning and balance between past and future in their 'ongoing present' (Schultz & Hernes, 2013).

### 2.5 Temporal brand agency

Taken together, these developments in the temporality of corporate branding indicate a much stronger focus on temporal agency in that both internal and external stakeholders are active co-creators of a corporate brand's temporality. This temporal agency refers both to the construction of the meaning(s) of the past and future and the enactment of connections between them in the present. In addition, these developments expand the scope of corporate branding in that a situated view allows stronger connections to multiple temporalities embedded in localized times and places. Although the chapters in the section focus more on (corporate) brand heritage and the expansion of past temporalities, their arguments are, in my view, equally relevant to future temporalities. The past and future are no longer external to corporate branding but are, rather, dimensions that are internalized and actively constructed. An active conception of how corporate branding is suspended between past and future temporalities creates new dilemmas for the management of corporate branding and invites new opportunities for future research.

## 3. New dilemmas in managing corporate branding

Almost by definition, corporate branding is riddled with dilemmas that managers must address, such as balancing a central coherent idea and local adaptations, or a long-term brand purpose and short-term brand marketing tactics. Moreover, the increased focus on temporal brand agency generates new dilemmas in the management of corporate branding, some of which are outlined below.

### *3.1 Balancing heritage sentiment and a one-directional future*

A recurrent theme of this Companion is the growth in co-creation of corporate brands, whether the co-creation comprises internal or external and enthusiastic or critical stakeholders (see Section B also). Thus, stakeholders bring many resources and expectations to co-creation processes. In my view, temporal brand agency both expands the queries that stakeholders bring to co-creation and enhances their expectations of how a corporate brand takes action. As scholars in this section argue, the increased focus on heritage brings new expectations to co-creation, whether heritage is embedded in narratives of a distant past or localized in places of the present. While research has shown that increased focus on heritage can be a source of innovation and strategic renewal (e.g., Brunninge, 2009; Hatch & Schultz, 2017; Suddaby et al., 2010), it may also be a source of nostalgia and resistance to future developments (e.g., Aeon & Lamertz, 2021). Together, these patterns may increase tensions between a 'heritage sentiment' among stakeholders engaged in co-creation and management's one-directional focus on a corporate brand's future. The early days of micro-brewing reflected this tension, when consumers and beer communities were much more concerned with brewing heritage, compared to most of the relevant corporations, which focused on their future timeless beer brands (e.g., Hatch et al., 2015).

### *3.2 Balancing localized connectivity with globalized 'nowhereness'*

Another temporal dilemma has emerged between a globalized presence 'from nowhere,' as Beverland argues in this volume, and the increased role of localness, whether it derives from local histories or specific places (see chapters by Burghausen and Kavaratsiz). All other things equal, corporate branding has been driven by forces of centralization and globalization in the pursuit of brand coherence and economies of scale. In contrast, brand heritage has been driven by a search for authenticity and connectivity. The increasing importance of localness will likely influence the expectations of stakeholders, particularly as they engage in co-creation, which will introduce dilemmas to brand managers still focused on achieving brand consistency across time and space. This, in turn, may compel managers to rethink what constitutes corporate brand equity (e.g., Iglesias et al., 2019), as the equity of localized heritage might be underestimated in current valuations of corporate brands' overall composition.

### 3.3 Balancing a contested past and heritage for the future

In general, heritage has been conceived as a resource to be evoked and/or reinterpreted for corporate brands, as the company behind the brand develops a new future. However, public reactions and debates about symbols of the past reveal that the past has become politicized. So far, past political leaders have been targets of severe criticism, such as when protesters spray-painted the statue of Winston Churchill at Parliament Square in London in 2020, accusing him of being a racist (see link in the following text), or the violent incidents related to removal of the Robert E. Lee monument in Charlottesville, Virginia, in 2017 (see link in the following text). Although historians have always debated controversial aspects of the past, these recent developments have made perceptions of heritage potentially controversial among broader audiences, including consumers and other stakeholders of corporate brands. For example, consumers criticized a classic ice-cream brand with a century-long history, called Eskimo, for exploiting the heritage of the Inuit people, and the product was eventually renamed. A contested past may become even more politicized as corporate brands increasingly articulate their purpose for the future, often by emphasizing how their contribution to society continues an authentic brand heritage. While most discussions of contested pasts have concerned the legacy of political leaders, often manifested in specific monuments or names of streets and places, this politicization may easily influence perceptions of corporate brands' heritages, as aspects of their past turn out to be more complicated than anticipated. The growing importance of localness to citizens and consumers may reinforce such scrutiny of brand heritage.

## 4. Avenues for future research

The move toward temporal brand agency suggests several avenues for future research.

### 4.1 Connecting the past and future

The active construction of connections between the past and future is an important assumption behind the temporal agency of corporate branding. The chapters in this section elaborate how different actors often hold multiple perceptions of the past and evoke resources from localized pasts. This multiplicity invites more research on connections to the future, in several ways. One set of questions concerns how multiple pasts influence the construction of the future in corporate branding. This issue is prevalent, for example, in mergers and acquisitions, where different perceptions of the past increasingly are expected to come together in a future purpose for a corporate brand. A second type of question addresses how ambitions for the future influence the selection of cues, events, artefacts, and so forth from the past. As Hatch and Schultz (2017) showed, the evoking of artefacts from a particular brewing past was driven by the Carlsberg Group's ambition to reposition the brand as a brewery opposed to being an FMCG company. Such internal historicizing processes may be even more controversial in corporate brands with multiple pasts. Finally, the movement toward a situated temporality questions how actors forge connections between the past and future through specific events or in specific localized settings. Rather than seeing connections between the past and future as created in central corporate communication and strategy units, a situated view also includes localized practices that aim to renew such connections. In that sense, corporate branding becomes a kaleidoscope of multiple connections between pasts and futures.

## 4.2 Intertemporal tensions

Another avenue for future research relates to increasing awareness of intertemporal tensions, defined as tensions between actors making different assumptions about time. This topic also indicates several research opportunities. One area concerns the intertemporal tensions between different generations. The Brundtland report's 1987 (see link) definition of intergenerational sustainability suggested this tension, stating 'development that meets the needs of the present generation without compromising the ability of future generations to meet their own needs.' These intergenerational tensions have gained increasing relevance given stakeholders' awareness of climate change and push for large corporations to take action. No doubt, new generations also expect to become involved in the co-creation of the corporate climate agenda. Such co-creation invites research on how next-generation climate movements and consumer activists interact with corporate brands and, perhaps, even research on specific activities or campaigns. Another area concerns tensions between actors from diverse units, functions, or cultures making different assumptions about time. Scholars have addressed these differences, for example, as actors refer differently to short and long-time horizons or different types of temporal orientations, e.g., between clock time and process time. Classic intertemporal choice theory treats these intertemporal tensions as trade-offs between benefits now versus benefits later (e.g., Kim et al., 2019). However, some scholars have taken a different view and scrutinized the conditions for a mutual 'temporal interplay' between different time horizons (Schultz & Hernes, 2020) or showed how 'temporal brokerage' may accommodate contradictory temporal orientations (Reinecke & Ansari, 2015). In relation to corporate branding, future research may reveal other tensions between time horizons and temporal orientations. For example, deep-seated references to corporate brand heritage may pave the way for other types of interplay among different time horizons. Also, as other sections of this Companion discuss, sustainability, and ethics are fundamental concerns in corporate branding, but adding an intertemporal dimension expands the types of questions raised in corporate brand research.

## 4.3 Addressing distant futures

A third avenue for future research emerged from the increasing focus on meaningful brand purpose along with consumers' and other stakeholders' push for corporate brands to engage in grand challenges. These developments imply that corporate brands increasingly must adopt an active stance toward a future that reaches beyond the time horizon of established brand strategies, let alone corporate brand campaigns. While the research in this section reflects the importance of the distant past to corporate branding, there is less research about how corporate brands cope with increasing pressure to address distant futures.[1] In recent, related research, Augustine and her co-authors (Augustine et al., 2019) show the dialectic process underpinning the emergence of geoengineering as an imagined concept in a distant future. Elaborating a situated view of temporality, Hernes and Schultz (2020) demonstrate how combinations of events enable actors to go beyond the time horizons within which they normally operate. These scholars stress the need to further explore how actors engage distant futures which are no longer perceived as an instrumental extension of current (brand) strategies. Distant futures challenge the established time horizons and temporal orientations of many corporate brands. This challenge is becoming

---

1 In making this argument, I am indebted to the research project: Making distant futures actionable at Copenhagen Business School, funded by Novo Nordisk Foundation (see link).

increasingly complex, as global leading brands increasingly commit to green ambitions reaching into 2050. In addition, corporate brands are confronting stakeholders' growing expectations that brands act upon such distant goals, if they are to maintain their credibility and legitimacy. These developments pave the way for research on how corporate brands address goals that reach into the distant future, along with research on the implications for product branding.

## 5. Conclusion

The scholars in this section show how corporate brands make connections to their past through deliberate selection and reinterpretation processes. These connections increasingly occur through co-creation processes with multiple stakeholders situated differently in time and space. At the same time, corporate brands confront stakeholders' expectations to articulate a compelling and meaningful brand purpose while taking a stance on grand challenges reaching into the distant future. Here, corporate brands must also consider consumers' increasing scepticism toward big corporate entities from nowhere and consumers' wish to reconnect with local communities, which they often perceive as more authentic. These developments together make corporate branding an exciting area for studying how temporal agency is enacted among multiple stakeholders. In many ways, corporate brands are constellations of numerous relationships reaching backward and forward in time. However, they only become brands if these relationships are guided by ideas and a sense of purpose which resonate with people across time. This section calls for more research on how a corporate brand purpose may connect distant pasts and futures while challenging conventional thinking in the company behind the brand. Finally, the increasing importance of co-creation not only includes relationships between stakeholders and a focal corporate brand but may create an ecosystem of interconnected brands, which together may initiate transformational change that increases the likelihood that corporate brands are able to contribute to resolve the grand challenges of our time.

## References

Aaker, D. A. (2004). Leveraging the corporate brand. *California Management Review*, 46(3), 6–18. https://doi.org/10.2307/41166218.
Adam, B. (2004). *Time*. Cambridge: Polity Press.
Aeon, B., & Lamertz, K. (2021). Those who control the past control the future: The dark side of rhetorical history. *Organization Studies*, 42(4). https://doi.org/10.1177/0170840619844284
Ancona, D. G., Goodman, P. S., Lawrence, B. S., & Tushman, M. L. (2001). Time: A new research lens. *Academy of Management Review*, 26, 645–663.
Augustine, G., Soderstrom, S., Milner, D., & Weber, K. (2019). Constructing a distant future: Imaginaries in geoengineering. *Academy of Management Journal*, 62(6), 1930–1960.
Balmer, J. M. T. (2009). Scrutinising the British monarchy: The corporate brand that was shaken, stirred and survived. *Management Decision*, 47(4), 639–675.
Balmer, J. M. T. (2011). Corporate heritage identities, corporate heritage brands and the multiple heritage identities of the British Monarchy. *European Journal of Marketing*, 45(9–10): 1380–1398.
Bluedorn, A. C., & Standifer, R. L. (2006). Time and the temporal imagination. *Academy of Management Learning & Education* 5, 196–206.
Brunninge, O. (2009). Using history in organizations: How managers make purposeful reference to history in strategy processes. *Journal of Organizational Change Management*, 22(1), 8–26.
Emirbayer, M., & Mische, A. (1998). What is agency? *American Journal of Sociology*, 103, 962–1023.
Hatch, M. J., & Schultz, M. (2008). *Taking brand initiative: How corporations can align strategy, culture and identity through corporate branding*. San Francisco, CA: Wiley/Jossey-Bass.
Hatch, M. J., & Schultz, M. (2010). Toward a theory of brand co-creation with implications for brand governance. *Journal of Brand Management*, 17(8), 590–604.

Hatch, M. J., & Schultz, M. (2017). Toward a theory of using history authentically: Historicizing in the Carlsberg Group. *Administrative Science Quarterly*, 62(4), 657–697.

Hatch, M. J., Schultz, M., & Skov, A. M. (2015). Organizational identity and culture in the context of managed change: Transformation in the Carlsberg Group, 2009–2013. *Academy of Management Discoveries*, 1(1), 58–90.

Hernes, T. (2014). *A process theory of organization*. Oxford: Oxford University Press.

Hernes, T., & Schultz, M. (2020). Translating the distant into the present: How actors address distant past and future events through situated activity. *Organization Theory* 1(1). https://doi.org/10.1177/2631787719900999.

Holt, D. (2004). *How brands become icons: The principles of cultural branding*. Cambridge. MA: Harvard University Press.

Iglesias, O., Markovic, S., Singh, J. J., & Sierra, V. (2019). Do customer perceptions of corporate services brand ethically improve brand equity? Considering the roles of brand heritage, brand image and recognition benefits. *Journal of Business Ethics*, 154(2), 441–459. doi: 10.1007/s10551-017-3455-0.

Iglesias, O., Ind, N., & Schultz, M. (2020). History matters: The role of history in corporate brand strategy. *Business Horizons*, 63, 51–60.

Ind, N., Iglesias, O., & Markovic, S. (2017). The co-creation continuum: From tactical market research tool to strategic collaborative innovation method. *Journal of Brand Management*, 24(4), 310–321.

Ind, N., Iglesias, O., & Schultz, M. (2013). Building brands together: Emergence and outcomes of cocreation. *California Management Review*, 55(3), 5–26.

Kim, A., Bansal, P., & Haugh, H. (2019). No time like the present: How a present time perspective can foster sustainable development. *Academy of Management Journal*, 62(2), 607–634. https://doi.org/10.5465/amj.2015.1295.

Mead, G. H. (1932). Chapter 3: The social nature of the present. In A. E. Murphy (Ed.), *The philosophy of the present* (pp. 47–67). Chicago; LaSalle, Ill.: Open Court. https://brocku.ca/MeadProject/Mead/pubs2/philpres/Mead_1932_03.html#:~:text=George%20Herbert%20Mead.%20%22The%20Social%20Nature%20of%20the%20Present%22%20Chapter%203%20in%20The%20Philosophy%20of%20the%20Present%2C%20edited%20by%20Arthur%20E.%20Murphy.%20LaSalle%2C%20Ill.%3A%20Open%20Court%20(1932)%3A%2047%20%2D%2067

Orlikowski, W. J., & Yates, J. (2002). It's about time: Temporal structuring in organizations. *Organization Science*, 13(6), 684–700.

Ramaswamy, V., & Ozcan, K. (2016). Brand value co-creation in a digitalized world: An integrative framework and research implications. *International Journal of Research in Marketing*, 33(1), 93–106.

Reinecke, J., & Ansari, S. (2015). When times collide: Temporal brokerage at the intersection of markets and developments. *Academy of Management Journal*, 58(2), 618–648.

Schroeder, J. E. (2009). The cultural codes of branding. *Marketing Theory*, 9(1), 123–126.

Schroeder, J. E., & Salzer-Mörling. M. (Eds.). (2006). *Brand culture*. London: Routledge.

Schultz, M., & Hernes, T. (2013). A temporal perspective on organizational identity. *Organization Science*, 24(1), 1–21.

Schultz, M., & Hernes, T. (2020). Temporal interplay between strategy and identity: Punctuated, subsumed and sustained modes. *Strategic Organization*, 18(1), 106–135.

Suddaby, R., Foster, W., & Quinn Trank, C. (2010). Rhetorical history as a source of competitive advantage. In J. A. C. Baum & J. Lampel (Eds.), *Advances in strategic management: The globalization of strategy research* (pp. 147–173). Bingley: Emerald.

## Links

Churchill Statue: www.theguardian.com/politics/2020/jun/13/removal-of-controversial-statues-winston-churchill-protest

Charlottesville monument: https://en.wikipedia.org/wiki/Robert_E._Lee_Monument_(Charlottesville,_Virginia)

Brundtland Commission Report Our Common Future: https://sustainabledevelopment.un.org/content/documents/5987our-common-future.pdf

Making Distant Futures Actionable:

https://www.cbs.dk/en/research/departments-and-centres/department-of-organization/centres-and-groups/centre-organization-and-time-cot/projects/actionable-futures-project

# F

# Branding inside-out

Corporate culture and internal branding

# 26
# BRANDING INSIDE-OUT
Development of the internal branding concept

*Rico Piehler*

## 1. Introduction

Internal stakeholders such as employees are either directly or indirectly responsible for delivering the externally communicated brand promise and are thus crucial to building and maintaining strong brands. Because they are key sources of sustainable differentiation and competitive advantages, they represent an important target group of corporate branding efforts. Consequently, internal branding has developed as a management concept that focuses on the internal perspective of branding. As a relatively young concept, it has gained widespread acceptance in mainstream branding literature over the past 20 years. Until the millennium, branding techniques and approaches applied mainly to external stakeholders, such as customers. Only with the rise of modern marketing and management concepts and theories, did the internal perspective of branding gain momentum through internal branding. This chapter briefly introduces the history of the concept by highlighting noteworthy contributions to developing the field. In addition to presenting the conceptual bases from different disciplines and integrating various definitions to create a shared understanding, this chapter also presents the elements (dimensions) of internal branding that have been investigated in internal branding literature. It concludes with future developments and directions for further research of the concept.

## 2. A brief history of internal branding

As with the emergence of the related concept of employer branding, which represents the application of branding principles to human resources management (Ambler & Barrow, 1996; Foster et al., 2010; Moroko & Uncles, 2008), the field of internal branding was not initially characterised by academics advancing the idea that employees are an essential target group of brand management. Practitioners mostly drove early internal branding literature with their book publications (Ind, 2001), as well as their publications in academic (Bergstrom et al., 2002; Ind, 2003) and practitioner-focused (Mellor, 1999; Mitchell, 2002; Zucker, 2002) journals. Following this stage, academics began to advance the field by defining and developing the internal branding concept. In addition to producing individual papers that shaped the development of the concept (Table 26.1), several clusters of academics from different regions of the world emerged, publishing a series of academic papers. These distinct research clusters made noteworthy contributions to developing the field of internal branding.

Table 26.1 Internal branding publications outside the identified research groups

| Author(s) | Contribution(s) |
|---|---|
| Aurand et al. (2005) | Discussion of human resource management's role in internal branding |
| Chong (2007) | Case study on how internal communication and training enable a company to deliver on its brand promise consistently |
| Mahnert and Torres (2007) | Identification of 25 key factors of failure and success in internal branding and introduction of a consolidated internal branding framework |
| Kimpakorn and Tocquer (2009) | Investigation of the effect of the employer brand dimensions on employees' brand commitment |
| Baumgarth and Schmidt (2010) | Introduction of internal brand equity and examination of its relationship with company-level and individual-level determinants and customer-based brand equity as a consequence |
| Hughes and Ahearne (2010) | Investigation of the impact of two types of salesperson identification and manager control system alignment on brand extra-role behaviours and (brand) performance |
| Raj Devasagayam et al. (2010) | Integration of the research streams of brand community and internal branding to investigate the viability of intraorganizational brand communities in internal branding |
| Chang et al. (2012) | Introduction of brand psychological ownership into internal branding and examination of organizational-level antecedents, individual-level and organizational-level outcomes and customer outcomes |
| Sharma and Kamalanabhan (2012) | Examination of the internal corporate communication (ICC) process and its effect on internal branding objectives |
| Sirianni et al. (2013) | Investigation of the effect of employee – brand alignment of frontline service employees on overall brand evaluations and customer-based brand equity as customer responses |
| Matanda and Ndubisi (2013) | Examination of the moderating role of goal congruence on the effects of internal branding and internal customer orientation on person-organization fit |
| Gelb and Rangarajan (2014) | Examination of employees' contributions to brand equity |
| Löhndorf and Diamantopoulos (2014) | Study of the mediating role of organizational identification on the effects of employee-brand fit, brand knowledge, and belief in the brand on employee brand-building behaviours |
| Du Preez and Bendixen (2015) | Examination of the effect of internal brand management on job satisfaction, brand commitment, and intention to stay |
| Erkmen and Hancer (2015) | Investigation of the effect of employees' brand citizenship behaviours on customers' evaluation of brand performance, brand trust, and brand commitment |
| Helm et al. (2016) | Study of the effect of brand self-congruity on employees' brand identification, brand pride, and brand-related behaviour |
| Kaufmann et al. (2016) | Development of a conceptual model for the effect of behavioural branding on customers' brand love and co-creation |
| Terglav et al. (2016) | Investigation of the mediating effect of employee brand knowledge, employee-brand fit, and psychological contract fulfilment on the relationship between brand-oriented leadership and brand commitment |
| Du Preez et al. (2017) | Analysis of the effect of internal brand management on brand citizenship behaviour and intention to stay through job satisfaction and brand commitment |
| Liu et al. (2017) | Examination of the processes whereby brand orientation affects in- and extra-role employee brand-building behaviour from the perspective of the attention-based view |

(Continued)

Table 26.1 (Continued)

| Author(s) | Contribution(s) |
| --- | --- |
| Anees-ur-Rehman et al. (2018) | Investigation of the relationship between brand orientation and financial performance through internal branding, brand communication, brand awareness, and brand credibility |
| Dechawatanapaisal (2018) | Examination of the relationships among internal branding, brand orientation, brand identification, brand commitment, and employees' intention to stay |
| Garas et al. (2018) | Analysis of the relationship between internal branding and employees' brand supporting in-role and extra-role behaviour, mediated by employees' role clarity, affective commitment, and continuance commitment |
| Iyer et al. (2018) | Investigation of the relationships between brand orientation, strategic branding, internal branding, and brand performance |
| Schmidt and Baumgarth (2018) | Identification of success factors of brand ambassador programs |
| Ngo et al. (2019) | Introduction of a cognitive-affective-behaviour model of internal branding proposing that internal brand knowledge triggers employee brand identification that influences brand- and customer-focused behaviours, which in turn foster employee performance |
| Boukis and Christodoulides (2020) | Development of a model of antecedents and consequences of employee-based brand equity (EBBE) via brand knowledge and brand identification |
| Iglesias and Ind (2020) | Holistic integration of the co-creation perspective into corporate brand management with multiple stakeholders helping to build and enrich the corporate brand |

The first three clusters come from the United Kingdom and the United States. Leslie de Chernatony and colleagues were among the first academics to bring attention to internal branding issues. Their publications deal with internal branding objectives (Thomson et al., 1999) and internal branding activities (Harris & de Chernatony, 2001; Vallaster & de Chernatony, 2005, 2006), particularly in the services branding context. The second research cluster from the United Kingdom formed around Khanyapuss Punjaisri, Alan Wilson, and Heiner Evanschitzky. This cluster developed a holistic internal branding model, comprising internal branding objectives, activities and moderators, and validated it empirically (Punjaisri & Wilson, 2007, 2011). Another cluster originates in the United States with Sandra Jeanquart Miles and W. Glynn Mangold conceptualizing and empirically examining the employee branding process (Miles et al., 2011; Miles & Mangold, 2004).

Two more clusters of internal branding researchers emerged in Germany and Switzerland. Together with their colleagues, Christoph Burmann, Sabrina Zeplin, and Rico Piehler introduced a holistic internal branding model comprising internal branding objectives, activities, moderators, and consequences (Burmann & Zeplin, 2005; Piehler et al., 2015). They validated the model in several studies across different contexts (Burmann et al., 2009; Piehler, 2018; Piehler et al., 2016). A German-Swiss cluster around Torsten Tomczak and Franz-Rudolf Esch introduced the behavioural branding concept. They outlined the brand behaviour funnel as the core of their approach in their edited book *Behavioral Branding*, proposing that internal branding activities affect internal branding objectives, leading to internal branding consequences (Tomczak et al., 2012). In addition, they published several journal articles on specific internal branding activities (Henkel et al., 2007; Morhart et al., 2009; Wentzel et al., 2010).

Finally, another cluster to develop internal branding emerged around Ceridwyn King and Debra Grace from Australia. Within the realm of services marketing, these authors investigated internal branding consequences, objectives, activities, and antecedents (King & Grace, 2005, 2008, 2012). Drawing from the concept of customer-based brand equity as 'the differential effect of brand knowledge on consumer response to the marketing of the brand' (Keller, 1993, p. 1), they also introduced the concept of employee-based brand equity, defined as 'the differential effect that brand knowledge has on an employee's response to internal brand management' (King et al., 2012, p. 269).

Table 26.1 presents examples of other academic publications outside those identified research clusters that have advanced specific internal branding research areas.

After the initial growth of the field, academics engaged in structuring and consolidating fragmented internal branding knowledge and extending that knowledge. They achieved structure and consolidation through the publication of literature reviews (Barros-Arrieta & García-Cali, 2020; Saleem & Iglesias, 2016) and special issues in branding journals (e.g., 2018 special issue 'Internal Brand Management' in *Journal of Brand Management*, 2021 special issue 'Internal Branding: In Search of a New Paradigm' in *Journal of Product & Brand Management*). Both forms of publication have contributed to the development of the field and delivered valuable insights for further research directions.

## 3. Conceptual basis and definition of internal branding

As a result of the diverse conceptual bases of internal branding research (Table 26.2), it is not surprising that the domain has been described as fragmented (Saleem & Iglesias, 2016). Internal branding authors not only rely on the marketing and management disciplines but also ground their research in psychology/sociology and organizational behaviour research. Services marketing and branding, corporate branding, internal marketing, corporate and brand identity management, brand orientation, brand equity, relationship marketing, co-creation, and service-dominant logic are among the most used foundations from the marketing discipline. From the management discipline, the resource-based and competence-based views of the firm, organizational communication, and human resources management are often cited as conceptual foundations. Social identity, social exchange, and social learning theories are among the most often-referenced theories from psychology/sociology. Finally, research on organizational commitment and organizational citizenship behaviour, organizational role theory, psychological contract, leadership, and job characteristics theory from the organizational behaviour domain are also frequently adapted to the internal branding context.

Due to the variety of conceptual bases, the understanding of internal branding in academic contributions differs with no generally accepted definition (Table 26.3). However, there are several commonalities among the definitions. First, almost all presented definitions explicitly mention employees as the target group of internal branding. Similarly, most definitions refer to the final objective of employees' living the brand and delivering on the brand promise. Other internal branding objectives mentioned in several definitions are brand understanding, brand commitment, and brand attitudes. The descriptions of what internal branding constitutes include process, effort, concept, strategy, management, practice, tool, activity, initiative, method, means, framework, orientation, and doctrine. Finally, some definitions also include specific internal branding activities, such as internal communications or internal promotion, human resource management, or training and leadership. Integrating the presented definitions and their components and considering not only externally oriented but also internally oriented behaviours of employees as well as other external stakeholders in addition to customers (e.g.,

*Table 26.2* Conceptual bases of internal branding research

| Discipline | Conceptual basis | Illustrative contributions |
|---|---|---|
| Marketing | Services marketing (Berry & Parasuraman, 1993; Grönroos, 1984; Zeithaml et al., 1996) and services branding (Berry, 2000; de Chernatony & Dall'Olmo Riley, 1999) | Aurand et al. (2005); de Chernatony (1999); de Chernatony et al. (2003, 2006); de Chernatony and Cottam (2006); Erkmen and Hancer (2015); Foster et al. (2010); Henkel et al. (2007); Judson et al. (2009); Kimpakorn and Tocquer (2009); King (2010); King et al. (2012, 2013); King and Grace (2005, 2006, 2008, 2010, 2012); Löhndorf and Diamantopoulos (2014); Morhart et al. (2009); Murillo and King (2019); Piehler et al. (2019); Punjaisri et al. (2008); Punjaisri, Evanschitzky, et al. (2009); Punjaisri, Wilson, et al. (2009); Raj Devasagayam et al. (2010); Sirianni et al. (2013); Terglav et al. (2016); Thomson et al. (1999); Vallaster and de Chernatony (2005); Wentzel et al. (2010) |
| | Corporate branding (Balmer, 1995; Balmer & Gray, 2003; Hatch & Schultz, 2003; Ind, 1997) | Anees-ur-Rehman et al. (2018); Baumgarth and Schmidt (2010); Chong (2007); de Chernatony (1999, 2002); Foster et al. (2010); Garas et al. (2018); Harris and de Chernatony (2001); Helm et al. (2016); Iyer et al. (2018); Kaufmann et al. (2016); Punjaisri, Wilson, et al. (2009); Punjaisri and Wilson (2007, 2011); Sirianni et al. (2013); Vallaster and de Chernatony (2006) |
| | Internal marketing (George, 1990; Rafiq & Ahmed, 2000) | Aurand et al. (2005); Du Preez et al. (2017); Du Preez and Bendixen (2015); King and Grace (2005); Mahnert and Torres (2007); Mangold and Miles (2007); Miles and Mangold (2004, 2005, 2007); Punjaisri and Wilson (2007); Thomson et al. (1999) |
| | Corporate identity (Balmer, 1998, 2001; van Riel & Balmer, 1997) and brand identity (Aaker, 1996; Burmann, Hegner, et al., 2009; de Chernatony, 1999; Kapferer, 1997) management | Baumgarth and Schmidt (2010); Burmann, Jost-Benz, et al. (2009); Burmann, Zeplin, et al. (2009); Burmann and Zeplin (2005); de Chernatony (1999); Dean et al. (2016); Harris and de Chernatony (2001); Judson et al. (2009); Vallaster and de Chernatony (2006) |
| | Brand orientation (Urde, 1994, 1999) | Anees-ur-Rehman et al. (2018); Dechawatanapaisal (2018); Iyer et al. (2018); King et al. (2013); Liu et al. (2017); Matanda and Ndubisi (2013); Schmidt and Baumgarth (2018) |
| | Brand equity (Aaker, 1991; Keller, 1993) | Baumgarth and Schmidt (2010); Burmann, Jost-Benz, et al. (2009); Gelb and Rangarajan (2014); King et al. (2012); King and Grace (2010) |
| | Relationship marketing (Berry, 1995; Gronroos, 1990; Morgan & Hunt, 1994) | Erkmen and Hancer (2015); King and Grace (2012); Punjaisri et al. (2008); Thomson et al. (1999) |
| | Co-creation (Hatch & Schultz, 2010; Prahalad & Ramaswamy, 2004) | Dean et al. (2016); Iglesias and Ind (2020); Kaufmann et al. (2016) |

(*Continued*)

Table 26.2 (Continued)

| Discipline | Conceptual basis | Illustrative contributions |
|---|---|---|
| Management | Service-dominant logic (Vargo & Lusch, 2004, 2016) | King and Grace (2008); Piehler et al. (2016) |
| | Resource-based and competence-based views (Prahalad & Hamel, 1990; Wernerfelt, 1984) | Burmann, Jost-Benz, et al. (2009); Iyer et al. (2018); King and Grace (2008); Piehler et al. (2016, 2018) |
| | Organizational communication | Baumgarth and Schmidt (2010); de Chernatony et al. (2006); Liu et al. (2017); Schmidt and Baumgarth (2018); Sharma and Kamalanabhan (2012) |
| | Human resources management | Aurand et al. (2005); Chang et al. (2012) |
| Psychology/ sociology | Social identity theory (Tajfel, 1982) | Boukis and Christodoulides (2020); Dechawatanapaisal (2018); Helm et al. (2016); Hughes and Ahearne (2010); Löhndorf and Diamantopoulos (2014); Morhart et al. (2009); Piehler et al. (2016); Punjaisri, Evanschitzky, et al. (2009); Punjaisri, Wilson, et al. (2009) |
| | Social exchange theory | Chang et al. (2012); Garas et al. (2018); Löhndorf and Diamantopoulos (2014); Xiong and King (2019) |
| | Social learning theory (Bandura, 1977) | Burmann and Zeplin (2005); Piehler et al. (2015, 2019) |
| Organizational behaviour | Organizational commitment and organizational citizenship behaviour | Burmann, Zeplin, et al. (2009); Burmann and Zeplin (2005); Chang et al. (2012); Dechawatanapaisal (2018); Du Preez et al. (2017); Du Preez and Bendixen (2015); Garas et al. (2018); Henkel et al. (2007); Hughes and Ahearne (2010); King and Grace (2012); Morhart et al. (2009); Piehler (2018); Piehler et al. (2015, 2016, 2019); Punjaisri, Wilson, et al. (2009); Punjaisri and Wilson (2011); Terglav et al. (2016); Xiong and King (2019, 2020) |
| | Organizational role theory (Kahn et al., 1964) | Garas et al. (2018); King (2010); King and Grace (2010); Piehler (2018); Piehler et al. (2016, 2019) |
| | Psychological contract | Mangold and Miles (2007); Miles et al. (2011); Miles and Mangold (2004, 2005, 2007); Terglav et al. (2016) |
| | Leadership | Burmann, Zeplin, et al. (2009); Burmann and Zeplin (2005); Morhart et al. (2009); Terglav et al. (2016); Vallaster and de Chernatony (2005, 2006) |
| | Job characteristics theory | Piehler et al. (2016); Sirianni et al. (2013); Xiong et al. (2013); Xiong and King (2019) |

suppliers, distribution partners, shareholders, investors, NGOs, regulators, policymakers, journalists, the general public), the following definition is provided:

> Internal branding is a management concept that implements a brand cognitively, affectively and behaviourally in the minds, hearts and behaviours of employees so that they

*Table 26.3* Exemplary definitions of internal branding in prior literature

| Author(s) | Definition/understanding |
|---|---|
| Aurand et al. (2005) | 'This engagement of employees in the brand, leading to their representation of brand qualities to outside constituents is often times referred to as internal branding' (p. 164). |
| Vallaster and de Chernatony (2006) | 'Internal brand building as a process to align staff's behaviour with a corporate brand's identity' (p. 761). |
| Mahnert and Torres (2007) | 'Internal branding is the concerted, interdepartmental and multi-directional internal communications effort carried out in order to create and maintain an internal brand. Internal branding attempts to achieve consistency with the external brand and encourage brand commitment and the propensity for brand championship among employees' (p. 56). |
| Foster et al. (2010) | 'Internal branding focuses largely on the adoption of the branding concept inside an organisation to ensure that employees deliver the brand promise to the external stakeholders' (p. 401). |
| Raj Devasagayam et al. (2010) | 'Internal branding is the process of engaging employees in the branding process, which enables them to more successfully represent the brand's qualities to outside constituents' (p. 211). |
| Punjaisri and Wilson (2011) | 'Internal branding describes the activities undertaken by an organisation to ensure that the brand promise reflecting the espoused brand values that set customers' expectations is enacted and delivered by employees' (p. 1523). |
| Chang et al. (2012) | 'Internal branding is regarded as the process of promoting the brand to employees, educating them what the brand value is . . . and then making employees' perception and behaviors transformed' (p. 629). |
| King and Grace (2012) | 'Internal brand management has been promoted to be the means to ensure employees are attitudinally and behaviourally ready to deliver the brand promise' (p. 471). |
| Sharma and Kamalanabhan (2012) | 'Internal branding represents a firm's internal communication efforts to promote both within the firm, a clear view of what makes it different and desirable as an employer' (p. 310). |
| Löhndorf and Diamantopoulos (2014) | 'Internal branding literature asserts that employees must behave in line with the brand when interacting with customers, to create and maintain a consistent brand image' (p. 311). |
| Erkmen and Hancer (2015) | '[I]nternal branding helps to promote brand supporting behaviors by integrating employees into the branding process to deliver a consistent quality service around brand promise so that the brand promise could be realized consistently during consumer brand experience' (p. 879). |
| Saleem and Iglesias (2016) | 'Internal branding is the process through which organizations make a company-wide effort within a supportive culture to integrate brand ideologies, leadership, HRM, internal brand communications and internal brand communities as a strategy to enable employees to consistently co-create brand value with multiple stakeholders' (p. 50). |
| Liu et al. (2017) | 'Internal branding refers to brand-building efforts that focus on promoting a brand inside an organization to motive the employees to transform the brand promise[1] into reality' (p. 1). |
| Anees-ur-Rehman et al. (2018) | 'Internal management processes by which employees understand the brand concept, commit to the brand and thus live the brand' (p. 315). |

(*Continued*)

Table 26.3 (Continued)

| Author(s) | Definition/understanding |
|---|---|
| Dechawatanapaisal (2018) | '[I]nternal branding engenders employees' attitudes and mindset toward the brand to ensure that brand messages are accurately delivered to external constituents' (p. 677). |
| Garas et al. (2018) | '[I]nternal branding, which is a tool for influencing employees to fulfil the external brand promise by ensuring that they transform the corporate brand values into reality when fulfilling the brand promise' (p. 80). |
| Iyer et al. (2018) | '[T]he organization's effort to align their employees and brands with each other, i.e., internal branding' (p. 202). |
| Murillo and King (2019) | '[I]nternal brand management (IBM) has identified several practices that service companies should adopt to ensure that their employees have the knowledge and attitudes that will enable them to champion the brand' (p. 893). |
| Piehler et al. (2019) | '[I]nternal brand management (IBM) as a concept for implementing the brand cognitively, affectively, and behaviourally at the employee level' (p. 445). |
| Ngo et al. (2019) | '[A]lignment of employees' knowledge, attitudes, and behaviours with brand values when delivering the brand promise to customers' (p. 277). |
| Barros-Arrieta and García-Cali (2020) | '[I]nternal branding as an internal orientation of brand management and its objective is to promote the brand internally to ensure that employees are willing to deliver the brand promise to external stakeholders, creating consistency between internal and external brand messages' (p. 4). |

live the brand towards internal and external stakeholders, thus consistently delivering on the brand promises to all target groups.

This definition enables differentiation from related yet distinct concepts such as internal marketing or employer branding (Barros-Arrieta & García-Cali, 2020; Foster et al., 2010; Saleem & Iglesias, 2016).

## 4. Elements of internal branding

Broadly, academic internal branding studies have responded to five questions relating to internal branding elements (or 'dimensions') (Figure 26.1).

### 4.1 Internal branding consequences: why is internal branding important for brands?

Despite authors arguing for the relevance of internal branding for companies by referring to diverse conceptual bases, most approaches emphasize employees' relevance in the delivery of the brand promise. Compared with the brand promise's development and communication to external target groups, fulfilling the brand promise represents a much more significant challenge for companies. Only when employees deliver on the brand promise can companies realize positive effects on internal branding consequences. For example, customers develop brand satisfaction if their brand experiences match or outperform their expectations. Only then can brand trust and strong customer-brand relationships, which are prerequisites of customer-based brand equity, develop. Internal branding literature has suggested numerous internal branding consequences that benefit the organization (Table 26.4).

*Branding inside-out*

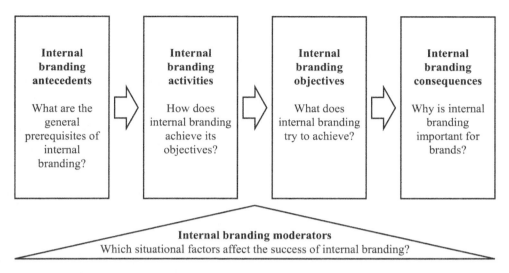

*Figure 26.1* Basic structure of internal branding research

*Table 26.4* Internal branding consequences and illustrative contributions

| Internal branding consequences | Illustrative contributions |
| --- | --- |
| (Brand) performance | Baker et al. (2014); Erkmen and Hancer (2015); Harris and de Chernatony (2001); Henkel et al. (2007); Hughes and Ahearne (2010); Iyer et al. (2018); Mahnert and Torres (2007); Ngo et al. (2019); Tuominen et al. (2016) |
| Service quality | Kaufmann et al. (2016); Kimpakorn and Tocquer (2009); King and Grace (2005, 2006, 2008); Mangold and Miles (2007); Miles and Mangold (2004); Terglav et al. (2016) |
| Brand strength | Burmann, Zeplin, et al. (2009); Burmann and Zeplin (2005) |
| Brand image | Chong (2007); Du Preez et al. (2017); Sirianni et al. (2013); Vallaster and de Chernatony (2006) |
| Brand reputation | Du Preez et al. (2017); Miles et al. (2011); Miles and Mangold (2005) |
| Brand credibility | Anees-ur-Rehman et al. (2018); Piehler et al. (2015) |
| Brand trust | Erkmen and Hancer (2015); Piehler (2018); Piehler et al. (2015, 2019) |
| Brands' position in customers' minds | Miles et al. (2011); Miles and Mangold (2005) |
| (Customer-based) brand equity | Baumgarth and Schmidt (2010); Burmann, Jost-Benz, et al. (2009); de Chernatony and Cottam (2006); Gelb and Rangarajan (2014); Judson et al. (2006); Miles et al. (2011); Ngo et al. (2019); Piehler (2018); Piehler et al. (2015); Sirianni et al. (2013); Vallaster and de Chernatony (2005) |
| Customer/brand satisfaction | Chang et al. (2012); de Chernatony (2002); Mangold and Miles (2007); Miles et al. (2011); Miles and Mangold (2005); Piehler et al. (2015, 2019) |
| Customer/brand retention/loyalty | Mangold and Miles (2007); Miles et al. (2011); Miles and Mangold (2004, 2005); Piehler (2018); Piehler et al. (2015) |

Empirical internal branding studies support these conceptual considerations by providing evidence of positive effects of internal branding activities and objectives on (brand) performance in many diverse contexts such as B2B (Baker et al., 2014, Hughes & Ahearne, 2010), the airline industry (Erkmen & Hancer, 2015), consumer goods, service, industrial goods, retailing, electronics, and technology industries (Henkel et al., 2007; Iyer et al., 2018; Ngo et al., 2019; Tuominen et al., 2016). Other empirical validations exist for internal branding effects on brand strength as the behavioural significance of a brand for stakeholders (Burmann, Zeplin et al., 2009), brand image (Sirianni et al., 2013), brand credibility as the ability and willingness of the brand to deliver its promises (Anees-ur-Rehman et al., 2018), brand trust as a psychological state resulting from confidence in a brand's reliability and integrity (Erkmen & Hancer, 2015), customer-based brand equity (Baumgarth and Schmidt, 2010; Sirianni et al., 2013), and customer satisfaction (Chang et al., 2012). In summary, there is plenty of evidence that treating employees as an important target group of branding efforts and engaging in internal branding increases brand and company success.

## 4.2 Internal branding objectives: what does internal branding try to achieve?

Among the many internal branding objectives that studies have considered, four merit explicit mention: brand-related behaviour, brand commitment, brand identification, and brand understanding (Table 26.5).

The ultimate objective of internal branding is to align employee behaviour with the brand. Therefore, numerous studies consider brand-related employee behaviour as an internal branding objective. Such behaviour has been variously described as brand-consistent behaviour, brand-supporting/supportive behaviour, brand-building behaviour, or brand citizenship behaviour. In addition to a basic distinction into intra-role and extra-role behaviours, with the former being related to the standards prescribed by employees' organizational roles as brand representatives and the latter going beyond their prescribed organizational roles (Liu et al., 2017), several more specific types of behaviours have been investigated in the literature. The first type is brand-consistent intra-role behaviour, also known as brand compliance and in-role brand-building behaviour, that manifests in behaviours such as following brand-related rules and instructions to support branding objectives and avoid damaging the brand (Baumgarth & Schmidt, 2010; Morhart et al., 2009; Piehler, 2018). The second type represents the willingness to help, also known as helping behaviours and brand consideration and brand acceptance, which relates to being helpful toward internal and external customers and taking over tasks outside employees' areas of responsibility (Burmann, Zeplin, et al., 2009; Chang et al., 2012; Porricelli et al., 2014). The third type of behaviour is brand enthusiasm, also known as brand endorsement, representing the conscious espousal of, and advocacy for, brands. It comprises behaviours such as recommending brands to prospective employees and customers, representing brands favourably and defending them from criticism (Burmann, Zeplin, et al., 2009; Piehler, 2018). The fourth type represents the willingness for further development, also known as willingness to support brand development, self-development of brand enhancement, and brand development, which enhances employees' brand-related knowledge, skills, and abilities or contributes to improving customers' brand experiences (Baumgarth & Schmidt, 2010; Burmann, Zeplin, et al., 2009; Chang et al., 2012; Porricelli et al., 2014).

Numerous internal branding studies have identified brand commitment, brand identification, and brand understanding as upstream internal branding objectives to encourage employees to fulfil brand promises and strengthen brands through their behaviours. Brand commitment

*Table 26.5* Internal branding objectives and illustrative contributions

| Internal branding objectives | Illustrative contributions |
| --- | --- |
| Brand-related behaviour | Baumgarth and Schmidt (2010); Burmann, Jost-Benz, et al. (2009); Burmann, Zeplin, et al. (2009); Burmann and Zeplin (2005); Chang et al. (2012); Chong (2007); de Chernatony et al. (2006); de Chernatony and Cottam (2006); Du Preez et al. (2017); Erkmen and Hancer (2015); Garas et al. (2018); Gelb and Rangarajan (2014); Helm et al. (2016); Henkel et al. (2007); Hughes and Ahearne (2010); Judson et al. (2006); Kaufmann et al. (2016); King (2010); King et al. (2012, 2013); King and Grace (2006, 2010, 2012); Löhndorf and Diamantopoulos (2014); Mahnert and Torres (2007); Morhart et al. (2009); Ngo et al. (2019); Piehler (2018); Piehler et al. (2015, 2016, 2019); Punjaisri et al. (2008); Punjaisri, Evanschitzky, et al. (2009); Punjaisri, Wilson, et al. (2009); Punjaisri and Wilson (2007, 2011); Sirianni et al. (2013); Vallaster and de Chernatony (2005, 2006); Xiong et al. (2013); Xiong and King (2019, 2020) |
| Brand commitment | Baumgarth and Schmidt (2010); Burmann, Jost-Benz, et al. (2009); Burmann, Zeplin, et al. (2009); Burmann and Zeplin (2005); de Chernatony et al. (2003, 2006); Dechawatanapaisal (2018); Du Preez et al. (2017); Du Preez and Bendixen (2015); Garas et al. (2018); Gelb and Rangarajan (2014); Kimpakorn and Tocquer (2009); King (2010); King et al. (2012); King and Grace (2008, 2010, 2012); Mahnert and Torres (2007); Morhart et al. (2009); Piehler (2018); Piehler et al. (2015, 2016, 2019); Punjaisri et al. (2008); Punjaisri, Evanschitzky, et al. (2009); Punjaisri, Wilson, et al. (2009); Punjaisri and Wilson (2007, 2011); Sharma and Kamalanabhan (2012); Terglav et al. (2016); Thomson et al. (1999); Vallaster and de Chernatony (2005, 2006); Xiong et al. (2013) |
| Brand identification | Dechawatanapaisal (2018); Helm et al. (2016); Hughes and Ahearne (2010); Ngo et al. (2019); Piehler et al. (2016); Punjaisri et al. (2008); Punjaisri, Evanschitzky, et al. (2009); Punjaisri, Wilson, et al. (2009); Punjaisri and Wilson (2007, 2011); Sharma and Kamalanabhan (2012); Vallaster and de Chernatony (2005) |
| Brand understanding | Baumgarth and Schmidt (2010); de Chernatony et al. (2006); de Chernatony and Cottam (2006); Gelb and Rangarajan (2014); Judson et al. (2006); Kimpakorn and Tocquer (2009); King et al. (2012); King (2010); King and Grace (2006, 2008, 2010); Löhndorf and Diamantopoulos (2014); Mahnert and Torres (2007); Mangold and Miles (2007); Miles et al. (2011); Miles and Mangold (2005, 2007); Murillo and King (2019); Ngo et al. (2019); Piehler (2018); Piehler et al. (2015, 2016, 2019); Punjaisri et al. (2008); Terglav et al. (2016); Thomson et al. (1999); Vallaster and de Chernatony (2005, 2006); Xiong et al. (2013); Xiong and King (2019) |

refers to the psychological attachment to a brand (Burmann & Zeplin, 2005); it is often conceptualized as an emotional attachment or affective commitment. Employees with psychological or emotional attachments to brands should strengthen them through their behaviour. Internal branding research has consistently validated this relationship (Burmann, Zeplin, et al., 2009; King & Grace, 2012; Piehler et al., 2016).

Brand identification represents an employee's sense of belonging to the brand (Punjaisri & Wilson, 2011). Employees who derive their identities from association with entities like brands should become more psychologically and emotionally attached to them. Also, social identity theory (Tajfel, 1982) proposes that employees who have a sense of belonging to brands are likely to engage in behaviours to strengthen those brands because they incorporate them into their self-concepts. Therefore, brand identification represents a basis for both brand commitment and brand-related employee behaviour (Hughes & Ahearne, 2010; Piehler et al., 2016; Punjaisri & Wilson, 2011).

Finally, brand understanding, also known as brand knowledge and knowledge of the desired brand image, represents an important cognitive internal branding objective. The literature has identified multiple dimensions of brand understanding (Piehler et al., 2016; Xiong et al., 2013). The first dimension is brand relevance, that is, employees' understanding that brands are important for their organizations' success, in that employees must perceive their brands as meaningful. The second dimension represents behaviour relevance, employees' realization that they contribute, with their behaviours, to their brands' perception and subsequent success. Brand knowledge, that is, employees' perceptions of what their brands represent, indicating they have sufficient knowledge of the brand identity and promise, is the third dimension. Finally, the fourth dimension represents brand confidence, that is, whether employees can confidently translate an abstract brand identity and brand promise into specific, brand-strengthening behaviours in their daily work. Internal branding studies repeatedly have delivered empirical evidence of the effect of brand understanding on brand identification, brand commitment, and brand-related employee behaviour (Ngo et al., 2019; Piehler et al., 2016; Xiong & King, 2019).

### 4.3 Internal branding activities: how does internal branding achieve its objectives?

To determine how to achieve the objectives of internal branding, internal branding literature has investigated managerial activities in four main areas (Barros-Arrieta & García-Cali, 2020; Piehler et al., 2018; Saleem & Iglesias, 2016): internal brand communications, external brand communications, brand-oriented human resource management, and brand-oriented leadership (Table 26.6).

Internal brand communications include all types of brand-related internal communications comprising internal mass communication tools (e.g., magazines, brand books, brochures, emails, newsletters, and intranet) and more personal and interactive tools (e.g., workshops, seminars, events, and supervisors). Internal brand communications help achieve building brand understanding (de Chernatony et al., 2006; Thomson et al., 1999), brand identification (Punjaisri & Wilson, 2011), brand commitment (Burmann, Zeplin, et al., 2009), and brand-related behaviour (Baker et al., 2014; Punjaisri & Wilson, 2011). When TUI, as one of the world's leading travel and tourism companies, implemented a new brand identity in its German business unit, it used mass communication tools, such as online newsletters, the staff magazine and the intranet, as well as an interactive workshop program consisting of 140 workshops to successfully build brand understanding and commitment among more than 1,500 employees in Germany. Internal branding literature has identified several success factors for internal brand communications to successfully achieve internal branding objectives (Burmann & Zeplin, 2005; Piehler et al., 2015; Punjaisri et al., 2008; Vallaster & de Chernatony, 2005). It should be integrated, multidirectional, interactive, personal, and characterised by high quality.

External brand communications comprising advertising, out of home media, digital communication, direct communication, public relations, sales promotions, fairs and exhibitions, event marketing, sponsoring, product placement, in-game advertising, and guerrilla marketing represent another powerful internal branding activity for achieving internal branding objectives. Although they aim primarily to build brand awareness and brand image among external stakeholders (such as customers) by communicating the brand identity and brand promise, internal stakeholders such as employees represent a critical 'second audience' (George & Berry, 1981,

*Table 26.6* Categories of internal branding activities and illustrative contributions

| Categories of internal branding activities | Illustrative contributions |
| --- | --- |
| Internal brand communications | Anees-ur-Rehman et al. (2018); Baker et al. (2014); Burmann, Zeplin, et al. (2009); Burmann and Zeplin (2005); Chong (2007); de Chernatony (1999, 2002); de Chernatony et al. (2006); Du Preez et al. (2017); Du Preez and Bendixen (2015); Garas et al. (2018); Gelb and Rangarajan (2014); Harris and de Chernatony (2001); Henkel et al. (2007); Judson et al. (2006, 2009); Kimpakorn and Tocquer (2009); King (2010); King and Grace (2005, 2006, 2008, 2010); Liu et al. (2017); Mahnert and Torres (2007); Mangold and Miles (2007); Miles et al. (2011); Miles and Mangold (2004, 2005, 2007); Piehler et al. (2015); Punjaisri et al. (2008); Punjaisri, Evanschitzky, et al. (2009); Punjaisri, Wilson, et al. (2009); Punjaisri and Wilson (2007, 2011); Sharma and Kamalanabhan (2012); Thomson et al. (1999); Vallaster and de Chernatony (2005) |
| External brand communications | Anees-ur-Rehman et al. (2018); Burmann and Zeplin (2005); de Chernatony et al. (2003, 2006); Du Preez et al. (2017); Du Preez and Bendixen (2015); Gelb and Rangarajan (2014); Henkel et al. (2007); Hughes (2013); Mahnert and Torres (2007); Mangold and Miles (2007); Miles et al. (2011); Miles and Mangold (2004, 2005, 2007); Piehler et al. (2015, 2019); Wentzel et al. (2010) |
| Brand-oriented human resource management | Anees-ur-Rehman et al. (2018); Aurand et al. (2005); Burmann, Zeplin, et al. (2009); Burmann and Zeplin (2005); Chang et al. (2012); Chong (2007); de Chernatony et al. (2006); de Chernatony (1999, 2002); de Chernatony et al. (2003); de Chernatony and Cottam (2006); Garas et al. (2018); Gelb and Rangarajan (2014); Helm et al. (2016); Kimpakorn and Tocquer (2009); King and Grace (2005, 2006, 2008, 2012); Liu et al. (2017); Mahnert and Torres (2007); Mangold and Miles (2007); Matanda and Ndubisi (2013); Miles et al. (2011); Miles and Mangold (2004, 2005, 2007); Murillo and King (2019); Piehler et al. (2015); Punjaisri et al. (2008); Punjaisri, Evanschitzky, et al. (2009); Punjaisri, Wilson, et al. (2009); Punjaisri and Wilson (2007, 2011); Sharma and Kamalanabhan (2012) |
| Brand-oriented leadership | Burmann, Zeplin, et al. (2009); Burmann and Zeplin (2005); de Chernatony et al. (2006); Gelb and Rangarajan (2014); Henkel et al. (2007); Kimpakorn and Tocquer (2009); King and Grace (2005, 2006, 2008); Mahnert and Torres (2007); Mangold and Miles (2007); Miles et al. (2011); Miles and Mangold (2004, 2005, 2007); Morhart et al. (2009); Murillo and King (2019); Piehler et al. (2015); Terglav et al. (2016); Vallaster and de Chernatony (2005) |

p. 52). Like internal brand communications, external brand communications can help to build brand understanding (Miles et al., 2011; Piehler et al., 2019), brand identification (Hughes, 2013), brand commitment (Piehler et al., 2019), and brand-related behaviour (Hughes, 2013; Piehler et al., 2019; Wentzel et al., 2010). Internal branding literature has identified several success factors for external brand communications to successfully achieve internal branding objectives (Gilly & Wolfinbarger, 1998; Wolfinbarger & Gilly, 1991; Piehler et al., 2019). It should ensure congruency of externally communicated brand benefits with actual brand benefits, congruency of externally communicated culture with actual culture, congruency of employees shown in external brand communications with actual employees and congruency of external brand communications with internal brand communications.

Brand-oriented human resource management ensures brand-oriented socialization of employees in all stages of their life cycles and helps achieve internal branding objectives. Internal brandings studies confirm its effect on brand understanding (de Chernatony et al., 2006; Miles et al., 2011), brand identification (Punjaisri & Wilson, 2011), brand commitment (Burmann, Zeplin, et al., 2009; Punjaisri & Wilson, 2011), and brand-related behaviour (Aurand et al., 2005; Punjaisri & Wilson, 2011). For each socialization stage, organizations can use specific brand-oriented human resource management practices (Aurand et al., 2005; Burmann & Zeplin, 2005; Miles et al., 2011; Punjaisri, Evanschitzky, et al., 2009). Before employees join, organizations can engage in brand-oriented personnel recruitment and selection practices. Exemplary practices in this anticipatory socialization stage include brand-oriented job advertisements, job interviews, and personnel selection. Organizations can communicate their brands and their brand identities to prospective employees in the recruitment process and select employees whose personal identities are congruent with those identities, with the recognition that it is more difficult to change employees' identities than to develop their job skills. Southwest Airlines has shaped this 'hire for attitude, train for skill' approach becoming one of the largest airlines in the world (Taylor, 2011). Once employees join, organizations can engage in brand-oriented induction practices. An exemplary practice in this encounter (i.e., entry) stage is brand-oriented orientation through training and events. Companies from many industries (e.g., Ritz-Carlton from the hospitality sector) start their onboarding processes by communicating their brand identity, values, or culture to new employees before engaging in job-specific training. Through these practices, organizations can build employee brand understanding and increase their brand identification with, and commitment to, the brands. In the metamorphosis stage, organizations can engage in brand-oriented personnel development practices and brand-oriented reward and remuneration practices. Exemplary practices include conducting brand-oriented coaching and mentoring to encourage development, as well as establishing brand-oriented personnel evaluation, promotion, and dismissal criteria for reward and remuneration. The German BMW Group has been educating its employees and partners within the BMW Group dealer organization since 2002 in the BMW Group Brand Academy and later in the BMW Group Brand and Customer Institute. In addition to increasing brand orientation through exercises and active discussions of practical examples, visitors learn about the group's brands in dedicated BMW, MINI, and Rolls-Royce brand worlds (BMW Group, 2005) and thus build brand knowledge and develop brand identification and commitment.

Brand-oriented leadership represents the fourth category of internal branding activities. By drawing on leadership concepts from organizational behaviour research, internal branding literature has investigated the effect of specific leadership styles on employees. In this context, transactional and transformational leadership styles have gained particular attention. Brand-oriented transactional leadership comprises leadership behaviours based on social exchange processes (Burmann & Zeplin, 2005). Leaders define not only behavioural standards for employees' roles as brand representatives but also undesired behaviours; they reward employees when expectations are met or punish them for not following specified standards (Morhart et al., 2009). In contrast, brand-oriented transformational leadership aims to transform employees' value systems and aspirations; it induces them to transcend self-interest for the sake of their brands (Burmann & Zeplin, 2005). Leaders motivate employees to act on behalf of brands by appealing to their values and personal convictions (Morhart et al., 2009). Empirical internal branding studies particularly confirm the effect of brand-oriented transformational leadership on brand understanding (Boukis & Christodoulides, 2020; Miles et al., 2011; Terglav et al., 2016), brand commitment (Burmann,

Zeplin, et al., 2009), and brand-related behaviour (Morhart et al., 2009). Internal branding literature suggests several specific leadership behaviours in this context. Successful transformational leaders act as role models and 'live' their corporate brands, articulate brand visions, and arouse employees' involvement and pride in brands, encourage employees to rethink their jobs from a branding perspective, and support them in interpreting brand promises and resulting implications for their daily work, as well as teach and coach employees to become brand representatives (Burmann & Zeplin, 2005; Morhart et al., 2009; Vallaster & de Chernatony, 2005).

## 4.4 Internal branding moderators: which situational factors affect the success of internal branding?

With regards to the moderators of the relationships between internal branding activities and objectives or among internal branding objectives, internal branding literature has investigated three levels of moderators: personal, organizational, and societal (Table 26.7).

The suggested personal variables include employee know-how/skills and demographic variables such as age, education, and length of service. Without necessary know-how/skills, employees cannot translate their brand understanding, identification, or commitment into brand-related behaviour. The results for demographic variables are mixed. Moreover, an organization only has limited control over them.

In contrast, considering organizational variables seems more promising from this perspective. As the alignment of employee attitudes or behaviours with the brand does not occur in a vacuum, identifying organizational internal branding moderators is essential as these variables might strengthen or weaken employees' ability to exhibit brand-aligned behaviour. Numerous organizational variables have been suggested in the literature: available resources, culture or culture fit, structure fit, process fit or systems and procedures, inter-functional communications, and the work environment, which includes relationships with colleagues and leaders, remuneration schemes, and perceived autonomy. However, many moderation hypotheses could not be empirically confirmed (Burmann, Zeplin, et al., 2009; Liu et al., 2017). Only Punjaisri and Wilson (2011) revealed a positive effect of employees' satisfaction with their work environment on the relationship between internal branding activities and objectives. Therefore, further research into boundary conditions regarding organizational variables is needed.

As an example of broader societal variables, Vallaster and de Chernatony (2005) raise the issue of culture with its influence on communicative, cognitive, and affective processes in the context of creating a shared brand understanding in the multicultural environment of international companies. They confirm that adequate knowledge of culture and its impact on the brand-building process are necessary to enable employees' brand-supporting behaviour.

*Table 26.7* Categories of internal branding moderators and illustrative contributions

| Categories of internal branding moderators | Illustrative contributions |
| --- | --- |
| Personal variables | Burmann, Zeplin, et al. (2009); Burmann and Zeplin (2005); Piehler et al. (2015); Punjaisri et al. (2008); Punjaisri and Wilson (2011) |
| Organizational variables | Burmann, Zeplin, et al. (2009); Burmann and Zeplin (2005); King and Grace (2005, 2006); Liu et al. (2017); Mahnert and Torres (2007); Piehler et al. (2015); Punjaisri et al. (2008); Punjaisri and Wilson (2011) |
| Societal variables | Vallaster and de Chernatony (2005) |

*Table 26.8* Internal branding antecedents and illustrative contributions

| Internal branding antecedents | Illustrative contributions |
| --- | --- |
| Brand orientation/ brand climate/ strategic branding | Anees-ur-Rehman et al. (2018); Baumgarth and Schmidt (2010); Iyer et al. (2018); King et al. (2013); Liu et al. (2017); Xiong and King (2020) |
| Market orientation | King and Grace (2006) |
| Relationship orientation | King and Grace (2010, 2012); Xiong and King (2019) |

## 4.5 Internal branding antecedents: what are the general prerequisites of internal branding?

Internal branding antecedents relate to more general aspects, such as orientations, that determine whether internal branding is considered in brand management or whether organizations engage in internal branding activities. Among the investigated antecedents are brand orientation (brand climate, strategic branding), market orientation, and relationship orientation (Table 26.8).

Brand orientation (i.e., 'a specific type of strategic orientation or corporate culture, characterized by high relevance of the brand as the basis of the business model,' Baumgarth & Schmidt, 2010, p. 1252), brand climate (i.e., 'employees' shared perceptions of the organization's emphasis, expectation, support, and rewards with respect to their brand-aligned performance that contributes to brand success,' Xiong & King, 2020, p. 575), and strategic branding (i.e., 'a process aimed at medium- to long- term maintenance of brands,' Iyer et al., 2018, p. 205) should result in companies engaging in internal branding activities, thus achieving internal branding objectives. Several empirical studies find evidence for the effects of brand orientation, brand climate, and strategic branding on internal branding activities and objectives (Table 26.8). Moreover, market orientation that involves putting the customer at the centre of all activities of the organization and relationship orientation as the extent to which organizations engage in positive behaviours towards employees have been identified as internal branding antecedents (Table 26.8). These orientations represent an organization's external and internal perspective, respectively. Therefore, organizations with a strong brand, market, and relationship orientation are more likely to engage in internal branding successfully.

## 5. Conclusion

As a management concept focusing on employees, internal branding represents an essential part of successful brand management. Many empirical studies have confirmed its positive effects on important customer-related and organization-related consequences. Within the 20 years of its existence, both practitioners and academics have advanced the field and built an extensive body of knowledge comprising internal branding antecedents, activities, objectives, moderators, and consequences. Figure 26.2 gives an overview of internal branding research findings regarding the internal branding elements. Based on prior research, the earlier presented definition of internal branding can be expanded:

> The concept comprises internal branding activities (e.g., internal and external brand communication, brand-oriented human resource management, brand-oriented leadership), internal branding objectives (e.g., brand-related behaviour, brand commitment, brand identification, brand understanding) and internal branding moderators (e.g., personal, organisational and societal variables). It is affected by internal branding

*Branding inside-out*

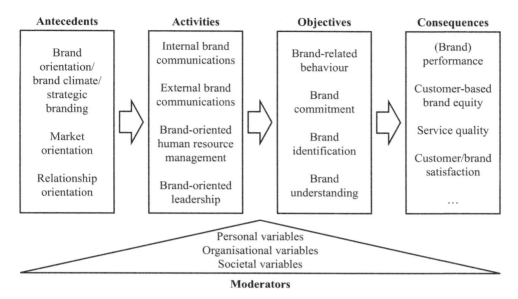

*Figure 26.2* Overview of internal branding elements

antecedents (e.g., brand orientation/brand climate/strategic branding, market orientation, relationship orientation) and results in internal branding consequences (e.g., brand performance, customer-based brand equity, service quality, customer/brand satisfaction).

While first attempts to consolidate the fragmented body of knowledge have been made with literature reviews and special issues, several directions for further research have been identified (Barros-Arrieta & García-Cali, 2020; Piehler et al., 2018; Saleem & Iglesias, 2016). They include investigations in other sectors than the service sector (e.g., B2B, public sector), using other methods, research designs, and data sources (e.g., longitudinal designs to validate causal relationships, experimental designs to investigate the effects of specific internal branding activities on internal branding objectives, multiple data sources), examining the effects of internal branding on other external stakeholders than customers (e.g., suppliers, distribution partners, shareholders, investors, NGOs, regulators, policymakers, journalists, the general public), building knowledge about moderators (e.g., organizational variables that support employees in building brand understanding, identification, and commitment, and delivering on the brand promise through their behaviour) and extending the framework to companies with multiple brands at different levels. More recent developments that have the potential to change the perspective of internal branding research and practice include integrating the co-creation perspective into corporate branding. It means considering the co-creation approach not only in relation to external stakeholders but also internal stakeholders within the organization (see the chapter 'A co-creative perspective on internal branding' by Holger J. Schmidt and Pieter Steenkamp in this section for details). Overall, it is expected that the field will continue to grow with contributions from both academics and practitioners, leading to knowledge generation and helping organizations to leverage one of their most important resources for building strong corporate brands – their employees.

# References

Aaker, D. A. (1991). *Managing brand equity: Capitalizing on the value of a brand name*. New York: The Free Press.

Aaker, D. A. (1996). *Building strong brands*. New York: Free Press.

Ambler, T., & Barrow, S. (1996). The employer brand. *Journal of Brand Management, 4*(3), 185–206. https://doi.org/10.1057/bm.1996.42

Anees-ur-Rehman, M., Wong, H. Y., Sultan, P., & Merrilees, B. (2018). How brand-oriented strategy affects the financial performance of B2B SMEs. *Journal of Business & Industrial Marketing, 33*(3), 303–315. https://doi.org/10.1108/JBIM-10-2016-0237

Aurand, T. W., Gorchels, L., & Bishop, T. R. (2005). Human resource management's role in internal branding: An opportunity for cross-functional brand message synergy. *Journal of Product & Brand Management, 14*(3), 163–169. https://doi.org/10.1108/10610420510601030

Baker, T. L., Rapp, A., Meyer, T., & Mullins, R. (2014). The role of brand communications on front line service employee beliefs, behaviors, and performance. *Journal of the Academy of Marketing Science, 42*(6), 642–657. https://doi.org/10.1007/s11747-014-0376-7

Balmer, J. M. T. (1995). Corporate branding and connoisseurship. *Journal of General Management, 21*(1), 24–46. https://doi.org/10.1177/030630709502100102

Balmer, J. M. T. (1998). Corporate identity and the advent of corporate marketing. *Journal of Marketing Management, 14*(8), 963–996. https://doi.org/10.1362/026725798784867536

Balmer, J. M. T. (2001). Corporate identity, corporate branding and corporate marketing – Seeing through the fog. *European Journal of Marketing, 35*(3–4), 248–291. https://doi.org/10.1108/03090560110694763

Balmer, J. M. T., & Gray, E. R. (2003). Corporate brands: What are they? What of them? *European Journal of Marketing, 37*(7–8), 972–997. https://doi.org/10.1108/03090560310477627

Bandura, A. (1977). *Social learning theory*. Englewood Cliffs, NJ: Prentice Hall.

Barros-Arrieta, D., & García-Cali, E. (2020). Internal branding: Conceptualization from a literature review and opportunities for future research. *Journal of Brand Management*, 1–19. https://doi.org/10.1057/s41262-020-00219-1

Baumgarth, C., & Schmidt, M. (2010). How strong is the business-to-business brand in the workforce? An empirically-tested model of 'internal brand equity' in a business-to-business setting. *Industrial Marketing Management, 39*(8), 1250–1260. https://doi.org/10.1016/j.indmarman.2010.02.022

Bergstrom, A., Blumenthal, D., & Crothers, S. (2002). Why internal branding matters: The case of Saab. *Corporate Reputation Review, 5*(2–3), 133–142. https://doi.org/10.1057/palgrave.crr.1540170

Berry, L. L. (1995). Relationship marketing of services – Growing interest, emerging perspectives. *Journal of the Academy of Marketing Science, 23*(4), 236–245. https://doi.org/10.1177/009207039502300402

Berry, L. L. (2000). Cultivating service brand equity. *Journal of the Academy of Marketing Science, 28*(1), 128–137. https://doi.org/10.1177/0092070300281012

Berry, L. L., & Parasuraman, A. (1993). Building a new academic field – The case of services marketing. *Journal of Retailing, 69*(1), 13–60. https://doi.org/10.1016/S0022-4359(05)80003-X

BMW Group. (2005, December 1). *BMW Group presents its brand academy*. Retrieved from www.press.bmwgroup.com/latin-america-caribbean/article/detail/T0050598EN/bmw-group-presents-its-brand-academy?language=en

Boukis, A., & Christodoulides, G. (2020). Investigating key antecedents and outcomes of employee-based brand equity. *European Management Review, 17*(1), 41–55. https://doi.org/10.1111/emre.12327

Burmann, C., Hegner, S., & Riley, N. (2009). Towards an identity-based branding. *Marketing Theory, 9*(1), 113–118. https://doi.org/10.1177/1470593108100065

Burmann, C., Jost-Benz, M., & Riley, N. (2009). Towards an identity-based brand equity model. *Journal of Business Research, 62*(3), 390–397. https://doi.org/10.1016/j.jbusres.2008.06.009

Burmann, C., & Zeplin, S. (2005). Building brand commitment: A behavioural approach to internal brand management. *Journal of Brand Management, 12*(4), 279–300. https://doi.org/10.1057/palgrave.bm.2540223

Burmann, C., Zeplin, S., & Riley, N. (2009). Key determinants of internal brand management success: An exploratory empirical analysis. *Journal of Brand Management, 16*(4), 264–284. https://doi.org/10.1057/bm.2008.6

Chang, A., Chiang, H., & Han, T. (2012). A multilevel investigation of relationships among brand-centered HRM, brand psychological ownership, brand citizenship behaviors, and customer satisfaction. *European Journal of Marketing, 46*(5), 626–662. https://doi.org/10.1108/03090561211212458

Chong, M. (2007). The role of internal communication and training in infusing corporate values and delivering brand promise: Singapore Airlines' experience. *Corporate Reputation Review*, *10*(3), 201–212. https://doi.org/10.1057/palgrave.crr.1550051

de Chernatony, L. (1999). Brand management through narrowing the gap between brand identity and brand reputation. *Journal of Marketing Management*, *15*(1–3), 157–179. https://doi.org/10.1362/026725799784870432

de Chernatony, L. (2002). Would a brand smell any sweeter by a corporate name? *Corporate Reputation Review*, *5*(2–3), 114–132. https://doi.org/10.1057/palgrave.crr.1540169

de Chernatony, L., & Cottam, S. (2006). Internal brand factors driving successful financial services brands. *European Journal of Marketing*, *40*(5–6), 611–633. https://doi.org/10.1108/03090560610657868

de Chernatony, L., Cottam, S., & Segal-Horn, S. (2006). Communicating services brands' values internally and externally. *The Service Industries Journal*, *26*(8), 819–836. https://doi.org/10.1080/02642060601011616

de Chernatony, L., & Dall'Olmo Riley, F. (1999). Experts' views about defining services brands and the principles of services branding. *Journal of Business Research*, *46*(2), 181–192. https://doi.org/10.1016/S0148-2963(98)00021-6

de Chernatony, L., Drury, S., & Segal-Horn, S. (2003). Building a services brand: Stages, people and orientations. *The Service Industries Journal*, *23*(3), 1–21. https://doi.org/10.1080/714005116

Dean, D., Arroyo-Gamez, R. E., Punjaisri, K., & Pich, C. (2016). Internal brand co-creation: The experiential brand meaning cycle in higher education. *Journal of Business Research*, *69*(8), 3041–3048. https://doi.org/10.1016/j.jbusres.2016.01.019

Dechawatanapaisal, D. (2018). Employee retention: The effects of internal branding and brand attitudes in sales organizations. *Personnel Review*, *47*(3), 675–693. https://doi.org/10.1108/PR-06-2017-0193

Du Preez, R., & Bendixen, M. T. (2015). The impact of internal brand management on employee job satisfaction, brand commitment and intention to stay. *International Journal of Bank Marketing*, *33*(1), 78–91. https://doi.org/10.1108/IJBM-02-2014-0031

Du Preez, R., Bendixen, M. T., & Abratt, R. (2017). The behavioral consequences of internal brand management among frontline employees. *Journal of Product & Brand Management*, *26*(3), 251–261. https://doi.org/10.1108/JPBM-09-2016-1325

Erkmen, E., & Hancer, M. (2015). "Do your internal branding efforts measure up?" Consumers' response to brand supporting behaviors of hospitality employees. *International Journal of Contemporary Hospitality Management*, *27*(5), 878–895. https://doi.org/10.1108/IJCHM-10-2013-0442

Foster, C., Punjaisri, K., & Cheng, R. (2010). Exploring the relationship between corporate, internal and employer branding. *Journal of Product & Brand Management*, *19*(6), 401–409. https://doi.org/10.1108/10610421011085712

Garas, S. R. R., Mahran, A. F. A., & Mohamed, H. M. H. (2018). Internal corporate branding impact on employees' brand supporting behaviour. *Journal of Product & Brand Management*, *27*(1), 79–95. https://doi.org/10.1108/JPBM-03-2016-1112

Gelb, B. D., & Rangarajan, D. (2014). Employee contributions to brand equity. *California Management Review*, *56*(2), 95–112. https://doi.org/10.1525/cmr.2014.56.2.95

George, W. R. (1990). Internal marketing and organizational behavior: A partnership in developing customer-conscious employees at every level. *Journal of Business Research*, *20*(1), 63–70. https://doi.org/10.1016/0148-2963(90)90043-D

George, W. R., & Berry, L. L. (1981). Guidelines for the advertising of services. *Business Horizons*, *24*(4), 52–56. https://doi.org/10.1016/0007-6813(81)90056-2

Gilly, M. C., & Wolfinbarger, M. F. (1998). Advertising's internal audience. *Journal of Marketing*, *62*(1), 69–88. https://doi.org/10.1177/002224299806200107

Grönroos, C. (1984). A service quality model and its marketing implications. *European Journal of Marketing*, *18*(4), 36–44. https://doi.org/10.1108/EUM0000000004784

Gronroos, C. (1990). Relationship approach to marketing in service contexts: The marketing and organizational behavior interface. *Journal of Business Research*, *20*(1), 3–11. https://doi.org/10.1016/0148-2963(90)90037-E

Harris, F., & de Chernatony, L. (2001). Corporate branding and corporate brand performance. *European Journal of Marketing*, *35*(3–4), 441–456. https://doi.org/10.1108/03090560110382101

Hatch, M. J., & Schultz, M. (2003). Bringing the corporation into corporate branding. *European Journal of Marketing*, *37*(7–8), 1041–1064. https://doi.org/10.1108/03090560310477654

Hatch, M. J., & Schultz, M. (2010). Toward a theory of brand co-creation with implications for brand governance. *Journal of Brand Management*, *17*(8), 590–604. https://doi.org/10.1057/bm.2010.14

Helm, S. V., Renk, U., & Mishra, A. (2016). Exploring the impact of employees' self-concept, brand identification and brand pride on brand citizenship behaviors. *European Journal of Marketing, 50*(1–2), 58–77. https://doi.org/10.1108/EJM-03-2014-0162

Henkel, S., Tomczak, T., Heitmann, M., & Herrmann, A. (2007). Managing brand consistent employee behaviour: Relevance and managerial control of behavioural branding. *Journal of Product & Brand Management, 16*(5), 310–320. https://doi.org/10.1108/10610420710779609

Hughes, D. E. (2013). This ad's for you: The indirect effect of advertising perceptions on salesperson effort and performance. *Journal of the Academy of Marketing Science, 41*(1), 1–18. https://doi.org/10.1007/s11747-011-0293-y

Hughes, D. E., & Ahearne, M. (2010). Energizing the reseller's sales force: The power of brand identification. *Journal of Marketing, 74*(4), 81–96. https://doi.org/10.1509/jmkg.74.4.81

Ind, N. (1997). The corporate brand. In *The corporate brand*. Palgrave Macmillan. https://doi.org/10.1057/9780230375888

Ind, N. (2001). *Living the brand: How to transform every member of your organization into a brand champion*. London: Kogan Page.

Ind, N. (2003). Inside out: How employees build value. *Journal of Brand Management, 10*(6), 393–402. https://doi.org/10.1057/palgrave.bm.2540136

Iglesias, O., & Ind, N. (2020). Towards a theory of conscientious corporate brand co-creation: The next key challenge in brand management. *Journal of Brand Management, 27*(6), 710–720. https://doi.org/10.1057/s41262-020-00205-7

Iyer, P., Davari, A., & Paswan, A. (2018). Determinants of brand performance: The role of internal branding. *Journal of Brand Management, 25*(3), 202–216. https://doi.org/10.1057/s41262-018-0097-1

Judson, K. M., Aurand, T. W., Gorchels, L., & Gordon, G. L. (2009). Building a university brand from within: University administrators' perspectives of internal branding. *Services Marketing Quarterly, 30*(1), 54–68. https://doi.org/10.1080/15332960802467722

Judson, K. M., Gorchels, L., & Aurand, T. W. (2006). Building a university brand from within: A comparison of coaches' perspectives of internal branding. *Journal of Marketing for Higher Education, 16*(1), 97–114. https://doi.org/10.1300/J050v16n01_05

Kahn, R. L., Wolfe, D. M., Quinn, R. P., Snoek, J. D., & Rosenthal, R. A. (1964). *Organizational stress: Studies in role conflict and ambiguity*. New York: Wiley.

Kapferer, J.-N. (1997). *Strategic brand management*. London: Kogan Page.

Kaufmann, H. R., Loureiro, S. M. C., & Manarioti, A. (2016). Exploring behavioural branding, brand love and brand co-creation. *Journal of Product & Brand Management, 25*(6), 516–526. https://doi.org/10.1108/JPBM-06-2015-0919

Keller, K. L. (1993). Conceptualizing, measuring, and managing customer-based brand equity. *Journal of Marketing, 57*(1), 1–22. https://doi.org/10.2307/1252054

Kimpakorn, N., & Tocquer, G. (2009). Employees' commitment to brands in the service sector: Luxury hotel chains in Thailand. *Journal of Brand Management, 16*(8), 532–544. https://doi.org/10.1057/palgrave.bm.2550140

King, C. (2010). "One size doesn't fit all." *International Journal of Contemporary Hospitality Management, 22*(4), 517–534. https://doi.org/10.1108/09596111011042721

King, C., & Grace, D. (2005). Exploring the role of employees in the delivery of the brand: A case study approach. *Qualitative Market Research: An International Journal, 8*(3), 277–295. https://doi.org/10.1108/13522750510603343

King, C., & Grace, D. (2006). Exploring managers' perspectives of the impact of brand management strategies on employee roles within a service firm. *Journal of Services Marketing, 20*(6), 369–380. https://doi.org/10.1108/08876040610691266

King, C., & Grace, D. (2008). Internal branding: Exploring the employee's perspective. *Journal of Brand Management, 15*(5), 358–372. https://doi.org/10.1057/palgrave.bm.2550136

King, C., & Grace, D. (2010). Building and measuring employee-based brand equity. *European Journal of Marketing, 44*(7–8), 938–971. https://doi.org/10.1108/03090561011047472

King, C., & Grace, D. (2012). Examining the antecedents of positive employee brand-related attitudes and behaviours. *European Journal of Marketing, 46*(3–4), 469–488. https://doi.org/10.1108/03090561211202567

King, C., Grace, D., & Funk, D. C. (2012). Employee brand equity: Scale development and validation. *Journal of Brand Management, 19*(4), 268–288. https://doi.org/10.1057/bm.2011.44

King, C., So, K. K. F., & Grace, D. (2013). The influence of service brand orientation on hotel employees' attitude and behaviors in China. *International Journal of Hospitality Management, 34*, 172–180. https://doi.org/10.1016/j.ijhm.2013.03.004

Liu, G., Ko, W. W., & Chapleo, C. (2017). Managing employee attention and internal branding. *Journal of Business Research, 79*, 1–11. https://doi.org/10.1016/j.jbusres.2017.05.021

Löhndorf, B., & Diamantopoulos, A. (2014). Internal branding: Social identity and social exchange perspectives on turning employees into brand champions. *Journal of Service Research, 17*(3), 310–325. https://doi.org/10.1177/1094670514522098

Mahnert, K. F., & Torres, A. M. (2007). The brand inside: The factors of failure and success in internal branding. *Irish Marketing Review, 19*(1–2), 54–63.

Mangold, W. G., & Miles, S. J. (2007). The employee brand: Is yours an all-star? *Business Horizons, 50*(5), 423–433. https://doi.org/10.1016/j.bushor.2007.06.001

Matanda, M. J., & Ndubisi, N. O. (2013). Internal marketing, internal branding, and organisational outcomes: The moderating role of perceived goal congruence. *Journal of Marketing Management, 29*(9–10), 1030–1055. https://doi.org/10.1080/0267257X.2013.800902

Mellor, V. (1999). Delivering brand values through people. *Strategic Communication Management, 5*(2), 26–29.

Miles, S. J., & Mangold, W. G. (2004). A conceptualization of the employee branding process. *Journal of Relationship Marketing, 3*(2–3), 65–87. https://doi.org/10.1300/J366v03n02_05

Miles, S. J., & Mangold, W. G. (2005). Positioning Southwest Airlines through employee branding. *Business Horizons, 48*(6), 535–545. https://doi.org/10.1016/j.bushor.2005.04.010

Miles, S. J., & Mangold, W. G. (2007). Growing the employee brand at ASI. *Journal of Leadership & Organizational Studies, 14*(1), 77–85. https://doi.org/10.1177/1071791907304287

Miles, S. J., Mangold, W. G., Asree, S., & Revell, J. (2011). Assessing the employee brand: A census of one company. *Journal of Managerial Issues, 23*(4), 491–507.

Mitchell, C. (2002). Selling the brand inside. *Harvard Business Review, 80*(1), 99–105.

Morgan, R. M., & Hunt, S. D. (1994). The commitment-trust theory of relationship marketing. *Journal of Marketing, 58*(3), 20–38. https://doi.org/10.1177/002224299405800302

Morhart, F. M., Herzog, W., & Tomczak, T. (2009). Brand-specific leadership: Turning employees into brand champions. *Journal of Marketing, 73*(5), 122–142. https://doi.org/10.1509/jmkg.73.5.122

Moroko, L., & Uncles, M. D. (2008). Characteristics of successful employer brands. *Journal of Brand Management, 16*(3), 160–175. https://doi.org/10.1057/bm.2008.4

Murillo, E., & King, C. (2019). Examining the drivers of employee brand understanding: A longitudinal study. *Journal of Product & Brand Management, 28*(7), 893–907. https://doi.org/10.1108/JPBM-09-2018-2007

Ngo, L. V., Nguyen, N. P., Huynh, K. T., Gregory, G., & Cuong, P. H. (2019). Converting internal brand knowledge into employee performance. *Journal of Product & Brand Management, 29*(3), 273–287. https://doi.org/10.1108/JPBM-10-2018-2068

Piehler, R. (2018). Employees' brand understanding, brand commitment, and brand citizenship behaviour: A closer look at the relationships among construct dimensions. *Journal of Brand Management, 25*(3), 217–234. https://doi.org/10.1057/s41262-018-0099-z

Piehler, R., Grace, D., & Burmann, C. (2018). Internal brand management: Introduction to the special issue and directions for future research. *Journal of Brand Management, 25*(3), 197–201. https://doi.org/10.1057/s41262-018-0096-2

Piehler, R., Hanisch, S., & Burmann, C. (2015). Internal branding – Relevance, management and challenges. *Marketing Review St. Gallen, 32*(1), 52–61. https://doi.org/10.1007/s11621-015-0506-8

Piehler, R., King, C., Burmann, C., & Xiong, L. (2016). The importance of employee brand understanding, brand identification, and brand commitment in realizing brand citizenship behaviour. *European Journal of Marketing, 50*(9–10), 1575–1601. https://doi.org/10.1108/EJM-11-2014-0725

Piehler, R., Schade, M., & Burmann, C. (2019). Employees as a second audience: The effect of external communication on internal brand management outcomes. *Journal of Brand Management, 26*(4), 445–460. https://doi.org/10.1057/s41262-018-0135-z

Porricelli, M. S., Yurova, Y., Abratt, R., & Bendixen, M. (2014). Antecedents of brand citizenship behavior in retailing. *Journal of Retailing and Consumer Services, 21*(5), 745–752.

Prahalad, C. K., & Hamel, G. (1990). The core competence of the corporation. *Harvard Business Review, 68*(3), 79–91.

Prahalad, C. K., & Ramaswamy, V. (2004). *The future of competition: Co-creating unique value with customers.* Boston, MA: Harvard Business School Press.

Punjaisri, K., Evanschitzky, H., & Wilson, A. (2009). Internal branding: An enabler of employees' brand-supporting behaviours. *Journal of Service Management,* 20(2), 209–226. https://doi.org/10.1108/09564230910952780

Punjaisri, K., & Wilson, A. (2007). The role of internal branding in the delivery of employee brand promise. *Journal of Brand Management,* 15(1), 57–70. https://doi.org/10.1057/palgrave.bm.2550110

Punjaisri, K., & Wilson, A. (2011). Internal branding process: Key mechanisms, outcomes and moderating factors. *European Journal of Marketing,* 45(9–10), 1521–1537. https://doi.org/10.1108/03090561111151871

Punjaisri, K., Wilson, A., & Evanschitzky, H. (2008). Exploring the influences of internal branding on employees' brand promise delivery: Implications for strengthening customer – brand relationships. *Journal of Relationship Marketing,* 7(4), 407–424. https://doi.org/10.1080/15332660802508430

Punjaisri, K., Wilson, A., & Evanschitzky, H. (2009). Internal branding to influence employees' brand promise delivery: A case study in Thailand. *Journal of Service Management,* 20(5), 561–579. https://doi.org/10.1108/09564230910995143

Rafiq, M., & Ahmed, P. K. (2000). Advances in the internal marketing concept: Definition, synthesis and extension. *Journal of Services Marketing,* 14(6), 449–462. https://doi.org/10.1108/08876040010347589

Raj Devasagayam, P., Buff, C. L., Aurand, T. W., & Judson, K. M. (2010). Building brand community membership within organizations: A viable internal branding alternative? *Journal of Product & Brand Management,* 19(3), 210–217. https://doi.org/10.1108/10610421011046184

Saleem, F. Z., & Iglesias, O. (2016). Mapping the domain of the fragmented field of internal branding. *Journal of Product & Brand Management,* 25(1), 43–57. https://doi.org/10.1108/JPBM-11-2014-0751

Schmidt, H. J., & Baumgarth, C. (2018). Strengthening internal brand equity with brand ambassador programs: Development and testing of a success factor model. *Journal of Brand Management,* 25(3), 250–265. https://doi.org/10.1057/s41262-018-0101-9

Sharma, N., & Kamalanabhan, T. J. (2012). Internal corporate communication and its impact on internal branding. *Corporate Communications: An International Journal,* 17(3), 300–322. https://doi.org/10.1108/13563281211253548

Sirianni, N. J., Bitner, M. J., Brown, S. W., & Mandel, N. (2013). Branded service encounters: Strategically aligning employee behavior with the brand positioning. *Journal of Marketing,* 77(6), 108–123. https://doi.org/10.1509/jm.11.0485

Taylor, B. (2011, February 1). *Hire for attitude, train for skill.* Harvard Business Review. Retrieved from https://hbr.org/2011/02/hire-for-attitude-train-for-sk.

Tajfel, H. (1982). Social psychology of intergroup relations. *Annual Review of Psychology,* 33(1), 1–39. https://doi.org/10.1146/annurev.ps.33.020182.000245

Terglav, K., Konečnik Ruzzier, M., & Kaše, R. (2016). Internal branding process: Exploring the role of mediators in top management's leadership – Commitment relationship. *International Journal of Hospitality Management,* 54, 1–11. https://doi.org/10.1016/j.ijhm.2015.12.007

Thomson, K., De Chernatony, L., Arganbright, L., & Khan, S. (1999). The buy-in benchmark: How staff understanding and commitment impact brand and business performance. *Journal of Marketing Management,* 15(8), 819–835. https://doi.org/10.1362/026725799784772684

Tomczak, T., Esch, F.-R., Kernstock, J., & Herrmann, A. (Eds.). (2012). *Behavioral branding.* Gabler. https://doi.org/10.1007/978-3-8349-7134-0

Tuominen, S., Hirvonen, S., Reijonen, H., & Laukkanen, T. (2016). The internal branding process and financial performance in service companies: An examination of the required steps. *Journal of Brand Management,* 23(3), 306–326. https://doi.org/10.1057/bm.2016.9

Urde, M. (1994). Brand orientation – A strategy for survival. *Journal of Consumer Marketing,* 11(3), 18–32. https://doi.org/10.1108/07363769410065445

Urde, M. (1999). Brand orientation: A mindset for building brands into strategic resources. *Journal of Marketing Management,* 15(1–3), 117–133. https://doi.org/10.1362/026725799784870504

Vallaster, C., & de Chernatony, L. (2005). Internationalisation of services brands: The role of leadership during the internal brand building process. *Journal of Marketing Management,* 21(1–2), 181–203. https://doi.org/10.1362/0267257053166839

Vallaster, C., & de Chernatony, L. (2006). Internal brand building and structuration: The role of leadership. *European Journal of Marketing,* 40(7–8), 761–784. https://doi.org/10.1108/03090560610669982

van Riel, C. B. M., & Balmer, J. M. T. (1997). Corporate identity: The concept, its measurement and management. *European Journal of Marketing,* 31(5–6), 340–355. https://doi.org/10.1108/eb060635

Vargo, S. L., & Lusch, R. F. (2004). Evolving to a new dominant logic for marketing. *Journal of Marketing*, *68*(1), 1–17. https://doi.org/10.1509/jmkg.68.1.1.24036

Vargo, S. L., & Lusch, R. F. (2016). Institutions and axioms: An extension and update of Service-Dominant Logic. *Journal of the Academy of Marketing Science*, *44*(1), 5–23. https://doi.org/10.1007/s11747-015-0456-3

Wentzel, D., Henkel, S., & Tomczak, T. (2010). Can I live up to that ad? Impact of implicit theories of ability on service employees' responses to advertising. *Journal of Service Research*, *13*(2), 137–152. https://doi.org/10.1177/1094670510363304

Wernerfelt, B. (1984). A resource-based view of the firm. *Strategic Management Journal*, *5*(2), 171–180. https://doi.org/10.1002/smj.4250050207

Wolfinbarger, M. F., & Gilly, M. C. (1991). A conceptual model of the impact of advertising on service employees. *Psychology and Marketing*, *8*(3), 215–237. https://doi.org/10.1002/mar.4220080306

Xiong, L., & King, C. (2019). Aligning employees' attitudes and behavior with hospitality brands: The role of employee brand internalization. *Journal of Hospitality and Tourism Management*, *40*, 67–76. https://doi.org/10.1016/j.jhtm.2019.06.006

Xiong, L., & King, C. (2020). Exploring how employee sense of brand community affects their attitudes and behavior. *Journal of Hospitality & Tourism Research*, *44*(4), 567–596. https://doi.org/10.1177/1096348020905360

Xiong, L., King, C., & Piehler, R. (2013). "That's not my job": Exploring the employee perspective in the development of brand ambassadors. *International Journal of Hospitality Management*, *35*, 348–359. https://doi.org/10.1016/j.ijhm.2013.07.009

Zeithaml, V. A., Berry, L. L., & Parasuraman, A. (1996). The behavioral consequences of service quality. *Journal of Marketing*, *60*(2), 31–46. https://doi.org/10.1177/002224299606000203

Zucker, R. (2002). More than a name change – Internal branding at Pearl. *Strategic Communication Management*, *6*(4), 4–7.

# 27
# A CO-CREATIVE PERSPECTIVE ON INTERNAL BRANDING

*Holger J. Schmidt and Pieter Steenkamp*

## 1. Importance and challenges of internal branding

### 1.1 The role of internal branding in corporate brand management

Corporate brands have become more significant over the past three decades (Iglesias et al., 2020; Balmer, 1995). Their primary role is to enhance trust (Kapferer, 2012; Balmer & Gray, 2003) and to add to a positive overall reputation. One of the main differences to managing corporate, as opposed to product brands, is the higher number of stakeholders that typically need to be considered (Schultz & de Chernatony, 2002; Roper & Davis, 2007). Among those stakeholders are the corporate brand's own employees. Brand, as a construct, entails the totality of all customer experiences with an organization and/or offering, which includes interactions with employees (Saleem & Iglesias, 2016). To intentionally *address* employees in brand related communications, to *involve* them in brand-building activities, and to *influence* their behaviour in a brand-related way is called internal branding (Punjaisri et al., 2009; Schmidt, 2017). In addition, Ahmad et al. (2014, p. 27) define internal branding as 'the set of strategic processes that align and *empower* employees to deliver the appropriate customer experience in a consistent fashion.' Supporting this view, Baumgarth and Schmidt (2010) and Burmann et al. (2009) state that internal branding refers to the activities involved in aligning employees to brands to create symbolic relationships that can lead to higher levels of brand identification, commitment, and citizenship behaviours. Based on an extensive literature review, Barros-Arrieta and García-Cali (2021, p. 145) define internal branding as a 'cross-functional process . . . which focuses on managing the brand within the organization through brand-centered human resources management, internal brand communications, and brand leadership, with the objective of achieving brand consequences in employees.' The definition of internal branding provided by Saleem and Iglesias (2016, p. 50), which is also based on a systematic literature review, incorporates the philosophy of co-creation and is formulated as: 'Internal branding is the process through which organizations make a company-wide effort within a supportive culture to integrate brand ideologies and values [brand vision, mission, goals, norms (p. 48)], leadership, HRM [human resource management], internal brand communications and *internal brand communities* as a strategy to enable employees to consistently *co-create brand value* with multiple stakeholders.' Scholars agree that due to the important role employees play in designing positive brand experiences for consumers, internal branding is essential for corporate brand management (Foster et al., 2010). Employee based brand equity, which is positively affected by internal branding, is an important part of brand equity (King & Grace, 2009; King et al., 2012).

## 1.2 The growing importance of internal branding

Generally, internal branding is strongly related to employee engagement (Suomi et al., 2019) as well as customers' brand experience and satisfaction (Benjarongrat & Neal, 2017). Undoubtedly, the discipline initially was a rather neglected practice (Burmann & Zeplin, 2005) and has gone a long way to be accepted as a relevant research stream within brand management science. Today, even if the discipline is still developing (Piehler et al., 2018), internal branding has become a very important field of corporate brand management (Schmidt & Baumgarth, 2018; Saleem & Iglesias, 2016). The importance of internal branding is due to several factors: First, in a hyper-connected and transparent world, the voice of employees, expressed through their behaviour, through direct communication or through social media, can be an important source of corporate brand meaning for external stakeholders, such as customers or potential employees (Ind & Schmidt, 2019). The former are increasingly critical towards classical marketing communication, and the latter are searching for workplaces that combine financial security and a sense of purpose. Second, as Orazi et al. (2017, p. 555) argue, 'digital media and multiple stakeholders increase the risk of misalignment between brand identity and brand image.' With the increase in online and offline touchpoints where stakeholders interact and negotiate a brand's meaning (Vallaster & von Wallpach, 2013), corporate brand managers need to secure a positive and consistent brand experience (Hesse et al., 2020). Therefore, they must rely on employees who are able to represent the brand. Third, employees value working for corporate brands that help them to construct their own identities (Guzmán et al., 2017) by offering a strong purpose, in addition to extrinsic rewards. Internal branding can help to clarify the brand's purpose internally (John et al., 2019). And fourth, organizations can 'benefit from internal branding as better relationships between employees and brands can lead to a more successful discovering of latent needs of customers . . . or a better understanding of how to satisfy the current needs of customers in a superior way' (Iyer et al., 2020, p. 11). On the contrary, poor brand practices might lead to demotivation and disengagement of employees and even sabotage (Wallace & de Chernatony, 2007; Suomi et al., 2019). Overall, it is commonly accepted that internal branding impacts companies' performance (Tuominen et al., 2016; Iyer et al., 2018).

## 1.3 Brand management changes – can internal branding change too?

Despite the discipline's major achievements, it can't be denied that the context of internal branding is changing (Ind, 2017) and faces severe challenges (Schmidt et al., 2021a). With Gen Z (born after 1995), a new generation with different demands compared to the older Gen Y is conquering the world of work (Gabrielova & Buchko, 2021). A new work culture, characterized by trust and a greater flexibility and mobility of the workforce (Chillakuri, 2020; Schroth, 2019), was already in the starting blocks before COVID-19, but was accelerated by the pandemic. And most important for the world of marketing, people are highly connected to their peers, and markets are exceedingly competitive and transparent. Consumers and employees feel empowered (Gill-Simmen et al., 2018) and expect a multifaceted and holistic relationship with their brands (Gobe, 2001), based on a partnership of equally distributed power. Customers search for brands that take a stand on socio-political issues (Schmidt et al., 2021b) and provide a purpose beyond the fulfilment of functional needs, and employees search for employers they can be proud of. But in an educated, critical, and demanding society, brands and their identity can't be predefined in small, inner circles of the branded company anymore, and their meaning can't be communicated in a unidirectional way to the market arena (Kornum et al., 2017; von Wallpach et al., 2017). Brand identity can therefore no longer be seen as 'a unique set of brand associations that the brand strategist aspires to create or maintain' (Aaker, 1996, p. 68) and that stays rather stable over a long period of time. On the contrary, Ind and Schmidt (2019, p. 170) define brand identity as 'an ever-evolving connotation, rooted in a brand's history, philosophy, practices and ambitions but subject to constant mediation and re-interpretation as its meaning is co-created by a brand's stakeholders.' If brand meaning is permanently negotiated among many stakeholders (Iglesias & Ind, 2020; da Silveira et al., 2013), brand management might still provide direction but is no longer in control of the brand management process (Iglesias et al., 2013). In order to stay relevant, it's the task of brand managers to initiate and to regulate social processes (e.g., managing branded online communities, creating and spreading stories around the brand, designing content for social networks, managing crowd sourcing activities) that involve multiple stakeholders including employees. In a nutshell: The rise of the 'co-creative school' (Schmidt & Redler, 2018) fundamentally changed the way researchers define and interpret key terms of brand management. It goes hand in hand that when brand management changes, internal branding needs to change as well. Therefore, a new approach to internal branding is needed: A co-creative approach.

## 1.4 The progression of internal branding

Iglesias and Bonet (2012, p. 251) argue that 'brand managers are progressively losing control over the multiple sources of brand meaning.' This implies the need that brand management teams transform from brand guardians to brand hosts who can only influence the various stakeholders involved with brand co-creation (Veloutsou & Delgado-Ballester, 2019). Based on this understanding, 'organizations need to approach employees as corporate partners in order to co-create employer-employee values' rather than seeing employees as only responsible to deliver organization-developed brand promises (Aggerholm et al., 2011, p. 105). In a study within the financial sector that investigated whether there was congruence between documented brand identities and how employees decoded it, Zwakala et al. (2017) recommend that banks invest in internal branding because employees deliver the brand identity – being involved in defining of a brand's identity could make it easier to bring the identity to life.

But the history of internal branding teaches us a different view: Internal branding has long been considered to be a managerial task that was predominantly done in a top-down approach (Mampaey et al., 2020). The meaning of the brand, as defined by its management, had to be communicated down the hierarchies, and the ultimate goal was to find triggers which would, in analogy to the stimulus-organism-response paradigm, influence employees so that they would behave in a way that management considered to be 'on brand' (Burmann & Zeplin, 2005). In brand management literature, this way of thinking is mirrored in what Merrilees (2016) calls the first and second phases of internal branding: To him, the first phase emphasized internal communication and employee training, while the second phase, already more open towards collaboration, focused on the role of the company culture and the empowerment of employees. Some leading research articles of phase 1 and 2 identified internal communication, a transformational leadership style and brand-related human resource management activities (e.g., training, onboarding, promotion, remuneration) as levers to brand commitment and brand-related behaviour (e.g., Burmann & Zeplin, 2005; Morhart et al., 2009). An insightful study of 20 business school brands found that internal brand communication did not lead directly to employee brand support, but rather that brand-centred training and development is the mediator between internal brand communication and employee brand support. Also, employees tried harder to align their work activities to the business schools' brand under immediate transformational leadership (Sujchaphong et al., 2020).

It is no surprise that in today's world, employees interact with customers in multiple ways that are often beyond the control of the company (Iglesias et al., 2013). In an environment like this, interactions must be inspired by the overall positioning of the brand, rather than by a rule book (Ind & Schmidt, 2019), the establishment of a psychological contract with existing and new employees and clarity regarding brand identity (Itam et al., 2020). A brand-oriented culture might contribute to a behaviour that is on-brand: As Anees-ur-Rehman et al. (2019, p. 303) argue, 'brand orientation improves the effectiveness of . . . internal branding,' and Zhang et al. (2016) show that brand-oriented business-to-business (B2B) service companies are likely to implement internal branding involving their employees, which improves the willingness and ability of employees to deliver excellent customer service. This perspective is considered in a third and very recent phase of brand management literature centring on relationships, networks, and co-creation (Merrilees, 2016), acknowledging that a brand is co-created in networks of multiple stakeholders (Iglesias et al., 2013), including employees.

In this context, it is important to note that co-creation can't be considered 'the new thing' anymore (Prahalad & Ramaswamy, 2002). Nevertheless, though co-creation is one of the emerging and, due to its managerial relevance (Gambetti & Graffigna, 2015), highly important themes of brand management (Schmidt & Redler, 2018), research on brand-co-creation remains limited (Merz et al., 2018). Specifically, literature on internal branding written from a co-creative perspective is still extremely scarce. An understanding of how brand meaning is created, shared, and co-created among the internal stakeholders before interacting with external stakeholders is limited (Dean et al., 2016). Research presented in this chapter strives to fill this gap and straddles internal branding and the co-creation literature.

## 2. Methodology

Building on the results of a literature review of the most common electronic databases, using the key words 'internal branding' and 'co-creation,' and limiting results to journal articles in English and a snowball literature review, where sources within these relevant papers lead to other important articles, we provide an overview of internal branding within the co-creative paradigm of brand management. This chapter contributes to the field by revealing how internal stakeholders engage in creating corporate brands and by examining how employees in corporate firms contribute to the co-creation of brand meaning. Though innovations are at the heart of brand management, our analysis does not cover co-creation in the context of (internal) innovation management. This would take us too far from our core concern: How do employees contribute to the co-creation of brand meaning?

In September 2020, we scanned the databases Emerald, Academic Search Premier (EBSCO), and Business Source Premier (EBSCO) for the aforementioned keywords 'internal branding' and 'co-creation.' Using 'advanced search' and selecting 'all content,' the Emerald database suggested 95 articles. In an online scan, we assessed the articles according to their relevance and whittled these down to 71. Then, by working through the articles one by one, more were eliminated because they didn't match our research intents. The process ended up with 19 articles. Academic Search Premier (EBSCOhost), using 'advanced search' and 'scholarly (peer reviewed),' identified no articles with the initial search query, but by using SmartText Searching the database suggested two articles. Even so, the articles found via SmartText were irrelevant to our field of interest. Business Source Premier, using 'advanced search' and 'scholarly (peer reviewed),' identified two articles of which one was relevant to our field of interest. During the review of the 20 articles four additional articles were found based on the snowball method, which brought the total to 24 articles. Then, in December 2020, we extended the literature analysis to the database ProQuest (including ABI/inform). Using the same keywords and again limiting the search to peer reviewed articles, we identified 55 articles. Three of them were already identified in the prior search. A quick scan of all abstracts showed that 21 of the remaining 52 were considered as relevant for our purposes. After a deeper analysis of the content, 7 out of those were included in our analysis, resulting in a total of 31 articles. The final list of articles identified by the structured literature analysis is summarized in Table 27.1 and is guided by the research question 'How do employees contribute to the co-creation of brand meaning?'

*Table 27.1* Literature analysis summary

| No. | Authors | Title | Journal | Article keywords |
|---|---|---|---|---|
| 1 | Aggerholm et al. (2011) | Conceptualising employer branding in sustainable organizations | Corporate Communications: An International Journal | Corporate communications, employers, branding, corporate social responsibility, human resource management |
| 2 | Ahmad et al. (2014) | The mediating role of employee engagement in relationship of internal branding and brand experience: case of service organizations of Dera Ghazi Khan | International Journal of Information, Business and Management 6(4): 26–41 | Customer services, brand loyalty, service industries, brands, employee involvement |
| 3 | Anees-ur-Rehman et al. (2019) | How brand-oriented strategy affects the financial performance of B2B SMEs | Journal of Business & Industrial Marketing | Brand orientation, brand awareness, B2B branding, brand credibility, financial performance, B2B SMEs |
| 4 | Babić-Hodović and Arslanagić-Kalajdžić (2019) | Perceived corporate reputation and pride as drivers of frontline employees' reputation impact awareness: mediating role of job satisfaction | Market-Tržište | Corporate reputation, frontline employees, employee pride, job satisfaction |
| 5 | Baumgarth and Schmidt (2010) | How strong is the business-to-business brand in the workforce? An empirically-tested model of internal brand equity in a business-to-business setting. | Industrial Marketing Management | Brand strategy, brand orientation, brand equity, business-to-business brand, internal branding |
| 6 | Benjarongrat and Neal (2017) | Exploring the service profit chain in a Thai bank | Asia Pacific Journal of Marketing and Logistics | Customer satisfaction, customer engagement, internal branding, convenience, courtesy, service profit chain |

*(Continued)*

*Table 27.1* (Continued)

| No. | Authors | Title | Journal | Article keywords |
|---|---|---|---|---|
| 7 | Braxton and Lau-Gesk (2020) | The impact of collective brand personification on happiness and brand loyalty | European Journal of Marketing | Brand loyalty, happiness, customer service, belongingness, brand authenticity, retail marketing, frontline employee, brand personification |
| 8 | Burmann and Zeplin (2005) | Building brand commitment: a behavioral approach to internal brand management | Journal of Brand Management | --- |
| 9 | Burmann et al. (2009) | Key determinants of internal brand management success: an exploratory empirical analysis | Journal of Brand Management | Internal branding, brand identity, brand commitment, brand citizenship behaviour, brand – customer relationship, brand strength |
| 10 | Chiang et al. (2018) | The attitudinal and behavioral impact of brand-centered human resource management | International Journal of Contemporary Hospitality Management | Customer satisfaction, customer citizenship behaviour, brand attitudes, brand-centred human resource management, person – brand fit |
| 11 | Chung and Byrom (2020) | Co-creating consistent brand identity with employees in the hotel industry | Journal of Product & Brand Management | Branding, brand identity, hospitality, case study, brand co-creation, five-star hotels, sensory elements |
| 12. | Dean et al. (2016) | Internal brand co-creation: The experiential brand meaning cycle in higher education | Journal of Business Research | Brand identity, co-creation, internal branding, brand meaning, higher education |
| 13 | Iglesias and Bonet (2012) | Persuasive brand management: how managers can influence brand meaning when they are losing control over it | Journal of Organizational Change Management | Brand management, rhetoric, narratives, storytelling, meanings, persuasive brand management |
| 14 | Itam et al. (2020) | HRD indicators and branding practices: a viewpoint on the employer brand building process | Journal of Training and Development | Qualitative study, HR managers, thematic analysis, employer brand, branding practices, HDR indicators |
| 15 | Iyer et al. (2018) | Determinants of brand performance: the role of internal branding | Journal of Brand Management | Internal branding, strategic brand management, brand orientation, brand management, brand performance |
| 16 | Iyer et al. (2020) | Market orientation, brand management processes and brand performance | Journal of Product & Brand Management | Market orientation, strategic brand management, internal branding, brand performance |

(*Continued*)

Table 27.1 (Continued)

| No. | Authors | Title | Journal | Article keywords |
|---|---|---|---|---|
| 17 | Juntunun (2012) | Co-creating corporate brands in start-ups | Marketing Intelligence & Planning | Corporate brand, corporate branding, stakeholders, process research |
| 18 | Kowalkowski (2011) | Dynamics of value propositions: insights from service-dominant logic | European Journal of Marketing | Offerings, value proposition, value-in-use, value-in-exchange, buying centres, service-dominant logic |
| 19 | Kuoppakangas et al. (2020) | Dilemmas in re-branding a university – 'Maybe people just don't like change': linking meaningfulness and mutuality into the reconciliation | Corporate Reputation Review | Re-branding, internal branding, dilemma theory, higher education, public sector |
| 20 | Liewendahl and Heinonen (2020) | Frontline employees' motivation to align with value propositions | Journal of Business & Industrial Marketing | Authenticity, autonomy, value propositions, bottom-up strategizing, co-activity, co-workership, frontline employee motivation |
| 21 | Lundholt et al. (2019) | Intra-organizational brand resistance and counter-narratives in city branding – a comparative study of three Danish cities | Qualitative Market Research: An International Journal | City branding, intra-organizational brand resistance, intra-organizational counter-narratives, administrative arena, brand resistance, political arena |
| 22 | Mishra et al. (2020) | The role of instructor experiential values in shaping students' course experiences, attitudes and behavioral intentions | Journal of Product & Brand Management | Higher education, brand experience, experiential value, normative influence, brand spokesperson |
| 23 | Ngo et al. (2020) | Converting internal brand knowledge into employee performance | Journal of Product & Brand Management | Internal branding, employer branding, employee performance, internal marketing, brand identification |
| 24 | Potgieter and Doubell (2020) | The Influence of Employer branding and Employees' personal branding on Corporate Branding and Corporate Reputation | African Journal of Business and Economic Research | Employer branding, employees' personal branding, corporate branding, corporate reputation |
| 25 | Saleem and Iglesias (2016) | Mapping the domain of the fragmented field of internal branding | Journal of Product & Brand Management | Employer branding, brand identity, internal branding |
| 26 | Schepers and Nijssen (2018) | Brand advocacy in the frontline: how does it affect customer satisfaction? | Journal of Service Management | Service encounter, customer satisfaction, frontline employees, brand advocacy behaviour, brand identification, product newness |

(Continued)

*Table 27.1* (Continued)

| No. | Authors | Title | Journal | Article keywords |
|---|---|---|---|---|
| 27 | Skaalsvik and Olsen (2014b) | Service branding: suggesting an interactive model of service brand development | *Kybernetes* | Interactive service brand model, service brand development, service branding |
| 28 | Sujchaphong et al. (2020) | A framework of brand-centred training and development activities, transformational leadership and employee brand support in higher education | *Journal of Brand Management* | Internal brand communication, brand centred training and development, transformational leadership, employee brand support, higher education institution branding |
| 29 | Veloutsou and Delgado-Ballester (2019) | New challenges in brand management | *Spanish Journal of Marketing – ESIC* | Brands, brand management, brand identity, brand image, brand reputation, brand meaning, brand co-creation |
| 30 | Zhang and He (2014) | Key dimensions of brand value co-creation and its impacts upon customer perception and brand performance: an empirical research in the context of industrial service | *Nankai Business Review International* | Service-dominant logic, stakeholders, brand performance, brand value, brand value co-creation, industrial services |
| 31 | Zhang et al. (2016) | How brand orientation impacts B2B service brand equity? An empirical study among Chinese firms | *Journal of Business & Industrial Marketing* | Brand orientation, empirical study, brand equity, Chinese firms, B2B services |

The following paragraphs will discuss the emerging main ideas of brand meaning when co-created by employees, based on the analysis of the identified articles.

## 3. Employees as co-creators of brand meaning: discussion of key themes

As is evident from the discussion within Section 1, employees are important stakeholders of brand management and of key importance for the creation of brand meaning. In congruence with Veloutsou and Delgado-Ballester (2019, p. 257), we define brand meaning as internal and external stakeholders' mind-set about a brand 'and, therefore, the term primarily incorporates both brand identity and brand reputation as well as brand image' (see also Vallaster & von Wallpach, 2013). But how do employees contribute to the co-creation of brand meaning? The literature review shows that co-creation occurs, explicitly or implicitly, at various levels: Employees can explicitly, by choice of the brand's management, be involved to co-create the formal brand identity ('the symbols and the set of the brand associations that represent the core character of the brand that the team supporting the brand aspire to create or maintain as identifiers of the brand to other people;' Veloutsou & Delgado-Ballester, 2019, p. 257), as part of the brand's meaning. Implicitly, they are central sources for the formation of the (external) brand image, understood as 'the perception formed to the mind of a member of the external audience about the brand' and brand reputation, understood as 'the aggregation of brand images' (Veloutsou & Delgado-Ballester, 2019, p. 257). Finally, employees also contribute to and therefore co-create the formation of brand meaning.

### 3.1 Employees co-creating a brand's identity

Brand management has often been described as a top-down process that requires a strong guidance by a brand's management (Skaalsvik & Olsen, 2014a). Managers, as so-called primary stakeholders (Henninger et al., 2016, p. 285), can then select other stakeholders, e.g., employees, to be potentially involved in the branding process. Nevertheless, various case studies have shown how corporate brands benefit from the early involvement of employees when the identity of a brand gets internally defined (Chung & Byrom, 2020; Ind & Schmidt, 2019; Kristal et al., 2020). The literature analysis drew our attention to the work of Liewendahl and Heinonen (2020) who, in an explorative case study, report on a Finland-based B2B company in the building and technical trade sector. The researchers used an abductive research strategy to identify co-creation of brand promises and value propositions as a motivator for employees to align to brand promises. Participants pointed out the logic that it makes sense for those that are to deliver or keep brand promises to be involved in developing the promises. In essence, co-creation would enhance awareness, understanding and buy-in to what was being promised. Forums, or what Chung and Byrom (2020) refer to as employee task force teams, were suggested as enablers of co-creation to contextualize promises and motivate employees through more meaningful work (Saleem & Iglesias, 2016). This aligns with Merrilees' (2016) second phase of internal branding. Furthermore, a multiple case study of start-up software businesses reveals that employees were involved in the co-creation of aspects of the brands' visual identity, namely the name before and after launch as well as updating the logo (Juntunen, 2012).

### 3.2 Employees co-creating internal brand meaning

Elaborating on Iglesias and Bonet's (2012) work, Dean et al. (2016) use the higher education sector as the context for a study into internal brand co-creation. The authors investigate 'the role of marketing and the internal market in realizing the brand identity' and 'developing a shared brand meaning' (p. 3041). The study considered employee brand meaning co-creation through their brand experiences and interactions with their networks. The study found that employees' brand meaning develops through their lived brand experiences and interactions with managers, other employees, and customers. Early seemingly insignificant brand experiences initiated brand meaning, which were added to through brand experiences and interactions with their networks. The authors develop what they call the 'experiential brand meaning cycle' conceptual framework (p. 3045). The framework consists of four stages, namely awareness, interpretation, appropriation, and communication.

Dean et al. (2016) found that the *awareness stage* is a passive stage and can start before being employed and continue into employment. This may be based on exposure to brand elements and in addition the employee absorbs brand communication and experiences from networks within the organization. If the passively absorbed brand awareness is meaningful, the employee moves to the *interpretation stage*. From here on the employee is no longer a passive absorber, but rather evaluates and interprets brand stories, the servicescape, etc. New experiences are interpreted by comparing it to the awareness knowledge base. Interestingly enough the authors found that close interaction between colleagues is important for brand meaning creation, which is challenging during periods of separation, as is the case with social distancing measures introduced due to COVID-19. It is during these interactions that employee brand meaning is co-created, which is referred to as the real brand identity and may differ to the corporation intended brand identity. When there is discord between historic brand experiences, official brand communication and actual experiences, the employee adapts the brand meaning based on his or her own experiences. The authors continue that when the brand meaning is internalized (the brand essence, value, and personality) the employee moves to the *appropriation stage*. This stage is characterized by brand commitment, trust, and ownership. During this stage and similarly to the interpretation stage, employees need to share their interpretation of brand meaning with colleagues, because if this is not done, engagement may be diminished. The final stage, according to the study, is the *communication stage* and refers to how the employee delivers brand meaning at the touch points. According to Dean et al.'s (2016) findings, the process repeats itself and the employee's brand meaning is altered over time. The results of a case study by Kuoppakangas et al. (2020) that analyses the rebranding of a university supports Dean et al.'s work and suggests that implementation should not rely solely on internal communication but also include enhanced engagement by involving employees. Employees should be involved in rebranding from the beginning to resolve 'core dilemma pairs: (1) new brand vs. previous brand; (2) voice at the organisational level vs. voice at the departmental level; and (3) voluntary down-up voicing vs. up-down voicing' (p. 23). Employee co-creation can 'produce meaningful re-branding results and mutuality, with shared values among employees' (p. 23).

## 3.3 Employees co-creating brand image

Dean et al. (2016) argue that in the *communication stage*, the employee has now moved past being an absorber and interpreter of brand meaning to being the brand meaning creator through the brand narrative. This shows the importance of employees in brand co-creation because it is the employees that convey their interpretation of the organization's brand meaning to consumers at the various touch points through brand stories. Burmann and Zeplin (2005, p. 282) support this point when they state that 'all sources of brand identity are based on the decisions and actions of employees.' The authors coined the term *brand citizenship behaviour* to refer to 'employee behaviours that enhance the brand identity' (p. 283). This means that the delivery of the brand identity at all customer-brand touchpoints will only happen if brand citizenship is present. They list seven dimensions of brand citizenship behaviour, namely (p. 284): helping behaviour, brand consideration, brand enthusiasm, sportsmanship, brand endorsement, self-development, and brand advancement.

Ngo et al. (2020) included Burmann and Zeplin's (2005, p. 283) 'brand citizenship behaviour' in a conceptual model of a descriptive study with a sample of 697 service providers. The study, which tested the conceptual model, found that it is not only employee/internal brand knowledge (cognitive brand understanding) that improves employee 'on brand' performance, but rather that employee/internal brand knowledge influences employee performance through employee brand identification (affective brand connection), brand citizenship behaviour, and customer-oriented behaviour (p. 275). In other words, there are 'self-driven positive brand-connection attitudes' or employee brand identification/connection that motivates employees to engage in brand- and customer-oriented behaviours (p. 273). These emotional connections that employees make with the brand are what Dean et al. (2016, p. 3045) refer to as appropriation, which potentially leads to brand advocacy and behaviours that are aligned to employees' self-image. Interestingly, research by Schepers and Nijssen (2018) in a B2B after-sales service context identified boundary conditions for brand advocacy, i.e., the promoting of products and services to potential customers, and concluded that brand advocacy behaviour can also harm customer satisfaction.

It is commonly accepted that employees have a decisive role on the emergence and development of the consumer-brand relationship (Iglesias & Saleem, 2015). Mishra et al. (2020), in a study positioned within the higher education context, express the novel view of the instructor as a brand spokesperson and the course offered as a brand. They argue that the instructor delivers experiential values that 'comprise appearance [attractiveness], entertainment [as a result of instructor showmanship], escapism [students becoming immersed in course], intrinsic enjoyment, efficiency [appropriate use of class time] and service excellence [instructor subject knowledge].' The course experiences are composed of sensory [involving the five senses of students], sentimental [effects on mood and emotions of students], behavioural [knowledge gained by students], and intellectual experiences [fosters continuous learning] (p. 1 with annotations from p. 3). The study reported the instructor experiential values strongly affected students' experience of the course. Higher education institutions' (HEI) hiring can thus be guided by the identified instructor experiential value dimensions, and it can be deduced that the HEI should channel institutional identity through these instructors, who personify the HEI brand, to establish the desired brand image within the minds of students.

A study by Steenkamp et al. (2020) that applied the brand resonance framework of Keller (2013, p. 108) to a B2B services context, elevates the importance of employees in the creation of customers' brand knowledge by including a service brand personification brand-building block in their conceptual servbrand framework. In line with this, but in the context of city branding, Lundholt et al. (2019) refer to the brand personification of municipal employees as an unexplored area. The authors suggest that branding efforts should not only focus on citizens, but they should include municipal employees and politicians as two individual stakeholder groups to increase the likelihood of long-term branding success. Alignment between the identity and core values of the brand and the frontline employees (FLE), via brand personification, leads to increased customer happiness and loyalty due to the customers' feelings of belongingness in relation to the brand as well as their perception of brand authenticity (Braxton & Lau-Gesk, 2020). HRM can contribute to achieving alignment between brand identity and employees by 'employing people whose values, morals and personality align with that of the organisation employer branding process' (Potgieter & Doubell, 2020, p. 110).

The idea that employees personify the organization's brand (Steenkamp et al., 2020) accords well with the views of Dean et al. (2016) and Burmann and Zeplin (2005). Aligned to this, Chung and Byrom (2020), focus on employee brand co-creation and conducted a qualitative longitudinal case study with document analysis and semi-structured in-depth interviews with 42 employees. The research focused on how employees of two five-star hotels within the same ownership structure, but with brand identities that were undifferentiated, contributed to brand identity co-creation. The authors found that employees that committed to the new brand identities generated positive guest perceptions towards the brand image and, as a result, employees' pride in their work improved. Additional benefits to employees included enhanced brand knowledge, emotional bonds with the brand, positive attitude, and motivation to deliver the brand identity. The authors state that: 'brand co-creation activities . . . are required to manage a brand with consistency.' The brand co-creation activities were structured as employee task force teams, which were formed with employees from various functional departments to co-create and communicate the brand identity with their colleagues. Over a period of more than four years, employees actively contributed to the hotels' visions, targeting guest identification and preferences and sensory identity elements such as floral arrangements and identity-specific scent. Key here is to note that employees were not only trained about a new brand identity that was developed by an external organization (what Merrilees [2016] calls the first phase of internal branding), but through their participation the understanding and ownership of the brand

and emotional connection to the brand were enhanced. Employees could live the brand identity for colleagues and guests to experience.

Based on the research, the authors developed a brand co-creation framework that shows the infinite loop of brand co-creation from 'learning the brand' to 'living the brand' to 'representing the brand' to '(re)discovering the brand.' In addition, the importance of aligning brand identity with brand image, which leads to brand reputation, is indicated. This accords with what Zwakala et al. (2017) propose as well as the advanced phases of Merrilees (2016).

Skaalsvik and Olsen (2014b) conducted a desk study and included employees and especially frontline employees, 'as active participants in service brand development' (p. 1215) and use the term 'empowered employees' (p. 1216) to describe this view. Zhang and He (2014) propose brand co-creation activities on the firm-employees interface, which will impact 'brand value and brand performance via value co-creation' (p. 65). In another study, involving managers, front line employees, and guests of 22 hotels in Taiwan, it was found that brand-centred human resources management had a positive effect on brand citizen behaviour. This is mediated by the employee and brand fit as well as employee commitment to the brand. As can be expected, employees who are committed to the brand displayed brand citizen behaviour and, if there was a good fit between the employee and brand, citizen behaviour improved. The study also found that brand citizen behaviour affected guest satisfaction and that guest satisfaction, in turn, affected guest brand citizen behaviour (Chiang et al., 2018). This means that recruitment and selection practices are important to select employees that fit brand values. In addition, 'Service employees play a crucial role in creating and sustaining the reputation of service firms' and 'FLEs are often perceived as the service itself' (Babić-Hodović & Arslanagić-Kalajdžić, 2019, pp. 171, 180). This supports the premise of the chapter that employees are not merely receivers of brand identity but rather co-creators of brand meaning. The authors further report that employees influence consumers' perceptions regarding the quality of the organization's offerings as well as their loyalty towards the brand. Front line employees' realization of their impact on brand image is to a large extent determined by their job satisfaction, and more experienced employees have a greater sense of their impact. This accords well with brand citizenship behaviour.

## 4. Conclusions, implications, and advice for future research

Iglesias and Ind (2020) illustrate the co-creative view of brand management and argue that it is the most modern and powerful approach to managing brands. Of course, this also applies in the context of corporate brands, where internal brand management traditionally plays a major role. Those who generally acknowledge the superiority of co-creative brand management over other, traditional perspectives, must also affirm that co-creation is important in internal branding. Top-down approaches, which seek to convey a brand identity developed in a closed management circle to employees, in order to create brand-oriented behaviour, are therefore doomed to failure under today's conditions. Internal branding, like brand management as a whole, must be co-creative.

Employees actively create the meaning of brands by influencing the definition of the brand identity, by affecting the brand image through their contact with external stakeholders (e.g., customers, suppliers, job candidates, general public) and by giving the brand meaning internally. However, positive stakeholder brand experiences across multiple brand touchpoints are difficult to ensure through command and control. Much more important than the management's setting of clear, brand-oriented rules of conduct is therefore a supportive corporate culture that focuses on the importance of the brand for the company's success and promotes an independent interpretation of the brand within predefined guidelines that align with corresponding human resource policies and practices (Iglesias & Saleem, 2015). A brand-oriented culture is therefore needed. Such a culture is based on brand-related values, norms, and symbols (Baumgarth, 2010, 2009; Urde et al., 2013). Values are defined as deeply embedded, taken-for-granted, and largely unconscious behaviours. They form the core of culture and determine what people think should be done. Norms, namely conscious brand strategies and brand-related goals, represent the explicit and implicit rules of behaviour. In a brand-oriented organization they determine how the members represent the corporate brand, both to themselves and to others. Symbols or artefacts are the most apparent element of a brand-oriented culture. They include any tangible, overt, or verbally identifiable element that represents the brand, for example, a brand-specific architecture, a dress code, or brand-related stories (Schein, 2006; Schmidt, 2017). Under a co-creative perspective, employees should participate in the definition of values, in the transformation of the committed values to norms, and in the establishment of brand-related symbols. Only then will corporate employees support the brand ideology with their behaviour.

Even though the co-creative school can't be considered to be the new kid on the block any more, we see plenty of open fields for research at the interface of internal branding and co-creation. Namely, we want to draw on three ideas that we consider to be of major interest for the co-creative perspective on internal branding. First, future research should clarify what brand-oriented behaviour ('on-brand-behaviour') means conceptually. What behavioural elements constitute on-brand-behaviour? If employees co-create a brand's meaning and if all brand-related actions of employees are relevant for the brand, how can, per definition, a behaviour be 'off-brand'? In a co-creative world, who makes this call? In the absence of narrow formal rules, who decides what behaviour is on- and off-brand? Only when more clarity on the nature of brand-related behaviour exists, can the conditions under which brand-oriented behaviour ('on-brand-behaviour') most probably occurs, be analysed. Second, two important questions in tackling this issue have been raised by Veloutsou and Guzmán (2017). They asked how brands can develop consistency throughout all brand touchpoints and for all stakeholders considering that the flow of brand meaning is multidirectional. The same authors also asked 'how brands develop an interactive, individualized but yet communal, brand experience throughout all brand touchpoints for all stakeholders, considering that not all stakeholders are actively involved' (Veloutsou & Guzmán, 2017, p. 6). Still, these issues have, at least to our knowledge, not been fully addressed yet. A third, but also important, research question was inspired by a point in the proposed research agenda of Iglesias and Ind (2020) when they recently commented on conscientious corporate brands: How can corporate brands reconcile potential conflicts of interest among their stakeholders? It may not be useful to talk of 'the employees' when discussing matters of internal branding. How can we, in the context of co-creating the corporate brand internally, better differentiate between various internal stakeholder groups and their own interests?

Overall, we urge researchers to focus more on a co-creative perspective on internal branding. The present chapter may have helped to emphasize this point.

# References

Aaker, D. A. (1996). *Building strong brands.* New York: Free Press.
Aggerholm, H. K., Andersen, S. E., & Thomsen, C. (2011). Conceptualising employer branding in sustainable organisations. *Corporate Communications: An International Journal, 16*(2), 105–123. https://doi.org/10.1108/13563281111141642
Ahmad, N., Iqbal, N., Kanwal, R., Javed, H., & Javed, K. (2014). The mediating role of emplcyee engagement in relationship of internal branding and brand experience: Case of service organizations of Dera Ghazi Khan. *International Journal of Information, Business and Management, 6*(4), 26–41.
Anees-ur-Rehman, M., Wong, H. Y., Sultan, P., Merrilees, B. (2019). How brand-oriented strategy affects the financial performance of B2B SMEs. *Journal of Business & Industrial Marketing, 33*(3), 303–315.

Babić-Hodovića, V., & Arslanagić-Kalajdžić, M. (2019). Perceived corporate reputation and pride as drivers of frontline employees' reputation impact awareness: Mediating role of job satisfaction. *Market-Tržište, 31*(2), 171–185. http://dx.doi.org/10.22598/mt/2019.31.2.171

Balmer, J. (1995). Corporate branding and connoisseurship. *Journal of General Management, 21*(1), 24–46.

Balmer, J., & Gray, E. (2003). Corporate brands: What are they? What of them? *Journal of Marketing, 37*(7–8), 972–997.

Barros-Arrieta, D., & García-Cali, E. (2021). Internal branding: Conceptualization from a literature review and opportunities for future research. *Journal of Brand Management, 28*, 133–151. https://doi.org/10.1057/s41262-020-00219-1

Baumgarth, C. (2009). Brand orientation of museums: Model and empirical results. *International Journal of Arts Management, 11*(3), 30–45.

Baumgarth, C. (2010). 'Living the brand'. Brand orientation in the business-to-business sector. *European Journal of Marketing, 44*(5), 653–671.

Baumgarth, C., & Kristal, S. (2019). The three theoretical pillars of brand co-creation. In N. Ind & H. J. Schmidt (Eds.), *Co-creating brands* (pp. 38–42) London: Bloomsbury.

Baumgarth, C., & Schmidt, M. (2010). How strong is the business-to-business brand in the workforce? An empirically-tested model of internal brand equity in a business-to-business setting. *Industrial Marketing Management, 39*, 1250–1260.

Benjarongrat, P., & Neal, M. (2017). Exploring the service profit chain in a Thai bank. *Asia Pacific Journal of Marketing and Logistics, 29*(2), 432–452. https://doi.org/10.1108/APJML-03-2016-0061

Braxton, D., & Lau-Gesk, L. (2020). The impact of collective brand personification on happiness and brand loyalty. *European Journal of Marketing, 54*(10), 2365–2386. https://doi.org/10.1108/EJM-12-2019-0940

Burmann, C., & Zeplin, S. (2005). Building brand commitment: A behavioral approach to internal brand management. *Journal of Brand Management, 12*(4), 279–300.

Burmann, C., Zeplin, S., & Riley, N. (2009). Key determinants of internal brand management success: An exploratory empirical analysis. *Journal of Brand Management, 16*(4), 264–284. https://doi.org/10.1057/bm.2008.6

Chiang, H.-H., Han, T-S., & McConville, D. (2018). The attitudinal and behavioral impact of brand-centered human resource management: Employee and customer effects. *International Journal of Contemporary Hospitality Management, 30*(2), 939–960. https://doi.org/10.1108/IJCHM-02-2016-0103

Chillakuri, B. (2020). Understanding generation Z expectations for effective onboarding. *Journal of Organizational Change Management, 33*(7), 1277–1296.

Chung, S-Y., & Byrom, F. (2020). Co-creating consistent brand identity with employees in the hotel industry. *Journal of Product & Brand Management*. https://doi.org/10.1108/JPBM-08-2019-2544

da Silveira, C., Lages, C., & Simões, C. (2013). Reconceptualizing brand identity in a dynamic environment. *Journal of Business Research, 66*(1), 28–36.

Dean, D., Arroyo-Gamez, R. E., Punjaisri, K., & Pich, C. (2016). Internal brand co-creation: The experiential brand meaning cycle in higher education. *Journal of Business Research*. (69), 3041–3048.

Foster, C., Punjaisri, K., & Cheng, R. (2010). Exploring the relationship between corporate, internal and employer branding. *Journal of Product and Brand Management, 19*(6), 401–409.

Gabrielova, K., & Buchko, A. A. (2021). *Here comes Generation Z: Millennials as managers*. Business Horizons. https://doi.org/10.1016/j.bushor.2021.02.013

Gambetti, R. C., & Graffigna, G. (2015). Value co-creation between the 'inside' and the 'outside' of a company: Insights from a brand community failure. *Marketing Theory, 15*(2), 155–178.

Gill-Simmen, L., MacInnis, D. J., Eisingerich, A. B., & Park, C. W. (2018). Brand-self connections and brand prominence as drivers of employee brand attachment. *AMS Review, 8*, 128–146. http://dx.doi.org/10.1007/s13162-018-0110-6

Gobe, M. (2001). *Emotional branding: The new paradigm for connecting brands to people*. New York: Allworth Press.

Guzmán, F., Paswan, A. K., & Fabrize, R. (2017). Crossing the border: Changes in self and brands. *Journal of Consumer Marketing, 34*(4), 306–318.

Henninger, C. E., Foster, C., Alevizou, P. J., & Frohlich, C. (2016). Stakeholder engagement in the city branding process. *Place Branding and Public Diplomacy, 12*(4), 285–298.

Hesse, A., Schmidt, H. J., & Baumgarth, C. (2020). Practices of corporate influencers in the context of internal branding: The case of Pawel Dillinger from Deutsche Telekom. *Corporate Reputation Review*. https://doi.org/10.1057/s41299-020-00103-3

Iglesias, O., & Bonet, E. (2012). Persuasive brand management – How managers can influence brand meaning when they are losing control over it. *Journal of Organizational Change Management*, 25(2), 251–264. https://doi.org/10.1108/09534811211213937

Iglesias, O., & Ind, N. (2020). Towards a theory of conscientious corporate brand co-creation: The next key challenge in brand management. *Journal of Brand Management*, 27(6), 710–720.

Iglesias, O., Ind, N., & Alfaro, M. (2013). The organic-view of the brand: Towards a brand value cocreation model. *Journal of Brand Management*, 20(8), 670–688.

Iglesias, O., Landgraf, P., Ind, N., Markovic, S., & Koporcic, N. (2020). Corporate brand identity co-creation in business-to-business contexts. *Industrial Marketing Management*, 85, 32–43. https://doi.org/10.1016/j.indmarman.2019.09.008

Iglesias, O., & Saleem, F. Z. (2015). How to support consumer-brand relationships – The role of corporate culture and human resource policies and practices. *Marketing Intelligence & Planning*, 33(2), 216–234.

Ind, N. (2017). The changing world of internal branding. In N. Ind (Ed.), *Branding inside out: Internal branding in theory and practice* (pp. 1–12). London: Kogan Page.

Ind, N., & Schmidt, H. J. (2019). *Co-creating brands*. London: Bloomsbury.

Itam, U., Misra, S., & Anjum, H. (2020). HRD indicators and branding practices: A viewpoint on the employer brand building process. *European Journal of Training and Development*, 44(6–7), 675–694. https://doi.org/10.1108/EJTD-05-2019-0072

Iyer, P., Davari, A., & Paswan, A. (2018). Determinants of brand performance: The role of internal branding. *Journal of Brand Management*, 25, 202–216. https://doi.org/10.1057/s41262-018-0097-1

Iyer, P., Davari, A., Srivastava, S., & Paswa AK. (2020). Market orientation, brand management processes and brand performance. *Journal of Product & Brand Management*. https://doi.org/10.1108/JPBM-08-2019-2530

John, J. K., Kilumile, J. W., & Tundui, H. P. (2019). Internal branding: An engine in building and sustaining brand equity – A conceptual paper. *American Journal of Management*, 19(5), 100–106. https://doi.org/10.33423/ajm.v19i5.2633

Juntunun, M. (2012). Co-creating corporate brands in start-ups. *Marketing Intelligence & Planning*, 30(2), 230–249. https://doi.org/10.1108/02634501211211993

Kapferer, J. N. (2012). *The new strategic brand management: Advanced insights and strategic thinking*. London: Kogan Page.

Keller, K. L. (2013). *Strategic brand management: Building, measuring, and managing brand equity* (4th ed.). Upper Saddle River, NJ: Pearson Education.

King, C., & Grace, D. (2009). Employee based brand equity: A third perspective. *Services Marketing Quarterly*, 30(2), 122–147.

King, C., Grace, D., & Funk, D. C. (2012). Employee brand equity: Scale development and validation. *Journal of Brand Management*, 19(4), 268–288.

Kornum, N., Gyrd-Jones, R., Al Zagir, N., & Brandis, K. A. (2017). Interplay between intended brand identity and identities in a Nike related brand community: Co-existing synergies and tensions in a nested system. *Journal of Business Research*, 70, 432–440.

Kowalkowski, C. (2011). Dynamics of value propositions: Insights from service-dominant logic. *European Journal of Marketing*, 45(1–2), 277–294. https://doi.org/10.1108/03090561111095702

Kristal, S., Baumgarth, C., & Henseler, J. (2020). Performative corporate brand identity in industrial markets: The case of German prosthetics manufacturer Ottobock. *Journal of Business Research*, (114), 240–253.

Kuoppakangas, P., Suomi, K., Clark, P., Chapleo, C., & Stenvall, J. (2020). Dilemmas in re-branding a university – "Maybe people just don't like change": Linking meaningfulness and mutuality into the reconciliation. *Corporate Reputation Review*, 23(2), 92–105. https://doi.org/10.1057/s41299-019-00080-2

Liewendahl, H. E., & Heinonen, K. (2020). Frontline employees' motivation to align with value propositions. *Journal of Business & Industrial Marketing*, 35(3), 420–436. https://doi.org/10.1108/JBIM-02-2019-0084

Lundholt, M. W., Jørgensen, O. H., & Blichfeldt, B. S. (2019). Intra-organizational brand resistance and counter-narratives in city branding – A comparative study of three Danish cities. *Qualitative Market Research: An International Journal*, 23(4), 1001–1018. https://doi.org/10.1108/QMR-01-2018-0012

Mampaey, J., Schtemberg, V., Schijns, J., Huisman, J., & Wæraas, A. (2020). Internal branding in higher education: Dialectical tensions underlying the discursive legitimation of a new brand of student diversity. *Higher Education Research & Development*, 39(2), 230–243.

Merrilees, B. (2016). Interactive brand experience pathways to customer-brand engagement and value co-creation. *Journal of Product & Brand Management*, 25(5), 402–408.

Merz, M., Zarantonello, L., & Grappi, S. (2018). How valuable are your customers in the brand value co-creation process? The development of a Customer Co-Creation Value. (CCCV). scale. *Journal of Business Research*, (82), 79–89. https://doi.org/10.1016/j.jbusres.2017.08.018

Mishra, A., Fha, S., & Nargundkar, R. (2020). The role of instructor experiential values in shaping students' course experiences, attitudes and behavioral intentions. *Journal of Product & Brand Management*. https://doi.org/10.1108/JPBM-11-2019-2645

Ngo, L. V., Nguyen, N. P., Huynh, K. T., Gregory, G., & Cuong, P. H. (2020). Converting internal brand knowledge into employee performance. *Journal of Product & Brand Management, 29*(3), 273–287. https://doi.org/10.1108/JPBM-10-2018-2068

Orazi, D. C., Spry, A., Theilacker, M. N., & Vredenburg, J. (2017). A multi-stakeholder IMC framework for networked brand identity. *European Journal of Marketing, 51*(3), 551–571.

Piehler, R., Grace, D., & Burmann, C. (2018). Internal brand management: Introduction to the special issue and directions for future research. *Journal of Brand Management, 25*, 197–201.

Potgieter, A., & Doubell, M. (2020). The Influence of Employer branding and Employees' personal branding on corporate branding and corporate reputation. *African Journal of Business and Economic Research, 15*(2), 109–135.

Prahalad, C. K., & Ramaswamy, V. (2002). The co-creation connection. *Strategy and Business 27*, 50–61.

Punjaisri, K., Evanschitzky, H., & Wilson, A. (2009). Internal branding: An enabler of employees' brand-supporting behaviors. *Journal of Service Management, 20*(2), 209–226.

Roper, S., & Davies, G. (2007). The corporate brand: Dealing with multiple stakeholders. *Journal of Marketing Management, 23*(1–2), 75–90.

Saleem, F. Z., & Iglesias, O. (2016). Mapping the domain of the fragmented field of internal branding. *Journal of Product & Brand Management, 25*(1), 43–57. https://doi.org/10.1108/JPBM-11-2014-0751

Schein, E. H. (2006). *Organizational culture and leadership*. New York: John Wiley & Sons.

Schepers, J., & Nijssen, E. J. (2018). Brand advocacy in the frontline: How does it affect customer satisfaction? *Journal of Service Management, 29*(2), 230–252. https://doi.org/10.1108/JOSM-07-2017-0165

Schmidt, H. J. (2017). Living brand orientation: How a brand-oriented culture supports employees to live the brand. In N. Ind (Ed.), *Branding inside out: Internal branding in theory and practice* (pp. 13–32). London: Kogan Page.

Schmidt, H. J., & Baumgarth, C. (2018). Strengthening internal brand equity with brand ambassador programs: Development and testing of a success factor model. *Journal of Brand Management, 25*(3), 250–265.

Schmidt, H. J., Ind, N., Guzmán, F., & Kennedy, E. (2021b). Socio-political activist brands. *Journal of Product and Brand Management*. https://doi.org/10.1108/JPBM-03-2020-2805

Schmidt, H. J., Ind, N., & Iglesias, O. (2021a). Internal branding – In search of a new paradigm: Guest editorial. *Journal of Product & Brand Management, 30*(6), 781–787.

Schmidt, H. J., & Redler, J. (2018). How diverse is corporate brand management research? Comparing schools of corporate brand management with approaches to corporate strategy. *Journal of Product & Brand Management, 27*(2), 185–202.

Schroth, H. (2019). Are you ready for gen Z in the workplace? *California Management Review, 61*(3), 5–18.

Schultz, M., & de Chernatony, L. (2002). The challenges of corporate branding. *Corporate Reputation Review*, 5(2–3), 105–113.

Skaalsvik, H., & Olsen, B. (2014a). A study of a service brand process in a cruise context: The perspective of the service employees. *International Journal of Culture, Tourism and Hospitality Research, 8*(4), 446–461.

Skaalsvik, H., & Olsen, B. (2014b). Service branding: Suggesting an interactive model of service brand development. *Kybernetes, 43*(8), 1209–1223. https://doi.org/10.1108/K-12-2013-0274

Steenkamp, P., Herbst, F. J., De Villiers, J. D., Terblanche-Smit, M., & Schmidt, H. J. (2020). Servbrand framework: A business-to-business services brand equity framework. *Journal of Business-to-Business Marketing, 27*(1), 55–69. https://doi.org/10.1080/1051712X.2020.1713560

Sujchaphong, N., Nguyen, B., Melewar, T. C., Sujchaphong, P., & Chen, J. (2020). A framework of brand-centred training and development activities, transformational leadership and employee brand support in higher education. *Journal of Brand Management*, (27), 143–159. https://doi.org/10.1057/s41262-019-00171-9

Suomi, K., Saraniemi, S., Vähätalo, M., Kallio, T. J., & Tevameri, T. (2019). Employee engagement and internal branding: Two sides of the same coin? *Corporate Reputation Review*, 1–16. https://doi.org/10.1057/s41299-019-00090-0

Tuominen, S., Hirvonen, S., Reijonen, H., & Laukkanen, T. (2016). The internal branding process and financial performance in service companies: An examination of the required steps. *Journal of Brand Management, 23*(3), 306–326.

Urde, M., Baumgarth, C., & Merrilees, B. (2013). Brand orientation and market orientation – From alternatives to synergy. *Journal of Business Research*, 66(1), 13–20.

Vallaster, C., & von Wallpach, S. (2013). An online discursive inquiry into the social dynamics of multi-stakeholder brand meaning co-creation. *Journal of Business Research*, 66(9), 1505–1515.

Veloutsou, C., & Delgado-Ballester, E. (2019). New challenges in brand management. *Spanish Journal of Marketing – ESIC*, 22(3), 255–272. https://doi.org/10.1108/SJME-12-2018-036

Veloutsou, C., & Guzmán, F. (2017). The evolution of brand management thinking over the last 25 years as recorded in the journal of product and brand management. *Journal of Product & Brand Management*, 26(1), 2–12.

von Wallpach, S., Hemetsberger, A., & Espersen, P. (2017). Performing identities: Processes of brand and stakeholder identity co-construction. *Journal of Business Research*, 70, 443–452.

Wallace, E., & de Chernatony, N. L. (2007). Exploring managers' views about brand saboteurs. *Journal of Marketing Management*, 23(1–2), 91–106.

Zhang, J., & He, Y. (2014). Key dimensions of brand value co-creation and its impacts upon customer perception and brand performance: An empirical research in the context of industrial service. *Nankai Business Review International*, 5(1), 43–69. https://doi.org/10.1108/NBRI-09-2013-0033

Zhang, J., Jiang, Y., Shabbir, R., & Zhu, M. (2016). How brand orientation impacts B2B service brand equity? An empirical study among Chinese firms. *Journal of Business & Industrial Marketing*, 31(1), 83–98. https://doi.org/10.1108/JBIM-02-2014-0041

Zwakala, K., Steenkamp, P., & Haydam, N. E. (2017). Brand identity: Theory versus practice in the South African banking sector. *The Retail and Marketing Review*, 13(2), 1–14.

# 28
# EXPLORING HOW TO BUILD A STRONG INTERNAL BRAND COMMUNITY AND ITS ROLE IN CORPORATE BRAND CO-CREATION

*Saila Saraniemi*

Acknowledgements: M.Sc. Hanna Nurkkala is gratefully acknowledged for her help in data collection.

## 1. Introduction

Corporate branding literature has increasingly adopted the view that brand value is interactively co-created with multiple stakeholders (Merz et al., 2009; Mäläskä et al., 2011). The approach thus views corporate brand value as created in the interactions between employees, managers, and external stakeholders (e.g., Saleem & Iglesias, 2016). Further, it is said that marketing has evolved towards a community-oriented approach, which is evident especially in social media where consumers produce organizational value in online collectives, that is, brand communities, constructed around common interests (Schembri & Latimer, 2016). These collectives enable consumers for example to share the meanings they ascribe to the brand and share their stories about it (Schembri & Latimer, 2016). Brand communities are thus important external stakeholders and co-creators of corporate brand value.

A company's internal stakeholders create a community as well. For example, a sense of community and support from a work community are important factors in employee engagement that apparently also influence the internal brand (e.g., Suomi et al., 2021.) However, research combining a community perspective with a corporate branding perspective as influenced by a company's internal stakeholders' interactions remains scarce. Such research would be valuable, for as Michel (2017) points out, we still know little about employees' role in the co-construction of a corporate brand identity, for example. The present study explores the phenomenon of internal brand communities in the co-creation of a corporate brand, and especially in remote working environments where the reduced physical proximity of employees creates an unique context to building a brand community. Saleem and Iglesias (2016) state that an internal brand community refers to a company's internal virtual or physical platform used to share brand values and brand-related ideas. Extant research does not specify whether these communities are necessarily formal, or company-led or part of the internal branding activities; although according to

Devasagayam et al. (2010), internal branding is a prerequisite for internal brand communities to exist. Accordingly, this study approaches the concept from a broad perspective and views the working community as an internal brand community, as far as it creates corporate brand value. The phenomenon is studied in a B2B project business, an industry where remote working environments are an intrinsic feature, but the COVID-19 pandemic has highlighted the importance of remote working environments across industries. Specifically, the qualitative interview data were gathered from an ICT consultancy company, a knowledge-intensive business services provider where it is typical for employees to work as subcontractors for lengthy periods at a client's premises. Such consultancy providers often have several B2B clients and the subcontracting chains can be long, with multiple corporate brands involved. Accordingly, from a corporate brand perspective, such remote or virtual working environments can be a challenging context in which to encourage internal branding.

Devasagayam et al. (2010) argued in their pioneering study of internal brand communities that it is in an employer's interest to enhance employees identification with the corporate brand, and moreover, that a firm supporting the creation of an internal brand community would encourage employees to socially negotiate the brand and involve to activities of the community. However, existing literature offers little knowledge on the dynamics that create and shape internal brand communities or on the role of those communities in corporate brand co-creation. Therefore, the objectives of the present study are to explore: (1) the dynamics of internal brand communities in remote working environments and (2) the roles played by remote internal brand communities in corporate brand co-creation. B2B project business is a relevant context for this study, as the internal aspect of the brand is central in B2B and services markets. In these companies, employees are in a pivotal role in branding interactions and corporate brands are a dominant brand strategy (see Schmidt & Baumgarth, 2018). Further, although project business marketing has evoked growing interest among researchers in recent decades, from a branding perspective, few studies address its characteristics (e.g., Jalkala et al., 2010; Sheikh & Lim, 2011).

Saleem and Iglesias (2016) state the aim of internal branding is to internally support brand value co-creation by stakeholders, which this study suggests is a role that can be adopted by an internal brand community, even in the absence of systematic internal branding activity. However, especially in the remote working environment, involving internal stakeholders in brand-related activities systematically advances the creation of an internal brand community and fosters a shared consciousness of the corporate brand, further positively impacting corporate brand co-creation. There are still gaps in the literature around co-creative perspectives on internal branding (Piehler et al., 2018). Through interviews with employees, founders, and managers on their brand-related interactions, and an analysis of the role of an internal brand community in the co-creation of a corporate brand, this study contributes to this emerging literature.

## 2. Literature review

### 2.1. Corporate branding in B2B

A strong corporate brand implies differentiating characteristics, trustworthiness, and quality among stakeholders of the company (e.g., Törmälä & Saraniemi, 2018). A reputable corporate brand means the company's products, services, and employees can more easily be perceived in a favourable light. Corporate brands act in networks with multiple meaningful stakeholders (e.g., Merz et al., 2009), a factor that has steadily amplified the role of corporate brands for businesses. The strategic and longer-term perspective of corporate brands (Balmer, 2001) reinforces the transformative objectives of companies regarding societal and environmental sustainability, for example (see Iglesias & Ind, 2020). For a growing number of firms today, the articulated purpose of the corporate brand (Gyrd-Jones, 2012) sets the direction the associated firm should take. At the same time, while being true to their purpose, corporate brands are constantly being adapted to reflect the needs of the firm's customers (Törmälä & Gyrd-Jones, 2017) and other stakeholders (Iglesias & Ind, 2020).

Interaction within networks and relationships is at the very heart of the business logics of B2B organizations (e.g., Mäläskä et al., 2011). Literature suggests that the benefits of a strong corporate brand include fostering trusting relationships with customers and other stakeholders (Leek & Christodoulides, 2011), swaying the decision-making processes of B2B customers (Bendixen et al., 2004) while reducing their perceptions of risk (Bengtsson & Servais, 2005). Research portrays the corporate brand as being co-created through dynamic, interactive social processes in multi-stakeholder networks (Merz et al., 2009), which signals that the interactions of the stakeholders constructing the corporate brand merit attention. Kristal et al. (2020) emphasized that these stakeholder interactions represent the key building blocks of the corporate brand. Further, as the heart of the corporate brand is its identity (see Iglesias et al., 2020); the interactions of internal stakeholders in corporate brand co-creation take a prevalent, yet not entirely understood, role. After all, the behaviour of internal stakeholders influences the perceptions held by external stakeholders (e.g., Sirianni et al., 2013). This is particularly the case in knowledge-intensive business services (KIBS), such as in engineering services, where the corporate brand's status is highly reliant on employee behaviour and professional knowledge.

## 2.2. Internal brand communities

As a co-creative approach to branding suggests, corporate brands are evolving entities owing to their symbiotic relationships with their founders, employees, customers, suppliers, and subcontractors in their internal and external environments (Iglesias & Ind, 2020) and consequently, there are myriad individuals and groups that enact the brand. The willingness to do so, and thus to co-create the brand, is most visible in brand communities where customers share their thoughts and interact with the brand alongside others interested in the development and well-being of the brand. Sometimes these individuals are so deeply involved with the co-creation of the brand that they start to behave like employees (see Ind et al., 2017).

Brand communities channel individuals' contributions to co-creating the brand, while at the same time also serving more individual motives such as the social and financial needs of their members (Veloutsou & Black, 2020; Ind et al., 2017). Studies considering online and offline brand communities reveal the power wielded by individuals and the groups to which they belong in corporate brand co-creation (Muñiz & O'Guinn, 2001; Hatch & Schultz, 2010). Through brand communities, consumers may influence the functional characteristics of the brand (Skålén et al., 2015), brand meaning (Cova & White, 2010), brand culture (Schembri & Latimer, 2016), and the transformation of brands (Cova & Paranque, 2016). For brand communities, brands are catalysts of social interaction and offer a sense of belonging. Brands evoke a shared consciousness, loyalty, engagement, common traditions, and even a sense of responsibility among members of communities (Muñiz & O'Guinn, 2001; Kaplan & Haenlein, 2010). In today's hyperconnected society, brand communities can help to combat loneliness and social isolation (Swaminathan et al., 2020).

However, the existent literature on brand communities focuses predominantly on consumer brands (e.g., Muñiz & O'Guinn, 2001; Black & Veloutsou, 2017), and only a few examples can be found in B2B contexts (e.g., Andersen, 2005; Mäläskä & Nadeem, 2012) and that latter group almost exclusively explores the actions of brands' external stakeholders in brand communities.

Moreover, although current literature is valuable for understanding the importance of brand communities and their social structures in facilitating the co-creation of corporate brands (see Veloutsou & Black, 2020), we know less about the relevance of the brand community concept to a company's internal actions in the co-creation of a corporate brand (see Devasagayam et al., 2010). A notion that is widely acknowledged in research on and the practice of internal branding (e.g., Saleem & Iglesias, 2016) is that of employees forming a work community, whose acceptance of and commitment to the corporate brand is reliant on its performance. Brand communities are in many ways similar to highly engaged work communities; their members act like employees and thus co-create the corporate brand. Therefore, it is perhaps surprising that research on work communities from the brand community perspective remains rare.

There is, however, some literature on internal brand communities. Saleem and Iglesias (2016, 48) defined them as 'virtual and physical communities that foster employee identification with the brand.' Devasagayam et al. (2010) suggested that only companies carrying out internal branding could have internal brand communities, while recognizing that internal brand communities could help align employee behaviour with brand values. Saleem and Iglesias (2016) remarked that the relevance of internal brand communities is growing with the increasing use of social network platforms that help to maintain communities. Furthermore, the immense rise of virtual and remote working environments due to the social distancing and restrictions in place during the COVID-19 pandemic has made the community aspect an even more important part of internal branding. Like members of consumer brand communities, (Nambisan & Nambisan, 2008; Schau et al., 2009) it is suggested that employees in internal brand communities can share practices of collective value creation, acquire information, socialize, and even enjoy hedonistic experiences, and even more so due to virtual interaction (see Saleem & Iglesias, 2016). However, although studies of internal branding have recognized the possibilities of internal brand communities (e.g., Saleem & Iglesias, 2016; Suomi et al., 2021), and several communal factors such as work community, sense of community, multi-professional cooperation, and workplace climate, are associated with internal branding in the literature (e.g., Suomi et al., 2021), we still know little about them, and particularly of their role in corporate brand co-creation in B2B companies with largely remote or virtual working environments that is, with a distributed, geographically dispersed, workforce.

## 2.3. Role of internal brand communities in B2B project business

The chosen context for this study is the project business and specifically the engineering consulting services area, which is distinguished by distributed, a sort of remote, working being a routine feature. The context of project has been extensively studied within the B2B marketing research field (e.g., Jalkala et al., 2010; Artto et al., 2015), and the literature features several contributions about the role of individuals and social interactions in business relationships (e.g., Alajoutsijärvi et al., 2000; Ojansivu et al., 2013). *Project business* refers to 'the part of business that relates directly or indirectly to projects, with a purpose to achieve objectives of a firm or several firms' (Artto & Wikström, 2005). The types of projects involve range from large construction projects to service-intensive projects, where in the latter case the role of a social dimension and personal relationships is usually strong, and not only because of the typical discontinuity of these business relationships (see Ojansivu et al., 2013). Among service-intensive projects, engineering consulting projects have their distinctive features (see Sheikh & Lim, 2011). They require close collaboration with the clients, high levels of technical knowledge and creativity, and an on-site presence by consultants, that is, a remote or virtual working environment for employees. Staff of project business providers working remotely will also be required to adhere to their clients' codes of safety and practice (see Downey & Lucena, 2004; Sheikh & Lim, 2011). Those particularities highlight the role of an internal brand community and engagement among employees of an engineering company to create common ground and identification with the employer and its corporate brand.

The study of Sheikh and Lim (2011) supports this perspective by showing that engineering consultants views of management's branding efforts are often less than favourable because corporate branding is often devised and implemented in a top-down manner. In line with these findings, Ojasalo et al. (2008) found that branding seemed to be a challenge internally for software companies. That is a result, for example, of the personnel not often being involved in brand-related decision-making and because getting technology-oriented personnel to cooperate with marketing- and management-oriented personnel can be a challenge. A particularly interesting insight in Sheikh and Lim's (2011, p. 1129) study was that engineers 'identified more readily with the specialist competencies they have been trained to deliver for clients rather than with brand personality and promise' and that strong personal brands among senior employees, in particular, were typical in these companies. These aspects suggest that the engineering profession drives an individualistic direction in the work of the engineers. Finally, when an engineering company grows there is a danger that the local contact points with a parent company are lost (Sheikh & Lim, 2011). This can also be an issue for geographically diverse sites and makes internal brand communities even more important from the perspective of company unity and corporate brand co-creation. In summary, several features of the B2B project business can provide insights into internal brand communities and their roles in co-constructing corporate brands, particularly in remote working environments.

## 2.4. The role of internal brand communities in co-creating the corporate brand

Existing research has shown that both internal and external stakeholders can co-construct, that is co-create a corporate brand (e.g., Iglesias et al., 2020; Mäläskä et al., 2011; von Wallpach et al., 2017). This constructivist and dynamic perspective on branding is evident in studies of the role of internal stakeholders (e.g., Schmeltz & Kjeldsen, 2019), although external stakeholders have had a more central role in recent studies of corporate brand co-construction (Törmälä & Gyrd-Jones, 2017; Iglesias et al., 2020). These studies have shown that internal stakeholders perform actions that impact the identity, image, or meanings of the corporate brand, and some of those actions are channelled by brand communities. For example, von Wallpach et al. (2017) investigated the LEGO brand community and found that, in addition to the actions of the strong consumer brand community, employees and managers of LEGO were also co-constructing the corporate brand identity through their actions as part of the brand community. Employees were facilitating the community, playing with LEGOs, liking others' actions in the community, and developing the marketplace for LEGO, both online and offline. Managers, in addition, acted as guardians or conductors of the co-construction of the corporate brand identity. Iglesias et al. (2020) suggested that both internal and external stakeholders co-construct the corporate brand through communicating, internalizing, contesting, and elucidating the corporate brand identity. Through those performative actions, internal stakeholders, as a community, may behave in a way that fosters their identification with the corporate brand (see Saleem & Iglesias, 2016), and moreover they co-construct the corporate brand.

Literature has demonstrated how members of consumer brand communities create their own identities when they enact the brand identity (e.g., Kornum et al., 2017). In a similar manner, the identities of employees depend partly on and contribute to the brand identity of their employer companies (e.g., Vallaster & von Wallpach, 2013). In knowledge-intensive business services, such as in engineering services, this interplay between corporate brand identity and employee identities can expand into a wider network encompassing the corporate brand to the employees' daily, often remote working environments, and also into the B2B clients' brand identities. Earlier studies suggest that especially in the service sector, employees have a critical role in building the corporate brand (e.g., Morokane et al., 2016). They are also expected to agree on the brand meaning (Schmeltz & Kjeldsen, 2019), an aspect often motivating a firm's internal branding activities. Elements of internal branding such as management and employees negotiating brand values are suggested to enhance employee engagement (Suomi et al., 2021.) On the other hand, studies suggest that multiple stakeholder voices may represent the same institution and its multifaceted identity. Even then, a certain level of consensus or compatibility between internal brand perceptions is needed, as all internal stakeholders are potential communicators of the brand (Schmeltz & Kjeldsen, 2019). Overall, literature seems to lean towards internal branding having a role in fostering internal brand communities and their actions in corporate brand co-creation. In this study, the focus is on interactions of professionals in a B2B project business, who according to the literature typically identify more with their tasks and profession than with their employer's corporate brand and who work mostly in a virtual or remote working environment, which would seem a challenging environment from an internal branding perspective. More precisely, the focus is on their dynamic interactions with regard to internal brand community building and their roles in corporate brand co-creation.

## 3. Methodology

This study draws from an empirical case of an ICT consultancy company with its headquarters in Northern Finland. It is referred to as The Company, and was founded at the beginning of the 2010s and has sites both in Northern Finland (City A) and in the area of the capital (City B), as well as individual employees in another city in southern Finland (City C). The Company has approximately 150 employees, and most of them worked at the headquarters when interviewed. As is typical of an ICT consultancy company, a significant proportion of the staff works on B2B clients' projects at the clients' premises, often for long periods and sometimes for years. Another aspect describing the company is that its sites in the North and South of the country differ somewhat in terms of the profile of the employees. As in many other ICT firms in the home city of the company, the four founders and several key employees have backgrounds in the Nokia mobile phone company and thus share a history. This is not a case for the capital area site, whose employees are on average also younger than in the northern City A. The Company has grown quite rapidly in the last 5 years and its ownership has also changed recently. The following quote describes the offering of the company:

> We offer our own projects, which means that we provide holistic solutions for clients from planning to implementation. We also hire out consultants to client companies, that is, in practice, a person goes to work at the client's premises.
> (User Experience (UX) Designer)

Since prior research on the topic is emergent, this study is a qualitative single case study that uses inductive reasoning (see Corley & Gioia, 2004). This approach allows to generate rich and contextual information about the phenomenon. The case company is chosen for this study, as it represents a typical B2B ICT consultancy company (see Stake, 1995). Altogether 12 semi-structured interviews were conducted in autumn 2020 among the case company's employees (Table 28.1). The informants represented employees from each site, and in various professions, managers, and

Table 28.1 Informants

| Informant's title | Informant's Site | Date | Duration |
|---|---|---|---|
| SW Specialist 1 | City A, headquarters | 1.10.20 | 34 min. |
| UX Designer | City A, headquarters | 1.10.20 | 40 min. |
| Content Designer | City A, customer's office | 5.10.20 | 52 min. |
| UX Specialist | City A, customer's office | 5.10.20 | 38 min. |
| Head Designer | City A, headquarters | 23.9.20 | 55 min. |
| SVP, Marketing & Sales, Founder | City A, headquarters | 5.10.20 | 60 min. |
| Sales Director | City B, company's office | 30.9.20 | 54 min. |
| HR specialist | City B, company's office | 1.10.20 | 53 min. |
| Data analytics consultant | City B, customer's office | 2.10.20 | 55 min. |
| Senior SW Specialist | City B, company's office | 16.10.20 | 51 min. |
| Cloud Engineer | City B, customer's office | 5.10.20 | 57 min. |
| SW Specialist 2 | City C, home/customer's office | 28.9.20 | 48 min. |

one of the founders. It is important to note that The Company's culture is based on a flat hierarchy, which was often stated throughout the interviews. Even the people in key management positions were reluctant to call themselves supervisors. Instead, informants emphasized the role of teams in organizing their work, teams that often included people from both main sites of the company. The interviews lasted between 34 minutes and an hour each and were conducted via Teams software, by two interviewers. The data were then transcribed and analysed to elicit the interactions that build an internal brand community and to reveal the roles of that community in corporate brand co-creation. The analysis started with open coding, for identifying initial concepts and resulting in an unstructured set of data extracts of branding and community interactions in the company (see Corley & Gioia, 2004; Törmälä & Gyrd-Jones, 2017). The analysis continued with theme-based coding, by first grouping interactions related to the internal brand community building and second, focusing to the action-based roles that the work community has in corporate brand co-creation (see Törmälä & Saraniemi, 2018). At this phase, the resulting categories were compared against existing research (Goulding, 2005) for providing a new theoretical framework. The whole research project was conducted as the COVID-19 pandemic was occurring, which helped the interviewers relate to their informants as both sides were working remotely at the time. At the beginning of the interview, this aspect acted as an icebreaker to prompt further discussion. Overall, the interviews followed an interview guide planned beforehand but that was subject to change along with the interview and the research process.

## 4. Findings

### 4.1. The dynamics of internal brand communities

#### 4.1.1 Dynamics that advance building the internal brand community

The data indicate that building an internal brand community in a remote working environment is advanced through five interrelated dynamic interactions of internal stakeholders: facilitating a sense of belonging, engaging with the community, boundary-spanning, sharing knowledge and stories, and upholding traditions and rituals. Figure 28.1 summarizes the dynamics of internal brand communities.

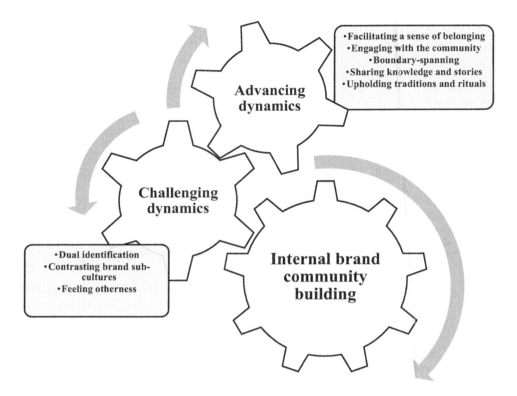

*Figure 28.1* The dynamics of internal brand communities

FACILITATING A SENSE OF BELONGING

Facilitating a sense of belonging involves internal stakeholders (founders, employees, and managers) uniting with a common purpose, which then advances understanding of a shared identity and the meanings of the corporate brand. The common purpose for an internal brand community is their raison d'être, which in this case was a shared understanding of the strong professionalism in The Company.

> I think that we still have a great community. No matter who you start to work with on some project from The Company, there is always a good atmosphere surrounding your work; an atmosphere, where it is easy to communicate. It is a mindset, that everybody who works for the company knows what they are doing.
>
> (UX Designer)

Employees facilitate a sense of belonging through developing and reinforcing mutual bonds. For example, visiting The Company's office regularly is important also in the remote and multi-local working environment, and reinforcing bonds with the community can be particularly important for an individual's working motivation during times of complicated client relationship, for instance. In the data, the sense of belonging, a sort of 'we-ness' was described as being even more important than the corporate brand elements and visuals:

Yes, I feel very strongly that I am a part of The Company. At this moment, it's not necessarily even related to the brand aspect of it because I feel like I can't support the brand very much as it is at the moment.... The important aspect for me at The Company has been the way we are as an employer and a work community. So that, we appear as a happy, good-spirited team, who have fun at work. That has always been a central aspect for me.

(UX Specialist)

The sense of belonging is also facilitated through developing and reinforcing formal and informal organizational behaviours, some of which concern the whole work community and some of which are more localized and concern a professional sub-group or team, such as designers' recurrent Design Friday event, for example.

The sense of belonging builds an internal brand community essentially through the positive and safe working climate that it creates. Employees used metaphors such as 'home' or 'family' when describing the working community in The Company: 'It is kind of family-like, very ordinary' (SW Specialist 1). Related to this, at the heart of the strong internal brand community seems to be the trust in colleagues' skills and a trusting atmosphere: 'The Company values us as we are' (UX Specialist). This affects the manner in which employees execute their duties and seems to be especially important in a remote working environment. However, working in the project business, employees of The Company could compare the firm's working environment against that of their client firm, which affected their level of identification with their consultancy client, sometimes over The Company's corporate brand.

### ENGAGING WITH THE COMMUNITY

Engaging with the community concerns interactions that create internal stakeholders' commitment to The Company and its corporate brand, as these interactions support internalizing the brand. The commitment of employees, that is, employee engagement, advances internal brand community development. Employee engagement flows from interactions, particularly those among co-workers and between employees and managers. Especially in the remote working environment, co-workers must communicate with their peers and make it known that their peers are appreciated. The feeling of being valued positively affects an employee's commitment to the company and its corporate brand and encourages employees' identification with their specific professional role in the community and thus affects the building of the internal brand community, as depicted in the following:

I feel that I'm appreciated in our work community, treated professionally. I'm trusted to handle a difficult client and that I can do intricate work.

(UX Specialist)The data show that offering training and opportunities for individual development fosters engagement with the community and is more important than remuneration from the perspective of developing an internal brand community.

It is not only a salary that attracts people. In The Company, you can get a very competitive one, but there are other aspects anyway, that become more important. For example, the possibility to develop yourself.

(Content Designer)

An important part of engaging with the internal brand community is the acculturation process that lets employees, and especially new recruits, internalize the company values and a certain mindset in their daily work. The data show that successful recruitment has much to do with acculturation. In this case, company recruitment targeted people with a certain kind of mindset: 'not extroverts in particular, but those who enjoy other people's company in general.' In a remote working environment, the same kind of mindset appears to be one of the most important aspects in building the internal brand community, as it integrates employees regardless of their location.

### BOUNDARY-SPANNING

Boundary-spanning means that an employee constantly crosses the boundaries of the internal brand community. Boundary-spanning is a special character of the remote working environment. Members of the working community engage with the corporate brand and other employees within and outside the boundaries of the community. Crossing the boundaries may happen either physically – as when an employee moves from one site to another – or mentally referring to the level of an employee's involvement in the client's working community, for example. This nature of consultancy work, characteristic of the B2B project business, gives a feeling of freedom for employees contributing positively to internal brand community development. It also permits employees working at the client's premises to distinguish between the internal brand community and the client's working community and, for example, to set limits on their involvement with certain discussions within the client's working community. This scenario supports their individual professional mindset, but as they are representatives of the corporate brand, it also differentiates and builds the internal brand community through adding a certain expertise-oriented mindset.

> But I like the setup when you are a consultant, you have certain kind of freedom . . . being a consultant [at the client's premises] lets me say things that I may not be able to question normally in a work community. . . . It is in a way my duty, as well. To highlight aspects based on my expertise.
>
> (UX Specialist)

Further, the data shows that especially in the context of B2B consultancy services, boundary-spanning that builds the internal brand community relates to identifying strongly as an employee of a provider company and a member of a provider's internal brand community, which offers a necessary outsider perspective when working at the client's premises. This special role of a consultant was emphasized by some informants. For example, there seems to be a line that how much a consultant can and should become involved in the client's internal discussions and when it is acceptable to ensure some distance. There is also a discernible limit to the kind of work-related conversations that can be had between, for example, designers of The Company. Obviously, discussions among employees not working at the same client premises must remain on the general level and not go into detail about the customer, which may create divisions and possible sub-groups within the internal brand community.

### SHARING KNOWLEDGE AND STORIES

Employees and founders play a significant role in building the internal brand community through sharing their knowledge and experiences of the company, the corporate brand, and their field of expertise among the community. This sharing can be informal or more formal, but voluntary activities in particular reflect the strength of the internal brand community. Such activities might include voluntarily writing a blog or content for a newsletter relating a person's expertise. In a remote working environment, digital platforms play an essential role by providing an arena for sharing.

The data show that the most important channel for sharing knowledge and stories internally is the team chat application that provides dozens of channels for conversations and communication between employees and thus, plays a key role in The Company's internal brand community building.

> The company's chat makes it possible to organize all kinds of things, through dozens of different conversations. Some of them are between a group of friends, while some focus on a certain topic. If you want to set up a free Friday afternoon sauna for everybody then you send a message on the chat or send a calendar invitation and then get the sauna ready.
> (SW Specialist 1)

The important role of the chat in channelling community building is visible in comments that relate to threats that the chat communication has recently addressed. For example, the growth of the company seems to be affecting communication through this platform, making it more fragmented than previously:

> We used to have more and unofficial discussions in the general channel. Now the company has grown, the amount of discussion in the chat has decreased and it is fragmented into several cliques.

(SW Specialist 2)The COVID-19 pandemic has further amplified sharing knowledge through channels such as remote, weekly meetings, that in part reinforce internal brand community development. This is important because the pandemic seems to reduce some employees' use of the chat. Sharing knowledge and stories about the company indicates an active membership in the internal brand community, and sometimes this activity extends to external stakeholders, as well. For example, the data show that employees repeatedly promote the positive working climate and good reputation of The Company as an employer to potential employees by word-of-mouth. This, in turn, reinforces internal brand community development.

### UPHOLDING TRADITIONS AND RITUALS

Upholding various traditions and rituals creates bonds between employees and thus advances the development of a strong internal brand community. Traditions encompass common events and hobbies that employees partake in together, for example, no matter where they physically work. Spending time together during leisure time also builds the community.

> Well, at The Company there have been a lot of fun parties. There are summer parties and usually during the fall a trip to the Levi ski resort, which is considered legendary.
> (Content Designer)

> We have had this old tradition from the beginning; a photo competition in the chat every Friday at 2 pm.
> (Head Designer)

However, this aspect can also create a distinction between different sites. The data show that the common leisure-time activities are more likely at City B than at Cities A or C, most probably due to the different age profiles of staff at the sites. Therefore, traditions and rituals can be common to all staff, or sometimes more local.

### 4.1.2. Dynamics that challenge building an internal brand community

Based on the data, building the internal brand community in a remote working environment is challenged through three interrelated dynamic interactions among internal stakeholders: dual identification, contrasting brand sub-cultures, and a feeling of otherness.

#### DUAL IDENTIFICATION

Dual identification, i.e., an employee identifying both with the company's and the client's brand, can be an issue that affects employees in the B2B project business in a remote working environment. It is a consequence of employees sometimes only rarely visiting The Company's site while working daily at a client's office, and its effects can hinder creating a clear perception of the corporate brand. Dual identification can therefore challenge the building of an internal brand community, and particularly among employees new to the organization. This special dual identification characteristic of consultancy services appeared strongly in the data.

> Primarily, I feel that I work for The Company. There is always this dual identity involved and I have to adopt those 'other hands' as part of my identity to be able to fulfil the client's wishes.
> (SW Specialist 1)

> At the beginning, I went to work full time at the client's office. At the time, my bond with the Company remained very thin. I went there mostly to sign the job agreement and collect luncheon vouchers, but I didn't feel any connection towards The Company, other than its name on the pay check.
> (Content Designer)

An employee's identification can appear on a continuum, sometimes veering more towards the client's community, even when there were other consultants from The Company at the same client's premises or regular work assignments with colleagues from The Company. Which end of the continuum was emphasized seemed to depend on the work environment at the client's site, with a welcoming and engaging atmosphere bolstering dual identification or even stronger identification with the client. Further, an aspect that may at least temporarily dilute an employee's identification with the corporate brand and the internal brand community, is their identification with the client's project, rather than a particular employer or their corporate brand.

#### CONTRASTING BRAND SUB-CULTURES

Contrasting brand sub-cultures are typified by interactions of internal stakeholders that highlight differences between organizational behaviour or manners of the diverse teams and groups in the company. Where brand sub-cultures clash, it can be challenging to build an internal brand community especially in a remote working environment and in a company that has different sites. The data show that different brand sub-cultures might have different conversational styles or different habits and even express the corporate brand differently.

> The sites in City A and City B are kind of separated. Sure, I know some people there [City A], and some might have projects in City B occasionally or in some other big firms that may have workers and offices in both cities. In that sense, I haven't been in touch with colleagues from City A, only with those that I have met somewhere else.
> (Data analytics consultant)

In The Company, the differences in the profiles and compilation of the teams at the geographically diverse sites seem to sometimes give rise to sub-cultures.

### A FEELING OF OTHERNESS

Internal stakeholders might have a feeling of otherness if they perceive themselves to be alienated from The Company's working community and its corporate brand. In a remote working environment, where the daily work is not always shared with the same colleagues in the same office, feelings of otherness can challenge building an internal brand community. The data show that when most of the daily work and related conversations are between the project team at the client's premises, an employee may feel alienated from The Company's internal brand community.

> It's usually always the client's project team who I am with and associate with. I don't usually talk about work-related issues with other colleagues at The Company. Of course, you can ask, if you need something technical or if you have worked with certain technology, you can ask for help [from the Company team].
> (Data analytics consultant)

In the remote working environment, and especially in the B2B project business, staying within the borders or outside of the internal brand community becomes sometimes critical as it is not rare that clients suggest moving as their employees from an external consultant's role.

> If you work as a consultant for many years for the same client, you are kind of integrated into their work community and it happens a lot that a consultant leaves the company to work for a client permanently. And that is the point, [when you evaluate] what is that thing that The Company offers that makes you want to stay there.
> (UX Specialist)

In summary, overcoming these challenges to building an internal brand community may make the community stronger and confer a more meaningful role in corporate brand co-creation, which is the focus of the next section. It should be noted that these challenging dynamics create diversity in the internal brand community, which at its most positive can help keep the community current and energetic.

## 4.2. The role of internal brand communities in corporate brand co-creation

Internal brand communities have an important role in corporate brand co-creation because it is the members of such communities – employees, founders, and managers – who experience the brand in their everyday work and actions and who represent the corporate brand to external stakeholders such as clients. A strong internal brand community will be united behind a common purpose and set of values and will offer a platform on which internal stakeholders can co-create the brand: 'Being a part of the team that has a common objective' (HR specialist). In particular, the internal brand community has a role in the co-creating corporate brand identity and meanings, which is then reflected in the co-creation of the brand image too. In a remote, physically dispersed working environment, realizing and nurturing the role of an internal brand community in corporate brand co-creation can be a critical factor in the performance of the corporate brand.

The data illustrate the role of The Company's internal brand community in corporate brand co-creation during the firm's recent rebranding, which involved adopting a new slogan and visual identity and redesigning its websites. As a special setting, this process highlights how the internal brand community co-creates identity, values, meanings, and the functional and emotional value of the corporate brand. The interview data reveal the internal brand community has the following roles in corporate brand co-creation: an enactor of corporate brand values, a negotiator of corporate brand meanings, a contributor to corporate brand design, a communicator of the corporate brand, and a maintainer of the corporate brand.

### 4.2.1 Enactor of corporate brand values

The data show that internally shared values can become an important guide for work routines. However, communicating the same values externally in a way that captures the essence of the internal enactment of those values can be challenging; especially if the internal community has not entirely internalized the corporate brand.

> To some extent, it is important what kind of values we are representing but there are two sides to this. The inner, how we interpret them and act accordingly and the other, how they are communicated outside. They should be the same values, but their focus is on the slightly different things. If you articulate those [values] and form them as words or sentences, they easily come across as fake.
>
> (SW Specialist 1)

> We have been working on those [values]. I'm not completely sure what was the outcome. If we have a brand promise, I don't remember it.
>
> (UX Designer)

For The Company, a clear shared value of employees, managers, and founders in their everyday work was trustworthy expertise. That ethos was strong.

### 4.2.2. Negotiator of corporate brand meanings

The data show how the corporate brand can become contested between internal stakeholders. The data depict that if only some sub-groups of the internal brand community are involved in the rebranding process, and some key figures feel alienated from the process, the meanings of the corporate brand might be disputed internally.

> This is an interesting question because I have been involved to some degree in the brand work myself due to text formatting. I know what it is that they want to showcase. One is a sense of community, which we have spoken about . . . caring for workers . . .

courage. Encouraging someone to take more initiative and focusing more on individualistic behaviour is what they want to focus on and showcase at The Company.

(UX Designer)

Some time ago we conducted a purpose survey among the employees. It explored how the employees saw The Company's purpose. I have read those answers a bit and I think that they should have formed the core of the brand development aims. How we employees experience our raison d'être. The new brand message does not relate at all to the results of that survey.

(UX Specialist)

It is also possible that some meanings are strengthened through common events, meetings, and online and offline conversations.

### 4.2.3. Contributor to corporate brand design

The data show that the internal brand community is an important contributor to and resource for the rebranding process and thus contributes to co-creating an authentic corporate brand. In particular, overreliance on external stakeholders, even marketing professionals for brand redesigns can alienate internal stakeholders from the corporate brand.

What happened is that the internal brand heroes weren't consulted that much; sure we were involved and commented but it got pushed through. You know the brand, the concept of it was created by the ad agency, which left me feeling like there could have been a phase where we could have made it more real, more like our brand. It was put in use as it was.

(UX Specialist)

When we designed the new core story for the brand with [the firm's advertising agency], we interviewed quite a lot of people . . . both our customers and employees. We wanted people to feel the brand was their own . . . but I guess we could have done it more precisely, to know where we are, and that we weren't making any assumptions.

(Founder)

In summary, the data illustrate that internal stakeholders can have different expectations and aims in regard to the level of their contribution to brand design.

### 4.2.4. Communicator of the corporate brand

According to the data, the way a brand concept is understood can vary within the internal brand community and that affects how the brand is ultimately communicated externally. In The Company, the changing focus of the brand message from describing *who we are* towards *how we do business* has generated contrasting responses among employees and there were doubts about the outcomes of the rebranding in different sub-groups of the community.

The colourways, typography, and visual logo describe the point in question. That has been one of the strengths [of rebranding], but if that is relevant and interesting externally, is, of course, another question.

(Founder)

The internal brand community communicates the corporate brand externally through its members who are thus tangibly co-creating the brand. They can communicate the brand elements and messages or their behaviours communicate the brand.

> Some discussions have been about promoting The Company's brand by using its visuals in our personal social media accounts, which could make the brand better known.
> (UX Designer)

> From the professional point of view, what The Company is like, is mostly based on the performance of individuals . . . people and teams. . . . [W]e have performed so well at our jobs that surely customers and competitors have formed their impressions based on that.
> (SW Specialist 1)

Employees have paid attention to the fact that communicating the corporate brand through their own personalities and stories gains attention in social media and increases awareness of the corporate brand. Overall, they felt that The Company could be more active in encouraging its employees in corporate brand communication.

### 4.2.5. Maintainer of the corporate brand

The internal brand community performs several activities that maintain the corporate brand. The potentially important role of the internal brand community in corporate brand co-creation is emphasized in the data in notions showing that although opinions on the recently revised brand communication are diverse, employees are willing to compromise on their opinions due to the strong sense of belonging to The Company and its community. In other words, the strong internal brand community can overlook some incomplete aspects of the corporate branding, thus maintaining the corporate brand. In addition, the interviews imply that promoting the corporate brand to external stakeholders maintains the corporate brand, a habit encouraged through The Company's remuneration system.

> At the client's office, we have promoted the good characteristics of The Company as an employer to client's employees.
> (Content designer)

> When we work at a client's office, we try to do additional selling ourselves as well. It is not only that coders code and sellers sell. We are in a way in the frontline to see where there is potential for additional sales.
> (Cloud engineer)

It is important to note that maintaining the brand does not imply stagnation, and the reality is that internal stakeholders have expectations and act to advance the development of the corporate brand. Some interviewees emphasized that, especially in a growing company, a remote working environment highlights the need for more systematic branding activities that also involve employees as much as possible. They have a stake in the brand and as individuals and, as members of a community, a motive to nurture it. In the B2B project business, a person's profession has an impact on how tangible and meaningful the corporate brand is, something the interviewees admitted. For engineers, the role of the brand is realized through an organizational

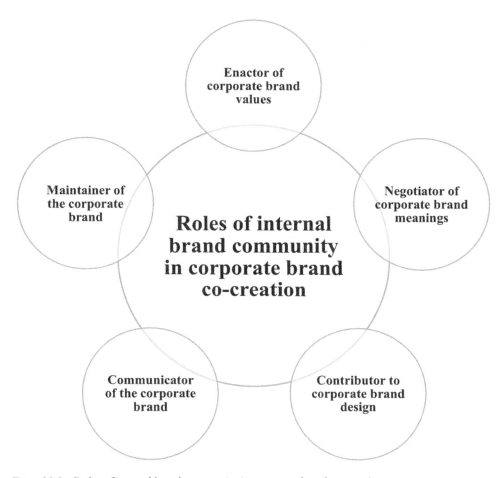

*Figure 28.2* Roles of internal brand community in corporate brand co-creation

culture and a shared mindset regarding work, whereas for designers and marketers, for example, the brand may have a more central role in their routine work.

Finally, the five roles for an internal brand community during corporate brand co-creation (Figure 28.2) were depicted here through an ongoing rebranding process. Those roles therefore also illustrate how an internal brand community can contribute to the transformation of a brand.

## 5. Discussion

This chapter explores and extends the rarely reported topic of a company's internal brand community. The study suggests that whereas brand communities in general have a commercial ethos (see Muñiz & O'Guinn, 2001), an internal brand community's ethos is professional, and at its core is an employer's corporate brand. In external brand communities, consumption binds communities together, whereas in internal communities the glue is professionalism, and a common employer. The study thus broadens the internal brand community concept (cf. Devasagayam et al., 2010; Saleem & Iglesias, 2016) to encapsulate working communities that create corporate brand value.

This is the first study to explore the dynamics of internal brand communities, in other words, internal stakeholders' interactions that advance or challenge the development of an internal brand community. Moreover, the study reveals the roles available to such an internal brand community in corporate brand co-creation. The study contributes to the literature on co-creative internal branding by drawing from community-oriented marketing (see Schembri & Latimer, 2016) and the co-creative corporate brand approach (e.g., Merz et al., 2009; Hatch & Schultz, 2010). The study focuses on the phenomenon in a remote working environment, typical of the B2B project business industry and ICT consultancy services because the absence of physical proximity of that context poses a challenge to building a community. The present study contributes to the literature in the following ways.

First, the findings shed light on five dynamic and interrelated interactions of internal stakeholders that advance building an internal brand community in a remote working environment: facilitating a sense of belonging, engaging with the community, boundary-spanning, sharing knowledge and stories, and upholding traditions and rituals. Although those interactions align with what is known of consumer brand communities and communities in general in terms of members' shared consciousness, shared rituals and traditions, and the moral responsibility towards the community (e.g., Muñiz & O'Guinn, 2001; Veloutsou & Black, 2020), this study reports their appearance in the B2B and remote/virtual working environment. For an internal brand community, employees' strong professionalism and expertise mindset are central for facilitating a sense of belonging and engaging with the community, regardless of the physical location. Those characteristics delimit the common ground and the purpose of the community, thus fostering the internal stakeholder's identification with the corporate brand. In the internal brand community in a remote working environment, 'we-ness' (e.g., Muñiz & O'Guinn, 2001), is more important than brand visuals and brand elements, an aspect that strengthens the bonds between members. We-ness contributes to establishing a trusted and safe working environment, further fostering voluntary activities and active membership in the community. For a remote working environment, a special interaction is boundary-spanning on the borders of the community. Boundary-spanning activity offers a consultant the experience of being an outsider when operating at a client's premises and bonding with an employer's corporate brand. This notion extends the earlier findings on members acting outside and borders of consumer brand communities (e.g., Veloutsou & Black, 2020). Further, as in online brand communities (e.g., Schembri & Latimer, 2016), in a remote working environment, the online communication platform plays a key role in ensuring the internal brand community remains active. The ways in which the platform is used mirror internal variations in organizational behaviour, in the brand's culture and its sub-cultures.

Second, the findings introduce three dynamic interactions of internal stakeholders that challenge the building of an internal brand community in a remote working environment: dual identification, contrasting brand sub-cultures, and feeling otherness. This is the first branding study suggesting that in the B2B project business, employees can experience dual identification with the corporate brand and with the client's brand. If the perception of the employer's brand is not clear, this dual identification becomes more likely. Moreover, the extent of identification with the corporate brand can vary temporarily. Törmälä and Gyrd-Jones (2017) suggested that corporate brand identity is subject to temporal variation, but they did not consider the employee's perspective as such. The finding extends Sheikh and Lim's (2011) notions that engineers identify with the competencies they have learned to deliver for clients rather than with employer's corporate brand promise. Further, this study suggests that a remote and virtual context may create sub-cultures that have their own organizational behaviours and that can also express the corporate brand differently. Sub-cultures are familiar from research into consumer brand communities (see Muñiz & O'Guinn, 2001), but in this study they are seen as potentially challenging an internal brand community building and suggesting employees engaging more with their team than the corporate brand. This study suggests that feeling otherness in the community challenges community building and an employee's identification with the corporate brand. The risk of a sense of otherness affecting employees is very real in the B2B project business and may even lead an employee to feel a stronger bond with a client's brand and to change employers.

The interactions identified in this study as building the internal brand community add to the findings of Iglesias et al. (2020) and von Wallpach et al. (2017) in that they represent communal interactions that support internalizing the corporate brand. This study also shows that these dynamics create diversity in the internal brand community, and therefore for the corporate brand. This diversity can have a positive impact for the community and the brand in that it ensures they continue to develop and stay alive.

Third, this study identifies five corporate brand co-creation roles of internal brand communities in the remote working environment: an enactor of corporate brand values, a negotiator of corporate brand meanings, a contributor to corporate brand design, a communicator of the corporate brand, and a maintainer of the corporate brand. Similar roles for internal and external stakeholders have been found in prior literature (e.g., Törmälä & Saraniemi, 2018; Veloutsou & Black, 2020), but this study considers internal stakeholders a community and finds a new role: a maintainer of the corporate brand. This study suggests that the internal brand community has a role in co-creating corporate brand identity and meanings, which then reflects on the co-creation of the brand image. As for brand communities in general (e.g., Schembri & Latimer, 2016), a strong internal brand community is united behind a common purpose and values, which differentiates such community from the client's community and acts as a platform on which internal stakeholders can co-create the brand. This study suggests that the community can also maintain the brand, especially if it is shifting in an unwelcome direction, which may also create tensions and conflicting meanings of the brand. This phenomenon is also familiar from consumer brand literature but has not previously been identified as a role in corporate brand co-creation. Iglesias et al. (2020), however, noted that founders may stabilize the corporate brand identity.

For managers of a remote working environment, the study shows that cementing a role for an internal brand community in corporate brand co-creation is important for enhancing the performance of the corporate brand. The current study suggests that although an online platform is a key channel through which the internal brand community communicates, other ways to enhance the sense of community are required too. Managers should provide employees opportunities to meet either online or offline and encourage voluntary interactions of the internal brand community. The study shows that a growing company benefits from the systematic involvement of employees in brand-related activities and that overlooking key figures in negotiating the brand's purpose, for example, can alienate them and create tensions that affect the corporate brand. The individual and communal aims interplay in the community, an aspect that managers should pay attention to especially in regards younger employees. A strong internal brand community may also forgive the incompleteness of the corporate brand, emphasizing its important role in corporate brand co-creation. Finally, the study reveals to managers the challenges of a growing company looking to maintain and enhance the internal brand and a sense of community around it. These challenges are emphasized in a remote working environment with employees with a strong sense of professionalism, but overcoming the challenges, and focusing on building trust and meaningfulness, makes the internal brand community stronger.

This study has its limitations, mainly owing to the interviews representing the views of the internal stakeholders in just one company; however, it does add to the rare empirical studies on the topic. In future, remote internal brand communities could be studied in different contexts.

For example, studying companies with only virtual offices would reveal more about the phenomenon. More research is needed about how multiple B2B customers influence corporate brand co-creation internally. It would be particularly interesting to know more about the level of intentionality and freedom of employees in internal branding for building a strong internal brand community.

## References

Alajoutsijärvi, K., Möller, K., & Tähtinen, J. (2000). Beautiful exit: How to leave your business partner. *European Journal of Marketing*, 34(11–12), 1270–1290.

Andersen, P. H. (2005). Relationship marketing and brand involvement of professionals through web-enhanced brand communities: The case of Coloplast. *Industrial Marketing Management*, 34(1), 39–51.

Artto, K. A., Valtakoski, A., & Kärki, H. (2015). Organizing for solutions: How project-based firms integrate project and service businesses. *Industrial Marketing Management*, 45, 70–83.

Artto, K. A., & Wikström, K. (2005). What is project business? *International Journal of Project Management*, 23(5), 343–353.

Balmer, J. M. T. (2001). Corporate identity, corporate branding and corporate marketing – seeing through the fog. *European Journal of Marketing*, 35(3), 248–291.

Bendixen, M., Bukasa, K. A., & Abratt, R. (2004). Brand equity in the business-to-business market. *Industrial Marketing Management*, 33(5), 371–380.

Bengtsson, A., & Servais, P. (2005). Co-branding on industrial markets. *Industrial Marketing Management*, 34(7). 706–713.

Black, I., & Veloutsou, C. (2017). Working consumers: Co-creation of brand identity, consumer identity and brand community identity. *Journal of Business Research*, 70, 416–429.

Corley, K. G., & Gioia, D. A. (2004). Identity ambiguity and change in the wake of a corporate spin-off. *Administrative Science Quarterly*, 49(2), 173–208.

Cova, B., & Paranque, B. (2016). Value slippage in brand transformation: A conceptualization. *Journal of Product and Brand Management*, 25(1), 3–10.

Cova, B., & White, T. (2010). Counter-brand and alter-brand communities: The impact of web 2.0 on tribal marketing approaches. *Journal of Marketing Management*, 26(3–4), 256–270.

Devasagayam, P. R., Buff, C. L. Aurand, T. W., & Judson, K. M. (2010). Building brand community membership within organizations: A viable internal branding alternative? *Journal of Product and Brand Management*, 19(3), 210–217.

Downey, G. L., & Lucena, J. C. (2004). Knowledge and professional identity in engineering: Code-switching and the metrics of progress. *History and Technology*, 20(4), 393–420.

Goulding, C. (2005). Grounded theory, ethnography and phenomenology. *European Journal of Marketing*, 39(3–4), 294–308.

Gyrd-Jones, R. (2012). Five ways branding is changing. *Journal of Brand Management*, 20(2), 77–79.

Hatch, M. J., & Schultz, M. (2010). Toward a theory of brand co-creation with implications for brand governance. *Brand Management*, 17(8), 590–604.

Ind, N., Iglesias, O., & Markovic, S. (2017). The co-creation continuum: From tactical market research tool to strategic collaborative innovation method. *Journal of Brand Management*, 24(4), 310–321.

Iglesias, O., & Ind, N. (2020). Towards a theory of conscientious corporate brand co-creation: The next key challenge in brand management. *Journal of Brand Management*, 27, 710–720.

Iglesias, O., Landgraf, P., Ind, N., Markovic, S., & Koporcic, N. (2020). Corporate brand identity co-creation in business-to-business contexts. *Industrial Marketing Management*, 85, 32–43.

Jalkala, A., Cova, B., Salle, R., & Salminen, R. T. (2010). Changing project business orientations: Towards new logic of project marketing. *European Management Journal*, 28, 124–138.

Kaplan, A. M., & Haenlein, M. (2010). Users of the World, Unite! The Challenges and Opportunities of Social Media. *Business Horizons*, 53(1), 59–68.

Kornum, N., Gyrd-Jones, R., Al Zagir, N. and Brandis, K. A. (2017). Interplay between intended brand identity and identities in a Nike related brand community: Co-existing synergies and tensions in a nested system. *Journal of Business Research*, 70, 432–440.

Kristal, S., Baumgarth, C., & Henseler, J. (2020). Performative corporate brand identity in industrial markets: The case of German prosthetics manufacturer Ottobock. *Journal of Business Research*, 114, 240–253.

Leek, S., & Christodoulides, G. (2011). A literature review and future agenda for B2B branding: Challenges of branding in a B2B context. *Industrial Marketing Management, 40*(6), 830–837.

Mäläskä, M., & Nadeem, W. (2012, June 17–20). Examining the nature of an online brand community as a B2B brand communication platform: A netnographic analysis of the CISCO LinkedIn Group. Proceedings of 25th BLED Conference (pp. 30–42). Bled, Slovenia.

Mäläskä, M., Saraniemi, S., & Tähtinen, J. (2011). Network actors' participation in B2B SME branding. *Industrial Marketing Management, 40*(7), 1144–1152.

Merz, M. A., He, Y., & Vargo, S. L. (2009). The evolving brand logic: A service-dominant logic perspective. *Journal of the Academy of Marketing Science, 37*(3), 328–344.

Michel, (2017). From brand identity to polysemous brands: Commentary on "Performing identities: Processes of brand and stakeholder identity co-construction". *Journal of Business Research, 70*, 453–455.

Morokane, P., Chiba, M., & Kleyn, N. (2016). Drivers of employee propensity to endorse their corporate brand. *Journal of Brand Management, 23*: 55–66.

Muniz, A. M., & O'Guinn, T. C. (2001). Brand community. *Journal of Consumer Research, 27*(4), 412–432.

Nambisan, S., & Nambisan, P. (2008). How to profit from a better virtual customer environment. *MIT Sloan Management Review, 9*(3), 53–61.

Ojansivu, I., Alajoutsijärvi, K., & Salo, J. (2013). The development of post-project buyer-seller interaction in service-intensive projects. *Industrial Marketing Management, 42*, 1318–1327.

Ojasalo, J., Nätti, S., & Olkkonen, R. (2008). Brand building in software SMEs: An empirical study. *Journal of Product and Brand Management, 17*(2), 92–107.

Piehler, R., Grace, D., & Burmann, C. (2018). Internal brand management: Introduction to the special issue and directions for future research. *Journal of Brand Management, 25*, 197–201.

Saleem, F., & Iglesias, O. (2016). Mapping the domain of fragmented field of internal branding. *Journal of Product & Brand Management, 25*(1), 43–57.

Schau, H. J., Muñiz Jr., A. M., & Arnould, E. J. (2009). How brand community practices create value. *Journal of Marketing, 73*, 30–51.

Schembri, S., & Latimer, L. (2016). Online brand communities: Constructing and co-constructing brand culture. *Journal of Marketing Management, 32*(7–8), 628–651.

Schmeltz, L., & Kjeldsen, A. K. (2019). Co-creating polyphony or cacophony? A case study of a public organization's brand co-creation process and the challenge of orchestrating multiple internal voices. *Journal of Brand Management, 26*, 304–316.

Schmidt, H. J., & Baumgarth, C. (2018). Strengthening internal brand equity with brand ambassador programs: Development and testing of a success factor model. *Journal of Brand Management, 25*, 250–265.

Sheikh, A., & Lim, M. (2011). Engineering consultants' perceptions of corporate branding: A case study of an international engineering consultancy. *Industrial Marketing Management, 40*, 1123–1132.

Sirianni, N. J., Bitner, M. J., Brown, S. W., & Mandel, N. (2013). Branded service encounters: Strategically aligning employee behavior with the brand positioning. *Journal of Marketing, 77*(6), 108–123.

Skålén, P., Pace, S., & Cova, B. (2015). Firm-brand community value co-creation as alignment of practices. *European Journal of Marketing, 49*(3–4), 596–620.

Stake, R. E. (1995). *The art of case study research*. Thousand Oaks, CA: SAGE.

Suomi, K., Saraniemi, S., Vähätalo, M., Kallio, T. J., & Tevameri, T. (2021). Employee engagement and internal branding: Two sides of the same coin? *Corporate Reputation Review, 24*, 48–63.

Swaminathan, V., Sorescu, A., Steenkamp, J-B. E. M., O'Guinn, T. C. G., & Schmitt, B. (2020). Branding in a hyperconnected world: Refocusing theories and rethinking boundaries. *Journal of Marketing, 84*(2), 24–46.

Törmälä, M., & Gyrd-Jones, R. I. (2017). Development of new B2B venture corporate brand identity: A narrative performance approach. *Industrial Marketing Management, 65*, 76–85.

Törmälä, M., & Saraniemi, S. (2018). The roles of business partners in corporate brand image co-creation. *Journal of Product and Brand Management, 27*(1), 29–40.

Vallaster, C., & Von Wallpach, S. (2013). An online discursive inquiry into the social dynamics of multi-stakeholder brand meaning co-creation. *Journal of Business Research, 66*(9), 1505–1515.

Veloutsou, C., & Black, I. (2020). Creating and managing participative brand communities: The roles members perform. *Journal of Business Research, 117*, 873–885.

Von Wallpach, S., Hemetsberger, A., & Espersen, P. (2017). Performing identities: Processes of brand and stakeholder identity co-construction. *Journal of Business Research, 70*, 443–452.

# 29
# CO-CREATING CONSCIENTIOUS CORPORATE BRANDS INSIDE-OUT THROUGH VALUES-DRIVEN BRANDING

*Galina Biedenbach and Thomas Biedenbach*

## 1. Introduction

What if, an organization, like a person, had a conscience? How would employees of a conscientious organization think, feel, and act in their professional and private lives? What roles would employees play in building a corporate brand with a conscience, or, in a worst-case scenario, in destroying it? While the literature on corporate branding does not provide definite answers to these questions, it indicates the importance of a conscientious approach to brand management in an ever-changing business environment (Rindell et al., 2011; Hutchinson et al., 2013; Iglesias & Ind, 2016). In general, conscience represents 'the disposition to integrate or harmonize moral knowledge or belief with the appropriate moral action' (Fuss, 1964, p. 116). Since conscience is closely linked to a subjective formation of moral knowledge by each person, organizations aiming to build conscientious brands can face challenges and often even difficulties in implementing their visions. The emerging theory of conscientious brand management proposes that conscientious brands can be built and enhanced by engaging multiple stakeholders, facilitating co-creation, and embracing sustainability (Iglesias & Ind, 2020). Undeniably, being relevant and attractive for many organizations across various sectors, the implementation of these principles entails a complete focus of an entire organization and genuine commitment of its every member.

In view of the fact that very few organizations can manage their operations without any employees, it is evident that employees have critical roles in enabling the functioning of organizations and determining their success, or sometimes even survival. From a branding viewpoint, the roles of employees extend beyond performing core operations, because, through their daily actions, employees actually 'live' a corporate brand and make it come 'alive' (Gotsi & Wilson, 2001; Burmann & Zeplin, 2005; Maxwell & Knox, 2009; Baumgarth, 2010). Confirming the ultimate importance of employees for corporate branding, prior research demonstrates that employees can make invaluable contributions by acting as brand ambassadors (Schmidt & Baumgarth, 2018) and brand champions (Morhart et al., 2009), but also cause enormous damage by behaving as brand saboteurs (Wallace & de Chernatony, 2007) and even brand killers (Olson & Thjømøe, 2010). Considering the variety of individual cognitive and affective responses, including those expressed by employees towards their employer, it is predictable that employees' perceptions about the corporate brand may vary from being negatively or positively polarized, as well as include indifferent states. Nevertheless, it is important to consider that these perceptions would lead to certain behavioural patterns occurring inside and outside an organization during employees' work and private times, which can potentially result in incredible success or catastrophic failure for a corporate brand.

In brand management practice and research, the early 2000s were marked by a paradigm shift when the wide use of the internet triggered the loss of direct control by managers over brands and facilitated the emergence of their co-creation by customers and other stakeholders (Christodoulides, 2009). Currently, in the early 2020s, environmental, socio-political, and technological changes indicate that contemporary brand management needs not only to embrace co-creation, but also to contribute effectively to accomplishing a sustainable future and to engage proactively in achieving the common good. Corporate brands with a conscience would naturally strive to achieve these goals. However, the success of these actions depends significantly on the devotion and efforts made by internal stakeholders, including employees, who would influence customers through their actions and would in turn be influenced by various internal and external stakeholder groups. Furthermore, in the case of moral dilemmas, individual and organizational values can be expected to affect moral judgements and consequently organizational conscience (Yagil & Shultz, 2017). As such, the values of an organization would facilitate an understanding about what is morally right and wrong, and also remind its members to act in a morally right way (Rasberry, 2000). Therefore, organizations committed to building conscientious brands can benefit from applying values-driven branding that aims to contribute to societal transformations. At the core of values-driven branding lies a transformative purpose, for example focusing on advancing sustainability, empowering customers, or committing to other forms of brand activism (Swaminathan et al., 2020; Hajdas & Kłeczek, 2021). Consequently, conscientious brand management based on values-driven branding would require an inside-out perspective empowering employees to co-create a corporate brand together with multiple stakeholders aiming to achieve a transformative purpose.

In this chapter, we aim to explore how conscientious brands can be co-created inside-out through values-driven branding. We start by discussing general issues related to establishing a conscientious organization. We continue with elaborating on the relevance of embracing values-driven branding. Consequently, we focus on internal branding with a conscience inside an organization. Finally, we reflect on how a conscientious corporate brand can be built inside-out. In addition to sharing research insights, we propose a framework that categorizes brands with a conscience in terms of the entire organization and its employees. We present a practical example illustrating how one organization, which is PwC, works with building a corporate brand with a conscience. We conclude the chapter by recommending that practitioners co-create conscientious corporate brands through values-driven branding and encouraging researchers to advance the current state of research on conscientious brand management and values-driven branding.

## 2. Establishing a conscientious organization

Although the notion of conscience has great potential to transform managerial practice and the current state of branding research significantly, it does not represent a new or unknown phenomenon. As individuals, we are driven by our conscience when we make moral judgements and, on some occasions, we might even refer to conscience when we need to justify our choices.

Historically, the first mentions of conscience appeared in the work of Greek playwrights dating back to the 5th century BCE (Sorabji, 2017). Over centuries, the notion of conscience evolved as a result of philosophical and religious debates on morality. Despite the lack of consensus about one unified definition of conscience, many proposed definitions emphasize the viewpoint that conscience triggers 'a general sense of moral obligation in the individual's consciousness' (Fuss, 1964, p. 116). A conscientious person does not only hold moral beliefs about what is ethically right and wrong, but also acts by following these beliefs (Wicclair, 2013). If a conscientious person cannot uphold individual moral beliefs, this person would experience mental discomfort and sometimes also decreased self-respect (Wicclair, 2013). Some philosophical theories propose that conscience has an innate nature being 'theologically implanted,' 'biologically evolved,' or 'axiologically inherent' (Bahm, 1965, p. 128). Other philosophical theories emphasize that conscience is influenced by the socialization process during which a person develops a moral character complying with social norms (Hogan, 1973). Nevertheless, conscience has a self-directed nature, where a person's conscience can only directly influence this person's ethical judgements and subsequent actions (Wicclair, 2013). Conscience is based on subjective perceptions, which are grounded in a person's moral standards (Childress, 1979). Therefore, the formation of conscience and moral judgements underlying it are impacted by the values held by a person, which might be similar to, or different from, the ones held by other people.

In an organizational setting, the nature of organizational conscience is even more complex and challenging than in the case of individual conscience. Organizational conscience depends on the moral knowledge of numerous people, their subjective judgements, and their actions, which are shaped by their own beliefs. Furthermore, for an organization, a common purpose, values, and identity can be seen as important moral obligations underlying organizational conscience and serving as a basis for moral judgements of employees, who must consider them in their actions (Sulmasy, 2008). To embrace conscience, corporate brands, which are by their nature attributed to organizational entities, need to rely on the morality of people within an organization and their actions impacted both by their individual values as well as organizational values. A lack of alignment, inconsistency, and even conflicts between individual values and organizational values can result in moral dilemmas leading to employees' actions, which can potentially undermine organizational conscience and damage the corporate brand (Yagil & Shultz, 2017). Thus, a conscientious organization requires a collective consciousness involving material, social, and spiritual aspects, which influence ethicality and morality of an organization (Pandey & Gupta, 2008). Notably, organizational conscience and morality cannot be expected to be stable, because they will be continuously reconstructed as a result of emerging societal changes, developing business practices, and shifting values (Garsten & Hernes, 2009). Therefore, organizations striving to build a corporate brand with a conscience need to create conditions supporting the formation of organizational conscience and to address conflicting contradictions between multiple individual consciences of their employees and organizational conscience.

In the branding literature, theoretical insights and empirical evidence about conscientious brands are still very limited. Despite the high managerial relevance and the urgent societal need, the complex nature of brands with a conscience and conscientious brand management were only investigated in very few studies. The most prominent contribution to advancing research in this area is a special issue of the *Journal of Brand Management* titled 'Conscientious Brands' that was published in 2011. An editorial to this special issue states that the idea about advancing research and managerial practice related to conscientious brands emerged in the early 2000s (Ind & Ryder, 2011). Almost two decades later, a recent conceptual article on conscientious corporate branding still acknowledges the lack of research in this area, and provides a comprehensive agenda detailing specific topics, which can be explored in future studies (Iglesias & Ind,

2020). With a continuously growing body of branding literature on multiple stakeholders, co-creation and sustainability, which represent the core themes contributing to conscientious brand management, we can expect that research focusing on brands with a conscience will increase in the future and provide fruitful insights for supporting practitioners and stimulating future studies.

In business practice, a conscientious corporate brand can be created simultaneously when a new organization is founded, or reinforced consequentially when an existing organization is committed to act in a conscientious way. Overall, independent of whether an organization is new or existing, a corporate brand with a conscience would require that 'ethical concerns and values are embedded in the company's entire business strategy, in its value and supply chain, as well as in its vision and culture over time' (Rindell et al., 2011, p. 710). Furthermore, a conscientious corporate brand would thrive in conditions where organizational leadership, the governance model, and the organizational culture would support the development of morality among organization's members and lead to their actions, which would facilitate a good conscience (Iglesias & Ind, 2020). To establish a conscientious organization embracing a corporate brand with a conscience, it is important to create awareness inside an organization about what is morally right and wrong, as well as to remind to owners, board members, and employees, including the ones in leadership, frontline, and other positions, to act in accordance with moral principles and to follow the 'moral compass' of their organization (Rasberry, 2000). The establishment of a conscientious organization would be challenging and most probably impossible without defining organizational values and complying with them in organizational practices, so that a corporate brand with a conscience will be not only visible in communication, but also that it will be 'lived' by employees on a daily basis.

## 3. Embracing values-driven branding

A strong corporate brand with a conscience undoubtedly requires a solid foundation in a form of unique, engaging, and powerful values, which would enable an organization to achieve its ultimate purpose and also guide its members in their long-term strategic decisions and short-term operational activities. Based on recent conceptualizations, values are 'individual and collective trans-situational conceptions of desirable behaviours, objectives and ideals that serve to guide or valuate practice' (Askeland et al., 2020, p. 3). The importance of values for building a strong corporate brand is recognized in seminal works on corporate branding (e.g., Balmer, 1995; Harris & de Chernatony, 2001; Balmer & Gray, 2003; Hatch & Schultz, 2003; Knox & Bickerton, 2003; Urde, 2003), as well as recent studies (e.g., Lahtinen & Närvänen, 2020; Ozdemir et al., 2020; Boukis et al., 2021; Maon et al., 2021). Prior research demonstrates that successful corporate brands have values that do not only support their differentiation and positioning but also impact a strategic vision, a corporate mission, and an organizational culture (Balmer, 1995; Knox & Bickerton, 2003; Hatch & Schultz, 2003). Therefore, in corporate branding, values serve as 'the guiding principles for all internal and external brand building processes' (Urde, 2003, p. 1035). Since internal and external stakeholders often perceive values as the ultimate promise (Balmer & Gray, 2003), undesirable or incongruent values can result in a negative corporate image, damaged reputation, and poor performance (Ozdemir et al., 2020). While in the past, owners and board members were seen as the primary decision-makers involved in defining values, contemporary corporate brand management recognizes the need to engage employees and other relevant stakeholders in the co-creation of these vital organizational characteristics (Harris & de Chernatony, 2001; Hatch & Schultz, 2003; Lahtinen & Närvänen, 2020; Boukis et al., 2021; Maon et al., 2021). Overall, the underlying values have not only a symbolic power to influence a corporate brand, but also actual power to shape the perceptions of diverse stakeholder groups about it.

Despite the high importance of values for successful corporate branding, the branding literature provides only scattered theoretical insights about the role of values in corporate branding and demonstrates limited knowledge about values-driven branding, which is also referred to as values-oriented branding or values-based branding. In the general marketing literature, the proposed conceptualization of values-driven marketing emphasizes organizations' 'sincere commitment to addressing customers' need for social, economic and environmental justice' (Kotler et al., 2019, pp. 140–141). According to the key principles of values-driven marketing, which endorse participation, collaboration, cultural resonance, and human spirit fulfilment, values support the implementation of these principles by representing a 'corporation's institutional standards of behavior' (Kotler et al., 2019, p. 146). Values-driven branding can build on these propositions and provide insights on how values can be integrated in a systematic and effective way in developing branding strategies and making tactical branding decisions. We envision that future research on values-driven branding can utilize the propositions originating from values-driven marketing and advance them by using the findings of previous studies on brand orientation, brand activism, purpose-driven branding, collaborative branding, participatory branding, stakeholder branding, and conscientious branding, among other areas. Additional inputs and inspiration for advancing research on values-driven branding can be acquired from management and organization studies, where notions of a values-driven organization and values-driven management are well-established, but still have a lot of potential to be further developed, as suggested by previous studies in these areas (e.g., Driscoll & Hoffman, 1999; Barrett, 2006; Bourne & Jenkins, 2013; Askeland et al., 2020).

One essential challenge in building a corporate brand with a conscience through values-based branding relates to selecting and endorsing values, which would be relevant, beneficial, and meaningful for an organization as well as for the entire society. The literature on corporate branding suggests that values should be distinct, clear, precise, and attractive for the key stakeholders (Balmer & Gray, 2003; Hatch & Schultz, 2003). Based on their temporal foci, an organization can embrace a set of diverse values, which would be oriented towards its past, present, and future (Yoganathan et al., 2018). Furthermore, in successful organizations, values would have a dynamic nature, where they will evolve over time depending on organizational, societal, and other changes (Bourne & Jenkins, 2013). Previous studies focusing on an emerging research area of purpose-driven branding suggest that contemporary brand management should be centred on achieving a transformative purpose that is based on the values of an organization (Hajdas & Kłeczek, 2021). The transformative purpose must extend beyond shareholder value and profit maximization, address societal challenges, and contribute to the societal good (Swaminathan et al., 2020). Considering ethicality and morality aspects, which are crucial for conscientious brands, already early works on business ethics emphasized that organizations, especially those having a great power, must "focus on right behavior rather than on avoiding wrongdoing, and on behavior rather than on motives or intentions" (Drucker, 1981, p. 36). Overall, genuine and authentic values reconciling the business interests of an organizational entity and its aspirations to achieving the societal good represent an important cornerstone for the effective implementation of values-driven branding.

Values-driven branding enables an organization to specify principles, in the form of values, and articulate them to the members of the organization, who would make their moral judgements in accordance with these principles and hopefully act with intentions to fulfil these values. Prior research on conscientious branding highlights additional considerations related to values endorsed by brands with a conscience. Following societal debates, earlier works emphasize values focusing on the natural environment, climate change, and ethical behaviours of all members in the supply chain (Rindell et al., 2011; Hutchinson et al., 2013). In general, the values of an organization are expected to lead to practices, which would ensure "long-term, consistent, and holistic socially responsible behavior" (Rindell et al., 2011, p. 710). Conscientious corporate brands should demonstrate an engagement that would extend beyond a limited CSR programme and commit to actions, which would be based on altruistic motives and benefit diverse stakeholder groups (Olsen & Peretz, 2011). Recent works on conscientious branding confirm that conscientious brands should have a strong sustainability focus and consider the interests of multiple stakeholders (Iglesias & Ind, 2020). Furthermore, conscientious brands must be genuinely co-created together with stakeholders, instead of being solely managed by the organization (Iglesias & Ind, 2020). Ultimately, conscientious organizations should lead public debates, contribute to environmental and societal well-being, and increase the public good together with various internal and external stakeholders (Lahtinen & Närvänen, 2020). One important reminder from seminal works on corporate branding is that it is critical not only to have desired values, which can be convincingly communicated by the organization, but also to ensure that they are practiced in the organization (Hatch & Schultz, 2003). Values-based branding can potentially enable conscientious organizations to make a great impact on society and lead to powerful transformations. However, organizations would need to create conditions that make it possible for the desired values to be really enacted by internal stakeholders inside organizations and that encourage external stakeholders outside organizations to contribute to the societal good.

## 4. Committing to internal branding with a conscience

Over the centuries, the understanding about brands and their nature has been extensively developed in business practice and academic research. The diverse emerging perspectives include conceptualizations of a brand as "(a) a passive object with utilitarian and symbolic meanings; (b) an active relationship partner and a regulator of, and venue for, interpersonal relationships; and (c) a creator of social identity with social group linking value" (Bagozzi et al., 2021, p. 588). The notion of a corporate brand followed historical patterns with its conceptualizations progressing from a corporate brand being seen as a simple visualization of an organization's name to a corporate brand being perceived as a complex representation of a socially constructed organizational reality. Even though the roles of different external stakeholders in co-creating a corporate brand are becoming increasingly acknowledged by organizations, unquestionably internal stakeholders cannot be ignored in corporate branding or mistreated as a result of it. In their strategic decisions and operational activities, owners, board members, and managers must consider one crucial fact that eventually "employees have the potential to make or break the corporate brand" (Ind, 1998, p. 324). Ideally, owners and managers of every organization would prefer that their employees are mainly brand enthusiasts, who are actively endorsing the brand and its values, or at least brand conformists, who are committed to delivering the brand promise (Boukis et al., 2021). However, in reality, many organizations also have brand deviants, who do not comply with the brand promise and even undermine values, and brand sceptics, who are passively fulfilling their duties in a barely satisfactory way (Boukis et al., 2021). Considerations about internal stakeholders are especially critical for organizations aiming to build corporate brands with a conscience, because employees' willingness to live up to the values of a corporate brand and their actual behaviours in shaping organizational practices determine whether the organization will succeed or fail in establishing and enhancing a conscientious corporate brand.

In the branding literature, the research stream on internal branding provides insights on how a strong corporate brand can be built inside-out by engaging and inspiring employees to co-create it together with multiple stakeholders. Prior research on internal branding closely followed the paradigm shifts in managerial practice and captured how the viewpoints on building a successful corporate brand changed from being a strictly controlled undertaking by senior level executives to a collaborative co-creation process engaging internal and external stakeholders. For instance, early works on internal branding highlight that a strong corporate brand can be built internally by using effective internal communication for achieving buy-in of employees (Thomson et al., 1999). In contrast to these views, recent studies emphasize that managers should be committed "to interact with all internal stakeholders, including volunteers and employees, to get these internal stakeholders engaged with the brand (thus, an interactive process) and, in turn, to motivate the same stakeholders to participate with and co-create the brand" (Merrilees et al., 2021, p. 9). The literature reviews focusing on internal branding research confirm that this relatively small, but a growing research stream provides fruitful findings about the dimensions of internal brand management, antecedents of internal branding, and its outcomes (Saleem & Iglesias, 2016; Barros-Arrieta & García-Cali, 2021). For example, in addition to internal communication, the findings of previous studies demonstrate the effectiveness of such dimensions of internal branding as brand ideologies, brand leadership, internal brand communities, and brand-centred human resource management, which includes brand-oriented recruiting, training, rewarding, and brand-based performance evaluation (Saleem & Iglesias, 2016; Barros-Arrieta & García-Cali, 2021). Considering the antecedents of effective internal branding, prior research has a strong focus on few variables, which are brand orientation and internal market orientation (Barros-Arrieta & García-Cali, 2021). The outcomes of internal branding are captured by a large variety of variables, for example, brand understanding, brand identification, brand loyalty, and brand citizenship behaviours, among many others (Barros-Arrieta & García-Cali, 2021). In general, the literature reviews and recent studies confirm the strong need to develop further research on internal branding and provide detailed suggestions about various topics, which can be investigated in future studies.

The emerging principles of conscientious brand management indicate areas, which, on the one hand, attract high interest among practitioners, because of a pressing need to incorporate these aspects in their managerial practices, but, on the other hand, need further inputs by the academic community, because of their novelty and complexity. First, *multiple stakeholders* with their unique perceptions about, and responses to, a corporate brand represent an important consideration for developing successful corporate branding strategies. However, the literature on internal branding predominantly focuses on internal stakeholders, mostly employees. Although some previous studies provide empirical evidence about critical interrelations between multiple stakeholders in a brand ecosystem, these propositions are relatively unexplored in internal branding research. For example, some previous studies show that interactions between various stakeholder groups can result in synergistic outcomes (Gyrd-Jones & Kornum, 2013) or in some cases in destructive consequences (Vallaster & von Wallpach, 2013). Other studies demonstrate that external communication can have a strong impact on employees' perceptions and outcomes of internal branding (Celsi & Gilly, 2010; Piehler et al., 2019), but also negative word-of-mouth by employees can trigger negative perceptions of external audiences (Lee & Suh, 2020). In addition, the calls for future research on internal branding confirm the need to advance this research area, for example, by exploring more holistic and dynamic models or integrating an inside-out approach to building a corporate brand with an outside-in approach considering multiple stakeholders (Veloutsou & Guzmán, 2017; Piehler et al., 2018).

Second, *co-creation* is acknowledged as the core focus of one of the most recent schools of thought in brand management, referred to as the co-creative school of thought (Kernstock & Powell, 2018; Schmidt & Redler, 2018). Prior research demonstrates the diversity of views on brand co-creation, which range from it being perceived as a "tactical market research tool" to a "strategic collaborative innovation method" (Ind et al., 2017, p. 310). From an internal branding perspective, brand co-creation enables capturing "behaviour that exceeds normal transactional expectations, something that goes beyond normal duties" (Merrilees et al., 2021, p. 3). Similar to the notion of multiple stakeholders, internal branding research addressing co-creation is very limited. Being of critical importance for contemporary brand management, the co-creation of a corporate brand from an internal perspective represents an important area for advancing research on internal branding (Saleem & Iglesias, 2016). Recent studies confirm the relevance of this area by presenting empirical evidence about the positive impact of co-creation by internal and external stakeholders on the effectiveness and success of the brand building process (Iglesias et al., 2020; Kristal et al., 2020; Mingione & Leoni, 2020; Merrilees et al., 2021). The calls for developing further the co-creative school of thought highlight opportunities for making significant theoretical contributions in this area and providing significant insights for managerial practice (Kernstock & Powell, 2018).

Last, considering *sustainability*, contrary to the increasing public awareness about sustainability issues and the growing attention of organizations to integrating CSR in strategic decisions and daily practices, a recent literature review demonstrates that there are very few previous studies on internal branding and sustainability (Barros-Arrieta & García-Cali, 2021). Nevertheless, considering the societal expectations about sustainability and CSR, and their vital role in achieving the common good, sustainability and CSR represent critical aspects, which must be considered by organizations aiming to build strong corporate brands (Maon et al., 2021). Prior research demonstrating the links between sustainability performance and internal branding outcomes highlights the relevance of addressing sustainability in future studies on internal branding (Biedenbach & Manzhynski, 2016). In addition, recent research provides a framework for integrating CSR and internal branding, which can be used as a starting foundation for future studies (Carlini & Grace, 2021). The calls for future studies on sustainability, CSR, and internal branding confirm the managerial and societal importance of advancing this research area (Golob & Podnar, 2019; Barros-Arrieta & García-Cali, 2021).

## 5. Building a conscientious corporate brand inside-out

A conscientious corporate brand requires not only a visible articulation of values in the mission, vision, or purpose of an organization, but also their integration in the organizational culture and their enactment in the organizational practices. Ideally, to build a conscientious brand, owners, board members, managers, and employees should have a true commitment to the values of their organization, act in good conscience in accordance with these values, contribute to the financial success of their organization, as well as make a transformative impact on society. In reality, where many of these idealistic expectations are not met, organizations face challenges in building conscientious brands. One challenge is, as philosophers warn in relation to individual conscience, that "even if a person's conscience *generally* provides reliable ethical guidance, it may not be *completely* reliable" (Wicclair, 2013, p. 7). For example, individual subjective judgements underlying the moral choices of one employee might differ from judgements of other employees or even contradict the social norms at an organization. Therefore, while one employee might have a good conscience about their own individual actions, these actions might be perceived as morally unjustified by other employees or even dimmish an organizational conscience, which would have a negative impact on a conscientious corporate brand. Although many employees would naturally be supportive of organizational actions related to achieving a common good, there might be also employees having indifferent opinions or even jeopardizing these efforts through their misbehaviours, which would damage the corporate brand. Considering the conscience of different organizations, moral judgements and consequent actions by one organization might differ from those of other organizations or mismatch the expectations of some stakeholder groups, which might question the intentions behind a conscientious corporate brand and may sabotage it. These hypothetical examples indicate only a few possible challenges, which might need to be addressed inside and outside a conscientious organization. Nevertheless, the benefits of building a conscientious corporate brand, in the form of opportunities to contribute to a better and more sustainable future, definitely outweigh the efforts needed for addressing problematic issues.

To overcome the challenges related to creating and enhancing a conscientious corporate brand, organizations need to devote resources and acquire the needed competence for establishing an effective values-driven organization. One important aspect, which is persistently emphasized in the research streams on corporate branding and internal branding is the alignment of values. Prior research demonstrates the importance of an alignment between the individual values of employees and the values of an organization, also an alignment between the values held by people in different roles in an organization, and in general an alignment between the desired and practiced values (Thomson et al., 1999; de Chernatony, 2001; Harris & de Chernatony, 2001; Balmer & Gray, 2003; Hatch & Schultz, 2003). As values represent "an integral facet of human decision-making" (Hemingway, 2005, p. 241), the alignment of values between employees and within an organization is central for building a strong conscientious brand. A literature review on corporate brand alignment notes the complexity of aligning various and sometimes contradictory values and indicates that it requires special considerations about the dynamic nature of a corporate brand, its context, and stakeholders (Mingione, 2015). Personal, organizational, and societal values can constantly evolve, and an organization will have to adjust to have a good conscience and to keep the strength of its corporate brand. For example, when in some industries a statement on diversity, equity, and inclusion became the norm, some organizations, which did not embrace these issues before, had to adopt these values and integrate them into their practices.

Taking into consideration the criticality of values, we find it important for future research to investigate the role of values and conscience in corporate branding by applying micro-, meso-, and macro-levels of analysis focusing on individuals, groups, organizations, and larger external forces. As a contribution to future research endeavours, we propose a categorization of corporate brands based on a conscience (see Figure 29.1). Presented in a matrix form, the categorization considers: (1) whether an organization is conscientious versus conscienceless, and (2) whether employees are conscientious versus conscienceless. The subjectivity of judgements about an organization or an employee being conscientious or conscienceless from an individual perspective and from an organizational perspective creates an interesting interplay in categorizing corporate brands with a conscience or without it.

Firstly, *a spiritual corporate brand* is a conscientious corporate brand whose ideology and organizational practices create a strong foundation and empower each member of this organization to act in a conscientious way. Owners, board members, managers, and employees live up to the values of the organization and have a good conscience in performing their roles. A spiritual corporate brand requires the evolution of organizational spirituality, which is conceptualized as "an organizational identity resulting from its values, practices, and discourse that is composed of workplace and individual spirituality guided by the leader and other members and influenced by the environment, organizational culture, and knowledge management" (Rocha & Pinheiro, 2021, p. 1). Previous research suggests that workplace spirituality captured by transcendence, sense of community, and spiritual values can be expected to have positive effects on the psychological conditions in an organization and consequently on employee engagement (Saks, 2011). A spiritual corporate brand is the ultimate outcome of successful conscientious brand management.

Secondly, *a hypocritical corporate brand* has a mission, a vision, and maybe even a purpose statement which communicate values of relevance for a conscientious corporate brand. Although

|  | *Conscienceless organization* | *Conscientious organization* |
|---|---|---|
| *Conscientious employees* | **Toxic corporate brand** | **Spiritual corporate brand** |
| *Conscienceless employees* | **Destructive corporate brand** | **Hypocritical corporate brand** |

*Figure 29.1* Categorization of corporate brands based on a conscience.

owners, board members, and managers might be committed to building a brand with a conscience, the organizational practices do not confirm these intentions. From an organizational perspective, employees can be characterized as lacking a conscience in their actions, which leads to an organization being perceived as hypocritical by external stakeholders. Corporate hypocrisy represents "a lack of integrity" and signifies "a negative social evaluation that results from the perception of a distance between an organization's claimed standards and actions" (Babu et al., 2020, p. 376). One potential reason that explains why the desired values are not enacted by employees in a hypocritical organization can be a lack of employee-organization alignment (Yang et al., 2020). Recent studies show that such a corporate brand can be perceived by multiple stakeholders as using "woke-washing," which is a form of inauthentic brand activism, for example when corporate claims do not match with prosocial practices (Vredenburg et al., 2020). Owners, board members, or managers can assess whether organizational conditions really enable the employees to live up to the desired values and make the needed changes in the work environment or current processes. They can also use brand-centred training and rewarding to increase the awareness of employees about the values of the organization and to motivate employees to enact them. Another alternative can be to search for new talents and cautiously use brand-oriented recruiting in hiring new employees who would have a better alignment with the organization.

Thirdly, *a toxic corporate brand* has a dysfunctional organization, where the majority of the employees act in a conscientious way, but these behaviours do not lead to the formation of perceptions about this organization as having a good conscience. One reason why some internal stakeholders might perceive that their organization lacks a conscience can be unclear and ineffective internal communication. In the case, when external communication contradicts internal communication, employees and other members of an organization might also develop negative perceptions about a corporate brand. Another reason can be the misbehaviours of owners, board members, or managers, which would have a negative impact on the reputation of an organization and trigger negative cognitive and emotional reactions among the employees. Previous studies demonstrate that toxic leadership has extremely negative consequences for an organization, its culture, practices, and the effectiveness of internal and external marketing

(Boddy & Croft, 2016). Toxic work environments, which might be caused not only by the toxic behaviours of managers, but also by the behaviours of some employees, would endanger the evolution of a conscientious corporate brand, even though the majority of employees would still act with a good conscience. Nevertheless, prior research indicates that even a few employees having individual values, which would motivate them to act in a conscientious way, can be a catalyst for transforming an organizational culture and the entire organization to being more conscientious (Hemingway, 2005). If owners, board members, and managers have a true aspiration to create a conscientious corporate brand in an organization, which is perceived as toxic, they need to explore whether these perceptions are caused by a misleading ideology, ineffective communication, the toxic behaviours of organizational members or are for other reasons. Consequently, problematic issues need to be addressed in an effective way for an organization to be able to evolve and to have stimulating conditions for building a conscientious corporate brand.

Finally, *a destructive corporate brand* is an extreme case of a conscienceless corporate brand. In such an organization, owners, board members, and managers do not have any real ambitions or interests in building a conscientious corporate brand. Lacking extrinsic motivation and maybe also intrinsic motivation to act in a conscientious way, the behaviours of the majority of employees can be characterized as being conscienceless. Prior research demonstrates that destructive practices in an organization can lead to harmful effects at the micro-level causing consumer dissatisfaction, or at the macro-level resulting in a harmful societal impact (Bertilsson & Rennstam, 2018; Padela et al., 2021). Even though a destructive corporate brand might have a financial success in the short term, it can experience challenges to survive in the long term. With evolving awareness about such an organization, its practices might be questioned by its stakeholders and its marketing offerings discarded by current and potential customers. In the case of a noticeable negative impact on the entire society, anti-brand or social movements can arise to stop the operations of a destructive organization and to destroy this conscienceless corporate brand (Krishnamurthy & Kucuk, 2009; Palmer et al., 2014). From a societal perspective, destructive corporate brands represent harmful corporate entities, which might be seen as distractions on the path to increasing the common good.

As an illustration of how an organization can use its values to communicate a conscientious ambition and embrace internal branding initiatives to facilitate the evolution of a spiritual organizational brand, we selected one exemplary case from the business-to-business market. PwC is a large professional services network, which is considered to be one of the top four leading organizations in this sector, known as the Big Four accounting firms. PwC operates in a sector which must be conscientious by its nature. Nevertheless, for many decades, this sector has been shaken by several scandals related to misbehaviours of employees as well as documented conflicts of interests involving many organizations in this sector and causing reputational damage to the entire profession. The commitment of PwC to building a corporate brand with a conscience is demonstrated in its purpose, which is "to build trust in society and solve important problems," and in its values, which are "Act with integrity. Make a difference. Care. Work together. Reimagine the possible" (PwC, 2017). PwC describes its organization as being "purpose led" and "values driven" (PwC, 2017). PwC's purpose and values lie at the core of the code of conduct that guides the behaviours of employees. In the code of conduct, PwC specifies that the purpose and values represent "our guiding principles in deciding the right thing to do" (PwC, 2017). The values of PwC were co-created together with partners and employees from different countries. The internal communication and external communication of PwC clarify and explain how these values should be enacted by employees when they provide services to clients and work with colleagues. The evolvement of organizational conscience within PwC is also supported by standards, policies, and guidance, which are continuously developed at the network and local levels (PwC, 2017).

One example of internal initiatives, which have a positive impact on the work and private lives of PwC's employees, is the strategic programme "Be Well, Work Well" which focuses on physical, emotional, mental, and spiritual well-being (PwC, 2021). Through this programme, PwC aims "to create an environment where our people are encouraged to bring their best selves to work and are supported in achieving greater well-being by fueling themselves across four dimensions of energy – physical, emotional, mental and spiritual" (PwC, 2021). By developing diverse educational materials devoted to increasing the well-being of individuals, teams, and communities, initiating well-being events, and supporting research projects on well-being, among many other actions, the programme "Be Well, Work Well" represents an important contribution to the evolution of a spiritual corporate brand with a good conscience. Another example of initiatives which have positive internal and external effects are the strategic actions of PwC focusing on diversity and inclusiveness. These initiatives, which the organization refers to as "the PwC diversity journey," started in 2004, when only 11% of partners at PwC were female (PwC, 2016). The initiatives still continue with PwC having in 2020 around 20% female representation among partners and 40% female representation in the global leadership team (PwC, 2020). For instance, one action among the diversity and inclusiveness initiatives of PwC, which complements the internal activities focusing on gender equality, is the participation of PwC in the United Nation's global solidarity movement for gender equality HeForShe (UN Women, 2021). As one of nine selected corporate impact champions, PwC shows dedication to making contributions which extend beyond one organization and have the potential to trigger societal transformation critical for gender equality. Within this partnership, PwC has three large impact commitments, which are: "(1) develop and launch innovative male-focused gender curriculum to reach millions of men around the world; (2) launch a Global Inclusion Index to further increase the representation of women in leadership role; and (3) raise the global profile of HeForShe with PwC people, clients, and communities, driving towards the 1B target" (UN Women, 2021). The participation of PwC in the movement for gender equality HeForShe is supported by active engagement of the CEO, managers, partners, and other employees.

These examples, which represent just a few instances among many other initiatives implemented by PwC, demonstrate how an organization can establish a long-term commitment to enhance continuously its conscientious brand inside-out by improving the well-being of employees and by endorsing diversity and inclusion in society across the world. In addition to PwC, which we selected as an illustrative case, there are many other large organizations with substantial resources and extensive brand ecosystems which are effective in using their values to lead positive transformation and to contribute to societal good. Furthermore, a conscientious organization can be also established even with limited resources. There are many small and medium-sized enterprises in which the values of their founders drove the creation of a corporate brand that was already born with a conscience and founded with an aim to contribute to the common good. While the evolution of a spiritual corporate brand represents a challenging process for an organization of any size, the societal impact made by such a brand is definitely worth the organizational resources devoted to building it.

## 6. Conclusions

As one German proverb suggests, "starting is easy, persevering is an art" (originally "*Anfangen ist leicht, beharren eine Kunst*"). This chapter demonstrates that organizations can begin their journeys towards building conscientious corporate brands in a multitude of ways depending on their organizational and contextual conditions. A new start-up can indicate a dedication to establishing a corporate brand with a conscience by focusing on values, which not only enable commercial success but also contribute to the common good. Based on these values, a new organization can develop its mission, vision, and organizational culture, which ultimately would form its organizational morality and ethicality underlying organizational conscience. Established organizations can also shape and advance their ideological foundations by applying values-based branding to accommodate their commitment to transformative purposes, which would increase the common good. While the process of building and enhancing conscientious brands might be more challenging for large established organizations, they do have larger brand ecosystems and often more resources than new organizations for utilizing the power of their corporate brands for making great societal transformations. In general, new and also established organizations with a conscience need to have a true and genuine commitment to addressing societal challenges, which requires the development of desired values as well as their implementation during interactions within and between multiple stakeholder groups. While starting the use of conscious brand management in an organization is relatively easy, the continuous long-term engagement in co-creating a corporate brand with a conscience is a rather challenging, but definitely rewarding, journey for a specific organization and also for society.

This chapter recommends that practitioners actively build and enhance corporate brands with a conscience. We suggest beginning by creating the conditions for a conscientious organization, continuing by using effectively values-based branding, and proceeding by empowering employees to co-create a corporate brand together with other internal and external stakeholders. The chapter provides guidance for practitioners on how to succeed in building a spiritual corporate brand with a conscience and how to avoid common failures, which can result in the corporate brand being perceived as hypocritical, toxic, or even destructive. In general, the chapter raises awareness among practitioners about conscientious corporate brand management and possibilities for implementing it inside-out, through values-based branding. This chapter invites researchers to contribute to the development of research on conscientious brand management and to explore the brand building process in conscientious organizations. We encourage researchers to consider investigating values-based branding and examining the principles of conscientious brand management, which are required for building a strong brand with a conscience. The chapter highlights various topics of relevance for future research on internal branding and indicates potential directions for advancing the current state of corporate branding research. To conclude, conscientious corporate brands require more dedication from practitioners and their further consideration in organizational practices. Conscientious corporate brands also need thought leadership from researchers to inspire future research and to facilitate the contributions by the academic community. The increased efforts devoted to corporate brands with a conscience by practitioners and researchers are necessary not only for increasing the effectiveness of corporate branding, but also for contributing to a better and more sustainable future.

# References

Askeland, H., Espedal, G., Løvaas, B. J., & Sirris, S. (2020). Understanding values work in organisations and leadership. In H. Askeland, G. Espedal, B. J. Løvaas, & S. Sirris (Eds.), *Understanding values work: Institutional perspectives in organizations and leadership* (pp. 1–12). Cham: Palgrave Macmillan.

Babu, N., De Roeck, K., & Raineri, N. (2020). Hypocritical organizations: Implications for employee social responsibility. *Journal of Business Research, 114*, 376–384.

Bagozzi, R. P., Romani, S., Grappi, S., & Zarantonello, L. (2021). Psychological underpinnings of brands. *Annual Review of Psychology, 72*, 585–607.

Bahm, A. J. (1965). Theories of conscience. *Ethics, 75*(2), 128–131.

Balmer, J. M. (1995). Corporate branding and connoisseurship. *Journal of General Management, 21*(1), 24–46.

Balmer, J. M., & Gray, E. R. (2003). Corporate brands: What are they? What of them? *European Journal of Marketing*, *37*(7–8), 972–997.

Barrett, R. (2006). *Building a values-driven organization: A whole system approach to cultural transformation*. New York: Routledge.

Barros-Arrieta, D., & García-Cali, E. (2021). Internal branding: Conceptualization from a literature review and opportunities for future research. *Journal of Brand Management*, *28*(2), 133–151.

Baumgarth, C. (2010). "Living the brand": Brand orientation in the business-to-business sector. *European Journal of Marketing*, *44*(5), 653–671.

Bertilsson, J., & Rennstam, J. (2018). The destructive side of branding: A heuristic model for analyzing the value of branding practice. *Organization*, *25*(2), 260–281.

Biedenbach, G., & Manzhynski, S. (2016). Internal branding and sustainability: Investigating perceptions of employees. *Journal of Product & Brand Management*, *25*(3), 296–306.

Boddy, C. R., & Croft, R. (2016). Marketing in a time of toxic leadership. *Qualitative Market Research: An International Journal*, *19*(1), 44–64.

Boukis, A., Punjaisri, K., Balmer, J. M., Kaminakis, K., & Papastathopoulos, A. (2021). Unveiling frontline employees' brand construal types during corporate brand promise delivery: A multi-study analysis. *Journal of Business Research*, *131*, 673–685.

Bourne, H., & Jenkins, M. (2013). Organizational values: A dynamic perspective. *Organization Studies*, *34*(4), 495–514.

Burmann, C., & Zeplin, S. (2005). Building brand commitment: A behavioural approach to internal brand management. *Journal of Brand Management*, *12*(4), 279–300.

Carlini, J., & Grace, D. (2021). The corporate social responsibility (CSR) internal branding model: Aligning employees' CSR awareness, knowledge, and experience to deliver positive employee performance outcomes. *Journal of Marketing Management*, *37*(7–8), 732–760.

Celsi, M. W., & Gilly, M. C. (2010). Employees as internal audience: How advertising affects employees' customer focus. *Journal of the Academy of Marketing Science*, *38*(4), 520–529.

Childress, J. F. (1979). Appeals to conscience. *Ethics*, *89*(4), 315–335.

Christodoulides, G. (2009). Branding in the post-internet era. *Marketing Theory*, *9*(1), 141–144.

de Chernatony, L. (2001). A model for strategically building brands. *Journal of Brand Management*, *9*(1), 32–44.

Driscoll, D. M., & Hoffman, W. M. (1999). Gaining the ethical edge: Procedures for delivering values-driven management. *Long Range Planning*, *32*(2), 179–189.

Drucker, P. (1981). What is "business ethics"? *The Public Interest*, *63*(2), 18–36.

Fuss, P. (1964). Conscience. *Ethics*, *74*(2), 111–120.

Garsten, C., & Hernes, T. (2009). Beyond CSR: Dilemmas and paradoxes of ethical conduct in transnational organizations. In K. E. Browne & B. L. Milgram (Eds.), *Economics and morality: Anthropological approaches* (pp. 189–210). Lanham: AltaMira Press.

Golob, U., & Podnar, K. (2019). Researching CSR and brands in the here and now: An integrative perspective. *Journal of Brand Management*, *26*(1), 1–8.

Gotsi, M., & Wilson, A. (2001). Corporate reputation management: "Living the brand". *Management Decision*, *39*(2), 99–104.

Gyrd-Jones, R. I., & Kornum, N. (2013). Managing the co-created brand: Value and cultural complementarity in online and offline multi-stakeholder ecosystems. *Journal of Business Research*, *66*(9), 1484–1493.

Hajdas, M., & Kłeczek, R. (2021). The real purpose of purpose-driven branding: Consumer empowerment and social transformations. *Journal of Brand Management*, 1–15.

Harris, F., & De Chernatony, L. (2001). Corporate branding and corporate brand performance. *European Journal of Marketing*, *35*(3–4), 441–456.

Hatch, M. J., & Schultz, M. (2003). Bringing the corporation into corporate branding. *European Journal of Marketing*, *37*(7–8), 1041–1064.

Hemingway, C. A. (2005). Personal values as a catalyst for corporate social entrepreneurship. *Journal of Business Ethics*, *60*(3), 233–249.

Hogan, R. (1973). Moral conduct and moral character: A psychological perspective. *Psychological Bulletin*, *79*(4), 217–232.

Hutchinson, D. B., Singh, J., Svensson, G., & Mysen, T. (2013). Towards a model of conscientious corporate brands: A Canadian study. *Journal of Business & Industrial Marketing*, *28*(8), 687–695.

Iglesias, O., & Ind, N. (2016). How to build a brand with a conscience. In N. Ind & S. Horlings (Eds.), *Brands with a conscience* (pp. 203–211). Amsterdam: Kogan Page.

Iglesias, O., & Ind, N. (2020). Towards a theory of conscientious corporate brand co-creation: The next key challenge in brand management. *Journal of Brand Management, 27*(6), 710–720.

Iglesias, O., Landgraf, P., Ind, N., Markovic, S., & Koporcic, N. (2020). Corporate brand identity co-creation in business-to-business contexts. *Industrial Marketing Management, 85*, 32–43.

Ind, N. (1998). An integrated approach to corporate branding. *Journal of Brand Management, 5*(5), 323–329.

Ind, N., Iglesias, O., & Markovic, S. (2017). The co-creation continuum: From tactical market research tool to strategic collaborative innovation method. *Journal of Brand Management, 24*(4), 310–321.

Ind, N., & Ryder, I. (2011). Conscientious brands editorial. *Journal of Brand Management, 18*(9), 635–638.

Kernstock, J., & Powell, S. M. (2018). Twenty-five years of the Journal of Brand Management. *Journal of Brand Management, 25*(6), 489–493.

Knox, S., & Bickerton, D. (2003). The six conventions of corporate branding. *European Journal of Marketing, 37*(7–8), 998–1016.

Kotler, P., Kartajaya, H., & Setiawan, I. (2019). Marketing 3.0: From products to customers to the human spirit. In K. Kompella (Ed.), *Marketing Wisdom* (pp. 139–156). Singapore: Springer.

Krishnamurthy, S., & Kucuk, S. U. (2009). Anti-branding on the internet. *Journal of Business Research, 62*(11), 1119–1126.

Kristal, S., Baumgarth, C., & Henseler, J. (2020). Performative corporate brand identity in industrial markets: The case of German prosthetics manufacturer Ottobock. *Journal of Business Research, 114*, 240–253.

Lahtinen, S., & Närvänen, E. (2020). Co-creating sustainable corporate brands: A consumer framing approach. *Corporate Communications: An International Journal, 25*(3), 447–461.

Lee, S. B., & Suh, T. (2020). Internal audience strikes back from the outside: Emotionally exhausted employees' negative word-of-mouth as the active brand-oriented deviance. *Journal of Product & Brand Management, 29*(7), 863–876.

Maon, F., Swaen, V., & De Roeck, K. (2021). Corporate branding and corporate social responsibility: Toward a multi-stakeholder interpretive perspective. *Journal of Business Research, 126*, 64–77.

Maxwell, R., & Knox, S. (2009). Motivating employees to" live the brand": A comparative case study of employer brand attractiveness within the firm. *Journal of Marketing Management, 25*(9–10), 893–907.

Merrilees, B., Miller, D., & Yakimova, R. (2021). Building brands through internal stakeholder engagement and co-creation. *Journal of Product & Brand Management, 30*(6), 806–818.

Mingione, M. (2015). Inquiry into corporate brand alignment: A dialectical analysis and directions for future research. *Journal of Product & Brand Management, 24*(5), 518–536.

Mingione, M., & Leoni, L. (2020). Blurring B2C and B2B boundaries: Corporate brand value co-creation in B2B2C markets. *Journal of Marketing Management, 36*(1–2), 72–99.

Morhart, F. M., Herzog, W., & Tomczak, T. (2009). Brand-specific leadership: Turning employees into brand champions. *Journal of Marketing, 73*(5), 122–142.

Olsen, L. E., & Peretz, A. (2011). Conscientious brand criteria: A framework and a case example from the clothing industry. *Journal of Brand Management, 18*(9), 639–649.

Olson, E. L., & Thjømøe, H. M. (2010). How bureaucrats and bean counters strangled General Motors by killing its brands. *Journal of Product & Brand Management, 19*(2), 103–113.

Ozdemir, S., Gupta, S., Foroudi, P., Wright, L. T., & Eng, T. Y. (2020). Corporate branding and value creation for initiating and managing relationships in B2B markets. *Qualitative Market Research: An International Journal, 23*(4), 627–661.

Padela, S. M. F., Wooliscroft, B., & Ganglmair-Wooliscroft, A. (2021). Brand externalities: A taxonomy. *Journal of Macromarketing, 41*(2), 356–372.

Palmer, M., Simmons, G., & Mason, K. (2014). Web-based social movements contesting marketing strategy: The mobilisation of multiple actors and rhetorical strategies. *Journal of Marketing Management, 30*(3–4), 383–408.

Pandey, A., & Gupta, R. K. (2008). A perspective of collective consciousness of business organizations. *Journal of Business Ethics, 80*(4), 889–898.

Piehler, R., Grace, D., & Burmann, C. (2018). Internal brand management: Introduction to the special issue and directions for future research. *Journal of Brand Management, 25*(3), 197–201.

Piehler, R., Schade, M., & Burmann, C. (2019). Employees as a second audience: The effect of external communication on internal brand management outcomes. *Journal of Brand Management, 26*(4), 445–460.

PwC. (2016). *The PwC diversity journey – Creating impact, achieving results*. Retrieved from www.pwc.com/gx/en/diversity-inclusion/best-practices/assets/the-pwc-diversity-journey.pdf

PwC. (2017). *Living our purpose and values – PwC's code of conduct*. Retrieved from www.pwc.com/gx/en/ethics-business-conduct/pdf/living-our-purpose-and-values-pwc-code-of-conduct-2017.pdf

PwC. (2020). *Global annual review 2020 – Working together to build a better tomorrow*. Retrieved from www.pwc.com/gx/en/about-pwc/global-annual-review-2020/downloads/pwc-global-annual-review-2020.pdf

PwC. (2021). *Be well, work well*. Retrieved from www.pwc.com/us/en/about-us/be-well-work-well.html

Rasberry, R. W. (2000). The conscience of an organization. *Strategy & Leadership, 28*(3), 17–21.

Rindell, A., Svensson, G., Mysen, T., Billström, A., & Wilén, K. (2011). Towards a conceptual foundation of 'Conscientious Corporate Brands'. *Journal of Brand Management, 18*(9), 709–719.

Rocha, R. G., & Pinheiro, P. G. (2021). Organizational spirituality: Concept and perspectives. *Journal of Business Ethics, 171*(2), 241–252.

Saks, A. M. (2011). Workplace spirituality and employee engagement. *Journal of Management, Spirituality & Religion, 8*(4), 317–340.

Saleem, F. Z., & Iglesias, O. (2016). Mapping the domain of the fragmented field of internal branding. *Journal of Product & Brand Management, 25*(1), 43–57.

Schmidt, H. J., & Baumgarth, C. (2018). Strengthening internal brand equity with brand ambassador programs: Development and testing of a success factor model. *Journal of Brand Management, 25*(3), 250–265.

Schmidt, H. J., & Redler, J. (2018). How diverse is corporate brand management research? Comparing schools of corporate brand management with approaches to corporate strategy. *Journal of Product & Brand Management, 27*(2), 185–202.

Sorabji, R. (2017). *Moral conscience through the ages: Fifth century BCE to the present*. Chicago, IL: The University of Chicago Press; Oxford: Oxford University Press.

Sulmasy, D. P. (2008). What is conscience and why is respect for it so important? *Theoretical Medicine and Bioethics, 29*(3), 135–149.

Swaminathan, V., Sorescu, A., Steenkamp, J. B. E., O'Guinn, T. C. G., & Schmitt, B. (2020). Branding in a hyperconnected world: Refocusing theories and rethinking boundaries. *Journal of Marketing, 84*(2), 24–46.

Thomson, K., de Chernatony, L., Arganbright, L., & Khan, S. (1999). The buy-in benchmark: How staff understanding and commitment impact brand and business performance. *Journal of Marketing Management, 15*(8), 819–835.

UN Women (2021). *HeForShe global champions for gender equality*. Retrieved from www.heforshe.org/en/impact

Urde, M. (2003). Core value-based corporate brand building. *European Journal of Marketing, 37*(7–8), 1017–1040.

Vallaster, C., & von Wallpach, S. (2013). An online discursive inquiry into the social dynamics of multi-stakeholder brand meaning co-creation. *Journal of Business Research, 66*(9), 1505–1515.

Veloutsou, C., & Guzmán, F. (2017). The evolution of brand management thinking over the last 25 years as recorded in the Journal of Product and Brand Management. *Journal of Product & Brand Management, 26*(1), 2–12.

Vredenburg, J., Kapitan, S., Spry, A., & Kemper, J. A. (2020). Brands taking a stand: Authentic brand activism or woke washing? *Journal of Public Policy & Marketing, 39*(4), 444–460.

Wallace, E., & de Chernatony, N. L. (2007). Exploring managers' views about brand saboteurs. *Journal of Marketing Management, 23*(1–2), 91–106.

Wicclair, M. R. (2013). Conscience. In H. LaFollette (Ed.), *The international encyclopedia of ethics* (pp. 1009–1020). Malden: Blackwell Publishing Ltd.

Yagil, D., & Shultz, T. (2017). Service with a conscience: Moral dilemmas in customer service roles. *Journal of Service Theory and Practice, 27*(3), 689–711.

Yang, L., Manika, D., & Athanasopoulou, A. (2020). Are they sinners or saints? A multi-level investigation of hypocrisy in organisational and employee pro-environmental behaviours. *Journal of Business Research, 114*, 336–347.

Yoganathan, V., McLeay, F., Osburg, V. S., & Hart, D. (2018). The core value compass: Visually evaluating the goodness of brands that do good. *Journal of Brand Management, 25*(1), 68–83.

# 30
# BRANDING INSIDE-OUT
## Corporate culture and internal branding

*Ceridwyn King*

## 1. Introduction

For many years, organizations and individuals alike have sought advantage in standing out from their crowded competitive landscape in pursuit of a variety of goals not limited to increased awareness, market share, and subsequently, profits. To this end, effective brand management continues to be a priority and has garnered appreciation in its endeavours to not only help an organization differentiate itself from competitors, but also being instrumental in helping guide organizational decision making. The growing appreciation of the latter underscores the emergence of a body of work with a strong focus on the role that employees play in the success of the brand. The currency of employee involvement in brand management was originally advanced by de Chernatony and Dall'Olmo Riley in 1998. However, it was not until the early 2000s that the label of *internal branding* was assigned in the academic literature to a practice that many successful brands, particularly in a service context, were already, somewhat by accident, practicing. With an almost an epiphanic type quality, academics and practitioners alike began a quest to be more intentional in applying and understanding such efforts, as evidenced in both practitioner and academic publications. It is from this evolutionary perspective that Piehler's Chapter 26 on the development of the internal branding concept comes to the fore. In doing so, the text provides a meaningful platform to consider the contributions of Chapters 27, 28, and 29 in seeking to charter new territory for the continued development of the internal brand management phenomenon.

## 2. The evolution of internal brand management

While consideration of internal brand management's contribution to a brand's overall success only emerged in the early 2000s, academics, inspired by practice, were quick to realize that such efforts lacked the necessary insight and understanding to solidify the concept of internal branding in traditional brand management frameworks. And so began a series of research clusters that dominate our early thinking of the concept. The early champions of internal branding emanate from the work of de Chernatony and colleagues as well as Burmann and his colleagues. However, for the most part, much of the foundational internal brand management research reflected in the research clusters identified by Piehler was developed somewhat simultaneously, as evidenced by publication date. Thus, it is noteworthy that these publications demonstrate a coalescing around the concept, with generated insights reflecting new and augmented learning in contrast to mere repetition or conflict of thoughts and ideas. While Piehler notes that previous literature reviews have commented that the internal brand management domain is fragmented, when looked at holistically, and supported by the comprehensive synthesis provided in his chapter, it is apparent that these early research clusters provided the architecture needed to explore this emerging concept.

In seeking to elucidate the contributions of the internal brand research, as well as solidify its relevance in the broader brand management framework, Piehler structures the extant literature in response to five questions relevant to both a practitioner and academic audience:

- Why is internal branding important for brands?
- What does internal branding try to achieve?
- How does internal branding achieve its objectives?
- Which situational factors affect the success of internal branding?
- What are the general prerequisites of internal branding?

In this way, not only does the chapter distinguish itself from other similar review papers, but it also helps to disentangle the literature from the perceived fragmentation. That said, the potential for the domain to become fragmented remains high if consensus is not reached on what has been established or agreed upon in the literature, thus mandating that attention turn to breaking new ground. For example, Piehler identifies the variety of definitions that have been advanced to capture the essence of internal branding (refer to Table 26.3). Yet he concludes that in most, if not all cases, the definitions seek to capture the essence of living the brand/delivering the brand promise with the target of such efforts being predominantly the employee. While some of the references captured in the table could be classified as more of an explanation of the concept of interest, rather than a specific definition, the desire for researchers to modify something in the spirit of contribution without really making new advances contributes to the fragmentation perception. This is also somewhat evident in the work that examines what internal branding is trying to achieve. Piehler emphasizes that the literature is replete with many internal branding objectives, but he chooses to highlight four. However, when looking at brand-related behaviour and brand understanding discussions, it is revealing how researchers have parsed those concepts into a variety of manifestations that contribute to the perceptions of fragmentation. It is also questionable whether all these nuanced constructs add further to our understanding of the concepts.

In contrast to the minutiae reflected in different definitions or articulation of internal branding objectives, work on internal branding activities and antecedents is relatively abstract or broad in nature and generally stagnate, if publication dates are an indication. It is suspected that this is because it is inextricably linked to organizational actions, which are varied and not easily observed, as well as the fact that beyond what has already been identified (communication, HR, leadership, and orientation), the extant marketing, management, and organizational behaviour literatures are not readily informative. Nonetheless, just as the external brand management literature provides integrative and detailed frameworks that are useful in guiding management practices, the internal brand management literature would benefit from a deeper dive into the nuances of these concepts and how they are manifested. For example, brand orientation's role in internal brand management is well established, yet there is currently no clear and detailed consensus of how an organization can create such an outcome, beyond the broad concepts identified previously.

In providing a framework to consider the internal branding literature, Piehler illuminates not only the conceptual process but also where research emphasis has been and where opportunities remain. Overall, in consideration of the literature review, it appears that the energy that drove the pioneering work of the original research clusters has dissipated. The volume of insight that emerged initially has slowed and the limited, more recent work appears to prefer re-packing of old insights as opposed to breaking new ground, which again adds to the idea that the literature is fragmented. Nonetheless, as Schmidt and Steenkamp allude to in Chapter 27, the world in which we operate is constantly evolving. This necessitates our understanding evolves too and thus brings new research opportunities.

## 2.1 Reimagining the focus of internal brand management

Whilst acknowledging that in all the internal branding chapters presented in this book and, for the most part, the internal branding literature, their focus is on the efforts of employees, new internal brand research ideas are challenged to broaden the target of our internal brand management efforts to consider all those that are responsible for living the brand and delivering the brand promise – the ultimate objective of internal branding. The reason is twofold. First there is already evidence in the literature that internal brand management is relevant outside of the traditional employee-organization relationship, extending to situations where the principle-agent relationship applies. Whether it be in franchising (King et al., 2013), destination management (Cox et al., 2014), or volunteerism (Liu et al., 2015), for example, previous research has shown that the desire to realize a brand aligned experience is not always relegated to the responsibilities of employees. Broadening our understanding of who can and should be the target of our internal branding efforts not only better aligns with the intent of internal brand management in the evolving landscape, but it also forces one to challenge our assumptions that what works for one brand experience provider group may not work for another. Thus, new models of internal brand management emerge.

The criticality of placing more emphasis on broadening the way we think about the target of internal brand management and thus informing how we understand the internal brand management process is also reflected in our understanding of the contemporary workforce, a notion that ignited the work presented in Schmidt and Steenkamp's chapter and is extrapolated in the case study presented in Saraniemi's. From a mere observational perspective, one can readily acknowledge that the way organizations and employees interact is undergoing fundamental change, an idea that has been supported in the literature (e.g., Subramony et al., 2018). These changes, as Schmidt and Steenkamp suggest, were present before the COVID-19 pandemic, but managers' response to the implications is more pressing now. A particular force that underscores the need to expand the internal brand management 'tent' relates to the workforce's desire for greater flexibility and mobility, the growing transactional nature of employment, and the rise of the 'gig' economy. With employees changing jobs more frequently as well as increasingly engaging in multiple roles or 'gigs,' not as an employee but as an independent contractor (Veen et al., 2020), continuing to think that the target of internal brand management remains confined to employees in the traditional sense may be to the detriment of the brand's success. When we think of a customer's experience with a brand today, and even more so in the future, these changes to the contemporary workforce suggest that it is less likely those experiences will be facilitated solely by employees of the organization. Nonetheless, the desire to deliver brand-aligned experiences will remain. So, the question may not be as simple as Schmidt and Steenkamp suggest when asking 'Can internal branding change, too?' but rather 'How will internal branding change to reflect the changing dynamics of the contemporary workforce?' From this perspective, there is great opportunity to explore the intersection of internal brand management evolution and that of contemporary work – an idea that is explored in Saraniemi's chapter.

## 2.2 Socially oriented internal brand management practices

One of the challenges that informs our thinking of how to develop internal brand management activities is ensuring the target audience (i.e., predominantly employees) sees relevance in the brand and their role in its success (e.g., King & Grace, 2006; Piehler et al., 2016; Xiong et al., 2013), that the employees' 'what's in it for me' threshold is reached (King & Grace, 2009). For the most part we have sought to achieve this largely through formal organizational practices, such as HR, communication, and training as well as leadership. However, as Saraniemi's work illuminates, when our workforce operates remotely and/or may not be a formal employee, these traditional channels may be ineffective. Rather it is the informal organizational factors, such as the social environment and relationships with co-workers, that may have greater influence on one's response to the brand. Such socially oriented influences have largely been neglected in the internal branding literature, the exception being Xiong and King (2018, 2019).

To the extent that social influences are considered in practice is unknown, however it is clear from Saraniemi's case study that they are critical in shaping a connection to the brand, particularly when the worker could be associated with more than one brand at the same time, which is the case for independent contractors or gig workers. Xiong and King's (2020) work on how an employee's sense of brand community affects their behaviour is particularly informative in this regard. Their work reinforces the need to understand how the social environment influences internal brand management outcomes. It illuminates how an employee's sense of brand community is a meaningful measure of their attitude toward the brand. In consideration of Saraniemi's work, and the changing nature of the contemporary workforce towards more fluidity and meaning in work relationships, sense of brand community may well be a more effective construct to measure workforce brand attitude, in contrast to brand commitment, for example, which suggests a monogamous employee-organization relationship. While both the work of Xiong and King (2020) and Saraniemi reinforce the significance of nurturing a sense of brand community internally, it is evident that how to enhance this remains a fruitful area for future exploration. This is consistent with the earlier observation that our understanding of internal branding activities and antecedents remains too broad or abstract and would benefit from a closer examination, particularly considering the changing landscape of the workforce as reflected by Saraniemi.

While changes to the contemporary workforce may be reflected in its composition, they are also having a significant influence on existing employee relationships. Schelichler and Baumann (2020) observe that today's employees see value not only in increased flexibility but also in opportunities for personal growth and skill development, as well as opportunities to share their opinions and have more informal feedback sessions with supervisors. Within this context, the arguments presented by Schmidt and Steenkamp in Chapter 27 that internal brand management needs to adopt a co-creation mindset regarding employees are timely. Further, Seligman and Csikszentmihalyi's (2014) observations that new generations of workers are increasingly seeking organizations that promote virtues of sustainability, altruism, and tolerance bodes well for the thinking advanced in Biedenbach and Biedenbach's Chapter 29. It seems that the organizational necessity to bring employees more into the brand development process and for them to champion the cause of conscientious branding aligns well with the desires of today's employee.

Schmidt and Steenkamp's contention that the internal brand management literature has, for the most part, assumed a top-down, organizationally guided approach to employees bares out Piehler's literature review chapter. However, this was not always the case. In the earlier work of King and Grace, intrigued by qualitative insights (King & Grace, 2006) and inspired by the internal market orientation work of Lings (2004) and Lings and Greenly (2005, 2010), employee involvement in the brand management process was considered a foundational element, an integral source of information necessary for brand success (King & Grace, 2010). Over time this seems to have been lost as researchers focused on better understanding the effects of internal branding, so the re-emergence of employee involvement, under the contemporary guise of co-creation, particularly as it relates to the creation of the brand's identity, is clearly needed.

In a service context, particularly high contact service experiences, employees are fundamental to the development of the brand image as they co-create the brand experience through their interactions with customers. It is this centrality of the service employee's role in delivering the brand experience that has seen service-related industries become the dominant context for the examination of internal brand management (King, 2017). Beyond the initial service brand work that illuminated the centrality of employees' role in shaping customer perception of the brand (Berry, 2000; Grace & O'Cass, 2004), more recent examinations attest to how employees' mannerisms, presentation, and engagement with customers have a significant impact on customers' evaluations and understanding of the brand (e.g., Sirianini et al., 2013; Wu et al., 2020; Garamoudi et al., 2020). With the body of work that supports the employees' role in co-creating the brand's image, the most meaningful take away from Schmidt and Steenkamp's chapter, in addition to re-imagining employee involvement in the creation of the brand's identity, relates to the co-creation of internal brand meaning. The evolutionary perspective of developing a shared brand meaning that the chapter describes emerging from the work of Dean et al. (2016) is reflected in Murillo and King's (2019) longitudinal study that examines how employees come to understand the brand. Of note in Murillo and King's work is the slow development of this process. Even after seven months, their research found that employees' understanding of the brand was still very much in flux, attributing this to, amongst other things, 'the inherent difficulty of transferring to new hires the tacit knowledge of the brand and the embodied performances required for the delivery of the brand-defined customer experience' (Murillo & King, 2019, p. 902). The longitudinal design of the study accounted for the co-creation element of the learning process, believing that in addition to deliberate organizational internal brand management actions, immersion in the brand community (i.e., co-workers, management, and customers) would facilitate a consolidation of the employee's brand understanding. However, this was not forthcoming over the examined period. It would seem, therefore, that progression from the interpretation stage to the appropriation stage promoted by Dean et al. (2016) can be prolonged. The criticality of a shared brand meaning/understanding by employees so that they can effectively deliver the experience suggests more work is needed to understand and facilitate this stage of the co-creation process.

In seeking to draw a contrast between traditional brand management practices and co-creation efforts, Schmidt and Steenkamp emphasize the former as being top-down, designed by a closed circle of managers versus the more open and interactive practices that enhance the brand experience for all stakeholders via a co-creative mindset. They underscore the need for co-creation is based on the premise that command and control of multiple stakeholders can be difficult. While this may be true, the real strength of the internal brand management co-creation mindset lies in the implicit or tacit knowledge perspective of what a brand stands for that makes it difficult to formalize and thus, communicate (King & Grace, 2009). Murillo and King (2019) emphasize that as a brand's identity has less to do with objective, easily measured characteristics as opposed to value based, personality-laden associations, understanding the brand is difficult in the absence of lived experiences with the brand.

The brand co-creation literature, whether it be from an employee or customer perspective, addresses the issue of involvement in the creation of the brand experience, with the goal of enhancing brand value (Vallaster & Von Wallpach, 2013). It acknowledges that multiple contributions of stakeholders are the ultimate determinants of brand value, with an emphasis on co-creating the brand's meaning that is both dynamic and continuous. While organizations/brand owners may not unilaterally control the communication of the brand's meaning to a passive audience as they once did, they nonetheless are still the ultimate arbitrators of what they want their brand to stand for. Therefore, co-creation is advanced to improve the brand experience for all stakeholders, not as a means through which a stakeholder can 'choose their own adventure' if that direction does not align with the brand owner's intentions.

This assertion is important when considering Schmidt and Steenkamp's question regarding employees co-creating a brand's meaning and if all brand-related actions of employees are relevant for the brand, then how can behaviour be off-brand. Just as King and Grace (2009) identified the need to distinguish between employees' knowledge of the brand and appropriate brand knowledge, it cannot be assumed that an employee's brand understanding and therefore brand behaviour, is as the organization intends. By suggesting that employees co-create the brand's identity, one does not believe the authors are suggesting that a brand is rudderless. While value derived from the brand is constantly negotiated between the brand's stakeholders, brand managers still need to provide direction (Iglesias et al., 2013). On-brand behaviour, conceptually, is behaviour that reflects the agreed upon positioning of the brand. Who decides what behaviour is on- and off-brand? – the brand's owner, based on insight that is garnered through the co-creation process. While brand owners may not specify explicit behaviours, they provide guideposts, in the form of brand values and brand experience stories, that imply what behaviour is on-brand. Co-creation is about bringing the brand experience to life in a meaningful and relevant way for the brand's stakeholders. As Chapter 27 reflects, this stakeholder/independent interpretation, however, is within predefined guidelines (Iglesias & Saleem, 2015) that are determined by the organization/brand's owner. So, while acknowledging what a brand means for one stakeholder group versus another may be different (i.e., for an employee the Ritz Carlton *brand* may mean the opportunity to serve ladies and gentlemen, while for a customer it means being served like ladies and gentlemen), it is equally important to acknowledge that these manifestations are derived from a single brand identity, albeit one that may organically evolve over time (Iglesias et al., 2013). It is only those brands that are not effectively managed by their owners where the brand takes on a fragmented and ill-defined identity, which makes enhancing brand value problematic, if not unachievable.

## 2.3 Brand values alignment

The idea that a brand experience, and subsequent brand value, maybe co-created yet directed/guided/championed by a brand owner is underscored in the final chapter by Biedenbach and Biedenbach. In seeking to illuminate not only the importance, but also the currency, of brands manifesting a conscience, the authors infer that such thinking is derived for the ultimate benefit or need of the organization (i.e., the brand's owner). While there is a moral element at play here in creating a conscientious brand, there is equally, if possibly not more, a business reason driving such a socially responsive brand management approach.

Acknowledging the authors' assertions that a conscientious brand extends beyond the mere adoption of corporate social responsibility programmes; the CSR brand literature is nonetheless informative with regard to how such a transformative purpose driven brand identity is successful. In both a consumer (e.g., Guzmán & Davis, 2017) and employee context (Carlini & Grace, 2021), extant literature has demonstrated that the success of such a strategy is determined by how this global phenomenon, that transcends product categorization, resonates with the brand's stakeholders. The extent to which the brand values promoted in a conscientious mindset align or fit with the stakeholders' perceptions of what the brand represents is critical for the desired outcomes to be attained, whether that be enhancing consumer brand equity or having employees embrace, and act on, those same values.

In advancing this contemporary approach to brand management, Biedenbach and Biedenbach's work raises an interesting question. If we consider the definition of conscientious being about harmonizing moral knowledge with moral action, to what extent is the consumer's or stakeholder's assumption today that all organizations act in this manner, in good faith, even if it is not explicitly stated in their mission? With Biedenbach and Biedenbach noting the high managerial relevance and social need of such an approach, is it reasonable to expect that as a society we are reaching a point when it is the expectation that all organizations conduct themselves in this manner. To that end, at what point is the adoption of a conscientious approach to business no longer considered a key point of differentiation and thus a brand-defining attribute? If this is how society demands business to be conducted, does focusing on developing a conscientious brand serve the purpose of brand management, which is to distinguish one brand from another, to develop a unique position in the minds of its stakeholders?

While this utopian view of the business community may be far away or potentially never realized, the positioning of conscientious branding as a value-led phenomenon reveals the real utility of this chapter's insights. As the authors indicate, unique, engaging, and powerful values are the foundation for a corporate brand with a conscience. But such value-laden thinking is not confined to conscientious brands, but rather all successful brands that seek to articulate what their brand stands for through their values. Thus, whether one is advancing a brand whose values are defined by a conscientious mindset or by other values that are different, but no less important to the organization and its stakeholders, the real insight lies in understanding how these values become an active contributor to the brand's success.

Acknowledging that employees are the primary custodians for bringing these brand values to life, the work of Löhndorf and Diamantopoulos (2014) along with Xiong and King (2015, 2019) emphasize the importance of seeking employee-brand value alignment for the ultimate benefit of the brand's success. In drawing from the person-organization fit literature (Helm et al., 2016), the important, yet limited employee-brand value fit examinations are underscored by the notion

that with higher levels of employee-brand value fit, information exchange is expected to be enhanced, stakeholder behaviour is more predictable, a more friendly organization environment may be realized, which in turn, all would contribute to a higher level of employee trust in the brand and contribution to achieving brand success.

(Xiong & King, 2015, p. 61)

Given the complexity with which Biedenbach and Biedenbach articulate the precarity of developing a corporate brand with a conscience, as reflected in their typology, more work needs to be done on not only understanding how to build such alignment between the brand's values and the employees, but also how to measure such alignment. Many researchers have adopted generic reflective measures to assess person-environment fit in both organizational behaviour and internal brand management literature. However, as values tend to be pluralistic in nature, current reflective measures do not identify which values are driving employees' congruence perception. Thus, an accurate measure of employee value fit cannot be determined. Further managers are not able to pinpoint which brand values, that are important to the organization, are, or are not, resonating with employees. Such insight is necessary to determine what, if any, remedial action is necessary to ensure employees are truly aligned with the brand's values as the organization intends. Enhanced measurement of employees' perceived fit with a brand's values will enhance practitioner understanding and the subsequent action that Biedenbach and Biedenbach call for when advancing the development and nurturing of conscientious brands – after all, what gets measured, gets done.

## 3. Conclusion

Despite its relative infancy when compared to external brand management, the body of work that reflects our understanding of 'insider' branding can be described as solid with opportunities to grow. Across the four chapters presented in this section, the case for the importance of internal brand management is strongly made. Not only do they underscore the need to consider the nuances involved when developing brand champions, they reaffirm that effective brand management is an evolutionary process that needs to morph with the market to survive. Whether it's seeking more detailed insight into how this process manifests, across different contexts, with stakeholders beyond traditional employees, or how the contemporary workforce and society is demanding how we create and present the brand experience, pioneering internal brand management research is still to be done. Through this work, internal brand management researchers will be able to meet the evolving needs of both practitioners and academics alike who seek to deliver an exceptional brand experience through an energized, informed, and committed internal brand community.

## References

Berry, L. L. (2000). Cultivating service brand equity. *Journal of the Academy of Marketing Science, 28*(1), 128–137.

Carlini, J., & Grace, D. (2021). The corporate social responsibility (CSR) internal branding model: Aligning employees' CSR awareness, knowledge, and experience to deliver positive employee performance outcomes. *Journal of Marketing Management*, 1–29. https://doi.org/10.1080/0267257X.2020.1860113

Cox, N., Gyrd-Jones, R., & Gardiner, S. (2014). Internal brand management of destination brands: Exploring the roles of destination management organisations and operators. *Journal of Destination Marketing & Management, 3*(2), 85–95.

de Chernatony, L., & Dall'Olmo Riley, F. (1998). Modelling the components of the brand. *European Journal of Marketing, 32*(11–12), 1074–1090.

Dean, D., Arroyo-Gamez, R. E., Punjaisri, K., & Pich, C. (2016). Internal brand co-creation: The experiential brand meaning cycle in higher education. *Journal of Business Research, 69*(8), 3041–3048.

Garmaroudi, S. A., King, C., & Lu, L. (2021). Social servicescape's impact on customer perceptions of the hospitality brand – The role of branded social cues. *International Journal of Hospitality Management, 93*. https://doi.org/10.1016/j.ijhm.2020.102774

Grace, D., & O'Cass, A. (2004). Examining service experiences and post-consumption evaluations. *Journal of Services Marketing, 18*(6), 450–461.

Guzmán, F., & Davis, D. (2017). The impact of CSR on brand equity: Consumer responses to two types of fit. *Journal of Product and Brand Management, 26*(5), 435–446.

Helm, S. V., Renk, U., & Mishra, A. (2016). Exploring the impact of employees' self-concept, brand identification and brand pride on brand citizenship behaviors. *European Journal of Marketing, 50*(1–2), 58–77.

Iglesias, O., Ind, N., & Alfaro, M. (2013). The organic view of the brand: A brand value co-creation model. *Journal of Brand Management, 20*(8), 670–688.

Iglesias, O., & Saleem, F. Z. (2015). How to support consumer-brand relationships: The role of corporate culture and human resource policies and practices. *Marketing Intelligence & Planning, 33*(2), 216–234.

King, C. (2017). Brand management – Standing out from the crowd. *International Journal of Contemporary Hospitality Management, 29*(1), 115–140.

King, C., & Grace, D. (2006). Exploring managers' perspectives of the impact of brand management strategies on employee roles within a service firm. *Journal of Services Marketing, 20*(6), 369–380.

King, C., & Grace, D. (2009). Employee based brand equity: A third perspective. *Services Marketing Quarterly, 30*(2), 122–147.

King, C., & Grace, D. (2010). Building and measuring employee-based brand equity. *European Journal of Marketing, 44*(7/8), 938–971.

King, C., Grace, D., & Weaven, S. (2013). Developing brand champions: A franchisee perspective. *Journal of Marketing Management, 29*(11–12), 1308–1336.

Lings, I. N. (2004). Internal market orientation: Construct and consequences. *Journal of Business Research*, 57(4), 405–413.

Lings, I. N., & Greenley, G. E. (2005). Measuring internal market orientation. *Journal of Service Research*, 7(3), 290–305.

Lings, I. N., & Greenley, G. E. (2010). Internal market orientation and market-oriented behaviours. *Journal of Service Management*, 21(3), 321–343. https://doi.org/10.1108/09564231011050788

Liu, G., Chapleo, C., Ko, W. W., & Ngugi, I. K. (2015). The role of internal branding in nonprofit brand management: An empirical investigation. *Nonprofit and Voluntary Sector Quarterly*, 44(2), 319–339.

Löhndorf, B., & Diamantopoulos, A. (2014). Internal branding: Social identity and social exchange perspectives on turning employees into brand champions. *Journal of Service Research*, 17(3), 310–325.

Murillo, E., & King, C. (2019). Examining the drivers of employee brand understanding: A longitudinal study. *Journal of Product & Brand Management*, 28(7), 893–907.

Piehler, R., King, C., Burmann, C., & Xiong, L. (2016). The importance of employee brand understanding, brand identification, and brand commitment in realizing brand citizenship behaviour. *European Journal of Marketing*, 50(9/10), 1575–1601.

Schleicher, D. J., & Baumann, H. M. (2020). Performance management and the changing nature of work. In *The Cambridge handbook of the changing nature of work* (pp. 340–363). Cambridge: Cambridge University Press.

Seligman, M. D., & Csikszentmihalyi, M. (2014). *Positive psychology: An introduction*. Heidelberg: Springer.

Sirianni, N. J., Bitner, M. J., Brown, S. W., & Mandel, N. (2013). Branded service encounters: Strategically aligning employee behavior with the brand positioning. *Journal of Marketing*, 77(6), 108–123.

Subramony, M., Solnet, D., Groth, M., Yagil, D., Hartley, N., Kim, P. B., & Golubovskaya, M. (2018). Service work in 2050: Toward a work ecosystems perspective. *Journal of Service Management*, 29(5), 956–974. https://doi.org/10.1108/JOSM-05-2018-0131

Vallaster, C., & Von Wallpach, S. (2013). An online discursive inquiry into the social dynamics of multi-stakeholder brand meaning co-creation. *Journal of Business Research*, 66(9), 1505–1515.

Veen, A., Kaine, S., Goods, C., & Barratt, T. (2020). The "Gigification" of work in the 21st century. In *Contemporary work and the future of employment in developed countries* (pp. 15–32). London: Routledge.

Wu, L., King, C. A., Lu, L., & Guchait, P. (2020). Hospitality aesthetic labor management: Consumers' and prospective employees' perspectives of hospitality brands. *International Journal of Hospitality Management*, 87. https://doi.org/10.1016/j.ijhm.2019.102373

Xiong, L., & King, C. (2015). Motivational drivers that fuel employees to champion the hospitality brand. *International Journal of Hospitality Management*, 44, 58–69.

Xiong, L., & King, C. (2018). Too much of a good thing? Examining how proactive personality affects employee brand performance under formal and informal organizational support. *International Journal of Hospitality Management*, 68, 12–22. https://psycnet.apa.org/doi/10.1016/j.ijhm.2017.09.007

Xiong, L., & King, C. (2019). Aligning employees' attitudes and behavior with hospitality brands: The role of employee brand internalization. *Journal of Hospitality and Tourism Management*, 40, 67–76.

Xiong, L., & King, C. (2020). Exploring how employee sense of brand community affects their attitudes and behavior. *Journal of Hospitality & Tourism Research*, 44(4), 567–596.

Xiong, L., King, C., & Piehler, R. (2013). "That's not my job": Exploring the employee perspective in the development of brand ambassadors. *International Journal of Hospitality Management*, 35, 348–359.

# INDEX

Note: page numbers in *italic* indicate a figure and page numbers in **bold** indicate a table on the corresponding page.

Abratt, Russell xiii, 13, 14, 27–28, 83–85, 171
action net perspective 111–112, 126–127; brand action nets in action 119–126, *119*, *124*; corporate brands as action nets 113–117, **113–114**; research context and methods 117–119
Actor-Network Theory (ANT) 115–116, 203–205
adaptive instability perspectives 140
agency: stakeholder 352–353; temporal 354–355, 411–412
alignment *see* brand values alignment; corporate brand alignment
all brand stakeholders 144
Andreassen, Tor W. xiii, 15, 215, 218, 250
Andreini, Daniela xiii, 9, 15, 203, 249, 250
applications *see* corporate brand applications
appropriating 349
Argenti, Paul A. xiv, 15–16, 339–341
artificial intelligence (AI) 195–196, 206–207; ANT perspective of brand experience co-creation at the time AI 203–205; application to brand management practice 200–202; and brand experience co-creation 196–197; definition and taxonomy of 198–200, **199**; theoretical and practical implications 205–206
attractiveness *see* relative brand attractiveness
audit *see* brand audit approach
augmenting 349
authentic internal brand strategies 378–380, 389–391, *389*; authenticity and corporate branding 380–389
authenticity: as conformity 383–386; as connection 386–389; as consistency 382–383; and corporate branding 380–389; *see also* authentic internal brand strategies; brand authenticity

Baumgarth, Carsten xiv, 15, 249–250, 253, 442
B★Canvas 2.0 177, 178–182, *179*, **180–182**, 190; use cases of 183–189, *184*, **186**, *187–188*, **189**
behavioural school 84
belonging, sense of 466–467
Beverland, Michael B. xiv, 17, 385, 409–412
Biedenbach, Galina xiv, 18, 499, 501–502
Biedenbach, Thomas xiv–xv, 18, 499, 501–502
boundary-spanning 119–123, 468
brand agency: temporal 411–412
brand attractiveness *see* relative brand attractiveness
brand audit approach 183–187
brand authenticity 33
brand building *see* corporate brand building
brand communities: co-creating value with 158–159; *see also* internal brand communities
brand differentiation 26–27
brand experience 33, 195–196, 206–207; ANT perspective of brand experience co-creation at the time of AI 203–205; application of AI to brand management practice 200–202; brand experience co-creation 196–197; and a definition and taxonomy of AI 198–200, **199**; theoretical and practical implications 205–206
brand foundation 179–180
brand heritage 29–30; in corporate branding 368–370; cross-fertilization between corporate heritage research and 370–371; in product branding 365–368; *see also* brand heritage research; corporate heritage branding

505

# Index

brand heritage research: and corporate heritage literature 372–373; and corporate heritage research 371–372
brand identification (BID) 336; dual 470; impact on CBE 325
brand identity (BI): employees as co-creators of 450; *see also* corporate brand identity
brand image: employees as co-creators of 451–453
branding *see* corporate branding; values-driven branding
brand innovativeness *see* innovation
brand loyalty (BLY): and co-creation 326; and customer brand engagement 326
brand management *see* B★Canvas 2.0; corporate brand management; internal brand management
brand meaning: employees as co-creators of 449–453; employees as co-creators of internal brand meaning 450–451; *see also* corporate brand meaning
brand performance 182
brand positioning 26
brands, hyperconnected 263–265
brands, start-up 187–188
brand strategy 395–396; heritage as always emergent 404–406; looking back to move forward 401–404; making history instrumental 398–401; why use history in place vs. corporate branding 396–398; *see also* authentic internal brand strategies
brand sub-cultures 470–471
brand touchpoints 181, 293–294
brand values 25–26
brand values alignment 501–502
building corporate brands *see* corporate brand building
Burghausen, Mario xv, 16–17, 29–30, 372, 410–412
Business Model Canvas 177–178; *see also* B★Canvas 2.0
business-to-business (B2B) 88; co-creating value with stakeholders 159–160; corporate branding in 460–461; role of internal brand communities in 462–463

cacophony 296; Danish National Gallery 294–295
Cankurtaran, Pinar xv, 17
capabilities, resourced 102–103
change 72–74; consumers' emotional reactions to 221–222; interpretations of 222; oscillations between stability and 123–126; perception of the distinctiveness of 221; role of context in perception of 222–223; role of managers in balancing stability and 143–144
character 341–342
character horizontal 77
co-creation 6–8, 13–14, 84–86, 89; B★Canvas 2.0 177–190; brand co-creation (BCO) 337;

brand experience 195–207; of conscientious corporate brands 480–492; and corporate brand management 42–53; and corporate brand narratives 338–342; and corporate heritage branding 345–359; Danish National Gallery 285; and destination brand engagement 321–329; key characteristics of 45–49; and internal brand communities 459–478; and internal branding 442–454; and leadership 86–87; and lived-experience ecosystem value creation 95–107; and the metaphor of voice 284; and polyphony 291; reconceptualizing corporate brand identity 131–146; stakeholder 35–36, 169–172; and temporality 410; of value 157–160
co-creative school 85
coherency 153–154
commercial innovations 211–213; building relative brand attractiveness 213–216; digital innovation 216–218; finding balance in brand innovativeness 223–225, *224*; juxtaposing manager and consumer views on innovativeness 218–219; social innovation 217–218; what managers do is not what consumers see 219–223, **220–221**
communication 61, 70–74; contents 305; of the corporate brand 473–474
communities *see* brand communities; community engagement; internal brand community
community engagement 270–272, 467–468
competence: enhanced competence base 102–103
conformity: authenticity as 383–386
connection: authenticity as 386–389
connectivity, local 412
conscientious corporate brands 480–481, 491–492; building brands inside-out 487–491; committing to internal branding with a conscience 485–487; embracing values-driven branding 483–485; establishing a conscientious organization 481–483
conscientious endeavour 10–12
conscious attention (CA) 336
consistency: authenticity as 382–383
'constant yet flexible' 134–136
constituencies *see* corporate brand constituencies
consumer engagement 266–270; *see also* customer engagement (CE) and customer brand engagement (CBE)
consumers: co-creating value with 158–159; emotional reactions to change 221–222; interpretations of change 222; views on innovativeness 218–219; what consumers see 219–223; *see also* consumer engagement
context: new market 136; research 117–119; role of context in perceiving changes 222–223
continuity 72–74
core competencies 31

# Index

core identity: communicating and positioning 70–74, *70*, *72–73*; the corporate brand 59–66, *60–61*, *63*, *65–66*; exercises 67–69, 78, 79; reputation 74–80, *75–76*, *80*
Cornelissen, Joep xv, 16, 32, 161–162
corporate brand alignment 32, 160–163, **161**; developing relationships to successfully co-create value with multiple stakeholders 157–160; fundamental underpinnings of 150–154; meta-paradigm perspective 154–157, *155*, *157*; philosophical premise 149–150
corporate brand applications 33–37
corporate brand building 32–33; the future of 251–253
corporate brand constituencies 151–153
corporate brand design 473
corporate brand experience management 8–10
corporate brand external alignment 158–160
corporate brand identity 131–132; from a co-creational perspective 136–139; implications and future research 144–146; reconciling the multi-stakeholder/dynamic and internal/static aspirations for 139–144; tensions in the conventional notion of 132–135, **133–135**
corporate branding 408–415; and authenticity 380–389; in B2B 460–461; as a co-creative process 6–8, 177; as a conscientious endeavour 10–12; as corporate brand experience management 8–10; cross-fertilization of heritage between product and 364–374; description of corporate brands 183; emergence of 3–4; history in 396–398; holistic evaluation of corporate brands 183–187; as a holistic management concept 177; paradigm shift 3–18; re-defining 4–12; *see also* building corporate brands; co-creation; conscientious corporate brands; core identity; corporate heritage branding; corporate services branding; external branding; internal branding; polysemic corporate branding; polysemic corporate brand narratives; strong corporate brands; temporality of corporate branding
corporate branding dynamics 111–112, 126–127; brand action nets in action 119–126, *119*, *124*; corporate brands as action nets 113–117, **113–114**; research context and methods 117–119
corporate branding gaps 378–380, 389–391, *389*; authenticity and corporate branding 380–389
corporate brand internal alignment 158
corporate brand management 12–13, 281–285, *283*; application of AI to 200–202; and brand touchpoints 293–296, *293*, *296*; building the corporate brand 32–33; characteristics of strong corporate brands 29–31; the core of the corporate brand 24–26; corporate brand applications and future directions 33–37; the emergence of the co-creation paradigm in 42–45; evolution of 28–29; fusing the layers of 61–65; implications of working with polyphonic branding 291–293; and internal branding 442–444; internal co-creation and polyphony 291; key characteristics of corporate brand co-creation 45–49; key facets of 83–84; managerial consequences of the co-creation paradigm for 49–52; new dilemmas in 412–413; and the origin of the metaphor of voice and polyphony 285–289; outcomes of 26–28, **28**; paradigm shift 83–89; and polyphonic brand voices 296; polysemy 302–306; potential future research 52–53; the role of the brand manager in the polyphonic brand approach 289–290, *290*; teaching 188–189; tools for applying 87–88; *see also* internal brand management
corporate brand meanings 472–473
corporate brand monitoring 52
corporate brand narratives 259–260, 338–342; benefits of engagement 265–266; consumer engagement techniques 266–270; employee and community engagement 270–272, *271*; frameworks 260–263, **261**, *261*; and hyperconnected brands 263–265, *264*; measurement 274–275; risks and mitigation 272–274, *272–273*; *see also* polysemic corporate brand narratives
corporate brands school 85
corporate brand symbolic connections 153–154
corporate brand values 472
corporate communications 32
corporate culture 17–18, 496–503
corporate heritage branding 345; background and context of 346–351, *350*; co-creation 351–359, *354*, *357*
corporate heritage literature 372–373
corporate heritage research 370–371; and brand heritage research 371–372
corporate identity 24–25
corporate services branding 228–229; content analysis and findings 241–244, **242**, **244**; descriptive analysis and findings 230–241, *230*, **231–239**, *240*, **241**; future research opportunities 245–246; method 229–230
corporate social responsibility (CSR) 31, 36–37, 89
corporate sustainability (CS) 36–37
credibility 27, 77
cross-fertilization of heritage 364–365, 373–374; brand heritage in corporate branding 368–370; brand heritage in product branding 365–368; cross-fertilization between brand heritage and corporate heritage research 370–373
cultural school 85
culture *see* corporate culture
curating 400

## Index

customer engagement (CE) and customer brand engagement (CBE) 323–324, 336; and brand co-creation 325–326; and brand identification 325; effect on brand loyalty 326; and social media involvement 325

Danish National Gallery 285, 294–295
da Silveira, Catherine xv, 14, 170–171
data collection 326–327
description of corporate brands 183
design: research 326–327; *see also* brand design
destination brand engagement 321–322; discussion 328–329; methodology 326–327; research model and hypotheses 325–326; results 327–329, **328**; theoretical background 322–325, *322*
destination brands: vs. corporate brands 324–325
differentiation 76; *see also* brand differentiation
digital 89; digitalized interactive platformization 102–103; hyper-connected digital environment 136; innovation 216–218; start-ups 187–188
dissonance: versus harmony 314–315
drivers of sustainability 244, 245
dual identification 470
dual orientation 133–134, 143
dynamic corporate brand identity 136–144; *see also* corporate brand identity
dynamics: that challenge building an internal brand community 470–471; of internal brand communities 465–471; *see also* corporate branding dynamics

ecosystems *see* lived-experience ecosystem value creation
embedding 400–401
emotion: emotional reactions to change 221–222
employee branding 32
employee engagement 270–272
employees: as co-creators of brand identity 450; as co-creators of brand image 451–453; as co-creators of brand meaning 449–453; as co-creators of internal brand meaning 450–451
enduring definition of BI 132–133
engagement: benefits of 265–266; employee and community engagement 270–272; engaging with the community 467–468; *see also* consumer engagement; customer engagement (CE) and customer brand engagement (CBE); destination brand engagement
enhanced competence base 102–103
enthused participation (EP) 336
environmental programmes 31
ethics 36, 89
evaluation of corporate brands: holistic 183–187
exercises: does your matrix measure up 67–69; does your reputational layer measure up 79; mapping the identity elements 64–65; mapping the reputational elements 78

experiences 15; co-creation of 353; *see also* brand experience; corporate brand experience management; lived-experience ecosystem value creation; sustainable experiences; valuable experiences
extended competition diagonal 76–77
extended interaction vertical 77
extended strategy diagonal 76
external alignment, corporate brand 158–160
external aspect of BI 133–134
external branding 51–52
external elements of identity 62–65
external focus: versus internal 316–317

fit: quest for 151–153
flexible: 'constant yet flexible' 134–136
focus: of internal brand management 498; internal versus external 316–317
foundation *see* brand foundation
functionalist paradigm 151–153

gaps *see* corporate branding gaps
Ghasemi, Mojtaba xvi
globalized 'nowhereness': and localized connectivity 412
goods-services 99–100
government 33–34
Guzmán, Francisco xvi, 14, 169, 454

harmony 296; versus dissonance 314–315; *see also* polyphony
Hemetsberger, Andrea xvi, 14, 44, 47, 170
heritage 89; as always emergent 404–406; contested 413; and history 401–403; and a one-directional future 412; and strategy 403–404; *see also* brand heritage; brand heritage research; corporate heritage branding; corporate heritage literature; corporate heritage research; cross-fertilization of heritage
high-control opportunities 266–268
history 89, 395–396; heritage as always emergent 404–406; looking back to move forward 401–404; making history instrumental 398–401; why use history in place vs. corporate branding 396–398
holistic approach 190; brand canvas 177–182, *179*, **180–182**; corporate branding as a holistic and co-created management concept 177; use cases of the B*Canvas 2.0 183–189, *184*, **186**, *187–188*, **189**
Hollebeek, Linda xvi, 46, 323, 327
hybrid school 85
hyperconnected brands 263–265
hyper-connected digital environment 136
hypothesis testing results 327–328

identification: dual 470; *see also* brand identification (BID)
identity: co-creation of 353; identity matrix 61; *see also* core identity; corporate brand identity; corporate identity
Iglesias, Oriol 7–8, 29, 112, 142–143, 158, 395–398, 405, 442–445, 450–454, 460–463, 477
image 27–28; *see also* brand image
Ind, Nicholas 15, 28, 44–47, 87, 102, 403–406, 444, 453–454
Industrial Age paradigm 282–284
innovation: digital 216–218; finding balance in brand innovativeness 223–225; juxtaposing manager and consumer views on innovativeness 218–219; locus of 99–100; social 217–218; vs. social responsibility 214–216; as a way to increase brand attractiveness 214
insights-based benefits 265–266
instability perspectives, adaptive 140
interactive platformization 102–103
internal alignment, corporate brand 158
internal aspect of BI 133–134
internal aspirations for corporate brand identity 139–144
internal brand community 459–460, 475–478; the dynamics of 465–471; literature review 460–464; methodology 464–465; role in corporate brand co-creation 471–475
internal branding 17–18, 32, 50–51, 434–435, 453–454; a brief history of 419–422, **420–421**; conceptual basis and definition of 422–426, **423–426**; and corporate culture 496–503; with a conscience 485–487; elements of 426–434, *427*, **427, 429, 431, 433–434**, *435*; employees as co-creators of brand meaning 449–453; importance and challenges of 442–445; methodology 445–449, **446–449**; *see also* authentic internal brand strategies
internal brand management: evolution of 496–502
internal brand meaning: employees as co-creators of 450–451; *see also* brand meaning
internal co-creation 291
internal definition of BI 132–133
internal elements of identity 62–65
internal focus: versus external 316–317
internal orientation 143–144
interpreting 349
interpretivist paradigm 153–154

Kavaratzis, Mihalis xvi–xvii, 17, 397–398, 400, 405, 410–411
Kernstock, Joachim xvii, 13
King, Ceridwyn xvii, 18, 422, 499–502
Kjeldsen, Anna Karina xvii, 16, 252, 339–341
knowledge 468–469
Koporcic, Nikolina xvii

Kukk, Jana xviii
Kurtmollaiev, Seidali xviii, 15, 250–254

lagging indicators 275
leadership: and co-creation 86–87
leading indicators 275
Lervik-Olsen, Line xviii, 15, 215, 218, 250
life journeys 100–102
listening 292
literature review 228–229, 460–464; content analysis and findings 241–244, **242, 244**; descriptive analysis and findings 230–241, *230*, **231–239**, *240*, **241**; future research opportunities 245–246; method 229–230; *see also* corporate heritage literature
lived-experience ecosystem value creation 95–96; co-creation paradigm 96–105, *97*, **98**; discussion 105–107
localized connectivity: and globalized 'nowhereness' 412
Locarno Film Festival 306–314
low-control opportunities 269–270
loyalty *see* brand loyalty
Lurati, Francesco xviii, 16, 249

maintenance of the corporate brand 474–475
management 366–367, 369–370; top management 49–50; *see also* corporate brand management; internal brand management
managerial trade-offs 314–317
managers: interpretations of change 222; role in balancing stability and change 143–144; role in the polyphonic brand approach 289–290; views on innovativeness 218–219; and what consumers see 219–223
Mangiò, Federico xviii, 15, 249–250, 252
manifesting 350
marketing: heritage in 346–347; *see also* social marketing
marketing school 85
Markovic, Stefan xix, 15, 251–252
meaning: co-creation of 353; *see also* brand meaning; corporate brand meaning
measurement 274–275; testing results 327; and variables 327
medium control opportunities 268–269
meta-paradigm perspective 154–157
metaphor 284–289; *see also* multiple voices; polyphony; voice
methods and methodologies 117–119, 229–230, 326–327, 445–449, 464–465
micro-boards for start-ups 187–188
Mingione, Michela xix, 13–14, 83–85, 159–160, 171
mitigation of risks 272–274
monarchy 34
monitoring *see* corporate brand monitoring

## Index

Mühlbacher, Hans xix, 13, 44, 47, 83–84
multiple stakeholders 13–14, 44–45, 169–172; involvement 32; multi-stakeholder corporate brand identity 137–138, 139–144; new multi-stakeholder and dynamic corporate brand identity definition 136–139; orientation 143–144; and value co-creation 157–160
multiple voices 259–260, 281–285, *283*; benefits of engagement 265–266; and brand touchpoints 293–296, *293*, *296*; consumer engagement techniques 266–270; employee and community engagement 270–272, *271*; frameworks 260–263, **261**, *261*; and hyperconnected brands 263–265, *264*; implications of working with polyphonic branding 291–293; internal co-creation and polyphony 291; measurement 274–275; the origin of the metaphor of voice and polyphony 285–289; and polyphonic brand voices 296; risks and mitigation 272–274, *272–273*; the role of the brand manager in the polyphonic brand approach 289–290, *290*

narratives 260–263; *see also* corporate brand narratives; polysemic corporate brand narratives
New Age paradigm 282–285
new market context 136
'nowhereness,' globalized 412

omni-brands school 85
online 89
operational activities 100–102
organization, conscientious 481–483; *see also* conscientious corporate brands
organizational studies 286–287
oscillations between stability and change 123–126
otherness 471
outcomes: experienced 103–105; of sustainability 244, 245–246
outputs-uses 103–105

paradigms: bridging boundaries between 154–157; co-creation 42–45, 49–52, 96–105; functionalist 151–153; interpretivist 153–154; meta-paradigm perspective 154–157; moving from Industrial Age to New Age 282–285; paradigm shift 3–18; traditional brand paradigm 42–43
Pecot, Fabien xix, 17, 366, 410
Pedeliento, Giuseppe xix–xx, 15, 249–250
performance 76–77; locus of 103–105; *see also* brand performance
performance school 85
philosophy 149–150; philosophical school 84
Piehler, Rico xx, 18, 421, 496–497, 499
place branding 34–35
place brands 395–396; heritage as always emergent 404–406; looking back to move forward 401–404; making history instrumental 398–401;

why use history in place vs. corporate branding 396–398
platformization 102–103
polyphony 285–289, 296; Danish National Gallery 294–295; implications of working with 291–293; and internal co-creation 291; versus polysemy 315–316; potential of 287–289; role of the brand manager 289–290
polysemic corporate branding 300–302; in corporate brand management 302–306, *303*; Locarno Film Festival case 306–314, *309*, *312–313*; and managerial trade-offs 314–317
polysemic corporate brand narratives 15–16
polysemy 338–342
positioning 61, 70–74; *see also* brand positioning
Powell, Shaun xx, 13
preservation: versus transformation 316
process: co-creation engagement as 45–46; process benefits 265
product branding 364–365, 373–374; brand heritage in 365–368; cross-fertilization between brand heritage and corporate heritage research 370–373
purpose 338–342

Qiu, Yuqian xx, 15, 251

Ramaswamy, Venkat xx, 9–10, 13–14, 95–107, 137, 170–171, 249, 324
Rather, Raouf Ahmad xx–xxi, 16
recognizability 77
reinterpreting 349
relationships: developing corporate brand-aligned relationships 157–160; relationship building 32
relative brand attractiveness 211–213; building 213–216; and digital innovation 216–218; finding balance in brand innovativeness 223–225, *224*; juxtaposing manager and consumer views on innovativeness 218–219; and social innovation 217–218; what managers do is not what consumers see 219–223, **220–221**
relevance 77
remembering 399–400
reputation 27–28, 61–62, 74–80
research *see* brand heritage research; corporate heritage research; methods and methodologies
resourced capabilities 102–103
responsibility 77
risks 272–274
rituals 469–470
role-related stakeholder participation 46–47

Sancha, Cristina xxi, 15, 251
Saraniemi, Saila xxi, 18, 47, 498–499
Schmeltz, Line xxi, 16, 249, 252, 339–341
Schmidt, Hoger J. xxi, 18, 178, 435, 442, 444, 498–501

*Index*

Schultz, Majken 17, 24, 28, 32, 47, 52, 86, 383, 388–389, 400, 403–404, 410, 413–414
service-dominant logic (SDL) 196–197
services *see* goods-services
Simões, Cláudia xxi–xxii, 14, 170–171
Smith, Dale L.G. xxii
social connection (SC) 336
social innovations 211–213, 217–218; building relative brand attractiveness 213–216; and digital innovation 216–218; finding balance in brand innovativeness 223–225, *224*; juxtaposing manager and consumer views on innovativeness 218–219; what managers do is not what consumers see 219–223, **220–221**
socially oriented internal brand management practices 499–501; *see also* internal brand management
social marketing 35
social media involvement (SMI) 336; impact on CBE 325
social responsibility: vs. innovation 214–216; *see also* corporate social responsibility (CSR)
space: in brand action nets 121–123
spanning boundaries *see* boundary-spanning
stability: oscillations between change and 123–126; role of managers in balancing change and 143–144
stakeholders 304–305; agency 352–353; all brand stakeholders 144; co-creation 35–36; drivers of stakeholder engagement 47; role-related stakeholder participation 46–47; stakeholder-focus brand era 136; *see also* multiple stakeholders
start-up brands 187–188
state: co-creation engagement as 45–46
static aspirations for corporate brand identity 139–144
Steenkamp, Pieter xxii, 18, 452, 498–501
stories 71–72, 468–469
strategic school 85
strategy: and heritage 403–404; locus of 102–103; strategizing 293; *see also* authentic internal brand strategies; brand strategy
strong corporate brands 249–254; characteristics of 29–31
student projects 188–189
sub-cultures *see* brand sub-cultures
sustainability 36–37, 228–229; content analysis and findings 241–244, **242**, **244**; descriptive analysis and findings 230–241, *230*, **231–239**, *240*, *241*; future research opportunities 245–246; method 229–230
sustainable experiences 15, 249–254

symbolic connections *see* corporate brand symbolic connections

teaching brand management 188–189
temporality and temporal concepts: co-creation and agency 354–355; developments 409–412; intertemporal tensions 414; in marketing 346–347
temporality of corporate branding 16–17
territorializing 292–293
theory 340–341
time: in brand action nets 119–121; and space in brand action nets 121–123
top management 49–50
touchpoints 306; *see also* brand touchpoints
tourism *see* destination brand engagement
trade-offs, managerial 314–317
traditions 469–470
transformation: versus preservation 316
trust 27
trustworthiness 77

universities 34
Urde, Mats xxii, 13, 25, 84, 88, 346, 365
use cases of the B★Canvas 2.0 183–189, *184*, **186**, *187–188*, **189**
uses-and-gratifications perspective 322–323

valorizing 349
valuable experiences 15, 249–254
value: co-creation of 157–160, 353; locus of 100–102
value creation 47–49; *see also* lived-experience ecosystem value creation
value destruction 47–49
values *see* brand values; brand values alignment; corporate brand values
values-driven branding 480–481, 491–492; building a conscientious corporate brand inside-out 487–491; committing to internal branding with a conscience 485–487; embracing 483–485; establishing a conscientious organization 481–483
variables 327
Visconti, Luca M. xxii, 16
voice 282, 285–289, 338–342; *see also* multiple voices; polyphony
von Wallpach, Sylvia xxii–xxiii, 14, 45, 46

Werkhaus case 183
willingness-to-support 76

Zamparini, Alessandra xxiii, 16, 249, 338–341

511

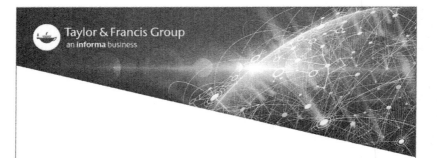